Research Methods and Statistics in Psychology

Sage Foundations of Psychology

Series editors:
Craig McGarty, Australian National University
Alex Haslam, University of Exeter

Sage Foundations of Psychology is a major new series intended to provide introductory textbooks in all the main areas of psychology. Books in the series are scholarly but written in a lively and readable style, assuming little or no background knowledge. They are suitable for all university students beginning psychology courses, for those studying psychology as a supplement to other courses, and for readers who require a general and up-to-date overview of the major concerns and issues in contemporary psycholgy.

Already published:

Doing Psychology: an introduction to research methodology and statistics
S. Alexander Haslam and Craig McGarty

Statistics with Confidence: an introduction for psychologists
Michael J. Smithson

An Introduction to Child Development
Thomas Keenan

Forthcoming:

An Introduction to Personality
Nick Haslam

An Introduction to Social Psychology
John Turner

Research Methods and Statistics in Psychology

S. Alexander Haslam and Craig McGarty

SAGE Publications

London • Thousand Oaks • New Delhi

© S. Alexander Haslam and Craig McGarty, 2003

First published 2003

Apart from any fair dealing for the purposes of research or
private study, or criticism or review, as permitted under the
Copyright, Designs and Patents Act, 1988, this publication
may be reproduced, stored or transmitted in any form, or by
any means, only with the prior permission in writing of the
publishers, or in the case of reprographic reproduction, in
accordance with the terms of licences issued by the
Copyright Licensing Agency. Inquiries concerning
reproduction outside those terms should be sent to the
publishers.

SAGE Publications Ltd
6 Bonhill Street
London EC2A 4PU

SAGE Publications Inc.
2455 Teller Road
Thousand Oaks, California 91320

SAGE Publications India Pvt Ltd
B-42, Panchsheel Enclave
Post Box 4109
New Delhi 100 017

British Library Cataloguing in Publication data

A catalogue record for this book is available from
the British Library

ISBN 0 7619 4292 0
ISBN 0 7619 4293 9 (pbk)

Library of Congress Control Number available

Typeset by Alden Bookset, Oxford
Printed in Great Britain by TJ International, Padstow

Contents

Online support material for lecturers and students, including PowerPoint lecture slides and sample exam questions can be found at: www.sagepub.co.uk/resources/haslam.htm

Preface to the First Edition (Doing Psychology)   xi
Preface   xiv
The Authors   xvi

1   Introduction   1
'Why do I have to do this?'   1
The structure of this book and an overview of the chapters   3
How to use this book   8
Discussion/essay questions   11

2   Research in Psychology: Objectives and Ideals   12
What is psychological research and why do it?   12
How does psychological research progress?   15
Principles of good research   20
Some notes of caution   26
Further reading   27
Objectives and ideals: A checklist for research evaluation
    and improvement   27
Discussion/essay questions   32
Exercises   32

3   Research Methods   34
Psychological measurement   34
The experimental method   43
The quasi-experimental method   51
The survey method   54
The case-study method   57
Overview   60
Further reading   62

Contents

Research methods: A checklist for research evaluation
   and improvement   62
Discussion/essay questions   65
Exercises   66

4   Experimental Design   67
Choosing an independent variable   68
Choosing a dependent variable   72
Choosing an experimental sample   75
Threats to internal validity   80
Threats to external validity   89
Further reading   95
Experimental design: A checklist for research evaluation
   and improvement   95
Discussion/essay questions   101
Exercise   101

5   Survey Design   102
The differences between surveys and experiments   102
Setting the question   107
Finding a sample   108
Types of survey   113
Constructing a questionnaire   120
Overview: Designing a survey   123
Further reading   125
Survey design: A checklist for research evaluation
   and improvement   125
Discussion/essay questions   129
Exercises   129

6   Descriptive Statistics   130
Different forms of research data   131
Describing a typical score: Measures of central tendency   134
The relationship between measures of central tendency
   and a response distribution   141
Describing the spread of scores: Measures of dispersion   144
Observed distributions and theoretical distributions:
   The difference between samples and populations   152
Further reading   162
Descriptive statistics: A checklist for research evaluation
   and improvement   162

Discussion/essay questions   164
Exercises   165

7   Some Principles of Statistical Inference   166
Statistical inference   169
Inferences about individual scores   176
Inferences about means   180
Overview   190
Further reading   192
Statistical inference: A checklist for research evaluation
     and improvement   193
Discussion/essay questions   196
Exercises   196

8   Examining Differences between Means: The *t*-test   198
Student's *t*-distribution   199
Comparing the results for a single sample to a specific value   203
Within-subjects *t*-tests   205
Between-subjects *t*-tests   209
The controversy about what to do with *t*-values   215
Handling the results of *t*-tests:
     The hypothesis-testing approach   216
Other ways of handling the results of *t*-tests:
     Probability-level, confidence-interval and
     effect-size approaches   227
Some notes of caution   234
Overview   239
Further reading   239
t-Tests: A checklist for research evaluation and improvement   240
Discussion/essay questions   244
Exercises   244

9   Examining Relationships between Variables:
     Correlation   246
Some basic principles of correlation   248
The measurement of correlation   250
Interpreting and making inferences about correlations   255
Some notes of caution   259
Conclusion   266
Further reading   266

Correlations: A checklist for research evaluation and
   improvement   267
Discussion/essay questions   270
Exercises   271

**10   Comparing Two or More Means by Analysing
   Variances: ANOVA**   273
Analysing variances   274
Comparing multiple means using one-way analysis
   of variance   277
Another way to explain analysis of variance:
   Sums of squares and mean squares   283
How big does a difference need to be?
   Significance testing and effect sizes   288
What does analysis of variance buy us? Some notes on
   comparing individual means   292
Using F-ratios with and without comparisons
   planned in advance   293
An introduction to analysis of variance with
   two independent variables   296
A final word   309
Further reading   310
ANOVA: A checklist for research evaluation
   and improvement   310
Discussion/essay questions   314
Exercises   314

**11   Analysing other Forms of Data: Chi-square and
   Distribution-free Tests**   316
Dealing with a single categorical variable that
   has two levels: The binomial test   320
Dealing with a single categorical variable that has more
   than two levels: The chi-square test of goodness of fit   324
Examining the relationship between two
   categorical variables: The chi-square test of independence
   for 2×2 tables   327
Distribution-free tests   335
Examining differences between two groups with relaxed
   assumptions: The Mann–Whitney test   337
Some options for other cases   340
Overview and checklist   343

Further reading 345

Other forms of data: A checklist for research evaluation
  and improvement 346

Discussion/essay questions 349

Practical problems 349

12 Qualitative Methods 351

Standard and radical critiques of quantitative approaches 353

Methods of collecting qualitative data 361

Some general principles for collecting and analysing
  qualitative data 364

Examples of qualitative research methods 368

Critiques of qualitative methods 388

Conclusion: The importance of responding to the challenge 392

Further reading 393

Qualitative research: A checklist for research evaluation
  and improvement 393

Discussion/essay questions 396

Practical problems 396

13 Research Ethics 398

Science and society 398

Participation in research 403

Research with animals 411

Final comment 414

Further reading 414

Research ethics: A checklist for research evaluation and
  improvement 414

Discussion/essay questions 419

**14 Conclusion: Managing Uncertainty in
    Psychological Research** 420

'Where has all this got us?' 420

Managing uncertainty in psychological research 420

Final comment 429

Further reading 430

References 431

Appendix A: Step-by-Step Guides to Key Statistical Tests 437

A.1 Working out a within-subjects *t*-test using the
    hyphothesis-testing method 437

A.2 Working out a between-subjects *t*-test using the
hyphothesis-testing method   439

A.3 Working out a correlation using both hypothesis-testing
and effect-size methods   441

A.4 Procedures for conducting one-way ANOVA with
equal cell sizes   444

A.5 Procedures for conducting two-way ANOVA with
equal cell sizes   448

Appendix B: Writing Research Reports in Psychology   451

Overview   451

Basic structure   451

The sections in detail   453

General stylistic issues   461

Presentational issues   463

Further reading   469

Sample laboratory report   469

Appendix C: Statistical Tables   477

Areas under the standard normal curve   477

Critical values of the *t*-distribution   481

Critical values of Pearson's *r*   483

Critical values of the *F*-distribution   485

Critical values of the χ^2-distribution   492

Appendix D: Answers to Exercises   495

Author Index   511

Subject Index   514

Preface to the First Edition (*Doing Psychology*)

Writing a book on research methodology and statistics is a lot of work, and library shelves sag with the weight of competing textbooks in the field (most of which are heavy in every sense). So why write another? Our impetus came from the fact that no existing textbook seemed to match up with what we were trying to offer students in our own introductory courses on these topics. In particular, we felt that most introductory books did little justice to the *research process* as we understand it – what *doing psychology* is all about. We believe that before you can do psychology you have to understand psychology, and that you cannot understand psychology unless you understand the process of conducting and interpreting psychological research. Hence the relatively stark title of this book.

We also wanted to write a book that conveyed our views using the same language, style and strategy as our own lectures. Our goal in this respect was to produce a down-to-earth text that treats the methodological and conceptual aspects of psychological research as the all-important gateway to statistical understanding rather than as an independent enterprise. We believe that if students can develop an understanding of the logic of research they will be able to see more clearly exactly what they need statistics for, and will then be motivated to understand more clearly what statistics can do for them – as well as what they cannot. Moreover, we suspect that unless statistics are dealt with in this way, they can do more harm than good – not least because they will turn otherwise eager students away in the belief that psychological research is about rote-learning, number-crunching and formulae that look like they come from outer space.

An unfortunate consequence of this approach is that some instructors may feel that this book covers more methodology and less statistics than they would like. We based our decision to omit a broad range of procedures from the present volume[1] (and our own introductory lecture courses) on the belief that it will be much easier for students to build knowledge of such statistical procedures on to a solid foundation in methodology and elementary procedures than to graft methodological knowledge on to bald statistical training. Our own experience suggests that the traditional emphasis can lead students to believe that statistics will get them out of any tight corner and will overcome any limitations in research design. Not only is this incorrect, but in our view it also leads to bad research. We would add, however, that plans are under way to commission a text that deals with more advanced statistical procedures in a manner that complements the approach we have taken here.

Although the present book does not deal with statistical procedures such as analysis of variance and chi-square, we were eager to ensure that our treatment of so-called basic techniques did not over-simplify the research process or make methodological and statistical issues seem easier to deal with than they really are. So, as we note in Chapter 1, the material that the book covers is often quite difficult – thereby reflecting the hard reality of doing psychological research. All the same, we hope that the book has still managed to convey our own enthusiasm for the research process and to *involve* readers in the many challenges it presents.

From our point of view, one very good thing about this undertaking is that even though it turned out to be much more work than we had expected, it also turned out to be more fun. In part this was due to our friends and colleagues who supported us while we were doing it. Many, including Mike Calford, Wolfgang Grichting, Judith Harackiewicz, Kate Reynolds and Jennifer Sanderson, provided comments on selected chapters for which we are extremely grateful. Others, including Mike Innes, Mike Platow and John Turner, provided very instructive input in specific content areas. Mariëtte Berndsen, Chris Cooper, Jason Mazanov, Richard Jennings, Penny Oakes, Rina Onorato and Russell Spears provided additional observations and suggestions that were helpful, too. Ziyad Marar at Sage also deserves to be singled out for his constant encouragement and his commitment to the *Foundations of Psychology* series as a whole. The editorial work of Lucy Robinson, Jane Evans and Richard Leigh was also superb. However, we would like to reserve our highest category of thanks to Michael Cook, Catherine Haslam, Duncan McIntyre and Mike Smithson. All four worked very long and very hard to provide detailed and extremely insightful comments on entire drafts of the text.

As is true of most scholarship and research, writing this book was therefore a genuinely collaborative enterprise. Ours, however, are the names on the book's cover and we, of course, take sole responsibility for its final form.

Alex Haslam and Craig McGarty (1998)

[1]This decision was revisited in preparing the second volume, leading to the addition of three new chapters.

Preface

It seems like a long time ago that we wrote the forerunner to this book, *Doing Psychology*. At the time we were relatively new to our lecturing jobs and to the process of developing and teaching courses on research methodology and statistics. In the interim, much has happened in our lives, but we have still retained our enthusiasm for psychology and the desire to engage students in the process of conducting psychological research. Consequently, when approached by the publisher, we were keen to thoroughly revise and update *Doing Psychology* in order to enhance its original content – in particular, by taking heed of the very generous feedback that we had received from colleagues around the world. For the most part this feedback encouraged us to write some new material that was pitched at the same level as the first volume (and retained its clarity and accessibility) but which tackled additional statistical, methodological and practical issues.

As a result, the present edition incorporates new chapters that provide introductions to (a) analysis of variance, (b) chi-square and distribution-free procedures, and (c) qualitative methods, as well as (d) an appendix on writing research reports. Each chapter now also includes practical exercises and discussion topics, as well as a checklist summarizing the key points that should inform relevant aspects of research practice. Partly as a reflection of the substantial nature of these changes, but also because we felt there was a need to disambiguate the original title, this second edition also goes by a more traditional name. The result of these changes, we hope, is a text that retains the freshness of the original volume (and which proves equally attractive to students and teachers), but which takes readers further down the road towards mastery of the many facets of research methods and statistics in psychology.

Our thanks to those people who helped us develop *Doing Psychology* remain as strong as ever. However, we would also like to thank our academic friends who played a part in bringing about this new volume: Steve Brown, Carole Burgoyne, Sue Burney, Kerry Chalmers, Barbara David, Nellie Georgiou-Karistianis, David Goble, Kristina Macrae, Elinor McKone, Annie Mitchell, Don Mitchell, Jonathan Potter, Kate Reynolds, Judy Slee, Janet Tweedie and Andy Wills. Michael Carmichael, Ziyad Marar and Zoë Elliott at Sage, and Bob Wilson at Footprint also deserve special mention for their continued commitment to the book and their unwavering confidence in our efforts. Richard Leigh and Lauren McAllister provided extremely helpful input at proof stage, as did Lucy O'Sullivan who also compiled the indexes. Finally, we would like to thank the many students who provided us with positive feedback on the first edition and who proved to us that there was a value to our endeavours. We hope that they are now enjoying the fruits of their study and that their success is an inspriation to those who will follow in their footsteps.

Alex Haslam and Craig McGarty

The Authors

Alex Haslam is professor of psychology at the University of Exeter. He is a former Associate Editor of the *British Journal of Social Psychology* and current Chief Editor of the *European Journal of Social Psychology*. He received an MA in psychology from the University of St Andrews in 1985. He spent a year as a Jones Scholar at Emory University before completing his PhD (1991) under the Commonwealth Scholarship and Fellowship Plan at Macquarie University. After lecturing at the University of Sydney, he was a post-doctoral researcher and then a lecturer at the Australian National University. He currently gives courses on social and organizational psychology and introductory research methodology and statistics. He is the author of *Psychology in Organizations*, *The Social Identity Approah* (2001) and the co-author of *Stereotyping and Social Reality* (1994; with Penny Oakes and John Turner) and the co-editor of *The Social Psychology of Stereotyping and Group Life* (1996; with Russell Spears, Penny Oakes and Naomi Ellemers) and *Social Identity at Work* (2003, with Daan Van Knippenberg, Michael Platow and Naomi Ellemers). Together with Craig McGarty he also co-edited *The Message of Social Psychology: Perspectives on Mind in Society* (1997).

Craig McGarty received his undergraduate training in psychology at the University of Adelaide and his PhD from Macquarie University in 1991 (where he was a tutor from 1985 until 1989). He spent 1990 as a lecturer in social psychology/social interaction at the University of Western Sydney and moved in 1991 to the Australian National University as a research associate. He is currently a Reader in the School of Psychology where he gives courses on group processes and advanced methodology and statistics. He has worked on a wide range of topics in experimental social psychology and is author of more than 20 research papers and book chapters. His most recent books are *Stereotypes as Explanations* (2002; with Vincent Yzerbyt and Russell Spears) and *Categorization and Social Psychology* (1999).

Introduction

'Why do I have to do this?'

Students are typically drawn to study psychology out of a sense of curiosity. They are interested in questions like 'What makes people love or hate each other?', 'How does our mind solve difficult problems?' and 'How do children develop a sense of morality?'. Such questions are potentially among the most interesting that can be explored in any academic setting. Not surprisingly, most students quickly find out that these and many other psychological topics can be fascinating to learn about and investigate.

The same can rarely be said for a student's first course on research methodology or statistics. When embarking on these courses most students often just ask themselves 'Why do I have to do this?'. The question is asked partly out of genuine confusion but also with a sense of foreboding – the study of methodology and statistics has the reputation for being dull, tedious, difficult and distressing. Few things have the same reputation for making people both bored and fearful at the same time.

Despite these concerns, the people responsible for laying down the guidelines for teaching in psychology continue to demand that students endure the trials and tribulations of a training in research methodology and statistics. Why spoil the fun? Why subject students to material which they may not only dislike, but which may lead to their disillusionment and turn them off studying psychology altogether?

It may be comforting to conclude that academic psychologists are sadists. Some probably are. But academics have little to gain from making students' lives miserable just for the sake of it. Nowadays almost all academic departments are keen to attract and retain as many students as possible. Accordingly, a number of very good reasons need to be put forward to encourage perseverance with this difficult material. So what are they? As we see it, the case for asking (indeed, demanding) psychology students to come to grips with issues of methodology and statistics rests on the following points.

First, it needs to be emphasized that one of the key transformations which students of psychology undergo in the course of their study is from being *consumers* of psychological knowledge to being *producers* of it. Before coming to university, most budding psychologists (like most other members of the general community) have been exposed to a range of relevant research. Psychology is the stuff of everyone's lives and for this reason it provides excellent material for television, radio, newspapers and everyday conversation. In the formal media journalists and commentators give us neatly packaged versions of the psychology of prejudice, fear, stress, physical attraction, memory and so on. Yet a key part of a person's academic training as a psychologist is to be able to participate *actively* in the research process. This role involves more than just supporting or challenging different versions of psychological truth with opinions and beliefs (something that any intelligent person should be able to do). It means being able to do so on the basis of carefully gathered and critically tested scientific evidence. Clearly we cannot do this unless we understand how to gather and how to test that evidence.

A second reason for studying methodology and statistics is related to the first. In order to understand and evaluate research conducted and reported by others, we need to have some insight into the procedures and assumptions by which their work has been guided. We may be suspicious of a person who uses a survey to make claims that eating a particular food will improve eyesight, or who concludes on the basis of an experiment that wearing a particular brand of jeans will make us more attractive to members of the opposite sex. By fully understanding the strengths and limitations of their research methodology we can find out whether our suspicions are well founded. Indeed, we can be fairly sure that it is precisely because so many people do *not* have this type of understanding that a great deal of important research continues to be misunderstood. It is also because so few people really understand these issues that certain research strategies continue to have appeal for those who want to use research to *conceal* truth rather than *reveal* it.

If the above reasons seem too idealistic and abstract, then a third reason is purely pragmatic. If you are reading this book you are likely to have one of two futures in mind. Either you are going to become a psychologist (in which case you will actually be doing research in the near future) or you are going to get a job where your psychological training will be very useful. In both cases, the ability to conduct, analyse and interpret psychological research is likely to serve you well. Indeed, of all the skills that a degree in psychology should impart, these are probably the most useful – and therefore the most marketable.

Of course psychology is not the only discipline which exposes its students to research methods and statistics. However, because psychology students approach these issues in an attempt to understand human behaviour, their expertise has a general and much sought-after relevance. This expertise is particularly relevant in fields such as advertising, marketing, teaching, politics, policy-making and in almost all managerial and executive roles.

This is not to say that studying research methodology and statistics will get you a well-paid job, or that you would necessarily want a job in which this knowledge played a central role. However, taking the above three points together, we believe that this knowledge should enhance your ability to make reasonable inferences about human behaviour and to evaluate critically the inferences drawn by others. These are probably the most directly applicable skills that can be imparted and developed through the study of psychology as a whole.

Finally, though, we would like to think that acquiring and mastering these skills could actually be intellectually rewarding and stimulating *in itself*. In light of the gloomy expectations with which you may have started reading this book, this may seem to be a tall order. A major objective of this book is to make the idea seem a little less outrageous than it might otherwise have been.

The structure of this book and an overview of the chapters

In writing this book our broad objective has been to take as much misery as possible out of studying research methodology and statistics. So in order to get our points across we have tried to use words and figures rather than numbers and equations wherever possible. Note, though, that it is not easy to do good psychological research. For that reason much of the material we have to deal with is challenging – sometimes extremely so.

Some people might suggest that one way to make the book more readable would be to take out *all* the numbers, *all* the equations, *all* the technical procedures and *all* the jargon. You may think this is a very attractive proposition. However, it will not be much help when you need to apply your knowledge, or when you progress to more advanced courses in which familiarity with this material is essential. Although the technical jargon we deal with is hard to understand at first, mastery of it

3

will ultimately make it much easier for you to communicate with other psychological researchers.

In this book we aim to provide a comprehensive examination of the research *process*. We have structured the chapters so that they present an ever-sharpening focus on the various aspects of research. We begin by asking very general questions about research motives and objectives. We then work through the main strategies that can be employed to reach those objectives. Finally, we consider the key statistical techniques typically associated with each strategy.

In this way, we address in sequence the key questions that are raised at different stages in the research enterprise: from the general ('What am I trying to do here?') to the specific ('How confident can I be that two groups of people really are different?'). We have outlined the structure of the next eight chapters in Figure 1.1.

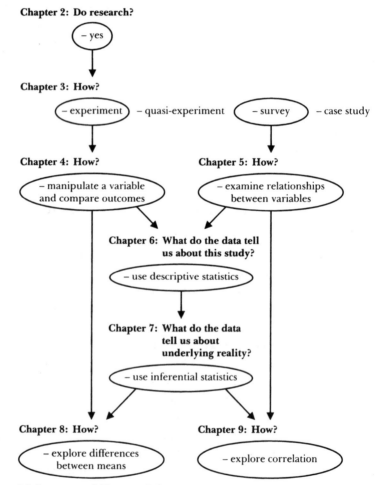

Figure 1.1 Structure of Chapters 2–9

In Chapter 2 we consider why people are motivated to conduct psychological research in the first place and the broad goals they set themselves when they do. We also identify properties which are generally considered the hallmark of good research and that are therefore most prized by members of the research community. Not surprisingly, because these properties can be viewed as prescriptions for research practice (effectively telling researchers what they should and should not aim for), there is controversy about their appropriateness and utility. For example, although we strongly endorse the view that psychology is a science, this scientific status is neither unproblematic (what does it mean?) nor uncontested (is it really?). In this chapter we outline these and other controversies, and some of the major camps into which researchers fall.

In Chapter 3 we discuss the main strategies which researchers employ to address different types of research question. We start by looking at precisely what psychologists measure and observe in their research and at the basis and consequences of measurement decisions. We then look at the aims of measurement in *experimental, quasi-experimental, survey* and *case-study* research. We outline the key features of each of these four methods and the kinds of conclusion each allows researchers to draw. We consider the factors that determine when each method is used and discuss the relative strengths and weaknesses of each.

In Chapter 4 we examine the experimental method in detail and explore how experiments are designed and conducted in psychology. In particular, we focus on the *choices* that using the experimental method involves, their consequences, and the factors to be considered when making them. These choices include decisions about who should participate in a study, what things should be controlled and what should be measured. Similar considerations are also central to Chapter 5 where we look at survey methodology and design. In both chapters we emphasize the types of *inference* which the various methods allow the researcher to make and consider how features of research design impact on our ability to make particular types of inference.

Chapters 6 to 9 introduce statistical concepts that are essential to almost all psychological research. These will form the backbone of the statistical knowledge that you will need to take from this book into more advanced courses or into a research setting. However, because our aim is to help you become a researcher rather than a mathematician, we generally downplay the algebraic and computational aspects of the statistics we introduce. It is our belief that the main obstacles to becoming a good researcher are conceptual not mathematical, so it is on overcoming these conceptual problems that we have chosen to expend most of our (and your) energy. For 99% of readers the mathematical (mainly algebraic) skills required to take you through this book will be ones that you acquired at high school (though your memory may need a bit of refreshing). We want to make it clear that statistics are not weapons of torture heralded from some alien world in order to confuse and deceive. Instead they are natural and sensible tools that are used in research (and other) contexts to make certain features of reality easier to grasp.

All the research methods discussed in Chapters 3 to 5 have one feature in common – they ultimately require the collection of research *data*. The first stage in handling almost all research data involves simply summarizing their most important features. In Chapter 6 we discuss the procedures most commonly used for describing data: those involved in representing typical data and the spread of data. This chapter thus includes our first attempt to make numerical statements about the properties of a given set of data. In other words, it introduces us to *descriptive statistics*.

Chapter 7 deals with a second class of statistics, those used to determine whether our *inferences* are sensible – that is, to make statements about what is going on in our research and about how our research findings relate to underlying reality. These inferences allow us to determine how likely it is that a given event has occurred by chance, and hence how 'special' it is. *Inferential statistics* allow us to establish, for example, how unlikely it is that if you asked a class of students to take a multiple-choice exam their average score would be above 65% if they were responding randomly. If this event is extremely unlikely and if you find that the average class score is above 65%, then this tells you that their performance is, in some sense, remarkable.

In fact, though, researchers do not (or should not) just ask endless questions and get people to do different things on the off chance that something remarkable will crop up. Instead, these types of activity are usually carried out in the context of a specific research question or *hypothesis* (a statement of what the effect of one thing should be on another). For example, a researcher may have a hypothesis that a particular class will perform well on an exam – perhaps because they are very bright, or have studied very hard, or have been well taught.

Inferential statistics are normally used as part of a *hypothesis-testing* exercise, as they allow the researcher to make qualified judgements about the degree of support for a particular hypothesis. Chapter 8 discusses these procedures as they are applied by researchers who are interested in comparing two sets of data that have been obtained in different situations (e.g., comparing the test performance of two different classes of students, or the same class at different times). Chapter 9 extends this analysis to examine situations in which more than two data sets are compared. Chapter 10 then discusses these procedures as they are applied to examine the *relationship* between *variables* (where a variable is simply a *dimension* on which people may differ, like age, mood or intelligence). Finally, Chapter 11 looks at a range of inferential statistics that are used to deal with categorical, proportional and ranked data (e.g., where researchers are not comparing two classes test scores but the proportion of people in the two classes who passed).

Having focused in the previous chapters on the way in which researchers collect and analyse numerical data, Chapter 12 provides an alternative perspective on the research process by looking at a class of techniques in which research findings are non-numerical. Here the emphasis is not on quantitative examination of psychological process (e.g., in terms of scores, speed or accuracy), but rather on *qualitative* approaches which attempt to discover and communicate the rich texture of particular forms of behaviour (e.g., language, movement and inter-action). Approaches like these are particularly useful when the essence of a phenomenon or process is at risk of being lost or changed through quantification. For this reason they are often used by researchers who are critical of quantitative approaches or who want to check that a quantitative approach does justice to the topic in which they are interested.

Chapter 13 steps back from the mechanics of conducting and analysing different forms of research to explore research *ethics*. Like the issues dealt with in Chapter 2, these are some of the most thorny in the research process. Leaving our consideration of these until the end of the book may appear to be inconsistent with the book's overall structure and the sharpening focus of the chapters. However, this chapter appears here not because it was an afterthought, but because we believe that it is necessary to have a full understanding of what the research process entails before one can reflect on its ethical implications and appropriateness.

Our concern in Chapter 13, as in all the others, is not so much to argue for one position over another (though we do express our opinions). Instead we set out the various considerations and positions with which researchers need to be familiar, and on which they need ultimately to take a stance themselves. This discussion also serves to take the book full circle, ending up by locating the research process within the world of people's values, perceptions and behaviour – the world that research sets out to understand and interpret. Sciences do not exist outside society but are a part of it, and scientific ethics express and reinforce the bond between science and society. This is especially apparent in psychology because the topics that it deals with are often quite sensitive and can sometimes be extremely controversial.

The concluding chapter attempts to bring together all the material discussed in the book in an integrated analysis of the research process as a whole. This analysis centres around the observation that when they conduct psychological research all researchers have to confront different forms of *uncertainty*. The chapter discusses what these forms are, and how each can best be dealt with.

A key point here is that it is generally impossible (and also undesirable) to eliminate all uncertainty from the research process. Nonetheless, one hallmark of a good researcher is the ability to *manage uncertainty appropriately*. Accordingly, a major objective of this book is to help you acquire this ability.

How to use this book

This is a book that we want you to *read*. That may sound rather obvious, but in many respects it is quite radical. This is because other methodology and statistics books often serve primarily as instruction manuals to which people turn only in times of crisis (either because they have forgotten how to do something or because they need to revise for an exam). There is nothing wrong with having books for this purpose and most seasoned researchers need to have a good one (for the same reasons that they will probably want a good dictionary or encyclopaedia). However, for someone coming fresh to the topic, this sort of text is not especially inviting. One would hardly seek to inspire literature students by giving them a reference book, so why would you do it for psychologists?

Indeed, it was the idea of writing a book that students could *read* that motivated us in the first place. So, as with most other books, we would recommend that the best way to use this one is to *start reading it at the beginning and work through to the end*. Having said that, it is quite likely that the instructor on any course you are taking will advise you that there are certain sections you should focus on and others that you can skim through. This will often be appropriate (depending on the course you are taking), but we think that as your career as a psychology student and researcher develops you will find it useful to return to the book to fill in any gaps in your knowledge. In this sense the book is designed to serve as a resource for researchers of all levels of sophistication.

It is clear, however, that, unlike most detective novels (and despite our best intentions), your reading is unlikely to be sustained simply by a desire to get to the end. We have deliberately avoided major twists of plot and we try to provide solutions to most of the mysteries on the spot. Partly to overcome any lack of intrigue, we have punctuated the text at regular intervals with relevant questions. These are designed to ensure that you process the material we present as actively as possible and that, as you progress, you understand the most important issues and concepts. All questions are asked in multiple-choice format and range in difficulty from those that are relatively easy (*) to those that are quite (and sometimes very) difficult (***).

We opted for the strategy of asking questions of different degrees of difficulty for three reasons. First, we hoped that this strategy would serve to vary the pace of the text and make it more engaging. Second, we thought that giving this form of graded feedback was more realistic as it will give you insight into how well you are progressing relative to the kinds of benchmark that your instructors are likely to apply in the exams and tests *they* set you. It is quite likely that these exam questions will not be of uniform difficulty, but will be designed to differentiate between students on the basis of how much they have learned. Finally, some of the concepts and issues we discuss *are* difficult so we felt it would be misleading to make questions about these artificially easy, just to make you feel good. Indeed, we suspect you may actually feel better if you are able to answer some of the more difficult questions.

Questions are presented in boxes set aside from the main text. In the shaded portion of each box we talk through the answer to the question, outlining both what makes one answer correct and what makes the others incorrect. In each case we recommend that if you get a question wrong (and we would be surprised if this never happens), you go back over the preceding text to identify the source of any confusion or misunderstanding. The following is an example of a fairly easy question:

Q1.1*

> How are the next eight chapters in this book organized?
>
> (a) Issues are discussed in no particular order.
> (b) Early chapters deal with broad methodological questions and later ones discuss more specific statistical issues.
> (c) Chapters start by discussing statistical procedures and then move on to examine the use of these in research settings.
> (d) The chapters are organized in terms of their difficulty, starting with the easiest topics.
> (e) None of the above.

The correct answer is (b). The book starts by considering broad issues such as why one needs to conduct psychological research at all. It then looks at the main ways of doing research, before going through the statistical procedures that this typically involves. Of the other responses, only (c) and (d) are really plausible, and although there may be some truth to (d) – at least for some readers – this was certainly not the basis on which the book's structure was devised.

To consolidate this process of continual active revision, at the end of each chapter we provide a set of three or four questions that deal with the major issues covered in each chapter. You can use these to test your understanding of the chapter as a whole before moving on.

At the end of some chapters we have also provided a list of some key references which you may want to look at if you are interested in pursuing certain issues further. Generally, though, we have been quite miserly in our referencing. This is mainly because we were keen not to clutter up the text with citations that would do little to help us communicate the particular point we were making. It is also the case that many of the views we present are widely held, so to attribute them to any one person (or a small number of people) would not be particularly appropriate. Yet where our ideas clearly derive from the work of a particular person or group of people, we have (as is necessary in all scholarly writing) endeavoured to acknowledge their source.

The only other main point to note is that, throughout the text, key concepts and terms are marked in **bold**. Definitions of each are provided in a box at the end of each section. Cross-references within the same box are indicated by terms that are in bold and italicized. We chose to place the definition of terms here, rather than in a glossary at the end of the book, to consolidate the learning process in an ongoing way. We would urge you to make sure that you are thoroughly familiar with these terms as about 90% of them will represent *assumed knowledge* in many later-year courses. Indeed, we explicitly based our decision about which items to place in these boxes on a survey of second- and later-year psychology instructors. The information in these boxes should also be useful if you are revising for an exam, or returning to the book after a long absence. So in many ways the boxes serve as the milestones with which our journey is marked out. Let's get on with it.

Discussion/essay questions

(a) Should the study of statistics and methodology be made optional in psychology courses?

(b) Discuss the proposition that the key to successful research is a sound understanding of methodology.

(c) Is the general public's limited understanding of research methodology and statistics a cause for concern?

(d) What are the main things to be learned from studying psychology?

(e) What general skills does a good psychologist need? To what extent are these skills related to an understanding of the research process?

2

Research in Psychology: Objectives and Ideals

What is psychological research and why do it?

In the previous chapter we attempted to justify the study of research methodology and statistics by arguing that it will allow you to conduct and understand psychological research. But this raises another question. Why do that research in the first place?

In order to answer this question we need to consider what the academic discipline of psychology *is* and what differentiates it from other disciplines. Broadly speaking, 'doing psychology' involves looking at all aspects of mental life and their impact on behaviour. Table 2.1 gives an indication of the different aspects of mental life that are examined by researchers in different fields of psychology.

Importantly, though, the difference between psychology and other academic disciplines is not just something to do with the topics that psychologists investigate. Many of the core issues addressed by work in fields referred to in Table 2.1 will also be examined by students of philosophy, art, literature, history, sociology and so on. This is true, for example, if someone is interested in the nature of sensation and perception, or in issues of self, consciousness and identity. Importantly, too, these other subjects provide significant and valuable insights into these topics. Indeed, one of our colleagues is fond of observing that anyone interested in learning about interpersonal relationships should start by reading a Dostoevsky novel.

What is customarily understood to differentiate psychology from these other disciplines is the *method* it uses to investigate these topics. In general, psychologists are committed to studying mental life and behaviour by using what is known as the **scientific method**. Just what the scientific method is, is itself a topic of great debate (particularly among philosophers of science), but in general terms it reflects *a commitment to test knowledge through observation and* (if possible)

Table 2.1 Fields of psychology

Different fields of psychology	Representative topics and issues
biological psychology	the brain's control over human and other animal behaviour
clinical psychology	the basis and treatment of mental disorders
cognitive psychology	the nature and basis of complex thought processes and reasoning
comparative psychology	animals' evolutionary adaptation to their environment
cross-cultural psychology	the impact of culture on social behaviour
developmental psychology	physical, intellectual and social development over the human lifespan
educational psychology	cognitive and social processes in a learning environment
environmental psychology	the impact of the physical environment on psychological well-being
health psychology	the contribution of psychological factors to illness
industrial/organizational psychology	cognitive and social processes in the work environment
neuropsychology	brain mechanisms underpinning cognitive processes
perception	processes that give coherence and unity to sensory input
personality psychology	individual differences in patterns of behaviour and temperament
psychophysics	quantitative relationships between physical stimuli and individuals' experience of them
social psychology	the impact of other people on individuals' thoughts, feelings and action
sport psychology	the impact of psychological processes and states on human performance

experimentation. In this sense it is an **empirical method** (i.e., an activity based on experiencing the world) that is used to discover truth, or at least *move towards* its discovery as we become more certain about what is true and what is false.

Psychologists, then, are not generally content to base their assertions simply on argument, opinion, gut feeling, or appeals to common sense or logic. Do not misunderstand this point, though. We are not saying that things like argument, common sense and logic have no place in psychology. They do, and their role is absolutely central. But this role relates largely to empirical evidence and its interpretation.

There are some heavy words in the preceding few paragraphs, and it is certainly true that the claims of anyone who uses concepts such as *science, knowledge* and *truth* should be closely examined to see if they deliver as much as they promise. It is worth noting, too, that on the basis of such examination some people have argued that these terms are really quite hollow and are used only to make particular views and practices sound serious and important. For example, Paul Feyerabend has argued that in modern Western society people who look up to science do so out of a quasi-religious faith that is blind and misdirected (e.g., Feyerabend, 1975). Others have argued that all truth is relative and that the quest for absolute scientific truth is therefore meaningless and futile.

Nevertheless, these complaints have had relatively little impact on what scientists do (or think they are doing). Moreover, some researchers have argued that these objections merely point to aspects of human behaviour which psychologists (and other social scientists) need to account for. One way in which they set about doing this is by trying to identify all the factors that contribute to truth and trying to understand their role.

These rather lofty (and really very complex) debates aside, though, there are three essential reasons for wanting to conduct psychological research using the scientific method: (a) to find out more about human behaviour and the mental processes associated with it; (b) to ensure that those findings are worthwhile; and (c) to ensure that our interpretation of those findings is correct.

To make this a little clearer, think of something that everyone reading this book has probably thought about at some stage or other – the effect that separation from a loved one will have on your relationship. As a casual observer or as someone who is keenly interested in the question (perhaps because your partner is about to go overseas on a long trip), you will probably think about lots of things which bear upon this issue (How long have we known each other? How much do we love them? How much do they love us? How many presents are they going to bring back?). Based on these observations you may conclude that 'absence will make the heart grow fonder'. The question though, is whether this conclusion is really appropriate.

Of course in one sense it is, because we all come to conclusions like this all the time in forming our opinions and deciding what to do in different situations. But the fact of the matter is that the same information inevitably leads different people to different conclusions. Indeed, we ourselves may reach different conclusions depending on our circumstances (our mood, our options, our state of inebriation). So, informal observation leads some people to conclude that 'absence makes the heart grow fonder', but others may lean towards the proverbial wisdom that 'absence leads the heart to wander'. Going back to the three points listed above, in order to understand *which* of these conclusions is true or *when* each is true we need to adopt a more systematic approach to the question. We also need to do this in order to understand exactly what is going on here – to answer the all-important question of *why* separation has these different effects.

Q2.1[*]

Which of the following is *not* associated with use of the scientific method in psychological research?

(a) A commitment to producing knowledge through observation and experiment.
(b) A commitment to basing knowledge exclusively on common sense and opinion.
(c) A commitment to basing knowledge on empirical evidence.
(d) A commitment to discovering truth.
(e) A commitment to ensuring that findings are correctly interpreted.

The correct answer is (b). Common sense and opinion play an important role in psychological research and its interpretation, but they are not all that is important. In particular, this is because use of the scientific method is associated with the attempt to base knowledge on systematic observation and measurement. The word 'exclusively' is therefore what makes statement (b) suspect. (a) and (c) are both statements of what the scientific method *is*, at least in part. (d) is the objective of all research using the scientific method and (e) is an important aspect of that objective.

empirical method A procedure for obtaining information on the basis of observation.
scientific method A procedure for acquiring and testing knowledge through systematic observation or experimentation (e.g., through use of empirical methods).

How does psychological research progress?

When we say that the key goal of psychological research is to understand *why* mental processes and behaviour have particular effects, we are essentially saying that we want to *explain* those phenomena. Ideally, psychologists achieve this by developing psychological **theory**. A theory is a set of explanatory principles used to make sense of and integrate a range of empirical findings. Theories can vary in specificity from broad explanatory frameworks comprised of abstract principles to sets of concrete hypotheses about particular structures and mechanisms. Not all psychologists actually use the word 'theory' to describe the forms of explanation they develop (some prefer terms like 'model', 'analysis', 'account', or – as we will discuss below – 'hypothesis'), but almost all use some form of explanatory system with similar properties.

Importantly, then, psychological research should not simply be conducted in an attempt to uncover more and more *facts* about relevant topics. As an example, research on a topic like memory does not just involve getting lots of different people to complete lots of different memory tasks.

Of course research using the scientific method *can* be conducted in this way (and in fact some of it is). But as Poincaré originally observed a hundred years ago, in the same way that a house is more than just a pile of bricks, so science is more than just the accumulation of facts. Similarly, in a recent book on astronomy and astrophysics, Gribbin and Rees (1990) open their discussion by noting that if science were only comprised of facts, it would have ground to a halt years ago. This is because it would have been weighed down by the burden of too much data. Instead Gribbin and Rees suggest that

> Science proceeds because of our ability to discern patterns and regularities in the natural world. As we come to see how previously unconnected facts hang together, we fit more data into laws of greater scope and generality, and we need to remember *fewer* independent basic facts, from which the rest can be deduced. The astonishing triumph of modern science . . . is its ability to describe so many of the bewildering complexities of the natural world in terms of a few underlying principles. (p. 3)

What is true of the laws of physics is also true of psychological theories. What perhaps separates psychologists from physical scientists is that they often *disagree* much more with each other about what these principles actually are. But this is not really the point. Even if they disagree about which theory is right, most psychologists still believe that their goal is to resolve these disagreements and settle upon one correct explanatory framework – a process which also goes on in many 'newer' areas of the physical sciences (e.g., debate on the role of 'cold dark matter' in the formation of galaxies).

In psychology, then, theory serves the same two important purposes that it does in other sciences – both of which are dealt with in the above statement by Gribbin and Rees. First, it should be capable of accounting for *multiple facts*. Second, it should allow researchers to generate predictions about what will happen in *novel* situations. The purpose of most psychological research is to test these predictions using scientific methods.

These predictions are often presented in the form of **hypotheses**. Hypotheses are statements about the **causal relationship** between particular phenomena. In other words, they are statements of *cause and effect* that say how one thing affects another. Broadly speaking, all psychological research is conducted in order to establish whether particular hypotheses are true or false. Often these hypotheses are derived from (or used to develop) psychological theory, but they do not necessarily have to be. They will often be tentative statements, too, particularly in the early stages of theory development.

To illustrate this process, we can think back to the case of someone contemplating the effects of separation on a relationship (let us call her Susan). We noted before that in contemplating this problem Susan could call to mind a whole series of cases where couples have been separated. She may remember that when Michelle went away to Greece her boyfriend left her, but that when Rita went to Bali her boyfriend missed her so much that he asked her to marry him the night she returned home. Furthermore, Susan may decide to observe some future separations very closely (perhaps monitoring a range of different kinds of relationship) to gather even more information about this topic. If she does she will clearly obtain a lot of data or facts and perhaps at the end of the process she will feel qualified to make a decision about whether or not she should go away. Perhaps she will conclude that absence really does makes the heart grow fonder and decide to journey to Patagonia after all.

We noted before that Susan's strategy will be of limited use if it is unsystematic (if it is not based on the scientific method). But *even if Susan did use the scientific method*, her research would still be severely limited if it was simply concerned with data-gathering. For one thing, when would she have enough data to know that she was right? Would it be enough to base her judgement on 5 relationships, or 50, or 5000? This is actually an intractable question for any scientist who wants to make conclusions only on the basis of raw observation (through a process known as **induction**). Even if every single relationship Susan observed (between couples of every conceivable type) survived separation, could she be sure that hers would?

A key feature of Susan's problem here is that her research is taking place in a theoretical vacuum – she does not have a theory to guide and structure her investigation (a theory that would suggest particular hypotheses to test). If she did, she could gather data which were *particularly* relevant to it. Alternatively, she could consider two competing theories and gather data which tested between them.

In this way, the advantage of having a theory is that it tells us *where to look* for evidence. For example, if Susan has a theory that 'absence makes the heart grow fonder', it may be more profitable to test this among people who have shaky relationships than among those who have strong relationships. This is because often the most useful way to examine a theory is to test it in a situation where it is least likely to be supported (though in practice most scientists do this quite rarely).

Progress in psychology is thus made not only by collecting evidence which supports a theory or hypothesis, but also by collecting evidence that *contradicts* it. When a theory is contradicted in this manner (through a process referred to as **falsification** or **refutation**), it generally has to be rejected or at least refined. According to Karl Popper, this is how most scientific progress is achieved (Popper, 1968; see also Magee, 1974).

In order to provide a critical test of her theory that 'absence makes the heart grow fonder', Susan may therefore want to see what happens to Martina (a friend with a very shaky relationship) when she is separated from her boyfriend. If Martina's boyfriend leaves her, this should force Susan to reject the simple version of her theory. At the very least she should modify it, perhaps by adding a *qualifying statement*, so that the revised theory (or hypothesis) becomes 'absence makes the heart grow fonder, but only if the initial relationship is already strong'.

One other point to note about Susan's theory is that it does not actually *explain* very much about the relationship between separation and feelings. The statement 'absence makes the heart grow fonder' is actually a **redescription** not an explanation. Strictly speaking, a psychological theory should *explain* and not just describe the findings from psychological research. It has to say *why* absence makes the heart grow fonder and not just *that* it makes the heart grow fonder. Related problems arise when psychological theory involves **circular argument** or **reification**, in which an empirical finding is purported to be explained simply by a process or state responsible for producing that finding. If, for example, a researcher attempts to explain students' good performance on a maths exam by saying that they have a high level of inherent mathematical ability we can see that the explanation does not necessarily tell us very much. Similarly, if we attempt to explain evidence that absence makes the heart grow fonder with reference to a 'separation-induced attachment mechanism' we run the risk of contributing more to psychological jargon than to psychological knowledge. Nonetheless, such strategies often prove tempting both for researchers and for their audience. Amongst other things, this is because they have the seductive capacity to explain *all* the available empirical data.

In Susan's case, then, a better theory might propose that 'separation strengthens attraction to someone you have a high opinion of (and weakens attraction to someone you don't) because memory preserves only the most salient (i.e., the most important or prominent) features of a person (or object)'. To avoid having to repeat the details of this explanation every time the theory is referred to, the theory will probably be identified by an abbreviated title. So this explanation might be referred to as 'salient feature theory'.

The advantage of this type of theory is that it allows researchers to examine *processes* and not just particular products or events. To illustrate this point, think about how people understand the operation of a car. Here we can formulate two kinds of theory: those of the type typically developed by drivers, and others of the type typically developed by engineers. As a driver you may develop (through empirical observation – i.e., driving) a descriptive understanding of the form 'if I depress the accelerator, then the car will go faster'. But an engineer may develop an explanatory theory of the form 'if I depress the accelerator, then the car will go faster because it increases the flow of oxygen to the engine and the engine then burns more fuel which in turn makes the engine go round faster'.

The advantage of the engineer's theory is that because it explains the observed relationship between the accelerator and the car's speed, engineers are not only able to drive a car but also to understand (and design) *other* machines where this principle operates. Clearly this is something that most drivers cannot do. So, going back to our relationship example, if it really is true that memory preserves the salient features of objects, then this may allow a psychologist not only to predict when separation will have a bad effect on a relationship but also to understand why it does and to apply this understanding to other things. For example, it might help us understand why as people grow older they start to think that summers were more pleasant when they were young, that milk used to taste better, or that the police used to be more honest.

Q2.2**

Which of the following contribute to the development of knowledge and theory in psychology?

(a) Evidence which supports a hypothesis.
(b) Evidence which contradicts a hypothesis.
(c) Evidence which tests a hypothesis.
(d) All of the above.
(e) Answers (a) and (c) only.

The correct answer is (d). All of these factors contribute to the development of knowledge in psychology. The most plausible alternative answer is (e), but it is important to recognize that evidence which contradicts (or refutes) a theory provides impetus for its revision or rejection.

causal relationship An association between two or more things, such that one causes (or brings about) the other.

circular argument An argument in which the thing to be explained is presented as the explanation (e.g., where memory ability is used to explain memory performance).

falsification The process of rejecting conclusions and theories on the basis of evidence that is inconsistent with them. A commitment to carrying out research with this objective is referred to as 'falsificationism'.

hypothesis Formally, a statement about the *causal relationship* between particular phenomena (i.e., in the form 'A causes B'). This is usually derived from a particular *theory* and designed to be tested in research. In statistics and in informal usage, a hypothesis can also be a statement of the expected results of a study.

induction The process of drawing conclusions and developing theories on the basis of accumulated observations.

redescription The process and outcome of attempts to explain an empirical finding by restating that finding (e.g., where fear of confined spaces is used to explain claustrophopia).

refutation Another word for *falsification*.

reification The process and outcome of treating an empirical finding in psychological research as if it were simply the expression of an underlying psychological process (e.g., to explain performance on intelligence tests as the expression of intelligence).

theory A system of explanation used to make sense of, and integrate, a number of empirical findings. A theory can vary in specificity from a broad explanatory framework comprised of abstract principles to a set of concrete hypotheses about particular structures and mechanisms.

Principles of good research

Although many of the ideas discussed in the previous two sections would be endorsed by a wide range of psychological researchers, they are often in the background when research is actually being done.

For this reason, most researchers would probably prefer to comment on research *products* rather than the research *process*. In their own research they would then strive to achieve the best product by adhering to some relatively down-to-earth principles that are widely endorsed by other researchers (e.g., Ray, 1993; Sternberg, 1995). In this section we will focus on five principles. These suggest that psychological research should be (a) reliable, (b) valid, (c) cumulative, (d) parsimonious and (e) public.

Two qualities which all psychologists strive for in their research are **reliability** and **validity**. These terms are easily confused with each other and with other things, but it is essential to have a clear grasp of both. Put simply, *reliability relates to our confidence that a given empirical finding can be reproduced* again and again and is not just a 'freak' or chance occurrence. If a finding is reliable it will be easy to reproduce or to **replicate**. A good way to remember what reliability refers to (and to avoid confusing it with validity) is to think about what it means to advertise a second-hand car as 'reliable'. If it really is reliable the engine will not just start once in a blue moon, it will start every time you turn the ignition. If after you buy the car you find that it only starts occasionally, you will think that you have been duped – and what's more you will be right. Similarly, if some psychologists suggest that a given finding is reliable but no one else can ever reproduce it, their research will be called seriously into question.

The concept of validity is slightly more difficult to grasp, largely because it can take a number of different forms. In the simplest terms, *validity relates to our confidence that a given finding shows what it purports to show*. Examining the validity of a **study** therefore involves seeing whether its findings have been correctly *interpreted*. If they have not then the research is *in*valid. Continuing with our car example, a car without an engine (and that therefore *never* starts) is actually *reliable* (because the same result is continually reproduced), but it is not a *valid* car because it is not what it seems or purports to be – if you like, it has been misinterpreted as a car when it is actually something else (perhaps a very cumbersome piece of modern art or a heap of scrap metal).

As a more psychological example, think of a study in which some researchers send a person overseas to see whether this makes that person think more favourably of his or her partner. Let us assume that it does (again and again – i.e., it is a reliable finding). If on this basis the researchers conclude that 'absence makes the heart grow fonder' their conclusion may not be *valid*. The study may show something else – and almost certainly does. It may just show that holidays make people feel better about things in general (including their partners).

21

Discussions about the validity of findings are some of the most common (and most heated) in psychological research. They contribute to many of the disagreements between researchers that we have alluded to already. This is partly because establishing the validity of research findings tends to be much more difficult in psychology than in other scientific fields (such as physics or biology). This is mainly because the things in which most psychologists are interested – mental processes or states – can *never* be observed or measured directly. It is never possible for psychologists to read someone's mind or know exactly what is going through it. We will discuss the implications of this point further in the next two chapters.

Disagreement about validity generally relates to assertions that findings which are said to show one thing can be *reinterpreted* in a way which suggests that they actually show something completely different. Debates about the validity of IQ testing are a good example. Some researchers have argued that studies using IQ tests 'show' that there are racial differences in intelligence. Their critics, however, argue that these studies only 'show' that IQ tests are culturally biased – that their construction reflects the values and prejudices of the test designers (see Gould, 1981).

A belief that research should be *cumulative* relates to the discussion of progress in the previous section. The basic idea here is that at any given time research into a particular issue or problem needs to be guided by research that has been conducted on it previously and to move forward by building on its insights. To the extent that it is cumulative, research should develop from a sound knowledge base, in which researchers learn from and avoid the mistakes of the past. It was to such a process that the physicist Isaac Newton attributed his own success when he remarked 'if I have been able to see further than others it is because I have stood on the shoulders of giants'.

Just how researchers choose what particular problem to address is itself a very important issue, and could be the topic of a whole book. In practice, though, the agenda of psychological research is governed by an array of factors including: (a) the work of other researchers in the field of interest; (b) the questions that are defined as important by both the general and the scientific community; and (c) the social, economic and political climate. All these factors actually affect each other. This can mean that sometimes the issues addressed by researchers will change dramatically in a very short period of time – a process which the philosopher Thomas Kuhn (1962) referred to as 'scientific revolution'. Nevertheless, during periods of stability (or what Kuhn called 'normal science'), groups of psychologists interested in a given topic will typically be engaged in the process of striving (both collaboratively and competitively) to explore and explain one particular issue as comprehensively as possible.

In thinking about this process of research development, one problem which may occur to you is how a researcher's ideas can ever be conclusively rejected. As we saw before, even when a hypothesis is refuted by a particular piece of evidence it is still possible to cling to the theory from which it was derived simply by continuing to add qualifying statements to the theory. So if the evidence from people who do not have strong relationships contradicts the theory that 'absence makes the heart grow fonder', then a researcher can propose a new theory such as 'absence makes the heart grow fonder, but only if the initial relationship is strong'. But what if this is true only of heterosexual relationships? And what then, if it is only true for couples without children? Exactly how long can researchers cling on to a theory (or another explanatory principle) before they are forced to give it up?

One answer is that they should hang on to the theory until a better one comes along. The question is, though, what makes a competing theory *better*? One commonly accepted answer appeals to the principle of **parsimony**. This asserts that the best theory (or other explanatory structure) is the one that provides the simplest, most economical and efficient explanation of the evidence. In these terms, the goal of psychology (and of science in general) is to *explain the largest number of facts in terms of the smallest number of principles*. This point in fact forms the basis of the statement by Gribbin and Rees that we discussed earlier.

To illustrate this point, we could develop three theories which might be used to explain the relationship between separation and attraction. Theory A (let us call it 'motivated nostalgia theory') might assert that separation from an object causes us to exaggerate the object's worth, because we are motivated to have positive memories of things encountered in the past (this explains the finding that 'absence makes the heart grow fonder'). Theory B ('physical reinforcement theory') could suggest that separation from an object causes us to devalue it because attraction has to be maintained by constant physical reinforcement (this explains the finding that 'absence leads the heart to wander'). Finally, Theory C ('salient feature theory') might argue that separation from an object causes us to exaggerate that object's qualities (whether good or bad) because memory tends only to preserve the most salient features of an object (this explains why 'absence makes the heart grow fonder' when we like someone and why 'absence leads the heart to wander' if we dislike them). According to the principle of parsimony, of the three theories, C should be preferred because it explains more empirical facts but still only involves one principle. So, in cases where researchers have to choose between two or more theories, if they apply this principle, they should favour the one that explains either more evidence, or the same amount of evidence (or more) with fewer principles.

All the above principles relate to how good research is done, but a final question concerns what one should do with good research. The short answer to this is that good research needs to be *public*. It is clear that keeping research findings secret will do nothing to advance scholarly debate. If Galileo had kept his observations to himself, the study of astronomy as a whole would have suffered. Similarly, it is important that research psychologists contribute to the scientific (and, where relevant, the general) community.

This participation takes many forms. Nowadays many psychologists are keen to discuss their research on television and radio, in newspapers and popular books. Here they have to justify their work to the general public. Just what qualifies as success here is quite a moot point, but the researchers would probably conclude that they had been successful if their research became widely known, if it had some impact on the policy of relevant bodies (e.g., government agencies) or if they benefited commercially (e.g., by selling a lot of books).

Researchers also commonly present their ideas and findings at conferences. These vary in terms of the composition both of the audience and of the speakers: from the most general (e.g., a conference on 'violence in the general community' that attracts people with different reasons for being there and from all walks of life) to the most specific (e.g., a workshop on 'cognitive development in early childhood'). Here the quality of the research might be gauged by the applause of the audience, the tone of the questions asked of the presenter, or the extension of an invitation to return next year. In some cases, too, the proceedings of these conferences are published, either formally or informally.

For most academic psychologists, however, the most important benchmark (or 'performance indicator') is their ability to publish their research in scholarly journals and books. The contributions to the more prestigious of these are handled by academic editors and the merits of the research are evaluated (often anonymously) by other experts in the field. On the basis of their judgement the editor will either reject the research or, usually only after revision, accept it for publication. Many journals publish less than 20% of the papers that are submitted to them.

This process of public exposure allows psychological research not only to be communicated, but also to be checked, both by the researchers' peers and by other scientists and members of the general public. This process of public scrutiny is a way of seeking to ensure that research satisfies the principles of good research that we have discussed above. For example, it allows other people to challenge the interpretation of research findings or to attempt to reproduce them themselves – thereby testing both the validity and the reliability of the research. This scrutiny can be uncomfortable and sometimes even humiliating, especially when it involves criticism. But opening research up to the *possibility* of such criticism is generally considered to be an important way of ensuring its integrity.

Finally, in an era when accountability (to both the public and the scientific community) is seen as an important means of justifying research funding, it is likely that researchers who are not prepared to make their work public will receive less support for doing research in the future.

Q2.3**

Which of the following statements is true?

(a) If a finding is reliable it should be easy to replicate.
(b) If a finding is reliable it will also be valid.
(c) If a finding is reliable it will be important.
(d) If a finding is reliable it must be an example of good scientific practice.
(e) If a finding is reliable it has been correctly interpreted.

The correct answer is (a). Reliability relates to the ability to reproduce or replicate a finding. Many reliable findings are incorrectly interpreted (i.e., invalid), so (b) and (e) are wrong. Reliability is also different from (though sometimes confused with) importance (a point we will discuss in more detail in later chapters), so (c) is wrong. Many examples of bad scientific practice produce findings that are reliable, too, so it is important not to fall into the trap presented by (d) – though many researchers do.

parsimony The goal of accounting for the maximum number of empirical findings in terms of the smallest number of theoretical principles. The most parsimonious theory is the one that accounts for the most findings using the fewest principles.
reliability The extent to which a given finding will be consistently reproduced. A reliable finding is one that is consistently reproduced

replication A research finding that reproduces another which has been
  obtained previously.
study A piece of empirical research.
validity The extent to which a given finding shows what it is believed to
  show. A valid finding is one that has been logically and correctly
  interpreted.

Some notes of caution

In writing this chapter we have tried to make it clear that few (if any) of
the practices we describe would be subscribed to by all researchers in
psychology. Most would agree with many of the criteria identified
above and with the use of the scientific method, but many would also
question the role of theory and other explanatory frameworks in the
discipline, or suggest that these serve very different purposes to those we
have outlined. Moreover, even if researchers *believe* that they adhere to
many of these principles, it is possible to argue that they do not in
practice.

In the case of parsimony, for example, many researchers have argued
that there are actually competitive pressures in the 'industry' of
psychological research that lead researchers to develop mini-theories
that address quite specific phenomena in preference to grand theories
with broader applicability (e.g., Aronson, 1997). One reason for this is
that mini-theories allow researchers to work in their own well-defined
territory and to have the prestige that goes with it, with less pressure
from rival theorists. On the other hand, grand theories (and grand
theorists) can be quite threatening and are often seen to be unnecessarily imperialistic.

So – as the title of this chapter suggests – the scientific principles we
have discussed are at the very best *ideals*. And even then they are ideals
that not all psychologists would endorse. Nevertheless, they are ideals
that most psychologists would *recognize* and as such they play an
important part in researchers' attempts to understand what they do
and to represent that understanding to other people.

At the heart of this point is a recognition of the fact that all science is
a profoundly *human* enterprise. In spite of attempts to represent science
as utterly impartial and objective, it is always shaped by the world in
which it takes place – a world of politics, economics, ideology and
history. The impact of the Second World War on the things psychologists studied and the kinds of explanation they developed makes this
point clear (a point which can also be made by thinking about the
things that physicists were doing around this time). In the wake of the

Holocaust in which millions of people from different groups were exterminated by the Nazis, people were much more concerned to investigate issues of prejudice and group hatred and to explain these either in terms of pathological personality factors (like propensity to Fascism) or in terms of the need for group members to justify and encourage social conflict.

Curiously, then, the processes which contribute to people's belief in a theory or which lead them to test a particular hypothesis are actually affected by many of the things which psychologists themselves study. For example, they may depend on how committed researchers are to the theory, their perceptions of the other people who endorse the theory, what makes sense to them, and their own self-interest. Many would argue that what psychologists believe (and what they do not believe) is as much to do with these human factors as it is to do with abstract principles like parsimony and validity. However, we raise this point more to urge you to think broadly and openly about the principles we have discussed in this chapter than to open the door on further debate.

Further reading

A large number of books provide useful discussions of the nature of research in psychology and the scientific status of that research. Valentine's (1982) book is typical of these and deals with a large number of important issues from the nature of explanation to the role of computer simulation in psychology. Chalmers (1978) provides an engaging discussion of the philosophy of science that has very broad relevance – not just to psychologists.

Chalmers, A. F. (1978). *What is this thing called science?* Milton Keynes: Open University Press.
Valentine, E. R. (1982). *Conceptual issues in psychology.* London: Allen & Unwin.

Objective and ideals: A checklist for research evaluation and improvement

Potential problem	Question to ask	Potential improvement
Empirical weakness	Do researchers have sufficient empirical evidence to back up their claims about particular psychological processes or states?	Consider carefully the relationship between the claims that researchers make and the empirical evidence they use to back up those claims. In particular, try to identify empirical gaps and to consider assumptions that are implicit in the arguments presented. Where gaps exist, or

27

Potential problem	Question to ask	Potential improvement
		assumptions appear questionable, consider conducting empirical research that clarifies matters and advances understanding of the relevant processes and states. The decision to conduct this research should be tempered by the importance of any problems you identify and of the research question as a whole.
Theoretical weakness	Have researchers integrated their empirical findings within a sufficiently broad and sufficiently plausible explanatory framework?	Consider how well researchers have succeeded in reconciling the range of empirical findings on a given topic and whether any integrated analysis they provide allows predictions to be made which extend beyond existing empirical work. Where necessary, seek to develop an appropriate theory that performs these functions and devise novel empirical studies that enable it to be tested.
Inductive reasoning	Have researchers developed an understanding of a particular issue simply by generalizing on the basis of prior empirical observations (i.e., without developing an appropriate theory)?	Develop a theory that explains previous findings and allows novel predictions to be tested.
Redescription; circular argument	Does a given psychological theory simply redescribe particular empirical findings rather than explain them?	Examine the content of psychological theory closely. If redescription is being presented as explanation, develop a critique along these lines and attempt to develop an alternative theory that explains why particular empirical findings arise and that can be tested in further empirical research.
Reification	Does a given psychological theory suggest that particular empirical findings are the	Examine the content of psychological theory closely. If you find evidence of reification, develop a critique along these lines and consider

Potential problem	Question to ask	Potential improvement
	unmediated expression of an underlying psychological process?	alternatives to the explanation provided. Devise research that tests between these alternative explanations and the one proposed in the original research.
Limited reliability	Can a particular empirical finding be replicated?	If the reliability of an empirical finding appears questionable, attempt to replicate it before proceeding to more elaborate tests or extensions of a theory.
Limited validity	Does a particular empirical finding show what researchers believe it to show?	Try to develop an alternative explanation of the empirical finding in question. If this alternative explanation appears plausible, devise empirical research that tests it competitively against the explanation proposed in the original research.
Non-cumulativeness	Does a particular piece of research draw from and attempt to develop existing knowledge?	Where a particular piece of research appears to have overlooked previous research or to have failed to draw connections with a relevant body of literature, point this out. If necessary, conduct additional research which clarifies the nature and importance of these links.
Lack of parsimony	Does a particular theory appear to be unnecessarily complicated or to contain too many qualifying statements?	If a theory appears to be unparsimonious, try to devise a simpler theory (one that contains fewer explanatory principles but explains as many, or more, empirical findings). Having done this, devise a study that subjects the two theories to a competitive test.
Lack of scrutiny	Has a researcher subjected their findings and conclusions to peer review?	If research has not been subjected to stringent peer review (e.g., by relevant psychological journals) it is prudent to treat it with some scepticism. When commentators on a particular topic assert that 'research has shown...', ask whether this is really the case and whether this is *all* that research has shown. Where you identify an error, attempt to correct it on the basis of evidence that is empirically and theoretically sound.

Potential problem	Question to ask	Potential improvement
Lack of accountability	Has a researcher endeavoured to promote an understanding of their research in the broader community?	Where relevant, psychologists have a responsibility to contribute to public debate by communicating their research findings to a non-academic audience. Consider ways of doing this which promote informed debate rather than reinforce popular myths or prejudices.

Q2.4*

Which of the following statements is true?

(a) The major goal of science is to identify as many facts as possible.
(b) The major goal of science is to develop as many theories as possible.
(c) The major goal of science is to explain as many facts as possible with the smallest number of theoretical principles.
(d) The major goal of science is to do as much research as possible with as little money.
(e) Both (a) and (b).

Q2.5**

Which of the following is *not* a widely accepted feature of good research?

(a) It should be public.
(b) It should be cumulative.
(c) It should be valid.
(d) It should be reliable.
(e) It should support a theory.

Q2.6***

Which of the following statements is true?

(a) All research in psychology is concerned with the development of explanatory theory.
(b) All research in psychology shows commitment to the scientific method.
(c) All research in psychology uses the scientific method even if researchers do not believe in it.
(d) The interpretation of all research in psychology is open to question, like that of all scientific research.
(e) None of the above.

Q2.7***

After reading some research on the topic of students' attitudes to university courses, Mark does some research to find out what students' favourite subject at university is. In this he finds that final-year psychology students prefer studying psychology to any other subject. On this basis he concludes that psychology is the most popular subject. However, Jane argues that this conclusion is wrong as the research actually shows that students prefer the subject they end up studying. What is the basis of her objection to Mark's research?

(a) The research is invalid.
(b) The research is unreliable.
(c) The research is non-cumulative.
(d) The research is unparsimonious.
(e) None of the above.

The correct answer to 2.4 is (c). This is the essence of the point made by Gribbin and Rees (1990) – and of the statement by Einstein that 'the grand aim of all science is to cover the greatest number of empirical facts by logical deduction from the smallest number of hypotheses or axioms'. If science were only concerned to generate more and more information (whether in the form of data or theory) it would grind to a halt under the burden – so (a), (b) and (e) are incorrect. (d) may be true for some scientists (and those who fund them), but it is not the major aim of science.

The correct answer to 2.5 is (e). Research should be public, cumulative, valid and reliable, but in order to be these things it does not necessarily have to support a theory, it may in fact contradict it.

The correct answer to 2.6 is (d). We noted at the end of this chapter that the conduct of psychological research is a human enterprise and that as such its output is always interpreted by people with particular values, beliefs and expectations. As these change, so too may the interpretation of even the most widely accepted wisdom. This is true of all science, so this fact does not make psychology any less scientific than, say, physics (although physical scientists are usually very keen to affirm the objectivity of what they do). Answers (a), (b) and (c) are true of much psychological research, but certainly not all of it. As we noted in the last section of the chapter, at best (a) and (b) are *ideals* to which some (but not all) researchers aspire.

The correct answer to 2.7 is (a). Jane is arguing that Mark's research does not show what he thinks it shows – i.e., that it is invalid. There is no reason to think either that if Mark did his research again he would not get exactly the same results, or that his research did not build on the previous research he had read about. So neither the reliability of his work nor its cumulative basis is being called into question. Jane's analysis is also no more parsimonious than Mark's – it still explains the findings in terms of one explanatory principle.

Discussion/essay questions

(a) What is the role of theory *in* psychological research?

(b) Is psychology a science or a pseudo-science?

(c) Does the scientific method unnecessarily restrict psychological enquiry?

(d) Can psychological research ever be completely valid?

(e) What role does the principle of parsimony play in psychological research and in science in general?

Exercises

(a) From the material you have studied in other psychology courses to date, identify an explanation of a phenomenon that has been proposed in the literature, and ask the following questions:

  (i) Is the explanation a theory?

  (ii) How many principles are involved in this explanation?

  (iii) Are there competing explanations that represent alternatives to this explanation?

  (iv) What form does the public evidence in favour of the explanation take?

  (v) Does the research conform to the ideals identified in this chapter?

(b) A widely replicated phenomenon is the 'cocktail party effect'. This refers to the fact that people can be listening to one conversation in a crowded and noisy room but nevertheless hear their own name mentioned in another conversation – even though they have no awareness of that conversation.

(i) Write down in 25 words or less an account of why you think this happens. Then look up 'selective attention' in the index of a psychology textbook to see what explanations previous researchers have proposed.

(ii) Does your account bear any resemblance to any of these explanations? What are the key differences between your account and the textbook explanation?

3

Research Methods

In the previous chapter we asked why researchers do research in psychology and what they are looking for when they do. If a researcher has decided to go ahead and conduct research, the next obvious question is 'What different research strategies are available?'.

Our response to this question starts with an examination of the things that psychologists measure and of the basic types of psychological measurement. We then look in turn at the four major research methods that psychologists employ in order to conduct research: (a) experimental, (b) quasi-experimental, (c) survey and (d) case study. The strengths and limitations of each of these methods are considered in separate sections in which we also discuss the basis on which researchers choose among them. This choice can be difficult to make and quite controversial. But as we shall see, it is often affected by factors over which the researcher has limited control.

Psychological measurement

In the previous chapter we noted that one of the things that differentiates psychology from other sciences is the fact that the things in which psychologists are typically interested – mental states and processes – can *never* be directly observed or measured. You cannot touch or see a mood, a thought, a disposition, a memory or an attitude. Instead, you can only observe things that are associated with these phenomena. This does not mean that the phenomena themselves are any less real, it simply means that they can be hard to get a handle on.

Of course the difficulty of observing and measuring phenomena of interest also exists in other sciences such as astronomy and chemistry, but in these fields this problem has often been solved by making relevant technological advances. For instance, difficulties that are caused by an inability to observe distant stars have led to the development of more powerful telescopes. Technology in psychology and related fields has made significant advances, too. It is now possible to monitor blood flow through the brain and a range of electrical signals within it. Similarly, technology exists to test reaction times and various other subtle and non-conscious responses. But these still only allow psychologists to study the *outcomes* of mental activity, or things that are *associated* with it – never the activity itself.

You might think that this constitutes such a serious impediment to research that it makes the whole enterprise of trying to study psychology futile. Indeed, just such a belief underpinned the emergence of **behaviourism** as a major approach to psychology in the 1920s. Proponents of this view (notably J.B. Watson and later B.F. Skinner) asserted that human behaviour could be understood without the need to examine, or even posit the existence of, internal states such as thoughts or emotions.

Nevertheless, the fact that something cannot be seen does *not* mean that hypotheses about its nature cannot be put forward and tested. Physicists have never seen sub-atomic particles or black holes, yet scientific analysis of their effects has been crucial to theoretical and practical advances in that field. The same is true in psychology, in which researchers generally use different forms of measurement to inform them about two types of psychological phenomenon: **stable psychological characteristics** (such as intelligence, personality or certain types of belief) and **dynamic mental processes** (such as memory, mood or judgement).

Both of these aspects of mental life are examined using similar measurement **instruments**. The primary difference is that when researchers examine dynamic processes they are usually interested in obtaining an on-the-spot measurement which they will compare with others obtained under different conditions. In contrast, to examine characteristics researchers usually administer particular **psychological tests**. These will either already exist or will be devised by the researchers. The tests generally seek to make judgements about any one individual by comparing their responses to those of the general population. They do this to make statements about an individual's relative position on the **dimension** in question (e.g., IQ, verbal reasoning, neuroticism, depression). In the case of widely used clinical and educational tests, the process of developing these tests in order to establish their reliability and validity is usually very extensive.

In conducting research into mental processes and characteristics, researchers have three main measurement options available to them. Most commonly, they can use **behavioural measures**. These study particular forms of behaviour and make inferences about the psycho-logical phenomena that caused or contributed to them. These measures come in a wide range of forms and are usually tailored to the specific question in which the researcher is interested. For example, the type of toy that children play with when given a choice (e.g., whether it is a gun or a teddy bear) can be used as a measure of their aggressiveness (Bandura, Ross, & Ross, 1961). Alternatively, finding out whether a person can recall more words that start with a 'k' than words that have 'k' as their third letter can tell a researcher something about the processes involved in the operation and organization of memory (Tversky & Kahneman, 1974). As a final example, discovering whether young children can imagine what a three-dimensional scene looks like from someone else's perspective might enable inferences to be made about the role which the self plays in the process of organizing and representing visual information (Piaget, 1952). By the same token, the performance of any individual child on this task may tell a researcher something about the state of the child's intellectual development.

A second measurement option is to use **self-report measures**, which ask people about their thoughts, feelings or reaction to a given issue. Providing that it is possible for people to reflect consciously on the relevant thoughts or behaviours, the responses they make can be used either to supplement other behavioural measures or as data in them-selves. Again these can be used to gain insight into both processes and states. So, the fact that people evaluate another person more favourably if they believe that that person belongs to the same group as themselves may tell us something about the process of stereotyping (Tajfel, 1970). On the other hand, people's responses to a large number of questions about their lifestyle and personal habits can be used to make inferences about their personality (e.g., Hathaway & McKinley, 1943). Here the unusual nature of a person's beliefs may lead a clinician to suspect that the person is psychologically disturbed (e.g., Eysenck & Eysenck, 1985).

Finally, researchers can use **physiological measures** to examine things that are believed to be directly associated with particular forms of mental activity. These can be thought of as measures of mental traces (i.e., of things associated with mental activity, whether conscious or not). For example, measures such as heart rate or galvanic skin response (GSR, a measure of the electrical conductivity of the skin) can serve as measures of anxiety or arousal (e.g., as associated with different emotional states such as anger, happiness or disgust; Ekman, Levenson, & Frieson, 1983). Similarly, measures of blood flow or electrical activity in the brain may tell us about the neural structures that are involved in particular forms of mental activity (e.g., reading aloud;

Lassen, Ingvar, & Skinhøj, 1978). These same data can also inform researchers about a person's enduring mental state – for example, informing them that they have generally low arousal levels or are suffering from a particular form of brain damage.

Although they are used primarily (but not exclusively) to make inferences about behaviour rather than psychological states or processes, it is worth adding here that **behavioural trace measures** are also widely employed in some areas of psychology (e.g., environmental, consumer and organizational). These involve obtaining physical traces of people's behaviour to inform researchers about what people are currently doing or have done in the past. Again, these measures take many different forms. For example, the amount of electricity being used in a town might be used to infer whether its residents are asleep or awake. Similarly, the sales of a particular edition of a newspaper could tell researchers something about the level of interest in a particular topic. More mundanely, an examination of people's garbage could provide information about their lifestyle or eating habits.

Decisions about which of the above measures to use will be dictated by a number of factors. Many of these are practical and will be linked to other methodological choices that we will discuss in the following sections. For example, self-report measures are relatively cheap and easy to administer, and so lend themselves to survey-based research examining large numbers of people in naturalistic settings. On the other hand, physiological measures can be difficult and expensive to obtain and so they are usually used only in experimental research using very few participants. However, decisions about which of these measures to use are guided as much by the particular question a researcher wants to address as by these pragmatic considerations.

Whatever choice a researcher makes, one point to emphasize about all these measurement options is that *none of them provides a pure or direct measure* of the variables in which researchers are interested. In all cases it is possible that the measures will be contaminated by other things, and that this may cloud interpretation of the data. For example, the toys that children play with may be a reflection of the aggressiveness of their parents, rather than their own aggressiveness. People's responses to a questionnaire may give insights into prevailing social norms (i.e., what people think is appropriate) rather than their personality. Skin conductance may measure people's excitement when it is intended to measure their anxiety.

These 'other things' in which the researcher is not immediately interested are referred to as **extraneous variables**. Because they adversely affect researchers' ability to interpret their findings correctly they can pose serious threats to the validity of a study or an entire research programme. This is a point to which researchers need to be continually alert. It is often dealt with either by using *multiple* measures or – as we will discuss below – by conducting controlled experiments to rule out the influence of a particular variable.

One other feature of psychological measurement that distinguishes it from measurement procedures in some other sciences is that it normally involves taking multiple observations. This might mean measuring more than one person or measuring the same person more than once. Some of the reasons for doing this are easy to see. If we were to base knowledge on one person's response to a single question or task, our research finding might tell us something about the particular characteristics of the person we chose to measure but very little about the **population** in general. For this reason we would probably be quite worried about the *reliability* of the finding.

To make the ramifications of this point clearer, imagine that you were concerned to find out how much reading ability 10-year-old children have. If you measured just one girl's ability you might get a distorted picture because you selected a child who had very high or very low ability. For reasons that we will explain in much greater detail in later chapters, you would want to guard against these possibilities by selecting a large **sample** of children to participate in your research. In order to get an accurate picture you would also want to avoid systematically selecting children of high or low ability.

You might argue that although you need to measure quite a few children to get an accurate picture of 10-year-olds' reading ability, a single measure of one child's ability would be sufficient to tell you what that particular child's ability is. In fact, though, were you to do this, the problem of reliability would come up again. Perhaps the child was having a bad day, or was ill on the day of the test, or was bad at the particular test chosen (but good in general), so that her score was not a good measure of her true ability. To guard against these possibilities there is no alternative but to take multiple measures.

In short, variability in responses means that psychological measurement normally involves taking large samples of observations from a population to reduce uncertainty about the conclusions we should draw. We also normally want to ensure that the sample is drawn from a population in a way that does not bias the results.

The easiest and best way to get an unbiased sample from a population is to draw a **random sample** from that population. One of the things that this means is that we need to select people to participate in our research in such a way that everyone in the population has an equal chance of being included. Often this procedure will also necessitate obtaining participants from a *sub-population* that is *available* to be studied. If we wish to **generalize** the results of our research to another situation we need to ensure that the sample we study is a random sample of any sub-population we have drawn it from, *and* that the sub-population is *representative* of the broader population on characteristics that we want to make generalizations about.

The extent to which we can do this varies from issue to issue. If we want to establish how colour perception works in humans then we need to sample from a sub-population that we believe has similar perceptual characteristics to the one we ultimately want to generalize to (the population in general). For example, a perceptual psychologist may believe that first-year university students are identical to the population in general in terms of their ability to perceive colour. Under this assumption the sampling procedure works in this way:

$$\text{sample characteristics} \approx \text{sub-population characteristics}$$

$$\approx \text{population characteristics}$$

This is represented in Figure 3.1. The proportions of black and white rectangles in the sample are the same as in the specific sub-population and in the population in general. If white squares represent people with good colour vision and black squares represent people with poor colour vision then we can see that the proportions of people with good and poor colour vision are the same in all three groups. In other words, the sample characteristics are approximately the same as those of the specific sub-population which are approximately the same as those of the population in general.

This strategy is reasonable providing we can assume that the sub-population is similar to the population in general. This seems a

Sample   Sub-population   Population in general

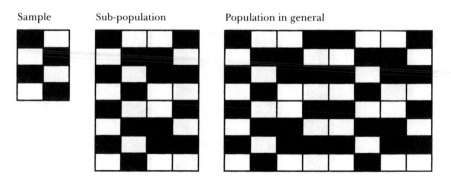

Figure 3.1 A sample with characteristics similar to those of the sub-population and the population

plausible assumption for colour vision and until somebody provides a plausible theory that would explain why the colour vision of university students should be different from the population in general, it makes sense for perceptual psychologists to continue to obtain research samples in this way.

However, for a researcher interested in estimating a population's attitudes to the environment or their IQ, this assumption would probably not hold. In particular, this is because university students might have more favourable attitudes to the environment and higher IQs than the population in general. For the example of attitudes to the environment, the following model would hold:

$$(\text{Sample characteristics} \approx \text{sub-population characteristics})$$

$$\neq \text{population characteristics}$$

If the black rectangles in Figure 3.2 represent negative attitudes to the environment, we can see that the prevalence of these negative attitudes is greater in the population than in the sub-population or the sample. Thus although the sample has similar characteristics to the sub-population it is quite different from the population in general. The implication is that if we want to find out about the nature of attitudes to the environment in the population then we need to study people from a sub-population that is more representative of the population in general. In fact the best strategy here is to take a random sample directly from the population.

The next question that one might ask is whether it is ever possible to generalize results about things like IQ or attitudes from a sample drawn from a sub-population that differs from the population in general. The answer is 'yes', but only where the population is similar in *relevant* ways. So although we might not be able to estimate the IQ of the general population from a sample drawn from a particular sub-population,

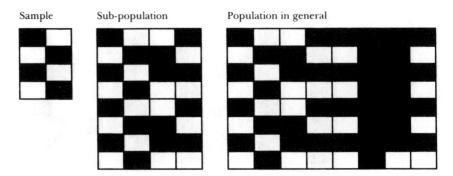

Figure 3.2 A sample with characteristics similar to those of the sub-population but different from those of the population

we *might* be able to estimate the effect of Wonder Drug X on the general population's intelligence by measuring the effect of the drug on a sample of university students. We are only able to do this, however, if we assume that the drug has the same *effect* on university students (or very intelligent people) as it does on everybody else. Clearly, these are quite complex issues and we will deal with them more thoroughly as we progress through the book.

Q3.1[**]

Which of the following statements is *not* true?

(a) Psychological measurement can involve the measurement of phenomena believed to be related to a given psychological state or process.
(b) Psychological measurement can involve the measurement of behaviour believed to result from a given psychological state or process.
(c) Psychological measurement can involve self-reports of behaviour believed to be related to a given psychological state or process.
(d) Psychological measurement can involve the self-reports of a sample drawn from a particular sub-population.
(e) Psychological measurement can involve direct examination of psychological states and processes.

The correct answer is (e). Although many people think that psychologists specialize in reading people's minds, this is not actually possible. Consequently, psychological research is based upon *in*direct measures of mental states and processes which include all of the possibilities outlined in statements (a) to (d).

behavioural measures Measures designed to gain insight into particular psychological states or processes that require participants to perform particular activities or tasks.
behavioural trace measures Measures designed to gain insight into behaviour that examine phenomena associated with that behaviour. For example, footprints in the sand could provide a behavioural trace of where people have walked, and this could be used to measure people's preference for particular parts of a beach.
behaviourism An approach to psychology which asserts that human behaviour can be understood in terms of directly observable relationships (in particular, between a stimulus and a response)

without having to refer to underlying mental states. Behaviourism was the dominant approach to psychology for most of the first half of the twentieth century.

dimension Any property of people or things on which they can differ (e.g., intelligence or height). Different people and things can therefore be situated or placed at different points along any dimension and it is possible to differentiate between them in terms of the positions they occupy (e.g., for measurement or assessment purposes).

dynamic mental processes Aspects of psychology that are seen to be common to people in general, but which are changeable over time (e.g., mood and judgement).

extraneous variable Any variable that is not of immediate interest to a researcher but which may pose a threat to validity because it compromises the interpretation of research findings. This is usually because it obscures the measurement of processes of interest.

generalization The process of making statements about the general population on the basis of relevant research (e.g., experiments or surveys).

instrument Any procedure or device used to assess or measure psychological or behavioural phenomena (e.g., intelligence, attitudes, eye movements).

physiological measures Measures of physiological states or processes (e.g., skin conductance and blood flow) used in psychological research to gain insight into particular psychological states or processes.

population The complete set of events, people or things that a researcher is interested in and from which any sample is taken.

psychological tests Measurement procedures used to identify a person's mental state relative to other people (or population norms). These typically involve large numbers of questions or tasks. Test reliability and validity are established through extensive research.

random sample A *sample* in which each member of the population has the same probability of being included. This is ensured by random selection methods (e.g., by drawing lots).

sample Either the group of participants from which a particular set of responses is obtained or that set of responses itself.

self-report measures Measures designed to gain insight into particular psychological states or processes that ask participants to reflect on their own mental processes or behaviour.

stable psychological characteristics Aspects of psychology that are seen to be relatively enduring over time and to be properties of particular individuals (e.g., personality and intelligence).

The experimental method

Using any or all of the above measurement strategies, psychologists often choose to investigate particular research questions by conducting **experiments**. These attempt *systematically to manipulate theoretically relevant variables and to examine the effect of these manipulations on outcome variables*. In order to clarify the meaning of the jargon in this statement (in particular, the terms **variable** and **manipulation**), we can state slightly less technically that experiments are attempts to change some aspect of a person's situation or mental state which is both of interest to the researcher (i.e., an aspect that is theoretically relevant) and capable of being altered (i.e., an aspect that is variable). The experimenters then look at the effect of this change on an aspect of the person's behaviour, which can also vary and on which the first aspect is believed to have some impact.

The most important point here is that experiments usually involve active intervention on the part of the researcher. Experimenters do not just sit back and watch what is going on in the world; instead they attempt to make some change to the world and then monitor the impact of that change. If a male friend of yours is feeling unhappy and you want to find out how to make him more cheerful, you could do one of three things. You could wait for him to cheer up and then see if you can infer what was responsible for his mood change, or you could ask him directly what would make him feel better. Alternatively, you could *intervene*. That is, you could actually do something to change your friend's circumstances (perhaps by taking him out for a meal) and see whether this intervention has any effect. This third strategy closely resembles the one that researchers adopt when they conduct experiments.

To examine what experiments involve more closely, we can refer back to the 'physical reinforcement theory' that we talked about in the previous chapter. As you may recall, this theory proposed that attraction to a person requires constant reinforcement if it is to be sustained. If a researcher were interested in human relationships, he or she might very well want to explore this idea in more depth. An experiment with this aim might involve manipulating the amount of physical reinforcement that a person received from someone else. The researcher would then look at the effects of different amounts of reinforcement on the person's feelings of attraction. In this example, then, physical reinforcement is the *theoretically relevant variable which is manipulated* and attraction is the *relevant outcome variable*.

To flesh out this example in more detail, one way in which such an experiment could be conducted would be to take a sample of 100 people who are in relationships from a given population and stop 50 of them seeing their partners at all for a given period (perhaps a month). These 50 people are an **experimental group** because they have been subjected to the relevant experimental **treatment** (in this case withdrawal of physical reinforcement). The other 50 people would not be deprived of their partner's company in this way, but would be allowed to continue interacting as normal. Because they are not subjected to experimental treatment, these 50 people represent a **control group**. Another way of describing the design of this study is to say that it has two **conditions** – that is, two different *levels of treatment* – in this case an experimental condition and a control condition. It should be noted, though, that an experiment does not necessarily have to incorporate a control group – it can consist of two experimental groups instead.

You may have noticed that the terms we have introduced here are also commonly used in other areas of scientific research. For example, in medical drug trials patients who receive a new treatment are referred to as the experimental group and patients who receive conventional treatment or no treatment are called the control group. Note, too, that the people who take part in an experiment (indeed, in any form of research) are usually identified by a special term that distinguishes them from members of the general population who do not take part. Traditionally such people have been referred to as **subjects**. However, the term **participants** is now recommended by major groups of psychologists (in particular, the American Psychological Association). These groups prefer the term 'participants' because it is seen to be less demeaning to the people it refers to. This is the term we shall use in this book.

Going back to our experiment, after the experimental manipulation (i.e., separation) had been implemented and given time to have some effect (in this case after a month in which the experimental group had undergone separation but the control group had not) the researchers would be interested in looking at how attracted to their partners all the participants in this study were. In other words, they have to measure attraction. They could do this in lots of ways – for example, by asking participants to fill in a questionnaire (a self-report measure) or by seeing how much time they wanted to spend together (a behavioural measure). A range of physiological measures could also be employed.

Let us say that on the basis of theory and past research the experimenters decided to measure attraction by monitoring how much time participants spend with their partners at weekends (by asking them to keep diaries). Here the researchers would be particularly interested to see whether the behaviour of participants in

the experimental group differed from the behaviour of participants
in the control group. Specifically, they would want to see if participants
in the experimental group were less attracted to their partners, as this is
what 'physical reinforcement theory' predicts – that a reduction in
actual contact should reduce attraction to a partner (that 'absence
leads the heart to wander').

In this example, then, there are two variables in which the researcher
is interested. In fact *all* experiments include these two different types
of variable and each is given a different name. The variable that is
systematically manipulated (in this case physical reinforcement) is
referred to as the **independent variable** (or **IV**). This can also be
thought of as the treatment variable. The outcome variable that is
measured after the manipulation has been carried out (time spent
together) is called the **dependent variable** (or **DV**). Because they
involve measurement of outcomes, dependent variables are sometimes
called 'dependent measures'.

It is important to have a clear grasp of these terms and what they
mean, because they are recurrent features of research terminology.
People often get the two terms confused (largely because they sound so
similar), but one way to think about the difference between them is to
remember that the dependent variable is measured *after* the independent variable has been manipulated. So the dependent variable *depends*
on the experimental manipulation. The letter 'd' is also a useful
memory aid as the *d*ependent variable provides the experimental *d*ata.

In experiments, independent variables are manipulated by the
experimenter. In general, independent variables are *causal* variables
and dependent variables are *effect* variables. In other words, change in
the independent variable is expected to cause change in the dependent
variable.

This point about the causal impact of the independent variable goes
to the heart of why researchers actually conduct experiments. This is
because in any experiment where there is a substantial change in the
dependent variable, this allows the researcher to make the logically
appropriate **causal inference** that this change *must* be due to manipulation of the independent variable. It also follows from points made in
the final section of the previous chapter, that if we can correctly *interpret*
the reasons for this change (i.e., if we can say exactly why the
independent variable had the effect it did), then our interpretation of
the experiment will be *valid*. If an interpretation of what causes change
in any dependent variable is correct, the experiment as a whole will
have what is referred to as **internal validity**. We will discuss these
points in more detail in the next chapter.

Q3.2*

A researcher conducts an experiment which tests the hypothesis that 'anxiety has an adverse effect on students' exam performance'. Which of the following statements is true?

(a) Anxiety is the dependent variable, exam performance is the independent variable.
(b) Anxiety is the dependent variable, students are the independent variable.
(c) Anxiety is the independent variable, students are the dependent variable.
(d) Anxiety is the independent variable, exam performance is the dependent variable.
(e) Students are the dependent variable, exam performance is the independent variable.

The correct answer is (d). In the experiment, the experimenter will be concerned to examine the impact that manipulations of anxiety have on students' exam performance. The independent (manipulated) variable is therefore anxiety and the dependent (outcome) variable is performance. This is because performance is hypothesized to be dependent on anxiety. Note, too, that students are not variables in this (or any other) study, they are the participants.

There is only one point which qualifies the above statements about our ability to draw causal inferences from experimental methods. However, this point is *extremely* important. It is that in order to have complete confidence in the correctness of a causal inference, conditions *must be identical in every respect* except for differences in the treatment (i.e., the independent variable). To be at least reasonably confident we must therefore take steps to equate the conditions.

Why must we equate the conditions in this way? The answer is that unless we know that the groups were similar *before* we manipulated the independent variable we cannot be sure that any differences between the groups that we observe later are due to that experimental manipulation. So, unless we equate the groups in this way, we cannot conduct a proper experiment.

The next obvious question is 'How should we equate the groups?'. There is one very good way. This is to allocate participants randomly to different conditions – through a procedure known as **random assignment**. Why randomly? The long answer appeals to a knowledge of some statistical principles that we will talk about in later chapters.

The short answer is that this procedure ensures that the experiment does not *build in differences* between groups – either on significant dimensions (their sex, wealth, age, intelligence or personality) or seemingly trivial ones (their eye colour, hair length or length of surname). Accordingly, randomization involves *strictly unsystematic* assignment of participants to conditions (e.g., based on the toss of a coin or the roll of a die).

We can use an extreme example to help make it clear why this is important. Imagine that in our separation and attraction experiment all the participants we assigned to the experimental condition were men and all the participants we assigned to the control condition were women. In this case if we found that participants in the experimental condition were less attracted to their partners than those in the control condition, this would not *necessarily* arise from the fact that participants in the experimental condition had been starved of company. Instead, it *could* be due to the fact that these participants were men and that men in general like their partners less than women do.

Even the most trivial systematic difference can undermine a researcher's ability to make an appropriate causal inference. For example, a researcher might place people into different conditions on the basis of their position on a roll: putting people whose names are late in the alphabet in the control condition and those with names early in the alphabet in the experimental condition. But by doing this the researcher may inadvertently build ethnic differences into the two groups – so that people from one geographical region (perhaps where names starting with Y and Z are common) are in one condition and people from another region in the other. In this case any difference observed on the dependent variable might therefore be due to differences in ethnicity rather than differences in physical reinforcement. It may, for example, reflect the fact that non-Caucasians (whose names may generally start with letters early in the alphabet) are more attracted to their partners than Caucasians. However, ethnicity is just one of the many dimensions on which people with different last names *may* differ and it is impossible to say that none of these will have any impact on attractiveness.

The primary strength of the experimental method, though, is that, *providing participants are randomly assigned to conditions*, researchers can be sure that effects observed on the dependent variable are due to one of two things: their manipulation of the independent variable or chance. In this way, it gives researchers **experimental control** over both what they investigate and the causal interpretation of their findings. Furthermore, as we shall see in later chapters, through appropriate use of statistics (which quantify chance) and by using sufficiently large experimental samples we can ensure that experimental research findings will generalize to the population at large.

As we discussed earlier, in order to generalize, the researcher must ensure that the participants in an experiment are *representative* of that general population on relevant dimensions – that they constitute a **representative sample**. For example, in our study of separation and attraction we might need to ensure that the social skills and physical attractiveness of the participants were similar to those of the general population. We will return to this point in the next chapter.

Yet while experimental findings allow researchers to be confident that there is something to explain, experiments do not always allow researchers to know how to interpret their findings. In other words, it can often be hard to establish an experiment's internal validity. This is because it is much easier to ascertain *that* an independent variable has had an effect than it is to ascertain *why* it has had an effect.

Problems in establishing an experiment's internal validity often occur when experimenters do not really manipulate what they think they are manipulating but actually manipulate something else. Thinking about our experiment on separation and attraction, it should be relatively easy to establish that separating participants from their partners reduces attraction to them, but it is much harder to conclude with certainty that this is due to a lack of physical reinforcement (the independent variable we wanted to manipulate). What we may have manipulated instead is just the participants' *opportunity to meet new people*, and it may be this variable that leads to the effects we observe. That is, participants in the experimental group may have become less attracted to their partners because they met lots of new people which participants in the control group did not have the opportunity to do. Where alternative explanations of experimental outcomes like this are identified it is often because the experiment involves an *unintended* manipulation of an extraneous variable. The technical term for unintentionally manipulating variables is **confounding**, and this is quite common in experimental research. It is certainly true that many disagreements between researchers are based on differing views about the existence of confounds and about what exactly experimenters have manipulated in their experiments.

We can use another example to reinforce this point. Imagine that some researchers are interested in the effect that a lack of space has on psychological distress. To investigate this they may put 50 people in a small room for 2 hours and 50 people in an open field for the same amount of time. As they expect, they may find that the people in the room get more distressed. The researchers may therefore want to conclude that crowding makes people distressed. However, a confound in this study may be the heat generated by having a lot of people in one room. So it may be the *heat*, not the crowding, that is producing effects on the dependent variable (distress). Another way of putting this is to say that in this study the two variables, space and temperature, are confounded.

Beyond these problems in establishing internal validity, one further reason why researchers may choose not to conduct experimental research is that they are interested in things that are unique to a particular individual. Experimental research is generally very useful in helping researchers test general theories about mental processes and human behaviour, but it does not necessarily help understand *idiosyncrasy*. So, coupled with the use of statistics, experiments enable us to say quite a lot about the behaviour of people *on average* and *as a general rule*. The same tools may be less useful in helping to understand the specific behaviour of one particular person at one particular point in time.

In practice, though, this last problem is less important than it might appear. This is because very few research psychologists are actually interested in drawing conclusions about individual people. Even if researchers were interested in the psychology of eccentricity, it is unlikely that they would only be interested in making statements peculiar to one individual, at one time and in one place. It is much more likely that they would be interested in understanding what eccentrics have in common and what makes them different from other non-eccentric people – and experimental research could play an important role in examining these issues.

Nevertheless, even if researchers are totally committed to experimental research, in some situations experimental methodology will not be an option. This is because some variables are impossible (or almost impossible) to manipulate. People's age and height cannot be changed, and the same routinely applies to their sex, cultural background and parents' birthplace. But even if a variable can be manipulated, it may not always be ethical to do so. For example, it may be highly inappropriate to conduct an experiment in which you attempt to manipulate people's physical and psychological health (points we will return to in Chapter 13). In such situations, psychologists usually have to resort to other research methods.

Q3.3*******

An experimenter conducts a study in which she wants to look at the effects of altitude on psychological well-being. To do this she randomly allocates people to two groups and takes one group up in a plane to a height of 1000 metres and leaves the other group in the airport terminal as a control group. When the plane is in the air she seeks to establish the psychological well-being of both groups. Which of the following is a potential confound, threatening the internal validity of the study?

(a) The reliability of the questionnaire that she uses to establish psychological health.
(b) The size of the space in which the participants are confined.
(c) The susceptibility of the experimental group to altitude sickness.
(d) The susceptibility of the control group to altitude sickness.
(e) The age of people in experimental and control groups.

The correct answer is (b). In answering this question it is important to remember that a confound is an unintended manipulation of an extraneous variable. So the question here is 'What has the researcher manipulated as well as altitude?'. There are many confounds here, but one answer to this question is that she has also manipulated the participants' personal space. It may be the case that just being in a confined space adversely affects well-being so that the effects that the experimenter ultimately observes have nothing to do with altitude at all. Note, too, that none of the things mentioned in the other answers (i.e., (a), (c), (d) and (e)) have actually been systematically manipulated in the experiment, so these could not represent confounds. Random allocation controls for possible differences in these and other variables.

causal inference Either the process of reaching conclusions about the effect of one variable on another, or the outcome of such a process.

condition A situation in which *participants* are all treated the same way (i.e., exposed to the same level of *treatment*) and where that treatment relates to something being investigated by the researcher.

confounding Unintended or accidental manipulation of an extraneous *variable* that occurs because that variable (called a confound) is associated with an *independent variable* in an experiment. A confound is thus a special case of extraneous variable.

control group *Participants* in an *experiment* who are not subjected to a relevant *treatment* (as distinct from an *experimental group*).

dependent variable (DV) The outcome variable on which a researcher is interested in monitoring effects.

experiment A piece of research in which one or more independent variables are systematically manipulated and all others are controlled.

Experiments assess the impact of manipulated (independent) variables on relevant outcome (dependent) variables.

experimental control The process of holding particular variables constant across different conditions of an *experiment* so that they have no impact on the results.

experimental group Participants in an experiment who are subjected to a particular level of a relevant *treatment* (as distinct from a control group).

independent variable (IV) The *treatment* variable manipulated by the experimenter in an experiment, or the causal variable which is believed to be responsible for particular effects.

internal validity The extent to which the effect of an independent variable on a dependent variable has been correctly interpreted.

manipulation The process of systematically varying an *independent variable* across different experimental conditions. This is sometimes referred to as the 'experimental treatment'.

participants The people who take part in a particular piece of research.

random assignment The process of assigning *participants* to conditions on a strictly unsystematic basis. When this occurs every participant has the same chance of being placed in any experimental condition.

representative sample A sample of research *participants* that is similar to the general population on characteristics that are relevant to the research question.

subjects Another word for *participants*.

treatment The experimental intervention that is the basis of the *independent variable* and therefore differentiates between *participants* in different conditions or phases of an *experiment*.

variable An aspect of a person or a situation which can change.

The quasi-experimental method

In situations where an independent variable is difficult or impossible to manipulate (such as the participants' age or sex), researchers sometimes choose to employ **quasi-experimental** methodology (Cook & Campbell, 1979). Quasi-experiments are identical to experiments, apart from one major difference: participants are *not randomly assigned to conditions* on one or more variables. So, as with proper experiments, quasi-experiments have both independent and dependent variables and the researcher is interested in observing the effect of differences in the independent variable on the dependent variable. However, the independent variable is not actually manipulated. Instead participants are assigned to different conditions explicitly on the basis of differences in that variable.

To illustrate this point, we can imagine some researchers who are interested in the effects of separation on attraction, but have developed a theory which suggests that separation has different effects on the relationships of young and old people. Perhaps they believe that for old people 'absence makes the heart grow fonder', but for young people 'absence leads the heart to wander'. In order to test this idea experimentally, the researchers clearly cannot assign some participants randomly to one experimental condition and *make them* old and assign some participants randomly to another experimental condition and *make them* young. So rather than manipulate the independent variable (age), they will probably just *find* some old people (e.g., 70-year-olds) and *find* some young people (e.g., 18-year-olds) and then compare the two age groups.

The process of conducting this quasi-experiment would be very similar to that of the experiment considered previously. Indeed, for this reason the researchers themselves would almost certainly refer to their study as an experiment rather than as a quasi-experiment. So, in the quasi-experiment the researchers might separate both groups of participants from their partners for an extended period and at the end of it see whether the two groups differ in their attraction towards their partners. Specifically, they would want to know if there was any support for the hypothesis that old people have stronger bonds with their partners. (Ideally, the experiment would also include two control groups who would not be subjected to separation, one made up of young people and one made up of old people.)

Although this strategy mimics that of proper experiments described in the previous section, it follows from our discussion of the importance of random assignment that the quasi-experimental method has a significant drawback compared to its experimental counterpart. As you may have foreseen, the systematic assignment of participants to different levels of the independent variable interferes with the researchers' ability to make conclusive causal inferences. In other words, where experiments involve systematic assignment of participants to conditions it *may not be valid* to conclude that any variation which is ultimately observed in the dependent variable has been caused by variation in the independent variable.

This point can be illustrated by referring back to our example. Imagine that the researchers find, as they predicted, that after a month of separation old people are more attracted to their partners than young people. Could they conclude that this is due to the fact that physical reinforcement is a more important component of younger people's relationships? Is it appropriate to conclude that this difference is due to the different age of the two groups of participants?

The answer to both questions is definitely 'no'. The reason for this blunt response is that although the age of the two experimental groups is different, so are a lot of other things which are associated with age but which the researcher was not able to *control*. Old people are not only older than young people, they may also be more wealthy, more cautious, more conservative, more happy, less restless, less healthy, less mobile, and so on – and any one of these uncontrolled differences *could* be responsible for the observed effects.

Any factors like this which are not (or cannot be) controlled for, and which impinge upon the researchers' ability correctly to interpret their findings and make valid causal inferences, are another form of *extraneous variable*. In this case the only way their influence can be fully controlled (and therefore ruled out) is by strictly random assignment of participants to conditions – that is, by use of fully experimental methodology. We will discuss this point further in the next chapter.

It follows from these points that quasi-experiments have one less advantage than experiments. However, because this deficit relates to the researcher's ability to make causal inferences (the single most important feature of experiments), it constitutes a serious drawback. Yet as we noted at the start of this section, random assignment of participants to conditions is often impossible. This fact alone makes quasi-experimental methods quite common.

Q3.4*

What distinguishes the experimental method from the quasi-experimental method?

(a) The scientific status of the research.
(b) The existence of an independent variable.
(c) The existence of different levels of an independent variable.
(d) The sensitivity of the dependent variable.
(e) The random assignment of participants to conditions.

The correct answer is (e). Quasi-experiments are like experiments in every respect but one – the fact that participants are not randomly assigned to conditions. They therefore contain independent variables with different levels (though level is not fully 'manipulated' for each participant) as well as dependent variables. Although experimental studies have the advantage of allowing researchers to draw conclusions about cause and effect they are no more scientific than quasi-experiments.

---

quasi-experiment A piece of research with the same features as an experiment but which does not involve the random assignment of participants to conditions on one or more variables.

The survey method

When people are not able to manipulate a given variable experimentally (or do not want to), the quasi-experiment is not the only option available to them. Indeed, the quasi-experiment can also be considered a special case of a methodology which is used extremely widely in psychological research – the **survey method**. This method is common to a lot of social scientific research and most of us encounter **surveys** quite frequently and in a number of different forms. These include opinion polls, market research, performance evaluations and censuses. They come in a range of guises – from structured telephone interviews to open-ended questionnaires.

Survey methodology typically *obtains information about a number of different variables in which the researcher is interested and identifies the relationship between those variables.* In other words, the methodology is used to identify the extent and nature of any association (or **correlation**) between different variables. For this reason what we have termed the survey method is often called the **correlational method**. The method does not necessarily require a response from participants at all. Instead, as with an experiment, it may merely involve *observations* of relevant variables on the part of the researcher.

Using surveys does not require a given variable to be examined outside its natural setting through manipulations conducted in a laboratory (a procedure common in experiments). On the contrary, one of the primary advantages and attractions of the survey is that it is usually quite easy to administer *anywhere*. In this manner, researchers can examine the relationship between variables that would be extremely difficult to isolate experimentally, such as wealth, age, socio-economic status, health, physical attractiveness and sexual preference. And while experiments are typically concerned with a limited number of different levels of a given variable, surveys usually include variables on which participants vary considerably and in many different ways.

In this way, using a survey to look at how age affects the relationship between separation and attraction is a clear alternative to using the quasi-experiment we discussed above. Researchers might include in such a survey participants who had undergone (or were actually undergoing) different amounts of separation – perhaps by studying scientists stationed in Antarctica. The survey might therefore involve participants of all ages rather than just the two ages of participants in the different conditions of the quasi-experiment (18 and 70). As well as asking participants how long they had been separated from their partner and how psychologically close they still felt to that person, the researchers might look at the relationship between these two variables and others that might be of theoretical interest – such as participants' health, intelligence and personality. Is attraction associated with good health or intelligence or introversion?

The clear benefit of this research strategy is that it allows researchers considerable scope to investigate many aspects of phenomena at the same time in the environment where they occur. For a number of reasons (ethical, financial, logistical) it can be extremely difficult to conduct experiments in people's place of work, on holiday, while they are waiting to see a doctor, or in other natural settings. It is usually easier, though, to administer a questionnaire or ask a series of questions in an interview. For this reason survey methodology is often used by researchers who want to examine important issues in the places that they arise (perhaps before seeking to explore them further in controlled experiments).

A further important feature of surveys is that, coupled with appropriate statistical methodology, they allow researchers to make *predictions* about the relationship between particular variables. For example, if researchers discover through a survey that older people feel more attracted to their partners, then they will be able to predict (with a quantifiable amount of uncertainty) both how attracted someone is to his or her partner if they know that person's age, and how old someone is if they know how attracted that person is to the partner.

This sort of descriptive and predictive information can be very useful for a range of people. This is one reason why surveys are so widely used by makers of social policy, consumer organizations, advertising agencies, government departments, prospective employers and so on. Information from our separation and attraction survey could, for example, prove invaluable to someone who has to decide how to distribute counselling resources among people of different ages. Similarly, surveys which identify relationships between people's lifestyle and various health risks can identify problems that require further investigation. They can also play a part in the development of advertising campaigns, intervention strategies and the training of health-care professionals.

A key problem with surveys, however, is that the applicability of their findings may be limited to the group of people that is actually studied. As with an experiment, it is therefore important that the participants in a survey are a representative sample of the population to which the survey will be generalized. Even so, it is likely to be the case that the relevance of the responses obtained will be restricted to a particular place and time. A survey conducted in the United States in the 1960s to examine the relationship between separation and attraction may have little to say about the relationship between these variables in Australia in the year 2000.

Yet by far the most severe limitation of survey methodology is that it does not allow researchers to draw causal inferences from their findings. This is the same problem that we have already discussed in relation to quasi-experimental methodology. Again, knowing that a relationship exists between two (or more) variables does not allow the researcher to say *what caused* that relationship.

In the case of the survey this can be a big problem because researchers are often extremely keen, or put under a lot of pressure, to provide *explanations* and not just descriptions. Journalists, grant-awarding bodies and the public in general often push researchers to explain what is going on in their research. And even if the researchers are unwilling to do so, others may jump to their own conclusions. If we hear that people's level of stress can be used to predict whether or not they will get a heart attack, we may conclude that 'stress causes heart disease'. But these statements are not justified and are often extremely misleading. This is because other explanations are just as likely to be true. For example, it may be that heart disease causes stress or that both stress and heart disease are caused by something else (such as diet).

The point here is that *correlation is not causation*. This is an extremely important point and it needs to be driven home because it is routinely overlooked by researchers in a wide range of fields (not just by psychologists). Accordingly, we will return to this point several times in later chapters.

However, the fact that survey (and quasi-experimental) research is limited in its ability to address causation does not mean that researchers should conduct experiments at every available opportunity. Experimentation is not a substitute for careful observation and description of behaviour. In psychology, as in all sciences, there is an important place for *both* descriptive *and* explanatory research procedures.

Which of the following is *not* an advantage of the survey/correlational method?

(a) It allows researchers to examine a number of different variables at the same time.
(b) It allows researchers to examine the relationship between variables in natural settings.
(c) It allows researchers to make predictions based on observed relationships between variables.
(d) It allows researchers to explain observed relationships between variables.
(e) It is often more convenient than experimental methods.

The correct answer is (d). The fact that researchers *cannot* make causal inferences is in fact the primary disadvantage of the survey method. The other statements all refer to advantages that survey research can have over experimental work in particular circumstances.

correlation A measure of the nature and strength of the relationship between two variables.
correlational method See *survey method*.
survey A research tool which obtains information about people's behaviour, mental states or environment.
survey method A procedure (also known as the correlational method) involving the collection of information about different variables in order to measure those variables and the relationship between them.

The case-study method

One of the things common to the three methods we have discussed so far is that they all typically involve quite a few participants. For reasons that we outlined at the start of the chapter, it is rare for fewer than half a dozen people to participate in an experiment and some surveys have thousands of respondents. Yet in some areas of psychological enquiry participants are extremely hard to come by. At one extreme a neuropsychologist may need to test theories of memory organization using participants who suffer from a very rare memory disorder, and at the other extreme researchers who want to investigate the social psychology of rioting may have trouble finding even one group of rioters in the city where they do research.

The questions addressed by these researchers may be extremely important, but any methodology that requires lots of participants is out of the question. Does this mean that these phenomena cannot be investigated? Thanks to the **case study**, it does not. Indeed, many of the most important insights gained by psychologists have come from researchers observing a single person or group. Freud's (1933/1964) analysis of Little Hans (a boy who had an intense fear of horses), Milner's (1966) work with HM (a patient with no apparent long-term memory) and Festinger, Riecken, and Schachter's (1956) studies of Mrs Kietch's religious cult (and how it dealt with the fact that the world did not come to an end when it said it would) provide a few of the best-known illustrations of this point.

Investigation of small samples is possible because the case study is simply a special instance of the methods that we have already considered. It is possible to apply experimental techniques to the investigation of a single case by experimentally manipulating a given variable *over time*. So, for example, over a period of days or weeks a neuropsychologist may vary the amount of practice a patient is allowed before being asked to recall a list of words, in order to see if this affects the patient's recall of those words. Similarly, a social psychologist may vary the task which a group has to perform to see if this affects the group members' mood. There are some precautions which need to be taken to eliminate particular confounds (in parti-cular, the influence of time and prior exposure – points we will discuss more in the next chapter). However, essentially the same principles (and precautions) apply to case studies as do to studies involving large numbers of participants. Nevertheless, one of the common complaints about case-study research is that the findings it produces can be unreliable because they are peculiar to the particular case being studied. For this reason researchers who base their conclusions on single cases are generally keen to replicate their findings wherever possible.

As with large-scale studies, sometimes manipulations of a given variable will be impossible or problematic. An experimenter may not be able (or want) to manipulate the behaviour of police at a riot or the treatment given to a patient suffering from a stroke. Accord-ingly, any study that is conducted may be based on the researcher's own *observations* of the participant's behaviour and environmental features. This scenario in effect corresponds to the survey method, where the researcher is able to monitor a large number of variables (the behaviour of the police, the crowd's mood, the physical conditions).

As one would expect, these two types of case study have broadly similar strengths and weaknesses to those that we have already identified in experiments and surveys. Experimental case studies allow the researcher to make appropriate inferences about causality, but the types of manipulation which are possible may be very limited. Observational case studies provide a good opportunity for detailed examination of a significant psychological phenomenon or event, but do not allow the researcher to make conclusive statements about cause and effect.

For these reasons case studies can generate data that are every bit as useful as those obtained in their full-scale counterparts. In particular, they often provide the opportunity for an in-depth exploration of theoretical ideas where the real-life manifestations of the phenomena in which a researcher is interested are either rare or complex (or both). In this capacity case studies play a key role not only in supporting theoretical predictions but also in *refuting* theories. You may remember from the previous chapter that a *single* piece of information which contradicts a theory can be enough to bring the value of that theory seriously into question. In a well-designed case study, such refutation can be achieved by the one case which demonstrates that something which a given theory predicts ought not to happen *does* happen.

*Q3.6**

Which of the following statements is true?

(a) Case studies have played no role in the development of psychological theory.

(b) Case studies have all of the weaknesses and none of the strengths of larger studies.

(c) Case studies have none of the weaknesses and all of the strengths of larger studies.

(d) Case studies should only be conducted if every other option has been ruled out.

(e) None of the above.

The correct answer is (e). The essential point to note about case studies is that most of their properties (including their weaknesses and strengths) are the same as those of larger studies. The primary difference is therefore one of sample size (i.e., the number of cases upon which conclusions are based). As a general statement, case studies are not universally superior or inferior to studies based on larger samples. They have played a major role in the advancement of psychological knowledge, and many researchers actually consider them to be a primary source of information rather than a 'last resort'.

case study Research (usually quite intensive) that involves a single participant or group of participants.

Overview

One of the points that emerges from this chapter is that despite the array of topics and issues that research in psychology can cover, researchers themselves actually have quite a limited number of tools available to them in order to conduct that research. The way these tools are used varies enormously, depending on both the topic itself and the underlying objectives of the researcher. Nevertheless, almost all psychological research could be classified as falling into one of the four categories we have discussed. The number of categories reduces to just two if quasi-experiments and case studies are seen merely as special cases of the other methods.

As we have seen, exactly which of these methods a researcher eventually decides to use depends on many things. Some of these relate directly to the applicability of the method to the topic at hand. In some situations it is not possible to manipulate a variable (e.g., abnormality or medical status) experimentally and in others it is not possible to examine a variable (e.g., reaction time or processing capacity) by using a survey. Other factors which influence a researcher's choice may be more a question of personal preference or established practice (either among a particular group of researchers or in the investigation of a particular issue).

Contrary to popular belief, choices about research *location* and research *participants* do not necessarily constrain the researcher's choice of methodology. Experiments do not have to be conducted in the laboratory and laboratory work need not be experimental. In fact many of the most significant psychology experiments have been **field studies**, using members of the general community in their natural environment. Similarly, a great deal of survey work is conducted on first-year psychology students in laboratory classes.

Regardless of the orientation researchers adopt, they should be aware of both the strengths of that approach *and* its limitations. This is important because researchers ultimately tend to classify themselves either as experimentalists or as survey-based researchers and then are inclined to emphasize the strengths of their preferred methods and the weaknesses of others. This will often be entirely appropriate as some methods are much more suitable for investigating certain topics than others. But no one method is *universally* superior. Part of any research psychologist's role is therefore to be able to make judgements about the appropriateness of any given method based on its suitability for investigating the issue at hand. Being a good researcher is not a question of *whether* you do experiments or surveys; it is more a matter of *when* and *how* you do them.

It is fair to add that many of the advances made in psychological knowledge have been gained through *innovation* at the methodological level – by researchers who were willing to explore old questions in new ways. Two cases in point would be Sherif's (1956) experimental field studies where experiments on group conflict were conducted using young boys who thought they were attending a normal summer camp and de Groot's (1965) quasi-experimental studies of chess masters' and novices' ability to encode and remember the positions of pieces on a chessboard.

In view of the potential limitations of any one method, many researchers use (or at least consider using) *multiple* research methods in order to explore the same issue in many different ways. In practice this is how knowledge in many areas of psychology has progressed over time – with the strengths of one approach correcting for the limitations of another. For this reason, the fact that psychologists have to make methodological choices should be seen more as an *asset* than as a basis for conflict. In the final analysis, the challenge faced by researchers is to demonstrate the merits of their own work by exploiting that asset appropriately.

---

field study A piece of research that is conducted in a natural (non-artificial) setting.

Further reading

Readings specific to the various methods covered in this chapter are provided in the chapters below. However, Leong and Austin (1996) and Sansone, Morf and Panter (in press) are advanced texts that provide detailed discussions of all of these methods and as well as discussions of a range of practical issues that confront researchers (e.g., designing a research programme, applying for grants).

Leong, T. L., & Austin, J. T. (1996). *The psychology research handbook: A guide for graduate students and research assistants*. Thousands Oaks, CA: Sage.

Sansone, C., Morf, C. C., & Panter, A. T. (Eds.) (in press). *Handbook of methods in social psychology*. Thousand Oaks, CA: Sage.

Research methods: A checklist for research evaluation and improvement

Potential problem	Question to ask	Potential improvement
Poor or limited choice of measure	Have researchers used an appropriate measure to investigate the psychological process or state in which they are interested?	Consider the different types of measure that could be used to investigate the issue at hand (e.g., behavioural, self-report, physiological). Consider the advantages and disadvantages (as well as the practicalities) of using different types of measure or different measures of the same type. If appropriate, design and conduct research that involves these alternative measures.
Extraneous variables	Are research findings contaminated by factors that are not of immediate concern to the researchers?	Think broadly about factors that are not addressed in the research but which may be affecting the findings (and their interpretation). Take steps to eliminate these (for more detail, see Chapters 4 and 5) or to compensate for them by using multiple methods.
Unrepresentative sampling	Is the experimental sample representative of the sub-population from which it is drawn and is the sub-population representative of the general population of interest?	Consider the implications of any unrepresentative sampling that has occurred. If necessary, take steps to improve the sampling procedure (e.g., by using random sampling; for more detail see Chapter 5) and then attempt to replicate the research findings.

Potential problem	Question to ask	Potential improvement
Confounding	Is assignment to experimental conditions associated with an additional variable that is not of immediate interest to researchers (and which they had not intended to manipulate) but which could be having an impact on the findings?	Take steps to eliminate the impact of confounding variables by controlling for them. This is typically done by manipulating the independent variable of interest under conditions where the level of the confound is held constant.
Lack of experimental control (in quasi-experiments and surveys)	Is the interpretation of a relationship between an IV and a DV compromised by a failure to manipulate the IV experimentally?	Consider ways in which it might be possible to manipulate an IV experimentally. If none is feasable, and an IV has not been manipulated experimentally, try to generate alternative explanations of the relationship and be careful to avoid the correlational fallacy of implying that the IV *caused* the DV (for more detail, see Chapter 10).
Poor or limited choice of method	Have the researchers used an appropriate method to investigate the psychological process or state in which they are interested?	Consider the different types of method that could be used to investigate the issue at hand (experimental, quasi-experimental, survey, case study). Consider the advantages and disadvantages (as well as the practicalities) of using alternative methods to supplement and extend the research. If appropriate, design and conduct research that involves these alternative methods.

Q3.7*

An experimenter conducts an experiment to see whether accuracy of responding and reaction time are affected by consumption of alcohol. To do this, she conducts a study in which students at university A react to pairs of symbols by saying 'same' or 'different' after consuming two glasses of water and students at university B react to pairs of symbols by saying 'same' or 'different' after consuming two glasses of wine. She predicts that reaction times will be slower and that there will be more errors in the responses of students who have consumed alcohol. Which of the following statements is *not* true?

(a) The university attended by participants is a confound.
(b) The experiment has two dependent variables.
(c) Reaction time is the independent variable.
(d) The experimenter's ability to draw firm conclusions about the impact of alcohol on reaction time would be improved by assigning participants randomly to experimental conditions.
(e) This study is actually a quasi-experiment.

Q3.8*
What is an extraneous variable?

(a) A variable that can never be manipulated.
(b) A variable that can never be controlled.
(c) A variable that can never be measured.
(d) A variable that clouds the interpretation of results.
(e) None of the above.

Q3.9*
Which of the following statements is true?

(a) The appropriateness of any research method is always determined by the research question and the research environment.
(b) Good experiments all involve a large number of participants.
(c) Experiments should be conducted in laboratories in order to improve experimental control.
(d) Surveys have no place in good psychological research.
(e) Case studies are usually carried out when researchers are too lazy to find enough participants.

Q3.10**
A piece of research that is conducted in a natural (non-artificial) setting is called:

(a) A case study.
(b) A field study.
(c) A quasi-experiment.
(d) A survey.
(e) An observational study.

The correct answer to 3.7 is (c). The independent variable in this study is alcohol consumption. The university that participants attend (A or B) has actually been manipulated along with alcohol consumption so, as (a) suggests, this is a confound. The experiment examines the impact of the independent variable on two dependent variables: reaction time and correctness of response, so (b) is true. As stated in (e), the fact that participants were not randomly assigned to conditions makes this a quasi-experiment. The problem of the confound could have been dealt with (and the study improved) by randomly assigning participants to conditions – thereby making this a proper experiment rather than a quasi-experiment (so (d) is also true).

The correct answer to 3.8 is (d). An extraneous variable is a variable that is not of immediate interest to a researcher but which poses a threat to validity because it compromises the interpretation of research findings. This usually occurs because the variable's impact upon the dependent variable has not been controlled for and so its influence upon that dependent variable cannot be ruled out. So if in a quasi-experiment participants are assigned to conditions on the basis of their intelligence, their wealth and socio-economic status may be extraneous variables that are confounded with intelligence. In this case the researcher cannot conclude that the effects that he or she wants to explain in terms of intelligence are not in fact due to these other variables. Under certain circumstances, extraneous variables of this type can be controlled (through random assignment of participants to conditions) and usually they can be studied in their own right, so answers (a), (b), (c) and (e) are all false.

Discussion/essay questions

(a) Compare the advantages and disadvantages of experimental and survey methodologies.
(b) Why does so much psychological research use quasi-experimental methodology?
(c) Are the benefits of experimental control overrated?
(d) Does an over-reliance on survey methodology compromise the scientific status of psychology?
(e) What are the strength and limitations of case studies?

Exercises

(a) Choose two topics that are covered in an introductory psychology textbook. Examples might be 'modelling of aggression in children' and 'long-term memory'. Classify the references used to explore each topic as (i) experimental studies, (ii) quasi-experimental studies, (iii) surveys, (iv) case studies or (v) presenting too little information for classification.

- Are there differences in the distribution of references into these categories for each topic?
- If so, what factors do you think have contributed to these differences?

(b) In dealing with these topics, do the authors of the textbook question the internal or external validity of any research reviewed? [*Hint*: This could be reflected in statements like 'the conclusions of this research have been challenged on methodological grounds' or 'it is difficult to know whether these results can be generalized to other settings'.]

- Is the validity of research on the two topics criticized on different grounds?
- If so, what factors do you think contribute to the different forms that criticism takes?

Experimental Design

In the previous chapter we noted that the experiment is one of the main research options available to people who want to do psychological research. We also dealt with some of the factors that dictate whether or not researchers decide to conduct experiments. However, we did not deal in any detail with the issues that confront them if they do. These details are the substance of this chapter.

Because we are going to deal with the *details* of designing experiments, we will tackle a number of quite difficult issues. Some of these are more fundamental than others and hence more immediately relevant to the first pieces of psychological research that you are likely to encounter or conduct. However, as you progress to more advanced courses and are exposed to a range of research articles, you will need to have a good understanding of all these concepts.

In essence the issues we are going to address are those of **experimental design** and **operationalization.** They concern the choices that the experimenter has to make about how to construct experiments in order to test hypotheses effectively. This effectiveness has two main bases: experimental components and experimental validity. We will treat these bases as if they were independent, but, as we will see, each actually exerts a strong influence on the other.

The first key to the effectiveness of experiments is an appropriate choice of experimental *components*. So, among other things, a researcher needs to select (a) an independent variable, (b) a dependent variable, (c) a participant sample, and (d) a method and criterion for establishing that the effects of manipulating the independent variable are sufficiently large to be taken seriously and of sufficient practical and theoretical interest. The first three of these components will be dealt with in the first half of this chapter and the fourth will be covered in Chapters 7 and 8.

Although participants and variables constitute the crucial ingredients of an experiment, their quality does not guarantee that the experiment will be effective. As with a cake, they have to be assembled appropriately – usually on the basis of a tried and tested recipe. And as any cook will attest, it is here that many of the secrets of their success (and failure) lie. Accordingly, a large part of any experiment's effectiveness derives from an experimenter's ability to construct a study in a way that allows its findings to be correctly interpreted. To do this the experimental design needs to avoid a number of potential *threats to internal validity*. Appropriate experimental design should also enable the researcher to *generalize* experimental findings to other non-experimental settings. However, this process is jeopardized by threats to **external validity**. In the latter part of this chapter we discuss some of the main forms which threats to these two types of validity take and some of the most common strategies which are employed to overcome them.

---

experimental design Both (a) the process of constructing experiments and (b) the resulting structure of those experiments.

external validity The extent to which a research finding can be generalized to other situations.

operationalization The process of deciding how to manipulate and/or measure independent variables and how to measure dependent variables. Note that this is quite a different meaning from methodologists' original usage of this term.

Choosing an independent variable

As we discussed in the previous chapter, in any experiment the independent variable (IV) is the variable that the researcher manipulates. On the basis of a theory or hypothesis, this variable is predicted to have a causal effect on a relevant outcome measure (the DV). The goals in selecting an independent variable to manipulate in an experiment are quite straightforward: to identify a variable which *can* be manipulated; and to ensure that this variable corresponds as closely as possible to the theoretical variable in which the researcher is interested. Satisfying these objectives can be quite difficult – partly because there is often an inherent tension between them.

To explain these points, we can develop a new example based on research into the cognitive aspects of depression (e.g., Abramson, Seligman & Teasdale, 1978; Seligman & Maier, 1967). A researcher interested in depression may have a general theory that whether or not people become depressed by failure depends upon how they explain that failure to themselves. The way in which people explain events can be thought of as their 'attributional style', so the theory suggests that depression depends upon people's attributional style. The theory might suggest that if people *internalize* failure (e.g., by saying to themselves 'it's my fault') they become depressed, but if they *externalize* it (e.g., by saying 'it's someone/something else's fault') they do not.

In this case, the key theoretical variable is attributional style. The goal of any experiment designed to test this theory would therefore be to manipulate people's attributional style to see whether it has any effect on their depression. But how can we manipulate something like attributional style *directly*? It is not possible to open up people's heads and turn a dial that changes 'attributional style' from 'external' to 'internal'. Even if it were, it would be ethically unacceptable to do so (as we noted in the previous chapter, such ethical considerations contribute considerably to many researchers' decisions to conduct correlational research).

The problem here is one that we first noted in Chapter 2 when we discussed the general issue of research validity and which we elaborated when discussing psychological measurement in Chapter 3. It arises from the fact that psychological research is generally concerned with making statements about theoretical variables – usually mental states or processes – that are not directly observable. This means that psychologists often have to manipulate theoretical variables *indirectly*, by using independent variables that they believe will have a specific impact upon a given mental process or state. In other words, they have to make decisions about how to *operationalize* the independent variable.

To manipulate people's mood a researcher may play them happy or sad music or ask them to think about something good or bad that has happened to them recently. We cannot just change their mood by flicking a switch. We have to manipulate variables which can be expected to change their mood. Similarly, in our example, the researcher may attempt to manipulate attributional style by exposing people to failure (e.g., in an exam) and then asking some of them to answer questions like 'Have you always been stupid?' or 'Can you explain why you did so much worse than everyone else in identical circumstances?' – questions which encourage them to reflect on their own contribution to their performance (i.e., to internalize). The researcher may ask other participants questions like 'Do you think that the fact that you weren't allowed to revise for the exam affected your performance?' or 'You were very unlucky, weren't you?' – questions which encourage them to reflect on the contribution of other factors to their performance (i.e., to externalize). We should note, however, that there would still be ethical concerns about aspects of this manipulation (concerns we will return to in Chapter 13).

Having performed indirect manipulations of this sort, it is often necessary for researchers to show that those manipulations have had the desired effect on the relevant theoretical variable. This demonstration is achieved by something referred to as a **manipulation check**. A manipulation check is a dependent variable. But unlike other dependent variables, it checks that manipulation of the independent variable has had an effect on a theoretically relevant *causal* variable. For this reason, obtaining an effect on this type of measure is a *prerequisite* in an experiment rather than an end in itself.

So, after making people listen either to Chopin's 'Funeral March' or to Beethoven's 'Ode to Joy', a researcher may ask them how they feel in order to check that the people who listened to Beethoven were in a better mood. Likewise, in our main example, having attempted to manipulate participants' attributional style by asking questions about their exam performance, the researcher could ask them a question like 'How much are you personally responsible for your failure?' (perhaps getting them to circle a number on a seven-point **scale** with end-points labelled 'not at all' (1) and 'completely' (7)). If participants who were asked 'internal' questions tended to mark higher numbers, then this suggests that the manipulation is working. Indeed, we can see that by this process the experimenter has successfully got to 'first base' and thereby overcome a major hurdle in psychological experimentation.

Researchers are usually keen to obtain very big effects on manipulation checks. If they do not they will probably be inclined to strengthen the manipulation of the independent variable. This might involve increasing its duration or intensity, reinforcing it with additional manipulations or simply using a different (superior) manipulation. Such steps are often necessary because it is a general rule of experiments that in order for them to have the best chance of working (i.e., for the manipulation to lead to an effect on the dependent variable), the researcher needs to ensure that the manipulation of the independent variable is *as strong as possible*.

In our examples so far we have often referred to experiments where one group of participants is exposed to one level of a particular independent variable and another group of participants is exposed to another (e.g., where the study contains two experimental groups or an experimental group and a control group). For example, we have discussed studies in which one group of participants is asked questions which lead them to externalize while another is asked questions which lead them to internalize; or where an experimental group is separated from their partners and a control group is not. When the independent variable is manipulated in this way it is a **between-subjects manipulation**. This is because levels of the independent variable differ between participants in different conditions.

However, the manipulation of independent variables does not have to involve different groups of participants. It is also possible to conduct experiments where the *same* participants are exposed to different levels of the independent variable but at different times. For example, one could conduct an experiment where the same group of participants were induced to internalize their failure at one point in time but to externalize it at another. When the independent variable is manipulated in this way it is referred to as a **within-subjects manipulation.** This is because levels of the independent variable differ *within* the same participants.

A number of factors determine whether the independent variable is manipulated within or between subjects. Two of the principal advantages of within-subjects manipulations are (a) that they reduce by at least 50% the number of people needed to participate in any given experiment, and (b) that they remove all of the differences between the participants in different conditions that are produced by chance as a result of the random assignment of different participants to different conditions. This is because the same people participate in each condition and their responses are directly compared across the two conditions. For this reason we say that each participant is being used as 'their own control'. This means that the differences between conditions that arise because different people are being measured (in between-subjects designs) are eliminated or controlled.

However as we will see below, within-subjects procedures can involve a number of quite serious threats to internal validity. This is mainly because other variables can change systematically between different phases of an experiment.

Q4.1*

What is a manipulation check and what is its purpose?

(a) A dependent measure used to check that manipulation of an independent variable has been successful.

(b) An independent variable used to check that measurement of a dependent variable has been successful.

(c) A measure used to check that an experiment has an independent variable.

(d) An independent measure used to check that the operationalization is relevant.

(e) A dependent measure used to check that an independent variable is sufficiently relevant.

The correct answer is (a). A manipulation check cannot check or ensure the relevance of any variable, so (d) and (e) are incorrect. It is a dependent measure used to check that the independent variable has actually been manipulated and so is operating in the experiment. (c) is therefore incorrect because unless the experiment includes an independent variable in the first place, a manipulation check is meaningless – indeed, without an independent variable there is no experiment. (b) is wrong because it completely reverses the logic of experimental design.

between-subjects manipulation Systematic change to an independent variable where different participants are exposed to different levels of that variable by the experimenter.

manipulation check A dependent measure which checks that manipulation of the independent variable has been successful (i.e., that it has changed the theoretically relevant causal variable that the experimenter wants to manipulate).

scale A system for deciding how to arrange objects or events in a progressive series. In this way scales are used to assign relative magnitude to psychological and behavioural phenomena (e.g., intelligence or political attitudes).

within-subjects manipulation Systematic change to an independent variable where the same participants are exposed to different levels of that variable by the experimenter.

Choosing a dependent variable

Of course the main 'prize' in any experiment is not to get effects on manipulation checks, but to get them on the other dependent variables – ones upon which the independent variable is hypothesized to have particular effects. So, in our depression experiment, the researcher is not going to be satisfied with the knowledge of having changed people's attributional style, but will want to know whether this change in attributional style has had any effect on the participants' mood.

In order to do this, the experiment has to include dependent variables – in this case measures of mood – on which such effects might emerge.

As with independent variables, the operationalization of these dependent variables can involve a trade-off between theoretical relevance and practical considerations. When they choose independent variables, experimenters often have to choose between what they would *like to manipulate* and what they *can manipulate*. Similarly, in the choice of dependent variables, there is sometimes a conflict between what experimenters would *like to measure* and what they *can measure*. This conflict creates a **relevance–sensitivity trade-off**. This means that when the dependent variable is highly relevant to a given issue, it may be less sensitive to changes in the independent variable.

As an example, we can think of a team of researchers interested in studying the effect of drivers' mood on the safety of their driving. In an effort to understand the phenomenon of 'road rage' the researchers might hypothesize that drivers who are in a bad temper are more dangerous. One way of manipulating the independent variable (mood) would be to get people to perform either very rewarding or very frustrating tasks. The experimenters could put some people in a good mood by asking them to complete an easy puzzle and others in a bad mood by asking them to solve an impossible one.

The most dramatic demonstration would then be to show that drivers in bad moods caused more accidents. We can see that there are serious ethical problems with this research, but even if they did not exist, one can imagine that it would be unlikely that any manipulation of the independent variable (mood) could ever be strong enough to bring about sizeable change in this dependent variable (number of road accidents) unless the study was going to include a massive number of drivers and be conducted over a very long period of time. The point here is that the dependent variable is not sensitive enough. To deal with this problem the researchers would have to design a study with a much more sensitive dependent variable.

For example, they could see whether drivers who were put in a bad mood drove faster or looked in their rear-view mirror less often. Although the dependent variable might now be sensitive enough to detect changes in the independent variable, its link to the theoretical variable of interest is less direct. Clearly, people might argue about whether accidents are really caused by fast driving or by not looking in the rear-view mirror. So in this case it could be argued that the researchers have simply replaced one research question with another.

This same point could be applied to our depression example. It is unlikely that any manipulation of an independent variable would ever produce really big differences in the number of participants who showed signs of clinical depression. On the other hand, the manipulation may produce differences on less dramatic dependent measures such as participants' responses to questions like 'How often do you feel sad?'.

The way in which researchers usually seek to deal with the tension between relevance and sensitivity in their choice of dependent variables is to select variables on which they can obtain effects (which are sensitive enough) and seek to ensure that these are as relevant as possible. However, in some cases this strategy opens their work up to a charge of *non-relevance* – and these charges are commonly made against experimentalists in all areas of psychology (educational, cognitive, social, clinical, etc.). This is particularly apparent where researchers justify their work in terms of variables which they never actually investigate. In the above examples the researchers might make claims about the relevance of their work to the reduction of road deaths and clinical depression (and obtain research funding on this basis), but never actually establish the link between their dependent variables and these phenomena.

Just how big a problem lack of relevance is for experimental research is a matter of some debate. Most researchers would agree that it is important to try to establish the relevance of an experiment's dependent measures to any phenomenon in which they are interested. This being the case, debate often arises because many researchers shy away from the task of establishing relevance, not because the task is an impossible one.

The main strategy for establishing the link between measured variables and variables more relevant to the issue being addressed is to back up experimental research that produces effects on a given dependent variable with additional research demonstrating a causal (not just a correlational) relationship between that variable and one of greater relevance. In the driver example, having found that mood affects driver speed, researchers could then conduct another experiment to address the question of whether speed affects safety. Indeed, ideally they (or someone else) would have established the relevance of speed to issues of safety *before* they conducted the experiment into the effects of mood on speed.

Q4.2**

Which of the following statements is true?

(a) Dependent variables that do not measure the most relevant theoretical variable are pointless.

(b) A study that employs dependent variables that are sensitive enough to detect variation in the independent variable is a quasi-experiment.

(c) Unless dependent variables are sufficiently sensitive they will not reveal the effects of manipulating an independent variable.

(d) Unless dependent variables are sufficiently relevant they will not reveal the effects of manipulating an independent variable.

(e) None of the above.

The correct answer is (c). Dependent variables that are not sensitive enough to reveal any of the effects of manipulating the independent variable can obviously tell you nothing about what those effects are (or may be) – so (a) is wrong. However, experiments *can* use dependent variables that are not sensitive enough to do this, they just will not reveal effects – which is one reason why (b) is wrong. Indeed, often the sensitivity of dependent measures can only be established *after* an experiment has been conducted. Dependent variables do not have to be the most theoretically relevant to have any purpose, as this relevance may be established by additional research. This relevance also has no bearing on the variables' ability to respond to change in the independent variable – so (d) is wrong.

relevance–sensitivity trade-off The principle that the more relevant a dependent variable is to the issue in which a researcher is interested, the less sensitive it may be to variation in the independent variable.

Choosing an experimental sample

As well as needing to decide what they are going to manipulate and measure in an experiment, researchers also need to decide who is going to participate in it. In many cases the choice of a sample is unproblematic. For example, if researchers are interested in looking at the impact of psychological therapy on anxiety, they will probably want to conduct their research on people who are anxious. Similarly, if researchers are investigating the impact of a given teaching method on the classroom learning of young children, then they will want to work with young schoolchildren in their study.

But what if a researcher is interested in examining normal psychological processes in the general ('normal') population? If you are a student of psychology, you will probably have been encouraged (or required) to participate in research of this nature. Testifying to this point, investigations by a number of researchers in a number of different sub-fields (experimental, social, personality) indicate that in around 80% of published research papers the participants in psychology experiments are first-year undergraduates (Cochrane & Duffy, 1974; Smart, 1966; West, Newsom, & Fenaughty, 1992). In these cases the choice of experimental participants appears to have been pretty straightforward.

However, first-year students themselves are often less willing to take their participation in experiments for granted. Quite reasonably, they often ask 'How can you possibly hope to make statements about human psychology in general when you only study a select subset of human beings in your research?'. This question (and the criticism it implies) appears more compelling when students learn that the researcher is interested in issues such as prejudice, depression or phobia. Such questions are asked even more forcefully when it is noted that student populations are usually studied in the laboratory rather than in the situations they encounter in their everyday lives. How can laboratory-based studies of people who are generally intelligent, healthy, assertive and tolerant tell us anything about the psychological make-up of the general population whose actions take place in a world of politics, poverty, oppression, struggle and intolerance?

Many non-experimental psychologists ask this same question, and go on to argue that the conclusions inferred from most experimental samples are necessarily flawed. Many experimentalists, too, would argue that research should not be based *solely* on student samples. Most would certainly encourage a researcher to conduct experiments using other samples wherever possible. However, the fact is that samples of certain types of participant (e.g., the chronically depressed, phobic, prejudiced or uneducated) are few and far between. Moreover, when they have been located there may be particular problems associated with studying them (e.g., it may be difficult for them to participate in the research).

More importantly, though, experimentalists generally argue that it *is* possible to gain significant insights into human nature on the basis of samples and situations that are not representative of the breadth of human society and experience. The arguments marshalled to support this point are quite complex, but they rest on two main points.

The first was noted in the previous chapter when we introduced the concept of a *representative sample*. We made the point there that in order to be able to apply research findings to a particular population (e.g., most 'normal' people), experimental samples and situations do not have to be representative of that population in *every* respect. Instead, the experimental sample only has to be representative of that population in *theoretically relevant* respects.

For example, if a perceptual psychologist is interested in how people with normal eyesight are able to locate objects in space, it would be appropriate to base his or her research on the perceptions of people with normal eyesight but not on those of people with a squint or astigmatism. However, it does not matter if those people are wealthier, taller or smarter than most other people. Similarly, if researchers are interested in how people form first impressions of other people and theorize that they do so on the basis of physical appearance, it only matters that their sample is representative of the population to which the research will be generalized on dimensions that relate to judgements of physical appearance. For example, they need to be able to detect differences in physical appearance and to be able to communicate those perceived differences.

A second point that is absolutely critical here is that researchers *have to have a theory* in order to make judgements about what is (and what is not) a relevant dimension of the experimental sample and the experimental situation. This also applies when the sample is directly relevant to the issue being studied. For example, in an educational study of pre-schoolers, researchers may need to ensure that those young children are representative of the population to which they wish to apply their research in terms of their intelligence and maturity.

If researchers do not attempt to ensure that their experimental sub-population is representative in this way, and they attempt to generalize any empirical findings they obtain straight to the larger world, then they are guilty of **naive empiricism**. For example, if a researcher conducts a study with some students and finds that their judgements of physical appearance are based primarily on hair colour then he or she may be tempted to (and often will) suggest that all people make judgements on this basis. However, this strategy is very dangerous largely because it is merely a form of *induction* – a form of scientific reasoning we discussed in Chapter 2.

Experimentalists argue that theory offers the scientific solution to this problem because it means that experiments can test theoretical ideas on any sample and in any situation where theoretically relevant variables can be manipulated (e.g., Turner, 1981). In this way we could test the theory that people's first impressions of others are based on their physical attractiveness by exposing *any sample* to people who differ in *what the sub-population from which that sample is drawn* defines as physical attractiveness (one aspect of which may be hair colour in a particular Western society, and neck length in a particular African society) and see if these different people are evaluated differently. Such a theory might predict that only Westerners would be more attracted to people with blond hair. In this way we would generalize our research to the larger world not on the basis of the experimental data themselves (which would almost certainly vary across samples, situations and cultures), but *on the basis of the theory* which they support. As we discussed in Chapter 2, it is then up to further research either to endorse or to challenge that theory.

Yet as we have already indicated, if they can, researchers often want to conduct experiments using specialized samples that are particularly relevant to the phenomena they are investigating. One reason for doing this is that it may be too difficult to manipulate a given variable using a non-specialized sample. In this case the researcher may resort to quasi-experimental methodology.

However, as we noted in the previous chapter, this strategy creates problems in establishing causality because participants in different experimental conditions may differ on more than just the independent variable of interest. One way in which researchers often try to deal with these problems is by **matching**. Matching involves ensuring that different experimental groups do not differ appreciably on dimensions that could be implicated in any effects obtained on the dependent variable (i.e., ensuring that they are *matched* on theoretically relevant variables).

Matching is very common in some areas of research (e.g., educational and clinical) where it is almost impossible (as well as unethical) to manipulate theoretically relevant variables such as intelligence, psychoticism or particular forms of brain damage. Researchers systematically assign participants to groups based on differences in the variable of interest (e.g., intelligence or psychoticism) but seek to ensure that they do not differ systematically on other key variables such as age, sex or socio-economic background.

Matching is also used in some fields to establish relevant *baselines* against which performance can be appraised. For example, in clinical studies a researcher may seek to obtain controls matched on variables such as age, sex and years of education, in order to gauge more accurately the amount of impairment in the performance of someone with brain injury or a particular clinical syndrome. This procedure allows the researcher to eliminate the variables on which the participants are matched as potential causes of differences in performance.

When we discussed the idea of randomly assigning participants to conditions in the previous chapter you may have thought that matching was another quite reasonable strategy that we ought to have considered as a means of eliminating systematic differences between groups. Yet although it sounds promising, matching is never as effective a means of removing differences between groups as randomization. This is partly because it is very difficult to do successfully, especially if the researcher is attempting to match participants on more than one or two variables.

For example, in our depression experiment if the researcher thinks it would be too hard to manipulate participants' attributional style, then he or she may decide to identify two sub-groups of participants: one of 'internalizers' and one of 'externalizers'. Yet by doing this the experimenter loses control over the independent variable. Perhaps internalizers are more intelligent, less imaginative, have unpleasant parents or received fewer Christmas presents as children. It may be any one of these factors – not attributional style – that is responsible for the greater depression that they ultimately display. The strategy of matching could eliminate some of these differences (e.g., if the researcher selected internalizers and externalizers of similar intelligence), but it could never eliminate them all.

Q4.3**

A team of researchers is interested in conducting an experiment in order to test an important theoretical premise. In order to draw appropriate conclusions from any experiment they conduct, which of the following statements is true?

(a) The experimental sample must be representative of the population to which they want to generalize the research on dimensions of age, sex and intelligence.
(b) The experimental sample must be representative of the population to which they want to generalize the research on all dimensions.
(c) The experimental sample must be representative of the population to which they want to generalize the research on all dimensions that can be measured in that population.
(d) The experimental sample must be representative of the population on all dimensions relevant to the process being studied.
(e) None of the above.

The correct answer is (d). In experimental research the concept of sample representativeness relates to the correspondence between the sample and the population to which the research is to be generalized on dimensions relevant to the processes the research addresses (rather than on all dimensions or a predetermined set of them). (a), (b) and (c) are wrong because it is not necessary for a sample to be representative of the relevant population on all dimensions (measurable or not) or on a universal subset of those dimensions.

> **matching** The process of attempting to remove systematic differences
>   between experimental groups on variables not of primary interest but
>   considered likely to produce differences in a dependent variable.
> **naive empiricism** The process of directly generalizing research
>   findings to other settings and samples, without basing that
>   generalization on a theory or explanation of the research findings.

Threats to internal validity

So far we have talked about the ingredients and purpose of experiments,
but we have not really touched upon exactly how experiments are put
together and conducted. As in any science, assembling and running
experiments are essential aspects of the experimental process – not least
because it is very easy to construct bad experiments and to conduct
experiments badly. In particular, there are a number of features of
design which can compromise the experiment's *internal validity*, leading
researchers to interpret incorrectly the effects they obtain. The seven
main forms which threats to independent validity take were originally
identified by Campbell and Stanley (1963), and we will discuss each in
turn, as well as the main ways to deal with them.

One of the main things which can cause problems in experiments is
the passage of time. This is a big problem in experiments that have within-
subjects designs where participants make a number of responses. As an
example, imagine a team of researchers who want to conduct an
experiment in order to look at the effects of a particular psychological
therapy on anxiety. One obvious way of doing this would be to obtain
some clinical participants, see how anxious they are, then administer
the therapy and see if their anxiety is reduced. This experimental design
thus involves two observations and an intervening experimental treatment.

If we were to represent the experiment schematically, one way to do
so would be as an O_1-X-O_2 design, where the Os indicate the
observations, the X represents the experimental treatment or manipulation, and the order (from left to right) and the subscripts indicate the
passing of time.

Now if in this study the experimenters find that the participants are
less anxious at the second observation (the **post-test** observation, O_2)
than at the first observation (the **pre-test** observation, O_1) they will
probably want to conclude that this was due to the effects of the
treatment. However, this conclusion is not necessarily valid because

between the two observations other things *apart from the manipulation* will have occurred. Basically both the participants and their circumstances will have changed – and these changes, *not the treatment*, may be responsible for the change between the two observations. The participants will all have grown older and greater maturity may itself serve to reduce anxiety. Time may also make people more uncertain, more sceptical or less healthy and so on. Any such changes in the participants that occur simply as a result of time passing are generally referred to as instances of **maturation effects**.

Two forms of maturation effect are particularly important. Both relate to the fact that by the time they complete the post-test, participants have already had some experience of the task they have to perform because they have completed the pre-test. So, on the one hand, any change in their performance over time may be due to the *practice* that they gained from doing the pre-test. If people do better the second time they take a particular test, their improvement may reflect the fact that they have done more work, but it may also reflect the fact that they know what is on the test. On the other hand, by the time they come to the post-test participants may have become bored or tired, and this *fatigue* may contribute to a falling off in their performance. These **practice effects** and **fatigue effects** are of particular interest to psychologists because they relate to the important topics of learning and motivation.

Maturation refers to the direct effects of time on the participants in experiments. However, time also exerts indirect effects on participants because it is associated with changes occurring in the world that those participants inhabit. So, between any two observations participants may be affected by any number of things going on in the world – change in the weather, the economy, the political climate and so on. For example, while our researchers were conducting their anxiety experiment the likelihood of nuclear war may have diminished (perhaps because an international peace treaty has been signed) and this may have reduced the participants' anxiety. More mundanely, the participants might have started watching a self-help video which had nothing to do with the treatment, or they may all have signed up for alternative therapy. Any changes to the participants' circumstances that take place over the course of a study are referred to as **history effects**.

Maturation and history effects pose threats to internal validity because they result in the participants not being completely identical at pre-test and post-test phases of an experiment. Indeed, they can lead to *systematic differences between observations* at different phases of a study. This is one reason why participants exposed to different levels of a within-subjects variable are not perfectly matched. And as we noted in the previous chapter, this fact clearly compromises our ability to interpret the results of an experiment correctly.

Other factors to do with the *experimental situation itself* may also mean that participants are systematically different at different phases of an experiment. For one thing, when participants are observed or asked to respond for a second time (i.e., at the post-test, O_2) they *already have experience* of being observed or having to respond (at the pre-test, O_1). Problems of this nature are referred to as **testing effects**. As an example of how these might adversely affect the interpretation of some results, think of an experiment in which researchers are interested in the effects of mnemonics on memory. They might hypothesize that teaching participants to use mnemonics to help them remember letter strings (for example, to develop a mnemonic like 'Every Good Boy Deserves Favour' to remember the string EGBDF) will improve recall. To investigate this idea they could conduct an experiment with a pre-test–treatment–post-test design (i.e., O_1–X–O_2). In this the participants could first be asked to remember some letter strings and have their memory measured, then be taught how to develop mnemonics, then come back a week later and have their ability to remember letter strings measured again.

As in the anxiety study, if the participants' memory has improved at the second phase of testing the researcher will probably want to attribute this to the effects of their mnemonic training. However, this may have had no effect at all. Perhaps the participants who did poorly at the first phase were so ashamed of their performance that when they came back a second time they were much more motivated to do well (perhaps this had also led them to develop alternative memory strategies before they were tested again).

Testing effects are actually one aspect of the more general issue of experimental **reactivity**. This refers to the fact that participants will often *react* to features of an experiment so that the process of *making observations can change observations*. As an everyday example, think what would happen if someone you disliked asked you 'Are you doing anything special tomorrow night?' You might say 'I'm not sure', even though you knew full well that you planned to do absolutely nothing. The response you provide the person is therefore not an accurate reflection of your intentions, but a reaction to the question and its assumed purpose (perhaps you fear the person wants to come round and bore you to death with some holiday photographs). Clearly, if reactivity affects participants' responses on dependent variables in experiments, it can cause serious problems of interpretation.

One of the best examples of reactivity at work was provided by a series of famous studies conducted in the Hawthorne Works of the Western Electric Company from 1924 onwards (e.g., Roethlisberger & Dickson, 1964). These studies were designed to investigate the effects that changes to working conditions had on the productivity, health and job satisfaction of the workers employed to perform a range of fairly unexciting tasks at the factory. To investigate these things the researchers set about trying to manipulate a number of features of the working environment. Among other things, they manipulated the illumination in the assembly rooms as well as their temperature and humidity. The experimenters went on to manipulate things like the management style of the supervisors, the control exerted over workers and the size of the work groups.

What the researchers expected was that these manipulations would have systematic effects. For example, they expected that workers would complain more about eye-strain and become less productive as the lighting in the factory was dimmed. What they found, however, was that *every* change in working conditions led to an increase in productivity and worker satisfaction. So, when the lighting was made brighter productivity went up and the workers felt happier, but workers were also more productive and happy when the lighting was reduced to a level similar to moonlight.

As you might expect, the researchers were perplexed by these results. Eventually, though, they figured out what was going on. They discovered that their findings were attributable not to the nature of the change in the work environment but to *change itself*. The workers in the factory were so used to being bored, ignored and taken for granted that they responded positively to the simple (but, for them, remarkable) fact that someone was paying attention to them and doing something different for a change. In other words, the participants' behaviour was changed by the process of participating in research and being made to feel important, rather than by the variables being deliberately manipulated. This effect is called the **Hawthorne effect** (after the factory where the above research took place) and it arises in any research where responses are affected by participants' sensitivity to the fact that they are participating in research.

Another way in which reactivity commonly manifests itself is through **order effects**. These arise if the responses to treatments change depending on the order in which the treatments occur. In the example of memory training, if all the participants were asked to remember letter strings using both multiple-choice questions and by writing down all the words they could remember (i.e., free recall), one might expect that participants would be better at the free-recall task if they did this after the multiple-choice task rather than before. This is because doing the multiple-choice task first would prepare them for the free-recall task.

Other features of the experiment may also change between any two observations, and these **instrumentation effects** undermine validity in much the same way. Instrumentation refers to *any* feature of the experiment related to the collection of data – for example, who it is collected by, where it is collected and the methods used for collection. So, in the above study of memory, if the data from the post-test were collected by a different experimenter than the one who collected it at the pre-test, this could have unforeseen effects on the participants' responses. For example, if the experimenter at the post-test was more attractive or pleasant than the experimenter at the pre-test, the participants might be motivated to perform better. By the same token, if the experimenters measured memory by different methods at the two phases this could have similar effects (e.g., if they used free recall at the pre-test and multiple choice at the post-test).

A final set of threats to internal validity relate to strategies for selecting participant samples and the effects of those strategies. The first of these are **selection effects**, and we have met and dealt with these before in our discussion of quasi-experimental designs. These effects arise when participants are assigned to different levels of an independent variable on the basis of some specific criteria (e.g., their age or their score on a particular test). So here any differences between groups on the dependent measures may exist *before* the manipulation occurs because different sorts of people have been selected for the groups.

As we have noted several times already, the basic problem posed by selection effects is that when participants are not randomly assigned to conditions, any change in the dependent variable may be due to things *associated with* the independent variable rather than due to the independent variable itself. So, in the example where participants were selectively placed into experimental groups on the basis of being externalizers or internalizers, if internalizers became more depressed after failure this may be due to things associated with their attributional style rather than due to their attributional style itself. Perhaps internalizers have generally experienced more failure in the past than externalizers, and this past experience of failure makes them more depressed when they confront it again. This, however, is only one of a large number of alternative explanations of such an outcome and, because the independent variable is not directly manipulated, all or none of these explanations *could* be valid.

A more subtle problem arises when an independent variable is manipulated within subjects and the participants are selected because of their extremity (or peculiarity) on the variable of interest. Imagine that the researcher who was investigating the effects of mnemonics on memory used participants who had performed particularly poorly on a previous memory test (imagine that none of them remembered more than one letter string out of 20). The problem here is that, *without any treatment taking place at all*, the likelihood of observing such poor performance again is very slight. This is because the performance is so bad it cannot get any worse. Therefore, *any* change can only be an improvement. As a result 'improvement' is quite likely to occur regardless of whether or not any experimental intervention occurs. This is due to a statistical phenomenon known as **regression to the mean**.

An example of how regression to the mean can cloud the interpretation of research data was provided by Tversky and Kahneman (1974). They noted the case of flight instructors who found that trainee pilots who made an excellent first landing generally performed less well on their second landing. The instructors thought that this deterioration in performance was a result of over-confidence on the part of these pilots. The instructors may have been right, but whether they were right or wrong, worse performance on average was almost *inevitable* as a result of regression to the mean. Pilots who are already performing extremely well cannot improve, so if there is any change in their performance at all they must do worse. Regression to the mean will occur whenever researchers attempt to compare scores from a sample that is extreme on one variable with scores from the same sample on another variable that is not perfectly related to the first. This point is quite complex but it will be easier to understand when you have read more about correlation, a topic we cover in Chapter 9.

One final threat posed by sampling strategies again arises where a variable is manipulated within subjects. This is the problem of participant **mortality effects**. It relates to the fact that in the time between any two observations, *particular* participants may withdraw from a study. In extreme cases (e.g., in animal and medical studies) this is because the participants die, which is where the term 'mortality' comes from. For example, in the study examining the effects of a psychological therapy on anxiety, it is quite possible that some participants will not turn up for the post-test (O_2) – possibly because they are too anxious. Clearly, though, if anxious participants were to drop out of the experiment or only those who feel the therapy is working turn up to be tested again, any conclusion about the effectiveness of therapy may be very misleading.

85

The problem posed by all of the above threats to internal validity is essentially the same. That is, they all produce systematic differences between different experimental observations over and above those caused by manipulation of the independent variable. It can be seen that in many cases these effects are quite subtle and, for that matter, quite intriguing. We should also add that, armed with an awareness of these problems, you will be in a position to identify faults in much of the research that you hear about every day – for example, a news item describing the latest medical 'breakthrough', or one which trumpets the new-found cause of a particular social problem. Faced with this list of potential experimental problems, you may also wonder if it is ever worth going to the trouble of trying to conduct valid experiments.

Well, the good news is that despite the subtlety of many of the problems we have identified in this section, all can be addressed (in many cases quite easily) by appropriate experimental design. Going through the details of all the possible ways in which this can be achieved would be a long and arduous task, so we will not. In fact, the ways in which researchers set about dealing with these problems differ enormously as a function of the type of research they are doing.

However, the basic principle used to eliminate these threats to validity is one that we have already talked about at length: *experimental control*. As we have pointed out, the main way in which experimental control is achieved is through randomization and/or matching. For example, an effective way of dealing with order effects, practice effects and fatigue effects is either (a) to randomize the order in which participants complete dependent measures, or (b) to make participants in both an experimental and control group complete all dependent measures in the same order, or (c) systematically to vary the order in which items are presented, through **counterbalancing**.

The point of the latter strategy can be demonstrated by thinking of an experiment in which participants have to perform two tasks, A and B. Imagine that they all perform Task A *then* Task B and their performance is found to be superior on Task A. This effect could occur because the participants have greater aptitude for Task A (or because Task A is easier) but it could also arise from the fact that participants were tired or bored by the time they came to do Task B. However, the second interpretation could be ruled out if the same effect emerged after counterbalancing such that half of the participants were randomly assigned to perform Task A first and the other half to perform Task B first. Counterbalancing is a simple strategy that allows researchers to neutralize or quantify any effects associated with the order in which tasks are completed.

These points about experimental control can be demonstrated by describing one of the main forms of what Campbell and Stanley (1963) call a *true experimental design*. This is a design that deals effectively with all of the above threats. It involves supplementing the basic pre-test–treatment–post-test design described above (i.e., O_1–X–O_2) with an additional pre-test–post-test control (i.e., O_1–O_2). This control condition involves different participants but a pre-test and post-test that are *identical in every respect* (e.g., including exactly the same measurement procedures and the same experimenters). This can be represented schematically as follows:

condition	time $\longrightarrow$		
experimental	O_1	X	O_2
control	O_1		O_2

If participants are randomly assigned to these two conditions, we can compare the results obtained at the post-test (O_2) in the experimental condition with those obtained at the post-test (O_2) in the control condition (as well as the change between pre-test and post-test in both cases). If there is a big enough difference, then this *must* be a result of the experimental treatment (manipulation of the independent variable) rather than any of the seven threats to internal validity described above.

As an example, in the case where researchers were interested in establishing the efficacy of a particular anxiety therapy they could randomly assign participants to experimental and control conditions and start by measuring the anxiety of each group of participants (due to random assignment there should not be any substantial difference between them). They could then treat one group of participants using the therapy but leave the other group alone (this constitutes the manipulation of the independent variable). Later they could measure the anxiety levels of both groups again. If the post-test shows that anxiety is much lower in the experimental group than in the control group (and there had been no difference between the groups before), then the researchers can correctly attribute this difference to the effects of the therapy. Similarly, if anxiety is now clearly greater in the experimental group than in the control group, they would have to conclude that the therapy is having a harmful effect.

Q4.4[***]

An experimenter conducts a study examining the effects of television violence on children's aggressiveness. To do this she asks 40 normal schoolboys to watch one violent video a week for 40 weeks. On a standard measure of aggressiveness, which she administers both before and after the

40-week treatment, she finds that the boys are much more aggressive at the end of the study. Without knowing anything more about this study, which of the following can be ruled out as a threat to the internal validity of any conclusions she may seek to draw?

(a) History effects.
(b) Maturation effects.
(c) Mortality effects.
(d) Regression to the mean.
(e) Testing effects.

The correct answer is (d). Regression to the mean could not contribute to the effects, because the boys participating in the study were selected on the basis of their being normal rather than extreme. This would not have been true, though, if she had selected as participants the 40 most aggressive boys in the city where the study was conducted. The other factors could all be responsible for the effects she observed. For example, the boys could have become more aggressive because they dislike a new government education policy initiative or because someone has told them what the study is about (*history effects*) or because boys in general may get more aggressive as they grow up (a *maturation effect*). Less aggressive boys may have withdrawn from the study because they did not enjoy watching violent films (a *mortality effect*). Finally, the boys may have become more aggressive because they were angry at being repeatedly tested (a *testing effect*).

counterbalancing Systematic variation in the order in which participants respond to dependent measures or receive treatments. This is designed to neutralize or help quantify ***order effects*** in within-subjects designs.

fatigue effects A special case of ***maturation effects*** where performance on a post-test deteriorates as a result of boredom or tiredness associated with having already completed a ***pre-test***.

Hawthorne effect A threat to internal validity posed by people's awareness that they are participating in research. As a result of this awareness, findings arise from the *fact* that research is being done, rather than from the nature of research manipulations. The effect is a special case of ***reactivity***.

history effects Threats to internal validity posed by events occurring between two experimental observations. These events can be of both major import (e.g., the outbreak of war) or relatively mundane (e.g., participants reading a newspaper article relevant to the research).

instrumentation effects Threats to internal validity arising from changes in dependent variables and materials used to record them.

maturation effects Threats to internal validity posed by the capacity for the passage of time to produce changes in the participants between two experimental observations.

mortality effects Threats to internal validity posed by the selective withdrawal of participants from an experiment.

order effects Experimental effects that result from the sequencing of experimental treatments or the completion of dependent measures.

post-test An observation made after an experimental treatment.

practice effects A special case of *maturation effects* where performance on a *post-test* is improved as a result of the practice gained from performing a *pre-test*.

pre-test An observation made before an experimental treatment.

reactivity Change in dependent variables caused by obtaining responses on those dependent variables. This threat to internal validity is often posed by participants' reactions to particular experimental procedures or measures (e.g., feeling that they are being observed).

regression to the mean The tendency for observations and responses at the extreme end of a scale on one measure to be closer to the mean on another measure. If this problem is not recognized it constitutes a threat to internal validity.

selection effects Threats to internal validity posed by assigning participants to conditions on a non-random basis.

testing effects Threats to internal validity that arise when responses on one dependent measure affect responses on another.

Threats to external validity

In the previous section we discussed how the addition of a between-subjects manipulation to a within-subjects experiment resulted in an almost perfect basic experimental design. There is only one real problem with the strategy we outlined, and this is that the effects of testing across the two observations (O_1 and O_2) may **interact** with the experimental manipulation, so that participants who are exposed to a particular level of a treatment react to the first phase of testing differently than those who are exposed to another level (e.g., in a control condition where they receive no treatment). This reactivity does not undermine the experiment's internal validity because the effect is still due to the experimental manipulation, but it does still constitute a problem. The problem is that the results of the study may only generalize to situations where people have been given the pre-test (O_1). In other words, the pre-test–post-test design can compromise *external validity*.

For example, in our anxiety study it may be the case that when participants receive therapy they become less anxious about being tested, so they perform less anxiously at the post-test (O_2). The results of this research would thus only tell us about the effectiveness of therapy as a means of reducing anxiety about testing. The results would not necessarily tell us anything about the effectiveness of therapy for the treatment of anxiety in general.

For this reason, one modification to the above design involves getting rid of the first observation, so that there is no pre-test for the experimental treatment to react with. This design can be represented as follows:

condition	time $\longrightarrow$
experimental	X O_1
control	O_1

This design in fact represents the basic building block of most experimental research. This is largely because it is simple, neat and effective.

However, experimental pre-tests are not the only things which threaten an experiment's external validity. You may remember that we discussed the issue of generalization both in the previous chapter and earlier in this chapter. We made the point that in order to generalize from an experimental sample to another population, the sample has to be representative of the population on theoretically relevant dimensions.

A related question concerns the process by which researchers seek to generalize from experimental situations to situations beyond the experiment. How, for example, can the effects of separation on attraction be studied in an experimental situation that manipulates features of relationships quite crudely and one at a time? Isn't separation a complex phenomenon shaped by the *interaction* of multiple factors (the many different things that contribute to any human relationship) so that each separation ends up having a more or less unique effect?

This is another complex issue, and one on which a multitude of opinions exist. Broadly speaking, though, debate centres around a number of features of experimental design which are seen to have the potential to compromise external validity. These include the *reactivity* of participants both to features of experimental design (as noted above) and to the experimenter's hypothesis, and the *artificiality* of experimental settings.

Commonly cited research by Rosenthal (e.g., 1966) is particularly relevant to problems of participant reactivity. Rosenthal's research suggested that even if researchers believe they are testing a hypothesis in an even-handed way, they may lead participants to behave in the way that the experimenters want. This can be because participants respond to cues in the experiment which tell them what is expected of them. For example, a question like 'Do you *really* want to do that?' may lead participants to assume that the correct answer is 'No' and to respond accordingly. These cues are known as the experiment's **demand characteristics** (Orne, 1962), and they can be thought of as *norms* that participants conform to because they appear to be appropriate guides to behaviour in the situation they confront. We are all motivated to seek out and act upon information of this sort in our everyday lives (indeed, these processes are routinely studied by social psychologists), so it is not surprising that normative information can exert a profound influence on people's behaviour in experiments.

Behaviour by the experimenter in the form of **experimenter bias** can have a similar effect. Experimenter bias is any behaviour by the researcher that prevents a fair test of the experimental hypothesis. As an example, the experimenter may react more positively to responses that are to his or her liking (e.g., by nodding or smiling). Less subtly, the researcher may 'prod' participants so that they behave in the desired way. Indeed, in a famous experiment where rats had to learn how to run through a complex maze, some experimenters were observed literally prodding the rats that they wanted to do well in order to make them run faster (Rosenthal & Fode, 1963).

The first point to make here is that the value of any research (experimental or non-experimental) will always be irretrievably compromised by any form of *cheating*. In practice, cheating can take any number of forms – from overtly prodding participants to fabricating data. If experimenters cheat it will be a lot easier for them to confirm their hypotheses, but the problems this creates will never be remedied by improvements to experimental design.

Cheating is a very serious problem in all science. But the problems it creates in psychology are moral and not methodological in origin, and their remedy lies well beyond the scope of this book. This is mainly because if scientists cheat they are not really conducting research at all.

However, the issue of *unintentional* experimenter bias can often be attended to quite straightforwardly – simply by using an experimenter who is **blind** to the condition in which participants are placed (a procedure that is very common in drug trials). Indeed, even if experimenters are not made blind in this way, there is some doubt as to whether experimenter bias is an especially serious problem (e.g., Barber & Silver, 1968). This is partly because it appears that even when participants are aware of an experimenter's hypothesis and so are sensitive to the experiment's demand characteristics, they may be at least as likely to seek to disconfirm that hypothesis as to confirm it.

Clearly, though, participants' awareness of an experimental hypothesis can jeopardize the external validity of findings. For this reason many researchers go to considerable trouble to conceal the purpose of any experiment they conduct. This can be done by means of **deception** – either misinforming participants about the purpose of an experiment or using **concealment** to avoid telling them the whole truth. Often this involves presenting participants with a plausible (but misleading) **cover story** which informs them that an experiment is about one thing when really it is about another.

Yet probably the most important threat to external validity concerns the ability of researchers to generalize on the basis of experiments that deliberately study psychology in laboratory situations. When researchers conduct experiments they try to manipulate theoretically relevant variables while holding all others constant. The question that arises is whether this inevitably deprives those variables of their meaning and richness.

The arguments which experimentalists use to defend their practices are similar to those that we presented in discussing the meaning of representative sampling. Most would agree that experiments simplify situations that confront people in their everyday lives. Indeed, the experimental control which produces this simplicity gives experimental research its explanatory power (as we noted in Chapter 3). But whether or not in any given case this practice constitutes *over*-simplification is an empirical and theoretical issue. In other words, it is something that can only be established by considering each case on its merits and doing additional research if necessary.

So, for example, if researchers argue that experimental research into separation and attraction has over-simplified the effects of separation by not looking at how it is affected by age (or any other variable, such as wealth or power or gender), they can conduct experimental research which supports this point and leads to a revision of the original researcher's theory. The examples we use in this book usually describe simple experiments involving only one independent variable, but in fact few experiments examine variables in isolation. Instead they usually explore complex interactions between *multiple psychological and situational* features. If a theoretical principle is challenged by the findings that such research produces, researchers can reject or modify that theory or principle accordingly. This should lead to a better theory on the basis of which it is more appropriate to generalize.

It is worth noting here that there is little or no research which has ever suggested that the operation of psychological processes and the impact of psychological states necessarily differ in experiments and in the so-called real world. This is because experimental settings – even those in a laboratory – are still a part of that real world. So, effects produced in experiments can be reproduced in the real world and real-world phenomena can be reproduced in experiments. As Turner (1981) puts it, there is no Great Wall of China between the two.

Indeed, it is possible to turn the argument about the irrelevance of psychological experiments on its head. In most sciences experiments are used for the purpose of creating ideal circumstances that would not otherwise occur in real life. In psychology, too, experiments are useful *precisely because* they control for the influence of extraneous variables that cloud the analysis of everyday behaviour. On this basis, some researchers have argued that the problem with many psychology experiments is that they are too uncontrolled and therefore *too similar* to everyday life, not that they are too artificial (e.g., Dawes, 1996).

Looked at in this way, where there is a problem with generalizing from experimental research to the real world it will often arise not from the fact that the research is invalid but from the fact that it is *irrelevant*. One of the main problems with experimental research is that researchers can easily be led to examine the impact of particular variables *because they can*, rather than because they should. For this reason, the relevance of experiments in psychology can be compromised more by a researcher's motivation than by his or her method. If topics are only studied because they are easy to investigate or because the findings are easy to publish it will often be the research *questions* that are at fault, not the *conclusions*.

Which of the following can increase a researcher's ability to generalize findings from a particular piece of research?

(a) Cheating.
(b) Experimenter bias.
(c) Deception and concealment.

Q4.5[*]

(d) Participants' sensitivity to demand characteristics.

(e) The use of unrepresentative samples.

The correct answer is (c). A researcher's ability to generalize a given set of research findings to other settings will often be *enhanced* by the use of deception (e.g., use of a cover story), because this can reduce the likelihood of participants reacting to the experimental hypothesis and deliberately behaving in a way that supports or undermines that hypothesis. (a) and (b) are wrong because the same is not true of any conduct by the experimenter which wittingly (e.g., in the form of cheating) or unwittingly (e.g., in the form of experimenter bias) contributes to support for an experimental hypothesis. Behaviour by the participants which is affected by their knowledge of the hypotheses (i.e., demand characteristics) may also make the research findings specific to that experimental situation – so (d) is wrong. (e) is wrong because the use of unrepresentative samples will also make research findings specific to that experimental sample.

blind (experimental) A control for experimenter bias achieved by ensuring that the experimenter is unaware of the condition to which participants have been assigned. This is often called a *double blind* if the participants are also unaware of which condition they are in (i.e., the level of treatment they are receiving).

concealment A research strategy similar to ***deception*** which involves giving participants limited information about a study (rather than misleading them with false information).

cover story Information about the supposed purpose of a piece of research which conceals its actual purpose.

deception The strategy of misleading participants in order to conceal the purpose of some research.

demand characteristics Cues which convey an experimental hypothesis to participants.

experimenter bias A threat to external validity that arises when experimenters construct or conduct an experiment in such a way that it unfairly tests (and usually is more likely to support) an experimental hypothesis.

interaction A situation where the effect of one independent variable depends on the level of another. If the effect of people's wealth on their happiness also depends on their intelligence (e.g., so that only intelligent wealthy people are happy), there is an interaction between wealth and intelligence.

Further reading

As indicated above, Campbell and Stanley's (1963) book represents a classic contribution to the field of experimental design and is well worth reading. Haslam and McGarty's (2003) chapter builds on the ideas discussed in this chapter, but uses examples from current research in social psychology and is pitched at a more advanced level.

Campbell, D. T., & Stanley, J. C. (1963). *Experimental and quasi-experimental designs for research*. Chicago: Rand McNally.

Haslam, S. A., & McGarty, C. (2003). Experimental design and causality in social psychological research. In C. Sansone, C.C. Morf & A.T. Panter (Eds.), *Handbook of methods in social psychology*: pp. 237–64 Thousand Oaks, CA: Sage.

Experimental design: A checklist for research evaluation and improvement

Potential problem	Question to ask	Potential improvement
No manipulation check	Have the researchers taken steps to ensure that a variable has been manipulated effectively?	If the efficacy of an experimental manipulation is in doubt, include a manipulation check to help clarify matters.
Insensitivity of the DV	Is the manipulation of the IV strong enough to produce discernable effects on the DV?	If the manipulation of the IV is too weak, try to identify ways of strengthening it or of making the DV more sensitive (bearing in mind how any changes may impact upon the theoretical relevance of the DV).
Irrelevance of the DV	Is the DV relevant to the phenomenon in which the researchers are interested?	If the DV is not relevant enough, try to identify ways of making it more relevant (bearing in mind how any changes may impact upon the sensitivity of the DV).
Sampling bias	Are the research participants representative of the population of interest on *theoretically relevant* dimensions?	If the sample is not representative of the population, conduct a replication with a more representative population.
Naive empiricism	Are the researchers seeking to generalize from experimental evidence without recourse to theory?	Work on theory development before conducting an experiment to ensure that experimental manipulations (and subsequent generalization) are informed by theory.
Maturation effects	Are responses affected by the fact that time has passed (and participants have matured) since	Consider whether effects attributable to maturation, practice, fatigue, history, testing, reactivity, order, instrumentation or mortality

	Potential problem	Question to ask	Potential improvement
		previous responses were obtained?	may be implicated in experimental findings. If this is the case, consider the relative merits of studies in which either (a) the order of measures and/or treatments is randomized, (b) the order of measures and/or treatments is counter-balanced or (c) different participants are randomly assigned to conditions in which they complete different measures and/or respond to different treatments (including a control condition).
	Practice effects	Are responses affected by the fact that participants had more practice at performing a task as a study progressed?	"
	Fatigue effects	Are responses affected by the fact that participants became more tired as a study progressed?	"
	History effects	Are responses affected by the fact that things have happened in the world since previous responses were obtained?	"
	Testing effects	Are responses affected by the experience of previous testing?	"
	Reactivity	Are responses affected by the fact that participants know they are taking part in research?	"
	Order effects	Are responses affected by the order in which responses are made?	"
	Instrumentation effects	Are responses affected by changes to features of the testing environment since previous responses were obtained?	"
	Mortality effects	Are responses affected by an inability to collect data from participants who	"

Potential problem	Question to ask	Potential improvement	
	took part in a previous phase of research?		
Selection effects	Are responses affected by the researchers' decision to assign particular participants to particular conditions?	If assignment to conditions is non-random, consider whether any differences in the populations from which participants in different conditions are drawn may be contributing to the observed effects. If this is the case, consider (a) matching participants on dimensions of potentially important difference or (b) randomly assigning participants to conditions.	
Regression to the mean	Are responses affected by the fact that in a previous phase of research participants were selected on the basis of their extremity on a dimension of interest to the researcher?	Consider using a between-subjects design where extreme participants are assigned randomly to treatment and control conditions. Alternatively, conduct research using a random sample of participants.	
Interaction between pre-test and IV	Are the effects of an experimental treatment restricted to situations in which this is coupled with a particular pre-test?	If validity is compromised by a pre-test (or there is no clear need for one) simplify the experimental design by removing it.	
Unnecessary pre-test	Is internal or external validity compromised by the use of a pre-test?	"	
Demand characteristics	Are particular responses encouraged by the researchers or by features of the research environment?	If responses are affected by participants' or researchers' awareness of (or beliefs about) experimental hypotheses, consider either (a) keeping participants blind to the conditions to which they have been assigned and/or to the hypotheses (e.g., through concealment or deception), (b) making the experimenters blind to the conditions to which participants have been assigned, or (c) conducting a double-blind study in which both participants and researchers are unaware of the conditions to which participants have been assigned.	

Potential problem	Question to ask	Potential improvement
Experimenter bias	Is the researchers' behaviour preventing a fair test of an experimental hypothesis?	"
Over-simplification; artificiality	Does an experimental design promote an over-simplified understanding of a psychological process or phenomenon?	If the conclusions drawn from experimental research appear to be over-simplified, develop a critique along these lines and design research (experimental or otherwise) which tests and promotes a more complex analysis.
Irrelevance	Are the processes examined in a particular experiment irrelevant to the broader issues in which the researchers purport to be interested?	If experimental research appears to be of questionable 'real-world' relevance, develop a critique along these lines and design research (experimental or otherwise) which *is* relevant.

Q4.6**

A researcher conducts an experiment to investigate the effects of mood on memory. In the experiment, before they are given any material to learn, half of the participants are given a box of chocolates, and the other half are given nothing. Which of the following statements is *not* true?

(a) Mood is a between-subjects variable.
(b) The experiment has two conditions.
(c) The experiment includes a control condition.
(d) The independent variable is manipulated within subjects.
(e) Experimental control eliminates potential threats to the internal validity of the experiment.

Q4.7*

Which of the following is a researcher's overall objective in using matching?

(a) To control for extraneous variables in quasi-experimental designs.
(b) To increase participants' enjoyment of correlational research.
(c) To ensure that participants are randomly assigned to conditions.
(d) To ensure that groups of participants do not differ in age and sex.
(e) To ensure that groups of participants do not differ in intelligence.

Q4.8**

Which of the following threats to validity can never be methodologically controlled?

(a) Maturation effects.
(b) Cheating.
(c) History effects.
(d) Sensitivity to demand characteristics.
(e) Experimenter bias.

Q4.9**

Some researchers decided to conduct an experiment to investigate the effects of a new psychological therapy on people's self-esteem. To do this they asked all their clients who were currently receiving treatment for low self-esteem to continue using an old therapy but treated all their new clients with the new therapy. A year later they found that clients subjected to the new therapy had much higher self-esteem. Which of the following statements is true?

(a) The greater self-esteem of the clients exposed to the new therapy resulted from the superiority of that therapy.
(b) The greater self-esteem of the clients exposed to the new therapy resulted from the fact that the new clients were more optimistic than those who were previously receiving treatment.
(c) The greater self-esteem of the clients exposed to the new therapy resulted from the fact that the new clients were less disillusioned with therapy than those who were previously receiving treatment.
(d) The greater self-esteem of the clients exposed to the new therapy resulted from the fact that the new clients were more intelligent than those who were previously receiving treatment.
(e) It is impossible to establish the validity of any of the above statements based on the results of this study.

The correct answer to 4.6 is (d). This experiment has two conditions: an experimental condition designed to create good mood and a control condition. As (a) suggests, mood is manipulated between subjects as participants are assigned to either the control condition or the experimental condition. Only if the same participants were exposed to different levels of the mood manipulation and completed a memory test after each would the independent variable be manipulated within subjects – so (b) is wrong. Note, however, that a within-subjects manipulation would pose a number of threats to internal validity. In particular, this is because the two tests would have to be different in order to rule out effects due to *reactivity*, and then any difference could be due to *testing effects*. As answers (c) and (e) suggest, these threats are eliminated in this design by the addition of an experimental control group.

The correct answer to 4.7 is (a). Matching is a procedure used to ensure that when participants have been assigned to groups on the basis of differences in an independent variable (e.g., age), they do not differ systematically on other variables which could plausibly lead to their being different on the dependent variable (i.e., extraneous variables such as wealth and level of education). Any variable other than the independent variable is extraneous, so these are not confined to differences in age, sex or intelligence as answers (d) and (e) suggest. Matching is normally carried out precisely when random assignment is not possible – so (c) is wrong. (b) is wrong because matching does not have any systematic impact on participants' enjoyment of research.

The correct answer to 4.8 is (b). Experimental design, however good, can never overcome dishonesty on the part of the experimenter. Maturation effects (a) and history effects (c) can be controlled by use of a control group to check for any spurious effects that arise from the passing of time. Participants' sensitivity to demand characteristics (d) may be eliminated through the use of an appropriate cover story, and experimenter bias (e) can be eliminated by not informing the experimenter of the experimental condition to which participants have been assigned (i.e., making them blind).

The correct answer to 4.9 is (e). The problem with establishing the validity of any interpretation of these results arises from the method of participant *selection*. This experiment is actually a quasi-experiment, and because the participants were not randomly assigned to treatment conditions, it is possible that the difference between groups arose from differences *associated* with the therapy they received, not from the therapy itself. It is quite possible that the clients who were receiving treatment before the experiment started and who continued receiving the old therapy were more jaded, more fatigued, less intelligent, more depressed and so on than the new clients assigned to receive the new therapy. They may even have had lower self-esteem to start with. Any one of these differences may have been responsible for the difference between the groups' self-esteem at the post-test. In other words, any of (a), (b), (c) and (d) *could* be true, but by the same token they could all be false.

Discussion/essay questions

(a) What factors govern the choice of an independent variable?
(b) What factors govern the choice of a dependent variable?
(c) How can experimental data obtained from students contribute to our understanding of general psychological process?
(d) What are the main problems associated with experiments that use within-subjects designs?
(e) What role does counterbalancing play in experimental research?

Exercise

(a) John wants to conduct an experiment to assess the effect of a new teaching technique (the treatment, X) on four-year-old children. In planning his research, he considers the designs below. What are the primary problems, if any, with each (assume participants are assigned randomly to conditions)?

   (i) O_1 X O_2

        O_2

   (ii) O_1 X O_2

             X O_2

   (iii)   X O_2

                  O_2

   (iv) O_1 X O_2

        O_1 O_2

   (v) O_1 X O_2

                  O_2

        O_1 O_2

             X O_2

   (vi) O_1 O_2

                  O_2

Survey Design

Many people are familiar with opinion polls or surveys, and just about everyone who reads this book will have participated in such a survey at some time or other. In an opinion poll the opinions of members of a sample are measured in order to estimate the amount of support for particular opinions in the general community. For example, pollsters might randomly select a sample of 2000 voters from around a country and try to establish which political parties and policies those people endorse. In this case the researchers conduct the poll not because they are more interested in the views of this sample of people than in the views of the rest of the population, but precisely because they want to use these people's responses to estimate what the opinions of the rest of the population are. In a political opinion poll, the aim is often to predict which candidate or party will win a forthcoming election.

The term 'survey' is therefore one that most people will have come across before. However, in this chapter we want to work with a precise definition that distinguishes surveys from experiments. The definition rests on the idea that in any piece of research you have to *measure* variables but you do not necessarily have to *manipulate* them. If you measure dependent variables *and* manipulate independent variables you are doing an experiment; if you measure both then you are doing a survey.

In this chapter we start by considering the differences between surveys and experiments in more detail. We then look at the sorts of question that surveys are used to answer. After that we examine the process of finding a sample or selecting participants to help answer research questions. Finally, we discuss some of the different types of survey technique available.

The differences between surveys and experiments

If they were asked to make a general observation about the difference between surveys and experiments a lot of people would say that surveys involve doing research in the community and that experiments involve doing research in the laboratory. This is often true, but it is not always the case. We have already noted that surveys can be done in places which have the words 'Psychology Laboratory' on the door, and that experiments can be done in the field.

The main differences between experiments and surveys relate to the sorts of question that surveys and experiments can answer. As we discussed in Chapters 3 and 4, experimental research tends to be concerned with establishing causal relationships between variables. Experimenters typically do this by comparing different groups which have been equated by randomization. If the differences between groups are big enough, they conclude that the difference arises from the manipulation of the independent variable.

In contrast, surveys tend to be concerned with measuring naturally occurring *relationships* between variables. The results from the sample surveyed are generalized to the population; that is, they are used to estimate the characteristics of the population of interest. It is important to note that any statement about the population is always an *estimate* and therefore statements about observed relationships are always made with some *uncertainty*.

Let us compare two studies of the same question to see how the experimental and the survey methods would treat them differently. We will look at the effect of televised violence on aggressiveness in children – a question of interest to social, developmental and personality psychologists. Some researchers would address this question using the experimental method. They might take a sample of 100 children, randomly divide them into two groups (experimental and control) and then show the experimental group a television programme containing some violence. The control group could be shown an episode from the same series that did not include violence. After the children had watched the programme the experimenters could measure the amount of violence that the children displayed in a specified period (e.g., the next hour).

Taking a rather different tack, survey researchers might measure (rather than manipulate) the amount of violent television that children watch and then measure the aggressiveness of the children. This research procedure might involve selecting a random sample of 1000 children and then giving their parents a **questionnaire** which asks them to list the television programmes that their children normally watch. The questionnaire would also ask the parents to describe their children's behaviour. The researchers would **code** the level of violence in the television programmes that each child watches and the parents' descriptions of the aggressiveness of their children's behaviour. There could be lots of variations on this research which would improve the methodology of the study, but this is a fair example of how this question could be addressed by survey techniques.

This example illustrates two key differences between experiments and surveys. First and foremost, the experiment allows researchers to manipulate variables and to use experimental control. Secondly, surveys tend to involve many more participants (often more than 10 times as many). This means that survey research can be much more expensive to conduct.

The fact that surveys require more participants is hard to get around. A major reason for this is that survey and experimental research often have different objectives. The key difference is in what they aim to generalize. As we noted in Chapter 3, survey researchers try to generalize from the sample directly to the population in order to make statements about the relationships observed in everyday life between psychological, behavioural and environmental characteristics. In order to do this they need to ensure that their sample is a **representative random sample** of the population.

Experimenters, on the other hand, try to establish controlled conditions where they show the immediate effect of some independent variable on a dependent variable. As we discussed in Chapter 4, they seek to establish controls so that they can generalize observed *processes* to a population where the same conditions are found. In contrast, survey research tries to generalize a particular result to the population.

Experiments are therefore well suited to investigate things that are believed to be changeable. In particular, they are used to examine the dynamic mental processes that we talked about in Chapter 3. Surveys are more suitable for studying things that are believed to be constant and enduring – like intelligence or personality.

We can illustrate these points by referring back to the example of research into televised violence. Let us imagine that the experimenters found that children in the experimental group were more likely to go out and hit another child than were children in the control group. The researchers might seek to generalize this finding by saying that their research shows that watching televised violence makes children more likely to commit *aggressive acts*. Survey researchers, however, might find that children who watched violent television programmes were more likely than those children who did not watch violent programmes to be rated as aggressive by their parents. They might then seek to generalize this finding by saying that *aggressiveness* is associated with watching TV.

Survey techniques thus lend themselves to examination of stable long-term states or conditions, while experiments are more suited to studying the immediate effects of psychological processes on behaviour. So, in the above example the survey and the experiment actually address related but subtly different questions. The experiment addresses the immediate effects of one television programme, and the survey addresses the long-term effect of televised violence on aggressiveness as a stable characteristic of the child.

As we also noted in Chapter 3, the main feature that distinguishes surveys from experiments is that the experiment allows us to infer causal relationships. In our example, the most that the survey researchers can hope to demonstrate is that watching violent television programmes is or is not associated with aggressive behaviour. Survey research never allows us to say that violent television causes aggressive behaviour because there are always other uncontrolled variables that could have produced any observed effect. Perhaps aggressive children like to watch violent programmes, or perhaps boredom leads people both to be aggressive and to watch violent programmes. That is, if children who watch more violent programmes are more aggressive it need not be the case that watching violent programmes *causes* aggressiveness. Again, the point here is that correlation is not causation. The fact that two things are associated with each other does not mean that one causes the other.

In experiments we can make such causal inferences. If we find a difference in aggressiveness between the experimental and the control conditions then this difference can only be due to one of two things: random error or the manipulation of the independent variable. This is because we have *controlled* everything else. In Chapters 7 and 8 we will discuss how we make the decision as to whether chance or the manipulation is the most plausible cause.

Given this enormous advantage that experiments offer the psychological scientist, one might reasonably ask why researchers bother doing anything other than experiments. The answer is that sometimes scientists are only interested in observing relationships. This is especially true in the initial stages of research where it is often useful to observe what is going on before launching into experimental manipulations – not least because we may have no detailed idea as to which variables to manipulate. Even if people do not conduct formal surveys before they do experimental research on the issue, they will often at least attempt to make some observations relevant to the process in which they are interested. Also, there are circumstances under which scientists are not allowed or not able to conduct experiments.

These issues apply to all sciences, not just psychology. Astronomers and geologists rarely do experiments, simply because it would be difficult or impossible to manipulate the independent variables of interest (such as the position of certain stars or the depth of the earth's crust). Instead they rely largely on the same logic of controlled observation that underpins psychological surveys. Clearly, this does not mean that astronomy and geology are unscientific. Similarly, an epidemiologist (who studies the spread of a disease) would not be allowed to release a disease into a human community. All the epidemiologist can do is study diseases that have already occurred. Psychologists often confront the same problem – one of the main reasons why they are unable to manipulate some important variables is that such manipulation would be unethical (*see Chapter 13*).

There are two complications in this overview of the differences between surveys and experiments. Some surveys actually involve manipulations (e.g., those that use **split-ballot techniques**), and if these involve full experimental control then they are really experiments. Some surveys also incorporate manipulations without random-ization and, as we discussed in Chapter 4, these are called quasi-experiments.

Another question you might reasonably ask is how surveys can have independent variables when no variables are actually manipulated. The answer is that in surveys independent variables are variables the researcher *believes to be* causal. If researchers do not manipulate variables they cannot prove that they *are* causal variables. They can, however, prove they are *not* causal variables. Understandably, there is quite a lot of confusion on this point: correlation cannot prove causa-tion, but a lack of a correlation can disprove causation. If our television survey found no relationship at all between the amount of violent television watched and aggressive behaviour (using valid and reliable measures) then aggressive behaviour cannot be caused by violent television. Thus, under certain conditions, survey methods can allow researchers to falsify causal hypotheses.

Q5.1*

Surveys are preferred in some areas of psychology for which of the following reasons?

(a) They are usually cheaper.
(b) They allow researchers to infer causal relationships.
(c) They are more scientific because similar methods are used in astronomy and geology.

(d) It is often impossible to manipulate the independent variables the researchers are interested in.

(e) They use randomization to achieve random sampling.

The correct answer is (d). (a) is wrong because surveys are often more expensive than other forms of research. (b) is wrong because surveys do not involve manipulations or experimental control and cannot establish cause. (c) is wrong because science involves both experimental and survey methods. (e) is wrong because although they sound the same, *randomization* and *random sampling* are quite different ideas. Random sampling relates to the procedure for selecting the sample; randomization is the process for assigning participants randomly to different conditions.

code A scheme for converting responses into numerical values. Researchers might write something like 'Sex was *coded* 1 = male, 2 = female'. All this means is that when describing the results, numbers are used rather than words. This is a useful thing to do for the purpose of analysing data.

questionnaire A set of questions to be answered by a research participant. These questions could be printed and given to the participant or asked by the researcher in an interview.

representative random sample A random sample of the population that has the same characteristics as the population.

split-ballot technique A survey research procedure whereby experimental manipulations are included. The most obvious form involves randomly selected participants receiving different *questionnaires*. In effect, split-ballot techniques are not surveys but experiments.

Setting the question

Many surveys are designed to estimate the level of one or more variables in the population. This is true of political opinion polls, for example. Psychological surveys are more commonly concerned to estimate relationships between variables. Just about any issue in psychology can be addressed in a survey design if a researcher has enough time and resources. As noted above, survey researchers normally try to establish the relationship between variables. The question might be what is the relationship between gender and verbal reasoning,

or between personality disorders and homelessness, or between age and
level of understanding of emotion. In each case we want to know if one
of the variables is related to the other – whether gender differences are
linked to differences in verbal reasoning, whether personality disorders
are associated with homelessness or whether children's understanding
of emotion changes as they grow older.

In all of these cases we cannot manipulate the relevant variables. We
cannot make people belong to different sexes, we cannot give people
personality disorders or make them homeless, we cannot make children
become older. Nevertheless, we can often *eliminate* the possibility that
some relationships are causal if it is the case that one thing can only
cause another if it occurs *before* the other. Children's eye colour could be
caused by their parents' eye colour (in fact it is), but parents' eye colour
cannot be caused by their children's. Similarly, it is silly to think that
improving children's understanding of emotion will increase their
physical age. Therefore in both of these examples if we were to observe
a relationship between these things, one possible causal explanation of
that relationship could be eliminated.

Researchers decide which relationships to investigate in their surveys
by a complex process (along the lines outlined in Chapter 2). The actual
questions they address are determined by events that occur within
scientific communities and within the general community. In this way
theoretical development and pressing social issues often come together
to determine the precise questions that survey researchers investigate.

Finding a sample

Once we have decided what research questions we want to address we
need to find some participants to help us answer them. That is, we need
to decide what population to sample from (Chapter 4). Most survey
researchers want to control sampling for two reasons. They want to
reduce the amount of uncertainty about their sample so that it is as
small as possible (see the discussion of sampling error at the end of
Chapter 6), and they want to be able to generalize the results of their
study to the relevant population.

A good example of this process is a political opinion poll where a
sample of people are asked which political candidate they are going
to vote for. Ethical researchers do not aim to produce a change in such
opinions, they want to find out what those opinions really are. They
want to eliminate uncertainty about whether the opinions really are
what they appear to be and they want to know that the methods they
use are *reliable* and that the opinions expressed are *valid* reflections

of people's real voting intentions (in fact, we can never be totally sure about this latter point). In this case, the poll is only useful if it can be generalized to the entire population of voters (in other words, the poll needs to have *external validity*).

When researchers are interested in any large population, if the sample they study is not representative of that population it does not matter if they have two dozen, two thousand or two million people in their survey. If the sample is not representative, the only thing a bigger sample does is lead researchers to draw the wrong conclusions more confidently.

One of the best examples of this point was provided by the *Literary Digest* survey of voter preference for the 1936 United States presidential election. This magazine conducted what was one of the largest ever political opinion polls. Its researchers contacted every US voter who was listed in the telephone directory or who was registered as owning a car. They obtained over 2 million responses (a typical opinion poll of the US population today will involve between 1000 and 2000 people). Despite their prodigious effort the pollsters got the result completely wrong. The poll said that the Republican candidate, Landon, would win by a land-slide when in fact President Roosevelt was re-elected. The apparent reason for this failure to predict the correct outcome was that the researchers had limited their sample to the wealthier segments of the population who owned cars and telephones. This population was *not* the same as the US voting population in 1936 (though it would be far more representative now). So although the researchers had a big sample it was a very biased (i.e., unrepresentative) sample. Similar problems would have occurred in the last US presidential election if pollsters had limited their sample to male voters, white voters or voters who were members of a golf club.

It is therefore essential that a survey sample is representative of the population of interest. If it is not, then the sample is useless for any purpose. We noted in Chapter 4 that for many psychological experiments the population in which researchers are interested is *all* human beings who display the psychological process they are investigating. For research into visual perception, the population of interest is usually people with normal vision. So for research in this area just about anybody with normal vision who can communicate what he or she sees and understands the experimenter's instructions can be part of the sample. No matter how narrowly people are chosen, they should be representative of people with normal vision. Similar sampling consid-erations are true for many other areas of psychology. This sampling procedure is called **convenience sampling**.

The alternatives to convenience sampling are **systematic sam-pling** methods, which can be divided into **probability sampling** and

non-probability sampling techniques. Probability sampling involves drawing people from the population so that any member of the population has a specifiable probability of being sampled. This sounds complex, but all it means is that when we select a probability sample we have to know what each population member's chance of being included in the sample is. In **simple random sampling** (a special case of probability sampling) every individual has exactly the same probability of being sampled.

Simple random sampling involves obtaining a complete listing of the population of interest, whether that be a class list, the voter roll, a telephone directory or something else. This listing is called a **sampling frame**. For the *Literary Digest* survey the telephone directory and the list of car owners constituted the sampling frame (the problem was that the sampling frame did not list the entire population of interest). To draw a simple random sample from the population the researchers would then attach a number to each person in the listing and if that number is chosen by a random process (e.g., pulling numbers out of a bucket, or using a table of random numbers) that person would be included in the sample. Simple random sampling is one method that makes it possible to obtain a representative random sample of the population.

Non-probability sampling includes all techniques where there is not an identifiable probability of each member of the population being included in the population. Convenience sampling is one form of non-probability sampling; another is **purposive sampling**. Purposive sampling involves obtaining a sample who all have a particular characteristic. For example, researchers who are interested in the effects of televised violence on children might take a random sample of the whole population and then exclude households where there were no children. But it might be more sensible just to go out and try to find a group of children. These children would suit the researchers' purpose but would not have been drawn randomly from the population. The same point applies if researchers are interested in studying mental illnesses and personality disorders. If they want to find out what the level of the mental illness schizophrenia is in the community, it makes sense to sample the entire population. However, if they want to find the relationship between schizophrenia and other mental illnesses (like depression) it makes sense to restrict their sample to schizophrenics.

Once researchers have decided on a sampling procedure they need to make a decision about the **sample size**. If the researchers eliminate systematic bias from the sample then the bigger the sample is, the better it will reflect the population and so the better it will be for the research. This is because, for reasons we will discuss in Chapter 7, a larger sample size reduces uncertainty about what conclusions it is appropriate to draw on the basis of data obtained from the sample.

The size of the chosen sample will be reduced by **non-response**. This occurs, for example, where people do not feel like participating in or forget to participate in the research, or their responses are lost in the mail. This is a problem because a smaller sample size reduces the ability of researchers to draw conclusions from the research. More importantly, though, it can also introduce threats to both internal and external validity. For example, if people choose not to respond because they are offended by the **survey instrument** then the sample will be unrepresentative of the population. For example, if a questionnaire in North America is called 'A Study of Housewives' Attitudes' then it might be the case that people who object to the term 'housewife' will refuse to fill in the questionnaire. This problem is one of *reactivity* – a threat to both internal and external validity that we discussed in the previous chapter. Similarly, it is conceivable that only highly motivated people will respond to the survey and not those who are too busy or too lazy (this is a problem of *mortality*). In both cases the survey might therefore systematically exclude a relevant part of the population (e.g., feminists or the unmotivated) and, as in the case of the 1936 *Literary Digest* survey, this would lead to biased results.

Q5.2[***]

A television news programme shows a murder case including video footage of the grieving parents of the victim. The television station then conducts an opinion poll in which it asks viewers to phone in and vote for or against the death penalty for murder. The results of the survey show that 83% of the 20 000 viewers who ring in are in favour of the death penalty. Which of the following statements is true?

(a) The results of this study can only be generalized to people who watch news programmes.

(b) The results of this study can only be generalized to people who own a television.

(c) The results of this study can only be generalized to people who care about the death penalty.

(d) The results of this study can only be generalized when we know much more about the sampling method.

(e) The results of this study can only be generalized if the bias created by showing the grieving parents is eliminated.

The correct answer is (d). Unless we know more about the way the sample is selected we cannot draw any conclusion about the true level of support for the death penalty in the community. In this case the sample selects itself from those who are watching the programme and who have access to a telephone. Nevertheless, we cannot say that (a) or (b) is true because only a subset of those who watch the programme or have access to phones will ring in. We do not know how that sample selects itself so we cannot conclude that it is a *representative* sample. It is likely that of the people who watch the programme, only those people who care a lot about the issue will phone in, but we cannot be sure. Perhaps only people who have faith in phone-in polls take part. Some people might also phone in several times. Answer (c) sounds plausible but it is only a hunch about a possible source of bias. Answer (e) also sounds plausible, but it is only a guess and not necessarily true. In short, people are well advised to treat the results of phone-in polls with a great deal of caution.

convenience sampling A sampling procedure where a sample is chosen from the people who are available to participate in research. Often just about any person who can understand the instructions and complete the task is acceptable. This is the technique used in many psychological experiments (often involving undergraduate students).

non-probability sampling A sampling technique where there is not a specifiable probability of a member of the population being sampled.

non-response The failure to obtain responses in circumstances where a person is selected from the population but does not actually participate in the survey.

probability sampling A sampling technique where there is a specifiable probability of each member of the population being sampled.

purposive sampling Selecting those members of a population who have a definable characteristic. For example, a study of depression might sample only those members of a population who are clinically depressed.

sample size The number of participants in a study. This is represented by the symbol N.

sampling frame A listing of all members of the population of interest.

simple random sample A random sample in which every member of the population has the same probability of being included.

survey instrument A means of collecting data from the sample. This could be a questionnaire form or an interview.

systematic sampling Sampling where participants are selected according to a specific plan or method (either ***probability*** or ***non-probability sampling***).

Types of survey

So far we have talked about survey design in very general terms. In fact there are many different survey methods and the wide choice reflects the many different interests, approaches and objectives of psychologists. We cannot, for example, expect that the same techniques would be applicable to studying adults and children, or for answering questions in cognitive and clinical psychology. It is difficult to say that one method is always better than another, though some techniques are certainly better than others for particular purposes.

Questionnaires are normally printed booklets with instructions and questions. These can be administered by researchers (i.e., handed out and then collected), mailed out to potential participants, or distributed by other means such as electronic mail or in a magazine.

Interviews are really just questionnaires where the questions are asked by researchers in person or over the phone. The interviewer writes down or records the response as he or she asks each question.

Computer-aided interviewing is used for telephone surveys. The computer assists the interviewers by telling them which question to ask next. Computer-aided interviewing allows researchers to conduct split-ballot surveys. That is, they can help to turn surveys into experiments by introducing manipulations. The computer achieves this because it is programmed either to produce different questions depending on pre-vious responses or to ask different people different questions (randomly assigning them to different conditions).

Naturalistic observational studies are widely used in both human and animal research and involve the observation of behaviour without any attempt to interfere with it. So, for example, comparative psychologists might study the behaviour of animals by observing them in the wild or environmental psychologists might study the movement of people through a shopping centre or the flow of traffic through an intersection. In neither case would any intervention take place (e.g., in the form of an experimental manipulation).

These observational studies can take many forms. One possibility is direct public observation where the participants are fully aware that they are being observed. This is normally true in *case studies* (as discussed in Chapter 3). For example, organizational psychologists might want to know how corporate boardrooms really work. Suppose they want to examine the hypothesis that male board members have more power than female members. The psychologists might obtain permission to attend a company's boardroom meetings for a few months in order to get a picture of what is going on. While attending meetings they would attempt to measure the amount of control over decisions that was exerted by males and females. To do this they might record the amount of time male and female board members spent talking during meetings, the number of times their suggestions were agreed to by other members, or the number of times males and females were interrupted.

Obviously, there are other possible research strategies that could be used in this case. For example, the researchers could give a questionnaire to the board members. The problem is that what people write down on their questionnaires would not necessarily correspond to their behaviour in their everyday lives. If the researchers ask male board members whether they give fair consideration to the proposals of female board members then they may well say that they do. They may say this because it is true, or they may say it because it is **socially desirable** (i.e., they think it is the right thing to say), or because they do not remember how they actually behave (can you remember which shoe you put on first every day?). The point here is that people do not have perfect memories and they are not always totally honest.

This problem is illustrated by attempts to establish the popularity of television programmes using questionnaires (ratings booklets). These usually obtain different results from those obtained by electronic devices attached to television sets (called 'people meters'). One inter-pretation of this discrepancy is that when people fill in the question-naires at the end of the week they forget, or lie about, what they have actually watched. Because of this it has been argued that questionnaires are an unreliable measure of viewer preference. Questionnaires may also be invalid measures if responses are biased. This could occur if people reported that they had watched particularly desirable or popular programmes. For example, it is easy to imagine that adoles-cents might not wish to report everything they had seen if they thought their parents would see the ratings book.

So, as in much psychological research, we are caught between two problems: that if we ask people to tell us what they think they may not be accurate (because they cannot tell us the truth or they do not want to tell us); and that if we simply observe behaviour we may also make mistakes (possibly due to experimenter bias). Another big problem is that if people know that they are being observed they may act differently. Think again of the case of the boardroom. Would male members be prepared to act in an aggressive or dominating manner if they knew their behaviour was being observed by outsiders? Perhaps not, because this behaviour would look bad to the observers.

These problems to do with the social desirability of responses apply to many types of research including experiments, questionnaires and observational studies. Again the problem reflects the more general issue of *reactivity* that we discussed in the previous chapter.

One way around this problem is to use **non-obtrusive measures**. These are research procedures which ensure that the participants are *not aware* that they are being involved in the research process (these methods are also called **non-reactive techniques**). The logic of such research is that people cannot change their behaviour in response to being observed if they do not actually know they are being observed. In observational studies this could be done by making audio recordings, by using secret video cameras or one-way mirrors, or by infiltrating organizations with researchers who pretended not to be researchers. There are serious ethical issues associated with conducting this sort of research (which we will discuss in Chapter 13) because the participants have not given their consent to be observed. Such hidden observation is always considered to be acceptable by scientists where the participants are animals (i.e., it is always acceptable to observe animals in their natural habitat, providing that that habitat is not disturbed by the research). Hidden observation is also acceptable where human participants are unable to give consent but someone else is legally able to (such as the parent or guardian of young children). However, a hidden camera in a boardroom or living room is extremely unlikely to be considered acceptable (however interesting the results might be).

Another alternative open to researchers who want to conduct non-reactive research is to use **archival records** or *behavioural trace measures* (see Chapter 3). Archival studies involve checking through records of behaviour such as books, videos, Internet sites and so on. These are non-reactive because the behaviour has occurred in the past so the participants cannot change it as a reaction to being observed. Rather than watching what goes on in a corporate boardroom, the researchers may obtain evidence of what has happened in boardrooms in the past (e.g., minutes and other records of meetings, the autobiographies of chief executives, and so on). The researchers might operationalize dominance as the number of times proposals brought by male and female board members were accepted. This technique is exactly the same as the methods that historians often use in their research.

Research examining physical traces of behaviour attempts to use evidence of a previous behaviour to define some dependent variable. These techniques are identical to the techniques used by archaeologists.

The researchers might look at which seats the female board members were assigned, perhaps assuming that more dominant board members would occupy seats closer to the chairperson of the meeting (naturally, they would need to establish that this was a valid and reliable measure of dominance). If females are allocated less dominant seats then this evidence would be consistent with the researchers' hypothesis (although it would not establish a causal relationship between gender and dominance).

As we noted earlier, a lot of survey research is concerned with variables that have long-term effects. Often it is not possible or appropriate for experimenters to control people's lives for extended periods of time, so it can be difficult to investigate variables which have long-term effects using experimental techniques. Thinking back to the example of televised violence, it is obviously the case that very few parents would allow experimenters to control the television diet of their children over a period of weeks or months. Surveys deal with these issues more effectively.

Research that examines long-term effects of ageing and maturation uses **developmental surveys**. A common type of developmental survey is the **cross-sectional study**. In this type of study a cross-section or slice of the population is taken at a particular point in time. If psychologists want to know whether the number of years of education has any effect on IQ scores then they need to study people who differ in the years of education they have received. Obviously they cannot *manipulate* the length of education. One possibility would be to take a sample of people with (say) 10 years of education and compare them to a sample with 12 years of education. A problem would arise, however, in the internal validity of this study. If a difference in IQ were found, we could not be sure that the difference was due to the number of years of education rather than some other difference between the samples. Any such differences are *confounds*, and this example can again be used to make the point that correlation does not establish causation. Perhaps people with higher IQ scores tend to stay at school longer (i.e., IQ could cause years of education and not the other way around).

The main alternative to the cross-sectional design is the **longitudinal study**. A longitudinal study involves taking a sample of participants and following them over a period of time. As an example, a longitudinal study into the effects of education on IQ might measure the IQs of a sample of students with 10 years of education and then measure them again 2 years later. Using the terminology that was introduced in Chapter 4, the difference between cross-sectional and longitudinal designs is that cross-sectional studies are conducted between subjects and longitudinal studies are conducted within subjects. The advantage of the longitudinal study is that it allows the researchers to use each participant as his or her own control and this serves to reduce uncertainty involved in deciding whether key variables are really having an effect (see Chapter 7).

However, longitudinal studies of this type can fall victim to a number of additional threats to internal validity in the form of testing, mortality and maturation effects (Chapter 4). In our example, the effects of all three problems can be seen quite clearly. First, it is apparent that repeated *testing* may produce changes in the participants. People may get better at doing IQ tests through practice. Alternatively, they may start to do worse on the tests because they become bored or lose interest. *Mortality* effects might be a problem because, due to the passage of time between measurements, it is quite likely that a number of people would drop out of the study (perhaps those who were least intelligent or least motivated). Finally, in this example education is actually confounded with *maturation*. Accordingly, IQ could increase with age rather than with education.

Most of these problems can be dealt with through appropriate controls of the form discussed in the previous chapter. However, in relation to the final point, it is worth noting that in developmental research *maturation* is actually the independent variable of interest. So rather than wanting to control for maturation, developmentalists actually want to examine it in its own right. This points to something that happens all the time in psychological research: what one researcher sees as a crucial variable another sees as an undesirable confound.

Yet another alternative to these cross-sectional and longitudinal strategies is to conduct a **successive cross-sectional study**. That is, rather than following the same sample (called a **cohort**) over time, the researchers would draw a different sample from the population at different times. This is the procedure normally used in opinion polling. It overcomes the problem of testing effects, but because it has a between-subjects design more participants are needed to draw conclusions with the same certainty. The differences between longitudinal, cross-sectional and successive cross-sectional studies are summarized in Table 5.1. The longitudinal design involves measuring the same sample twice, the cross-sectional study involves measuring two different samples at the same time and the successive cross-sectional study involves selecting two different samples at two different times. Of course, these principles can be applied to studies that involve more than two observations.

Table 5.1 Types of developmental survey

	Time 1	Time 2
Longitudinal	Select and measure sample	Measure sample again
Cross-sectional	Select and measure Sample A	
	Select and measure Sample B	
Successive cross-sectional	Select and measure Sample A	Select and measure Sample B

Although this chapter (like those before it) has focused on procedures that all involve attempts to quantify mental states and behaviour, there are also observational studies that do not attempt to *measure* variables in the way that is implied throughout most of this book. This research uses techniques called **qualitative research methods**, and we will discuss these in more detail in Chapter 12. These methods are often similar in appearance to the observational techniques used in certain types of case study, and they are becoming increasingly popular in some areas of psychology. The techniques typically involve reporting behaviour and commenting on it, without attempting to quantify the behaviour – that is, without attempting to express it in numbers. These techniques are often used by **critical psychologists** who challenge conventional approaches to psychological research. In turn, many mainstream psychologists are critical of qualitative methods. Again, we will explore the basis and nature of this debate in Chapter 12.

Q5.3**

Which of the following can be a threat to the internal validity of longitudinal studies?

(a) Testing effects.
(b) The IQ of the participants.
(c) Sample size.
(d) Maturation effects.
(e) Both (a) and (d).

The correct answer is (e). As (a) suggests, testing effects are a problem in longitudinal studies because the participants are tested on more than one occasion. As (d) suggests, maturation effects are potentially a problem, but it is worth noting that they can also be the independent variable of interest. (b) is a nonsense answer, as IQ does not have a consistent effect on internal validity (we chose IQ as a variable because we included it in the example we used to explain longitudinal designs – people writing exam questions often use this ploy to see whether students can separate the general concept from the details of the specific example). (c) is also wrong because sample size is unrelated to internal validity.

archival records Written or other records that are stored and are available for study. Sometimes these are stored in institutions called *archives*, but any record that is not in current use is also called an archive.

cohort A group of participants who take part in a particular piece of research at the same time.

computer-aided interviewing A research procedure where the researcher is prompted by a computer to ask questions over the telephone in a particular order. The order of questions is set by the chief researchers.

critical psychologists Psychologists who are critical of the conventional methods and approaches of mainstream psychology. For this reason, they tend to use alternative methods.

cross-sectional studies Studies that sample a cross-section of the population at a particular time. In developmental psychology the sample normally comprises a number of different age groups (***cohorts***).

developmental surveys Surveys conducted into the effects of ageing and maturation. Such surveys may be conducted by developmental psychologists or others interested in changes in psychological processes and behaviour over time.

interview A series of questions asked by a researcher and answered by a research participant.

longitudinal studies Studies where the same sample of participants is measured on more than one occasion.

naturalistic observational studies Non-experimental studies in which the researcher observes behaviour and makes no attempt to interfere with the participants.

non-obtrusive measures Measurements that are obtained without the participants being aware that they are participating in research.

non-reactive techniques Research procedures that use ***non-obtrusive measures*** to reduce the reactivity of participants' behaviour.

qualitative research methods Procedures for studying psychological and behavioural phenomena that do not involve their quantification.

social desirability The extent to which people's behaviour appears acceptable to other people. If behaviour is affected by people trying to behave in ways that they perceive to be desirable to the researcher then this threatens both the internal and external validity of research.

successive cross-sectional studies Studies that take repeated samples from a cross-section of the population at different times. These combine the features of ***cross-sectional*** and ***longitudinal studies***.

Constructing a questionnaire

We noted above that questionnaires are one of the most common forms of survey instrument. It is worth noting, too, that the use of questionnaires is not restricted to survey research. For example, in many of the experimental designs we have discussed, the effect of an independent variable would be assessed by using a questionnaire to collect data on relevant dependent variables. In light of the questionnaire's importance as a tool in psychological research, it is therefore worthwhile outlining some general principles of questionnaire design.

Perhaps the most important feature of a questionnaire is that it needs to be user-friendly and welcoming. Remember that the respondent is doing you a favour by responding, so you want to do everything you can to make their task as easy and pleasant as possible. You should start by providing a clear introduction to the questionnaire that explains what it is about, why it is worthwhile, and provides key information that the participant needs to know (e.g., who is going to use the information, and what it will be used for) and which may reassure them (e.g., that their responses are anonymous and will be confidential).

The questionnaire as a whole then needs to be set out clearly, to avoid using jargon, and to ask questions in as straightforward a way as possible. It should be easy to read, pleasing on the eye, and create a positive impression (e.g., it should not contain typographic errors or bad grammar). It should not be any longer than it needs to be, as the longer it is, the more off-putting it is likely to be. Moreover, even if someone goes to the trouble of completing a long questionnaire, it is likely that by the time they get to the end, their concentration will have lapsed and hence the responses they give will be less valuable.

Nonetheless, sometimes a questionnaire needs to be long and in such cases it is worthwhile paying careful attention to the way it is structured. In particular, the questionnaire as a whole should be organized so that the process of responding makes as much sense as possible. Sub-headings can help in this process, and, as far as possible, there should be a logical sequence to the questions.

The fact that people's attention can wander while completing a questionnaire is also a factor to bear in mind when thinking about the order in which questions are asked. For this reason it is often best to put the most important questions towards the start of the questionnaire, and to place open-ended questions towards the end (as these take longer to complete and are often more fatiguing). Questions which ask for demographic information (e.g., about a person's age and sex) are also usually placed at the end of a questionnaire because they can be quite *reactive*. For example, if you ask people whether they are hetero-sexual or homosexual, this may lead them to believe that the research is 'about' sexuality and hence affect their responses. Generally, then, reactive and sensitive items are placed at the end of a questionnaire.

It is also very common for researchers to ask respondents to provide answers to questions using **response scales** where the nature of a response is indicated by selecting one of a number of options that are sequentially ordered on a scale. An example of this was provided in Chapter 4 where we discussed a manipulation check in which partici-pants were asked to respond the question 'How much are you person-ally responsible for your failure?' on a seven-point scale with end-points labelled 'not at all' (1) and 'completely' (7). When using such scales it is important to attach meaningful labels to the numbers. This can be done either by providing *anchors* in which only the end-points are labelled (as in this example), or by attaching labels to all scale points, as in the following example:

- Was this year's exam more difficult than last year's?

1	2	3	4	5
much less difficult	slightly less difficult	the same	slightly more difficult	much more difficult

Indeed, here the numbers need not be included at all, and can simply be added by the researcher when they set about performing quantita-tive analysis at a later stage.

Labelling all scale points reduces some of the ambiguity in a scale and makes it easier for participants to understand what a particular response means. However, this procedure takes up more space and can create problems if the labels do not correspond to the particular response that the participant has in mind. A general principle of scale labels is that they need to be non-overlapping and discrete, and this can sometimes be hard to achieve if all points are given separate labels.

It is also a mistake to use a response scale with too many points. There is little to be gained by using more than nine, and five- or seven-point scales are the norm. Note that scales typically have an odd number of points because this means that they have a clear mid-point. On the other hand, under certain circumstances, using a scale with an even number of points can be useful, as the absence of a clear mid-point makes it impossible for respondents to 'sit on the fence'. At their simplest, such scales take the form of two-option **forced-choice responses** (e.g., 'yes–no').

If a questionnaire contains a large number of such scales, this may also increase the likelihood of a respondent simply making an identical response to each scale. To check for and to discourage response bias of this form, it can be useful to measure the same psychological state using multiple items where some items require **reverse scoring**. This involves asking questions so that a person with a given psychological state would answer some by marking a higher score and others by marking a lower score. For example, a questionnaire to measure depression might include the normally scored item 'Do you ever feel low or depressed?' as well as the reverse-scored item 'Do you feel positive about the future?'. On the second item a higher score would indicate *lower* depression, and so responses on it would need to be reversed when creating a single depression score. However, in constructing reverse-scored items, it is important to avoid the need for double-negative responses (e.g., the response 'not at all' to the statement 'Are you never happy?'), as these are very confusing.

Q5.4**

Which of the following statements is true?

(a) Questionnaires should not ask people to provide personal information.
(b) Questionnaires should aim to obtain as much information from people as possible.
(c) The order of items in a questionnaire is not particularly important.
(d) Questionnaires should contain a mixture of open-ended and forced-choice items.
(e) None of the above.

The correct answer is (e). All of these statements are false. (a) is incorrect because, in some sense, all questionnaires require people to provide personal information. Note, however, that steps need to be taken to deal with sensitive personal information appropriately (e.g., by assuring respondents that their responses are anonymous and confidential, if this is true) and the broad ethical implications of a particular questionnaire need to be addressed *before* it is administered (see Chapter 13). (b) is incorrect because it is important to ensure that a questionnaire only collects information which is of use to the researcher. There is no justification for simply collecting information 'for the sake of it', and it is likely to be counterproductive (e.g., in inducing response fatigue). (c) is incorrect because the order of questionnaire items is very important. For example, more reactive items need to be asked last. (d) is incorrect because there is no formula for the type of items questionnaires contain — the mix of items depends on a number of factors, including the nature of the research question and the form of analysis that is going to be performed (e.g., qualitative or quantitative; see Chapter 12).

> **forced-choice responses** Questionnaire items where a respondent has
> to select one response from two or more options.
>
> **response scale** An ordered sequence of responses to a particular
> questionnaire item. These responses can be numbered, or numbers
> can be attached to them prior to quantitative analysis.
>
> **reverse scoring** The practice of having some of the items that measure
> a particular construct worded so that a *higher* score is associated with a
> *lower* level of the construct. For example, on a scale designed to
> measure happiness, if a question asked 'Are you sad?' higher
> agreement would indicate less happiness. So, before calculating an
> overall score for the construct, scores on these particular items are
> transposed so that on all measures a higher score is associated with a
> higher level of the construct. This is done by (a) subtracting the
> participants' response from the scale mid-point and (b) adding the
> resulting score, including the + or − sign, to the scale mid-point to
> provide a new score.

Overview: Designing a survey

One thing that is clear from this chapter is that there are many options
open to researchers who wish to use survey methods. Despite this, we
should add that our coverage of survey strategies has been far from
exhaustive and we have only hinted at the richness of possible survey
designs. However, most of the strategies that we have not dealt with
build upon the core principles and practices outlined above. In order to
summarize these, we felt that it would be instructive to highlight the
main steps involved in designing a survey.

1 *Formulate the research question.* Before researchers can begin to collect
  data they must be clear about the question they want answered. In
  survey research the question is often about the relationship between
  two (or more) variables. Survey methods cannot be used to tell us
  whether one variable causes another. However, they can be used to
  falsify causal relationships by showing that certain variables are not
  related. This is because one variable cannot cause another if it is not
  related to it.
2 *Decide on the measurement of dependent and independent variables.* Measuring
  the variables often involves complex steps of operationalization
  (Chapter 4). The variables should be both relevant and sensitive
  and every effort should be made to eliminate extraneous variables
  (Chapter 3).

3 *Decide on the population of interest.* This involves deciding exactly which population the results will be generalized to.

4 *Decide on the sample size.* Other things being equal, the larger the sample size is, the less uncertainty there will be about what is going on in the population from which the sample is drawn. This is because large surveys have a greater probability of revealing relationships between variables that exist in the population. However, increasing the sample size does not increase the validity of a survey if there is any bias in the methods or the sampling. In this case a large sample will only increase the chance of drawing the wrong conclusions.

5 *Decide on the sampling method.* The key choice of sampling method is between a probability and a non-probability sample. In order to obtain a representative random sample of the population, probability sampling methods have to be used.

6 *Decide on the technique.* There are many ways of administering a survey. These include observational, questionnaire, interview, archival and other techniques. Choices of which to use will be dictated by a number of factors, including the ease and likelihood of obtaining appropriate responses and established practice in the research area.

7 *Consider possible experimental manipulations.* Researchers should always consider the possibility of using some experimental manipulations in surveys (the split-ballot technique). Experimental manipulations allow researchers to make causal inferences, and help them to be more certain about the reasons for any effects they obtain. These are massive benefits that are sometimes overlooked by survey researchers. One possible reason for this is that when some researchers conduct surveys, they believe they are collecting pure measures of psychological variables and thus do not feel there is a need to complicate the research with experimental manipulations. Some researchers also believe that such manipulations are artificial. This cuts to the heart of the distinction between surveys and experiments in psychology. Of course, many interesting variables cannot be manipulated experimentally (for ethical or other practical reasons), but that is not a reason to rule out experimental manipulations if they are possible. Even if it is not possible to manipulate the main independent variable of interest it may still be possible to control experimentally for some confounds (e.g., order effects).

In conclusion, we should note that none of the above decisions can be made in isolation, and that it is not always possible (or necessary) to make decisions in the order they are presented here. Researchers may decide that they will measure the dependent variable using a particular psychological test and then find that the test is too long to include in a telephone interview and that they have to change the measure. For this reason, we often liken designing any piece of research (whether it be an experiment or a survey) to a juggling act. As you get further into the act you pick up new balls. Each step in the design of the research is like a new ball that has to be worked seamlessly into the act, lest everything comes crashing down around your ears. Because of this, when dealing with a new problem, even the most experienced researchers often need to conduct many preliminary studies (and to reveal many errors) before they get their research procedures to work well.

Further reading

There are a number of very good volumes dedicated to issues of survey design. However, the book chapter by Schuman and Kalton (1985) provides an accessible, comprehensive and relatively succinct treatment of the topic. Frazer and Lawley's (2000) text is also very user-friendly and provides multiple worked examples of appropriate survey practice.

Frazer, L., & Lawley, M. (2000). *Questionnaire design and administration*. Brisbane: Wiley.

Schuman, H., & Kalton, G. (1985). Survey methods. In G. Linzey & E. Aronson (Eds.), *The handbook of social psychology* (3rd ed., Vol. 1, pp. 635 – 697). Reading, MA: Addison-Wesley.

Survey design: A checklist for research evaluation and improvement

Potential problem	Question to ask	Potential improvement
Unrepresentativeness; sampling bias	Have the researchers collected data from a sample that is representative of the population of interest?	Think about the characteristics of people included in the survey and of those *not* included. If they differ, this suggests the sampling process was not representative (and was not random). Reflect on the impact that this may be having on the research findings. If this impact is significant, take steps to improve the sampling process (e.g., by making it truly random).
Limited consideration of options	Could the research have been improved by conducting a split-ballot survey?	Think of ways in which it may have been possible to investigate the impact of a relevant variable by systematically varying

Potential problem	Question to ask	Potential improvement
		the form and content of the survey instrument.
Inappropriate sampling	Is the researchers' sampling strategy appropriate?	Think about the range of sampling options available to the researchers in addition to the one that they have chosen (e.g., convenience sampling, purposive sampling). If any of these options would have had appreciable benefits (e.g., in saving time without compromising external validity) consider implementing it.
Inappropriate sample size	Is the sample size large enough?	If a sample is too small to reduce uncertainty about a particular finding to a tolerable level, increase the sample size.
Reactivity	Has the nature of the survey instrument affected who responds or the way they respond?	Think about ways in which the nature or content of the survey may be encouraging participants either (a) to respond in particular ways or (b) to avoid responding. Reflect on the impact that this may be having on the research findings. Consider trying to assess the extent of this impact by conducting a split-ballot survey. If the impact is significant, modify the survey instrument appropriately (e.g., by rewording the rubric or particular questions).
Inappropriate survey choice	Have the researchers used the appropriate type of survey?	Think about the survey techniques that the researchers might have used but did not (e.g., archival, observational, non-reactive). If any of these have obvious advantages, design a study that incorporates them.
Poor questionnaire design	Is the questionnaire polished, clear, and in a form suited to obtaining information that will allow researchers to address the research	Think about how the question-naire will appear to potential respondents. Why might they not want to complete it? What might they mis-understand? Also, think about the nature of the

Potential problem	Question to ask	Potential improvement
	question(s) in which they are interested?	information the questionnaire will yield. Will it allow you to answer your research question? Make changes in light of your reflections on these questions.

Q5.5**

In a survey where the results are obtained from a representative random sample of a population, which of the following is true?

(a) The results can be generalized to that population.
(b) The sample can only be obtained by simple random sampling.
(c) The sampling procedure is similar to that used in most experimental research.
(d) Both (a) and (b).
(e) None of the above.

Q5.6**

Which of the following statements about convenience sampling is true?

(a) It should always be avoided.
(b) It is appropriate providing the sample size is extremely large.
(c) It can be used under some circumstances.
(d) It is a non-probability sampling technique.
(e) Both (c) and (d).

Q5.7***

Which of the following is likely to be a problem for non-reactive studies that use non-obtrusive measures?

(a) Social desirability effects.
(b) Defining the probability of maturation for each member of the population.
(c) Appropriate operationalization of variables.
(d) Behavioural traces.
(e) Both (c) and (d).

Q5.8**

A team of researchers conduct a study in which they ask boys and girls from a local high school to complete a battery of psychological tests that investigate their social skills and levels of sociability. Ten years later they ask boys and girls from the same school to perform the same tests. Which of the following statements is *false*?

(a) The study has a successive cross-sectional design.
(b) The research is invalid because developmental studies should not include psychological tests.
(c) Testing effects are eliminated by using a between-subjects design.
(d) Mortality effects are eliminated by using a between-subjects design.
(e) Maturation effects are eliminated by using a between-subjects design.

The correct answer to 5.5 is (a). (b) is not correct because there are other probability sampling techniques that will produce representative random samples. (c) is wrong because representative random samples are rarely used in experiments. Because (a), and only (a), is correct, both (d) and (e) must be wrong.

The correct answer to 5.6 is (e). If (a) were correct only a very small proportion of published research in psychology (and almost no experiments) would ever have been conducted. (b) is not true, as the 1936 *Literary Digest* survey shows. (c) must be true if (a) is not true. Convenience sampling makes sense where you can generalize the findings from a convenience sample on the basis of a theory to a population of interest (e.g., all people with normal vision). (d) is correct because there is not a definable probability of being sampled for each member of the population.

The correct answer to 5.7 is (c). Appropriate operationalization of variables is always a major problem in any research. In non-reactive, non-obtrusive studies social desirability and other reactive effects are eliminated because the participants do not know that they are being observed – so (a) is incorrect. (b) is a meaningless string of jargon. Behavioural traces are not problems as such, instead they are a potential source of the dependent variables. Because (d) is therefore wrong, (e) must also be wrong.

The correct answer to 5.8 is (b). Developmental studies and surveys can involve any form of measurement instrument (as outlined at the start of Chapter 3), and certainly are not restricted to questionnaires or interviews. (a) is true because this study includes a different sample of participants at the two stages of testing. Because of this between-subjects design (c), (d) and (e) are all true, too – noting that problems arising from testing, mortality and maturation effects are all associated with within-subjects designs.

Discussion/essay questions

(a) What are the main differences between the surveys typically used in psychological research and opinion polls?

(b) Under what conditions should researchers consider using non-obtrusive measures?

(c) Discuss the strengths and limitations of the various sampling strategies available to researchers using surveys.

(d) Is the inability to draw causal inferences an insurmountable limitation of the survey method?

(e) Discuss the strengths and limitations of telephone-based survey techniques.

Exercises

(a) Researchers want to find out whether men and women have the same level of colour vision. They select 100 men and 100 women by giving volunteers a test of colour vision in a shopping centre.
   (i) What sort of sampling method have the researchers used?
   (ii) Is the sample likely to be representative of the population in general?
   (iii) Is the sampling method appropriate given the research question?

(b) An economic psychologist conducts a survey into people's spending habits and financial plans. The questionnaire she designs contains the following items. What are the problems with these, and how might they be improved?

```
  (i)  How much do you earn?...............
 (ii)  Do you ever worry that you haven't got enough
       money? (tick one) yes no
(iii)  Are you in a pension plan and a superannuation
       scheme? (tick one) yes no
 (iv)  Do you have an ISA? (tick one) yes no
  (v)  On the scale below indicate your level of agreement
       with the following statement (circle one number)
       I do not always organize my finances as well as I
       might
       disagree  1  2  3  4  5  6  7  agree
 (vi)  How much are you agree with the following statment
       (circle one)
       I organize my fiancesquiet well
       disagree completly  1  23  4  5  6  7agree
       completly
```

6

Descriptive Statistics

So far in this book we have looked at a number of the processes that go on behind the scenes in psychological research. We have discussed why people conduct research, what they want to achieve when they do, and how research is designed in order to achieve particular objectives. In doing this we have tackled some of the most complex issues that a researcher can ever confront. One thing we have not done, however, is actually talk about the process of *handling and making sense of research data*. If you like, we have dealt with executive and managerial issues, but we have not actually got our hands dirty at the data coal-face. To do this we need to enter the domain of **statistics**.

Although in some fields researchers are able to keep their hands relatively clean by leaving statistical problems to other people, no research psychologist will ever be able to avoid them completely. This is because a large amount of psychological training is focused explicitly on providing psychology students with statistical skills, and an understanding of statistics is essential to the appropriate interpretation of any research finding. A research psychologist cannot get by simply with a knowledge of psychological principles for the same reason that an artist cannot get by simply with a knowledge of artistic principles. Psychologists need to know how to deal with data in its many forms in the same way that artists need to be familiar with the properties of different paints.

Two forms of statistics are essential to the appropriate handling of research data. **Descriptive statistics** enable a researcher to *describe* the properties of a particular **data set** (e.g., responses to an experiment or survey). **Inferential statistics** enable a researcher to make appropriate *inferences* from those descriptions in order to decide whether those descriptions can also be applied to a population from which the sample is drawn. We will deal with the main forms of inferential statistics that are used to examine experimental and survey data in Chapters 7, 8 and 9.

In this chapter we will look at how we can appropriately summarize the properties of a given data set using descriptive statistics. Our discussion focuses on two key properties: the description of a *typical* piece of data; and the description of the *spread* of data. However, before we can address these issues we need to discuss the different forms that the data obtained from psychological research can take.

---

data set A specified body of numerical information obtained from a given piece of research.

descriptive statistics Numerical statements about the properties of some data.

inferential statistics Numerical statements that represent conclusions about populations on the basis of sample data.

statistics Numerical statements about data from a sample, and the discipline associated with making and understanding those statements.

Different forms of research data

In Chapter 3 we noted that there are three types of psychological measure: behavioural, self-report and physiological. Having decided upon which one (or which combination) of these measures to use, the actual measure employed by researchers can vary immensely. A behavioural measure could be the number of times a person has visited a doctor in the last year or the amount of money that the person spends on food. A physiological measure could be the volume of blood flow in a particular region of the brain or a person's skin conductance. A self-report measure might be a person's response to a statement on a rating scale or a stated preference for one of three candidates in an election.

Despite this vast array of possible measures, the data from any piece of psychological research always take one of four different forms. **Nominal measures** simply identify the category or class of events to which a particular response belongs. As the term suggests, they involve giving different levels of a variable different names. Nominal variables describe people and their behaviour in terms of *categories* – as male or female, young or old, depressed or non-depressed, Australian, French or American, or as occupying a particular position in a soccer team. Nominal data like this can still be coded numerically (e.g., Australian = 1, French = 2, American = 3; goalkeeper = 1, left-back = 2, centre-back = 3,...), but the numbers here do not express a quantity, they simply serve as convenient tags. In this way the levels of nominal variables differ in kind or type, not in degree or amount.

Ordinal measures place responses on a single measurement continuum where different values indicate the relative magnitude (i.e., the strength or amount) of a particular response. In other words, they involve a relative *ordering* of responses. The position students come in a class exam (i.e., their rank in the class) is an ordinal variable, as is the grade they get in a course (e.g., A, B, C). Unlike nominal variables, the levels of ordinal variables differ in degree and amount, and they can be numerically coded in a way that reflects this (for example, by giving an A grade a score of 4, a B grade a score of 3 and so on).

However, ordinal measures only represent an ordering or ranking of responses. Nothing at all is implied about how far apart the various responses on that measure are. For example, the difference between an A grade and a B grade need not be the same as the difference between a B grade and a C grade. The same is not true of **interval measures**, where there is a *specific and constant quantitative relationship* between the various outcomes that are measured. In the case of interval measurement, the various scores or responses obtained correspond to an equal quantity of the measured variable (like marks on a ruler). As a result, the distance between any two points that are a given number of scale positions apart will be equivalent to the distance between any other two points the same number of scale positions apart (in the way that the amount of time or difference between 1 o'clock and 4 o'clock is the same as the difference between 8 o'clock and 11 o'clock). However, there is no true zero point and therefore we cannot compare ratios of variables. It makes little sense to say that 2 o'clock is twice as late as 1 o'clock and it is just wrong to say that 40°C is twice as hot as 20°C. This is because 0°C is not a true zero point, it is an arbitrary point chosen for convenience.

The distinguishing feature of **ratio measures** is that they clearly specify a zero point (like absolute zero on the kelvin temperature scale). Measures such as weight, height and speed are all ratio measures. They have the same properties as interval measures (so that the difference between 10 miles per hour and 20 miles per hour is the same as the difference between 40 miles per hour and 50 miles per hour), but they can be directly compared as ratios. That is, it is possible to say that 20 miles per hour is twice as fast as 10 miles per hour.

It is very common for psychology textbooks to include this system of classifying measures and this is partly because the sort of mathematical operation one can perform on data depends on the form that those data take. In practice, however, it is often more convenient to distinguish between just two types of measure. One form (nominal) involves placing observations (e.g., scores, responses) into distinct categories that have no quantitative relationship to each other. Other measures (ordinal, interval and ratio) differentiate between observations along a numerical dimension. These non-nominal measures can take the form of either **discrete variables**, where responses fall into a limited number of separate categories measured in whole numbers (e.g., the number that a person circles on a rating scale), or **continuous variables**, where any response can be treated as if it were measured in terms of an infinite number of points on a continuum and there is no clear gap between positions on the scale (e.g., a person's weight or reaction time).

It is worth noting that the investigation of most psychological phenomena can involve either discrete or continuous measures and that the type that is employed depends upon the researcher's objectives and circumstances. For example, reaction time, intelligence and personality can all be measured either along a single continuous quantitative dimension (milliseconds, IQ scores, level of extroversion) or in terms of discrete categories (such as fast or slow, intelligent or unintelligent, extroverted or introverted). Nevertheless, most of the statistical principles that we are going to discuss in the remainder of this chapter (and in the following chapters) apply to the analysis of non-categorical data where responses are *quantitatively differentiated* on either a continuous or discrete dimension. It is also fair to say that this is by far the most common form of data encountered in psychological research.

Q6.1[**]

A researcher conducts an experiment in which she assigns participants to one of two groups and exposes the two groups to different doses of a particular drug. She then gets the participants to learn a list of 20 words and 2 days later sees how many they can recall. In the experiment the dependent measure is simply the number of words recalled by each participant. What type of dependent measure is this?

(a) Nominal.
(b) Ordinal.
(c) Interval.
(d) Ratio.
(e) None of the above.

The correct answer is (d). The number of words recalled is a ratio measure, because all the possible scores that it is possible to obtain $(0, 1, 2, 3, \ldots, 20)$ are separated by equal intervals and there is also a true zero. The dependent variable could be made into a nominal measure if the participants were scored only as having good or poor memories (e.g., if they remembered 10 or more words, or less than 10 words, respectively). It could also be made into an ordinal measure if participants were simply ranked in terms of the number of words they remembered (so that the person who remembered the most words was given a ranking of 1, etc.).

continuous variable A variable that can be treated as if there were no breaks or steps between its different levels (e.g., reaction time in milliseconds).

discrete variable A variable with clear breaks or steps between its different levels (e.g., responses on a rating scale).

interval measure A measure on which the obtained scores stand in a quantitative relationship to one another so that adjacent scores are separated by an equal interval, but where there is no true zero value.

nominal measure A measure on which the obtained scores reflect distinct categories that stand in no quantitative relationship to one another.

ordinal measure A measure on which the obtained scores reflect the ordering of responses on a continuum, but where the intervals between scores are not necessarily equal.

ratio measure A measure on which the obtained scores stand in a quantitative relationship to one another so that adjacent scores are separated by an equal interval and where there is a true zero value.

Describing a typical score: Measures of central tendency

To provide a concrete example around which to structure our introduction to statistics, let us go back to one of the studies we described a few chapters ago where a researcher was interested in looking at the impact of attributional style on depression. Conceivably, before the researcher examined this issue in any depth he or she might want to find out how a control sample of students respond to failure on an exam. The researcher might want to do this to see whether students generally attribute their failure to internal factors (such as their lack of intelligence or motivation) or to external factors (such as bad luck or the exam conditions). To do this, the researcher might ask a number of students (say 25) to respond to the question 'How much was your failure due to things beyond your control?' by getting them to circle a number on a seven-point scale with end-points labelled 'not at all' (1) and 'completely' (7). Let us imagine that the numbers circled by the 25 participants in this study were as follows:

$$3, 5, 6, 5, 2, 3, 6, 4, 6, 7, 6, 4, 5, 5, 1, 2, 5, 4, 4, 5, 5, 7, 3, 3, 4$$

These scores constitute the data set in this study, and when presented in this untreated form they are often referred to as the **raw data**. However, it makes sense that in trying to manage these data the researcher would try to organize them in some way. With this in mind, the first obvious thing to do is to put the numbers in some sort of order (either ascending or descending) as follows:

$$1, 2, 2, 3, 3, 3, 3, 4, 4, 4, 4, 4, 5, 5, 5, 5, 5, 5, 5, 6, 6, 6, 6, 7, 7$$

This ordering begins to tell us how the data are *distributed* across the continuum of possible responses.

The data could be summarized further by noting the frequency with which the different responses were made. So, in this case there is one response of '1', two of '2', four of '3', five of '4', seven of '5', four of '6', and two of '7'. For ease of presentation, this information about the **distribution** of responses could be presented in a table that would summarize the data in numerical form. In particular, a **frequency table** reporting the number of times each different response was made would take the form shown in Table 6.1.

Alternatively, the response distribution could be represented pictorially in a graph. One common way of doing this is to use a **frequency graph**, where the area of each bar or column is proportional to the frequency of any given response (or group of responses). These are called

Table 6.1 Frequency table for attributional style study data

Response	Frequency
1	1
2	2
3	4
4	5
5	7
6	4
7	2

bar charts for discrete variables and **histograms** for continuous variables. The bar chart for our exam data is shown in Figure 6.1.

All of the above methods offer very useful ways of representing *all* the data that the researcher has obtained in the study. But if researchers had to reproduce data in one of the above forms every time they wanted to communicate what they had found, this could be quite a time-consuming task. It might also be completely impractical if the data set were much larger (with many more different levels of response) or if researchers had multiple sets of data to report.

The same would be true if a friend were to ask us a question like 'What do your colleagues think about the government?'. In response we could provide a very detailed answer to the question. We could, for example, reply that three of our colleagues are enthusiastic about the government, that eight are relatively neutral, that four are opposed to its policies and that two are vigorously opposed. However, by doing this we would risk missing the point, and it might easily detract from our friend's ability to get a clear indication of what our colleagues thought in general. Indeed, our friend might think that we were trying to be funny or being deliberately evasive.

What our friend would probably be looking for, then, is some statement of what our colleagues *typically* thought about the government. Similarly, in dealing with the above data on attributional style, the researcher may want to know what constitutes *a typical response* to failure. The descriptive statistics that provide answers to this sort of question are known collectively as **measures of central tendency**.

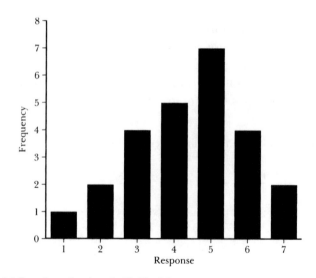

Figure 6.1 Bar chart for data in Table 6.1

In everyday interaction when someone asks us to describe any typical thing, this can have three distinct meanings. A typical reaction to the government, for example, could be either (a) the *average* reaction, (b) the reaction of an *average person*, or (c) the *most common* reaction. These three distinct meanings of typicality are also reflected in the three main descriptive statistics used to measure central tendency.

The first and most commonly used of these statistics is the **mean**. The mean is a measure of the average score. It is calculated by adding up all the different scores and dividing this total by the number of scores. So in the case of the data from the attributional style study (on page 119), the sum of the 25 responses is 110 and the mean, or average response, is therefore 110 divided by 25. This comes to 4.40 exactly. In other words, the mean is the *arithmetic average* of a given set of numbers, whether those numbers be responses, scores or values (terms that we will use more or less interchangeably in what follows).

We should also point out in passing that when a computation does not work out to be an exact number, the number of figures reported after the decimal point depends on the amount of accuracy that is possible given the measurement taken. In this way the reported result generally depends on the number of **significant figures** that it is appropriate to report – that is, the number of digits that are accurately measured and therefore provide meaningful information.

On the basis of this principle, when a calculation produces more numbers after the decimal than are warranted, researchers usually report a value with a specified number of digits after the decimal place – the value that is closest to the one obtained. As an example, 1807 divided by 21 comes to 86.047619, but this would be written as 86.05 if the researcher had decided to report just two digits after the decimal place. This procedure is known as **rounding**. If the obtained number falls exactly half-way between two such numbers the higher number is normally reported (this is known as **rounding up**). As an example, 100 divided by 32 comes to 3.125, but when reporting this figure you would round it up to 3.13. The strategy of reporting just two digits after the decimal place – 'rounding to two decimal places' – is one that is widely used by research psychologists and journals.

Something else that we need to alert you to is that as this chapter progresses it will get increasingly difficult to describe the mathematical operations we are performing by using words alone. For this reason we are going to start introducing some statistical notation. This may make you feel slightly nervous. However, the reasons for doing this are much the same as the reasons for introducing specialized terminology and jargon in previous chapters (terms such as independent variable, reactivity and between-subjects manipulation). First, statistical notation is so widely used by other researchers that if we did not introduce you to it a large amount of what other people have to say on important issues would remain completely incomprehensible. Second, it should be emphasized that although statistical notation is often difficult to master at first, once it is understood and learned it allows researchers to communicate very complex ideas succinctly and efficiently. This book would be about twice as long (and far more exhausting to read) if at every relevant point we had not used jargon but instead substituted the definition that is provided in the boxes at the end of each section. The same point is true for statistical notation.

So, if we wanted to represent the formula for the mean in words, we could do so as follows:

$$\text{mean score} = \frac{\text{sum of all scores}}{\text{number of scores}}$$

However, this formula could also be written using the following statistical notation:

$$\text{mean score} = \frac{\text{sum}(X)}{\text{number}}$$

If we replace the words 'mean score', 'sum' and 'number' with the symbols $\bar{X}$, Σ and N we get:

$$\bar{X} = \frac{\Sigma X}{N}$$

Each of the terms in this formula relates to the corresponding phrase in the long-hand version above. More specifically, X refers to the scores on variable we have measured (i.e., responses on the rating scale – in this case, 1, 2, 2, etc.). $\bar{X}$ (pronounced 'X-bar') refers to the mean value of that variable X. Σ (the Greek letter sigma or S) means that everything that is referred to in what follows needs to be added together or summed. So ΣX is shorthand for 'the sum of all the scores' (i.e., $1 + 2 + 2 + \cdots + 7$). Finally, N refers to the total number of scores obtained (i.e., the sample size).

As we have suggested, however, the mean is not the only way to represent central tendency. A second way to represent a typical score in a given data set is simply to identify *the middle score* (equivalent to the score obtained by the average person). The technical term for this is the **median**. Where scores are ordered sequentially (ranked from either lowest to highest, or highest to lowest) this is the value which has an equal number of values above and below it. So, in the attributional style data (on page 135) the median response is 5 as this has 12 responses above it and 12 below it.

In fact, in any data set where the scores are ordered sequentially the median value can be worked out by adding 1 to the number of scores (N) and halving it (dividing ($N + 1$) by 2) and then identifying the score that falls at this point in the sequence. In the attributional data there are 25 responses, so the median is the 13th value in sequence (because half of ($25 + 1$) is 13). Expressed in mathematical terms, the median score in a sequence of a given number of scores (N) is the $((N + 1)/2)$th value. Note that the positioning of the brackets in this or any other formula is vital, because we must *complete all the computations inside the brackets before we do anything else.*

Returning to our discussion of how to calculate a median value, the only slight complication in the procedure outlined above arises when there is an even number of scores in a data set. In this case the median is simply a score that falls exactly half-way between the *two* middle values. Let us imagine, for example, that the research into attributional style yielded only 24 responses because one of the highest responses (a '7') had not been collected. Here the median value (the $(24 + 1)/2$th or 12.5th value) would fall between the 12th and 13th values (4 and 5, respectively) and so it would be 4.5 (even though 4.5 does not correspond to an actual or possible response).

The third and final measure of central tendency corresponds simply to the *most common value* in a particular data set. This is referred to as the **mode**. In any given set this is the response or score that occurs most frequently, so it will always correspond to the tallest column in a frequency graph. In the attributional style data, the modal response is 5, as this response was made by more participants than any other. Of course, sometimes it will happen that two or more scores are observed with equal highest frequency. In this case all modes are reported.

Q6.2[**]

A researcher conducts a study to find out how many times people had visited a doctor in the previous year. Five people participated in the study and the numbers of visits they had made were 2, 5, 7, 4 and 2. Which of the following statements is true?

(a) The mean number of visits is 2.
(b) The median number of visits is 2.
(c) The median number of visits is 4.
(d) The modal number of visits is 4.
(e) The modal number of visits is 7.

The correct answer is (c). The median number of visits (i.e., the $((5+1)/2)$th, 3rd in sequence) is 4 – not 2 as (b) suggests. (a) is wrong because the mean number of visits is equal to the total number or sum of visits (20) divided by the number of scores (5) which also equals 4. (d) and (e) are wrong because the mode refers to the most common number of visits, and this is 2.

bar chart A *frequency graph* for discrete variables in which the length of bars or columns indicates the frequency with which different levels of a variable have been observed.

distribution The spread of scores across levels of a variable.

frequency graph A graph which shows the number of times that the different levels of a variable have been observed. Among other things, this can take the form of a *bar chart* or *histogram*.

frequency table A table which reports the number of times that the different levels of a variable have been observed.

histogram A *frequency graph* for continuous variables in which the area of bars or columns is proportional to the frequency with which different levels of a variable have been observed.

mean The average of a set of scores $(\bar{X})$. It is equal to the total of all the scores (ΣX) divided by the number of scores (N).

measures of central tendency Statistics which describe a typical score.

median The middle score of a set of scores. It is equal to the $((N+1)/2$th$)$ value, where N is the number of scores in the data set.

mode The most commonly occurring score in a data set.

N Statistical notation for the number of scores obtained on a given measure and also the total number of respondents to a measure (i.e., the sample size).

raw data Data that have not been summarized or transformed in any way.

rounding (up) The procedure for reducing the number of digits reported after a decimal point where a calculation produces more digits than necessary. Rounding up involves increasing the last reported digit by 1 when the first deleted digit is greater than or equal to 5 (e.g., so that 3.665 becomes 3.67).

Σ (sigma) Statistical notation indicating summation (i.e., 'the sum of...').

ΣX (**sigma X**) Statistical notation for the sum of all the scores of a given
variable (X).

significant figures The number of digits that are accurately measured
and that are considered to convey meaningful information about a
numerical value.

X Statistical notation for (a) the scores on a given variable and (b) the
variable itself.

$\bar{X}$ (**X-bar**) Statistical notation for the mean of X. The mean of Y would
be $\bar{Y}$.

The relationship between measures of central tendency and a response distribution

It is clear from our calculations of the mean, median and mode for
the attributional style data that these three statistics can differ. You
may recall that the mean was 4.40, but the median and mode were
both 5.00. For this reason, one question that you may have asked
yourself is which measure we should use. For many statistical
purposes, the mean is the preferred measure of central tendency.
Consequently, it is perhaps more appropriate to ask under which
circumstances we should *not* use the mean as a measure of central
tendency.

To start with, we can see that the mean is of no use when we are
dealing with nominal data. For example, there is no way that we can
meaningfully say what a mean surname or town is. The mean can also
be of dubious value for ordinal data, like the mean level of education in
a country (primary, secondary or tertiary) or people's ranking on an
aptitude test. If we have an interval or ratio scale, however, we can set
about answering this question by looking at how measures of central
tendency vary depending on the shape of a response distribution. The
important point is that this variation is *systematic*, so that if we know how
a given set of scores is distributed we will also know which of the three
measures will have the highest value without having to work them all
out.

The first thing we need to do, then, is to describe the different shapes
that a response distribution can have. If we return to consider the data
presented in Figure 6.1, you will recall that the columns of the bar chart
were based on the *actual* responses of our experimental sample of 25
participants.

Now just by looking at this distribution of responses we can see
that it is off-centre or **skewed**. In fact it is clear (both from this figure

and our previous calculations) that the mode is displaced to the right, or towards more positive responses. When this is the case a distribution is said to be **negatively skewed**. This is because the direction of skew (positive or negative) refers to the position of the tail of the distribution – its longer end.

At first this description will probably strike you as being a bit odd. It seems counter-intuitive because you might assume that the direction of skew would refer to the position of the distribution's peak (i.e., its mode) rather than its tail. However, the terminology reflects the fact that *when a distribution is skewed the mean often provides an ambiguous measure of central tendency*. More specifically, when the peak of a distribution is displaced towards more positive values (as it is in this case), the mean will tend to be an unduly *negative* measure of central tendency. By the same token, when the peak of a distribution is displaced towards more negative values, the mean will tend to be an unduly *positive* measure of central tendency, and so in this case the distribution will be described as **positively skewed**.

When a distribution is skewed the mean is an ambiguous measure of central tendency as it will tend to differ (sometimes quite considerably) from the mode and from the median. This is true, for example, if a researcher wants to make a statement about typical salaries or personal wealth in a given country. The distributions of wealth and wages are both positively skewed, because in all countries a very small proportion of people earn exceedingly large amounts of money. Accordingly, mean wage and mean salary levels are often misleading statistics because they tend to exaggerate wealth and earnings (which is one reason why these statistics are normally preferred by governments and employer groups).

By the same token, people's self-evaluations tend to be negatively skewed as most people tend to have quite a high opinion of themselves (e.g., Svenson, 1981). This is reflected in the data in our attributional style example where the participants prefer not to blame themselves for their failure. In such a case the mean will tend to underestimate people's sense of their self-worth and the extent to which they deflect blame from themselves.

In cases of severe skewness the median will usually be a more appropriate measure of central tendency than the mean because it will fall *between* the mean and the mode. The median is also the best measure of central tendency if we do not know the shape of a distribution. However, the mean, median and mode will be identical when the distribution of data is symmetrical (providing there is only one mode), and of the three the mean is usually the preferred measure.

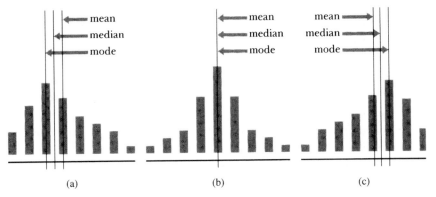

Figure 6.2 Relative position of mean, median and mode in: (a) positively skewed distribution; (b) symmetrical (non-skewed) distribution; (c) negatively skewed distribution

In order to clarify the above points, the three types of distribution we have discussed are represented in Figure 6.2. This also indicates the relative position of the mean, median and mode for each distribution.

Q6.3*

Which of the following statements is most likely to be true if the distribution of a variable is severely skewed?

(a) The mean will be the best measure of central tendency.
(b) The median will be as misleading as the mean.
(c) The mode will no longer be the most common response.
(d) The median will be the best measure of central tendency.
(e) The mode will be the best measure of central tendency.

The correct answer is (d). If the distribution of some data is severely skewed both the mean and the mode can be misleading statistics. If a distribution is positively skewed (so that scores tend to be relatively negative) the mean will tend to be too positive a measure of central tendency and the mode will be too negative. On the other hand, if a distribution is negatively skewed (so that scores tend to be relatively positive) the mean will tend to be too negative a measure of central tendency and the mode will be too positive. Thus statements (a), (b) and (e) are incorrect. As (d) suggests, in both cases the median will fall between these values and so will often be a more appropriate measure. (c) is incorrect because, regardless of skew, the mode is always the most common score or response.

negative skew The shape of a response distribution in which a high
 proportion of responses are above the mean. In such cases the mean
 tends to be too negative a measure of central tendency.

positive skew The shape of a response distribution in which a high
 proportion of responses are below the mean. In such cases the mean
 tends to be too positive a measure of central tendency.

skewness The degree of non-symmetry in the distribution of scores on a
 given variable.

Describing the spread of scores: Measures of dispersion

When we want to summarize the properties of a given data set it is clear
that being able to convey information about what constitutes a typical
score or value will be extremely useful. However, in many ways it is
only half the story. Knowing the average height of people in a basketball team will be useful, but we would consider a team in which every
player was almost exactly the same height to be very different from one
in which some players were extremely tall and others extremely short.
Similarly, we would consider the psychological health of people in two
cities to be very different if the people in one city were all moderately
happy, while in the other city a large proportion were extremely happy
but the remainder were clinically depressed.

   The point here is that knowledge about the *distribution of data around a
typical value* can be every bit as important as knowledge of that value
itself. For a start, if the data are tightly clustered around a central value
this will make it much easier to make a reasonably accurate prediction
about what any one value is likely to be compared to a situation where
the data are more scattered. For this reason researchers generally use
two summary statistics to characterize a given data set: a measure of
central tendency and a measure of *dispersion*. However, researchers are
sometimes guilty of neglecting dispersion and concentrating too much
on central tendency.

   One of the most obvious statistics that could be used to measure
dispersion is the **range** of scores contained in a data set. This is simply
the difference between the maximum and minimum scores in any given
case. So, for our attributional style data (see page 135) the range is 6.00
as this is the difference between the highest and lowest observed
responses (7 and 1, respectively).

   However, it is not hard to see that range could be an extremely
misleading statistic in certain circumstances. For example, imagine

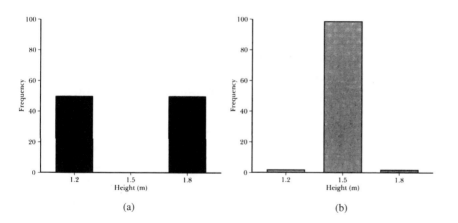

Figure 6.3 Heights of (a) Blacktown residents and (b) Greytown residents

we measured the height of people who lived in two towns (Blacktown and Greytown), and found that 50 people in Blacktown were 1.20 metres tall and 50 were 1.80 metres tall, but that in Greytown one person was 1.20 metres tall, one was 1.80 metres tall and the other 98 were 1.50 metres tall (Figure 6.3). The range and mean are the same in both towns (i.e., range $= 0.60$ m; $\bar{X} = 1.5$ m) but, as we can see by comparing the frequency graphs, the height of the Blacktown residents is generally quite different from the mean, while the height of Greytown residents is generally quite similar to the mean. If we want to convey more information about important differences of this type, we need to use a more sophisticated measure of dispersion, which would allow us to say how *certain* we were that a typical score describes the sample.

One of the first things that we should note here is that scores which lie a long way from the typical value for a distribution will contribute a great deal to the dispersion of a distribution. Such scores are called **outliers** and they can have a profound – sometimes unduly pro- found – impact. We can see this from the above example for the distribution of Greytown residents' heights. Here if we were to remove the outliers from the distribution (the person who is 1.2 m tall and the one who is 1.8 m tall) there would actually be no dispersion at all. For this reason, researchers often take steps to eliminate outliers. This can be done either through **transformation** of the entire data set (e.g., taking the square root of every score) or by dealing with each outlier individually (e.g., by deleting or recoding them; see Tabachnick & Fidell, 1996). The decisions as to what to do about outliers are often difficult, but before we can make those decisions we need to find out whether they are present.

In order to quantify dispersion more precisely, the first thing that we could do is measure *the average distance of all the scores from the mean score*. This statistic is commonly referred to as the **mean deviation**. Clearly in the case of the height of people from our two towns, mean deviation would be much higher in the case of people from Blacktown than it would be for people from Greytown.

To measure mean deviation in the case of our attributional style data we would compute the distance between every single score and the mean (4.40) and then average these distances. So, we would subtract the first response (1) from 4.40, the second response (2) from 4.40, and so on until we subtracted 4.40 from the 25th response (7). We would then add up all these distances and divide them by 25 (the total number of scores). You might want to do this yourself as an exercise. If you do you will find that the sum of the distances between the scores and the mean is 31.60. The mean deviation is therefore 31.60 divided by 25, which is 1.26.

A point to notice here is that the distance between two scores is worked out by subtracting the lower value from the higher value, not by always subtracting each individual score from the mean score. If you were to do the latter (and so recorded negative differences, like −2.60, when the mean (4.40) was lower than the individual score (e.g., 7)), you would actually find that the mean deviation was always zero.

So, along the lines that we did for the mean, we could express the formula for mean deviation in words as follows:

$$\text{mean deviation in scores} = \frac{\text{the sum of the unsigned differences between all scores and the mean}}{\text{number of scores}}$$

Using statistical notation (elements of which were contained in the formula for the mean), the same ideas can be expressed in the following compact formula:

$$\text{mean deviation } (X) = \frac{\sum |X - \bar{X}|}{N}$$

Again, then, in this formula X refers to the scores on variable we have measured (i.e., responses on the rating scale – in this case, 1, 2, 2, etc.). $\bar{X}$ refers to the mean value of that variable. Σ means that everything that is referred to in what follows needs to be summed. N refers to the total number of scores obtained (in this case 25). The only new thing here is the two vertical lines either side of the Xs on the top line. These indicate that when a subtraction is performed we need to disregard any minuses that result from that subtraction (this is referred to as the unsigned or **absolute difference**).

It is certainly the case that the formula for mean deviation looks quite unfriendly. However, it looks more complex than it really is, and in the case of our attributional style data it could be worked out quite simply by putting all the values (1, 2, 2, 3, etc.) in one column (under the heading X), putting the mean in a column to the right of them (under the heading $\bar{X}$) then subtracting the numbers in the left column from those in the right column and putting the resulting values in a third column leaving out any minus sign that arises from the subtraction (under the heading $|X - \bar{X}|$). The values in this third column can then be added together and divided by the number of rows (25) to provide the mean deviation. Such a procedure would look like this:

X	$\bar{X}$	$|X - \bar{X}|$
1	4.40	3.40
2	4.40	2.40
2	4.40	2.40
3	4.40	1.40

and so on for each of the next 18 scores down to

6	4.40	1.60
7	4.40	2.60
7	4.40	2.60

$$\text{Total } (\Sigma) = 31.60$$

Therefore,

$$\text{mean deviation} = \frac{\Sigma |X - \bar{X}|}{N}$$

$$= 31.60/25$$

$$= 1.26$$

However, as we have already observed, unless we get rid of the minus signs that are produced by subtractions in this procedure (i.e., unless we compute absolute differences), the mean deviation of any set of scores is always going to be equal to zero. Because the procedure of removing minus signs is quite clumsy, it would be preferable if we could use another more elegant procedure to ensure that every difference between a score and the mean was positive.

One of the best ways to get round the problem caused by minus signs is to *square* all the deviations from the mean – in other words, to multiply each deviation by itself. This gets rid of negative values because a negative number multiplied by a negative number always results in a positive number. So, for example, $-3.48 \times -3.48 = 12.11$.

The **variance** of a given variable is similar to the mean deviation, but its calculation incorporates this procedure of squaring deviations from the mean rather than computing absolute differences. This statistic is therefore calculated by summing together the squared deviations of each score from the mean and dividing this sum by the number of scores. Variance, then, is the *mean squared deviation from the mean* (sometimes referred to as the *mean squared deviate*).

The procedure for calculating the variance of any variable (X) is summarized in the following formula:

$$\text{Var}(X) = \frac{\sum (X - \bar{X})^2}{N}$$

If we compare this formula with the one for mean deviation presented above, we can see that it is very similar. The only difference is that the terms to be summed (i.e., those after the Σ) are the squared differences between each score and the mean (i.e., $(X - \bar{X})^2$) rather than the absolute differences (i.e., $|X - \bar{X}|$). What the formula essentially says, then, is that the variance of any variable (X) is equal to the sum of the squared differences between each score and the mean, divided by the total number of scores.

We can use a fairly similar procedure to that which we used to calculate mean deviation to work out variance in the case of our attributional style data. As we did when calculating mean deviation, we can put all the values (1, 2, 2, 3, etc.) in one column (under the heading X), put the mean in a column to the right of them (under the heading $\bar{X}$), then subtract the numbers in the left column from those in the right column and put the resulting values in a third column (under the heading $X - \bar{X}$). Finally, in a fourth column (under the heading $(X - \bar{X})^2$) we can square each of the values in the third column (i.e., multiply them by themselves). Having done all this, the values in this fourth column can then be added together and divided by the number of rows (25) to provide the variance. This procedure would look like this:

X	$\bar{X}$	$X - \bar{X}$	$(X - \bar{X})^2$
1	4.40	−3.40	11.56
2	4.40	−2.40	5.76
2	4.40	−2.40	5.76
3	4.40	−1.40	1.96

and so on for each of the next 18 scores down to

6	4.40	1.60	2.56
7	4.40	2.60	6.76
7	4.40	2.60	6.76

$\Sigma = 58.00$

$$\mathrm{Var}(X) = \frac{\sum(X - \bar{X})^2}{N}$$

$$= 58.00/25$$

$$= 2.32$$

Variance is a very commonly used measure of dispersion. Like the mean, its primary advantage over alternative measures is that it is useful when working with inferential statistics. One other handy feature of this measure is that in order to compute it, we do not necessarily have to go through the elaborate process of calculating the square of every score's deviation from the mean. Instead it is possible to use a **computational formula**, for which we only have to know the sum of all the scores $(\sum X)$ and the sum of all the squared scores $(\sum X^2)$.

The computational formula for variance is as follows:

$$\mathrm{Var}(X) = \frac{\sum X^2 - \frac{(\sum X)^2}{N}}{N}$$

Expressed in words, this formula tells us that variance is equal to (the sum of all the squared scores) minus ((the sum of all the scores) squared and then divided by the number of scores) *all* divided by the number of scores.

In order to obtain the information necessary to use this computational formula to calculate the variance of our attributional style data, all we have to do is to list all the scores in one column (under the heading X) then square all these scores and put the resulting number in a second column (under the heading X^2). Summing these two columns will provide us with $\sum X$ and $\sum X^2$, respectively. This procedure would look like this:

X	X^2
1	1
2	4
2	4
3	9

and so on for each of the next 18 scores down to

6	36
7	49
7	49

$\Sigma = 110$	$\Sigma = 542$

$$\mathrm{Var}(X) = \frac{\Sigma X^2 - ((\Sigma X)^2/N)}{N}$$

$$= \frac{542 - (110^2/25)}{25}$$

$$= \frac{542 - (12\,100/25)}{25}$$

$$= (542 - 484)/25$$

$$= 58/25$$

$$= 2.32$$

Applying the computational formula: variance is therefore equal to (the sum of all the squared scores; i.e., 542) minus ((the sum of all the scores) squared and divided by the number of scores; i.e., 110^2 divided by $25 = 12\,100/25 = 484$) *all* divided by the number of scores (25). It is therefore equal to $(542 - 484)/25$. This is equal to 58 divided by 25, which comes to 2.32 – the same number that we obtained previously. This is a much quicker method for computing variance than the one we first used. It ends up being even faster if you put a calculator into statistical mode and then enter all the scores (following steps described in the calculator's operating manual). This will provide you with values for ΣX and ΣX^2 without you having to work them out yourself.

Although we have noted some of the advantages of variance as a measure of dispersion, this statistic in fact has one drawback. This arises from the fact that its calculation is based on squaring the difference between individual scores and the mean. Because of this, the variance of any variable (X) is represented in *squared units of X* (i.e., X^2). If we wanted to know the dispersion of the height of people in a basketball team, calculating the variance would therefore give us that measure in terms of centimetres squared (cm^2) rather than just centimetres. However, centimetres squared is actually a measure of *area* rather than *height*, so it does not give us exactly what we are looking for.

The way that we can get around this problem is to compute the *square root* of the variance. Like the mean deviate, this statistic is measured in the same units as the variable in which we are interested and we can refer to it as the *root mean square deviate*. This statistic has everything we are looking for in a measure of dispersion. Accordingly, it is the statistician's and the research psychologist's measure of choice. It is called the **standard deviation** (or SD).

In the case of our attributional style data, the standard deviation of responses is simply equal to the square root of the variance (2.32) which is 1.52. The only difference between the formula for standard deviation and the one for variance is that for standard deviation the whole variance formula is qualified by a square root sign ($\sqrt{}$) as follows:

$$\mathrm{SD}(X) = \sqrt{\frac{\sum(X - \bar{X})^2}{N}}$$

Similarly, the computational formula for standard deviation is the same as the one for variance apart from the fact that it is preceded by a square root sign:

$$\mathrm{SD}(X) = \sqrt{\frac{\sum X^2 - \frac{(\sum X)^2}{N}}{N}}$$

Q6.4[**]

If X is a variable, which of the following is *not* measured in the same units as X?

(a) The mean of X.
(b) The range of X.
(c) The standard deviation of X.
(d) The variance of X.

The correct answer is (d). Variance is measured in units of X^2 as it is the average *squared* difference between a set of scores and the mean of those scores. All other measures of dispersion (including range, mean deviation and standard deviation) as well as all measures of central tendency (including the mean) are measured in units of X.

absolute difference The unsigned difference between two scores. It is the score that is obtained if the smaller of two values is subtracted from the larger value (so that no negative scores are produced).

computational formula A formula developed for ease of calculation and which does not necessarily describe the mathematical processes most relevant to a particular procedure.

mean deviation The average absolute difference between a set of scores and the mean of those scores.

outliers Scores that are very different from the typical value for a distribution. Because they are very different from the central tendency of a distribution they contribute a great deal to the amount of dispersion in the distribution.

range The difference between the maximum and minimum scores on a given variable.

standard deviation The square root of variance. Otherwise known as the *root mean squared deviate*.

transformation A systematic arithmetic change to a variable that alters its distribution (e.g., the process of taking the square root of each score in a sample.

variance The average squared difference between a set of scores and the mean of those scores. Otherwise known as the *mean squared deviate*.

Observed distributions and theoretical distributions: The difference between samples and populations

Up to this stage we have been talking about statistics for samples. These relate to observations or measurements of things that have taken place at particular times in particular places. Although these observations are vital, scientists are often even more interested in things *in general* rather than just the observed details of the sample. This is true for two reasons that relate to the issues we discussed in Chapters 2, 3 and 4. First, the observations we make are more interesting if they generalize to a population – that is, if we are confident of their external validity. But perhaps even more fundamentally, knowing something about things in general enables us to say something about the particular sample. For example, knowing about things in general allows us to say whether our observations are unusual and interesting.

Working with statistics is thus a two-way process because we are trying to do two different things. We are trying to say something about things in general (the population) on the basis of the sample, and we are trying to say something about the sample based on what we know about things in general. We will discuss how we do these two things more in the next chapter. For present purposes we need only accept that we need to be able to describe things in general, as well as particular samples.

Even if you have never studied statistics before you already know quite a bit about the difference between the distribution of things in general and particular observations. We can illustrate this with the example of rolling a fair six-faced die. You know that if you were to roll a die like this many times that you would tend to get approximately equal proportions of 1s, 2s, 3s, 4s, 5s and 6s. More specifically, about one-sixth of your throws would be 1s, one-sixth would be 2s, and so on.

You also know that you would not always get exactly equal proportions. If you roll a die 12 times you are unlikely to get two of each number. Think, for example, of the times that you have waited for what seems like hours before throwing a 6 to get started in a board game. This difference between what we expect and what we find in any given case is the difference between **observed** and **theoretical distributions**.

The problem is that we only very rarely measure the entire population because to do so would take too much time and effort. The scientific solution to this problem is to theorize. That is, if we do not know what the characteristics of the population are and we are unable to obtain these characteristics empirically (i.e., through observation or measurement), what we have to do is to estimate these characteristics on the basis of a set of plausible and public assumptions. We assume that if certain conditions hold then the population will be expected to have particular properties. In this way we create a theoretical distribution of the population to go along with the empirically observed distribution of the sample. When we do this we find that we can use concepts that describe our observed distributions (e.g., central tendency, dispersion and skewness) to describe the likely shape of the theoretical population distribution. However, we also find that we need to develop some new terms and concepts.

The first of these terms and concepts is **expected frequency**. We discussed what a frequency is when we talked about frequency graphs earlier in this chapter. If we assume that any sample is drawn randomly from a given population then we would *expect* the *frequency* of responses in the sample to match the proportions of those responses in the population. In our die-rolling example we would expect the distribution of a sample of 12 throws to be similar to the distribution of all throws that have ever been made. For example, about one-sixth of our throws should be 6s and about one-sixth of all the die rolls ever made should have been 6s. In our sample of 12 rolls the expected frequency of 6s is therefore 2 (i.e., $1/6 \times 12$).

An expected frequency like this is directly related to the concept of **probability**. Probability refers to the likelihood of events under certain conditions (e.g., the likelihood of throwing a 6 under conditions where a die is thrown once and that die is unbiased and has six sides). As we have seen, if we know what the probability of an event is we can convert this into an expected frequency by multiplying the probability by the sample size. On the other hand, if we know what the expected frequency of an event is we can convert this into a probability by dividing the expected frequency by the sample size, and thereby generating a number between 0 and 1.

So, returning to our experiment on attributional style, if the probability of a response of '5' on a rating scale were 0.4, this would mean that in a sample of 25 people we would have an expected frequency of 10 such responses (i.e., 25×0.4) and in a sample of 40 people an expected frequency of 16 (i.e., 40×0.4). In this case though, you may be wondering exactly how we originally identify either probabilities or expected frequencies. In the die-rolling example it is relatively easy to see that the probability of throwing a 6 is 1/6 (or 0.167), but it is not so obvious how we could generate the same sort of figure for psychological data. We deal with the answer to this question in Chapter 7 when we discuss the concept of the statistical model.

All that we need to know for the present is that it is often very useful to estimate the expected frequencies of the various outcomes from some research – that is, to develop an estimated frequency distribution. This distribution represents estimations about the population of all the similar people that might have been included in any piece of research with a given sample size. In contrast to frequency distributions obtained from actual data (which are presented in frequency graphs), this distribution is typically represented as the area under a curve. This in effect represents the outline of a fine-grained histogram. Returning to the attributional style data, if we assume (a) that our responses are in fact drawn from a continuous dimension so that fractional scores (e.g., 1.1, 1.2, 1.3 etc.) are included within each category (e.g., '1') and (b) that the population's responses mirrored those of our sample (a big assumption that may in fact be unjustified), then the estimated frequency distribution of the population – known as the *population distribution* – would be represented by the area under the curve in Figure 6.4.

As well as being able to estimate how a variable is likely to be distributed in a population, researchers often need to be able to estimate the central tendency and dispersion of that variable. Usually they want to estimate its mean and standard deviation. Such characteristics are referred to as **population parameters** rather than population statistics. To distinguish between sample statistics and population parameters, the latter are usually identified by Greek letters. So we use the symbol SD or s_x to identify the *sample* standard deviation but the Greek letter σ (sigma) for the *population* standard deviation. Similarly, we use the symbol $\bar{X}$ for the *sample* mean but the Greek letter μ (mu) for the *population* mean.

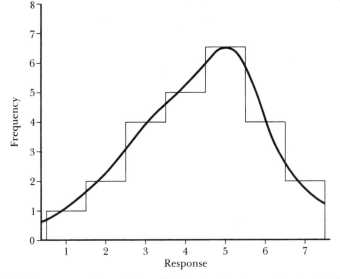

Figure 6.4 Frequency and population distributions for the attributional style study

If we do not know what the population mean is (and we usually do not), the best estimate of it is the sample mean. Similarly, if we do not know what the population standard deviation is, then the best estimate we have available is the sample standard deviation. So, if we have sampled randomly from the population, then for a reasonably large sample size, the mean and standard deviation of our sample data will provide a reasonable estimate of the population mean and standard deviation.

However, there is one complication with the formula we gave for the standard deviation above as a means of estimating the population standard deviation. This is that the sample standard deviation is a *biased* estimate of the population standard deviation. In fact it can be shown that the sample standard deviation is an *underestimate* of the population standard deviation. In other words, the sample standard deviation tends to be smaller than the population standard deviation. To correct for this, we need to make a slight adjustment to the statistic. We do this by dividing the numerator (i.e., the top half) of the equation by $N - 1$ rather than N.

Having made this correction, the formula for sample standard deviation can therefore be written as follows:

$$s_x = \sqrt{\frac{\sum(X - \bar{X})^2}{N - 1}}$$

You will notice that the only difference between this equation and the one for the sample standard deviation is that there is an $N - 1$ term on the bottom line of the equation (the denominator) rather than an N. Similarly, the computational formula for standard deviation is the same as the one previously presented apart from the fact that it has a denominator of $N - 1$:

$$s_x = \sqrt{\frac{\sum X^2 - \frac{(\sum X)^2}{N}}{N - 1}}$$

Calculating the values in this way will tend to give an unbiased estimate of the population standard deviation, providing that sampling is random. Note that whenever we refer to or need to calculate standard deviation in the remainder of this book, this is the formula we will apply.

We now have some useful tools for describing the shape and parameters of theoretical distributions. We can use these concepts of expected frequency and population mean and standard deviation to describe the shapes of such theoretical distributions. By knowing the shapes of these distributions we can examine the observed data from a sample and compare them to what they should look like if the sample is drawn from a specific population.

To illustrate how this process works we can think back to the example where we throw a die many times and record the number. The theoretical distribution for this case is called a **uniform** or **flat-rectangular distribution**. For such a distribution every outcome has an equal probability of one-sixth or 0.167 (see Figure 6.5).

Imagine now that we decide to toss two dice and add the scores together. Instead of having six possibilities we now have 11 possibilities. What is more, these possibilities are not equally likely. In fact you have a much better chance of getting a combined score of 7 (one chance in six) than a combined score of 12 (1 chance in 36). This is shown in Figure 6.6.

What happens as we add more and more dice to the theoretical distribution is that we start to get a particular form of bell-shaped curve. This curve is almost certainly the most useful and important of all the distributions observed in psychological research and is known as the **normal distribution**. The normal distribution is reasonably common in psychological data. It is observed, for example, in the distribution of such things as people's IQ scores, their height and pulse rate. The distribution is symmetrical about its mean, so its mean, median and mode are all equal (see Figure 6.7).

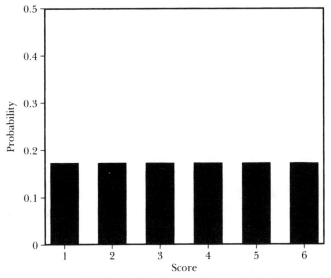

Figure 6.5 Theoretical distribution for the score from a single die

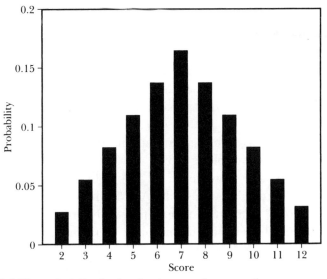

Figure 6.6 Theoretical distribution for the score from two dice

The question you are probably asking yourself here is why this distribution is so common. Why do so many theoretical distributions of variables follow a bell-shaped curve? There are at least three answers to this. The first can be seen in our dice example. Most things in life are not decided from a few discrete alternatives like the faces of a die. Instead they are based on a complex sum of lots of different factors. Most of us do not lead our lives by tossing coins

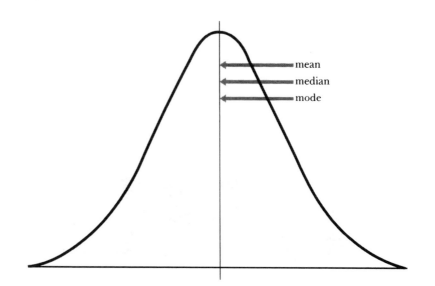

Figure 6.7 The normal distribution

or rolling dice. Instead most of our decisions and actions are
determined by the interaction of many different factors, each one
of which might be reduced to a simpler set of choices. Adding all of
these complex events together will tend to produce a range of events
that vary in their likelihood, so that extreme occurrences that rely
on the conjunction of many specific events will be very unlikely
indeed.

In the case of rolling two dice and adding the scores together a 12
can only be obtained by rolling a 6 on the first die (die A) *and* a 6 on
the second die (die B). However, a 7 can be obtained by rolling any
one of six different combinations: (die A = 1, die B = 6); (2, 5); (3, 4);
(4, 3); (5, 2); (6, 1). Similarly, people may only grow up to become
extremely tall if they have an unusual genetic make-up *and* their
mothers have good health during pregnancy *and* they have good
nutrition and health during childhood. If height does depend on this
simple model (the full explanation is of course much more complex
than this) then it will be approximately normally distributed because
very few people will meet *all* these conditions. To think of something
more psychological in nature, extreme behaviours such as reacting
violently to somebody might also be determined by a complex interaction of different factors. Perhaps people only react violently when
they are very angry *and* they do not fear retaliation *and* they have
previously been exposed to violent role models. If violent behaviour
follows this very simple model then there is quite a good chance that it
too will be normally distributed. This is the case with many variables

that relate to individual differences (such as intelligence and some personality traits).

The second, related, answer to the question of why so many phenomena are normally distributed is that most measurements in psychology are associated with a degree of uncertainty. That is, most measurements actually involve **measurement error**. These measurement errors can be seen as deviations from the true value that would have been obtained if we could have measured a value with perfect accuracy. These deviations from the true score are likely to reflect complex processes like those that we have discussed in the previous paragraph. Deviations from accurate measurement should therefore be normally distributed. If the deviations are normally distributed then there is a good chance that the measurements themselves will be normally distributed.

These measurement errors occur in all sciences. If you studied the published height of the tallest mountain in the world (Mt Everest) over the last 100 years you would find that the statistics have changed as measuring techniques have changed. We would also expect that if a team of researchers set out to measure the height of Mt Everest on a number of different occasions using an unbiased measuring technique they would produce a number of different results and that these would be normally distributed about the true height of the mountain. Similarly, if psychologists were to measure a person's IQ using many different unbiased measuring techniques we would expect that the measurements would be normally distributed about the true IQ score. This variation between different tests of the same thing is quite distinct from variation between different people's IQs (individual differences) and is also distinct from variation within the same person's IQ (e.g., variation due to maturation). In fact, though, it is often hard to distinguish between these things empirically. For this reason, individual differences, measurement error and maturation get rolled into one measure of dispersion.

One important way in which error is introduced into measurement is via **sampling error**. Let us imagine that statisticians want to find out what the level of unemployment in a country is (as they regularly do in most developed countries). They could survey the entire population of that country and find out whether each person is employed or not. However, statisticians find this takes too long and costs too much. So instead what they do is take a representative random sample of the population and measure the level of unemployment in that sample. When you hear the unemployment rate reported in the news this is the figure that is actually being used. But of course, even if the sampling is done perfectly we can never be sure that the sample corresponds to the population exactly – and it rarely will. However, if the sample is representative and random the differences between the sample and the population will be due to complex processes that are normally distributed around the true value.

The third reason why so many variables are normally distributed is perhaps more surprising. Normal distributions are so mathematically useful that, even if variables are not actually normally distributed to begin with, it is worth using mathematical procedures to make them normal. This is something that psychologists often do.

We will consider issues to do with population parameters and normal distributions in a lot more detail in Chapter 7. For now, though, we will only note that if we are interested in a variable (e.g., the responses of our control sample on the attributional style response scale) and we know (a) the *mean* of that variable together with (b) its *standard deviation*, and we also know (c) that that variable is *normally distributed*, then armed with this knowledge we can make a number of incredibly powerful statements about the behaviour of that variable in the population. For example, we can confidently make statements about (a) the proportion of scores on that variable that will fall within a given range (e.g., above a certain value), (b) how unusual any given observation is, and (c) the difference between this sample and others with which we want to compare it and for which similar information is available. It should be clear from the material we have covered in previous chapters that these are precisely the sorts of thing that research psychologists want to know.

Q6.5[**]

If scores on a variable are normally distributed, which of the following statements is *false*?

(a) All scores on the variable will have been observed with equal frequency.
(b) The distribution of scores is symmetrical about the mean.
(c) Similar distributions are commonly observed in data obtained from psychological research.
(d) There will be relatively few extreme scores.
(e) The mean, median and modal scores will be equal.

The correct answer is (a). When every score on a variable is observed with equal frequency, the distribution of scores on that variable will be uniform (i.e., flat and rectangular), not bell-shaped. As statement (d) suggests, when a variable is normally distributed, the more extreme a score is the less likely it is to be observed. Statements (b) and (e) are true because a normally distributed variable is symmetrical about its mean, and its mean, median and mode are equal. As (c) suggests, the normal distribution is commonly observed in data obtained from psychological research. This is because many psychological variables are normally distributed (e.g., IQ scores, personality variables).

expected frequency Formally, the *probability* of some event multiplied by the sample size. That is, it is the likely total number of events of a particular type resulting from a random process (e.g., drawing a random sample of a given size from the population). For example, the expected frequency of heads when you toss an unbiased coin 10 times is 5 (i.e., $.5 \times 10$).

flat-rectangular distribution Another name for a *uniform distribution*.

measurement error Deviations between a true score and an observation produced by inaccuracies in measurement. This can arise from inaccuracies in the measurement instrument or from other sources.

normal distribution The symmetrical spread of scores that is obtained when scores on a variable are randomly distributed around a mean in a bell-shaped curve. The term is applied to *observed* and *theoretical* distributions.

observed distribution A distribution obtained by empirically observing a set of scores (a sample). It is assumed that the observed distribution is drawn from a *theoretical distribution* of scores in a population.

population parameter Some characteristic of the population that is estimated on the basis of data from a sample.

probability (*p*) The likelihood of an event. Probabilities are expressed as a number between 0 and 1, where 0 indicates that an event definitely will not occur and 1 indicates that an event definitely will occur. The sum of all probabilities (corresponding to all possible events) equals 1, and any given probability corresponds to a fraction of this total. Under certain circumstances, probability can be thought of as the sample size divided by the *expected frequency*.

sampling error Differences between a sample and the population. It is therefore error associated with estimating the true value of some characteristic of a population.

theoretical distribution An expected or hypothesized distribution of what scores should be like in general. Population distributions are usually theoretical distributions (except where every member of the population has been measured).

uniform distribution A distribution where there is an equal frequency (or equal expected frequency) of each possible event. Also known as a *flat-rectangular distribution*.

Further reading

A number of excellent texts deal with the consequences of not mastering the concepts in this chapter – pointing, in particular, to the ways in which statistics can be misused and misinterpreted. The short books by Huff (1973) and Paulos (1990) are particularly good examples of this genre and they are both well worth reading.

Huff, D. (1973). *How to lie with statistics*. London: Penguin.
Paulos, J. A. (1990). *Innumeracy*. London: Penguin.

Descriptive statistics: A checklist for research evaluation and improvement

Potential problem	Question to ask	Potential improvement
Inappropriate measurement of central tendency	Have the researchers used an appropriate measure of central tendency (in particular, is the use of the mean appropriate)?	Because the mean is often used as a default measure of central tendency, it can be useful to consider whether use of this measure is unjustified or misleading. This is most likely to be the case if data are highly skewed, in which case you should consider the implications of reporting an alternative measure (the median or mode).
Inappropriate measurement of dispersion	Have the researchers used an appropriate measure of dispersion (in particular, is the use of standard deviation appropriate)?	Because standard deviation is often used as a default measure of dispersion, it can be useful to consider whether using this measure is unjustified or misleading. This is most likely to be the case if a data set includes outliers (a problem that can also contaminate other measures).

Potential problem	Question to ask	Potential improvement
Outliers	Have the researchers tested for the presence of outliers?	Examine the distribution to see if it contains outliers. If it does, see if this can be corrected by an appropriate statistical transformation of the data. If this is not possible, consider (a) removing individual outliers or (b) recoding them to the same value as the nearest non-outlier. Ensure you report any transformations that you make.

Q6.6*

Which of the following is *not* a measure of central tendency?

(a) The mean of a distribution.
(b) The mean deviation of some data.
(c) The modal value of a set of values.
(d) The median response on a scale.
(e) An average score.

Q6.7***

If the shaded bars in the histogram below represent the times (rounded to the nearest 10 milliseconds) that 50 people take to react to a loud noise, which of the following statements is *not* true?

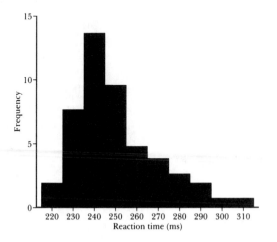

(a) The distribution of reaction times is negatively skewed.
(b) The modal reaction time is 240 ms.
(c) The median reaction time is greater than 240 ms.

(d) The mean reaction time will be greater than the modal reaction time.

(e) The mean is an ambiguous measure of central tendency.

Q6.8*

'Root mean squared deviate' is another name for which measure of dispersion?

(a) Range.
(b) Mean deviation.
(c) Variance.
(d) Standard deviation.
(e) Squared deviation from the root.

The correct answer to 6.6 is (b). The mean, median and mode are all measures of central tendency (i.e., attempts to describe a typical value), and average is just another word for central tendency. However, mean deviation is a measure of dispersion (it is the average absolute difference between a set of scores and the mean of those scores).

The correct answer to 6.7 is (a). This distribution is actually positively skewed. Because of this the mean will tend to be an ambiguous measure of central tendency (as (e) suggests). Both the median and the mean will also be greater than the mode (which, as (a) suggests, is the most common reaction time of 240 ms). Note that by understanding the relationship between measures of central tendency and a response distribution we can deduce that statements (c) and (d) are correct *without* having to compute these measures.

The correct answer to 6.8 is (d). The answer to this question is given away by the term 'root'. Standard deviation is the square root of the variance, which is the mean squared deviate (the average squared difference between a set of scores and the mean of those scores). Range is just the difference between the highest and lowest scores. Mean deviation is the average absolute difference between a set of scores and the mean of those scores. There is no such term as squared deviation from the root.

Discussion/essay questions

(a) What are the advantages and disadvantages of different measures of central tendency?

(b) What are the advantages and disadvantages of different measures of dispersion?

(c) Which descriptive statistics would you use to summarize information about wage levels in different countries? Discuss the reasons for your answer.

(d) Why does the normal distribution play such an important role in psychological research?

Exercises

(a) Draw a frequency graph for each of the following data sets (from scores on a response scale):
  (i) 7, 6, 5, 1, 5, 5, 6, 4, 7, 5, 3, 2, 4, 6, 4
  (ii) 1, 2, 4, 3, 5, 3, 5, 3, 2, 3, 6, 7, 3, 4, 2, 2, 1, 2, 4, 2

(b) Are these distributions skewed at all? If so, in what direction?

(c) Work out the mean, median and mode for each of the above data sets.

(d) Work out the range, mean deviation, variance and standard deviation (s_X) for each of the above data sets.

(e) One of the factors that often leads to distributions which would otherwise be normal being skewed is the existence of a floor or a ceiling at one end of a distribution. A ceiling is a point that scores cannot exceed and a floor is a point that all values must exceed. For example, in the case of reaction time, the floor is 0 milliseconds because a person cannot respond before a stimulus is presented.
  (i) Based on the principles we have discussed in this chapter, what should be the impact of floors on the relative position of mean, median and modal values for a distribution?
  (ii) Why do floors have this impact?

(f) Having answered the previous question:
  (i) Would you expect the mean number of cars people in America own to exceed the median number of cars owned? Why?
  (ii) Would you expect the mean score on a very easy exam to exceed the median score on the same exam? Why?

(g) In his book *Life's Grandeur*, Stephen Jay Gould (1997) notes that over the past century the performance of the *best* baseball hitters has declined (so that the batting averages of the best players are lower than in the past). Does this imply that the overall performance of baseball batters has decreased? Why (or why not)?

7

Some Principles of Statistical Inference

As we outlined in Chapter 2, a major part of research in psychology involves making decisions about how confident we should be in the conclusions we draw from research data. Statistics allow us to express this degree of confidence in numerical terms. This is a useful thing to do because it allows us to say clearly when we have great confidence in the pattern of findings we observe and when we are not so sure about them.

In this chapter we are concerned with how we go about making those decisions. Imagine that you have done a piece of research where you have followed all the steps we have outlined in the book so far. The research might be an experiment with a control condition and a theoretically interesting experimental condition. Imagine you have eliminated all confounds and have a dependent variable that is both relevant to the question in which you are interested and sensitive to changes in the independent variable. You have collected the data and calculated the means and standard deviations, and you now want to know if the theory you set out to test is supported or not. If there is a difference between the mean scores obtained for the experimental and control groups, you will want to know whether you should take that difference seriously, or just consider it as a chance event. So, the critical question is 'Exactly how confident should I be that the difference between the groups is big enough to take seriously?'

Alternatively, the research you conducted could have been a survey investigating the relationship between two variables. Imagine you have drawn a representative random sample from the population of interest, you have measured the variables in a valid and reliable manner and now you want to know whether the variables are related in the sample. If they are related in the sample you want to be able to draw a conclusion about the relationship between the variables in the popula-tion. In both the experiment and the survey, you want some way of expressing your confidence that what you have found is interesting or unusual, and not just some uninformative random event.

Why is this necessary? Why is it that psychologists cannot just accept the results they observe, without resorting to statistical analysis in order to make statements about confidence? In fact, when they use statistics to make statements about confidence psychologists are no different from anybody else. Before they decide whether they should believe that something is true, they simply want to know what the evidence for that belief is. For example, most people will choose not to carry an umbrella unless they are reasonably sure that it could rain. Similarly, if the share price of a company drops slightly, the shareholders do not immediately rush off and sell all their shares in the company, unless they believe that the fall in price is a sign of further falls to come. Perhaps neither the umbrella-holder nor the shareholder will perform a statistical test before making their decisions. However, both will definitely base their decision on the evidence available and will take steps to reduce any uncertainty they may have about that evidence (e.g., by listening to weather forecasts or stock market reports). The fact that psychologists use statistics to make these decisions is simply a reflection of the controlled and systematic manner in which scientists make observations and draw conclusions in their work.

Even without statistical training we can all make quasi-statistical decisions in everyday life. Imagine you go to a casino and play a game of chance where you win if any tails are tossed and the house wins if every coin toss comes up heads. If a coin is tossed 10 times and heads comes up 10 times, you will be left with two possible conclusions. Either something funny is going on and the game has been rigged (e.g., because the coin is biased) or the casino has been very lucky. *This is exactly the same type of decision as we make in statistics.* If we find a difference between the means of an experimental and control condition then we have to decide between two possibilities: either there really is something going on (and the independent variable is having an effect) or the difference is due to chance.

There is yet another reason why we cannot just say that any observed difference between means is 'big enough' for us to be interested in it, or that any observed relationship between variables is a 'big enough' relationship. The reason is that, if we use accurate measuring techniques, we will almost always find a difference between means or a relationship between variables. If you were to measure the IQs of a sample of 20 males and a sample of 20 females you would almost certainly find a 'difference' between the mean IQs of your male and female participants. Let us imagine that you find that the males have

an IQ that is one point higher than that of the females. How confident
would you be in concluding that males are more intelligent than
females? While you are thinking about that, let us also imagine that
you measured the heights of 20 males and 20 females, and found that
the mean height of the males was 10 cm more than that of the females.
How confident would you be that males are taller than females? We
suspect that most people would be happy to say that the first data set
does not *prove* that males are more intelligent than females, because the
difference is so small. Others would say that evidence from just 40
people proves nothing. Yet most people would accept the difference
in heights as evidence that males are taller than females. Indeed, if
someone tried to tell you that males *were not* taller than females you
might seriously question their powers of observation. As a scientist you
might well tell the person to have a good look around and measure the
heights of the people they see.

But what if this trouble-maker were to follow your advice and
measure the heights of 20 men and 20 women, and come back to you
and simply say 'Here are the data. I have calculated the means and
standard deviations as per the instructions in Chapter 6. I want to
know, what *makes you so sure* that men are taller than women?' What
possible answer could you give?

It would be unsatisfactory to say 'Look, I just *know* that men are
taller than women'. Doing research is not so much about reaffirming
what we already know, as about adding to that knowledge by enquir-
ing into what we do not know. If we restrict our enquiries to what we
already know with absolute certainty then there is no point in doing
research. It is also true that few of the interesting statements we can
make about psychological processes can be made with *absolutely no
uncertainty*. When we say that 'men are taller than women' or 'males and
females are of equal intelligence', we acknowledge some uncertainty in
those statements. We know that some women are taller than some men
and that some men are more intelligent than most women and that
some women are more intelligent than most men. That being the case,
we try to make statements that are true on average, on the balance of
evidence available to us. What inferential statistics help us to do is
decide how confident we should be that some statement is true *on
average*.

What of the question posed by our height-measuring trouble-maker?
How can we be sure that men really are taller than women? Although it
might be tempting to tell the person to go away and stop bothering us,
it would actually be well worth attempting to grapple with the
substance of such questions. This is because they actually touch

on the key concepts in inferential statistics that we confront in psychology, and the next time you are confronted by similar questions might be when you are doing research or a class test. The aim of this chapter is to help you answer questions of *exactly* this form.

Statistical inference

Throughout this book so far we have suggested that a key objective of research is to reduce uncertainty so that we can confidently draw conclusions. If we are not sure about something we need to collect evidence that will enable us to be more certain. It is always worth looking first to see whether somebody else has already answered the question we are interested in, but in practice we often need to collect new data.

In this chapter we want to distinguish between two types of **statistical uncertainty**. The first is the type of uncertainty that we talked about in the previous chapter when we discussed *dispersion*. We call this **descriptive uncertainty**. A normally distributed variable can be expressed as a mean plus a certain amount of variability around that mean. In this case the mean will be the best summary of the scores for a given sample. If most of the scores are close to the mean then this will be reflected in a small standard deviation – that is, the mean will be a good indicator of each score and there will be relatively little uncertainty about the position of the score. But if the other scores are spread out a long way from the mean, there will be quite a lot of uncertainty about where each score lies. Thus descriptive uncertainty is uncertainty in our ability to know, or to predict, individual scores on the basis of a measure of central tendency.

The idea of uncertainty about the degree to which the mean is a good summary of all of the scores contains within it the notion of **random error**. As we discussed in Chapter 6, theoretically speaking, random error arises from two main sources: imprecision in the measurement instrument and other kinds of measurement error; and sampling error. There are important differences between these two things, and researchers who are concerned to reduce random error will take different steps to deal with each of them. For example, to deal with measurement error they may try to devise a more reliable dependent measure, and to reduce sampling error they may take a larger random sample from the population. In practice, however, none of these things can be eliminated completely, and in a great deal of psychological data there are also differences between individual people which cannot be removed by accurate measurement or representative sampling.

For practical purposes, as we noted in the previous chapter, measurement and sampling error are therefore usually lumped together with individual differences because they are all things over which the researcher does not have total control.

The other type of statistical uncertainty relates to the conclusions we draw from research, and this is our primary focus in the present chapter. This sort of uncertainty arises from not knowing whether the patterns we observe in the data (e.g., a difference between means) are *informative* because they reflect some process of interest or whether they are due to a series of **chance** events. We call this **inferential uncertainty**. If we eliminate all alternative explanations of experimental results through good research design there are still always two possibilities: the results could reflect the impact of the independent variable and hence provide meaningful information, or they could be due to sampling error. If we can reduce or control uncertainty in the form of random error then we can reduce inferential uncertainty about our conclusions. Although inferential uncertainty and descriptive uncertainty are related to each other – inferential uncertainty will be higher when descriptive uncertainty is high – they are actually quite different concepts.

We can see the difference between the two types of uncertainty in the following example. Imagine that you had conducted the study where you measured the heights of 20 men and 20 women. If you wanted to answer the question 'How tall are men?' then the best answer you could give would be the mean height for your sample of men. However, there would be some uncertainty in your response because not all men are the same height (if they were the standard deviation would be zero). This type of uncertainty is descriptive uncertainty. On the other hand, if you wanted to answer the question 'Are men taller than women?' then the obvious thing you need to do is to compare the mean height of the men with the mean height of the women. If you were to answer this question 'yes' or 'no' there would still be inferential uncertainty because you could never be entirely sure that the results were not due to chance rather than due to a real difference. The difference may reflect the fact that there just happened to be a difference in the heights of the particular samples of men and women that you chose to measure. Thus descriptive and inferential uncertainty are different because they reflect uncertainty about the answers to quite different questions.

As we will see, however, the amount of inferential uncertainty does depend upon the amount of descriptive uncertainty (or variability).

To take the most extreme example, if the standard deviation of two groups in a study were zero (so that there was no descriptive uncertainty) then there would be no inferential uncertainty. However, it is possible for descriptive uncertainty to be low, but for inferential uncertainty to be high. This would occur when the standard deviations were small but the means of two groups *were very similar*. It is also possible for descriptive uncertainty to be high and for inferential uncertainty to be low, and this is more likely to be the case when the sample size is very large.

The other key difference between these forms of uncertainty is that they are measured in different ways. Random error – descriptive uncertainty – is measured in terms of dispersion or variability (e.g., standard deviation). Uncertainty about whether our results are due to chance – inferential uncertainty – is normally thought of as a probability. When the probability that our results could have been produced by chance or random error is very low then our uncertainty about our conclusions is low. That is, inferential uncertainty will be low.

In fact, though, we can *never* calculate the probability that our results are due to chance. Instead what we can do is calculate the probability that a **random process** (such as coin tossing) could produce results as dramatic as the ones we have obtained. If this probability is very low then we can conclude that it is unlikely that our results are due to chance. This is a fine technical point, but it is a mistake for researchers to lose sight of the fact that the statistics they use express uncertainty in this form (Tukey, 1991). If we want to know whether our results are due to chance or to some meaningful process, we need to work out the probability that a random process could have produced results like ours. Once we know how plausible it is that our results are due to chance, we can decide whether we think they *are* due to chance or to the meaningful process. In other words, although we can never tell whether our results have been produced by a random process, we can decide how *plausible* that possibility is. Inferential uncertainty relates to precisely this sort of decision.

Sometimes we can calculate this probability exactly, but most of the time in psychology it is necessary first to work out a **test statistic**. Once we have calculated that statistic we can then determine the probability of a random process producing a result as dramatic as that which we have obtained. The two possible conclusions – that something is going on (representing meaningful *information*) and that the results are due to chance or random *error* – are related to

inferential statistics that we calculate using equations of the following
form:

$$\text{test statistic} = \frac{\text{information}}{\text{error}}$$

What this sort of equation tells us is that as the ratio of information to
error gets larger the calculated statistic will be larger. Also, as the statistic
becomes larger, the probability that chance or random error could have
produced results of this size becomes smaller. This means that if we want
to reduce uncertainty about our conclusions, we need good evidence to
support the conclusion (i.e., high information) and/or a very small
amount of random error. To understand statistical equations we recommend that you always think about what the **information term** and the
error term are in each equation. You will find the expression 'error
term' in many statistics books. The idea of an 'information term' is less
widely used. But by introducing this term we can express the key idea of
inferential statistics quite succinctly: to the extent that the information
term is much larger than the error term, the probability that results of the
observed size (or greater) could have been due to chance will be low.
Thus uncertainty about inferences will be low.

It is worth returning to the example of a game of chance in order to
see how these random processes work. Remember that the casino
employee tossed the coin 10 times and obtained 10 heads. This is a
simple example where we are able to calculate exactly the probability
of a random process producing an outcome that unusual (without
needing to calculate an information and error term to obtain the
statistic). We suggested that if you saw this happen you could explain
this in one of two ways, concluding either that the coin was biased or
that the casino had just been very lucky. If we conclude that the result
is due to a biased coin then we are saying that the behaviour of the coin
is both meaningful and important. If we say that the casino was just
lucky we are saying that the behaviour of the coin was due to random
error or chance. The best way to make this decision in a systematic way
is to imagine how an ordinary, fair coin would behave in the same
circumstances.

This process of imagining how an ordinary coin would behave over a
run of 10 tosses is called creating a **statistical model** of coin tossing. In
this case we use a simple but reasonable statistical model that assumes
that there is an equal chance of getting a head or a tail. We say that
the probability of a head or a tail is .5. This model also allows us to
calculate what is called the **expected value** of the distribution. The
expected value is really just another name for the *mean* of a population.

For a sample of 10 coin tosses with a probability of .5 the expected value for the number of heads is 5 (i.e., $10 \times .5 = 5$).

Can we now make the decision as to whether the casino has cheated? Well, we could compare the expected value of 5 with the obtained value of 10. These outcomes are obviously different but we still do not know *how* different. After all, it is *possible* (but unlikely) to obtain 10 heads from 10 tosses of a fair coin. In order to decide how confident we can be that the coin is biased we need to extend our statistical model a bit to consider not just the expected value of the distribution, but also the uncertainty or variability associated with that distribution. What we need to do is map out all the probable outcomes that we could obtain from tossing that coin. We are able to do this using the **binomial distribution**. This allows us to calculate the probability of any possible outcome when we toss a fair coin 10 times. This binomial distribution tells us that the chance of obtaining 10 heads is $.5^{10}$ which is .0009765. In other words, there is less than a 1 in 1000 chance of a fair coin doing what the one in the casino did. It is your decision as to whether you would say the casino was cheating on the basis of this evidence, but it might be unwise to keep betting in that casino.

The binomial distribution for 10 coin tosses is shown in Figure 7.1. You can see that the distribution is symmetrical around five heads (which is the mean, median and modal response) and that the probability of this outcome is .246. This distribution is chunky like a frequency graph rather than smooth like a normal distribution because

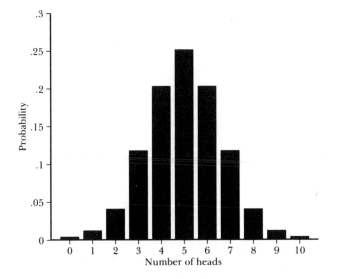

Figure 7.1 Theoretical distribution for 10 fair coin tosses

there is a small and discrete set of outcomes (11 in fact). If there were a thousand possible outcomes the distribution would be a lot smoother.

All other statistical inferences involve a similar process to this. In order to decide whether we have observed a chance event or a meaningful event we create a statistical model of what *could* happen by chance. This statistical model describes the likelihood of each of the events that could occur if there is nothing special going on – that is, when we are observing a random process like tossing a fair coin. The statistical model takes into account the variability and uncertainty in the situation, and tells us what the chance of obtaining an effect as large as the one we have observed would be if the process were random. If this probability is very small then we can be more confident that something is going on, in the same way that we can be reasonably certain that something funny is going on in the casino.

In the previous chapter we showed you how to calculate means and standard deviations. We also suggested that, compared to other measures of central tendency and dispersion, means and standard deviations are especially useful in inferential statistics. This is mainly due to the properties of the normal distribution. So, if we know that a variable is normally distributed with a given mean and standard deviation, then we know just about everything we need to about that variable. This is especially true when we want to make inferences about relationships between variables, because we can create detailed statistical models about how random variables behave.

Q7.1**

Imagine a coin-tossing experiment in which a coin is tossed 10 times and the researcher records the number of heads obtained. Which of the following statements are true?

(a) The binomial distribution helps provide a statistical model for this coin-tossing experiment.
(b) The binomial distribution gives the probability that the coin is biased.
(c) Very rare events are always random.
(d) The information term of the statistic used in this experiment will be a measure of chance, or random error.
(e) Both (a) and (b).

The correct answer is (a). (b) is wrong because the binomial distribution cannot give us the probability that a coin is biased, rather it gives us the probability that a fair coin would behave in some specified manner.

binomial distribution The distribution of the possible outcomes from a *random process* where there are two possible events (event p and event q) so that the probability of one or other occurring is 1 (and the probability of p occurring is 1 minus the probability of q occurring – i.e., $p = 1 - q$). An example would be the process of tossing an unbiased coin, where the probability of getting heads is .5 and the probability of getting tails is .5.

chance Another word for luck or *random error*.

descriptive uncertainty *Statistical uncertainty* arising from variation in observations around any measure of central tendency for which the researcher proposes no explanation. It is uncertainty in knowing or predicting individual scores on the basis of a measure of central tendency. This uncertainty is quantified by dispersion measures (e.g., standard deviation, variance, range).

error term In an equation for a test statistic, the mathematical expression that estimates how much *random error* there is in the data.

expected value The mean value of a probability distribution. For example, the expected value for the number of heads when a fair coin is tossed 50 times is 25.

inferential uncertainty *Statistical uncertainty* relating to the possibility that an observed result is due to *random error* or *chance*. This uncertainty is estimated by a probability value, where a low probability indicates low uncertainty.

information term In an equation for a *test statistic*, the mathematical expression that tells us how much evidence there is that the results are not due to *chance* or *random error*.

random error The amount of *descriptive uncertainty* or *chance* variation associated with statistical statements and observations.

random process A process which generates a range of different events which are independent of each other. When this is the case the occurrence of one event is not dependent on the occurrence of another.

statistical model A detailed statement about the likelihood of a particular set of events.

> **statistical uncertainty** Doubt about statistics arising from the
> presence of ***random error***. Generally speaking, such uncertainty is
> easier to estimate than to reduce.
>
> **test statistic** A numerical statement about a population based on
> ·sample data.

Inferences about individual scores

When we conduct research, what sort of inferences can we make from
the results we obtain? Most importantly perhaps, if we know the mean
and standard deviation of a variable and that it is normally distributed,
we can say how likely some individual score or event is. An example of
just such a variable is IQ. This is because IQ scores are actually
constructed so that they are normally distributed and have a mean of
100 and a standard deviation of 15.

Let us say someone does an IQ test and obtains a score of 120. We
might want to know if that is a high or average score compared with the
rest of the population. By knowing the shape of the normal distribution
we are able to say exactly where that score lies in relation to the rest
of the population. What we are able to do is express the difference
between that score and the population mean in terms of **standard
deviation units**. In this case 120 is 20 IQ points away from the
population mean of 100. More informatively, we can say that it is 20/15
or 1.33 standard deviation units away. This process of converting scores
into units that express differences from the mean in standard deviation
units is called **standardization**. This is done to make different scores
comparable. To standardize a score all you need to do is subtract the
mean from the score and divide by the standard deviation.

As a student, you may have already encountered the term 'standardization' in relation to test scores. It is very common for instructors to
standardize the results of class tests. This can be puzzling for students
when they find that the scores that they have obtained on a test have
gone up or down. If you are a student and you are not already clear
what standardization is, then the next few paragraphs are probably
worth paying particularly close attention to.

The reasons for standardizing scores are quite easy to grasp, but it is
harder to understand why standardization involves the particular
mathematical operations that it does. Let us take an example of two
students who do different tests. They both obtain 75% (i.e., they both
have the same raw score of 75 out of 100) but student A is in a class
where the class mean is 50 (with a standard deviation of 10) while

the mean for Student B's class is 80 (also with a standard deviation of 10). Which performance would you be more impressed by? Most people would say Student A because this person is performing at a level 25 points better than the class mean, while Student B is actually 5 points worse than the class mean.

The main point about standardization is therefore that it is useful to express individual scores in terms of a difference from a mean in order to compare them. This explains the mathematical operation of subtracting the mean from the score. Why do we then divide this difference by the standard deviation? The answer is that if we want to know how well a person has done relative to the class on average, it is helpful to express the difference from the mean relative to the amount of dispersion (of which the standard deviation is one measure). This difference can be thought of as a *statistical difference* or distance. Dividing the difference by the standard deviation tells us how distinctive or remarkable a score is. We know that Student A has done better than the class mean, but we would also like to know what sort of proportion of the class was doing that well. Is it the case that 10% or 5% (or even less) of the class have done as well as this student? Ideally we would want a score that tells us this information without having to remember what the distribution of all the scores was. This is what standardization allows us to do. It gives us a single number which expresses the difference from a mean relative to the standard deviation (which is related to average deviation from the mean).

So, in the examples above, Student A has a standardized score of 2.5 (i.e., $(75 - 50)/10$) and Student B has a standardized score of -0.5 (i.e., $(75 - 80)/10$). Providing that they believed that the classes were of equal ability (and this is crucial), most people would be much more impressed with Student A's performance.

For this sort of purpose, standardization is a useful procedure that has a sound statistical basis. This is not to say that standardization has always been used sensibly and well. Indeed, on occasion it has been seriously misused by educators and social policy-makers. It is fair to say, though, that it is much more likely to be misused by those who do not understand its statistical rationale.

Standardizing scores will create a distribution of scores with a mean of 0 and a standard deviation of 1. A normal distribution with a mean of 0 and a standard deviation of 1 is called a **standard normal distribution**. A score that has been subtracted from the mean and then divided by the standard deviation is called a **z-score**. A variable whose values have been converted to z-scores has a mean of 0 and a standard deviation of 1. Putting these ideas into the form of an equation:

$$z_x = \frac{score_x - mean}{standard\ deviation}$$

In this equation the top line on the right is the information term and the bottom line is the error term. To work out the z-score associated with an IQ of 120, we would do the following calculation:

$$z_{120} = \frac{120 - 100}{15}$$

$$= 1.33$$

To set these standard scores to another mean and standard deviation, all you need to do is multiply them by the new standard deviation and then add the new mean. The order in which you do these calculations is very important. For example, if you wanted to create a new 'height quotient' with a mean of 100 and a standard deviation of 15, you would multiply people's standardized heights (which would have a mean of 0 and standard deviation of 1) by 15 and then add 100.

Another reason for wanting to describe scores in standard deviation units is that if we know the variable is normally distributed then we know exactly what proportion of scores will be greater than any given z-score. We can get an insight into how this works by referring to Figure 7.2 which shows a standard normal distribution.

In a figure like this any z-score corresponds to a point on the horizontal axis of the graph. As you can see, if we draw a vertical line through the distribution at that point we divide it into two regions or areas

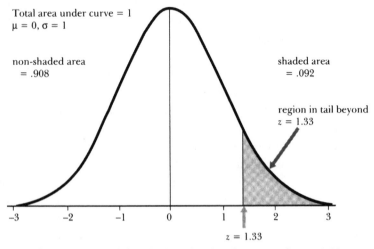

Figure 7.2 Standard normal distribution, showing the z-score for $z = 1.33$

(shaded and non-shaded), so that the line cuts off a certain part of that distribution. Remember that the distribution is actually a representation of what the total population of everybody's IQ would look like. So when we divide the curve into two areas we divide this population into two groups, those who lie at 120 or below, and those who lie above 120.

We can use this distribution to work out exactly what proportion of people have scores above or below any particular value. So, in this case we can work out what proportion of people have IQs above and below 120. This is because different z-scores correspond to points that cut off different, *specifiable* proportions of the population.

The way we work out the area under the curve to one side of the line cut through it by a z-score is complex. The good news is that you do not have to do any of the complicated calculations. The areas under the curve have already been worked out and are given in Table C.1 of Appendix C.

To use this table look down the left-hand column (labelled z) for the z-score 1.33. The area under the curve that lies in the tail beyond this z-score is then provided by the value in the 'Area in tail beyond z' column. In this case the value associated with a z-score of 1.33 is .092. Because the total area under the curve corresponds to all the events that could occur, this total area equals 1: the sum of all probabilities. The value associated with the area of the curve beyond any particular z-score therefore indicates the probability (between 0 and 1) of obtaining a score above this value. In this example the probability of a score greater than 1.33 is .092. Another way of putting this is to say that 1.33 cuts off .092 × 100% of the total area under the curve. Accordingly, we can say that 9.2% of the population have an IQ of 120 or more and 90.8% have an IQ of less than 120.

$Q7.2^{**}$

Jane has an IQ of 145. The area beyond a z-score of 3.0 (the z-score associated with her IQ) is .001. If we took a random sample of 1000 people from the population (which is known to have a mean of 100 and a standard deviation of 15) then which of the following statements is true?

(a) Jane's z-score will be 3.0.
(b) We can expect about 1 person in the sample of 1000 to have an IQ the same as or higher than Jane's.
(c) Both (a) and (b).
(d) Jane's z-score is obtained by dividing the binomial distribution by the error term.
(e) Both (a) and (d).

The correct answer is (c). The z-score is given in the question as 3.0, so (a) is correct. (b) is also correct because the proportion of the normal curve beyond Jane's z-score is also the proportion of the population with her IQ or higher. If it is a random sample we should expect .001 of the sample (or 0.1%) to have an IQ this high (i.e., 1 person in 1000). (d) is incorrect because the binomial distribution has nothing to do with this case. The z-score is obtained by dividing the difference between the score and the mean by the standard deviation.

standard deviation units The units in which *z-scores* are expressed.

standard normal distribution A normal distribution with a mean of 0 and a standard deviation of 1. *z-scores* correspond to different points of the horizontal axis of the standard normal distribution, cutting off regions of different sizes.

standardization Setting the mean and standard deviation for a variable to new values that are useful in a particular setting. In order to do this, we subtract the original mean from each value and divide it by the standard deviation, then multiply this value by the new (or desired) standard deviation and add the new mean.

z-score The difference between a score and the mean divided by the standard deviation. These scores have very useful properties when they are drawn from a normally distributed population.

Inferences about means

It seems reasonably easy to find out where an individual lies in relation to the rest of the population when we know that the population is normally distributed with a specified mean and standard deviation. Can we make similar statements about groups? Imagine we gave an IQ test to a class of 30 children and obtained a mean IQ for the class of 120. Could we find out whether the class mean differed from the expected population mean? The answer is 'yes', but, as you can probably imagine, things now start to become a bit trickier.

Things become trickier as a result of a statistical principle that just about everybody understands and uses in their everyday life. It is called the **law of large numbers**. For those who have not studied statistics in the past, it may seem strange that we say that you already under-stand something that you have never heard of. Part of the reason for this is that statistical ideas often sound more complex when it becomes necessary to express them technically.

The principle with which you are already familiar is that, other things being equal, uncertainty is reduced by taking many measurements of the same thing. We are more confident about something that we have lots of evidence for than about something we have little evidence for. This is why the mean score will be a more reliable indicator of what is going on in a sample than any individual score: the mean is the position in the sample which describes the sample with the least uncertainty because it is the average of many observations.

Thus, although around 9% of the population have IQs over 120, far fewer than 9% of classes of 30 randomly selected students will have a *mean* IQ over 120. We claimed a moment ago that you already understand this principle. To illustrate this, suppose that we offered you two choices: $20 if you could toss a fair coin five times and obtain five heads, or $20 if you could toss a fair coin 10 times and obtain 10 heads. Most people would take the first option (especially if they have been reading this chapter carefully so far). What if we offered you $200 if you could toss 10 heads? You would still be better off taking $20 for tossing 5 heads. By calculating the values from the binomial distribution we can show that you have 31 in 1000 chances of winning the $20 prize but only a 1 in 1000 chance of winning the $200. To make the offers of equal value we would have to offer you about $620 for tossing 10 heads.

Thus, obtaining the same extreme proportion of 100% heads with a small sample happens fairly regularly, but obtaining an extreme proportion with a larger sample is very rare if the process is truly random. We know that if we toss a coin 1000 times we can be reasonably confident that there will be something like 500 heads and 500 tails, even though we do not know what any given coin toss will yield. If we ask what the outcome of tossing a coin 10 times will be, then we can still expect there to be around 50% heads, but the variation in the proportion of heads will actually be much larger than with 1000 tosses. If you repeatedly perform the experiment of tossing a coin 10 times you will eventually have an example of all 10 tosses being heads (you can expect one every 1024 trials or so). On the other hand, we can expect that you will be tossing a coin a very long time before you get 50 out of 50 heads (at 2 minutes per 50 coin tosses you could expect to get 50 heads out of 50 tosses once every 4 billion years or so – so get tossing). We know it sounds a bit paradoxical, but this is the good thing about random processes: even though each **random event** is unpredictable we can have a pretty good idea of how random processes will behave in the long run, providing we know what the probability of a relevant event is. This long-term predictability is what makes random processes useful in statistical models.

Non-random processes are quite different in this respect. Suppose that instead of tossing a coin 1000 times we asked a person to *place* a coin on a table 1000 times. Now we might *hope* to do a better job of predicting how the person will place each coin than of predicting a random coin toss, but the possibility also exists that we could do *far worse* than chance. It is so unlikely that the possibility is not even remotely worth considering that someone could toss a fair coin 1000 times and obtain 1000 heads, but it would be a trivially simple exercise for somebody to place a coin heads up 1000 times. This illustrates what we mean about random processes being predictable (even though random events are not).

Let us take another example to explore some additional issues related to the law of large numbers. Imagine that the mean height of the men from a city is 175 cm and the standard deviation is 10 cm. If we were to take random samples of 10 men from the population and also take random samples of 100 men from the same population we would find that a larger proportion of the 10-man samples would have high means such as 185 cm. We would also find that a larger proportion of the 10-man samples would have low mean heights such as 165 cm. This is because there is greater variability in smaller samples as fewer scores need to be extreme in order to make the mean extreme. In other words, the process of dividing up exactly the same population in different ways provides a different distribution of means. More specifically, the law of large numbers implies that the *means* of large samples will be more tightly clustered around the population mean than the *means* of small samples. In other words, there will be less random error with large samples because the means will be less spread out. Of course, the overall population mean would not change, nor would the population standard deviation. It is the *same* population being divided up in each case – all we are doing is dividing it up randomly into samples of different sizes. However, the larger random samples provide more reliable **estimates** of the *population parameters*. In other words, they are more likely to provide summary statistics (e.g., means and standard deviations) which are close to those of the population the sample is drawn from.

The law of large numbers is a fundamental principle on which the inferential statistics that we use in psychology are based. We will not have too much difficulty in finding one person who has an IQ of 120 (as we have seen about 9% of people have an IQ of over 120), but we will be looking for a long time before we randomly draw a sample of 30 people who have a *mean* IQ of 120.

This statistical knowledge makes us more confident that if we *do* find a class (i.e., a sample) of 30 students with a mean IQ of 120 then this is unlikely to be a chance event (though it is always possible that it could be). In other words, we can be reasonably sure that we have discovered an intelligent group of students, and that there is probably some reason, other than chance, for their being so intelligent on average (perhaps particularly intelligent students have all been put in one class). It will be easier to decide whether or not the sample is a random sample from the population if the sample size is large, because extreme events such as randomly drawing a sample with a very high or very low mean will be more unlikely. The law of large numbers suggests that larger sample sizes should reduce uncertainty in the form of random error and consequently reduce uncertainty about our decision as to whether observed patterns are due to chance.

To calculate how confident we can be about such decisions we need to introduce some new ideas. The first of these is the idea of a **sampling distribution**. A sampling distribution is a theoretical distribution like those we discussed in Chapter 6. Its shape is derived from our understanding of the statistical model we are using. What we do is determine theoretically what would happen if we drew a sample of a particular size from a population. For example, we determine what the distribution of IQ scores in a sample of 30 people drawn randomly from the general population might look like based on knowledge that the population of IQ scores has a mean of 100 and a standard deviation of 15. Of course, in practice any sample is unlikely to have exactly this mean and standard deviation, and its exact mean and standard deviation will depend on the people that are sampled.

The sampling distribution we use does not exist in reality because it is not based on actual observations. However, we can specify what the sampling distribution would look like if it did exist. This is where our knowledge of the properties of the normal distribution becomes really useful. If the sampling distribution is a normal distribution then we know pretty well exactly what it would look like, so long as we know the population mean and standard deviation.

This might sound a bit mystical, in so far as we are relying on a sampling distribution that we have never actually seen but we believe that we know what it would look like if we could see it. Nevertheless, these ideas work. What we are doing is no different from what we did with the binomial distribution for the coin-tossing example. To create the sampling distribution for some normally distributed variable we simply calculate what would happen if we drew a sample of a particular size from the population. We could do that empirically (e.g., by going out and collecting the data from different groups), but we do not need to do that if we have a good statistical model (in the same way that we have a good model of how a fair coin behaves over a long run of tosses).

The second concept we need to introduce is the **sampling distribution of the mean**. This is the sampling distribution that would be obtained if we repeatedly sampled from the population and calculated the means. In the coin example we could compute such a sampling distribution for the number of heads obtained for sample sizes of 10 and 20. They are shown in Figure 7.3.

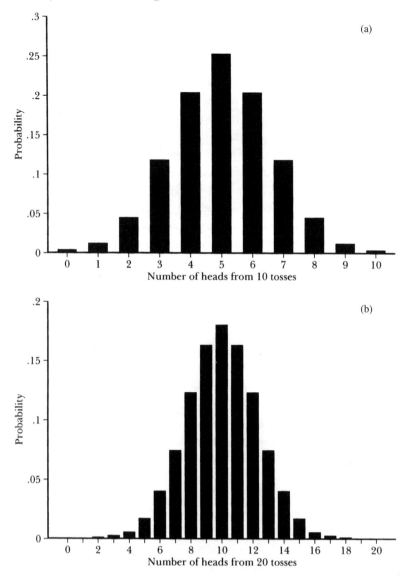

Figure 7.3 Sampling distribution of the mean for (a) 10 and (b) 20 fair coin tosses

We can see that the sampling distribution for 20 coin tosses is much more steeply peaked about the mean than that for 10 coin tosses. This is another way of saying that the sampling distribution for 20 coin tosses has less variance.

We could also construct a theoretical sampling distribution of the means from a normally distributed population of men with a mean height of 175 cm and a standard deviation of 10 cm (assuming random sampling). We have not actually done this but instead have approximated the sampling distribution by generating some random data where the population is divided first into samples of 10 men and then into samples of 100 men (Figure 7.4). What this involves is selecting a random sample of a given size (10 in Figure 7.4(a), 100 in Figure 7.4(b)) and calculating the mean for each sample. The histograms therefore do not show distributions of heights, instead they show distributions of the *means* of heights. About 300 samples were taken in each case. If we did this exercise again we would obtain distributions with slightly different shapes.

There are two things to note about Figure 7.4. First, we can see that the distributions are shaped rather like a normal distribution (even though they are not smooth, we can say that they are approximately normally distributed). Second, as the sample size gets larger the mean of these distributions stays the same, but the amount of dispersion of these sampling distributions decreases (even though the population standard deviation of the original sample must remain the same). In Figure 7.4 it can be seen that when the sample size is 10 the means range from 167 to 183, but that when the sample size is 100 the means only range from 172 to 177. In effect this is a statistical demonstration of the law of large numbers.

Two extremely useful properties of the sampling distribution of the mean are that it has a mean equal to the population mean, and a standard deviation equal to the population standard deviation divided by the square root of the sample size. Furthermore, for very large samples the sampling distribution of the mean will tend to be normally distributed. The last of these properties is a statement of a statistical principle called the **central limit theorem** and it tends to hold for large sample sizes even if the distribution that we are sampling from is not normally distributed. The standard deviation divided by the square root of the sample size is called the **standard error.** The **standard error of the mean** is the standard deviation of the sampling distribution of the mean:

$$\text{standard error of the mean} = \frac{\text{standard deviation}}{\text{square root of sample size } (N)}$$

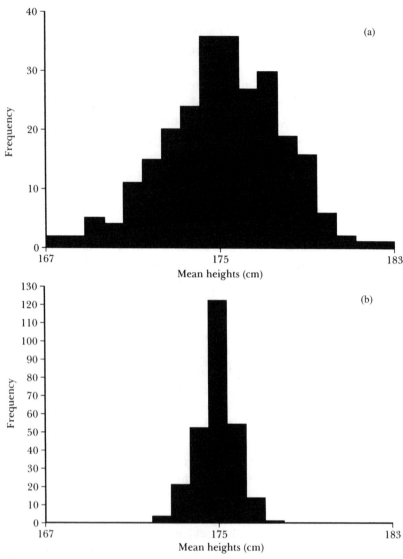

Figure 7.4 Mean heights for samples of (a) 10 and (b) 100 men

Now we know that all this jargon sounds very confusing. However, don't panic. We are still working with just two statistical principles, the law of large numbers and the idea of random sampling. Just about everything else follows from these relatively simple points. This is not to say that it will not take some hard work to get these ideas clear in your own mind.

What we think we do need to do at this point is convince you it is worth doing that hard work. The ideas that we are discussing here are extremely useful for answering questions like 'When is an observed difference worth taking seriously?' and 'Can we be confident about decisions based on our data?'. This makes them intriguing and interesting in themselves (or at least when compared to many other statistical concepts). By using these theoretical sampling distributions we are able *to go beyond the data given* and say something about certainty (or uncertainty). That is, by comparing our data with what we would expect to happen by chance, we are able to answer questions like 'How sure are you that men *are* taller than women?' or 'How sure are you that a class of 30 people with a mean IQ of 95 really is below average?'.

The statistical principles outlined above thus put us in a very strong position when it comes to answering interesting questions of this form. Let us take the case of the schoolteacher who gives an IQ test to her class of 30 students and finds that their mean IQ is 95. Should the teacher draw the conclusion that the IQ of her class is lower than the population mean?

There are two answers to this. First, there is the obvious answer that it is lower – in fact, five points lower. We do not need inferential statistics to tell us that. The more interesting answer, however, is somewhat more sophisticated, and draws on the concepts that we have been introducing here. We can tell the teacher where her class of 30 students lies in comparison to other samples of the same size drawn randomly from the population. That is, we can do for her class scores what we did previously for the individual score of 120.

From the discussion above we know a number of things about the theoretical sampling distribution of the mean. We know that samples of size 30 drawn from a population with a mean of 100 and a standard deviation of 15 will have a mean of 100 and standard deviation of $15/\sqrt{30}$. That is, they will have the population mean as their mean and the standard deviation of the sampling distribution of the mean as their standard error (which is the population standard deviation divided by the square root of the sample size). In this case, the standard error of the mean $= 15/\sqrt{30} = 2.74$.

$$z = \frac{\text{sample mean} - \text{population mean}}{\text{standard error of the mean}} \quad \begin{array}{l}\text{(information term)}\\ \text{(error term)}\end{array}$$

$$z_{class} = \frac{95 - 100}{15/\sqrt{30}}$$
$$= \frac{-5}{2.739}$$
$$= -1.83$$

With this information we can calculate the value of z for the entire class in the following way. In essence, what we want to know is how many **standard error units** the class mean of 95 is from the population mean:

The mean of 95 is 5 points from the population mean, and 5/2.74 is 1.83 standard error units *below* the mean, which gives us a z-score of -1.83. From Figure 7.5 we can see that 1.83 standard error units cuts off a small amount of the population. Indeed, from Table C.1 in Appendix C, we can see that the area beyond a z-score of 1.83 is .034 (i.e., 3.4% of the population). What this is telling us is that if we were to repeatedly draw random samples of 30 people from the population and measure the IQ of each group, only 3.4% of those groups would have a lower mean IQ than the class in question. Put another way, around 96% of all the other samples of the same size in the world can be expected to have a higher mean IQ than this class.

The thing to point out here (the law of large numbers again) is that around 37% of all the individuals in the world have IQs of 95 and lower. So, although it is not at all unusual for an individual (a sample of one) to have an IQ of 95, it is much more unusual for a sample of 30 to have an IQ this low. In this case the teacher can be fairly confident that her class has a lower IQ than the population average.

We can use this example to illustrate how the process of inferences for individual scores is actually a special case of inferences about groups. It is just that inferences for individual scores are based on a sample size of one. We said that when comparing one individual's score to the population mean we express the scores in standard deviation units and when

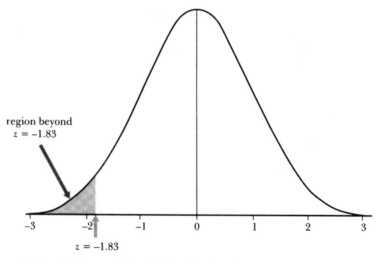

region beyond
$z = -1.83$

$z = -1.83$

Figure 7.5 Standard normal distribution, showing the z-score for $z = 1.83$

we compare a group's score we express it in standard error units. In fact, we use standard error units in both cases, but when $N = 1$, the standard error is the same as the standard deviation because the square root of 1 is 1 and dividing a quantity by 1 does not have any effect on the quantity.

We can summarize the process here as one of deciding where the sample mean lies in relation to the population mean. If there is a very low chance of sampling that mean from the population we conclude that the sample is probably not drawn from that population but instead belongs to another population. Perhaps less intelligent students were assigned to that teacher's class by the school authorities. We cannot be sure *what the explanation is*, but we can be sure that *there is something to be explained* and this is the purpose of conducting statistical tests. The tests can reduce inferential uncertainty but they cannot directly reduce methodological uncertainty – a point we will return to in Chapter 14.

In these examples we know the population mean for IQ and we know the population standard deviation. This is a very unusual case because most of the time we do not know the population parameters. Although we know the population mean and standard deviation for IQ we do not know what they are for other variables such as height unless we go out and measure the entire population. When we do not know the population mean and population standard deviation we have to estimate them. To do this we have to use a different sampling distribution. We will consider this case in the next chapter.

Q7.3***

Which of the following is true of the sampling distribution of the mean?

(a) It is an observed distribution of scores.
(b) It is a hypothetical distribution.
(c) It will tend to be normally distributed with a standard deviation equal to the population standard deviation.
(d) The mean will be estimated by the standard error.
(e) Both (b) and (c).

The correct answer is (b). The sampling distribution of the mean is an assumed distribution that we imagine we are sampling from. It is not observed unless we measure the entire population – therefore (a) is wrong. (c) is wrong because although the sampling distribution of the mean will tend to be normally distributed, the standard deviation will be approximated by the *standard error* (i.e., $SD/\sqrt{N}$). If (c) is wrong (e) must also be wrong. (d) is wrong because the mean is equal to the population mean, and the standard error expresses dispersion and not central tendency.

central limit theorem The statistical theorem that for large samples the *sampling distribution of the mean* will be approximately normally distributed.

estimate A statistic used to approximate a population parameter on the basis of the sample data. For example, the sample standard deviation is often used as an estimate of the population standard deviation.

law of large numbers The idea that the average outcomes of random processes are more predictable with large samples than with small samples. In other words, large samples are associated with less uncertainty in their estimates of population parameters.

random event An event which is an outcome of a random process.

sampling distribution A hypothetical distribution of the values of some statistic (e.g., the mean). This provides information about the pattern of values that would be expected to arise from repeated sampling from a particular population.

sampling distribution of the mean A sampling distribution obtained by calculating the means for samples of a given size. Where the sample size is large, it has a mean which is equal to the population mean and a standard deviation which is equal to the standard error of the mean.

standard error The standard deviation of any *sampling distribution*. This is an estimate of random error in estimates of population parameters.

standard error of the mean The standard deviation of the *sampling distribution of the mean* (i.e., the standard deviation divided by the square root of the sample size).

standard error units Units that quantify random error in estimates of population parameters. If we calculate the difference between two scores and divide this difference by the standard error the result is expressed in standard error units.

Overview

There are many important points in this chapter, and we think that you will almost certainly need to read it several times before they all make sense. You will also probably find that in years to come you need to come back and refresh your understanding of these very important principles. We hope that when you engage in this process of revision the following summary is useful.

Doing inferential statistics is all about making decisions about how confident you should be in conclusions made on the basis of data. There are two major factors which help us to make decisions about confidence: the information we have obtained and the amount of descriptive uncertainty about that information (random error). If the information is pretty clear despite the descriptive uncertainty, then we can be confident in the conclusion (there is low inferential uncertainty). The inferential statistics used in psychology tend to involve comparing the evidence that 'something is going on' to a measure of uncertainty or random error. Where the ratio of information to error is very large we are more confident that something is going on.

Thus, the statistics that we will describe in the next two chapters of this book are of the form:

$$\text{test statistic} = \frac{\text{information}}{\text{error}}$$

Where information is large and error is small, the ratio of information to error will be large and the corresponding probability that a random process could have produced results like the ones obtained will be small. Where this probability is small we can be relatively confident that our results are not due to chance.

The next question concerns how we obtain the information and error terms. The process by which we go about deciding how confident to be about our observations involves creating a model of what would happen if there were no information and only uncertainty. This is another way of saying that we create a model which describes what would happen if the process we are observing is random. The main advantage in treating the process as random is that random processes are highly predictable *in the long run*. If we know something behaves like a random variable then we will have a good idea of what its distribution will look like, even though we almost never really have all the information about each member of the population (if we did we would not have to do research).

The model we create is represented by a *sampling distribution*. The *sampling distribution of the mean* is what we would obtain if we kept on taking random samples of a particular size from a population for ever and calculated the mean for each sample. The sampling distribution of the mean has a mean that is equal to the population mean, but it has a standard deviation that is equal to the population standard deviation divided by the square root of the sample size. The sampling distribution of the mean will tend to be normally distributed even if the population distribution is not normally distributed. Dividing the standard deviation by the square root of the sample size means that the sampling distribution of the mean involves less uncertainty than the population of individual scores, and this is particularly true when the sample size is large. This follows from the law of large numbers, as it is far less common to select random samples with extreme means (either high or low) if you have a large sample rather than a small one.

In statistical inference the law of large numbers is reflected in the fact that the standard deviation is divided by the square root of the sample size to obtain the *standard error*. The larger the sample size, the smaller the standard error will be. Standard error is a measure of random error. The effect of the division by the square root of the sample size is to reduce random error (uncertainty about the values of parameters) and by reducing this error we reduce uncertainty relating to the question of whether the sample is a random sample of the population.

What the sampling distribution of the mean enables us to do is compare our obtained mean with the expected value of the sampling distribution. From this comparison we work out the probability that, for a sample of a given size, we could have obtained a mean at least as big by taking a random sample from the population. This probability is *not* the chance that our results are due to random error, but is our best guess of this probability. If this probability is very small then we can be more confident that the results reflect something of interest and not just random error.

In other words, constructing ratios of information to error allows us to *compare models* or to *test hypotheses*. These two approaches to statistical inference are presented in more detail in the next chapter.

Obviously, there are many difficult ideas in this summary, but the really important thing is to make sure that you (a) understand the difference between the two types of uncertainty we have discussed (descriptive uncertainty and inferential uncertainty), and (b) remember that everything else follows from the principles of random sampling and the law of large numbers.

Further reading

Most statistics textbooks that are pitched at a more advanced level than this one include a more elaborate discussion of statistical inference than we have provided here. Smithson's book in this series is as good a place as any to start.
Smithson, M. (2000). *Statistics with confidence*. London: Sage.

Statistical inference: A checklist for research evaluation and improvement

Potential problem	Question to ask	Potential improvement
Descriptive uncertainty	Is the researchers' ability to describe a given population compromised by the amount of variation in their sample data?	Examine the data and try to ascertain (or hypothesize about) the cause of any unduly high levels of variation. This may be a true reflection of the population(s) from which the sample data are drawn. However, if the variation appears to reflect empirical limitations (e.g., measurement inaccuracy, uncontrolled extraneous variables) you may be able to reduce this through appropriate refinements (e.g., better measurement, improved experimental control).
Inferential uncertainty	Is the researchers' ability to make statistical statements about a given population compromised by the amount of random error (relative to information) in their sample data?	Examine the data and try to ascertain (or hypothesize about) the basis of the high ratio of random error relative to information. This may be a true reflection of the population(s) from which the sample data are drawn, but it may also arise from either (a) measurement and other problems (e.g., associated with high descriptive uncertainty) that can be addressed through empirical refinement or (b) a lack of statistical power that can be addressed by conducting a study with a larger sample.
Inferential uncertainty about individual scores	Do the researchers want to compare scores or to understand how a single score stands in relation to a population with a known mean and standard deviation?	Standardize scores by subtracting the population mean from them and dividing by the population standard deviation. This procedure turns raw scores into z-scores and Table C.1 can be used to provide information about the proportion of scores in the population that would be expected to be larger than any obtained z-score.
Inferential uncertainty about sample means	Do the researchers want to compare means or to understand how a sample mean stands in relation to a	Standardize means by subtracting the population mean from them and dividing by the standard error of the mean (the population

Potential problem	Question to ask	Potential improvement
	population with a known mean and standard deviation?	standard deviation divided by the square root of the sample size). This procedure turns raw means into z-scores and Table C.1 can be used to provide information about the proportion of scores in the population that would be expected to be larger than any obtained z-score.

Q7.4**

Which of the following statements about descriptive uncertainty and inferential uncertainty is true?

(a) Both are types of statistical uncertainty.
(b) Only descriptive uncertainty is a form of statistical uncertainty.
(c) They are unrelated.
(d) Both are measured by the information term of any statistic.
(e) They provide different answers to the same questions.

Q7.5*

Which of the following statements about z-scores is true when they are used to make inferences about individual scores?

(a) They are produced by random processes.
(b) They are calculated by dividing the difference between the score and the mean by the standard deviation.
(c) They can only be used to make inferences about groups.
(d) They follow the central limit theorem.
(e) None of the above.

Q7.6***

Which of the following statements about statistical inferences in psychology is *false*?

(a) Statistical inferences usually involve calculating a statistic that is obtained by dividing an information term by an error term.
(b) Statistical models allow us to calculate the probability that our results are due to chance.

(c) The sampling distribution of the mean is a useful concept for making inferences about groups.

(d) Statistical inferences about the mean can often make use of the z-distribution when the population standard deviation is known.

(e) The law of large numbers implies that, other things being equal, it is easier to be confident when making inferences using large samples.

Q7.7***

Which of the following follows from the law of large numbers?

(a) If you are unlucky in roulette you should stick with the same number because it has to come up eventually.

(b) The mean of a small random sample of the population is more likely to be a reliable estimate of the population mean than that of a large sample.

(c) In the long run we can expect similar numbers of heads and tails from a fair coin.

(d) The mean of a large sample will be larger than the mean of a small sample.

(e) The standard deviation of a large sample will be smaller than the standard deviation of a small sample.

The correct answer to 7.4 is (a). If (a) is true, (b) must be wrong. (c) is wrong because inferential uncertainty actually arises as a result of descriptive uncertainty. (d) is wrong because descriptive uncertainty is reflected in the error term, not in the information term. (e) is wrong because although the two are related (because inferential uncertainty increases with descriptive uncertainty), they are not the same thing. Indeed, descriptive and inferential uncertainty reflect uncertainty about the answers to quite different questions. Descriptive uncertainty is uncertainty about the extent to which the sample is accurately described by a measure of central tendency (e.g., the mean). Inferential uncertainty is uncertainty about whether a relationship between variables or a difference between means is meaningful.

The correct answer to 7.5 is (b). z-scores involve the standard deviation and not the standard error. (a) and (d) are nonsense answers based on other terms used in the chapter. (c) is wrong because z-scores are also used for inferences about individual scores.

The correct answer to 7.6 is (b). This statement is false because statistical models actually allow us to calculate the probability that a random process (or chance) could have produced results as dramatic as ours. Statistical models cannot tell us whether a random process is actually operating. The former is our best way of estimating the probability that the results are due to chance but it is not the same thing. All of the other statements are true and are explained in this chapter.

The correct answer to 7.7 is (c). (a) is wrong because if the game is fair, then random events are independent and do not depend on what has occurred in the past. (b) is wrong because the statement is the wrong way around – the mean of a large random sample will be a more reliable estimate. (d) is wrong because if both samples are drawn from the same population then their means should both be estimates of the same population mean. There is no reason for one to be larger or smaller than the other (though the larger sample will tend to have a mean that is closer to the population mean). (e) is wrong, but would be correct if we replaced 'standard deviation' with 'standard error'.

Discussion/essay questions

(a) How does knowledge of random processes contribute to our ability to make statistical inferences?

(b) Why is standardization a useful statistical procedure?

(c) What is the law of large numbers? Discuss some everyday situations which demonstrate people's general awareness of the law.

(d) What is the difference between a sample statistic and a population parameter? What are the implications of this distinction and why is it important?

Exercises

(a) Janet obtains a score of 18 on an exam where the population mean level of performance is 15.2 and the standard deviation is 2.6 and the distribution of scores is normal. What is her standardized score on this test?

(b) What percentage of exam-takers would be expected to obtain a score higher than Janet's?

(c) A lecturer observes that his current class of 190 students obtains a mean score of 15.6 on this exam. How many standard error units is the class mean from the population mean?

(d) What percentage of similar-sized classes would be expected to obtain a higher mean exam score than that of this particular class?

(e) The principal of a school randomly divides her school into two teams for a sports day. The red team has 100 students and the blue team has 900 students. The prize goes to the team with the ten fastest runners in the 1500 m race (i.e., for a team to win its 10th fastest runner must beat the 10th fastest runner on the other team). The school population mean time for the 1500 m is known to be 7 minutes and the standard deviation is known to be 1 minute (60 seconds). All students enter the 1500 m race, and the running times are normally distributed.

  (i) How many runners from the blue team would you expect to finish in the top 20 places?

 (ii) Why is question (i) a trick question?

(iii) What time would you expect the 10th fastest member of each team to complete the race?

(iv) What principle tells us that the contest is unfair? What should we infer if the red team wins the prize?

F. Geoff is trying to find the best candidate to fill a vacancy in his architecture office in New York. He is given information about a field of three overseas applicants. Unfortunately, they all took their architectural exams in different places. Adam obtained a score of 145 on his exam in Adelaide (where the mean score on the test was 110, with a standard deviation of 15), Bill obtained a score of 240 in his exams in Brisbane (where the mean score on the test was 180, with a standard deviation of 30), and Charles obtained a score of 50 in his exam in Christchurch (where the mean score on the test was 35, with a standard deviation of 7).

  (i) Assuming that the population of candidates for the exams in the three cities is normally distributed and of equivalent ability, who appears to be best qualified for the job?

 (ii) What percentage of architecture students would perform better than the best candidate for this job?

(iii) If Geoff randomly selected three architects from the cities and standardized their scores, what proportion of those groups would have standardized means that were greater than the lowest standard score of any of the present applicants?

(iv) What does this tell us about the field of applicants for this job?

8

Examining Differences between Means: The *t*-test

In the previous chapter we dealt with some statistical inferences under conditions where we knew quite a few things about the dependent variable. We used two examples: coin tossing and IQ test scores. At the risk of revealing trade secrets, we should point out that these two examples are pretty common in this sort of book.

The reasons for the popularity of these examples are worth looking at: the example of coin tossing is widely used because it relates to people's experiences in their everyday lives, but it is also an example where we can directly calculate an *exact* probability for each possible outcome. However, this state of affairs is pretty rare in psychological statistics. As we made clear in Chapter 7, most of the time we first have to calculate a test statistic (involving dividing an information term by an error term) and then identify the probability associated with that statistic by working it out or looking it up in a table.

The example of IQ scores is also widely used in books like this one, in order to provide an introductory example of statistical inference. In part this is because IQ is a psychological variable that most people will have heard of before, but an even better reason is that we know that in the population the mean IQ is 100 and the standard deviation is 15. How do we know this? You might think that there is a mysterious process at work here, but in fact we know these things because the people who design IQ tests actually go to some trouble to ensure that IQ tests yield a mean of 100 and a standard deviation of 15. Once the test designer has ensured that the test is a valid and reliable measure of intelligence through extremely extensive sampling of the population and rigorous comparison with other measures, the mean of the test is reset to 100 and the standard deviation is set to 15 (following the process called *standardization* that we explained in Chapter 7). When all this is done the results of the test are then said to be IQ scores.

But this is actually quite an unusual set of circumstances. This extensive process of measurement and validation has been carried out for only a limited number of psychological variables, and in many cases there are still residual disputes about the validity of these measures. This means that, most of the time, psychological researchers do not know the population parameters of the measures they use. Instead they have to *estimate* these parameters. Along these lines, you will remember that we discussed how to estimate the population standard deviation in Chapter 6.

If we can estimate the population standard deviation we are in a position to conduct a ***t*-test.** A *t*-test is a test for differences between means under conditions where the population standard deviation is not known and therefore has to be estimated. In this chapter we first discuss the case where we are comparing the mean of a single sample to a known value. This is very similar to the case in the previous chapter where we compared the mean IQ of a sample of children in a particular class to the population mean of 100. We then deal with within-subjects experiments where we compare the mean response of a sample at one point in time, or on one measure, with the sample's mean response at another time or on another measure. Finally, we discuss the two-sample or between-subjects *t*-test. Here we compare means of two different samples of people. At that stage we will finally be able to answer the sort of question that we posed at the start of the previous chapter: how certain can we be that the scores for two groups of people on some psychological variable are really different?

> ***t*-test** A test for differences between means under conditions where the population standard deviation is not known but has to be estimated.

Student's *t*-distribution

The ***t*-distribution** describes a sampling distribution used to test the difference between means when the population standard deviation (σ) is unknown. It has a mean, or expected value, of zero. The reason why the expected value is zero is that the **sampling distribution of differences between means** is based on a statistical model where we imagine that we are continuously drawing *two* random samples from the same population and comparing their means. Because the two samples are drawn from the same population, their means should both be estimates of the same population mean. Thus, saying that the expected value of the sampling distribution of the difference between the means is zero is just a technical way of saying that we would expect no difference between the means if they are in fact estimates of the same population mean. If we find a large enough difference between the means of the two samples we draw, we start to question whether both means are actually estimates of the same population mean. We would go through the same process if we saw a coin come down heads or tails too many times and started to wonder if the coin was fair.

Put simply, the *t*-distribution describes the statistical model of what happens when you take random samples of a certain size from the population and subtract one mean from the other and divide the result by an estimate of the standard error. We are able to compare empirical results with the results we obtain from this statistical model and, what is more, the *t*-distribution tells us how likely the observed difference between means would be if that *t*-distribution's statistical model did apply. In the same way that the binomial distribution can tell us how likely a run of heads is with a fair coin, the *t*-distribution can tell us what the chance is of drawing two random samples from the same population with a difference between them of a certain size or bigger. However, what the model can never do is tell us whether the two samples are from the same population or from different populations. That is a decision researchers have to make for themselves, guided by the results of the statistical test.

The shape of the *t*-distribution changes as the sample size increases. This is once again a consequence of the law of large numbers. As we take larger and larger samples we obtain a statistic that actually becomes closer and closer to the normal distribution. This is largely a result of the fact that as samples become larger we obtain better estimates of the unknown population standard deviation. Indeed, with infinitely large samples t becomes normally distributed and equivalent to z.

There is thus a different *t*-distribution for every different sample size. Each *t*-distribution shows what the probability of any given difference between means is, expressed in standard error units. For example, if we found a difference between mean heights for a sample of three men and a sample of three women of 10 cm and a standard error of 5 cm then this would correspond to 2.0 t units (i.e., 10/5). This would cut off the region of the *t*-distribution that is marked in Figure 8.1(a). We can see that only a small proportion of all the possible differences between the means lies beyond this point.

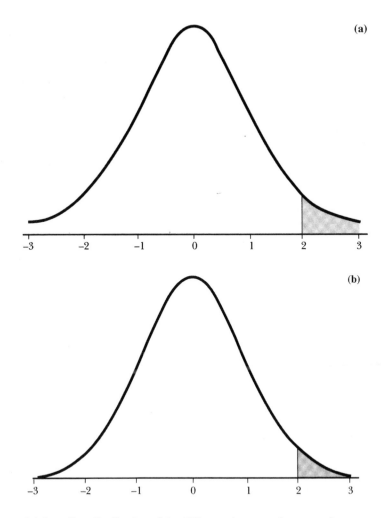

Figure 8.1 Sampling distribution of the difference between the means for two samples
of size (a) 3 and (b) 30

What this distribution does is map out all the possibilities that could
occur if you were to calculate the mean for random samples of three
people from the population and subtract the means for another random
sample of three people and express the differences between the means in
standard error units. We can contrast this to the *t*-distribution for two
samples of 30 people (Figure 8.1(b)).

The overall shapes of these distributions are pretty similar, but you
can see that the tails of the sampling distribution as a whole are much
smaller with the larger sample size. This is reflected in the fact that
the area beyond 2.0 *t* units is even smaller than it was in Figure 8.1(a),
so that it contains an even smaller proportion of possible difference
between means.

Rather than corresponding to sample size exactly, however, the sampling distribution of t depends on something called the **degrees of freedom**. The degrees of freedom are the number of scores in a given set that are free to vary. To explain what this means, think of a waiter in a restaurant who forgets which customer ordered what at a table of five people. Here he has four degrees of freedom because if he can remember what four people ordered, he must get the fifth right. If he has one table of five people and one of two, providing that he knows which table placed the orders he has five degrees of freedom – i.e., $(N_{\text{table 1}} - 1) + (N_{\text{table 2}} - 1) = 4 + 1$.

Returning to Figure 8.1, the first is actually the t-distribution for 4 degrees of freedom and the second figure is t for 58 degrees of freedom. The calculation of the number of degrees of freedom varies a bit depending on what sort of t-test you are doing, so we explain the calculation for each case below. The issue of degrees of freedom is the major difference between the z-distribution and the t-distribution. There is only one z-distribution for z-tests, the standard normal distribution, but for t-tests there is a different distribution for each different number of degrees of freedom.

Q8.1**

Which of the following statements is/are true about the t-distribution?

(a) Its shape changes with the number of degrees of freedom.
(b) Its expected value is zero.
(c) It can be used to test differences between means providing that the population standard deviation is known.
(d) Both (a) and (b).
(e) All of the above.

The correct answer is (d). Answers (a) and (b) are both true of the t-distribution. (c) is wrong because it is not necessary to know the population standard deviation in order to use the t-distribution. Indeed, the t-distribution was specifically developed to apply to sampling situations where the population standard deviation is unknown.

---

degrees of freedom (df) The number of scores that are free to vary.

sampling distribution of the difference between means The hypothetical distribution of differences between the means of two random samples drawn from the same population. It has a mean of zero and a standard deviation that decreases with the square root of the sample size.

t-distribution The hypothetical distribution of expected differences between the means of randomly chosen samples drawn from the same population divided by an estimate of the standard error.

Comparing the results for a single sample to a specific value

Often psychologists collect a set of data from a sample and then want to know whether the results are greater or less than some specified value. Let us imagine that 10 students do a multiple-choice test in psychology. Imagine, too, that the mean number of correct responses is 25 out of 100 and that there are five choices for each question. We might want to know whether the students are performing better on the test than they would if they had just randomly chosen an answer. Given that there are five choices the expected number of correct answers is 20.

Some example data are shown below:

Participant	Test score
1	18
2	22
3	30
4	28
5	25
6	22
7	24
8	25
9	27
10	29

$N = 10$ $\sum X = 250$
$\bar{X} = \sum X / N = 25.0$

Here the mean, $\bar{X}$, is 25.0 and the standard deviation, s_X, is 3.68.

We use s_X as an estimate of the population standard deviation σ in order to work out the probability that, if the students had just answered the questions by randomly choosing a number, they could have obtained a mean value as high as 25.

To find out whether students are performing better than chance we construct the test statistic t as a ratio of information over error (in fact we could do an exact probability calculation in this case as we did in the coin-tossing example, but we chose not to do that here). In this example the *information term* is the difference between the mean (i.e., the observed mean of the 10 students: 25) and the value we want to test against (i.e., the value expected by chance: 20). The difference is therefore $25 - 20 = 5$. The error term is an estimate of the standard error of the mean which is the standard deviation of the sample divided by the square root of the sample size ($N = 10$). Next we need to know the degrees of freedom. For a single-sample *t*-test the degrees of freedom are equal to $N - 1$. In this case $N = 10$, so there are nine degrees of freedom. The value we are trying to find here is referred to as $t(9)$ – that is, *t* with nine degrees of freedom (df).

$$t(9) = \frac{\bar{X} - \text{value}}{s_X/\sqrt{N}} \qquad \frac{\text{(information term)}}{\text{(error term)}}$$

$$= \frac{25 - 20}{3.68/\sqrt{10}}$$

$$= 4.3$$

We have thus obtained a value of *t*. Remember that if the value of *t* is very large (either positive or negative) then the probability that a random process could have produced a difference this large will be very small. If the probability is very small then this means that we will have low *inferential uncertainty*: that is, we can be confident that our results are not due to random error or chance. What we need to do now is find out what probability the value of *t* we have obtained corresponds to.

To find that probability we have to calculate it or look it up in a table. It can be calculated by hand, but it is easier to look up the values in a table like the one given in Appendix C (Table C.2). As the instructions given there indicate, you should first find the row that corresponds to the number of degrees of freedom. If the degrees of freedom you are looking for do not appear, go to the row with the nearest lower number of degrees of freedom. Then look along that row until you find the largest value of *t* that is smaller than the one you have just calculated. Look back up to the top of the column and find the probability that corresponds to this value of *t*. The actual probability will be less than the one in that column. For the example above with nine degrees of freedom the largest value of *t* that is smaller than 4.3 is 3.69. This corresponds to a probability of .005 so we write that $p < .005$.

In this case the value of *t* corresponds to a very small probability – one that is less than 5 in 1000. In other words, providing we have an accurate estimate of the population standard deviation, there is less than 1 chance in 200 that a sample of 10 students who randomly answered the questions would have obtained or exceeded an average of

25 correct answers out of 100. We can therefore be quite confident that our results are not due to chance or random error. In other words, we can conclude that it is very unlikely that the students were responding randomly.

The mean height of a sample of 100 men in 1997 is 180 cm, with a standard deviation of 10 cm. The mean for the same population in 1926 was 170 cm. Imagine that we want to use the 1997 sample to test whether the height of the population has changed over the intervening 71 years. Which of the following statements is true? (You may need to refer to Table C.2 in Appendix C.)

(a) The degrees of freedom for the test in this case is 99.
(b) The t-value is 10.0.
(c) The t-value corresponds to a probability of less than 1 in 1000 of a random process producing a difference this size or larger.
(d) All of the above.
(e) Answers (a) and (b) only.

The correct answer is (d). Answers (a), (b) and (c) are all correct here. The degrees of freedom are equal to $N - 1 = 99$. The t-value is $(180 - 170)/(10/\sqrt{100}) = 10$, so (b) is correct. Turning to Table C.2 in Appendix C, you will also see that a t-value of 10.00 far exceeds the t-value for 95 degrees of freedom associated with a probability level of .001 (i.e., 3.396). In other words, there is less than a 1 in 1000 chance that a random process would produce a difference this size or larger.

Within-subjects t-tests

The within-subjects t-test is used when we are comparing means based on sets of data that are collected in pairs from the same participants. Let us go back to the example used in Chapter 2 where we talked about the process of testing a 'physical reinforcement theory'. This simple theory explained the observation that 'absence leads the heart to wander' by proposing that attraction to another person is dependent on physical reinforcement achieved through interaction with them. Let us imagine we do an experiment to test this theory where participants have to make attractiveness ratings of two people – one with whom they have interacted (Person I, for *I*nteraction) and one with whom they have not (Person N, for *N*o interaction). In this experiment physical reinforcement has been manipulated *within subjects* because all participants are in both conditions. Our theory predicts that attraction will be greater for ratings of Person I than Person N. The dependent variable is ratings of the attractiveness of these two people on a nine-point scale from 1 to 9 (where 1 = 'do not like at all'; 9 = 'like a great deal').

Suppose our data were as follows:

Participant	Target person	
	I	N
1	7	5
2	6	6
3	5	2
4	6	3
5	5	4
6	7	5
7	3	6

Note that these are *pairs* of data. For example, Participant 1 responded '7' when rating the person they had interacted with (Person I) and '5' when rating the person they had not interacted with (Person N).

Just by looking at these results we can see that the pattern of data is generally consistent with our hypothesis, but the question is whether the ratings of I and N are *sufficiently different* to infer that they reflect a real underlying difference. As we have already noted several times, inferential statistics cannot answer this question directly, but they can tell us how likely it is that two sets of responses as different as this would have been drawn randomly from the same population. To find out, we take the five steps set out below.

1. Convert each pair of scores into a *difference score*, D, by subtracting the second score from the first for each participant.

In this case:

Participant	I	N	$D(I - N)$
1	7	5	2
2	6	6	0
3	5	2	3
4	6	3	3
5	5	4	1
6	7	5	2
7	3	6	-3

2. Calculate the mean, $\bar{D}$, and standard deviation, s_D, of the N difference scores (do not ignore the minus sign in front of any of the differences).

In this case we can do this by hand as follows:

Participant	I	N	$D(I - N)$	D^2
1	7	5	2	4
2	6	6	0	0
3	5	2	3	9
4	6	3	3	9
5	5	4	1	1
6	7	5	2	4
7	3	6	-3	9
$N = 7$			$\sum D = 8$	$\sum D^2 = 36$

$$\bar{D} = \sum D/N = 8/7 = 1.14$$

$$s_D = \sqrt{\frac{\sum D^2 - \frac{(\sum D)^2}{N}}{N - 1}} = \sqrt{\frac{36 - \frac{8^2}{7}}{6}} = \sqrt{\frac{26.86}{6}} = 2.12$$

Here you can see that we have calculated the mean and standard deviation following the steps described in Chapter 6. In fact, though, both statistics can be worked out very quickly using a calculator. For this reason in the remainder of this book we will not routinely go through the details of their calculation.

3. Compute a *t*-value, using the formula

$$t = \frac{\bar{D}}{s_D/\sqrt{N}} \qquad \begin{array}{l} \text{(information term)} \\ \text{(error term)} \end{array}$$

So here:

$$t = \frac{1.14}{2.12/2.65}$$

$$= 1.43$$

4. Compute the *degrees of freedom* for the test from the number of participants, where $df = N - 1$.

Here $N = 7$, so $df = 6$. We write that $t(6) = 1.43$. We actually say this as '*t* with six degrees of freedom equals 1.43'.

5. Look up Table C.2 in Appendix C to see what probability corresponds to the value of *t* for that number of degrees of freedom. In the table find the largest *t*-value for the degrees of freedom that the obtained value exceeds, and identify the corresponding probability level. If you have an exact calculation of *p* from a computer package, you can report that instead, but in other circumstances

the convention is to report the 'upper bound on p'. This is the value of p corresponding to the largest t-value that is exceeded.

From the table we can see that for six degrees of freedom 1.43 is greater than 1.134 but less than 1.440. The tabulated value 1.134 corresponds to a probability of .3 and the value 1.440 corresponds to a probability of .2. Accordingly, $t(6) = 1.43$ corresponds to a probability that is less than .3 (but greater than .2). This can be written as $p < .3$. In other words, a random process would have less than a 3 in 10 chance of producing a difference this large.

To summarize, our t-test would look like this:

Participant	I	N	$D(I - N)$
1	7	5	2
2	6	6	0
3	5	2	3
4	6	3	3
5	5	4	1
6	7	5	2
7	3	6	−3
$N = 7$			$\sum D = 8$

$$\bar{D} = \sum D/N = 8/7 = 1.14$$

$$s_D = 2.12$$

$$t = \frac{\bar{D}}{s_D/\sqrt{N}}$$

$$= \frac{1.14}{2.12/\sqrt{7}}$$

$$= \frac{1.14}{2.12/2.65}$$

$$= 1.43$$

$$df = N - 1$$

$$= 6$$

The obtained t-value is greater than the tabled value of t with 6 df for $p = .3$ (i.e., 1.134), so

$$t(6) = 1.43, p < .3$$

Between-subjects *t*-tests

The above case dealt with a situation where we had two sets of data from the same sample of participants. So, by using difference scores, we could use one mean and one standard deviation to represent both sets of scores. Let us now consider a between-subjects case where we are comparing means obtained from *different* groups of participants. In essence, our decision as to whether those means are likely to have been drawn from the same population comes down to a statement about the difference between two means *relative* to the variation of scores around each of those means and the number of responses on which the means are based.

This may sound complex, but the underlying logic is quite simple and can be illustrated in the following scenario. In this diagram each 'e' is a response on a scale from 1 to 7 by a person in an experimental condition, and each 'c' a response on the same scale by a person in a control condition.

Case 1

c	c	c	c				Mean c = 2.5
			e	e	e	e	Mean e = 5.5
1	2	3	4	5	6	7

Case 2

	c	c					Mean c = 2.5
				c	e		Mean e = 5.5
1	2	3	4	5	6	7

Case 3

	cc	cc					Mean c = 2.5
				ee	ee		Mean e = 5.5
1	2	3	4	5	6	7

In which of these cases would you be most confident that the responses of people in the two conditions reflected a real underlying difference between groups? Your confidence should be greatest in Case 3. This is for two reasons. First, in Case 3 the dispersion of the two sets of responses is smaller than in Case 1 (and the **overlap** in the response distributions is smaller). Secondly, Case 3 provides more evidence of a real difference than Case 2 because it is based on more data. So here, even though the means are the same in each case, we would be more confident that the population mean for the experimental condition really was greater than that for the control condition in Case 3 because the *difference in means relative to the amount of error* is greater.

Going back to our example of research on 'physical reinforcement theory' which was exploring the basis of attraction between people, let us consider a new experiment. In this experiment instead of each participant rating two target people (the within-subjects case), let us imagine that some participants in an experimental condition interact with and then rate a target person and that *other* participants in a control condition do not interact with the target person they are asked to rate. Participants might then rate their attraction to the target person they are asked to consider on a nine-point scale (where $1 =$ 'do not like at all' and $9 =$ 'like a great deal'). Here we would obtain two independent sets of 'attractiveness ratings': one from participants in the experimental condition and one from participants in the control condition. Let us imagine that the data looked liked this:

	Participant										$\bar{X}$	s_X	s_X^2
	1	2	3	4	5	6	7	8	9	10			
Experimental	4	5	7	8	6	9	7	8	5	5	6.40	1.65	2.71
Control	4	4	6	5	7	3	4	2	5	4	4.40	1.43	2.04

Our physical reinforcement theory predicts that participants in the experimental condition should like the target person more. This would appear to be the case: the mean rating of the target's attractiveness is higher in the experimental condition ($\bar{X}_1 = 6.4$) than in the control condition ($\bar{X}_2 = 4.4$).

The question, though, is whether this difference is big enough to allow us to conclude that the two means are unlikely to have been drawn from the same population. In other words, what we really want to know is whether the two samples are drawn from the same population (with the same population mean) and are just different by chance or whether the samples are drawn from two different populations. As you should be sick of reading by now, we can never tell this exactly. So instead we determine the chance that a difference this large could be obtained by drawing random samples from the same population. To do this we need to perform the following five steps.

1. Compute the mean and variance of the data in each experimental condition.
2. Compute a **weighted average** of the two variances. This is called a **pooled variance estimate**. We compute this because the average of the two variances should give us a more accurate estimate of the population variance if both samples are in fact drawn from a population with the same mean and variance. This is done using the following formula:

$$s_{pooled}^2 = \frac{(N_1 - 1)s_1^2 + (N_2 - 1)s_2^2}{N_1 + N_2 - 2}$$

In this formula N_1 is the number of participants in the first group, s_1 is the standard deviation for the first group (and s_1^2 the variance for the first group) and so on.

This formula looks a bit frightening but is really quite simple. In words, what it is saying is that the pooled variance for two sets of scores is equal to (the variance of one set of scores multiplied by that set's degrees of freedom) plus (the variance of the other set of scores multiplied by that set's degrees of freedom) *all* divided by the total number of degrees of freedom. So in our example

$$s_{pooled}^2 = \frac{(9 * 2.71) + (9 * 2.04)}{10 + 10 - 2} = 2.38$$

Note that because this variance is a weighted average it must fall between the variances for each of the two conditions (in this case, between 2.71 and 2.04). If it does not, a computational error has been made somewhere. Note, too, that if $N_1 = N_2$ (i.e., there are the same number of participants in each group) then the pooled variance is simply the average of the two sample variances.

3. Now compute a *t*-value using the following formula:

$$t = \frac{\bar{X}_1 - \bar{X}_2}{\sqrt{s_{pooled}^2 \left(\frac{1}{N_1} + \frac{1}{N_2} \right)}} \qquad \text{(information term)} \atop \text{(error term)}$$

In this case

$$t = \frac{6.4 - 4.4}{\sqrt{2.38 \left(\frac{1}{10} + \frac{1}{10} \right)}} = \frac{2.0}{0.69} = 2.90$$

4. Compute the degrees of freedom for the test from the sample sizes, where

$$df = N_1 + N_2 - 2$$

So here $df = 10 + 10 - 2 = 18$. We therefore write that $t(18) = 2.90$.

5. Look up Table C.2 in Appendix C to see what probability corresponds to the value of *t* for that number of degrees of freedom. In the table find the largest *t*-value for the degrees of freedom that the obtained value exceeds, and identify the corresponding probability level.

In this case 2.90 is greater than 2.878 corresponding to a *p*-value of .01, but it is less than 3.197 corresponding to a *p*-value of .005. We say here that the probability level is less than .01 (i.e., $p < .01$). In other words, there is less than 1 chance in a 100 that a random process could have produced a difference between means this large.

To summarize, the calculations for this t-test would look like this:

$$\bar{X}_1 = 6.40; \quad s_1^2 = 2.71; \quad N_1 = 10$$

$$\bar{X}_2 = 4.40; \quad s_2^2 = 2.04; \quad N_2 = 10$$

$$t = \frac{\bar{X}_1 - \bar{X}_2}{\sqrt{s_{pooled}^2 \left(\frac{1}{N_1} + \frac{1}{N_2} \right)}}$$

where

$$s_{pooled}^2 = \frac{(N_1 - 1)s_1^2 + (N_2 - 1)s_2^2}{N_1 + N_2 - 2}$$

$$= \frac{(10 - 1)2.71 + (10 - 1)2.04}{10 + 10 - 2}$$

$$= \frac{9(2.71) + 9(2.04)}{18}$$

$$= \frac{24.39 + 18.36}{18}$$

$$= 2.38$$

So

$$t = \frac{6.4 - 4.4}{\sqrt{2.38 \left(\frac{1}{10} + \frac{1}{10} \right)}}$$

$$= 2.0 / \sqrt{2.38 * 0.2}$$

$$= 2.0 / \sqrt{0.48}$$

$$= 2.90$$

$$df = N_1 + N_2 - 2$$

$$= 18$$

The obtained t-value is greater than the tabulated value of t with 18 df for $p = .01$ (i.e., 2.878), so

$$t(18) = 2.90, p < .01$$

Before moving on, it is worth noting that one of the most confusing things about t-tests is the wide variety of different terms that are used to describe the different types of tests. If you were to read another textbook after this one, you might be forgiven for thinking that there are lots of different types of t-test. In fact there are only two types that you really have to worry about – the within-subjects t-test and the between-subjects t-test. We have chosen to use these names because they relate directly to the methodological terms that psychologists use, and because they match the usage of these terms in other statistical tests (in particular, analysis of variance, an advanced procedure for comparing more than two means, also referred to as ANOVA; see Chapter 10).

Table 8.1 is intended to help you work out what the different types of t-test are when you see the terms used in other books and in the research literature.

Table 8.1 Terms used to describe t-tests

Terms for within-subjects t-tests	Terms for between-subjects t-tests
single-sample t-test	two-sample t-test
dependent t-test	independent groups t-test
related samples t-test	
paired t-test	
repeated measures t-test	
correlated samples t-test	

Q8.3*

Which of the following is *not* relevant to a between-subjects t-test?

(a) The pooled variance estimate.
(b) A difference score D.
(c) An information term.
(d) A sampling distribution of the differences between means.
(e) A probability that a difference of the observed size or larger could have been obtained by a random process.

The correct answer is (b). The difference score D is used in the within-subjects t-test where we deal with the difference between pairs of the scores from the same participant. The features referred to in answers (a), (c), (d) and (e) are all aspects of between-subjects t-tests discussed in this chapter.

Q8.4***

If an experimenter conducts a *t*-test to see whether the responses of participants in a control group differ from those of an experimental group, which of the following outcomes will yield the highest *t* value?

(a) If there are 10 participants in each condition and the difference between the mean responses of the control group and the experimental group is 2 and both have standard deviations of 1.

(b) If there are 10 participants in each condition and the difference between the mean responses of the control group and the experimental group is 2 and both have standard deviations of 2.

(c) If there are 20 participants in each condition and the difference between the mean responses of the control group and the experimental group is 1 and both have standard deviations of 1.

(d) If there are 20 participants in each condition and the difference between the mean responses of the control group and the experimental group is 2 and both have standard deviations of 1.

(e) If there are 20 participants in each condition and the difference between the mean responses of the control group and the experimental group is 2 and both have standard deviations of 2.

The correct answer is (d). The value of *t* is largest when you have small standard deviations, large samples and a large difference between means. All of these conditions apply in answer (d). The largest samples contain 20 participants per condition, the smallest standard deviation is 1, and the largest difference between means is 2. Based on these principles, we can conclude that the value of *t* will be greater in (a) than (b), greater in (d) than (a), greater in (d) than (c) and greater in (d) than (e). Of course we could actually calculate the *t*-values for each of the alternatives but this would take quite a bit of time. The point of this question is to get you thinking about what the formula for *t* actually means.

overlap of distributions The degree to which two distributions share the same range of values. The overlap of the two distributions in the following figure is shown by the shaded region.

overlap of distributions

pooled variance estimate An estimate of the variance of the population made by averaging the variances of the two samples to provide the error term for the between-subjects *t*-test.

weighted average An average where the result is modified to take account of differing sample sizes. A weighted average tends towards a given sample mean in proportion to the sample's size relative to the size of other samples being compared. If one group of 10 people has a mean score of 10 and another group of 100 people has a mean score of 20, the weighted average will therefore be much closer to the mean of the larger sample. In this case it is not 15 but $[(10 * 10) + (100 * 20)]/110 = 19.09$.

The controversy about what to do with *t*-values

At this stage you might be feeling that the process of statistical inference is a bit clumsy. After all, we are interested in two possibilities: whether the results we have obtained are due to chance or whether they represent a real difference between two means. These possibilities seem pretty obvious to most people when they are explained, but confusion arises because inferential statistics never allow us to reach either conclusion with complete certainty. Statistical tests never allow us to say that our results are due to a random process. All they can ever do is tell us how likely they would be if they *were* due to a random process. Similarly, the results of statistical tests can never tell us that our findings are not due to chance.

The inability of statistics to answer particular questions can be confusing and frustrating for both students and experienced researchers – not least because in order accurately to convey the truth of what statistical tests are telling us we have to use very awkward forms of expression. However, *attempts to simplify the way we express statistical ideas lead to inaccuracy*. Because the temptation to simplify statistical test results is quite strong, many psychologists and statisticians have argued that statistical tests are poorly understood and poorly used. This problem can be traced back to the fact that statistical tests do not answer *exactly* the questions that research scientists want to answer.

Problems with reporting and interpreting statistics have been around for a long time. But recently in psychology there has been a great deal of argument about exactly how to use inferential statistics (e.g., as reflected in the initial report of the Task Force on Statistical Inference of the Board of Scientific Affairs of the American Psychological Association, released December 1996). For the purposes of this chapter, the controversy relates to what to do with *t*-values once we have obtained them. The next few sections offer *choices* to students and instructors about how to conduct statistical tests and make statistical inferences. *We suggest that all students should be familiar with the hypothesis-testing approach and with one or more of the alternative approaches.* This follows the advice of many psychological statisticians who argue that we should compensate for the limitations of the hypothesis-testing approach by employing (or at least considering) other methods (Cohen, 1994, 1995; Hammond, 1996; Judd, McClelland, & Culhane, 1995; Syvantek & Ekberg, 1995).

Handling the results of *t*-tests: The hypothesis-testing approach

Once we have obtained the value of *t* and worked out the corresponding probability value we have some more decisions to make. What we have effectively done so far is turn an observed difference between means into a probability value. We then have to decide whether that probability is small enough for us to conclude that the two means were unlikely to have been drawn from the same population. You might reasonably ask whether this process has got us very far. After all, we only did the *t*-test so that we could make a definitive statement about whether the difference between the means was large or small, and now it seems that we have to decide whether the *p*-value is big or small.

The answer is that we have indeed made some progress because, rather than simply talking about differences between means, we now have a probability value that is comparable across research situations. The probability value is comparable because it depends on both the difference between the means and the amount of dispersion or random error in the sample.

The **hypothesis-testing** or **significance-testing** approach to *t*-tests is an attempt to come up with definitive answers to the question of whether we have observed an informative difference between means or not. The logic underpinning this approach is to develop a statistical model which assumes that both means are based on random samples from the same population (i.e., the samples share the same population mean and standard deviation). The sampling distribution provided by the *t*-distribution is just a mathematical way of expressing this statistical model of no difference between means, and, as we have discussed, the expected value of the *t*-distribution is zero. That is, if the means are both drawn from the same population then there *should be* no difference.

This statistical model that there should be no difference between the means is called the **null hypothesis**. In all psychological research the null hypothesis is really a statement about what we would expect if there is nothing dramatic going on in our research (and in the population to which it relates). That is, it is a statement of what should occur if we are simply observing a random process. The null hypothesis is often called H_0 (pronounced 'H nought').

When testing for a difference between means using a *t*-test, the null hypothesis is:

$$H_0 : \quad \mu_1 = \mu_2 = \mu$$

What this says is that the null hypothesis assumes that μ_1, the population mean associated with Sample 1 (in the between-subjects case) or with Variable 1 (in the within-subjects case) is the same as μ_2, the population mean associated with Sample 2 or Variable 2, and that they are both equal to the same value (μ). This model also assumes that the standard deviations of each sample are estimates of the population standard deviation (and should therefore be similar).

The model is just like imagining that we have programmed a computer to repeatedly produce means for pairs of samples of a given size from a population with a certain mean and standard deviation. Imagine that we then get the computer to calculate the *t*-values obtained and draw these differences as a frequency graph. If the null hypothesis is true then our data should look like a typical distribution of *t*-values randomly generated by the computer (i.e., a normal distribution). In fact, because random variables are so well behaved in the long run, we do not need to write such a computer program to do statistics, we can use equations and look up values in a table.

When we use a hypothesis-testing approach to test for differences between means we contrast this null hypothesis model with the alternative that there actually *is* a difference between the means. This is called the **alternative hypothesis** or H_1 and is a statement to the effect that something dramatic *is* going on in our research – reflecting something going on in the population from which our samples are drawn. In this case we assert that the two means are really drawn from two different populations with different means. When testing for a difference between means using a *t*-test, the general form of the alternative hypothesis is therefore:

$$H_1 : \quad \mu_1 \neq \mu_2$$

This says that the alternative hypothesis is that μ_1, the population mean associated with Sample 1 (in the between-subjects case) or with Variable 1 (in the within-subjects case) is *not* the same as μ_2, the population mean associated with Sample 2 or Variable 2. An alternative hypothesis like this is normally based on a theory which provides the rationale for our research.

The logical process of the hypothesis-testing approach involves testing between the null hypothesis and the alternative hypothesis. We do not accept the null hypothesis when inferential uncertainty is high, but we reject it and accept the alternative hypothesis when inferential uncertainty is low. *In other words, we never say that the null hypothesis is true, but under certain circumstances we conclude that it is probably false, and so accept the alternative hypothesis.* Researchers and students often forget the fact that, regardless of the results of statistical tests, we can reject or not reject the null hypothesis but we are never entitled to accept the null hypothesis. Again, this is because statistics can never *prove* that a random process has produced the results. We do not know whether the null hypothesis is actually true or whether our study was just not sensitive enough to detect a real difference between means.

In order to make the decision about whether we will reject the null hypothesis or not, we take our *t*-distribution and divide it into three regions. A large region in the middle contains most possible values of *t* and two small regions in the tails of the distribution contain only a few extreme values of *t*. These small regions are called the **rejection regions**. If the obtained value of *t* falls in one of these rejection regions then we say that the difference between means is

statistically significant. In other words, statistical significance is another way of saying that inferential uncertainty is low. The process is shown in Figure 8.2.

You will note that for each tail there is a value that cuts off the rejection region. These values are called **critical values**. If the obtained *t*-value falls in the tail beyond either critical value, it falls in the rejection region. Under these conditions we *reject* the null hypothesis (hence the name 'rejection regions') and conclude that the difference between means is significant – thereby accepting the alternative hypothesis.

How large should these rejection regions be? Well, that depends on how much inferential uncertainty you are prepared to live with. Most psychologists follow the suggestion that a 5% or less chance that a random process could produce the same results is sufficiently low to conclude that the results were not produced by a random process. This figure is commonly used in psychological research, but people also use 1% and 0.1% chances. We call these values **alpha levels** (or, to use the Greek letter for alpha, α levels). Alpha levels correspond to the size of the rejection region, and because we can never be completely sure that our results are not due to chance, an alpha level is essentially just a researcher's statement about the level of inferential uncertainty that he or she is prepared to live with. Rather than use percentages as alpha levels we quote them as probability values, so a rejection region of 5% corresponds to an alpha level of .05. When the obtained *t*-value exceeds

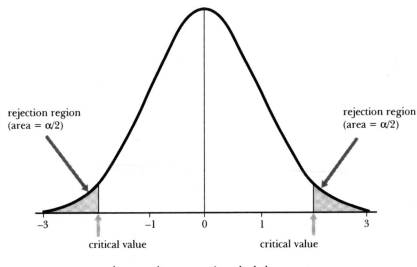

Figure 8.2 *t*-distribution showing rejection regions

the critical value and the value falls in the rejection region, we say 'p is less than α' where α is an alpha level such as .05 (so here we would write $p < .05$).

As an analogy to the process of working with alpha levels, imagine that you and a friend want to drive to the coast 500 km away. Your car is not particularly new and lately you have heard a few rattles coming from somewhere near the engine. Your natural inclination is to assume that the rattles mean nothing, that they are just randomly generated noise that you need not pay attention to. This, in effect, is a null hypothesis – a statement of the view that the noise does not amount to much. On the other hand, you at least entertain the possibility that there may be something to the noise after all. Maybe the engine is about to self-destruct. This, in effect, is an alternative hypothesis – a statement of the view that the rattle is *not* just a random noise, but a signal that you should pay attention to and probably do something about.

Faced with these two possibilities (the only logical alternatives) you then have to decide which one to go with. It is not an easy decision to make, but one way to do this would be to decide on an alpha level for your car before you set out on your trip. This amounts to a statement of the amount of uncertainty about whether the car is fit for the journey that you are prepared to accept – a statement of when you are going to take the mysterious noise seriously. The alpha level you set will depend on a large number of factors including the importance of the journey, the cost of a breakdown and the weather. You might be prepared to start the journey if you thought that the chance that there was really something wrong with the engine was less than 10% (an alpha level of .10). However, your friend might only be prepared to travel with you if there was no more than a 1% chance of the engine breaking down ($\alpha = .01$). Obviously, in everyday life we do not go around quantifying uncertainty like this in numbers. We express our everyday doubts by saying things like 'I'm pretty sure we'll make it' or 'I don't want to seem rude, but I'd feel happier taking the bus'.

In reflecting on this process, it is important to point out that alpha levels are criteria that researchers set *before* they conduct research in much the same way that high jumpers set the height of the bar before they run up and make a jump. If their obtained result yields a value that falls in the rejection region associated with a given alpha level then they reject the null hypothesis. How much they exceed the critical value by is not particularly important. On the other hand, if their obtained value falls outside the rejection region then they do not reject the null hypothesis. Again this decision should not be affected by the distance between the obtained and critical values. The point here is that if you adopt the hypothesis-testing approach then you either clear the bar (the critical value associated with your alpha level) or you do not.

There are just two further complications to the process we have described so far. You will note there are two rejection regions in the figure above. This is because *t*-values can be positive or negative. This occurs because the first mean can be larger than the second, or the second can be larger than the first. Because the obtained value of *t* can fall in either tail, we call this a **two-tailed test**.

The total rejection region is divided into two tails. If $\alpha = .05$ (5%) then each of the two rejection regions will be 2.5% (i.e., $\alpha/2$) of the total distribution. Under some circumstances, however, we can take a slightly different approach where we test a different alternative hypothesis. Think for a moment about H_1:

$$H_1 : \quad \mu_1 \neq \mu_2$$

This can be re-expressed in the following way:

$$H_{1a} : \quad \mu_1 > \mu_2$$

and

$$H_{1b} : \quad \mu_1 < \mu_2$$

That is, if the two means are not equal then one has to be larger than the other. Sometimes we might want to test both those possibilities, but under other circumstances this does not make sense. If we compare the heights of men and women we might want to know whether men are taller or not, but it is not particularly useful or relevant to test the idea that men are shorter than women. Thus, under some circumstances we only have:

$$H_1 : \quad \mu_1 > \mu_2$$

That is, we hypothesize that one mean will be greater than the other. If this is the case, rather than using two rejection regions, it can be appropriate to use a single rejection region at one end of the distribution, as shown in Figure 8.3. You will note that the critical value cutting off the rejection region is closer to zero (i.e., smaller) in this case. This test with only one rejection region is called a **one-tailed test** or a **directional test**.

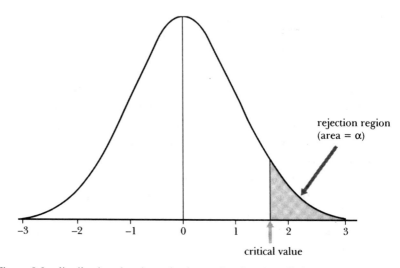

Figure 8.3 *t*-distribution showing rejection region for one-tailed test

Opinions about when one-tailed tests should be used vary, but they are most appropriate under circumstances where researchers know that one mean cannot possibly be larger than the other. So unless they have a good reason not to, researchers should use the two-tailed test described above, where there is a rejection region in each tail. Using one-tailed tests to make non-significant results become significant is particularly inappropriate – this is equivalent to high jumpers lowering the height of the bar when they have just failed to clear it with their one and only attempt.

A second complication is that sometimes when we make a statistical inference we find that we have made a mistake. Either we have said that there is a difference between means when there is not really a difference, or we have said that there is no difference when there is. When we say there is a difference between means when there is none – in other words, when we *reject the null hypothesis when it is actually true* – this is called a **Type I error**. The second type of error – where we *do not reject the null hypothesis when it is false* – is called a **Type II error**.

In the language that we have been using to deal with issues of statistical inference, these two types of error relate to the *appropriateness* of a researcher's certainty. A Type I error occurs when researchers are wrong in saying that something is going on. A Type II error occurs when researchers are wrong in saying that something is not going on.

As you can probably see, these two types of error are actually inter-related. This is because as researchers seek to reduce the likelihood of making a Type I error (by reducing their alpha level and being prepared to tolerate less inferential uncertainty), their chances of making a Type II error are increased. In fact both errors arise because we make all-or-none decisions about information which is not clear-cut but is based on probability. However, as we have been at pains to point out, if the data were clear-cut we would not need to use statistics in the first place.

The chance of making these errors is something that we have to take very seriously. An acute problem arises where certain statistical tests or methodological circumstances are more likely to lead to one type of error than the other. Because we are always liable to make some errors we need to know whether those errors will be of a particular kind so that we can correct them. Furthermore, some types of error are more undesirable than others in particular circumstances. For example, if clinical psychologists were testing the effectiveness of a therapy which has the possibility of harmful side-effects they would want to avoid Type I errors because they would not want to expose clients to these risks if the therapy does not actually help.

We are more likely to make Type II errors when the sample size or the effect is small, when we are investigating effects of a small size, where there is a lot of random error, or where the alpha level is very small. It is worth looking at the terms in the equation for the t-statistic to see why this is the case. Type II errors can only occur when the obtained test statistic is smaller than the critical value of t – that is, when we do not reject the null hypothesis. Type II errors are therefore associated with factors that reduce the value of the calculated t-value and with those that increase the critical t-value. A small value of calculated t will be obtained when there is a small sample size, a large error term or a small information term (i.e., a small difference between means). A large critical value of t will be obtained when the alpha level (not the p-value) is very small.

When the likelihood of making a Type II error is inflated for one or more of these reasons, the t-test will be unlikely to reveal any relationships that may be present in the data. This is analogous to looking at stars with a very weak telescope. To avoid these problems we can use a more powerful test, in the same way that an astronomer would use a more powerful telescope. Powerful tests have a greater ability to reveal relationships that are present in the data. It is thus possible to distinguish between tests in terms of their **power**. Saying that a test is powerful is the same as saying that the test has a low chance of producing a Type II error. Formally, we can therefore define power as $1 - \beta$, where β (the Greek letter beta) is the probability of a Type II error.

In general, we should use the most powerful test of a hypothesis that is appropriate for the data we are dealing with (a point we will return to below when we discuss the assumptions of statistical tests). A test that is not powerful is called a *conservative* test. In the example of testing the effectiveness of a therapy with harmful side-effects, we would probably wish to use a conservative test. However, in order to identify those side-effects in the first place, we should definitely use a powerful test.

We can summarize the process of hypothesis-testing as follows:

1. Decide on an alpha level before you commence the research. This is the amount of inferential uncertainty that you see as acceptable.
2. Calculate the *t*-statistic and obtain the corresponding probability value by looking it up in Table C.2 of Appendix C.
3. If the probability value is less than the alpha level then reject the null hypothesis and conclude that the difference between means is statistically significant. If the probability value is greater than the alpha level you should conclude that the result is not statistically significant and should make no inferences about differences between the means.

When you report the results you should do so in the following way (assuming an alpha level of .05). To report a significant result:

The difference between the means was significant

$(t(18) = 2.90, p < .01)$

To report a non-significant result:

The difference between the means was not significant

$(t(20) = 1.75, p < .10)$

or

The difference between the means was not significant

$(t(20) = 1.75, p > .05)$

Obviously in these examples the values of *t* and *p* and the degrees of freedom vary. When doing your own research you need to use the values that you have calculated for the data you are working with.

Note here that you should report the *p*-value that corresponds to the highest *t*-value in the relevant row of the table that has been exceeded (or the exact *p*-value if, for example, it is available from a computer program). Some textbooks advise researchers simply to report whether the obtained *p*-value is less than the alpha level (e.g., with an α of .05 to report '$p < .05$' even when p is much smaller than .001). However, we advise against this practice simply because it reduces the amount of information available to the reader about the inference that is being made.

If there are no *t*-values in the relevant row that have been exceeded (and hence no tabled *p*-value that the obtained *p* falls below), then report the significance level with the letters *ns* (for 'not significant') in the following way:

The difference between the means was not significant

$(t(30) = 0.40, ns)$

Some researchers use this form of notation for all non-significant results (i.e., whenever an obtained probability is greater than the alpha level).

The whole process of using the hypothesis-testing approach to conduct *t*-tests is summarized in Appendix A. Examples of how to write these tests up formally are presented there, too.

Q8.5[**]

Which of the following must be true of a statistically significant result of a *t*-test?

(a) The probability that a difference at least as large as the observed difference could have been produced by a random process will be less than the alpha level.

(b) The obtained value of *t* will exceed the alpha level.

(c) The rejection regions must be significantly different from each other.

(d) Both (a) and (c).

(e) Alpha must be set at .05.

The correct answer is (a). A significant *t*-test yields a *p*-value that is less than a predetermined alpha level. (b) is wrong because the value of *t* must exceed the critical value, not the alpha level. However, if *t* is greater than the *critical value* then *p* will be less than the alpha level. Answer (c) is a nonsense answer – we want the means to be significantly different from each other, not the rejection regions. If (c) is wrong, (d) must be wrong. Although an alpha of .05 is a popular alpha level, it is only one possible choice, so (e) is wrong.

alpha level The largest probability that the researcher is prepared to accept in order to reject the **null hypothesis**. The probability of a random process producing a result as big as the one obtained has to be smaller than this for a statistical test to be significant. It is equal to the probability of making a **Type I** error and should be set before research is carried out.

alternative hypothesis The hypothesis that the research reveals an effect (e.g., that two samples are drawn from different populations and that there is an informative difference between their means). Also referred to as H_1. This is normally the hypothesis that the research was designed to test.

critical value The value associated with a statistical test (e.g., t) that cuts off the *rejection region*. If the obtained value exceeds this value then the test result will be significant. This is because the probability of the obtained value will be less than the *alpha level*.

directional test A *one-tailed* statistical test, where the *alternative hypothesis* specifies the direction of any effect (e.g., hypothesizing that one particular mean will be greater than another).

H_0 The *null hypothesis* that the research reveals no effect.

H_1 The *alternative hypothesis* that the research reveals an effect.

hypothesis-testing approach The process of making decisions as to whether the pattern of obtained results (e.g., differences between means) is due to chance (H_0) or to significant effects (H_1).

null hypothesis The hypothesis that the research reveals no effect (e.g., that two samples are drawn from the same population and that there is no informative difference between their means). Also referred to as H_0. This is the hypothesis that statistical procedures allow researchers to reject.

one-tailed test A *directional test* with a single *rejection region*. Such a test has a rejection region whose area is twice as large as that for a *two-tailed test*, and is based on the *alternative hypothesis* being *directional* (e.g., hypothesizing that one particular mean is larger than the other).

power The ability of a statistical test to reveal effects that exist in the data. Increasing power reduces inferential uncertainty. Formally, power is equal to $1 - \beta$, where β is the probability of a *Type II error*.

rejection region The area of the sampling distribution associated with a statistical test (e.g., the t-distribution) that is cut off by the *critical value(s)*. The size of these regions depends upon the *alpha level*. For example, an alpha level of .05 corresponds to a rejection region (or regions) taking up 5% of the total distribution.

significance-testing approach Another name for the *hypothesis-testing approach*.

statistical significance An outcome where the probability that an effect at least as large as that observed could be produced by a random process is less than a predetermined *alpha level*. Where a result is

statistically significant it is implausible that a random process could
have produced the effect.

two-tailed test A test with two *rejection regions* that is based on the
alternative hypothesis that research reveals an effect (e.g., that two
means are different). The nature of any departure from randomness
(e.g., which mean will be larger) is not specified.

Type I error Making the statistical inference that an effect exists (e.g.,
that there is a difference between means) when the effect is actually
due to a random process. Here the *null hypothesis* is rejected when
it is actually true.

Type II error Making the statistical inference that there is no effect
(e.g., that there is no difference between means) when the effect does
actually exist. Here the *null hypothesis* is not rejected when it is
actually false.

Other ways of handling the results of *t*-tests: Probability-level, confidence-interval and effect-size approaches

Despite its popularity, the hypothesis-testing or significance-testing
approach is only one way to make decisions about inferential uncertainty. There are several alternatives which are preferred by statisticians who do not like the all-or-nothing nature of the hypothesis-testing
approach. In this section we present three alternative methods for
dealing with inferential uncertainty. All of them are acceptable in
different areas of the psychological research literature. However,
different instructors will have preferences about which one they want
students to use in their work.

The probability-level approach
The **probability-level approach** is the technique that we presented
in the sections above where we first explained how to do a *t*-test. This
involves simply calculating and reporting both a *t*-value and an
associated probability level. If this approach is taken the results are
not described as being significant or non-significant – or at least hard-
and-fast significance levels are not used. Instead the researcher simply
states the probability that a random process could have produced a
difference as large as the one obtained. The disadvantage of this
method is that it is a bit clumsier to express in words. One advantage
is that other people can look at your results and use another approach if
they choose.

The confidence-interval approach

When we estimate parameters we can do one of two things. We can estimate a parameter by suggesting a particular value. This is called a **point estimate**. However, when we do this we still have a degree of uncertainty about the correspondence between this point estimate and the true parameter value. To deal with this uncertainty we could therefore specify a range of values around the point estimate within which we expect the true value to lie. Such a range of possible values is called a **confidence interval** (or sometimes an interval estimate). Confidence intervals can be constructed for a variety of parameters, including the mean and the difference between means.

When examining differences between means, the **confidence-interval approach** involves reporting a probable range of differences between population means. This is the likely range of differences that would be obtained by taking random samples from the same population and subtracting one mean from the other.

The size of the confidence interval depends on the amount of inferential uncertainty that researchers are prepared to accept and the amount of random error present. The less uncertainty they are prepared to live with, the larger the confidence interval will be. As a result, more and more of the possible differences between means that would be obtained from a random process will lie within the confidence interval.

The probability of including the true value in the confidence interval is used to name the confidence interval. A 95% confidence interval for the sample mean would contain the true population mean 95% of the time if many samples of the same size as the empirical sample were drawn randomly from that population. A 95% confidence interval for a difference between means would contain the true difference between means 95% of the time.

To find a confidence interval for the difference between means we need to go through the following steps:

1. Decide on the alpha level for the desired confidence interval. A confidence interval has an alpha level that corresponds to $1 - (\text{confidence interval} / 100)$.

So, for a 95% confidence interval:

$$1 - (\text{confidence interval}/100) = 1 - (95/100) = .05$$

2. Find the critical value of t for the appropriate number of degrees of freedom. This involves consulting Table C.2 in Appendix C and looking for the critical value of t for a given alpha level.

For the example given earlier of a two-tailed between-subjects *t*-test with 18 *df*, the critical value for a 95% confidence interval is 2.101.

3. Multiply the value of *t* by the standard error. For a between-subjects *t*-test the standard error is $\left(s_{pooled}\sqrt{1/N_1 + 1/N_2}\right)$. For a within-subjects *t*-test the standard error is $\left(s_D/\sqrt{N}\right)$. This is the confidence interval for the difference between the means.

In the example we are using, the standard error is

$$\sqrt{2.38} * \sqrt{1/10 + 1/10} = 1.54 * \sqrt{0.2} = 0.69$$

The confidence interval is therefore $2.101 * 0.69 = 1.45$ units either side of zero.

4. When we have constructed our confidence interval we can examine whether the observed differences lie within or outside the confidence interval.

The last of these steps is contentious because many would argue that it simply reproduces the logic of the *t*-test (see Frick, 1995). This is because there is a simple relationship between these confidence intervals and *p*-values. A difference with a *p*-value of less than .05 will lie outside the 95% confidence interval, a difference with a *p*-value of less than .01 will lie outside the 99% confidence interval and so on. For this reason confidence intervals can be seen as a means of rewriting statistical tests, because if a difference is significant with $p < .05$ then it will also lie outside the 95% confidence interval. This is because the *t*-test and the confidence interval involve the same three terms: the difference between the means, the standard error and the critical value. However, the two approaches use these terms in different ways. As Figure 8.4 illustrates, the confidence interval corresponds to the region of the *t*-distribution that is between the tails that would be cut off by the critical values. So, a 95% confidence interval includes all the possible outcomes that would lead us not to reject the null hypothesis at an alpha level of .05.

If we follow Step 4 with the data from our example, any difference between the means that is greater than 1.45 or less than -1.45 will lie outside the 95% confidence interval. Here the difference between means was 2.0, so this difference lies outside the 95% confidence interval. In other words, we can conclude that 95% of differences between means produced by a random process would not be this large.

Confidence intervals are a very good way of making the level of inferential uncertainty associated with a given test clear. By alerting the

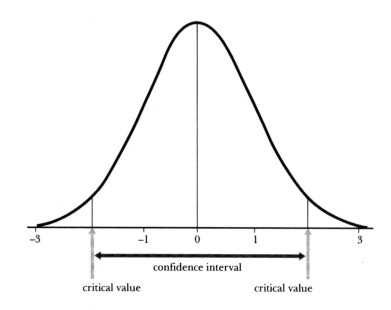

Figure 8.4 *t*-distribution showing confidence interval

researcher to the range of possible outcomes associated with the process of doing the research, the calculation of a confidence interval puts results in perspective by comparing our obtained result directly to a range of possible results that would be produced by a random process. This avoids the trap that can occur when researchers using the hypothesis-testing approach lose sight of the idea that their results are being treated as one possible sample from a specified population and are being used to estimate parameters of that population. Nevertheless, most of the thorny issues associated with statistical inference are as evident in the use of confidence intervals as they are when using the hypothesis-testing approach.

However, one additional benefit of the confidence-interval approach is that even when an observed difference between means lies within a specified confidence interval, the confidence interval itself provides information about how large an effect would need to be in order to make us certain that something was going on in our research. This information can be very useful as it may give researchers insight into the ability of their tests, measures or manipulations to reveal effects. As we discussed in Chapter 4, this is an important methodological consideration.

The effect-size approach
One of the things about the approaches to the results of *t*-tests that we have discussed so far is that inferential uncertainty is reduced by

increasing the sample size. This follows again from the law of large numbers. This means that we can do exactly the same study twice (where the second study is a *replication*) and obtain a significant difference in the first study and not in the second, simply because the second study has fewer participants – even though the differences between the means and the variances are the same in each case. So, the fact that a result is significant does not mean that it is large enough to be important or interesting. The important point here is that statistical significance is not the same as **psychological significance**. This is true partly because if the sample size is large enough then just about any difference can be significant. The mistaken belief that a statistically significant finding in a psychological study necessarily tells us something important about the psychological processes or states under investigation (i.e., that statistical significance *implies* psychological significance) can be referred to as the **significance fallacy**. This fallacy is made all the more potent because it is one to which researchers easily succumb – particularly if they are under pressure to make as much of their research as possible.

To address this problem many psychologists who use statistics prefer to base their interpretation of results on an **effect-size approach**. **Effect sizes** are not affected by the sample size and simply tell us whether the difference between the means is large compared to the amount of dispersion (or descriptive uncertainty). These effect sizes help us to compare results across studies.

A number of proposals have been made about how to measure effect size. One measure is *d*. This is essentially the difference between means divided by the standard deviation. Unlike the *t*-statistic, the standard deviation is not divided by the square root of the sample size, so the size of *d* does not depend on the sample size. The measure of effect size that we will use here is *r*, largely because we use this statistic again in the next chapter. The formula for *r* is:

$$r = \sqrt{t^2/(t^2 + df)}$$

This value of *r* can vary between 0 and 1. And as with all measures of effect size, the value of *r* can be compared across studies. Following the advice of Cohen (1977), if *r* is at least .1 it can be considered to be a weak effect, if it is at least .3 it is a moderate effect and if it is at least .5 it is a strong effect. In the examples we used previously, the size of the effect for the between-subjects *t*-test in the 'physical reinforcement theory' experiment would be presented as follows:

$$r_{between} = \sqrt{t^2/(t^2 + df)}$$

$$= \sqrt{2.90^2/(2.90^2 + 18)}$$

$$= \sqrt{8.41/26.41}$$

$$= .56$$

This is a strong effect. In the within-subjects example used to examine the same theory, the effect size would look like this:

$$r_{within} = \sqrt{t^2/(t^2 + df)}$$

$$= \sqrt{1.43^2/(1.43^2 + 6)}$$

$$= \sqrt{2.04/8.04}$$

$$= .50$$

This is a strong effect.

Our use of these examples makes it clear that the different approaches to statistical tests lead to different conclusions about the importance or interest of studies – remember that the hypothesis-testing approach would have suggested that the within-subjects test results yielded no effect (by any conventional choice of alpha level). Results can be highly statistically significant but of small size, or of large size but not significant. This is because effect sizes are not estimates of inferential uncertainty. They do not tell us whether the results could have been due to chance, they simply tell us the size of those results relative to error but ignoring sample size. To address the issue of inferential uncertainty, effect sizes need to be accompanied by other measures. Before taking the results of a piece of research that showed a large effect size too seriously, most researchers would want to be confident that the results were not a chance occurrence. In other words, effect sizes are very useful but they complement rather than replace the other approaches.

Q8.6***

Researchers conduct a *t*-test and obtain a *p*-value of .0012. Which of the following is an appropriate conclusion on the basis of the information provided?

(a) The result is significant.

(b) The effect size will be large.

(c) Both (a) and (b).

(d) A 99% confidence interval for the differences between the means will include the observed difference.

(e) A 95% confidence interval for the differences between the means will not include the observed difference.

The correct answer is (e). We cannot say whether a result is significant or not unless an alpha level is specified, so (a) is wrong. (b) is wrong because a small p-value does not necessarily correspond to a large effect size. If (a) and (b) are wrong, then (c) must be wrong. Answer (d) is wrong because if the p-value is less than .01 the 99% confidence interval cannot include the observed difference. The confidence interval would have to be 99.9% before it included the observed difference. Answer (e) is correct for the reasons that make (d) incorrect.

confidence interval An estimated range of values for a population parameter. The size of the confidence interval is expressed as a percentage. If sampling is random, a 95% confidence interval has a 95% chance of containing the population parameter.

confidence-interval approach An approach to inferential statistics based on the use of *confidence intervals* rather than *point estimates*.

effect size A measure of the size of an effect that ignores the sample size.

effect-size approach An approach to inferential statistics based on the calculation of *effect sizes* rather than probability levels.

point estimate A single value used to estimate a population parameter. For example, the sample standard deviation is a point estimate of the population standard deviation.

probability-level approach A procedure whereby the researcher calculates the probability that a random process could have produced a difference of the observed size. No hard-and-fast inferences about statistical significance are made.

psychological significance An outcome of research which produces important knowledge about psychological processes or states. This should not be confused with statistical significance.

> **significance fallacy** The mistaken belief that a statistically significant
> result in a psychological study constitutes a ***psychologically
> significant*** finding.

Some notes of caution

All of the procedures described in this chapter are based on statistical models. Statistical models allow us to make inferences so long as the principles they are based on are applicable. These principles are called **assumptions**. Assumptions are the foundations upon which everything else we do with statistics is based. If the assumptions do not hold (where we say there is a **violation of assumptions**) then the process of doing inferential statistics can be very risky because we can make the wrong inferences.

Given that assumptions are so important, you may well ask why we are talking about them now, towards the end of the chapter. That is a very good question, and the answer is that we have, in fact, been talking about assumptions all the time up to this point, without calling them assumptions. This may become clearer when we point out that the assumptions of the between-subjects *t*-test are that our samples are *independent* random samples from a population with a normal distribution, and that the standard deviations of both samples are estimates of the same underlying population standard deviation.

Let us go through these assumptions one at a time. There is only one new term that has been introduced here, and that is 'independent'. **Independence** refers to things being separate and standing on their own. Events are independent if the occurrence of one has no effect on the probability of the other. Coin tosses are independent events. If we toss a coin and obtain a head then the chance of the next coin toss being a head is the same regardless of what has occurred in the past. This point is often misunderstood. One way in which it is misunderstood is in the **gambler's fallacy** – the belief that luck has to change (see Question 7.7 at the end of the previous chapter). Samples are independent if the probability of one participant's being included in the sample is not affected by the probability of any other person being sampled. In other words, the samples are selected randomly from the population.

Whenever researchers do anything to bias the selection procedure – for example, if they deliberately select participants to be in one particular group (rather than randomly allocating participants) or if they use the same participants twice in a between-subjects *t*-test, the **assumption of independence** is violated. Under these conditions *t*-tests can give misleading results. For within-subjects *t*-tests the assumption of independence is relaxed. This is for the obvious reason that if the same sample is used for both measures these samples *cannot* be independent. However, the participants that comprise the sample still need to be independent of each other.

The use of *t*-tests also assumes that the samples are drawn from a normally distributed population. This is known as the **assumption of normality**. This is a very important idea in those areas of psychological statistics which rely on **normal theory tests**. We will provide no detailed justification for this idea here, but just point out that the mathematical solutions to statistical problems become much easier if we are able to assume that the variables are normally distributed. It is easy to see why this would be the case given the advantages of a normal distribution that we have already identified. If we know that a variable is normally distributed and we know its mean and variance, we know a great deal about it. Not surprisingly, it is easier to develop statistical tests for variables that are well understood in this way.

Finally, a third assumption is that the samples must both have standard deviations which are estimates of the same population standard deviation. This is called the **assumption of equal variance**. Where this is not true we cannot be sure that our procedures for deciding the level of inferential uncertainty will be accurate. If the standard deviations are not equal then we should treat the results of the *t*-test with caution. In fact, there are correction procedures that can be used under these circumstances involving the transformation of variables (see Chapter 6).

As we mentioned in Chapter 6, one thing that can contribute a great deal to the amount of variance in a distribution is the presence of one or more outliers. This means that if we have outliers in one sample and not in the other the assumption of equal variance is likely to be violated. The effect of this will normally be to reduce the power of the test. The only way to check whether outliers could be affecting your results is to look at your data. This could involve constructing a frequency graph.

For example, the bar charts for the between-subjects *t*-test that we used as an example earlier are shown in Figure 8.5. If instead the distribution of data from the experimental condition had been like that in Figure 8.6 (i.e., if the response of Participant 1 had been '1' rather than '4') we would have evidence of an outlier. The presence of this outlier increases the standard deviation of the data in this condition

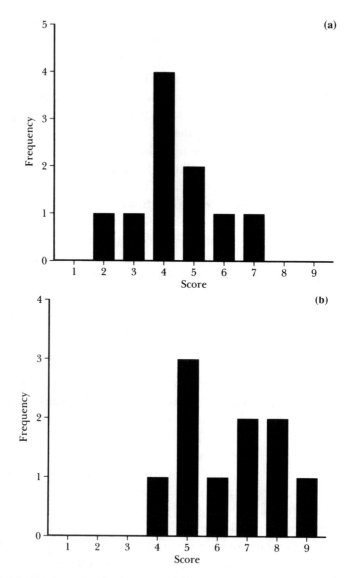

Figure 8.5 Bar charts for the between-subjects *t*-test carried out in Chapter 6 (see pp. 210–12): (a) control condition; (b) experimental condition

from 1.65 to 2.28. As a result, the assumption of equal variance could be violated and, if it was, the power of a *t*-test would be dramatically reduced. That is because a larger standard deviation makes it more difficult to demonstrate differences between the means. Outliers like this can be present for all sorts of reasons, including mistakes in recording the data. As we noted in Chapter 6, outliers can sometimes be corrected by appropriate statistical transformation, but sometimes it is better to remove or recode individual outliers.

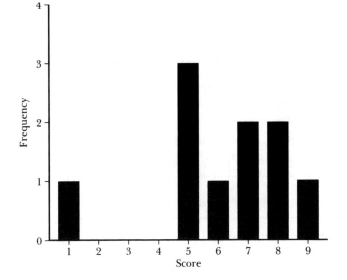

Figure 8.6 Bar chart showing evidence of outlier

Where the assumptions of the *t*-test do not hold we must proceed with caution. By far the best option is to use **non-parametric** and **distribution-free** tests. These do not make the same restrictive assumptions as the *t*-test and we will consider them in detail in Chapter 11. There is a tendency in psychology to assume that statistical tests are **robust** to violations of assumptions (particularly the assumption of equal variance). However, these assumptions are considerably less robust than is commonly believed. In general, it is *highly desirable* to look for violations of assumptions in your data – for example, by using a frequency graph to explore its distribution. One of the major benefits of this inspection process is that problems or other interesting features of the data are likely to reveal themselves. There is little to lose and much to gain from looking carefully at data before subjecting them to statistical tests.

Q8.7*

Researchers conduct a *t*-test to compare two groups and find that one of the groups has a much larger standard deviation than the other. Which of the following statements is true?

(a) The variances are robust.
(b) The assumption of equal variance may have been violated.
(c) The researchers should make sure that their distributions are free of parameters.

(d) The standard deviations are not normal.

(e) Both (b) and (d).

The correct answer is (b). Answers (a) (c) and (d) are all nonsense answers involving mixing up other terms from this section. In particular, with respect to (a), *tests* can be robust, not *variances*; and with respect to (d), *distributions* are normal, not *standard deviations*. If (d) is wrong, then (e) must also be wrong.

assumption of equal variance An assumption of the *t*-test procedure that the variances of the samples that are compared are both estimates of the same population variance and thus are similar.

assumption of independence An assumption of the *t*-test procedure that sampling of the underlying population is independent and can be treated as random.

assumption of normality An assumption of the *t*-test procedure that the samples are random samples drawn from a normally distributed population.

assumptions The conditions that must be satisfied before we can use a statistical test with confidence. The assumptions of the *t*-test are that the samples are independent and randomly sampled from a normally distributed population which has the same variance for all samples.

distribution-free tests Tests that make no assumptions about the theoretical distribution of variables in the population from which a sample is drawn (i.e., the sampling distribution).

gambler's fallacy The mistaken idea that random events are not independent. A gambler may believe that a long run of good or bad luck has to change. The gambler's fallacy arises from a misunderstanding of the law of large numbers. The idea that a random process will behave in a predictable way on average over a long run of observations can be misunderstood to imply that there is 'a law of averages' that serves to *change* the probability of random events based on past events. However, coins, dice and other things that generate random outcomes do not have memories.

independence A term with numerous meanings in statistics. Two events are independent where the probability of one occurring does not depend upon the probability of the other occurring.

non-parametric tests Generally similar to ***distribution-free*** tests,
but, technically speaking, these tests do not involve hypotheses related
to a population parameter.

normal theory tests Statistical tests, like the *t*-test, that assume that
samples are drawn from a population that is normally distributed.

robust test A statistical test that tends to yield valid results even when
the assumptions underpinning that test are violated.

violation of assumptions Threats to interpretation of the results of
statistical tests that arise when the conditions required for the test to
work properly do not hold.

Overview

This chapter began with a consideration of how to compare means
when the population standard deviation is unknown. We covered three
situations where the *t*-test can be used: for testing the difference
between the mean of a single sample and some hypothesized population
mean; for testing the difference between the means for a single sample
on two different variables; and for testing the difference between two
samples on a single variable.

In each case we find a value for *t* which corresponds to a probability
that the results are due to random error. This probability corresponds
to the level of inferential uncertainty. However, once we have obtained
that probability we have some additional decisions to make.

Having computed a *t*-value and a probability level, there are several
choices as to how to treat, interpret and use these. The traditional
approach has been to perform significance tests. To understand much
of the literature that has already been published in psychology you will
need to have some familiarity with this approach. Nowadays, however,
important alternatives are available. These techniques include the use
of confidence intervals and effect sizes.

Further reading

There is little more to discover about *t*-tests through further reading.
However, a distinctive – indeed, almost unique – feature of Smithson's book is
that it explains how these can be conducted using a confidence-interval
approach.

Smithson, M. (2000). *Statistics with confidence*. London: Sage.

t-Tests: A checklist for research evaluation and improvement

Potential problem	Question to ask	Potential improvement
Inferential uncertainty about an individual sample mean	Do the researchers want to compare a sample mean with another score when the population mean and standard deviation are unknown?	Subtract the comparison score from the sample mean and divide by the standard error of the mean (the sample standard deviation divided by the square root of the sample size). This procedure creates a *t*-score and – having calculated the degrees of freedom (the sample size minus one) – Table C.2 can be used to provide information about the probability of observing by chance a *t*-score as large as the one obtained.
Inferential uncertainty about means from the same sample	Do the researchers want to compare means associated with data that have been obtained from the same sample on two occasions when the population mean and standard deviation are unknown?	As set out in Section A.1 of Appendix A, convert each pair of scores into a difference score by subtracting the second score from the first. Calculate the mean and standard deviation of the difference scores. Divide the mean difference score by the standard error of the mean difference (the standard deviation of the difference scores divided by the square root of the sample size). This procedure creates a *t*-score and – having calculated the degrees of freedom (the sample size minus one) – Table C.2 can be used to provide information about the probability (p) of observing by chance a *t*-score as large as the one obtained.
Inferential uncertainty about means from different samples	Do the researchers want to compare means associated with data that have been obtained from two independent samples when the population mean and standard deviation are unknown?	As set out in Section A.2 of Appendix A, compute means and variances for the scores in each sample. Compute a pooled variance estimate (a weighted average of the two variances). Divide the difference between the means by the standard error of the difference between means (the square root of the product of the pooled variance and the sum of the reciprocal sample sizes). This procedure creates a

Potential problem	Question to ask	Potential improvement
		t-score and – having calculated the degrees of freedom (the sum of the two sample sizes minus two) – Table C.2 can be used to provide information about the probability (p) of observing by chance a t-value as large as the one obtained.
Significance fallacy	If the researchers are using a hypothesis-testing approach to t-tests, have they distinguished appropriately between psychological and statistical significance?	Consider significance levels in conjunction with effect sizes (e.g., compare p and r). Be alert to the dangers of making too much of statistically significant t-values when effect sizes are low.
Violation of the assumption of independence	Do the means that are being compared relate to independent sets of observations?	If sample scores are not independent (and dependent scores are not being compared in a within-subjects t-test) it can be misleading to compare them using a t-test (or any other statistical test) if, in effect, the same piece of data is being counted more than once. Accordingly, if possible, any source of dependence (e.g., the fact that the same participant responded twice) should be removed before collecting data. If this is not possible, the nature of the violation should be noted and results treated with caution.
Violation of the assumption of normality	Do the means that are being compared relate to observations that are normally distributed?	If the distribution of sample scores is non-normal (e.g., severely skewed or U-shaped) and the cell sizes are unequal, or there are reasons to believe that the mean is a misleading indicator of central tendency, you should seriously consider using a non-parametric test (Chapter 11) or correct the distribution by transformation (see Chapter 6).
Violation of the assumption of equal variance	Do the means that are being compared relate to samples that have equal variance?	If sample variances are unequal (e.g., one is more than four times bigger than the other) you should seriously consider using a non-parametric test (see Chapter 11). This is only

Potential problem	Question to ask	Potential improvement
		worth doing if the size of one sample is much larger than the other.
Outliers	Is the distribution of scores (especially its shape and variance) dramatically affected by the presence of outliers?	Examine the distribution of scores to see if it contains outliers. If it does, see if this can be corrected by an appropriate statistical transformation of the sample data. If this is not possible, consider (a) removing individual outliers or (b) recoding them to the same value as the nearest non-outlier. Ensure you report any transformations that you make.

Q8.8*

If an experimenter were to conduct an experiment in which participants were randomly assigned to either a control condition or an experimental condition, which of the following statements would be true?

(a) It will be appropriate to analyse results using a between-subjects t-test.
(b) Any statistical analysis will be based on pairs of responses.
(c) If a t-test is performed to analyse the results, it will have $N - 1$ degrees of freedom.
(d) The experiment involves two related samples.
(e) Both (a) and (c).

Q8.9**

John, a second-year psychology student, is using the hypothesis-testing approach and an alpha level of .05 to examine a difference between two means. He discovers that this difference is associated with a t-value of 3.46. If the critical t-value with $\alpha = .05$ is 2.056 what should he conclude?

(a) That the difference between the means is statistically significant.
(b) That the alpha level is too high.
(c) That the alpha level is not high enough.
(d) That the experiment did not contain enough participants to draw a strong conclusion.
(e) That no conclusion can be made about the nature of the underlying populations.

Q8.10**

Which of the following suggests that the assumptions underlying a
between-subjects *t*-test have been violated?

(a) Evidence that the dependent variable is normally distributed.
(b) Evidence that the samples being compared have unequal variances.
(c) Evidence that the manipulation of the independent variable had no
effect.
(d) Evidence that sampling was random, and that scores were
independent.
(e) None of the above.

Q8.11***

Which of the following increases the likelihood of a Type II error when
conducting a *t*-test?

(a) A high alpha level.
(b) A large sample size.
(c) High power.
(d) Low random error.
(e) A small difference between means.

The correct answer to 8.8 is (a). Between-subjects *t*-tests are used for
between-subjects designs like this. (b) is wrong because pairs of responses
are used in within-subjects *t*-tests. (c) is wrong because there will be
$N_1 + N_2 - 2$ degrees of freedom. (d) is wrong because the two samples
are independent and not related. Because (c) is wrong, (e) must also be
wrong.

The correct answer to 8.9 is (a). There are no grounds to support any of
the other conclusions. (b) and (c) are wrong because the alpha level is a
criterion that is set before the research is carried out. The alpha level
quantifies the amount of inferential uncertainty the researcher is prepared
to tolerate and is a decision to be made by the researcher (as always, these
decisions should be influenced by an evaluation of past practice in that
area of research). In short, decisions about the appropriate size of alpha
levels are not made on the basis of the results of the study they are applied
to. (d) is wrong because the test has yielded a significant result. We would
only suspect that (d) were correct if a significant result were not obtained
with a small sample size. (e) is wrong because if the result is significant the

experimenter should conclude that the means belong to samples drawn
from different populations.

The correct answer to 8.10 is (b). Evidence that the samples being
compared have unequal variances violates the assumption of equal
variance. Other assumptions of the *t*-test are that the variable under
investigation is normally distributed (as (a) suggests) and that scores on
that variable are independent (as (d) suggests). The outcome of a *t*-test
cannot tell us about the appropriateness of that statistical procedure – so
(c) is wrong.

The correct answer to 8.11 is (e). A Type II error involves making an
inference that no effect exists when it actually does – accepting the null
hypothesis when it is false. When we do a *t*-test, Type II errors are
associated with factors that reduce the value of the calculated *t*-value and
with those that increase the critical *t*-value. A large critical value of *t* will
be obtained when the alpha level (not the *p*-value) is very *small*, so (a) is
wrong. A small value of calculated *t* will be obtained when there is a *small*
sample size (so (b) is wrong), a *large* error term (so (d) is wrong) or a *small*
difference between means (as (e) suggests). Power is increased by any
factor that reduces the likelihood of a Type II error, so (c) is wrong.

Discussion/essay questions

(a) Why is the hypothesis-testing approach to statistical inference
controversial?

(b) Has a reliance on hypothesis-testing techniques had a detrimental impact
on the study of psychology?

(c) Discuss the relative advantages and disadvantages of a confidence-
interval approach to statistical inference.

(d) In what way does the presence of outliers affect the results of *t*-tests?

Exercises

(a) An experimenter conducts a study in which participants try to remember
a number of digits. Some participants do this after consuming 3 litres of
beer, others do it after drinking a litre of milk. The data from the study
were as follows:

		Participant number									
	1	2	3	4	5	6	7	8	9	10
Milk	7	6	7	7	8	8	9	5	6	7
Beer	6	5	6	7	5	3	7	6	7	5

(i) What form of *t*-test is appropriate to analyse these data?

(ii) What value of *t* does the appropriate test yield?

(iii) Is this effect statistically significant with α set at .05?

(b) Imagine that the data in the above table were obtained from examination of the same participants under different conditions (i.e., that the researcher collected pairs of data from each participant).

(i) What form of *t*-test is appropriate to analyse the data?

(ii) What value of *t* does the appropriate test yield?

(iii) Is this effect statistically significant with α set at .05?

(c) A parapsychologist wants to know whether a person claiming to have psychokinetic powers can produce higher numbers throwing red dice than throwing blue dice. The results are analysed by *t*-test. Why is it more appropriate to test this hypothesis by comparing scores obtained when the person throws many dice at the same time and adds them up rather than just comparing the scores when a single die is thrown? (Hint: What shape would the distributions of scores be in each case?)

(d) A psychotherapist consults you (as an expert statistician) to see whether an expensive new therapy they have developed is working and whether it has any side-effects. For this purpose they provide you with two sets of scores for 200 patients. One set of scores measures psychological functioning pre- and post-treatment and the other measures the presence of self-reported side-effects pre- and post-treatment.

(i) What form of *t*-test is appropriate to analyse these data?

(ii) What alpha levels would you recommend?

(iii) In the course of your discussion with the therapist, you find out that many of the participants in their study discussed amongst themselves how they should respond on the self-reported side-effect measure. Why does this make it inappropriate to analyse the data using a *t*-test?

(e) A personality researcher asks you whether 10 students in his class have a mean score significantly greater than the population norm on a standard personality test (with alpha set at .05). The population norm on the test is 100, and the students' scores are 111, 101, 94, 131, 120, 98, 114, 113, 132 and 109. What answer would you give him?

Examining Relationships between Variables: Correlation

A lot of what we have talked about in the last two chapters relates to comparisons between means, and comparing means is what psychologists typically do when they use experimental methodology. However, in a great deal of research investigators confront another interesting question: what is the *relationship* between two variables? For example, how is stress related to heart disease? How is socio-economic status related to intelligence? How is personality related to the judgements people make?

This type of question can be addressed by experiments (as in the previous chapter, where we used an example of the relationship between the amount of physical contact and attraction), but is more typically examined in surveys. In surveys the researchers collect information about variables where there may be many different values for each variable (in the attraction study, for example, lots of different levels of contact, not just two, and lots of different levels of attraction). Surveys also often measure two or more variables, each with multiple levels. We can contrast this with the case of a *t*-test where we have an independent variable with just two levels (a categorical variable) and a dependent variable with multiple levels.

In survey research we often want to know whether two variables vary *together*. In other words, we want to determine whether there is an association between the variables. This is quite different from the example of the within-subjects *t*-test, where we are interested in the question of whether there are informative differences between participants' scores on different measures. In this chapter we want to look at pairs of scores to see whether high scores are consistently associated with high scores (and low scores with low scores) *or* whether high scores are consistently associated with low scores. Where there is a relationship between variables that takes either of these two forms we say there is a *correlation* between the variables.

For any given participant in a correlational study we do not just have that participant's responses on one dependent measure (X). This would be **univariate** data. Instead, we have participants' responses on *pairs of* measures (X and Y). The technical term for this type of data is **bivariate.** The idea of correlation is useful because it helps us make **predictions**. Knowing that there is a relationship between two variables enables us to predict (with some degree of uncertainty) the score on one variable if we know the score on the other variable. This reason for doing statistical analysis is quite different to those we considered in Chapter 8.

Nevertheless, while *t*-tests and correlations are used to address different questions, they can also be seen to be closely related. In fact a between-subjects *t*-test and a correlation can be used for exactly the same purpose. This makes sense if we think of the *t*-test as a way of examining the relationship between an independent and dependent variable – trying to see if variation in the independent variable is associated with variation in the dependent variable.

As an example of some data that we might conduct correlational analysis upon, we can imagine research where we recorded both people's reaction time and the amount of alcohol they consumed in the last three hours. If there is a relationship between these two variables in the sample, then it is possible to predict the score on one variable as long as we know the score on the other variable.

When discussing the relationship between these variables, we would be interested in knowing whether increasing alcohol consumption (AC) is related to longer or shorter reaction times (RT), or whether there is no discernible relationship between these variables. If there is no relationship, then we cannot predict reaction time from knowledge about the amount of alcohol a person has consumed (or vice versa).

---

bivariate Involving the relationship between two variables (roughly speaking, 'variate' is another word for variable).
prediction A common statistical purpose or goal of correlational analyses. The aim is to be able to estimate (with some uncertainty) a person's score on one variable by knowing that person's score on another variable (or variables).
univariate Involving a single variable.

Some basic principles of correlation

One useful way to set about looking at the relationship between any two variables is to draw a **scatterplot**. This is a two-dimensional graph displaying each pair of observations (e.g., each participant's RT and AC). So, let us say our data were as shown in Table 9.1 (where AC is standard units of alcohol consumed in the last 3 hours and RT is reaction time in milliseconds). These data can be represented graphically as in Figure 9.1. Note too, that we could also draw the relationship as in Figure 9.2.

Now just by looking at either of these graphs we can see that there is an obvious relationship between alcohol consumption and reaction time: the higher one of these variables is, the higher the other is. We call this

Table 9.1 Observations from reaction-time study

Participant	AC	RT
1	9	172
2	2	112
3	4	132
4	6	163
5	3	139
6	5	170
7	6	139
8	7	157

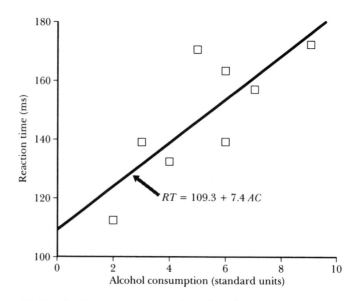

Figure 9.1 Graph of reaction time against alcohol consumption based on data in Table 9.1

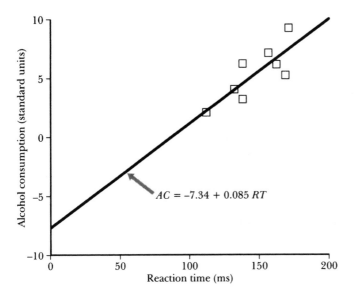

Figure 9.2 Graph of alcohol consumption against reaction time based on data in
Table 9.1

a **positive correlation**. A **negative correlation** is obtained where the
values of one variable decrease as values of the other increase.

These sorts of relationships are **straight-line relationships**. A
straight-line relationship is one where it is possible to draw a straight
line through the scatterplot showing how the variables are related on
average. For this purpose, a straight line and its equation are shown in
Figures 9.1 and 9.2 (although the two lines are different, as we will see,
there is only one value for the correlation).

Two points are important to note here. First, the stronger a positive or
negative relationship is, the less the various points will depart from the
straight line. Second, the smaller such departures are, the more confidently we can estimate or predict one variable on the basis of the other.
So if a perfect positive correlation were found between RT and AC, the
points on the graph would all lie on a straight line going upwards and we
would be able to know from someone's reaction time *exactly* how much
that person had drunk. If we knew how much a person had drunk, we
would also know *exactly* what that person's reaction time would be.

Q9.1*

Which of the following statements is true?

(a) A negative correlation is the same as no correlation.
(b) Scatterplots are a very poor way to show correlations.
(c) If the points on a scatterplot are close to a straight line there will be a
positive correlation.

(d) Negative correlations are of no use for predictive purposes.

(e) None of the above.

The correct answer is (e). All of the other alternatives are nonsense answers. (a) is wrong because a negative correlation involves one variable decreasing as the other increases; this is very different to no relationship. (b) is wrong because scatterplots are in fact an excellent way to show correlations. (c) is wrong because a negative correlation (or even no relationship) is also possible where points fall on a straight line. (d) is wrong because negative relationships are just as useful for predictive purposes as positive ones. The amount people smoke is a predictor of their general physical health, but the relationship between smoking and health is negative.

negative correlation A relationship between variables where high scores on the first variable are associated with low scores on the second variable, and low scores on the first are associated with high scores on the second. Spelling ability and number of spelling errors are negatively correlated because the more spelling ability a person has, the fewer spelling mistakes he or she will make.

positive correlation A relationship between variables where high scores on the first variable are associated with high scores on the second variable, and low scores on the first are associated with low scores on the second. Reading ability and IQ are positively correlated.

scatterplot A two-dimensional graph plotting the scores on one variable against the scores on another.

straight-line relationship A relationship between two variables that can be described by a straight line. The equation for such a line is $y = a + bx$, where b is the slope of the line (its gradient) and a is the y intercept (where it cuts the vertical axis). In Figure 9.1, the equation for the straight line is $RT = 109.3 + 7.4AC$. Accordingly, you can see that the line cuts the vertical axis at 109.3 and that for every two standard units of alcohol consumed, reaction time increases by about 15 milliseconds (i.e., about $2 * 7.4$).

The measurement of correlation

Correlations are generally measured in terms of statistics called **correlation coefficients** and the most commonly used of these is the **Pearson product-moment correlation**. This usually goes by the more user-friendly label, **Pearson's r**. The value of r indicates how strong a correlation is, and it can vary between −1.00 (a perfect negative correlation) and +1.00 (a perfect positive correlation). If there is no correlation the value of Pearson's r will be close to zero.

As with t-tests, computation of Pearson's r involves going through a series of standard steps. In essence, these allow us to establish the extent to which high scores on one variable are associated with high scores on the other, and low scores on one variable are associated with low scores on the other.

The formula for Pearson's r is:

$$r_{xy} = \frac{\sum(X - \bar{X})(Y - \bar{Y})}{\sqrt{\sum(X - \bar{X})^2 \sum(Y - \bar{Y})^2}} \quad \begin{array}{l} \text{(information term)} \\[1em] \text{(error term)} \end{array}$$

This is called the mean-deviation version of the formula for correlation. The terms on the top line of this formula, the information term, express **covariance**. Covariances reflect how much scores vary in the same way. As you can see by inspecting the top line of the equation closely, the covariance term is the sum of the product of differences between each participant's score and the mean score for each variable.

Each participant's contribution to covariance will therefore be close to zero when the difference between each score and the mean is close to zero for both variables. The contribution to covariance will have a large positive value when scores on both variables are well above the mean or when scores on both variables are well below the mean (because multiplying two negative numbers gives a positive number). The contribution to covariance of a pair of scores will have a large negative value when the participant has a score on one variable that is well below the mean and a score on the other variable that is well above the mean.

The sum of all these contributions to covariance for the sample will be a large positive number when there are lots of positive contributions, and will be a large negative number when there are lots of negative contributions. It will be close to zero where there is a balance of positive and negative contributions or where there are lots of small contributions.

The bottom line of the equation is an error term relating to the variances of the two variables (remember from Chapter 6 that variances are related to the sum of the squares of the deviation). Correlation is therefore an expression of *covariance relative to dispersion*. In effect, correlation is a *standardized* covariance. If there is large positive or negative covariance we can still have a correlation coefficient that is close to zero if the amount of random error (descriptive uncertainty) is large. Note also that the error term does not contain a $\sqrt{N}$ term. For this reason the law of large numbers or sample size does not affect the size of the correlation.

Although this appears quite complex, we can summarize the 'message' of the mean-deviation formula for correlation as follows. The correlation coefficient will have a large positive value when *both* scores for a participant tend to be above the mean or below the mean, and the size of the deviations relative to the mean are large compared to the standard deviations for the variables. On the other hand, the correlation coefficient will tend to have a large negative value when participants tend to have a score that is below the mean for one variable and a score that is above the mean for the other variable, and the size of the deviations is also large relative to the standard deviations.

It is useful to illustrate these points with some data. Let us imagine that we ask three women how many times they went to the theatre last year (variable X) and how many hours they spent watching television yesterday (variable Y). Imagine that their responses were respectively 11 times and 1 hour, 6 times and 5 hours, and once and 6 hours. The mean for X ($\bar{X}$) is 6.0 times and the mean for Y ($\bar{Y}$) is 4.0 hours. The other calculations we need to carry out are shown in the following table:

Participant	X	$(X - \bar{X})$	$(X - \bar{X})^2$	Y	$(Y - \bar{Y})$	$(Y - \bar{Y})^2$	$(X - \bar{X})(Y - \bar{Y})$
1	11	5	25	1	−3	9	−15
2	6	0	0	5	1	1	0
3	1	−5	25	6	2	4	−10
$\sum =$			50			14	−25
Mean =	6			4			

From the final column in this table, we can see that Participant 1 contributes negative covariance because her score on Variable X (i.e., 11) is larger than the mean for X (6) and her score on Variable Y (1) is lower than the mean for Y (4). Similarly, Participant 3 contributes negative covariance because her score on Variable X (1) is smaller than the mean (6) and her score on Y (6) is greater than the mean (4). On the other hand, Participant 2 contributes zero covariance because although there is a positive difference between her score on Variable Y and the mean for Y (in this case, $5 - 4 = 1$), her score for Variable X is equal to the mean for Variable X (both $= 6$). Zero multiplied by any number yields zero. However, as a result of the high negative contributions to covariance yielded by Participants 1 and 3, and providing that random error is small for the sample, the overall data for the three women will yield a sizeable negative correlation.

Although it is possible to work out Pearson's *r* by comparing each score on a variable to the mean score on that variable, it is actually much easier to obtain values of this statistic by applying a computational formula. This only requires calculation of the sums and of the sums of squares for X and Y (i.e., $\sum X, \sum X^2, \sum Y$ and $\sum Y^2$) and the sum of products ($\sum XY$). Using these summed terms, Pearson's *r* may be calculated from the formula:

$$r = \frac{N \sum XY - (\sum X \sum Y)}{\sqrt{(N \sum X^2 - (\sum X)^2)(N \sum Y^2 - (\sum Y)^2)}}$$

This formula looks like a bit of a monster, but it is relatively straightforward to apply, as we shall illustrate using the data from Table 9.1 (denoting alcohol consumption as X and reaction time as Y). Our calculation would look like this (see also Section A.3 in Appendix A):

Participant	X	X^2	Y	Y^2	XY
1	9	81	172	29 584	1548
2	2	4	112	12 544	224
3	4	16	132	17 424	528
4	6	36	163	26 569	978
5	3	9	139	19 321	417
6	5	25	170	28 900	850
7	6	36	139	19 321	834
8	7	49	157	24 649	1099
$N = 8$	$\sum X = 42$	$\sum X^2 = 256$	$\sum Y = 1184$	$\sum Y^2 = 178\,312$	$\sum XY = 6478$

$$r = \frac{N \sum XY - (\sum X \sum Y)}{\sqrt{(N \sum X^2 - (\sum X)^2)(N \sum Y^2 - (\sum Y)^2)}}$$

$$= \frac{(8 * 6478) - (42 * 1184)}{\sqrt{(8 * 256 - (42)^2)(8 * 178\,312 - (1184)^2)}}$$

$$= \frac{51\,824 - 49\,728}{\sqrt{(2048 - 1764)(1\,426\,496 - 1\,401\,856)}}$$

$$= \frac{2096}{\sqrt{284 * 24\,640}}$$

$$= \frac{2096}{2645.33}$$

$$= .79$$

We have now obtained a value for a correlation coefficient (*r*). The further away from 0 this value is, the more highly correlated two scores are. The maximum value the correlation can have is 1 and the minimum value is −1. The obtained value of *r* is a descriptive statistic like a mean or standard deviation. The only difference is that whereas the mean and standard deviation describe a single variable, the correlation coefficient describes the relationship between two variables. In the next section we discuss how to interpret this statistic.

Although in this section we have only discussed the product-moment correlation coefficient, it is worth noting that there are in fact many other types of correlation. Some of these are special cases of Pearson's *r* and produce the same results, so we have not discussed them for reasons of brevity and clarity. Others are useful where particular assumptions associated with this form of correlation are violated or where the data take a different form (e.g., where they are nominal or ordinal). We will talk about these assumptions later in this chapter.

Q9.2**

If a calculation of Pearson's *r* yields a value of −.96, which of the following statements is *false*?

(a) The observed correlation between variables is negative.
(b) There is a small amount of negative covariance between variables relative to random error.
(c) A high score on one variable is associated with a low score on the other.
(d) This correlation is useful for predictive purposes.
(e) Points on a scatterplot would resemble a straight line.

The correct answer is (b). The observed correlation between variables is negative (as the sign indicates) which means that high scores on one variable are associated with low scores on another. The maximum absolute value *r* can have is 1.00, and as this correlation is quite close to this maximum it will be very useful for predictive purposes and clearly resemble a straight line on a scatterplot (this point is actually demonstrated by the example in Section A.3). Furthermore, the high value of *r* indicates that the information to error ratio is *high* – in other words, there is a *large* amount of negative covariance between variables relative to random error.

correlation coefficient A measure of the degree of linear association between two variables.
covariance The degree to which scores above the mean on one variable are associated with scores above the mean on another variable.

A negative covariance arises where scores above the mean on one variable are associated with scores below the mean on the other variable. ***Correlation coefficients*** are standardized covariances, that is, correlation coefficients also take random error into account.

Pearson's product-moment correlation coefficient A commonly used measure of association between variables that involves the ratio of the ***covariances*** of scores and the product of the standard deviations of the variables.

Pearson's *r* Another name for ***Pearson's product-moment correlation coefficient***.

Interpreting and making inferences about correlations

We have already noted that an *r*-value of +1 indicates a perfect positive correlation, and an *r* value of −1 indicates a perfect negative correlation. In both these cases the value of one variable can be predicted precisely for any value of the other variable. On the other hand, an *r*-value of 0 indicates there is no reliable relationship between the variables at all. These points are demonstrated in Figure 9.3.

As in Chapter 8 when we discussed the interpretation of effect sizes, Cohen's (1977) overview provides a useful guide for interpreting correlations with absolute values that lie between 0 and 1. If *r* has an absolute value between .1 and .3 then the effect can be said to be of small size. If the absolute value of *r* is between .3 and .5 it is of moderate size, and if it is greater than .5 it is of large size. With a reasonable number of participants (e.g., more than 100), correlations of .3 and greater should be apparent to the naked eye in a scatterplot.

As well as allowing us to say how strong a relationship between two variables is, correlations also provide us with additional information about

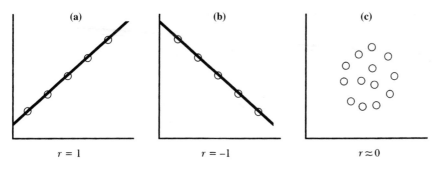

Figure 9.3 Graphs showing *r*-values of (a) +1.00, (b) −100 and (c) 0.00

the proportion of variance in one variable that is associated with variation in the other variable. This is illustrated in Figure 9.4, where the total amount of variation in each variable is represented by a circle. The overlap of these circles represents correlation between the variables.

This representation makes sense when we think about what a relationship between the variables means. If two variables are correlated then that means they are varying in the same way. This is the same as saying that if you know the value of one variable you know something about the value of the other. This is true of both positive and negative correlations. The degree to which two variables vary in the same way is called **common variance**. In fact, the square of the correlation (r^2) provides a measure of the common variance in two variables. This is the amount of overlap between the variables in Figure 9.4.

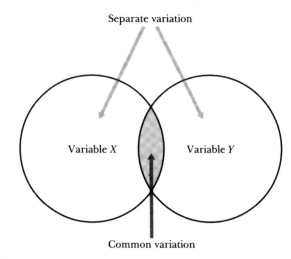

Figure 9.4 The common variance between two variables

Because r is squared we have a measure of common variance that works for positive and negative correlations (because r^2 is always positive). We can then multiply this by 100 to express it as a percentage. For the example above, using the alcohol consumption/reaction time data, a correlation of .79 is associated with $.79^2 = .63$ or 63% of the common variance. What this tells us is that variation in the number of alcoholic drinks a person has consumed in the last 3 hours is associated with 63% of the variation in a person's reaction time.

A correlation of this size is large enough to be very useful in many circumstances. In the hypothetical study of alcohol consumption and reaction time the researchers knew how much each participant had drunk. But imagine that they did not have this information and wanted to estimate how much alcohol a person had consumed when the only thing they knew was the person's reaction time. This is exactly the situation that a police force might find itself in if it were developing a test to discover whether drivers had consumed too much alcohol. The test would only be useful if it could be shown that it was associated with a high proportion of the variation in alcohol consumption.

On the other hand, low correlations mean that variation in one variable is only associated with a very limited amount of the variation in the other variable. Put another way, if the correlation between two variables (say, shoe size and IQ) is less than .1 then variation in one variable is associated with less than 1% of the variation in the other. This means that more than 99% of changes in the value of one variable will be associated with things *other than* change in the second variable. Similarly, a correlation of .3 between two variables means that they have less than 10% of variance in common (because $.3^2 = .09$ or 9%), implying that more than 90% of the variation in one variable is associated with things other than variation in the other variable.

In these two examples the percentages 99% and 90% represent separate variation. One way of thinking about what these numbers mean is to note that they represent the amount of variation in one variable that would still be observed if the other variable were held constant (i.e., fully controlled). So if you conducted research with people of identical shoe size, those people's IQ would still vary almost as much (99% as much) as it would if you sampled from the entire population (when shoe size was not controlled). However, if two variables are perfectly correlated (i.e., $r = \pm1$) then when one variable is held constant there will be no variation in the other at all.

Under some circumstances, as well as wanting to know how large a correlation is, we will want to make inferences about correlations. These inferences are similar to those we seek to make when conducting *t*-tests. In particular, if we are using a hypothesis-testing approach like that outlined in the previous chapter, we will want to know whether any relationship we observe is a chance event (the null hypothesis) or whether it represents a relationship so strong that it is unlikely to have occurred by chance (the alternative hypothesis).

In other words, we want to make an inference about the correlation coefficient for the *population* (this coefficient is denoted by the Greek letter ρ, pronounced 'rho'). Following the logic outlined in the previous chapter, the null hypothesis is that there is *no* relationship between the variables in the population (i.e., $H_0 : \rho = 0$), and the two-tailed alternative hypothesis is that there *is* a relationship ($H_1 : \rho \neq 0$). A one-tailed alternative hypothesis would be either that there is a positive correlation (i.e., $\rho > 0$) or that there is a negative correlation (i.e., $\rho < 0$).

In order to see whether the obtained value of r is significantly different from one produced by chance we first calculate the degrees of freedom. For correlations, the degrees of freedom are equal to the number of observations minus two (i.e., $df = N - 2$). We then look at Table C.3 in Appendix C for the largest tabulated value of r which our obtained value of r exceeds for that number of degrees of freedom and see whether the corresponding probability level is less than a pre-determined alpha level. In our worked example, the obtained correlation of .79 with 6 degrees of freedom is greater than the critical value of r for $\alpha = .02$ (i.e., .789) but it is less than the critical value of r for $\alpha = .01$ (i.e., .834). So in this example, the correlation would be significant – and we would reject the null hypothesis that there was no relationship between the variables in the population – if our alpha level were .05 or .02. However, it would not be significant – and we would not reject the null hypothesis – if our alpha level were .01.

Following common usage, we recommend that the results of these significance tests should always be assessed alongside their effect sizes. To be useful, correlations normally need to be of at least moderate size (i.e., with an absolute value of at least .3) and unlikely to have arisen from random error (in other words, they should be statistically significant). In itself, statistical significance is not really sufficient. This is because with large sample sizes a very small correlation will be statistically significant. For example, with a sample size of 1000 an r greater than .081 in absolute value will be significant at an alpha level of .01, even though, for reasons we have already outlined, this correlation is associated with less than 1% of the total variance. The whole process of using hypothesis-testing and effect-size methods to deal with correlations is summarized in Section A.3 of Appendix A.

Q9.3*

As part of a psychology assignment, Kate has to calculate Pearson's r to measure the strength of association between two variables. She finds that $r = -.2$ and that this is significant at an alpha level of .05. What should she conclude?

(a) That there is a significant but small relationship between the two variables.

(b) That there is a non-significant but large relationship between the variables.

(c) That there is a significant and moderate relationship between the variables.

(d) That the two variables are unrelated.

(e) That variation in one variable is associated with most of the variation in the other.

The correct answer is (a). A correlation with an absolute value between .1 and .3 is a small relationship by Cohen's (1977) criteria, but the relationship is also significant (by the criterion of $\alpha = .05$). It follows, then, that (b) is wrong. (c) is wrong because a moderate correlation needs to have an absolute value greater than or equal to .3 (and less than .5). (d) is wrong for the reasons that make (a) correct. (e) is wrong because the amount of variation in one variable associated with variation in the other is only $-.2^2$ (i.e., .04). Therefore the common variance between variables is associated with only 4% of the total variance. In other words, 96% of the variation in one variable is associated with factors other than variation in the other variable.

common variance The amount of variation in one variable associated with variation in another variable (or variables). In the bivariate case this is given by r^2.

Some notes of caution

When we calculate correlations there are quite a few things that we need to be wary of. This is partly because, as with t-tests, the process of making inferences from correlations involves *assumptions*. If these are violated it will be imprudent to proceed without first taking steps to rectify the problem (if that is possible). The values you obtain for correlations are also affected by the sizes of the variance and the range of scores that are included in the analysis. Similarly, when we do research using correlation we must always be wary of the *correlational fallacy*.

An assumption of correlation is that there is a straight-line relationship between y and x of the form $y = a + bx$ (where a is the y intercept and b is the slope of the line). These straight lines are called *regression lines* and the slopes of these lines are called **regression coefficients**. An associated assumption is that the variables will jointly have a **bivariate normal distribution**. In practice, this means that a scatterplot of the relationship between the variables will have a cigar-shaped (i.e., elongated oval) form like that in Figure 9.5.

A particular problem arises when the overall pattern of the data is distorted by a few points that are very different from the others.

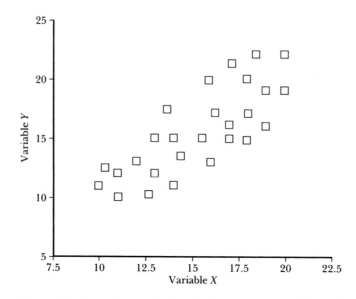

Figure 9.5 Cigar-shared relationship between two variables, characteristic of the bivariate normal distribution

These points are outliers, and in scatterplots we refer to them as *bivariate outliers* (because they are outliers in a plot of two variables and not just one). These outliers can have a disproportionate influence on the size of the correlation coefficient. In particular, if the outliers do not fit the straight-line relationship then a lower correlation coefficient will result – essentially because the outliers increase the amount of variance in the data.

Bivariate outliers are best detected by plotting the data. Indeed, the need to check that outliers are not present is another reason for starting any correlational analysis by drawing a scatterplot. The black square in Figure 9.6 gives an example of a bivariate outlier that would result in a lower correlation coefficient.

The bivariate normal distribution will not apply, and therefore this assumption of the correlation procedure does not hold, where there is a *nonlinear* relationship between the two variables. What happens, then, when variables are not related to each other by a function of the form $y = a + bx$ but instead $y = a + bx^2$? As you may recall from high-school mathematics, this is a simplified version of the equation for a parabola, which results in a curve like that in Figure 9.7.

Where we encounter a **curvilinear relationship** like this, our procedures for computing the product-moment correlation coefficient break down. If a curvilinear relationship exists in the scatterplot then it is inappropriate to compute the correlation coefficient. Sometimes it is

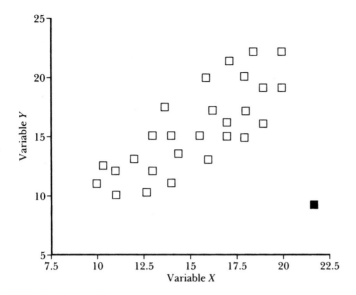

Figure 9.6 A bivariate outlier

possible to transform one of the variables (e.g., by taking the square root of all the Y-values) so that the relationship becomes linear. Having done this, we can compute r.

Another case where the relationship between variables will not yield a scatterplot with the desired cigar-shaped distribution occurs where we sample only a narrow band of participants from a wide population. Even though the bivariate normal distribution may apply to

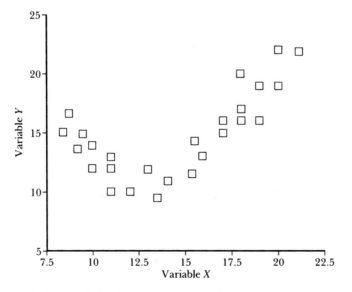

Figure 9.7 Nonlinear relationship between two variables

the relationship between the variables in the population in general, the
relationship may not be shown in our particular sample. This is because
correlations can be greatly changed if participants are sampled from a
restricted part of the range of the scores. This principle of **restricted
range** is illustrated in Figure 9.8 which shows a hypothetical correlation between the number of hours of study for a statistics test (Variable
X) and the mark obtained (Variable Y) for a sample drawn from the
entire class (the whole graph) and for a sample restricted to those who
studied less than 15 hours (the left portion of the graph). In the whole
graph there is a very strong correlation of .87. However, when we
restrict the sample to participants who studied for 15 or fewer hours
(those to the left of the vertical line), we find that the correlation is now
.53, and this is much harder to detect just by looking at the graph.

What is happening in the second case is that the sample is restricted
to a small part of the population – those who did less work. The
relationship between hours of study and the mark obtained is very
strong for the entire class, but for those who studied only a relatively
small amount the relationship is much weaker. The point here is that
even though a bivariate normal relationship can exist for the entire
population, that relationship need not be evident for all sub-popula-
tions. Similarly, what looks like a linear relationship for a restricted
range could really be a curvilinear relationship for the entire population. This applies in Figure 9.9 where the relationship across all values
of X is curvilinear, but becomes linear if we restrict the sample to those

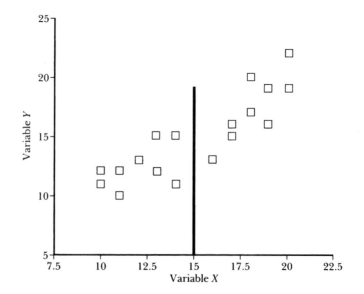

Figure 9.8 The effect of restricted range on correlation

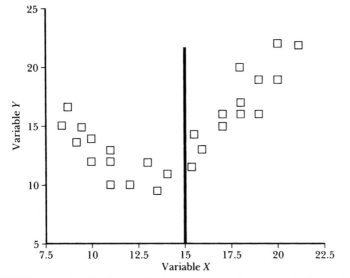

Figure 9.9 Two restricted sub-samples showing strong linear correlations, where the relationship across both samples is curvilinear

with scores over 15. The only way to deal with these potential difficulties is to sample over as wide a range of the population as possible.

One of the consequences of making predictions based on the linear approach is that when we sample a restricted range of scores on one variable we may forget the effect of that restriction. Let us say that we took a group of people with a full range of scholastic achievement at high school and sent them all to a local university. After a semester at university we would probably find that the top 10% at university were not the same as the top 10% at school. On average, relative to the rest of the class, the ranking of those who were in the top 10% at school would have declined. The good news, however, is that the people in the bottom 10% at school would have improved (on average) relative to the rest of the class.

Having obtained such results it would be tempting to think of possible explanations for these changes in performance. Perhaps the top 10% were over-confident and did not try as hard at university, or perhaps university and school performance are based on different skills. These and other explanations are quite plausible, but they are more specific versions of a more general phenomenon – the phenomenon of *regression to the mean* that we discussed when dealing with issues of sampling and experimental design in Chapter 4.

This problem rears its head in this case because the top 10% in the class at school *cannot do any better* at university than the top 10%

of positions that they already have. If there is any variation whatsoever, then it can only lead to their doing worse on average (if there is absolutely no variation their performance will only stay the same). The effect of this is that mean performance on the second measure – in this case, university performance – will be closer to the mean for the sample. This applies to extreme scores wherever variables are not perfectly correlated. If it affects extreme scores at the top of the scale it is an example of one type of **ceiling effect** (referring to the fact that scores cannot get any higher) and if it affects scores at the bottom of the scale it is an example of a **floor effect** (referring to the fact that scores cannot get any lower).

Regression to the mean will occur wherever we take extreme scores from a sample and examine the participants' scores on correlated variables. As we noted in Chapter 4, if proper controls are not in place, this comprises a serious threat to internal validity.

One of the ways that restricted range affects correlations is by changing variance. Correlations are very sensitive to changes in variance. If you look back at the main equation for the correlation coefficient you will see that the error term (the bottom line) contains terms for the standard deviations of each variable. This relationship will be weaker if the standard deviations of the variables are larger. For example, this can occur if measurement in one setting is less reliable than in another. Therefore, before comparing correlations across situations you should be certain that the variances are comparable.

Moving beyond issues of how to conduct correlational procedures, we return to the most common mistake made by researchers when they come to *interpret* correlations. This is the **correlational fallacy** which leads researchers and consumers of research to assume that, because two variables are highly correlated, one must be *responsible* for variation in the other. The important point to reassert is that *correlation does not imply causation*.

To drive this point home, imagine that researchers have conducted a study which reveals a strong positive correlation between the consumption of chocolate and aggressiveness. On this basis it *cannot* be concluded that chocolate causes aggressiveness. This is because the causal relationship between these variables may be *reversed* (aggressiveness may cause people to eat more chocolate), or the relationship may be the product of a *third factor* such as a person's upbringing. That is, certain styles of upbringing (e.g., a totally permissive style of parenting) may encourage chocolate consumption *and* aggressiveness, without each having a direct effect on the other.

There are many examples of spurious correlations that arise from the influence of a third factor like this. One example is the old story about researchers who found that there was a high correlation between the presence of 'spongy tar' in children's playgrounds and the incidence of polio. On this basis the researchers misguidedly claimed that 'spongy tar' caused polio. They urged the schools to dig up their playgrounds to get rid of the offending tar. However, this was a complete waste of time and money, because the researchers' causal analysis was wrong. In fact both spongy tar and polio were caused by a third factor: temperature. Excessively high temperature led to an increase in *both* polio and the sponginess of the tar. To reduce polio, schools needed to control the effects of temperature and not the type of tar in their playgrounds.

This inability to draw strict causal inferences (and the associated temptation to do so) is by far the most serious problem associated with correlational and survey methodology. Even if you learn nothing else from this book, by understanding this vital point you will have learned something that is sometimes forgotten by even the most eminent researchers.

Q9.4[*]

The correlational fallacy refers to which of the following?
(a) The idea that a correlation can be statistically significant without being psychologically meaningful.
(b) The idea that a strong correlation between variables does not mean that one predicts the other.
(c) The idea that a correlation between variables does not mean that one variable is responsible for variation in the other.
(d) The idea that correlation does not justify prediction.

The correct answer is (c). (a) is true, and is an important point, but it is not the correlational fallacy. (b) and (d) are false because a strong correlation does imply that one variable predicts the other and that prediction is justified.

bivariate normal distribution A straight-line relationship between two variables with a cigar-shaped dispersion.

ceiling effect A barrier to the correct interpretation of results that arises when scores cannot increase because they are already clustered in the region of the maximum scale value.

correlational fallacy The mistaken belief that because two variables are related one variable must cause the other.

curvilinear relationship A curved relationship between variables
   that is not well described by a straight line.

floor effect A barrier to the correct interpretation of results that arises
   when scores cannot decrease because they are already clustered in the
   region of the minimum scale value.

regression coefficient The slope of a regression line (b in the equation
   $y = a + bx$). For a two-variable case, the standardized regression
   coefficient (β) will be equal to the correlation coefficient. This means
   that the correlation between two variables will be the same regardless
   of the regression line.

restricted range Selecting part of the sample so that there is not a full
   range of scores on a variable being measured.

Conclusion

In this chapter we have only scratched the surface of the uses and
possible forms of correlational analysis. We have, however, mapped out
the basic principles necessary for calculating and interpreting correlations. We have also suggested some of the pitfalls that correlational
research needs to avoid, such as changes in variance, restricted range,
regression to the mean, and the correlational fallacy.

The last of these things is by far the most important. It is easy to
overlook, but when designing your own research and evaluating that of
other people you should always look to see whether causal inferences
are being made on the basis of correlational evidence. You should do
this regardless of whether the research under consideration is referred to
as a survey or an experiment – remembering that many experiments
are really quasi-experiments.

Further reading

Over the past few years correlation and regression techniques have become
much more popular as a means of analysing psychological data. Cohen's
(1988) book provides a very good introduction to this area which underlines
the importance of looking beyond statistical significance. Miles and Shevlin's
(2001) text provides a good user-friendly introduction to the possibilities of
such analysis and to the various ways in which it can be conducted.

Cohen, J. (1988). *Statistical power analysis for the behavioral sciences* (2nd ed.).
   Hillsdale, NJ: Erlbaum.

Miles, J., & Shevlin, M. (2001). *Applying regression and correlation: A guide for
   researchers and students*. London: Sage.

Correlations: A checklist for research evaluation and improvement

Potential problem	Question to ask	Potential improvement
Inferential uncertainty about a relationship between variables	Do researchers want to examine the relationship between scores on one variable and those on another variable when the population parameters are unknown?	As set out in Section A.3 of Appendix A, divide the sum of the covariances (the sum of the product of differences between each participant's score and the mean score for each variable) by the square root of the error variance (the product of the squared differences between each participant's score and the mean score for each variable). This procedure creates an r-score and – having calculated the degrees of freedom (the sample size minus two) – Table C.3 in Appendix C can be used to provide information about the probability (p) of observing by chance an r-score as large as the one obtained.
Significance fallacy	If the researchers are using a hypothesis-testing approach to correlation, have they distinguished appropriately between psychological and statistical significance?	Consider significance levels in conjunction with effect sizes (e.g., compare p and r). Be alert to the dangers of making too much of statistically significant correlations when effect sizes are low.
Bivariate outliers	Have the researchers tested for the presence of bivariate outliers that might be affecting the correlation?	Draw a scatterplot to identify bivariate outliers. If any are present and they appear likely to have an undue influence on the correlation, consider either (a) removing them or (b) recoding them so that they have the values of the nearest non-outlier. Ensure you report any transformations that you make.
Non-linearity	Is the relationship between variables linear?	Draw a scatterplot and see if data fall on a straight line. If they do not, be

Potential problem	Question to ask	Potential improvement
		alert to the limitations of tests for linear relationships.
Restricted range	Have the researchers sampled across a full range of potential values for a given variable?	Consider values of variables that have *not* been sampled and consider whether the study is compromised by failing to include these.
Ceiling effects	Is a relationship between variables affected by the fact that scores on one or both variables cannot get any higher?	Try to understand what is constraining responses on the affected variables. If possible, suggest alternative measures.
Floor effects	Is a relationship between variables affected by the fact that scores on one or both variables cannot get any lower?	Try to understand what is constraining responses on the affected variables. If possible, suggest alternative measures.
Correlational fallacy	Have the researchers implied that one variable causes another on the basis of a correlation?	Suggest alternative interpretations of the correlation. Consider conducting experimental studies that might address isssues of causality.

Q9.5*

A group of researchers conduct some research in which they identify a significant positive correlation ($r = .42$) between the number of children people have and their life satisfaction. Which of the following is it *inappropriate* to conclude from this research?

(a) That having children makes people more satisfied with their life.
(b) That someone who has children is likely to be more happy than someone who does not.
(c) That the causes of life satisfaction are unclear.
(d) That the consequences of having children are unclear.
(e) That it is possible to predict someone's life happiness partly on the basis of the number of children they have.

Q9.6**

Which of the following statements is true of the problem of restricted range?

(a) Restricted range can reduce the size of correlations.
(b) Restricted range can lead to a violation of the assumption of bivariate normality.
(c) Restricted range can produce regression to the mean.
(d) All of the above.
(e) Answers (a) and (b) only.

Q9.7**

If an experimenter observes a correlation of −1 between two variables which of the following is *false?*

(a) One variable is completely predictive of the other.
(b) One variable is completely responsible for variation in the other.
(c) Knowledge of the value of one variable allows one to know with certainty the value of the other.
(d) A higher score on one variable is associated with a lower score on the other.
(e) All the variation in one variable is associated with variation in the other.

Q9.8**

If the correlation between people's wealth and a measure of their psychological well-being is .40, how much of the variation in their scores on the well-being measure will be associated with variation in their wealth?

(a) 60%
(b) 40%
(c) 16%
(d) 4%
(e) It is impossible to say without information about how psychological well-being is defined.

The correct answer to 9.5 is (a). This statement is an expression of the correlational fallacy. Answers (c) and (d) are true because they recognize that correlation does not imply causation. Answers (b) and (e) are true because they merely point out that the existence of a correlation can be a basis for making predictions.

The correct answer to 9.6 is (d). (a) and (b) are correct because restricted range can lead to violations of the assumption of bivariate normality and the effect of this can be to reduce correlations. This is primarily because the cigar shape across the entire distribution can be lost over a shorter range. (c) is correct because although regression to the mean is often thought of as a different sort of problem, if the range is restricted to the extreme end of the population then scores on a second measure will be closer to the mean. If (c) is correct, (e) must be incorrect.

The correct answer to 9.7 is (b). This statement is false because it implies that correlation (even when it is perfect) allows researchers to infer causality. Although perfect correlation does not allow people to make causal inferences, it does allow them to know with absolute certainty scores on one variable on the basis of scores on the other (as suggested by statements (a) and (c)). In other words, 100% of the variation in one variable is associated with variation in the other (as suggested in statement (e)). Because the correlation is negative, a high score on one variable will be associated with a low score on the other – so statement (d) is true.

The correct answer to 9.8 is (c). The square of the correlation coefficient (r^2) is a measure of the common variance between two variables. This gives a direct indication of the amount of variation in one variable that is associated with variation in the other. In this case $r^2 = .4^2$, which comes to .16, or 16% of the total variance. It is certainly true that a researcher might want to question the validity of a particular measure of psychological well-being, but this does not affect the correlation between that measure and another and thus does not affect their amount of common variance – so (e) is not an appropriate answer.

Discussion/essay questions

(a) Why is it helpful to create scatterplots in preliminary analysis of correlations?

(b) What is the difference between a statistically significant and a psychologically significant correlation? Is this distinction important?

(c) If correlations allow researchers to say nothing about causation, why are they of any interest?

(d) In the wrong hands, few statistics are more dangerous than a correlation. Discuss.

Exercises

(a) The data in the table below were obtained from 12 participants in an experiment. The participants were of different ages, and scores were obtained on three dependent variables (speed, attention and accuracy). Draw scatterplots and calculate the correlation between the participants' age and each of these three dependent variables.

Age	Speed (m/s)	Attention	Accuracy
10	150	2	2
11	160	1	3
11	165	1	2
12	155	2	4
12	140	4	1
12	130	3	5
13	120	4	3
13	135	1	7
14	130	3	3
14	115	3	5
15	110	2	6
16	120	3	5

(b) Use the hypothesis-testing method to establish whether each of the above three correlations is statistically significant at the .01 level.

(c) Based on Cohen's criteria, how would you describe the effect size of each of the above three correlations?

(d) Based on these data, how much of the variation in a child's response speed is associated with variation in their age?

(e) A researcher conducts a longitudinal study and administers a test of reading ability to 10 children at age 9 and then three years later at age 12. The data are shown in the table below:

	Age	
Participant	9 years	12 years
1	10	13
2	10	15
3	11	12
4	11	9
5	14	17
6	15	18
7	12	17
8	14	16
9	11	15
10	9	12

(i) The researcher wishes to find out whether there has been a change in the reading ability of the children as they have grown older. She expects a large change. Is she correct?

(ii) She also wishes to know whether there is a relationship between reading ability at age 9 and age 12. She expects the two reading ability scores to be highly correlated. Again, is she correct?

(iii) How is it possible for reading ability to change over time but the scores of the children at the different ages to be correlated?

10

Comparing Two or More Means by Analysing Variances: ANOVA

In Chapter 8 we saw how it was possible to compare two means. The statistical procedure that we addressed in some detail was the *t*-test. We saw in that chapter, though, that this procedure is limited to comparing just two means at a time. The *t*-test is fine for giving us an insight into whether the mean scores of two groups are plausibly different or whether the mean scores of the same group on two variables are different, but it has its limits.

In particular, what should we do when we need to compare more than two means? The typical case where we might to do this is where we have conducted an experiment involving many conditions. Participants in each group have been randomly assigned to a particular condition of an experiment. The conditions (representing different levels of the experimental **factors**) can be considered as levels of a categorical independent variable (or variables) and we want to know whether this variable (or variables) has affected some dependent variable which we have measured. That is, does our independent variable have an effect on the dependent variable – in other words, does the treatment make a difference?

One solution that might occur to you is that because you have lots of means to compare you could perform lots of *t*-tests. Thus, if we had the means for three groups (we can call them groups A, B and C) we could do three *t*-tests comparing A with B, A with C, and B with C. This approach has two problems that we can address here, the first of which is quite easy to see. Each of the three *t*-tests combined gives us a clue as to whether two means are different (e.g., that memory is better with high practice than with low practice), but no single test helps us to establish whether there are differences between the three conditions in general. Often it is helpful to try to reach one overall conclusion about whether there are such overall differences.

The second problem is much less obvious, and it relates to the logic of significance testing. As we have been at pains to point out, significant results are never open-and-shut cases for the simple reason that they do not directly answer the questions we are interested in. Instead they only give us clues to those answers. They involve making decisions one way or the other on the basis of fuzzy evidence. This means that sometimes results are significant when they should not be (remember from the previous chapter that this is called a Type I error) and sometimes they are not significant when they should be (Type II errors). The problem is that when you do lots and lots of significance tests the chance of making a Type I error increases.

If we use an alpha level of .05 then the probability of a Type I error if we only do one test is also .05. Now think of a Type I error as one bad apple in a constantly replenished fruit bowl that always contains 20 apples. Each statistical test is like drawing an apple from the bowl. If we only draw one apple then our chance of getting a bad one on that draw is .05. However, as we do more tests then the chance that at least one of them will be significant increases. If we draw enough apples then, unless we are really lucky, sooner or later we are going to get a bad one. Similarly, if we did lots of *t*-tests on means sampled from the same distribution then we would find that some of them would be significant purely by chance (equivalent to a bad apple — and as with apples, one bad test can spoil all the others). Now we could protect against this possibility by reducing our alpha level (e.g., from .05 to .01) but this creates the opposite problem — we may miss detecting differences that should be significant.

This is quite a tricky problem and we will return to it later in the chapter. In order to get to that point, however, we need to explain some procedures for comparing more than two means that get around these problems. These procedures involve analysing variance.

> **factors** Another term for independent variables. The term is used to describe design features of studies whose data are subjected to analysis of variance.

Analysing variances

If we are interested in comparing means, why do we need to analyse variances? The answer is that variances are highly informative about the way variables behave. After all, they are called 'variables' and not 'meanables'.

Why are variances so informative then? Remember that the variance is the square of the standard deviation and reflects the amount of dispersion in the variable. There is more dispersion when the scores all tend to be quite different from the mean and there is less dispersion when the scores are all similar to the mean. Another way of saying this is to refer to variance as the descriptive statistical uncertainty in the variable (which can be considered to be due to random error). The mean is simply the position that describes scores on the variable with the least uncertainty. This way of thinking of the relationship between the mean and the variance makes most sense when the variable is normally distributed.

The previous paragraph gives us a hint as to one reason why we might want to compare variances. We might be interested in knowing whether one variable has a bigger variance than another. That is, is variable X associated with more dispersion, error and descriptive uncertainty than variable Y?

Imagine that we wanted to compare the variances of two variables. One obvious way to compare them is to form a ratio. To do this all we need to do is to divide the variance of one variable by the variance of the other. It is convenient to divide the larger variance by the smaller one. A ratio of this form gives us information about whether one variance is larger than another and by what amount. Values close to 1.0 tell us that the variances are about equal, and values much bigger than 1.0 tell us that one variance is much bigger than the other.

As usual, we have the problem that we need to know how big the statistic has to be before we can conclude that it is big enough to be meaningfully different. And again, as usual, statistics are unable to tell us what we would really like to know: 'Is one variance really bigger than the other?' However, statistics might be able to answer another question that gives us a clue to the answer to the question we are interested in.

The related question in this case is this: how plausible is it that the variances we have observed are really estimates of the same population variance? That is, can they be treated as if they were two different samples drawn in the same way (i.e., randomly) from the same population? If the variances are both estimates of the same population variance then they should both be pretty similar and any difference between them will be due to chance variations. That is, if one variable has a higher variance it might be because a few more observations which were quite different from the mean happened to occur on one variable and not the other (just as when digging for gold in the same hole we might turn up dirt one day and a gleaming nugget the next).

In order to examine this issue further we need to know how this ratio-based statistic behaves. More specifically, we need to know more about its sampling distribution. In fact, virtually all of the decisions we make in life are based on our knowledge of sampling distributions, and statistics just formalizes this fact. For example, the fact that you know something about the sampling distribution for gold digging (if you dig in most places you are likely to find a lot of dirt and very little gold) explains why you are currently reading this book rather than digging up your backyard. In the case of comparing variances, we need to know about the sampling distribution of the ratio of variances. As it happens, the behaviour of this sampling distribution is quite well understood, and providing that certain assumptions hold, it follows a particular pattern. This pattern is called the **F-distribution**.

Unlike the normal and the *t*-distribution, the *F*-distribution is not symmetrical. It is positively skewed, so that it has a tail at the right-hand end. If you think about it, it is easy to see part of the reason why the distribution has this shape: it is impossible to have a ratio of variances that is less than zero (a variance is an average sum of squares and a square of a number cannot be negative).

Like the *t*-distribution, the *F*-distribution varies in shape with the number of degrees of freedom. However, there is another complexity here: because the *F*-distribution involves the ratio of two variables we have to worry about degrees of freedom for both the numerator (the top line) *and* the denominator (the bottom line) of the ratio. The degrees of freedom for the numerator and denominator are here both equal to the number of people in the group minus 1 (i.e., $df = n-1$). To compare the variances of two samples each containing 10 observations, the *F*-distribution we need has 9 degrees of freedom in the numerator and 9 in the denominator. *F*-distributions for many combinations of degrees of freedom are given in Table C.4 in Appendix C.

Once we have calculated a value for *F* we can compare this to the distribution and ask what proportion of the *F*-distribution this cuts off. Consider the data from Chapter 8 where we computed the variances for two different groups (control and experimental) to conduct a between-subjects *t*-test. The variance (s_X^2 in the table on page 210) of the experimental group was 2.71 and the variance of the control group was 2.04. We can turn these two variances into a ratio and obtain the *F*-value 1.33. We write *F*-values in the form $F(df_1, df_2)$, where df_1 refers to the numerator degrees of freedom and df_2 to the denominator degrees of freedom, so here $F(9, 9) = 1.33$.

If we assume that these two variances are drawn from a normal population, what we now need to do is check what proportion of the

F-distribution is cut off by this value. We can see from Table C.4 that this value is quite a bit smaller than the critical value given for $F(9, 9)$ with $\alpha = .05$ of 3.18. This suggests that this ratio would not be a particularly unusual one to obtain if the samples really were both drawn from a population with the same variance. A large region is cut off and this implies that it is certainly not implausible that they are estimates of the same population variance.

This procedure has allowed us to compare variances. In doing so it gives us some guidance about the extent to which the assumptions that we made in Chapter 8 about doing the *t*-test hold. That is, there is no reason to believe that the variances are unequal (though having said that, the actual test for inequality of variances that we used in this case is itself over-sensitive to the assumption of normality that we discussed in Chapter 8).

But having followed all this, you may still be wondering why a discussion of comparing variances is helpful when this chapter is supposed to be about comparing means. The answer is that we can use the *F*-distribution to compare means if we do something rather clever. This clever thing is to recognize that variances are simply average squared deviations. If we choose the right average squared deviations and form the *F*-ratio from them then this ratio can be very informative.

> **F-distribution** The hypothetical distribution of the expected ratio of variability between group means divided by variability within group means.

Comparing multiple means using one-way analysis of variance

In order to use the *F*-distribution to compare means we need to construct a ratio of two variances. Remember that variances are just the average of a sum of squares of the difference between a mean and some observations. So what we want to do is to transform the variances of these two variables into the classic ratio that underpins test statistics. This is of the form:

$$\frac{\text{Information}}{\text{Error}}$$

But what exact ratio do we want to examine here? The short answer is that we want to compare the differences between groups (information) with the differences within groups (error; see the scenario on page 273). If that ratio behaves in an unusual way then we may have something interesting to talk about.

In analysis of variance, though, we do something even more cunning than usual. We actually create a ratio of two estimates of the *same* population variance. If a certain assumption holds true then these estimates should give us similar answers. However, if these estimates are very different then we really have to doubt whether our assumption was correct.

The assumption in question is a null hypothesis that there are no differences between means (they are all estimates of the same population mean). If this assumption is correct then we can estimate the population variance in two ways. The first estimate is quite straightforward and involves an assumption that the population variance should be equal to the pooled variances of the **cells** we are comparing (remember we saw how to calculate the pooled variance in Chapter 8).

The second estimate requires more subtlety. If the null hypothesis is true then the samples are drawn from the same population and any differences between means reflect chance variation. If this is true then all of the means should be estimates of the same population mean (and any differences between them reflect random error). If that is the case the central limit theorem that we discussed in Chapter 7 tells us what this distribution of means should look like.

This distribution of means will have a mean that is equal to the population mean and a variance $(s_{\bar{X}}^2)$ that is equal to the population variance divided by the sample (cell) size (n). It is the variance we are trying to estimate here. If

$$s_{\bar{X}}^2 = s^2/n$$

then if we multiply both sides of the equation by N we see it is also true that

$$s^2 = Ns_{\bar{X}}^2$$

So if we find the variance of the sample means and multiply it by the sample size we will have an estimate of the variance in the population means.

Providing that there are the same number of observations in each group it is reasonably straightforward to come up with this estimate. The variance of the sample means is based on the deviations between means of the groups we are comparing. We find the sum of the squared deviations between the mean for the entire sample and the mean of each group and divide by the number of groups (less one to obtain an unbiased estimate) and then multiply by the number of people in each group.

We can then compare this estimate of the population variance with the estimate of the population variance obtained from pooling the within-cells variances by forming an F-ratio. If the ratio is close to 1.0 we have no reason to reject the null hypothesis, but if the number is much bigger than 1.0 we may be confident in rejecting the null hypothesis and conclude that the means are more variable than they should be if they are indeed drawn from the same population. Clearly, the logic behind the above ideas is quite difficult to follow, so let us make them more concrete with an example.

To start off let us stay with the example we used to discuss the between-subjects t-test in Chapter 8. These data are shown below:

Control group	Experimental group	
4	4	
4	5	
6	7	
5	8	
7	6	
3	9	
4	7	
2	8	
5	5	
4	5	
$\bar{X}_i = 4.40$	6.40	(Grand mean $\bar{X} = 5.40$)
$s_{\bar{X}}^2 = 2.04$	2.71	

We will first look at a very simple way to calculate the F-ratio. We need to estimate the variances of two things (variables) and form a ratio of these variances. The first thing we need to estimate is the variance estimated from the means. We can construct such an estimate by taking the average deviations between the overall or **grand mean** and the cell means.

The unbiased estimate of the variance of the means (with equal cell sizes) is:

$$\Sigma(\bar{X}_i - \bar{X})^2/(k - 1)$$

where k is the number of cells, $\bar{X}_i$ is the mean for each group and $\bar{X}$ is the grand mean. The only problem with this (as noted above) is that the variance of the means will tend to be smaller than the actual variance of the deviations as implied by the central limit theorem (the law of large numbers again). To correct for this we simply need to multiply this variance by the cell size. Such variance estimates are also called **mean squares** or **MS** because the sums of squares are averaged. The mean square we calculate here is called the **between-cells mean square** (the shorthand is MS_B)

$$MS_B = \Sigma n(\bar{X}_i - \bar{X})^2/(k-1)$$

In this case the mean for the control group is 4.40 and the mean for the experimental group is 6.40. Here we can work out that the grand mean pooled across the two groups is 5.40 (because the cell sizes are the same the grand mean is just the average of the cell means – try it and see). So

$$
\begin{aligned}
MS_B &= (10 * (4.40 - 5.40)^2 + (10 * 6.40 - 5.40)^2))/1 \\
&= (10 * 1^2 + 10 * 1^2)/1 \\
&= 20
\end{aligned}
$$

This value is associated with df_B degrees of freedom.

$$df_B = k - 1$$

where k is the number of cells.

As we noted above, the bottom line is an error term, involving the average difference *within* groups. We can find this by just pooling the variances we obtained previously. In Chapter 8 we saw this value was 2.38. It is associated with degrees of freedom df_W

$$df_W = N - k$$

This is the total number of participants minus the number of cells. Where we are only comparing two groups it is the same number as the degrees of freedom used in the between-subjects t-test. In this case

$$df_W = 20 - 2 = 18$$

The F-ratio is found by dividing MS_B by MS_W:

$$F = 20/2.38 = 8.41$$

In order to evaluate this F-ratio we can compare it to the F-distribution with 1 and 18 degrees of freedom given in Table C.4. We can see that this value is larger than the tabulated value for $F(1, 18)$ with $\alpha = .05$ of 4.41. Indeed, it is larger than the value with $\alpha = .01$. If there really were no difference between the groups then we would expect to find a difference that big on less than 1 in 100 random selections of two samples of that size.

Referring back to Chapter 8, we see this gives us a similar answer to the between-subjects t-test. Indeed, providing that there are only two groups to be compared (that is, the numerator has one degree of freedom) there is an exact relationship between t and F in that $F = t^2$ (squaring the t-value of 2.90 gives us 8.41, which is the same value as we obtained from the F-ratio).

It is reassuring that F and t tell us the same thing under these circumstances, but the F ratio really comes into its own when we have more than two groups. So let us imagine that there were another two groups in our design and now go through the same process again. The new groups involve increased interaction between the participant and the target person they are rating, with the result that our extended (four-condition) study is now helping us to see not just whether interaction increases attraction, but whether the amount of interaction increases attraction. If we assume that our standard experimental condition involves a single session (and is renamed the 'one-session condition') then we can see that we now have two more conditions: one in which the participants have two interaction sessions and the other in which they have three interaction sessions.

	Exposure to Target			
	No sessions (control)	One session (experimental)	Two sessions	Three sessions
	4	4	5	9
	4	5	8	6
	6	7	9	9
	5	8	9	7
	7	6	5	6
	3	9	8	6
	4	7	8	7
	2	8	9	9
	5	5	8	8
	4	5	9	8
Mean $\bar{X}$	4.40	6.40	7.80	7.50	Grand mean = 6.525
Variance s_X^2	2.04	2.71	2.40	1.61	Pooled variance = 2.19

In this case because the cell sizes are all the same the grand mean of 6.525 is obtained by averaging the four condition means (4.40, 6.40, 7.80 and 7.50). For the same reason the pooled variance is obtained by averaging the four variances (2.04, 2.71, 2.40 and 1.61).

We now have an experimental design that involves four different conditions. Each of these conditions is made up of a group of participants who have been randomly allocated to that condition. And each condition or cell can be thought of as a level of our independent variable.

In order to compute the F-ratio we need a top line (the numerator or information term) and bottom line (the denominator or error term). Again, our top line here is based on the deviations between each of the cell means and the grand mean multiplied by the number of observations in each cell, divided by the number of groups minus 1. Thus:

$$MS_B = (10 * ((4.4 - 6.525)^2 + (6.4 - 6.525)^2 + (7.8 - 6.525)^2$$
$$+ (7.2 - 6.525)^2))/3$$
$$= (10 * (4.52 + 0.02 + 1.63 + 0.95))/3$$
$$= 10 * 7.11/3$$
$$= 23.69$$

The within-cells variance estimate (the **within-cells mean square**, MS_W) is simply equal to the pooled variance (i.e., 2.19).
Hence

$$F = MS_B/MS_W = 23.69/2.19$$
$$= 10.81$$

The critical value of F with an alpha level of .01 with 3 degrees of freedom in the numerator and 36 in the denominator is 4.38. The fact that our obtained F-value is larger than this suggests that it is implausible that differences between cells as big as those we have obtained would be generated by taking random samples from the same population.

Q10.1[***]

Which of the following is a pooled variance estimate which constitutes the denominator of an F-ratio?

(a) The between-cells mean square (MS_B).
(b) The mean of the sampling distribution.
(c) The sum of the deviations from the grand mean.
(d) The grand mean.
(e) The within-cells mean square (MS_W).

The correct answer is (e). Population variance is estimated using within-cells mean square (MS_W) and between-cells mean squares (MS_B), but it is MS_W which constitutes the denominator. (a) is wrong because the between-cells mean square (MS_B, which is equal to the sum of the squared deviations (SS_B) multiplied by mean cell size and divided by the degrees of freedom for the numerator) constitutes the *numerator* of an *F*-ratio. (c) is wrong because variances are means not sums and in any case deviations from the grand mean are involved in the numerator. The most obvious reason why (b) and (d) are wrong is that *F*-ratios are ratios of *variances* not means.

---

between-cells mean square (MS_B) This is an estimate of variance between cells and provides the numerator of an *F*-ratio.

cells The independent conditions in an experiment. The data in a given cell are thus based on responses from people who are all exposed to identical experimental treatment, and whose treatment differs in some way from that which has contributed to responses in other cells.

grand mean The mean response across all the cells in a given experiment.

mean squares (MS) The average of the sums of squares.

within-cells mean square (MS_W) A measure of variance within groups that is equal to the pooled variance. This is an estimate of population variance and provides the denominator of an *F*-ratio.

Another way to explain analysis of variance: Sums of squares and mean squares

In the previous section we explained analysis of variance as a way of making comparisons between means. Indeed, given the complexity of the material covered, you may be surprised by the claim that we have only introduced one genuinely new concept in this chapter so far, and that is the idea of the *F*-distribution.

This sort of explanation is slightly unusual in a book like this one. Most texts start with a treatment of ANOVA in terms of sums of squares and then move to mean squares (which are the variance estimates we have been talking about). However, we need to cover this terminology too (and not just so that you can have something interesting to say at parties when conversation strays onto the topic of sums of squares in ANOVA). This is because sums of squares have interesting properties and the idea of sums of squares has an extremely wide application in statistics.

A sum of squares is just that. It is the sum of all the squared deviations between a relevant mean and a set of scores. To see what this implies, we can express every score in our data set as the deviation between the score and the overall mean of all the scores. As we saw above, this mean is referred to as the grand mean, and the grand mean is the position that describes the whole set of scores with the least uncertainty.

Why would we express the data in this way? The answer is that once we have identified the grand mean then all of the variability in the data set can be understood as deviations from the grand mean. This gives us a new way of thinking about the score. It is not just a single number with a certain value but it is a deviation from the average position. It is true that thinking about numbers as a mean plus a deviation makes them more complex but it also allows us to do things with those numbers, in particular, to calculate variances.

Where we sum the squares of all the deviations from a grand mean we get a single number that expresses all of the variability that exists in our data set. This single number is the **total sum of squares**. If the data contain lots of values that are smaller than and/or larger than the grand mean then the total sum of squares will tend to be large.

The total sum of squares is useful primarily because it can be divided up in a number of ways. This process is called **partitioning the sum of squares**, and ANOVA can be thought of as a set of procedures for deciding how to do this.

The method for partitioning sums of squares involves deciding on the types or **sources of variation** that you are interested in and then breaking up the total sum of squares into these types. Once we have done this we turn the sums of squares into variance estimates by dividing them by the degrees of freedom. As we saw above, we refer to these new qualities as *mean squares* and we can conduct statistical tests by forming ratios of these mean squares (which, after all, are variances).

In one-way ANOVA we are normally interested in partitioning the total sum of squares into two main sources of variation. The first of these is the **sum of squares between cells** (SS_B, also referred to as the *treatment source*) and the second is the **sum of squares within cells** (SS_W, also referred to as the *error source*).

In fact, the total source (SS_T) is exactly equal to the sum of the between-groups source and the within-groups source so that

$$SS_T = SS_B + SS_W$$

It is easy to see that this is the case by asking what other sort of variation there could be. We have deviations between the scores and their individual group means and we have variations between those group means. What other source of variation could there be that was not completely included within these two? None.

Each of these effects is also associated with a certain number of degrees of freedom. These values are the numbers you divide the sums of squares by to turn them into variance estimates (mean squares). The degrees of freedom can be partitioned in exactly the same way as the sums of squares. Thus:

$$df_T = df_B + df_W$$

As noted earlier in the chapter, the between-cells degrees of freedom (df_B) are equal to the number of cells (minus one to make it unbiased). The within-cells degrees of freedom (df_W) are equal to the total number of observations (minus one per cell to make it unbiased).

To see how all this works, we will return to the two-group example used previously. We have already calculated the between-groups sum of squares $(SS_B = 20)$. The within-cells sum of squares is equal to the average squared deviation between each score and its own group mean. These need to be pooled across all the groups involved. The table below shows the calculation of these average deviations for this example;

Control group, $\bar{X} = 4.40$			Experimental group, $\bar{X} = 6.40$		
X	$X-\bar{X}$	$(X-\bar{X})^2$	X	$X-\bar{X}$	$(X-\bar{X})^2$
4	−0.40	0.16	4	−2.40	5.76
4	−0.40	0.16	5	−1.40	1.96
6	1.60	2.56	7	0.60	0.36
5	0.60	0.36	8	1.60	2.56
7	2.60	6.76	6	−0.40	0.16
3	−1.40	1.96	9	2.60	6.76
4	−0.40	0.16	7	0.60	0.36
2	−2.40	5.76	8	1.60	2.56
5	0.60	0.36	5	−1.40	1.96
4	−0.40	0.16	5	−1.40	1.96
	Σ	18.40			24.40

In order to pool the two contributions to the sum of squares we compute the total sum of all the deviations from group means. The sum of the squared deviations within cells (SS_W) is the sum of the squared deviations within the control group (let us call it SS_{WCG}) and the sum of the squared deviations in the experimental group (SS_{WEG}). Expressed algebraically:

$$SS_W = SS_{WCG} + SS_{WEG}$$

Here

$$SS_W = 18.4 + 24.4 = 42.8$$

To turn this into an unbiased variance estimate we need to divide by the number of observations (minus one for each group that we are pooling a variance from). In the example there are 20 observations, subtracting 2 gives us 18 (which is the number of degrees of freedom in the error term). When we have done this we now have an estimate of variance within groups that we can use as an error term called MS_W.

$$MS_W = 42.8/(20 - 2) = 2.38$$

Notice that this is exactly the same as the pooled variance that we obtained in Chapter 8 for these data. We have just calculated that value by another method.

Once we have divided by the appropriate degrees of freedom we have mean squares for both sources and can form the F-ratio to examine how plausible it is that between-group differences of this size would have been obtained by randomly sampling groups from a single population.

The outcomes of these various steps can be formally summarized in an **ANOVA table**. This has one row for each effect as well as a row for the total. It also has a column for the name of the effect (this is called the **source of variation**), as well as columns for the sum of squares, degrees of freedom, mean square, and F-ratio. We can also include columns for the level of significance and the effect size which we discuss below.

An ANOVA table for the above example would look like this:

Source	SS	df	MS	F	p <	R^2
Between cells (Condition)	20	1	20	8.41		
Within cells	42.8	18	2.38			
Total	62.8	19				

As we will find out later in this chapter, there are other ways to partition the total sum of squares, but for the time being this is sufficient. Any partitioning, however, is only useful to the extent that it allows us to evaluate models. We consider this in the next section.

Q10.2[**]

Which of the following statements is true?

(a) In one-way ANOVA the total sum of squares is comprised of two main sources of variance: within-groups variance and between-groups variance. Each has the same number of degrees of freedom.

(b) In one-way ANOVA the total sum of squares is comprised of two main sources of variance: within-groups variance and between-groups variance. Each has its own number of degrees of freedom.

(c) In one-way ANOVA the total sum of squares is comprised of three main sources of variance: within-groups variance, between-groups variance and error variance. Each has the same number of degrees of freedom.

(d) In one-way ANOVA the total sum of squares is comprised of three main sources of variance: within-groups variance, between-groups variance and information variance. Each has the same number of degrees of freedom.

(e) In one-way ANOVA the total sum of squares is comprised of three main sources of variance: within-groups variance, between-groups variance and information variance. Each has its own number of degrees of freedom.

The correct answer is (b). In one-way ANOVA we are normally interested in partitioning the total sum of squares into two main sources of variation: the between-groups or treatment source (SS_B) and the within-groups or error source (SS_W). Each of these sources has its own degrees of freedom: for the between-groups source it is equal to the number of conditions minus 1 (i.e., $df_B = k-1$), for the within-groups source it is equal to the total number of responses minus 1 for each conditions (i.e., $df_W = N-k$). (a), (c) and (d) are wrong because these degrees of freedom are not the same, but different. Like (e), (c) and (d) are also wrong because there are only two sources of variation; error variance is the same as within-subjects variance and information variance is the same as between-subjects variance.

ANOVA table A summary table that provides key information arising from analysis of variance. Its rows relate to the various *sources of variation* and columns relate to the corresponding sums of squares, degrees of freedom, and mean squares, as well as values of F, p and R^2.

partitioning the sum of squares The process of dividing up the *total sum of squares* in order to identify *sources of variance* in a data set.

sources of variation Components of the *total sum of squares* that are associated with particular features of a research design and partitioned out on this basis. In one-way ANOVA the two sources of variation are within-groups variance (error) and between-groups variance (information).

sum of squares between cells (SS_B) The sum of the squared
    difference between all cell means and the grand mean multiplied by
    the cell size.
sum of squares within cells (SS_W) The sum of the squared difference
    between each individual score and its cell mean.
total sum of squares (SS_T) In analysis of variance, the sum of all the
    squared deviations between individual cells means and the grand
    mean.

How big does a difference need to be? Significance testing and effect sizes

In the case of one-way ANOVA the model which is being evaluated is
that the total sum of squares can be partitioned in a particular way and
that in fact it is desirable to consider it in this way when compared to
the null model that all the variance can be treated as error variance. We
will tend to be less convinced by this null model when our statistical
tests reveal that it is implausible.

In general, the models we are comparing take the following forms.
First, the null hypothesis model is that

$$X = \mu + e_{ij}$$

This says the score for participant j in group i is equal to the grand
mean (μ) plus the deviation of that participant from the grand mean
(assumed to be error). Where this model holds, the expected values of
the ratio of mean squares (the ratio of the average level of the mean
squares over a long run if we were to sample repeatedly) will be distributed according to the F-distribution and will tend to be around 1.0.

The alternative model that we can test asks whether our experimental treatment has an effect. That is, do the groups to which participants are assigned make sufficient difference for us to consider this to
be worthy of comment, attention and explanation? If they do then the
following model would apply:

$$X = \mu_i + e_{ij}$$

That is, the scores will be expressed by the mean for the condition i plus
error. In this case the treatment effect is also expressed as a deviation
from the grand mean. Where this model holds, the ratio of the expected
value of the ratio of mean squares will tend to be greater than 1.0. If it is
sufficiently large we conclude that it is not plausible that the different
groups have all been sampled from the same population, and we can
therefore be more confident that there are differences between groups.

The significance-testing approach to making these decisions involves comparing the support for an alternative hypothesis that there are differences between the means with a null hypothesis of no difference. These have the form

$H_0: \mu_1 = \mu_2 = \mu_3$ etc.

That is, the null hypothesis is that the population mean for Group 1 is the same as that for Group 2 which is the same as that of Group 3 and so on. This is compared with the alternative hypothesis (called the **effects model**)

H_1: not all μs are equal

These hypotheses are evaluated by comparing the observed value of F with the critical value of F for a certain number of degrees of freedom in the numerator and denominator for a particular alpha level (such as .05).

As suggested in the previous section, to find the critical value of F we need to consult Table C.4. If the observed value is greater than the critical value of F then we conclude that the test is significant and we reject the null hypothesis. In the case of the two-group example above, if we set α at .05, then the critical value of $F (1,18)$ is 4.41. Our obtained value $(F = 8.41)$ exceeds this, so we conclude that the test is significant and we reject the null hypothesis. Indeed, our grounds for doing this are especially strong as the obtained F-value exceeds the critical F-value for an α of .01 (8.29).

Alternatively, the same statistics can be considered as placing a confidence interval around F (for a detailed exposition of this point see Smithson, 2000). The 95% confidence interval for F lies between 0 and $F_{.05}$. If the obtained value lies within this range we cannot reject the null hypothesis, but if the obtained value lies outside the range we can be confident in rejecting the null hypothesis.

However, this information is most useful if it is supplemented by information about the *size* of effects. For the case of ANOVA the information we are interested in here is the extent to which the effects model is superior to the null model. This can be measured by examining the degree to which differences between groups make up a large proportion of the total amount of variance in the data. It is estimated by comparing the between-subjects sums of squares with the total sum of squares. This yields a statistic called R^2:

$$R^2 = SS_B/SS_T$$

Remember that SS_B must be less than SS_T (because $SS_T = SS_B + SS_W$, and because SS_W and SS_B are squared values they must be positive). Thus, where this ratio is large (close to 1.0) that means that most of the variance in the data is actually *variance between groups*. Where the value of R^2 is close to zero (it can never be negative, again because both SS_B and SS_T are always positive) this means that most of the variance is actually within groups and not between groups (because any variance not associated with SS_B must be associated with SS_W).

All of this means that R^2 is a measure of the degree to which the treatment makes a difference, that is, of whether it matters which experimental condition participants were placed in. The particular thing they make a difference to is accounting for variance. R^2 tells us how much better we are doing than the null model by taking the conditions into account, and in particular it gives us an indication of the proportion of variance that is accounted for by taking groups into account (or alternatively, the proportion of variance that we would have to treat as error if we did not take groups into account).

We can examine this in relation to the example of our four-group experiment. We have already calculated MS_B and found that it was 23.69. We multiply this by df_B to obtain SS_B, which is $23.69 * 3 = 71.075$. To find SS_T we need to know SS_W. We know that

$$MS_W = SS_W/df_W$$

and therefore

$$SS_W = MS_W * df_W$$

We previously calculated MS_W and we know that $df_W = 36$ (the total number of observations, 40, less one for each group) so:

$$SS_W = 2.19 * 36 = 78.9$$
$$SS_T = 71.075 + 78.9 = 149.975$$
$$R^2 = SS_B/SS_T$$
$$= 71.075/149.975$$
$$= .47$$

In other words, differences between groups account for 47% of the variance in this sample. This says that the effect was significant and is associated with a large proportion of the variance. Only 53% is associated with variance within groups and so, by Cohen's (1988) criteria (discussed on page 231), we can classify the effect size as large because R^2 is greater than .25 (the values on page 231 actually give effect sizes for r so, as discussed in that chapter, we need to square these to get R^2).

If we go through the same process with our two-group example, we can compute R^2 very quickly from the values in our ANOVA table. Here $SS_B = 20$ and $SS_T = 62.8$, so $R^2 = SS_B/SS_T = 20/62.8 = 0.32$. Here, then, not only is the effect significant but it is also of large size (i.e., $R^2 > .25$). This agrees with the conclusion we arrived at in Chapter 8. Moreover, we can now fill in the two empty spaces (for p and R^2) in the ANOVA table so that it looks like this:

Source	SS	df	MS	F	p <	R^2
Between cells (Condition)	20	1	20	8.41	.01	.32
Within cells	42.8	18	2.38			
Total	62.8	19				

It is important to report these measures of effect size along with any inferences made on the basis of statistical tests. We normally need to know not just whether it is plausible that the differences are due to chance but that the differences are sufficiently large to be concerned about. Are first born children more intelligent that their younger siblings? If we took a sufficiently large sample we may find that they are, but the difference in intelligence would be very small. Accordingly, this difference might be of interest to those who study the influence of birth order on intelligence, but it might be so small as to be irrelevant for most everyday considerations. As noted in the previous chapter, effect size measures therefore play an important role in helping us to put our results in perspective.

Q10.3[**]

What is the point of calculating the value of R^2 in relation to particular F- and p-values?

(a) R^2 is a hypothesis-testing measure that can tell us whether a particular F-value is significant.

(b) R^2 is the square of α and can tell us whether a particular p-value is significant.

(c) R^2 is a measure of effect size that can tell us whether a particular F-value is significant.

(d) R^2 is a measure of effect size that can tell us whether a particular p-value is significant.

(e) R^2 is a measure of effect size that can tell us how much variance a particular effect accounts for.

The correct answer is (e). R^2 is a measure of effect size that quantifies the amount of variance between conditions in an experimental design as a proportion of the total amount of variance. This information is used in conjunction with information about the probability of an effect of the observed size (i.e., a p-value), to give an indication of the effect's psychological (not just statistical) significance. All other answers are wrong because R^2 is not a measure of probability or statistical significance. Note too that (a) and (b) are particularly wrong because R^2 has nothing to do with hypothesis testing and the square of α is a completely irrelevant value (for any purpose).

effects model A hypothetical model in which mean responses *differ* across the conditions of an experimental design. This represents an alternative to the null hypothesis that the mean response is the same in all conditions.

What does analysis of variance buy us? Some notes on comparing individual means

Once we have calculated the F-ratio and made the inference that chance variation is not a plausible way to explain the pattern we have observed, and that the effect size is sufficiently large to be concerned about, we have a new problem. We are prepared to accept that there are differences between conditions, but we have no idea *which* individual means are different.

What? Why have we gone to this amount of trouble to calculate F-ratios if we still have not answered this very simple question? This is quite a complex problem and there are several answers, we will address three of them.

The first answer is that once we have calculated the F-ratio and found that it is indicative of a statistically significant effect we can be confident that there is some relationship between our independent and dependent variables (i.e., the conditions make a difference or there are differences between conditions). Armed with this knowledge, we can then explore the data further to find out where the differences lie (paying close attention to the number of tests we do and the possibility of the inflation of alpha). However, we know that there is no point in going further if the F-ratio is not significant. Thus, a non-significant

F-ratio is a stark 'Keep out!' sign, while a significant one is an invitation to explore further.

The second answer is that a significant F-ratio is indeed not all that useful when we are comparing many different means (i.e., in a multiple-condition experiment). Instead of worrying too much about the F-ratio, researchers should instead plan to make comparisons of *particular* means in advance of collecting the data (again taking account of inflation of alpha). The trick here is to work out which means to compare and what differences between those means reflect. This then raises the important question of where exactly the plans that lead us to make the comparisons come from. The answer is that they are given by our experimental hypotheses and predictions. Where we expect in advance that two means should be different (or that they should not be different) then we should plan to compare them.

The third answer to our problem is really a combination of the first two. This view says that we should calculate the F-ratio and if it is significant then proceed to test any comparisons that we considered in advance and/or any other comparisons that might occur to us on the basis of a discovery of significant F-ratios. This view is actually fairly common in psychological research but it should be avoided as it rests on a statistical misunderstanding (which we will explain further below). In this book we will briefly discuss the first two views here.

Using *F*-ratios without comparisons planned in advance

If you find a significant F-ratio and have no comparisons planned in advance you should now proceed to conduct all possible **pairwise comparisons**. This simply means comparing every mean with every other mean. If we have three means, for example, there are three possible comparisons (A with B, A with C, and B with C) and if there are four means there are six possible comparisons. Such comparisons are called **post hoc comparisons** (*post hoc* is Latin for 'after this') because they were not planned in advance. There is a wide variety of methods available for doing these multiple comparisons. One of the best known is the Scheffé method which uses the F-ratio obtained from the ANOVA, and details are provided in more advanced ANOVA texts (e.g., Keppel, 1982; Maxwell & Delaney, 1990).

If we know in advance that we wish to compare particular pairs of means then we can conduct planned (also called **a priori**) comparisons. There are many methods for doing planned comparisons (such as orthogonal polynomial contrasts); one simple method is to perform *t*-tests but to make an adjustment to the alpha level of the *t*-test to take account of the inflation of alpha and adjust the error term used in the *t*-test to take account of the full set of data available.

The first adjustment relates to the problem that we referred to at the start of the chapter. It is always possible that some differences which we find to be significant actually reflect chance variation (i.e., they are not really valid). If we draw random samples from the same population then the probability that two will be significantly different is equal to the alpha level (often .05). If we do lots of comparisons we are more likely to find significant differences by chance (for the same reason that we are more likely to choose at least one bad apple over a long run of choices). One way to deal with this problem is to adjust the alpha level to take account of the number of comparisons we need to do (this is called the family of comparisons). Doing this will allow us to maintain an **experimentwise alpha level** that is the same as our intended alpha level. Each comparison, however, will be conducted using a lower (protected) alpha level.

Protecting the alpha level is quite simple to do. First, you count up the number of comparisons that you plan to calculate. Then you simply divide your alpha level by the number of comparisons you need to perform. This gives you the new alpha level to be used for each comparison.

As an example, let us say that we hypothesized that one or two exposures to a target person would increase their attractiveness but that an additional session would have no effect. In the design above that would mean that we would need to compare the no-exposure condition with the single-exposure session, the single session with the two-exposure session and the two-session condition with the three-session condition. That is, we have three comparisons (A with B, B with C, and C with D). To find our protected alpha level we simply divide by 3 (the number of comparisons) and use this as our alpha level. This is called the **Bonferroni adjustment**.

We can then perform our *t*-tests using this protected level of .017. In order to do this, however, the error term (denominator) comes from the pooled variance across all our cells. To find this, calculate the square root of MS_W and then multiply this by the square root of $2/n$, where n is the number of participants in each cell.

Thus to compare the mean of group i with the mean of group j, subtract the first mean from the second and divide by the error term:

$$t = \frac{\bar{X}_i - \bar{X}_j}{\sqrt{MS_W * \frac{2}{n}}}$$

Critical t is not shown in Table C.2 for this value, but it is close to the level of .02 for a two-tailed test. This indicates that for 18 degrees of freedom an observed t of around 2.6 will be significant.

There are some quick points to make here. To follow this method you do not actually have to calculate an analysis of variance. If somebody advises you to perform an analysis of variance and check to see whether that is significant before conducting *planned comparisons*, they are simply giving you bad advice (see Maxwell & Delaney, 1990, p. 200). They are essentially advising you to reduce the power of your test to reveal what is going on in the data. However, ANOVA is actually very useful for estimating error terms (especially if variances are homogeneous) as we have done above. It is also worth noting that the Bonferroni adjustment becomes very conservative when the number of comparisons is large. As a rough rule of thumb, you should include no more comparisons between cells than you have cells unless you have a large number of cells (more than four) and a large sample size (at least 40).

There is obviously quite a bit to do when conducting one-way ANOVA. To help summarize this process, Section A.4 of Appendix A shows the steps to follow and a worked example.

$Q10.4^*$

A researcher conducts one-way analysis of variance in which they compare the final marks of students who have studied psychology at one of five different institutions, A, B, C, D, and E. The study looks at the marks of 100 students, 20 from each institution. On the basis of a given theory, the researcher plans to make four comparisons: between A and B, A and C, C and D and C and E. Three other researchers make the following observations:

X: 'If the researcher used an experimentwise alpha level of .01, a Bonferroni adjustment would mean that each of these tests had an alpha level of .0025.'

Y: 'If the researcher used an experimentwise alpha level of .05, a Bonferroni adjustment would mean that each of these tests had an alpha level of .0025.'

Z: 'If the researcher used an experimentwise alpha level of .05, a Bonferroni adjustment would mean that each of these tests had an alpha level of .0125.'

Who is correct?

(a) Only X.
(b) Only Y.
(c) Only Z.
(d) X and Y.
(e) X and Z.

The correct answer is (e). In this case the Bonferroni adjustment simply involves dividing the experimentwise alpha by the number of comparions (i.e., 4). Thus when this alpha is .01, adjusted alpha is $.01/4 = .0025$, and when it is .05, adjusted alpha is $.05/4 = .0125$. Therefore both X and Z make correct observations, and only Y is incorrect.

a priori comparisons Comparisons between cells that a researcher has planned to perform prior to a study being conducted. These constitute a subset of all possible comparisons and have usually been identified as important on the basis of a particular theory.

Bonferroni adjustment An adjustment to alpha that takes into account the number of comparisons that are being made (and hence the number of t-tests that are being conducted).

experimentwise alpha level The overall alpha level that informs hypothesis testing in a given study. When specific tests are conducted, this may be adjusted to take into account the number of comparisons that are being made.

pairwise comparisons Comparisons between every pair of cells in a given experimental design.

post hoc comparisons Comparisons between cells that a researcher has not planned to perform prior to a study being conducted.

An introduction to analysis of variance with two independent variables

So far we have dealt with techniques for examining differences between levels of a single experimental manipulation. The chief question that we can answer here is whether that manipulation makes a difference. If we reject the null hypothesis then we are expressing some confidence that there are meaningful differences between experimental conditions.

Both the null model and the effects model can be thought of providing answers to questions. One key question that the models give different answers to is 'what is the best guess for the score of a participant in Group i?' If we are convinced by the effects model, then the best guess will be the mean for Group i. If not, the best guess is the grand mean. A slightly different way to state the question is to ask 'what is the effect of the treatment on the scores participants obtain?'. The answer that the effects model gives is 'people in some groups tend to get higher scores than other groups'; the answer that the null model gives is 'people get roughly similar scores in different groups'. In even simpler terms, the effects model answers 'yes' to the question 'Does the treatment make a difference?' and the null model answers 'no'.

We all know that the world is not always quite as clear-cut as this. In many situations we are unable to give straight answers to questions like 'Does the treatment make a difference?' Our answers often take the form 'That depends on some other factor' or 'Yes, but only in some circumstances'. Take the example we have been considering of the test of the physical reinforcement theory. The conclusion suggested by the effects model is that the treatment does make a difference – exposure to targets leads people to regard those people as more attractive. Here, though, we are more than likely to ask just how widely we would expect this conclusion to hold. Would we expect the same pattern to hold with target people we already knew, or if the people the participants were exposed to could not speak the same language?

Assuming that we do not expect exactly the same relationship, the sorts of hunch that we could have in those cases fall into three classes: 'no', 'yes, but not to the same degree', and 'yes, even more so'. Regardless of which of these we suspect, in any case we are doing something quite special. We are hypothesizing an *interaction* between the treatment variable and some other variable (see Chapter 4).

This sounds like a complex thing to do (and it certainly does lead to statistical complexities), but in everyday life we hypothesize interactions between variables all the time. Let us imagine that while writing this text one of us remembers that he needs to phone someone in another town about some pressing matter to obtain some information for a colleague here. Will I ring the person now or wait until later? One would hope that this would be determined by how pressing the matter was. If it was really urgent I would probably do it now, but there are other possibilities. Some of the answers you might give could be 'It depends on whether your colleague is really desperate for the information' or 'It depends on whether you think the person will be at their phone', or 'It depends whether you remember' and so on. All of these involve positing an interaction between the urgency of the matter and other variables.

Imagine a friend asks if you are likely to go to a party on Saturday night. If you give just about any answer other than 'yes' or 'no' you are proposing a statistical interaction (and in this example maybe even a social one). For example, if you say 'It depends who else is going' or 'It depends on whether I can get a lift there' then you are saying that your likelihood of going is not just determined by whether you want to go, but by other factors. One interesting thing about these everyday exercises of logic, which we can all perform, is that they only become difficult to grapple with when we put them into statistical and mathematical terms.

Analysis of variance involving more than one categorical variable basically exists to answer the question of whether there is statistical evidence of interaction. It can still answer other questions, about whether other variables have effects on their own, but these effects, known as **main effects**, follow exactly the same ideas as one-way ANOVA. It is interaction which is the tricky part, but we will deal with the main effects first.

Let us consider a straightforward example. Imagine we measured biscuit eating in four people, two of whom were hungry when they started eating and two who were not. We provide one of the hungry people with chocolate biscuits and one with plain biscuits and do the same with the people who are not hungry. We wish to find out the effect of hunger and type of biscuit (plain or chocolate) on the number of biscuits eaten in the pack. We can represent these data in a 2 by 2 table, and we might do that by treating hunger as the **row variable** and flavour as the **column variable**. Each row will have its own **row mean** (the average of means in that row) and each column will have a **column mean**.

	Plain	Chocolate	(Row means)
Not hungry	5	15	10
Hungry	10	20	15
(Column means)	7.5	17.5	Grand mean = 12.5

By examining this table we can work out the effect of flavour and hunger on biscuit consumption. By examining the difference between the column means we can see that chocolate increases biscuit consumption by 10 and that hunger increases biscuit consumption by 5.

There is another useful but less obvious way to think about these data, though. We can consider each row or column mean as a deviation from the grand mean of 12.5. Why would we do this? The answer is that in many cases we want to know not only how large some score is in absolute terms, but also whether it is bigger or larger than the average. This is especially important when we are trying to work out whether some variable or combination of factors has an effect, that is, whether it makes a difference. Thus:

Chocolate coating = grand mean + 5

Plain = grand mean − 5

Not hungry = grand mean − 2.5

Hungry = grand mean + 2.5

If we are prepared to believe these data then they suggest a model to us. Note that the difference between hungry and not hungry biscuit consumption is the same for chocolate and plain biscuits (+5), and that the difference between chocolate and plain biscuit consumption (+10) is the same for hungry and less hungry people (these two statements are identical in this case). That is, even though the effect of flavour is stronger than the effect of hunger, the effect of flavour is the same for both levels of hunger. This need not always be the case (see below), but it is the case here. The model these data suggest to us is called a **main effects model** and it holds that the cell means are given by the sum of the effect of the row variable and the column variable at that cell. Will a person who is not hungry eat more or fewer chocolate biscuits than the grand mean of all biscuit eaters? The answer is found by adding the effect for chocolate (+5) to the effect for not being hungry (−2.5). This gives us a score of 2.5, suggesting that the person will consume 2.5 more biscuits than average under these conditions.

We can write this model in the following way:

$$X = \mu_{ij} + e$$

where

$$\mu_{ij} = \mu + \alpha_i + \beta_j$$

That is, the score for a participant is given by μ_{ij}, the mean for the particular cell they belong to, plus error, and this cell mean is given by the grand mean plus an effect α_i and an effect β_j, where α_i is the row effect for cell i and β_j is the column effect for cell j. The row and column effects can be thought of as the deviations from the grand mean that occur at a particular level of a factor. Under this main effects model we can find the effect of the row and column by just *adding* these together (it can also be termed the **additive model**).

The biscuit example we used involved observations of only a single participant in each cell and not cell means calculated for several participants. Now consider some more realistic psychological data. These data come from an imaginary experiment that involved measuring the amount of distress (rated on a 10-point scale) experienced in a group of adults who were exposed to very loud or very soft noises that were controllable or uncontrollable (they could switch them off by pressing a button). Each cell mean is based on measuring the responses of 12 participants who were randomly assigned to conditions. For simplicity's sake, we will assume that the variances in all cells are equal to 8.0.

	Uncontrollability		
Noise intensity	Controllable	Uncontrollable	(Row means)
Soft	4.3	5.4	4.85
Loud	6.7	7.8	7.25
(Column means)	5.5	6.6	(Grand mean) 6.05

Here there are two levels of noise intensity (soft and loud) and for each of these there are two levels of uncontrollability (controllable and uncontrollable). We will refer to noise intensity as the row variable and uncontrollability as the column variable. Such a set up is called a **2 × 2 factorial design**. In this notation each of the factors has two levels. In this book we will only consider **fully factorial designs**, where all levels of each factor occur within each level of the other factor.

In the above example the main effects model seems to hold. Uncontrollable noises are more distressing than controllable ones and loud noises are more distressing than quiet ones. We can compute the deviations from the grand mean (in this case 6.05) for each level of the two factors in exactly the same way that we did for the biscuits.

Controllable = grand mean − 0.55

Uncontrollable = grand mean + 0.55

Soft = grand mean − 1.20

Loud = grand mean + 1.20

We can then evaluate these effects in exactly the same way as we did for one-way ANOVA. All we need to do is create a variance estimate based on the row means and divide this by an estimate of the error variance (variance within cells). This gives us an F-ratio that tests the main effect of the row. If there is a lot more variance between rows than within cells, then we are more likely to be convinced that the row variable (uncontrollability) has an effect.

The top line here is easy to create. Ignore the fact that the columns exist for a moment. Simply take the sum of the squared deviations between the mean for each row and the grand mean and divide their sum by the number of means (less one to create an unbiased variance estimate) and then multiply by the number of people in each cell. In this case this gives us:

$$MS_R = 12 * (-1.2^2 + 1.2^2)/1 = 34.56$$

The bottom line is the same as for one-way ANOVA. Calculate the variance within cells by computing the pooled variance across the four cells. We could do this from the raw data (if they were available) or by pooling the within-cells variances, which in this case gives us 8.0 (which means that $SS_W = 44 * 8 = 352$).

This gives us

$$F = 34.56/8 = 4.32$$

This is more than the critical value of $F_{.05}(1,40)$ of 4.08 so we reject the null hypothesis that there is no row effect.

We can perform exactly the same test for the column effect. The top line is given by taking the sum of the squared deviations between the mean for each column and the grand mean and dividing by the number of means (less one to create an unbiased variance estimate) and multiplying by the number of people in each cell.

In this case this gives us:

$$F = 7.26/8 = 0.91$$

This F-ratio is less than 1.0 so we certainly cannot reject the null hypothesis.

We see, then, that we have a significant row effect and a non-significant column effect (we could also compute R^2 to find the size of these effects, which would show us that the row effect although significant, is actually quite small). We say here that there is a main effect for uncontrollability but no effect for noise intensity.

When the main effects model does not hold we have a statistical interaction. It is best to explain interaction in two ways: graphically and numerically. Obviously to get a graphical understanding of interaction we need to draw what the interaction looks like. We do this by plotting the interaction on a graph. The conventions for doing this in psychology rely on column graphs of the form that we introduced in Chapter 6. Unfortunately this convention is particularly unhelpful for explaining interaction. A better option is provided by the line graph, and this involves drawing one line for each level of one of the two factors

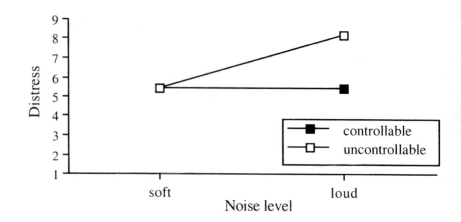

Figure 10.1 Line graph showing interaction

we are interested in. We have done this in Figure 10.1 for a different set of means which do in fact suggest an interaction. We can see from the graph that very loud noises were associated with a higher level of distress but only when they were uncontrollable. If we were to ask 'What is the effect of noise intensity on distress?' the answer would be 'it depends on whether the noise is controllable or not.'

Let us now consider one of a number of other possible patterns of results. Imagine that we found that the soft noise was more distressing when it was controllable (perhaps participants were distressed by the fact that they found the noises difficult to detect). In this case the data might look like this:

| Noise intensity | Controllability | | (Row means) |
	Controllable	Uncontrollable	
Soft	8.2	5.4	6.80
Loud	5.8	8.0	6.90
(Column means)	7.0	6.7	(Grand mean) 6.85

When we plot these data in a line graph (Figure 10.2) we can see that we still have an interaction, but the form of the interaction is what we call a **crossover interaction**. Whereas in the previous case being uncontrollable made loud noises more distressing but had no effect on soft noises, we now see that being controllable makes soft noises more distressing.

As the next step in our statistical analysis of this data, we can apply the formulae we have already learned and quickly work out a number of quantities such as the following:

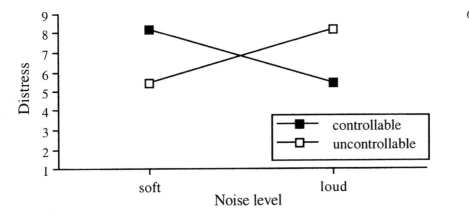

Figure 10.2 Line graph showing crossover interaction

$SS_B = 76.2$ with 3 degrees of freedom (the number of cells, k, minus one)

$SS_W = 352$ with 44 degrees of freedom (the number of observations, N, minus one for each group)

$SS_R = 12[(6.80 - 6.85)^2 + (6.90 - 6.85)^2] = 0.06$ with 1 degree of freedom (the number of rows minus one)

$SS_C = 12[((7 - 6.85)^2 + (6.7 - 6.85)^2)] = 0.54$ with 1 degree of freedom (the number of columns minus one)

$SS_T = SS_B + SS_W = 76.2 + 352 = 428.2$

The first thing to notice about the sums of squares for SS_R and SS_C is that they are very small. This is interesting because SS_B is large and SS_B is made up of SS_R and SS_C and other variation between cells. Accordingly, if SS_R and SS_C are small and SS_B is large this means that the other variation must be very large.

What other type of variation could this be? It is not variation between rows *or* between columns (we have already measured that) so it must be variation involving rows *and* columns. This other type of variation is the interaction effect that we have discussed so far. In the case of a two-way design there is no other type of variation between cells that makes sense: we can have variation across rows *or* variation across columns, or we can have variation across rows within a column or variation across columns within a row. The interaction effect is what is produced by (the product of) combining our row and column effects.

We can call this new sort of sum of squares the **interaction sum of squares** or the row and column sum of squares (involving rows and columns) which we can write as SS_{RC}.

As there are no other sources of between-cell variation, the following relation holds:

$$SS_B = SS_R + SS_C + SS_{RC}$$

Therefore

$$SS_{RC} = SS_B - SS_R - SS_B$$

So in this case

$$SS_{RC} = 76.2 - 0.06 - 0.54 = 75.6$$

This effect must be associated with one degree of freedom as

$$df_B = df_R + df_C + df_{RC}$$

And thus

$$df_{RC} = df_B - df_R - df_C$$

so

$$df_{RC} = 3 - 1 - 1 = 1$$

There are actually four logically distinct forms of interaction for a two-way factorial design like this one. All of them can be detected graphically as they involve different combinations of the main effects for the independent variables. In simple terms, though, an interaction can exist whenever one of the lines we have drawn is not parallel to another line and in each case, we decide whether it is plausible that the interaction exists by doing a statistical test.

How do we make that decision? Given that we know what an interaction would look like if we were to graph it, what sort of numerical or computational evidence would we need to be convinced an interaction exists? The rough and ready answer is that for the case of two independent variables (such as the 2×2 design we have been discussing) an interaction exists when there is a bigger difference between two levels of one variable than there is between another two levels. This is the same as saying the lines representing the two different conditions are not parallel or that the size of the difference between two means depends on the level of the other factor.

The extent of this interaction is calculated by examining the differences between the cell means and the value that would be expected if there were no interaction effect. This expected value is the one given by the main effects model discussed above that says that the variables have independent effects. The difference between this expected value and the actual cell mean gives us our interaction effect. Using the terminology adopted by Smithson (2000), this can be thought of as the product of the row and column effect so that the relation

$$X = \mu_{ij} + e$$

still holds, but now

$$\mu_{ij} = \mu + \alpha_i + \beta_j + \alpha_i\beta_j$$

where $\alpha_i\beta_j$ is given by the deviation between the actual cell mean and the expected value for the cell mean based on the main effects model, that is:

$$\alpha_i\beta_j = \mu_{ij} - (\mu + \alpha_i + \beta_j)$$

We can write this again as:

$$\alpha_i\beta_j = \mu_{\text{adj}} - \mu$$

where $\mu_{\text{adj}} = \mu_{ij} - \alpha_i - \beta_j$

The interaction term involves variance in the adjusted cell means. If the cell means adjusted for the row and column effects are highly variable (when compared to the variation within cells) then we have evidence of interaction. Thus, if the cell means adjusted for the row and column effects are pretty similar to the grand mean then we have little evidence of interaction. Another way of saying this is that where the cell means are quite different from the values we would expect given the rows and columns they belong to, then we have evidence of interaction. To return to our earlier biscuit example, given the main effects that people eat more chocolate than plain biscuits *and* eat more biscuits when they are hungry, to then find that the cell mean is somewhat higher than the grand mean when a hungry person is allowed to gorge themselves on chocolate biscuits is not surprising, and it is not evidence of interaction. We would expect it to be higher (due to the presence of these two main effects). However, if we find that the cell mean is substantially higher or lower than the grand mean that we would expect after adjusting for (i.e., adding) the row and column effects, then that *is* evidence of interaction.

Computationally, finding the interaction term involves finding a sum of squares of the deviations between the adjusted cell mean and the grand mean (multiplied by the number of people in each cell). This sum is then averaged to form a mean square or variance estimate (in this case variance in the cell means in each column pooled across the various columns, or variance in the cell means in each row pooled across the various rows – these two are identical). If this mean square is large relative to the error mean square, we will be more confident that there is an interaction.

There is an even easier way to calculate this two-way interaction effect, and we will focus on this for current purposes because it helps to reinforce a basic point about sums of squares. The interaction effect represents all variance between cells that is not accounted for by the row and column effects. Remember we have already calculated SS_{RC} and found that it equals 75.6.

We can turn this into a variance estimate by dividing by the interaction degrees of freedom. In general, this is the number of rows (minus one) multiplied by the number of columns (minus one). For a 2×2 design the interaction degrees of freedom (df) are equal to

$$df_{RC} = (2 - 1) * (2 - 1) = 1$$

So

$$MS_{RC} = SS_{RC}/df_{RC}$$
$$= 75.6/1 = 75.6$$

We can construct the F-ratio by dividing by the within-cells mean square that we obtained previously to give us:

$$F = 75.6/8 = 9.45$$

This is larger than the critical $F_{.05}$ (1, 44) of 4.06. Indeed, it is larger than the critical value $F_{.005}$ (1, 44) of 8.74, so we can see that this is a significant interaction effect. It also has an R^2 of SS_{RC}/SS_T of .18, suggesting that this is a larger effect than many of the ones we have considered so far. The statistical inference we would make here, then, is that it is implausible that such a pattern would be obtained by taking random samples from the same population. We can conclude both that the effect of noise intensity on distress probably does depend on whether it is uncontrollable or not, and that the effect of uncontrollability of noises on distress depends on how loud the noise is.

Designs and interactions can involve many more cells as additional factors are added. Providing researchers design their experiments carefully, ANOVA can deal with these complexities (including repeated observations of the same participants). However, such considerations are well beyond the scope of this book. What is more important for present purposes is that you have some grasp of the underlying logic of ANOVA techniques. If you have, you will be very well equipped to handle the issues that arise from more complex experimental designs when the need arises.

We do not expect that you will be conducting many two-way ANOVAs by hand. Nevertheless the steps to follow for two-way ANOVA are given in Section A.5 of Appendix A.

An experimental psychologist conducts a study examining whether the speed with which two shapes can be identified as similar or different depends on whether the stimuli are (a) of equal or unequal size and (b) symmetrical or asymmetrical. The mean reaction times for the four cells of the design are as follows: equal symmetrical ($M = 132$ ms), unequal symmetrical ($M = 148$ ms), unequal asymmetrical ($M = 142$ ms), unequal asymmetrical ($M = 182$ ms). Which of the following is true?

(a) A line graph in which these data are plotted suggests that there might only be a main effect for size.

(b) A line graph in which these data are plotted suggests that there might only be a main effect for symmetry.

(c) A line graph in which these data are plotted suggests that there might only be a main effect for size and an interaction between size and symmetry.

(d) A line graph in which these data are plotted suggests that there might only be a main effect for symmetry and an interaction between size and symmetry.

(e) A line graph in which these data are plotted suggests that there might be main effects for size and symmetry and an interaction between size and symmetry.

The correct answer is (e). A line graph of these data would look like this:

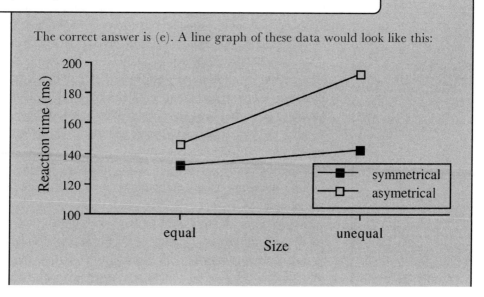

From this we can see that there is the suggestion of a main effect for size (such that equal-sized objects are judged faster than unequal-sized objects), a main effect for symmetry (such that symmetrical shapes are judged faster than asymmetrical shapes), and an interaction between size and symmetry (which means that the combined impact of these variables is not simply the sum of the two main effects). The interaction is suggested by the fact that the lines are not parallel. (a), (b), (c) and (d) are wrong because they each overlook one or two of these three effects. Of course, we would be more confident in answering the question of whether there was an interaction after performing an analysis of variance.

2 × 2 factorial design A study with a *fully factorial design* in which each of two independent variables (factors) has two levels. An example would be an experiment that includes the factors age (with two levels: young and old) and sex (with two levels: male and female).

additive model Another term for a *main effects model*.

column mean When mean scores from a two-factor study are represented in a table, the mean of all the mean scores in a particular column.

column variable When data from a two-factor study are represented in a table, the variable whose different levels are presented in different columns.

crossover interaction A pattern of two-way interaction, in which, when a line graph is drawn, the lines connecting the means for different levels of the same factor cross over each other. This pattern indicates that at one level of one of the factors (A) the mean is higher for one level of the other factor (X will be greater than Y), but that at another level (B) this pattern is reversed (Y will be greater than X).

fully factorial designs Experimental designs in which all levels of each factor occur within each level of the other factor. If an experiment involves the factors age (with two levels: young and old) and sex (with two levels: male and female), the old group will contain males and females, the young group will contain males and females, the male group will contain young and old, and the female group will contain young and old.

interaction sum of squares In a two-factor design, that part of the total sum of squares which is due to the interaction of column and row variables. In such a design this is the between-cell variance that is left over after accounting for column and row variance.

main effects Effects which reflect the impact of one independent variable averaged across all levels of other independent variables, rather than the impact of an interaction between two or more independent variables.

main effects model A hypothetical data model in which the combined effect of two or more independent variables results from their being added together.

row mean When mean scores from a two-factor study are represented in a table, the mean of all the mean scores in a particular row.

row variable When mean scores from a two-factor study are represented in a table, the variable whose different levels are presented in different rows.

A final word

In this chapter we have only touched on the procedures for conducting ANOVA. There is much, much more that can be done even with designs as simple as the ones we have discussed here, and designs that ANOVA can be applied to are often much more complex than these.

Indeed, even though ANOVA can become mind-numbingly complex, it is worth alerting you to the main ways in which this complexity presents itself. First, two-way designs can involve many more than four cells, and there can be more than two factors in a given design. Secondly, ANOVA can include within-subjects measures as well as between-subjects manipulations (noting that in this chapter we have only dealt with the analysis of between-subjects designs). Thirdly, ANOVA can involve more than one dependent variable (this is called multivariate ANOVA or MANOVA). Fourthly, the procedures for making planned and post hoc comparisons are enormously diverse. Fifthly, there are many ways to partition sums of squares depending on the features of the design and the cell sizes (especially where these are unequal). Sixthly, there are different procedures that need to be applied when the levels of the factors are not determined experimentally (i.e., where there is not random assignment to conditions).

Even without these complexities there are some points to be wary of. ANOVA is subject to the same assumptions as is the t-test: homogeneity of variance, normality and independence. With equal cell sizes, ANOVA is quite robust to violations of the assumption of equal variances. It is also robust to violations of normality but the picture is more complex, because although ANOVA may still work well in comparing means, the decision to compare the means is dubious if the mean is a dubious measure of central tendency (due to extreme skewness). The assumption of independence is particularly important. Where these assumptions do not hold we face new choices, and we will consider some of these in Chapter 11.

Further reading

If you plan to do a lot of research using analysis of variance you would be well advised to read an advanced statistics text that deals with this and related techniques in much more depth than the present chapter. Of these, Maxwell and Delaney's (1990) volume is one of the most comprehensive and up to date. We also recommend Keppel (1982). However, if you want an intermediate step up in complexity, we recommend Smithson's (2000) text which provides discussions of confidence intervals and other features not dealt with in this book.

Keppel, G. (1982). *Design and analysis: A researcher's handbook* (2nd Ed). Englewood Cliffs, NJ: Prentice Hall.

Maxwell, S. E. & Delaney, H. D. (1990). *Designing experiments and analyzing data: A model comparison perspective.* New York: Harper Collins.

Smithson, M. J. (2000). *Statistics with confidence.* London: Sage.

ANOVA: A checklist for research evaluation and improvement

Inferential uncertainty about means from more than two different samples	Do the researchers want to compare means associated with data that relate to one independent variable and have been obtained from more than two independent samples?	Conduct one-way analysis of variance following the steps laid out in Section A.4 of Appendix A in order to provide information about the probability (p) of obtaining by chance differences between means as large as the ones obtained. Conduct any planned comparisons to identify the source of the difference.
	Do the researchers want to compare means associated with data that relate to two independent variables	Conduct two-way analysis of variance following the steps laid out in Section A.5 of Appendix A in

	where data relating to each variable have been obtained from two or more independent samples?	order to provide information about the probability (p) of obtaining by chance main effects and interactions as large as the ones obtained. Conduct planned comparisons to identify the source of the difference.
Significance fallacy	If the researchers are using a hypothesis-testing approach to ANOVA, have they distinguished appropriately between psychological and statistical significance?	Consider significance levels in conjunction with effect sizes (e.g., compare p and R^2). Be alert to the dangers of making too much of statistically significant F-values when effect sizes are low.
Violation of the assumption of independence	Do the means that are being compared relate to independent sets of observations?	If sample scores are not independent it can be misleading to compare them using ANOVA (or any other statistical test) if, in effect, the same piece of data is being counted more than once. Accordingly, if possible, any source of non-independence (e.g., the fact that the same participant responded twice) should be removed before collecting data. If this is not possible, the nature of the violation should be noted and results treated with caution.
Violation of the assumption of normality	Do the means that are being compared relate to observations that are normally distributed?	If the distribution of sample scores is non-normal (e.g., severely skewed or U-shaped) and the cell sizes are unequal, or there are reasons to believe that the mean is a misleading indicator of central tendency, you should seriously consider using a non-parametric test (Chapter 11) or correct the distribution by transformation (see Chapter 6).
Violation of the assumption of equal variance	Do the means that are being compared relate to samples that have equal variance?	If sample variances are unequal (e.g., one is more than four times bigger

Outliers	Is the distribution of scores (especially its shape and variance) dramatically affected by the presence of outliers?	Examine the distribution of scores to see if it contains outliers. If it does, see if this can be corrected by an appropriate statistical transformation of the sample data. If this is not possible, consider (a) removing individual outliers or (b) recoding them to the same value as the nearest non-outlier. Ensure you report any transformations that you make.

than the other) you should seriously consider using a non-parametric test (see Chapter 11). This is only worth doing if the size of one sample is much larger than the other.

Q10.6*

Which of the following statements is *false*?

(a) One difference between ANOVA and *t*-tests is that ANOVA allows researchers to compare responses of more than two groups.
(b) One difference between ANOVA and *t*-tests is that ANOVA does not make assumptions about homogeneity, normality and independence.
(c) One difference between ANOVA and *t*-tests is that ANOVA can be used to simultaneously examine the impact of more than one variable.
(d) One difference between ANOVA and *t*-tests is that ANOVA is based on analysis of the ratios of variances.
(e) One difference between ANOVA and *t*-tests is that ANOVA uses two separate degrees of freedom (one for between-cells variance, one for within-cells variance).

Q10.7**

A researcher conducts a study examining the impact of social support on depression in which she studies how four independent groups that each receive a different type of social support (financial, emotional, intellectual, none) react to a stressful experience. There are 20 people in each group. Which of the following statements is true?

(a) There are 4 degrees of freedom for the between-cells variance.
(b) There are 78 degrees of freedom for the within-cells variance.
(c) If ANOVA yielded a between-groups F-value of 2.18 this would be significant with α set at .05.
(d) If ANOVA yielded a between-groups F-value of 3.18 this would be significant with α set at .01.
(e) None of the above statements is true.

Q10.8***

Which of the following statements about the F-distribution is *false*?

(a) The distribution is asymmetrical.
(b) The distribution is one-tailed.
(c) Higher values of F are associated with a higher probability value.
(d) The distribution is positively skewed.
(e) If the amount of between-cells variance is equal to the amount of within-subjects variance, the value of F will be 1.00.

The correct answer to Q10.6 is (b). As noted at the end of the chapter, ANOVA requires exactly the same assumptions to be satisfied as a t-test: equal variances, the normal distributions, and independent observations. (a) is wrong because the main feature of ANOVA is that it allows researchers simultaneously to examine data from more than two groups (something that cannot be done with a t-test). (c) is wrong because, unlike t-tests, ANOVA can be multi-factorial, (d) is wrong because analysis of variance relies upon the F-distribution and (e) is wrong because it involves a comparison of between-cells (treatment) variance and within-cells (error) variance, and each of these is associated with a different number of degrees of freedom ($N-k$ and $k-1$, respectively).

The correct answer to Q10.7 is (e). All of these statements are untrue. (a) is untrue because there are 3 degrees of freedom for the between-groups variance (i.e., $k-1$). (b) is untrue because there are 76 degrees of freedom for the within-groups variance (i.e., $N-k$). (c) is untrue because (as we can see from Table C.4) with α set at .05 the critical value of $F(3,70)$ is 2.74 and the obtained value (2.18) is lower than this. (d) is untrue because (as we can see from Table C.4) with α set at .01 the critical value of $F(3,70)$ degrees of freedom is 4.07 and the obtained value (3.18) is lower than this.

The correct answer to Q10.8 is (c). A higher value of F is associated with a lower probability value, so that the larger the ratio of between-subjects variance to within-subjects variance becomes, the less plausible it is that the ratio is the result of a random process. (d) is the wrong answer because it is in fact positively skewed – and if it is skewed it cannot be symmetrical, so answer (a) is wrong too. Answer (b) is wrong, because, unlike the t-distribution, the F-distribution is not two-tailed (i.e., there is only one rejection region). Answer (e) is wrong because an F-ratio is the ratio of between-*cells* variance (the numerator) divided by within-cells variance (the denominator) and when these two are equal this ratio equals 1.

Discussion/essay questions

(a) Why are procedures for examining statistical interactions so important in psychological research?

(b) What are the advantages of performing ANOVA by hand rather than using a computer package?

(c) Some people argue that the prevalence of ANOVA techniques as a basis both for designing research and for analysing data has led researchers to construct artificial models of human behaviour because phenomena tend to be simplistically understood in terms of main effects and interactions. Do you agree?

(d) What problems of data analysis are encountered in studies in which

Exercises

(a) A team of developmental psychologists measure the moral reasoning of children giving each a score from 0 to 100 (where 100 indicates a higher state of reasoning). The moral reasoning of 10 children in four age groups is assessed in this way and the scores are as follows:

age 10–11:	32	43	54	31	29	27	33	43	49	35
age 12–13:	35	44	56	65	71	62	61	48	39	47
age 14–15:	54	57	62	70	49	61	55	55	60	64
age 16–17:	56	65	75	66	77	81	87	75	63	68

The researchers hypothesize that older children will have higher levels of moral reasoning, but before they can conduct specific tests of this hypothesis they want to conduct analysis of variance to see

whether there is any evidence of overall effect such that moral
reasoning differs across age groups.

(i) What would an ANOVA table for this analysis look like?

(ii) Would analysis of variance provide the researchers with the
evidence they require? (base your answer on levels of p and R^2).

(b) Imagine that instead of being from four groups of different
ages, the above data had been gathered from 10–11-year-olds
and 12–13-year-olds from two different areas: one with a high
crime rate (HCR), one with a low crime rate (LCR) as follows:

HCR	age 10–11:	32	43	54	31	29	27	33	43	49	35
	age 12–13:	65	64	56	75	71	68	63	68	69	77
LCR	age 10–11:	54	57	62	70	49	61	55	55	60	64
	age 12–13:	56	65	75	66	77	81	87	75	63	68

The researchers again hypothesize that older children will have
higher levels of moral reasoning, but they also expect that there might
be differences in the moral reasoning of children who live in areas
with different crime rates, and that these might interact with
children's age.

(i) What would an ANOVA table for this analysis look like?

(ii) Would analysis of variance provide the researchers any evidence
to support their hypotheses? (Base your answer on levels of p
and R^2.)

Analysing other Forms of Data: Chi-square and Distribution-free Tests

So far in this book we have dealt with several methods for analysing quantitative data: these include within- and between-subjects t-tests, correlation and ANOVA. It should be obvious by now that different techniques are used in different circumstances (and this should be apparent even if you are not completely confident about what those circumstances are). To take an example, we know from Chapter 10 that you should use ANOVA (and not a t-test) when you wish to compare three or more means.

The different circumstances that lead us to use different tests can be broken down in terms of three dimensions. The choice of technique depends upon (a) the form of data, (b) the question we are trying to answer, and (c) the assumptions we are willing to make about the data we are dealing with.

By the *form of the data* we are simply referring to the number of levels of each variable. We are assuming that there are always one or two variables (i.e., that the data are univariate or bivariate) because **multivariate statistics** are beyond the scope of this book. For example, in previous chapters we have dealt with situations where we have either (a) two variables with many levels (continuous variables as in the case of correlations and within-subjects t-tests), or (b) one variable with a small number of levels (a categorical variable) and another with many levels (as in the case of between-subjects t-tests and ANOVAs). However, there is one other important form of data, and that is where both variables are *categorical*.

In the case of within-subjects t-tests (Chapter 8) and the Pearson product-moment correlation (Chapter 9) the form of the data is identical: we need two continuous variables. Nonetheless, *the question we are trying to answer* with the two statistics is very different. We use a correlation when we want to know whether the two variables are related, and a within-subjects *t*-test when we want to compare the means of the two variables.

However, there are many other questions that could be asked, and sometimes questions like 'are the means of the two variables different?' do not make much sense. This is often because the form of the data does not lend itself to answering that kind of question. For example, it makes sense to calculate the mean age of the people in your class, but it does not make much sense to calculate the mean sex. Sometimes, too, we are not able to make the necessary assumptions about the data that would allow us to perform the test in which we are interested. For example, as we discussed in Chapter 6, it is not appropriate to compare means if the skewed distribution of our data makes the mean a misleading statistic.

To start our discussion, let us imagine, for example, that we wanted to know whether adolescent males or females were more likely to have eating disorders. Imagine that we had data from samples of 20 males and 20 females who were receiving therapy and that the data told us whether these clients had been diagnosed with an eating disorder by the clinical psychologist they were seeing. Some hypothetical data are shown in the table below:

	Male	Female
Do not have eating disorder	15	12
Have eating disorder	5	8

With these data we cannot ask whether the means are different. There are no scores from which to calculate means because both variables are categorical. Nevertheless, we could still ask whether the *proportion* of people with eating disorders is the same amongst the males and females. In this case 25% of the males have eating disorders, compared to 40% of the females. Clearly, a greater proportion of females have eating disorders. But we are faced with a familiar problem: just how should we make sense of this difference? In this case we would like to know whether sex is related to the frequency of eating disorders. In particular, it would be helpful if there were a statistical test that told us how plausible it would be that proportions of eating disorder as different as this would be found if these samples of males and females were drawn from the same population (i.e., if there were no real differences between males and females in the level of eating disorders). As it happens, there is such a test – the χ^2 (chi-square) test of independence – and we will discuss this in some detail in this chapter.

Now imagine that instead of just a diagnosis of eating disorders we had a measure of the level of eating disorders for each participant. Let us assume that eating disorders were measured on an 11-point scale (from 0 to 10) but that the majority of participants scored 0 (indicating that they had no eating disorder at all). Reminding ourselves of the assumptions that should be satisfied before t-tests are performed (see pp. 234–6), under these circumstances it might not be safe to conclude that the scores for the two groups were drawn from a normally distributed population or that the variances of the two populations from which they were drawn were equal. If that were the case it might not be wise to use a between-subjects t-test because it would be questionable whether the assumptions of that procedure hold.

The question we would be left with here is whether or not there is a procedure that allows us to compare the scores of two groups when we are unable (or at least reluctant) to presume that these assumptions hold. As you might imagine from the fact that we are asking the question, there is such a test. Indeed, there are a number of them, and one example – the Mann–Whitney test – is discussed in this chapter.

To see the scope of the alternative situations that we need to be able to deal with, it is helpful to start by summarizing the relevant features of the procedures that we have already covered in previous chapters (Table 11.1).

In this chapter we will deal with a range of other cases that are not covered in Table 11.1. Before we do, it is worth noting at the outset that these cases do not occur as commonly in the psychological literature as the other techniques that we have discussed in earlier chapters. This is one reason why they are located together in this chapter rather than each given separate chapters of their own.

At the same time, though, the fact that these alternative ways of analysing data are bundled together does not mean that they are inherently less relevant or important for psychological research. Instead, the fact that they are used relatively infrequently simply reflects features of the standard research training that psychologists receive and which orients them towards particular research designs and particular data management strategies.

Accordingly, when we outline these various alternative techniques, we think you will agree that it is important to be equipped to deal with the situations they relate to. When you conduct your own research in the future, we would also strongly encourage you to explore the limitations and possibilities of your data, to see whether or not the tests described below could be of any use to you. Like the joker in a pack

Table 11.1 Statistical tests and when to use them

Form of data	Question of interest	Assumptions about data*	Test used
One variable with many levels	Does the mean differ from some value (e.g., zero)?	(i) Population variances are unknown; (ii) observations are independent; (iii) the sample is drawn from a normally distributed population.	One-sample t-test
One variable with two categories; one variable with many levels	Are the means of the two categories different?	(i) Population variances are unknown; (ii) observations are independent; (iii) the two categories are drawn from populations with the same variance; (iv) the categories are drawn from normally distributed populations.	Between-subjects t-test
One variable with more than two categories; one variable with many levels	Are the means of the categories different?	(i) Population variances are unknown; (ii) observations are independent; (iii) the categories are drawn from populations with the same variance; (iv) the categories are drawn from normally distributed populations.	ANOVA
Two variables with many levels	Are the means of the two variables different?	(i) Population variances are unknown; (ii) observations are independent; (iii) variables are correlated; (iv) variables are drawn from normally distributed populations.	Within-subjects t-test
Two variables with many levels	Are scores on the two variables related?	There is a linear and bivariate normal relationship between the variables.	Pearson product-moment correlation coefficient

* We assume in each case that each observation of a different person is independent.

of cards, it may be the case that you use them only on special occasions, but when you do, they will be very useful indeed.

> **multivariate statistics** Statistical procedures which simultaneously examine relationships between more than two variables. Bivariate statistics – which examine the relationships between two variables – constitute a particular class of these.

Dealing with a single categorical variable that has two levels: The binomial test

The first case we will examine is one in which we have a single categorical variable with two levels (e.g., 'yes' or 'no'; 'present' or 'absent'; 'right' or 'wrong') and we want to get some insight into the different responses we have obtained. The only question that statistics can really help us with here is whether or not there are differences between the frequencies of the two responses that are large enough to be interesting.

In Chapter 7 we discussed the dilemma of being in a casino and trying to decide whether some game of chance was fair. That is, if we were playing such a game we would want to be confident that we are as likely to win as often as we should (which admittedly is probably less than we would like) given the rules of the game. We discussed briefly the way in which the binomial distribution could be used to help us decide how plausible it was that the game was fair. As we have been at pains to point out, statistics cannot tell us whether the game really is fair, they can simply give us a guide as to how confident we should be that it is not fair. In this section we give the barest taste of the possibilities involved in using the binomial test. The more advanced book in this series by Smithson (2000) provides a much more detailed treatment.

The binomial test involves calculating the expected outcomes or probabilities of two alternatives (such as winning and losing) and comparing these to the observed outcome. This is easy (but uninteresting) to do for a single trial or event. If the casino tosses a coin and it comes up heads then there is not much we (or anybody else) can say about it. The event (heads) had a probability of .5 and was just as likely as the other possible event (tails).

Things become more interesting if we observe the same process over many trials. If the casino kept tossing heads then it would be useful to know the chance of that run of events occurring. This is what the binomial distribution makes it easy for us to do. Amongst other things, it tells us that the probability of obtaining heads four times in a row with a fair coin is 1 in 16. That is, every 16 times you do the experiment of tossing a coin four times you can expect to get all four heads on one of those occasions (remembering everything we said earlier about the gambler's fallacy).

Let us call the outcome of getting four heads x, and the probability of this outcome $P(x)$. The value of this or any outcome based on the combination of multiple events, each with just two possibilities with known constant probabilities, is given by the formula for the binomial distribution:

$$P(x) = \frac{N!}{x!(N-x)!} p^x q^{N-x}$$

where a term like 3! (pronounced '3 factorial') is equal to 3 multiplied by 2 multiplied by 1 (i.e., 6) and $N!$ is N multiplied by $N-1$ multiplied by $N-2$ and so on down to 1 (with the special case that 0! is equal to 1), and p is the probability of one alternative and q is the probability of the other alternative (as these are the only two alternatives their probabilities must sum to 1).

In this case

$$P(x = 4 \text{ heads}) = \frac{4!}{4!(4-4)!} = 0.5^4 \, 0.5^{4-4}$$
$$= 0.5^4$$
$$= .0625 \text{ (which is 1 in 16)}$$

We can use this procedure for any set of circumstances where we want to compare an observed proportion with what we would have expected. Let us imagine that a school had a population with an equal number of boys and girls and the school offered an after-school special activity programme which attracted 4 boys and 2 girls. If we assume that boys and girls are equally likely to attend the programme, is this an unlikely outcome? Put another way, what is the likelihood that if 6 people attend 4 or more of them will be boys (assuming that boys and girls are equally likely to attend)? If this probability is very low, the school might conclude that it needs to investigate the reasons for girls' low interest in the programme (or the high interest of boys).

To calculate the probability, we simply calculate $P(x)$ for each of the cases we are interested in (4 boys, 5 boys, and 6 boys) and add these together. To do this we need a calculator and the formula for the binomial expansion. Here $p(\text{boy}) = .5$ and $p(\text{girl}) = .5$. Using the formula above, we find $P(4)$ to be .2344. We can easily calculate $P(5)$ and $P(6)$ as well, and sum them to find $P(\geq 4)$ to be .3438. That is, it is not very unlikely that the group would be made up of four or more boys. Certainly, the probability is not so small that we would describe it as statistically significant at conventional levels (e.g., $\alpha = .05$).

Let us imagine instead, though, that the school population did not contain an equal number of boys and girls but a majority of girls (80%). Now $p(\text{girl})$ is .8 and $p(\text{boy})$ is .2. Under these conditions, the combined probability of an outcome such as 4 or more boys is .0170.

This suggests that it is far less plausible that boys and girls are equally likely to attend. Accordingly, the reasons for boys' and girls' attendance patterns may be worth exploring.

The binomial test becomes tricky to calculate when there are multiple outcomes (we have to sum a large number of very small probabilities). Fortunately, however, there is a normal approximation that works very well when $N > 25$ and p (the probability of one alternative) and q (the probability of the other) are not very dissimilar in size (e.g., where both p and q are greater than .1). This is given by the equation:

$$z = \frac{x - N_p}{\sqrt{Npq}}$$

This gives us the z-score corresponding to the probability that at least x cases are drawn from one category. Assume that the after-school programme attracts 30 students from a population with equal numbers of boys and girls, and that 19 are boys and 11 are girls. How plausible is an outcome like this if the programme is equally attractive to boys and girls? Using the formula,

$$z = \frac{19 - (30 * .5)}{\sqrt{30 * .5 * .5}}$$

$$= \frac{4}{\sqrt{7.5}}$$

$$= 1.46$$

We can see from Table C.1 in Appendix C that this z-score corresponds to a one-tailed probability of .072. However, if the same pattern had occurred in a school with 80% girls, the z-score would have been 5.93 (as an exercise, you may want to check this yourself). This z-score corresponds to a p value much smaller than .001.

This normal approximation works less well when $N < 25$ or where the probability of one or the other alternative is close to zero (e.g., less than .1). Nevertheless it gives us a powerful tool for making quick assessments about the likelihood of different events. If you invite an equal number of your friends and your partner's friends to a party and you find that more of their friends turn up than yours then you could calculate whether the assumption that both sets of friends are equally likely to turn up is plausible or implausible. More seriously, if a psychotherapist discovers that more cases treated by one common therapy have recurring problems than do cases treated by another rarer therapy, she could assess the hypothesis that the two therapies are equally likely to produce the same rate of recurring problems.

In order to use these procedures sensibly, though, we need to bear one additional factor in mind – the **base rate** of the phenomena in question (i.e., those that constitute the independent variable). That, is we need to be aware of situations in which it is inappropriate to assume that two alternatives (p and q) are equally likely. We remember a (hard-drinking) comedian who used to observe that half of all road accidents were not caused by drunk drivers. His joke, of course, was 'Who's doing anything about all those sober drivers then, and what's their excuse?'. The humour (such as it is) rests here on equating the expected frequencies of sober and drunk drivers. The vast majority of drivers at any one time do not have excessive amounts of alcohol in their blood, so in order to decide whether it is dangerous to drive while drunk we need to compare the number of accidents for sober and drunk drivers *bearing in mind* the proportions of drunk drivers. If, for example, drunk drivers represent only 5% of the population but are involved in 50% of the accidents then that is clearly important.

We see how important expected frequencies are in the next case we consider. This also involves dealing with more than two levels of a variable.

Q11.1[**]

A team of researchers conducts a large study looking at factors that predict poor health in the workplace. They find that more men than women have heart attacks at work. They plan to analyse their data using a binomial test, but are aware of the need to take into account relevant base-rate information. Which of the following constitutes relevant base-rate information for this purpose?

(a) The proportion of people in the workplace who are men.
(b) The proportion of people in the workplace who have heart attacks.
(c) The proportion of men in the workplace who have heart attacks.
(d) The proportion of women in the workplace who have heart attacks.
(e) None of the above, as base-rate information is irrelevant here.

The correct answer is (a). Unless the researchers take into account the proportion of employees who are men, they will not be able to establish whether their results simply reflect the fact that men are more likely to work than women. This base-rate information is very important, so (e) is wrong. The other three answers are all incorrect because base-rate information is relevant to the independent variable (in this case, sex) not the dependent variable (incidence of heart attacks).

> **base rate** The incidence of a particular phenomenon among a
> population of interest. Information about base rates is required in
> order to establish the significance of the incidence of the phenomenon
> within a subset of that population (e.g., people who have been
> subjected to a particular treatment).

Dealing with a single categorical variable that has more than two levels: The chi-square test of goodness of fit

Imagine that instead of having one categorical variable with two levels
(e.g., participants' sex with levels male and female) we had a categorical variable with three levels such as Therapy A, Therapy B and
Therapy C. Imagine, too, that we conducted research in which we
recorded the number of patients who were given a particular therapy
and independently assessed as having had a successful outcome. If we
did this research, the sort of data we might obtain are as follows:

Therapy A	Therapy B	Therapy C	Total (N)
35	27	13	75

Let us assume that all therapies have been used equally often. If
this is the case, and if the therapies were equally effective, we would
expect that the incidence of a successful outcome would be the same
for each. This idea of the expected outcome or expected frequency
(see Chapter 6) is critically important. If the **observed frequencies**
(f_o) are clearly different from the expected frequencies (f_e) then this
would be important evidence that the therapies differ in their effectiveness.

In this case, because the therapies are equally common, the expected
frequency is simply the total ($N = 75$) divided by the number of
therapies (3) which gives us 25. The table below shows these expected
frequencies as well as the difference between the observed and expected
frequencies.

	Therapy A	Therapy B	Therapy C	Total (N)
Observed	35	27	13	75
Expected	25	25	25	
Observed−Expected	10	2	−12	

We can see from this table that Therapy A is associated with more successful outcomes than expected, that Therapy C is associated with fewer successful outcomes, and that Therapy B does not differ much from the expected frequency.

Beyond this observation, though, it would clearly be useful if we were able to assess these differences to find out whether the observed outcomes are plausible in relation to a model which assumed that the rate of success was the same for every therapy. In doing this we are assessing how well the model *fits* these data. To use some statistical jargon, we are testing the **goodness of fit** of the model.

The **chi-square distribution** is extremely useful for testing goodness of fit. In order to use it in this way, we first need to calculate the χ^2 (chi-square, pronounced 'ky square') statistic by applying the following formula:

$$\chi^2 = \frac{\Sigma(f_o - f_e)^2}{f_e}$$

What this formula is saying is that the value of χ^2 increases to the extent that the sum of the squares of the differences between observed and expected frequencies (divided by expected frequencies) is greater than zero. So, in our example:

$$\chi^2 = ((35 - 25)^2 + (27 - 25)^2 + (13 - 25)^2)/25$$
$$= (10^2 + 2^2 + 12^2)/25$$
$$= (100 + 4 + 144)/25$$
$$= 248/25$$
$$= 9.92$$

It can be seen that Therapy B has made almost no contribution to this value of 9.92 as $4/25 = 0.16$ is only 1.6% of the total. Indeed, if all therapies had had an observed value equal to 25 then the value of χ^2 would have been 0. On the other hand, if all the cases with successful outcomes had occurred with one therapy then the value we obtained would have reached its maximum possible value for this sample size of 150. As a result, our obtained value lies somewhere in the range 0 to 150, and we need to find some way of specifying where this position is and what meaning it has.

As with the techniques discussed in previous chapters, in order to assess the meaning of a calculated statistic we can compare it to a value of a theoretical distribution. In this case, as noted above, the distribution of interest is the chi-square distribution. This is shown in Table C.5.

As with the *t*-distribution, this distribution varies with the number of degrees of freedom. However, in the case of the chi-square distribution, the degrees of freedom (*df*) depend on the number of categories rather than N (the number of participants). In general $df = k-1$, where k is the number of categories. In this example $df = 3-1 = 2$.

From Table C.5 we can see that a χ^2 of 9.92 exceeds the critical value for χ^2 with 2 degrees of freedom of 9.21 for $\alpha = .01$. Accordingly, we can conclude that there is a less than 1 in 100 chance that a distribution like the one observed would be randomly sampled if the therapies were in fact equally successful. The logic of hypothesis testing would therefore lead us to conclude that the therapies have different success rates.

It is worth observing in passing that the maximum possible value of χ^2 was 150, but that our obtained value (9.92) was associated with a small probability even though it was relatively close to the minimum value of 0. This is a reflection of the fact that the χ^2 distribution is not symmetrical but is skewed with a long positive tail (like the *F*-distribution).

It is also worth noting that the sorts of categorical outcomes that make up the data set in this example are actually quite common in applied settings. Indeed, the example has a ring of truth about it in light of the fact that in clinical, health and organizational contexts a psychologist or other professional may not be able to obtain outcome measures that can be treated as continuous variables. Sometimes such data simply do not exist, and sometimes they do exist but cannot be obtained for ethical or practical reasons. Nonetheless, the example is an illustration of the point that very simple statistical techniques can be used to tackle quite substantial issues, and that they can be applied quickly and effectively in a variety of situations.

Q11.2[**]

A researcher is interested in seeing whether families who go to a particular coastal town for their holiday are more likely to come from some towns than from others. In his research he looks at the visitors' books of three hotels and finds that together they have been visited by 1204 families over the past year. Of these, 261 are from Town A, 403 are from Town B, 312 are from Town C and 228 are from Town D. Which of these towns makes the greatest contribution to χ^2?

(a) Town A.
(b) Town B.
(c) Town C.
(d) Town D.
(e) All make an equal contribution.

The correct answer is (b). To answer this question we need first to compute the expected frequency (f_e) for number of visiting families. In this case this is $1204/4 = 301$. The town that makes the greatest contribution to χ^2 is then the town whose observed frequency (f_o) of visits is most different from this expected frequency. This difference between observed and expected frequency (f_o-f_e) is $261-301 = 40$ for Town A, $403-301 = 102$ for Town B, $312-301 = 9$ for Town C, and $228-301 = 73$ for Town D. The difference (f_o-f_e) is therefore greatest for Town B.

chi-square distribution (χ^2) The sampling distribution of the chi-square statistic (χ^2). The distribution varies as a function of the degrees of freedom, it can only have positive values, and is positively skewed. A larger value of the statistic indicates that a model based on expected frequencies has a worse **goodness of fit**, implying evidence against the null hypothesis.

goodness of fit An assessment of the correspondence between an observed pattern of data and a particular model of that data.

observed frequency The number of times that a particular outcome is observed. This is compared to the expected frequency in order to assess how well a particular model fits the data.

Examining the relationship between two categorical variables: The chi-square test of independence for 2×2 tables

The previous case dealt with a single categorical variable. Where we have two categorical variables then we can use very similar principles. In many ways this development is akin to moving from one-way to two-way ANOVA, but it is actually much simpler.

Let us look at the data on eating disorders again. Imagine we had 40 people, 20 of whom were male and 20 were female. We saw before that there was a different rate of eating disorders for males and females, but the question we would like to be able to answer is whether this is a remarkable event. A more formal way of asking this question is to imagine that males and females were equally likely to experience an eating disorder, that is, does the likelihood of an eating disorder *depend* on sex or is it *independent* of sex. Under such circumstances how likely is it that a pattern as unusual as the one we have obtained would occur by chance? Recall that our data were as follows:

	Male	Female
Do not have eating disorder	15	12
Have eating disorder	5	8

The format in which this data set is presented is called a **contingency table**. It shows the frequencies for a set of combinations of events or **contingencies**. This particular 2×2 table shows the frequencies of four contingencies: being male *and* having no eating disorder, being female *and* having no eating disorder, being male *and* having an eating disorder, and being female *and* having an eating disorder.

There are several ways that we could try to make inferences about the data in this table. One thing we could do is compare the proportion of people with eating disorders for males and females using the binomial test (and its normal approximation). This procedure would be fine, but in this section we will consider another approach using the χ^2 distribution. Our reasons for doing this are simply that the χ^2 distribution can be applied to a much wider set of circumstances – including ones in which there are more than two levels of the variable in question.

To calculate a value of χ^2 we simply compare the expected frequencies with the observed frequencies as we did for one-way χ^2. The only slightly tricky feature of this task is the calculation of the expected frequencies. To do this we simply need to imagine for a moment what the table would look like if the *same* proportion of males and females had eating disorders. Put another way, we want to know how many people could be expected to have an eating disorder if sex was irrelevant (i.e., eating disorders are independent of sex).

You might think that the obvious way to do this would be to assume that the expected frequencies were all the same. However, we cannot do this because some contingencies are more common than others due to a higher base rate. To illustrate this, imagine that the contingency table looked like this:

	Male	Female
Do not have eating disorder	15	120
Have eating disorder	5	80

In this case there are obviously more women with eating disorders but this is partly because there are more women in the sample. What we need to do therefore is to calculate expected frequencies in a way that takes into account base-rate information concerning the overall preponderance of events in the categories that make up the table — in this case men versus women, and people who have eating disorders versus people who do not.

To calculate these expected frequencies we first need to compute the **marginal totals** for both the rows and columns. These are shown for the original data in the table below:

	Male	Female	(Row totals)
Do not have eating disorder	15	12	27
Have eating disorder	5	8	13
(Column totals)	20	20	$N = 40$

With these row and column totals we can compute the expected frequency (f_e) of each contingency. This is done for each contingency using the following formula:

$$f_e = (\text{row total} * \text{column total})/N$$

For both males and females who do not have an eating disorder this expected frequency is as follows:

$$f_e = (27 * 20)/40$$
$$= 13.5$$

And for both males and females who have an eating disorder:

$$f_e = (13 * 20)/40$$
$$= 6.5.$$

We can now elaborate on our initial contingency table by including the expected frequencies in parentheses next to the four contingencies:

	Male	Female	(Row totals)
Do not have eating disorder	15 (13.5)	12 (13.5)	27
Have eating disorder	5 (6.5)	8 (6.5)	13
(Column totals)	20	20	$N = 40$

As we did with the previous case, we can then calculate the sum of squares of the differences between observed and expected frequencies for the four contingencies, dividing each one by the expected frequencies:

$$\chi^2 = \frac{\Sigma(f_o - f_e)^2}{f_e}$$

$$= ((15 - 13.5)^2/13.5) + ((12 - 13.5)^2/13.5)$$
$$+ ((5 - 6.5)^2/6.5) + ((8 - 6.5)^2/6.5)$$
$$= ((1.5)^2/13.5) + ((-1.5)^2/13.5) + ((-1.5)^2/6.5)$$
$$+ ((1.5)^2/6.5)$$
$$= (2.25/13.5) + (2.25/13.5) + (2.25/6.5) + (2.25/6.5)$$
$$= 0.17 + 0.17 + 0.35 + 0.35$$
$$= 1.03$$

We can then compare this value with the critical value of χ^2 for the given number of degrees of freedom. In two-way tables the degrees of freedom are equal to the number of rows minus one multiplied by the number of columns minus one. Accordingly, if there are two rows and two columns this gives us 1 degree of freedom.

We can see from Table C.5 that our obtained value of χ^2 is smaller than all the tabulated values for one degree of freedom. On this basis we therefore cannot conclude that our observed data is inconsistent with the assumption that the rows and columns are *independent*. In other words, the results provide no basis for rejecting the null hypothesis that a person's sex is unrelated to eating disorder.

As an interesting exercise, we can compare this result with the outcome of the binomial test in order to calculate the approximate probability that a sample of 13 people (the number of people with eating disorders in our contingency table) would include 8 or more girls if the probability of including a boy or a girl were both .5. This is a slightly different question than the one we asked above, but it is clearly related.

The binomial probability for this comparison is relatively large (.291). In other words, the event would not be particularly unlikely to occur if it were the result of a random process. Happily, then, we can see that these two statistical techniques would lead us to the same conclusion about our data.

There are a couple of important additional things to note. The first is that the chi-square procedure does not work as well if the expected frequencies are small. In particular, where the expected frequency of any contingency is less than 5 it is best *either* not to employ this procedure *or* to make adjustments to the data or to the calculation of the statistic. This can be done using the **Yates correction**, but this procedure is not recommended for general use, so we will not discuss it further here.

Second, in addition to the chi-square statistic, 2×2 contingency tables can also be used to obtain a measure of association between variables. This is done very simply by dividing χ^2 by N. This produces a value between 0 and 1 that we call **phi** or ϕ (pronounced 'fy'). This is a correlation coefficient and can be interpreted just like any other correlation coefficient (e.g., Peason's r that we discussed in Chapter 10).

For the eating disorder data that we were working with above this calculation would produce phi $= 1.03/40 = .026$. Indeed, we can use phi as an indication of effect size (in the way that we discussed in Chapter 8), and by squaring phi we obtain a measure of the amount of variance shared by our variables. In this case, then, the correlation is small, and the effect is very weak. Certainly, this analysis would indicate that the relationship revealed in these data is not sufficiently strong to warrant taking it too seriously as evidence of a difference in the incidence of eating disorders among males and females.

A further point to note is that when it comes to assessing the outcomes of contingency tables it can often be helpful to calculate **odds**. Odds represent a particular way of expressing the likelihood of some event, and anyone who has ever placed a bet on a horse is likely to have some familiarity with this concept. If we decide a horse in a race has true 3 to 1 odds then we are saying that three out of four times the horse will lose, or in other words, that the horse has a 1 in 4 chance of winning (or put another way, it has a probability of winning of .25).

Bookmakers' odds are slightly different from true **betting odds** in that they are designed by the bookmaker to make money out of gamblers. Fortunately, then, experience at gambling is not the only way to learn about the principles of odds. With betting odds what happens is that the bookmaker estimates the true odds of each event and then offers some odds that give a higher probability of each horse winning than it actually does. For example, if the bookmaker thinks that the horse has a 1 in 4 chance of winning he may 'quote' the horse at 3 to 1 odds or lower. A further complication is that if the odds are better than 1 to 1 they are referred to as 'odds on'. A horse that has true odds of 3 to 1 *on* has a probability of winning of .75.

To convert true betting odds to probabilities we simply divide 1 by the odds plus 1, so that

$$p(e) = \frac{1}{\text{betting odds} + 1}$$

Plugging in odds of 3 to 1, we get $1/(3 + 1) = .25$.

To convert probabilities to true betting odds we reverse this operation by subtracting the probability of the event from 1 and dividing by the probability of the event, thus:

$$\text{Odds} = \frac{1 - p(e)}{p(e)}$$

A probability of .25 thus becomes $(1 - .25)/(.25) = 3$ (to 1).

As a further twist, in technical settings researchers usually drop the expression 'to 1' and invert these fractions. Betting odds of 3 to 1 would therefore be expressed as technical or **statistical odds** of .333 and odds of 3 to 1 on are expressed as 3.

For contingency tables we can also calculate **conditional odds**. These are statements of the likelihood of one event occurring given that another has occurred. They are calculated by dividing the frequency of one alternative by the frequency of the other alternative. For example, if we return to the eating disorders data, given that a person is female, the conditional odds of having an eating disorder are $8/12 = .666$, and given that a person is male, the conditional odds of having an eating disorder are $5/15 = 0.333$.

Once we have calculated conditional odds we can use these to create **odds ratios**. These are the ratios of the conditional odds of two alternatives, dividing the larger odds by the smaller odds (so that the ratio is capable of varying between ∞ and 1). In this case:

$$.666/.333 = 2$$

In other words, the odds of having an eating disorder for a female are double those for a male. Although this sounds like a large effect, the result of our χ^2 test gives us reason to doubt that the association is particularly remarkable.

Note, however, that if we had found the same relationship with a sample of 400 rather than 40 people we would have reached a different conclusion:

	Male	Female	(Row totals)
Do not have eating disorder	150 (135)	120 (135)	270
Have eating disorder	50 (65)	80 (65)	130
(Column totals)	200	200	$N = 400$

$$\chi^2 = \frac{\Sigma(f_o - f_e)^2}{f_e}$$
$$= ((150 - 135)^2/135) + ((120 - 135)^2/135) + ((50 - 65)^2/65)$$
$$+ ((8 - 6.5)^2/6.5)$$

$$= ((15)^2/135) + ((-1.5)^2/135) + ((-15)^2/65) + ((15)^2/65)$$
$$= (225/135) + (225/135) + (225/65) + (225/6.5)$$
$$= 1.67 + 1.67 + 3.46 + 3.46$$
$$= 10.26$$

In this case $\chi^2 = 10.26$, and we can see from Table C.5 that this cuts off less than .005 of the χ^2 distribution, suggesting that there is a small probability that a pattern as extreme as this would occur if males and females are equally likely to have eating disorders. Remember, though, that the phi coefficient will still be exactly the same (.026). So even though this pattern may now be considered to be statistically significant it is still a very weak effect. Again, if we had real data suggesting effects of this small size then we would be very cautious in reading too much into them.

These calculations do show, however, that χ^2 depends heavily on the value of N. In line with our earlier discussion of the importance of information about effect sizes, phi and the odds ratio can therefore be seen as providing useful additional indicators to help interpret this statistic.

Finally, we should note that χ^2 can be calculated for tables with many more contingencies than the four shown for a 2×2 table. However, the principles of such analyses are exactly the same as those described above – they just involve more calculations. For more complex contingency tables, a set of procedures called **loglinear analysis** is also available, but these procedures are beyond the scope of this book.

Q11.3[**]

The statistical odds of an event occurring are .25. Which of the following statements is true?

(a) The probability of the event occurring is .25.
(b) In four independent tests the expected frequency of the event is 1.
(c) The probability of the event occurring is .2.
(d) We cannot make a statement about probability or expected frequency, because odds are only ever calculated by bookmakers who are trying to make a profit.
(e) None of the above.

The correct answer is (c). Statistical odds can be converted into probabilities by converting them into betting odds and then using the formula $p(e) = 1/(\text{betting odds} + 1)$. Statistical odds of .25 represent betting odds of 4 (to 1), so $p(e) = 1/(4 + 1) = .2$. The easiest mistake to make here is to confuse odds with probability and hence to select (a). If one does this, one might also mistakenly select answer (b) because an expected frequency of one event in four tests is equivalent to a probability of .25. (d) is wrong because odds are frequently used by statisticians to make statements about probability or expected frequency.

betting odds Statements of the likelihood of a given event occurring expressed in terms of the expected frequency of it not occurring and the expected frequency of it occurring. For example, if a die is expected to fall on a '3' one time out of six (i.e., where $p = .167$), the betting odds of obtaining a '3' are 5 to 1.

conditional odds Statements of the likelihood of one event occurring given that another has occurred. These are obtained from the data in specific rows or columns of *contingency tables*, and are expressed in terms of the frequency with which the event occurs in a given row or column divided by the frequency with which it does not occur in the same row or column.

contingencies Events which are the combination of two or more categories of event. For example, the contingency of being a female with an eating disorder is the consequence of being both (a) female and (b) having an eating disorder.

contingency table Tables which present information about the frequencies of all possible contingencies associated with two or more categories of event.

loglinear analysis A statistical procedure for analysing data in complex contingency tables.

marginal totals The sum of the *contingencies* in a given row or column of a *contingency table*.

odds Statements of the likelihood of a given event occurring expressed as the ratio of the expected frequency of two alternatives: that the event occurs and that it does not occur.

odds ratios Ratios of conditional odds. These indicate the relative likelihood of one event rather than another occurring given that another has occurred.

phi A correlation coefficient that measures the association between two sets of dichotomous scores (e.g., male–female, yes–no).

statistical odds Statements of the likelihood of a given event occurring expressed in terms of the expected frequency of it occurring divided by the expected frequency of it not occurring. For example, if a die is expected to fall on a '3' one time out of six, the statistical odds of obtaining a '3' are $1/5 = 0.20$. Note that this is *not* the same as the probability of the event occurring.

Yates correction A statistical procedure used when calculating the chi-square statistic and the expected frequency of any ***contingency*** is very small. It was once very common to use this, but in fact it has been shown to be appropriate in only a very limited set of circumstances (where ***marginal totals*** are known in advance – which is rare).

Distribution-free tests

In previous chapters we have discussed tests that make reasonably restrictive assumptions about the shape of the population distributions that we sample from. For example, we assume in performing a between-subjects *t*-test that the samples are drawn from populations that are normally distributed and have equal variances. We noted before that it is customary (but not always correct) to believe that procedures like the *t*-test and ANOVA are robust to the violation of assumptions. In other words, it is widely believed that these tests produce similar results regardless of whether or not the assumptions hold.

However, sometimes it is not convenient or sensible to assume that these assumptions hold, and sometimes the violation of assumptions can compromise the inferences that we make about our data. As we noted earlier, if it can be true that the mean is sometimes a misleading statistic for describing a distribution then it must also be the case that a test that compares the means of two distributions can be comparing two misleading indicators. Clearly, we need alternatives to deal with such situations. **Distribution-free statistics** provide such alternatives.

Roughly speaking, distribution-free statistics involve procedures that are relatively free of restrictive assumptions about the *shape* of the distribution of the population that the sample was drawn from. They still involve distributions (such as distributions of the test statistic and the observed sample distribution) and they still involve assumptions about the sampling distribution, but the assumptions they make about the shape of the population distribution are generally quite relaxed. Distribution-free statistics have many similarities to, and overlap with, a family of procedures called **non-parametric statistics**. The term non-parametric refers to the fact that such statistics do not make assumptions about the parameters of particular distributions.

In what follows, we will stick with the term distribution-free because, although the term 'nonparametric' is more common, it refers less obviously to the key feature of such tests: that they are free of restrictive assumptions about the shapes of distributions. The term '**tests with relaxed assumptions**' can also be used to convey this central idea more clearly.

Q11.4**

Which of the following statements is true?

(a) Distribution-free tests do not involve distributions.
(b) Nonparametric tests do not involve distributions.
(c) Nonparametric tests are very different from distribution-free tests.
(d) Distribution-free tests are free of assumptions about the parameters of the distribution from which a sample is drawn.
(e) None of the above.

The correct answer is (e). (a) and (b) are false because both distribution-free and non-parametric tests involve distributions (e.g., of a test statistic and the observed sample). (c) is false because there is considerable overlap between distribution-free and non-parametric tests. (d) is false because it confuses the definition of distribution-free and non-parametric tests. Distribution-free tests are free of strong assumptions about the *shape* of the distribution from which a sample is drawn; *non-parametric tests* are free of assumptions about the parameters of the distribution from which a sample is drawn.

---

distribution-free statistics Statistics which involve procedures that are relatively free of restrictive assumptions about the shape of the distribution of the population that a sample is drawn from.
non-parametric statistics Statistics which do not make assumptions about the parameters of the distribution of the population that a sample is drawn from.
tests with relaxed assumptions Another term for *distribution-free statistics* that conveys more clearly the idea that such tests still involve distributions, but simply make relaxed assumptions about them.

Examining differences between two groups with relaxed assumptions: The Mann–Whitney test

In this chapter we discuss one distribution-free statistic in detail: the **Mann–Whitney test.** This is an alternative to the between-subjects t-test but it has the great advantage that it can be used when the assumptions of the t-test do not hold or when the data are not measured in a form that allows direct numerical comparisons (i.e., where data are not obtained using ratio or interval scales).

A good example would be a case where our data represented the rankings of people from two groups. Let us imagine that some sports psychologists had developed a new coaching method for athletes and then entered the runners trained under traditional and new methods into a race. The dependent variable of interest here is not the time taken to complete the race but the placings or rankings of athletes in the race.

Imagine that the data for 26 athletes looked like this:

Group	Place	
Old	1	
New		2
New		3
Old	4	
New		5
Old	6	
New		7
New		8
New		9
Old	10	
New		11
Old	12	
Old	13	
New		14
New		15
Old	16	
New		17
Old	18	
Old	19	
New		20
New		21
New		22
Old	23	
Old	24	
Old	25	
Old	26	
Σ rank	197	154
Mean rank	15.2	11.8

We can see from this table that athletes trained under the new method came 2nd, 3rd and 5th and so on, and that athletes trained under the old method came 1st, 4th and 6th etc. The mean rankings for each group and the sums of rankings are also shown as we will use these in the calculations below.

The question we would like to answer (but that a *t*-test cannot help us with) is whether the average ranking of one of the groups is better or worse than we would expect by chance. If one group is better than expected we know that the other must be worse (as there are only two groups). In this case it is worth finding out whether the mean ranking obtained by athletes with the new training method is clearly better than we would expect if training method makes no difference. If training makes no difference then the mean rankings of both groups should both be estimates of the expected (i.e., mean) population ranking of both groups. As we noted when discussing the calculation of the median in Chapter 6, this mean rank is 13.5 (it is not a whole number because the total, 26, is even).

The Mann–Whitney test gives us information that helps us to answer the above question. For the sake of simplicity we will focus on the normal approximation of this test that can be used where $N > 25$ (or where the N for at least one group is 20). However, it is worth noting that if $N < 25$ then a slightly different procedure is used (one that involves using special statistical tables).

To calculate the normal approximation we compare the total (rather than mean) rankings of one of the groups with the expected total ranking of that group. If that total ranking is relatively small (when judged against the amount of error in estimating those rankings) then this would suggest that that group has done very well in the race (i.e., that it has more rankings near the top).

The expected sum of rankings is obtained by calculating:

$$U_e = N_1((N_1 + N_2 + 1)/2)$$

where N_1 is the number of people in group 1 and N_2 the number of people in group 2. The standard error of the U-statistic is given by:

$$S_U = \sqrt{\frac{N_1 N_2 (N_1 + N_2 + 1)}{12}}$$

We then calculate z in the following way:

$$z = \frac{U_1 - U_e}{S_U}$$

where U_1 is the sum of rankings for group 1.

To show how this works when dealing with the data from our athletics race, let us nominate the new training method as group 1. As we saw in the above table, this group has a total ranking (U_1) of 154. Here

$$U_e = 13((13 + 13 + 1)/2) = 13 * 13.5 = 175.5$$

and

$$S_U = \sqrt{\frac{13 * 13 * (13 + 13 + 1)}{12}}$$
$$= 19.5$$

It therefore follows that

$$z = (154 - 175.5)/19.5$$
$$= -1.10$$

This z-value can be compared to the values in Table C.1. Ignoring the sign, we can see that it cuts off a relatively large proportion of the normal curve, corresponding to a probability of .136. This suggests that such a difference in rankings would not be remarkably rare if it were the result of chance. Accordingly, we do not have a sound basis for concluding that type of training makes a difference to athletic performance.

In the example that we have just used we relied on data that already existed as rankings (placings in a race). However, it is worth noting that the Mann–Whitney test can also be used where our data exist as scores (e.g., as the times that the individual athletes took to complete the race). To use scores of this form we need to convert them into ranks and then use these in the analysis. As discussed in the previous section, this strategy is especially useful where we have scores but we do not want to make assumptions associated with a particular statistical procedure (e.g., a *t*-test).

One complication with the above procedure arises where two scores are identical (and therefore have equal rankings – these are called ties or tied rankings). Where this happens the calculation of the value of the statistic is problematic. The simplest, if not always the best, solution is to give both scores the same rank. The easiest way to do this is to give each their median rank. For example, if the 4th and 5th ranked scores are equal both could be given a ranking of 4.5.

A more serious complication is that although the Mann–Whitney test is normally used to compare the central tendencies of two groups (and it is differences in the central tendencies that the test is most sensitive to) it also tests differences in the *dispersion* of the distributions.

Q11.5***

Accordingly, it may be the case that the null hypothesis of no difference between the two groups is rejected because they have a different spread rather than a different mean (or mean rank). The test does not tell us whether this is the case and so this is clearly something to bear in mind when interpreting test results.

The Mann–Whitney test is the distribution-free analogue of which of the following tests?

(a) The between-subjects *t*-test.
(b) The within-subjects *t*-test.
(c) One-way ANOVA.
(d) Two-way ANOVA.
(e) Pearson's *r*.

The correct answer is (a). Like the *t*-test, the Mann–Whitney test compares scores that are obtained from two independent groups and is used to establish whether the central tendency of those two groups is different. (b) is incorrect because a within-subjects *t*-test is used to analyse data from the *same* sample on two occasions. (c) is incorrect because one-way ANOVA can be used to analyse data from *more than two* groups. (d) is incorrect because two-way ANOVA is used to simultaneously analyse data that relates to *two* independent variables. (e) is incorrect because Pearson's *r* is used to analyse the *relationship* between two variables.

Mann–Whitney test A distribution-free test that is usually used to compare the central tendency of two independent groups. In this regard it is the distribution-free analogue of a between-subjects *t*-test.

Some options for other cases

In this section we will briefly discuss some other cases that you might encounter and suggest options that you might take. However, because each of these tests is quite different (and each requires a specific table to interpret their outcomes) we will not provide details or examples of how to calculate them. These are available in other sources (e.g., a specialist text on distribution-free statistics such as Siegel, 1956).

Examining differences between two related samples with relaxed assumptions: The Wilcoxon test

In the previous section we discussed the Mann–Whitney test for comparing two groups and noted that this was analogous to the between-subjects *t*-test. There are also analogues of the within-subjects *t*-test. These can be used when the samples are related (e.g., when comparing measurements of the same sample on two measures). The best known of these is the **Wilcoxon matched-pairs signed-ranks test**. This works in much the same way as the Mann–Whitney test in that it involves computing a sum based on ranks. However, unlike the Mann–Whitney test, the sum computed is the sum of the signed ranks of the differences between the two variables. If this sum has a large absolute value (either negative or positive) then we are more likely to conclude that there is a difference between the variables.

The Wilcoxon test also assumes that the differences in scores represent an ordinal scale. This assumption may not hold (and it is often difficult to tell whether it does). In this regard it is worth noting that alternatives such as the **sign test** and the **McNemar test** can be used in these circumstances, but that these are less powerful.

The sign test is a straightforward application of the binomial test presented at the start of this chapter. Calculate the signed difference between each pair of scores (i.e., the scores for the same participant on the two measures). If the proportion of positive or negative scores is very small when compared with the binomial distribution, then this is evidence against the null hypothesis of no difference.

McNemar test A distribution-free test that is used to compare the central tendency of sets of data that are collected in pairs from the same participants. It is particularly applicable to 'before' and 'after' designs in which data are obtained from the same source on two occasions.

sign test The binomial test when used to compare the central tendency of sets of data that are collected in pairs. The test is based on attaching plus and minus signs to differences between pairs of data. It makes no assumptions about the distribution from which those data are drawn.

Wilcoxon matched-pairs signed-ranks test A distribution-free test that is used to compare the central tendency of sets of data that are collected in pairs from the same participants. In this regard it is the distribution-free analogue of a within-subjects *t*-test.

Examining differences between more than two groups with relaxed assumptions: The Kruskal–Wallis test

Distribution-free comparisons between groups are also possible when there are more than two groups. This is a direct analogue of one-way within-subjects ANOVA and it is called the **Kruskal–Wallis test**. It works in much the same way as the Mann–Whitney test. Unfortunately, it is far more difficult to find distribution-free alternatives for testing statistical interactions. However, a **Friedman test** can be used to compare more than two related samples.

> **Friedman test** A distribution-free test that is usually used to compare the central tendency of more two related groups. In this regard it is the distribution-free analogue of one-way within-subjects ANOVA.
>
> **Kruskal–Wallis test** A distribution-free test that is usually used to compare the central tendency of more than two independent groups. In this regard it is the distribution-free analogue of one-way between-subjects ANOVA.

Using ranked data in correlations

Many older statistics texts suggest that the **Spearman's correlation** (r_S) should be used when judging whether ranked data are correlated. However, although the data take the specific form of ranks, this procedure is actually identical to the Pearson product-moment correlation that we discussed in Chapter 9 (and the **point biserial correlation**). As a result, it is not helpful to consider it further (even though its calculation can be made easier by application of a special formula). However, it is worth noting that when dealing with ranked data, tied ranks still present something of a tricky issue. As we discussed in relation to the Mann–Whitney test, the easiest way to deal with scores that have the same rank is to assign them the same value (their median rank).

> **point biserial correlation** A correlation coefficient used to assess the degree of association between two variables when one is dichotomous (e.g., male–female; right–wrong).
>
> **Spearman's correlation** (r_S) A correlation coefficient used to assess the degree of linear association between two sets of ranked data.

Choosing the most powerful test

Given the wide variety of tests that are available for answering related questions, this implies a choice of test. It is important to have rules for making those choices as clear as possible.

As it happens, there is a reasonably straightforward rule that we can suggest. The test that should be applied is the most powerful test that can appropriately answer the question of interest. You will recall that by power we are referring to the ability of the test to reveal relationships if they actually exist. By 'appropriately answer' we mean that the assumptions of that test are not grossly violated in ways that threaten the interpretation of the test. As a simple rule of thumb, the classical or parametric tests that we have discussed in earlier chapters will be more powerful than the distribution-free alternatives that we have considered in this chapter and hence they will be more appropriate *provided that the assumptions of these tests hold.*

Overview and checklist

It is now possible to return to the table at the start of this chapter and present an extended range of alternatives. This is the purpose of Table 11.2.

Table 11.2 Statistical tests (including those with relaxed assumptions) and when to use them

Form of data	Question of interest	Assumptions about data*	Test used
One variable with many levels	Does the mean differ from some value (e.g., zero)?	(i) Population variances are unknown; (ii) observations are independent; (iii) the sample is drawn from a normally distributed population.	One-sample *t*-test
One variable with two categories; one variable with many levels	Are the means of the two categories different?	(i) Population variances are unknown; (ii) observations are independent; (iii) the two categories are drawn from populations with the same variance; (iv) the categories are drawn from normally distributed populations.	Between-subjects *t*-test
One variable with more than two categories; one	Are the means of the categories different?	(i) Population variances are unknown; (ii) observations are	ANOVA

Table 11.2 Continued

Form of data	Question of interest	Assumptions about data*	Test used
variable with many levels		independent; (iii) the categories are drawn from populations with the same variance; (iv) the categories are drawn from normally distributed populations.	
Two variables with many levels	Are the means of the two variables different?	(i) Population variances are unknown; (ii) observations are independent; (iii) variables are correlated; (iv) variables are drawn from normally distributed populations.	Within-subjects t-test
Two variables with many levels	Are scores on the two variables related?	There is a linear and bivariate normal relationship between the variables.	Pearson product-moment correlation coefficient
One variable with two levels	Is one level of the variable more common than the other?	None	Binomial test
One variable with more than two levels	Do the levels occur with the frequencies we would expect?	None	χ^2 test of goodness of fit
Two variables with two or more levels	Are the two categorical variables related?	None	χ^2 test of independence
One variable with two categories; one variable with many levels	Do the two categories have different central tendencies?**	None	Mann–Whitney test
Two variables with many levels	Is the central tendency of the two variables different?	None	Sign test
One variable with more than two categories; one variable with many levels	Do the categories have different central tendencies?	None	Kruskal–Wallis test

* We assume in each case that each observation of a different person is independent.
** As noted in the text, this is the question of interest rather than the question the test is necessarily informative about, as the test also provides information about differences in dispersion.

Obviously the complexity of the range of matters that we can address has greatly increased. Indeed, armed with an understanding of the ideas contained in this table you are in a position to tackle a mind-boggling array of different situations. In many cases you will actually choose to proceed using a computer package such as SPSS to help you. Nonetheless, you can see that the simplicity of the tests we have dealt with in this chapter means that this can often be done just as effectively (and with far greater risk of error) using a calculator and a sheet of paper.

There remains one final point to stress. Despite the diversity and sophistication of statistical tests, and the enormous lengths we all have to go to in order to understand how these tests work, they still do not normally answer the questions that we are interested in. A statistical test cannot tell us whether or not there is a real difference between groups or a relationship between variables, it cannot even tell us the probability that some relationship we have observed is true or due to chance. All the test can tell us is how likely the result we have observed would be if we make certain assumptions about the way the data were sampled from the population. This is why distribution-free statistics in particular are so important: precisely because they allow us to be somewhat more relaxed in our assumptions about the population (which we generally know very little about in most psychological research).

For this and other reasons, distribution-free statistics should really be used more widely in psychological research than they are. As we noted at the start of the chapter, the fact that we have spent so little time on them compared to the parametric alternatives is thus a reflection of the way the science of psychology is practiced rather than a statement about the value of these procedures. Bear in mind, then, that the most complex statistical analysis is not necessarily the best. Sometimes, less is more.

Further reading

There is a long tradition of using non-parametric statistics to analyse data from psychological research. In testament to this fact, Siegal's (1956) book remains one of the classic texts in this area. It contains details of a large number of non-parametric tests that can be used to tackle a broad range of research situations. Smithson's (2000) text includes detailed discussions of a number of the statistics discussed here and also includes a treatment of confidence intervals.

Siegel, S. (1956). *Non-parametric statistics for the behavioural sciences*. New York: McGraw-Hill.

Smithson, M. J. (2000). *Statistics with confidence*. London: Sage.

Other forms of data: A checklist for research evaluation and improvement

Potential problem	Question to ask	Potential improvement
Inferential uncertainty (see Chapter 7) about the frequency of two events, where only two are possible	Do the researchers want to compare the frequencies?	Conduct a binomial test to compute the probability of observing frequencies as extreme as the ones observed if both events occurred with their expected frequency. If $N > 25$ use the normal approximation to this test.
Inferential uncertainty about the frequency of more than two events, where there is one independent variable		Conduct a χ^2 test of goodness of fit to compare observed frequencies with expected frequencies. Unless the base rate of events differs, expected frequency equals the frequency of observations divided by the number of events. χ^2 is computed by summing the squares of the difference between observed and expected frequencies and dividing by the expected frequency. Table C.5 can be used to provide information about the probability of observing by chance a χ^2 score as large as the one obtained.
Inferential uncertainty about the frequency of more than two events, where there are two independent variables	Do the researchers want to see if there is a relationship between the variables, such that one event is more likely to occur when another event has also occurred?	Conduct a χ^2 test of independence to see whether the observed frequencies differ from the frequencies that would be expected if the same proportion of events occurred in the two levels of both variables. χ^2 is computed by summing the squares of the difference between observed and expected frequencies and dividing by the expected frequency. Table C.5 can be used to provide information about the probability of observing by chance a χ^2 score as large as the one obtained.
Significance fallacy	In testing for independence, have the researchers distinguished appropriately	Compute a phi-coefficient by dividing χ^2 by the total number of events, N. Consider significance levels for χ^2 in conjunction with effect sizes

Potential problem	Question to ask	Potential improvement
	between psychological and statistical significance?	(e.g., compare p and ϕ). Be alert to the dangers of making too much of statistically significant correlations when effect sizes are low.
Inferential uncertainty about the central tendency of scores obtained from two samples, where assumptions about the distribution of scores are violated	Do the researchers want to compare the scores?	Conduct a Mann–Whitney test by ranking all scores and comparing the expected sum of rank scores (U_e) with the sum of rank of scores in one sample (U_1). If $N > 25$ use the normal approximation to this test in which a z-score is obtained by subtracting U_e from U_1 and dividing by the standard error of the ranks. Table C.1 can be used to provide information about the probability of observing by chance a z-score as large as the one obtained.
Inferential uncertainty about the central tendency of scores obtained from the same sample, where assumptions about the distribution of scores are violated		Conduct a sign test by computing the differences between the two sets of scores. Use the binomial test to evaluate the probability of observing frequencies of positive and negative scores like the ones you have observed if there is really no difference between the variables.

Q11.6***

An organizational psychologist conducts a piece of research in which he tests the hypothesis that companies that have a pension plan retain more employees than companies that do not have a plan. To test this hypothesis he collects data from 60 companies recording (a) whether or not they have a pension plan and (b) what percentage of their employees are still working for the company after a year. However, on inspecting his data, the researcher finds that most companies retain a very high proportion of their employees and that scores on this measure are therefore very highly skewed. Which of the following tests would be most appropriate for comparing central tendencies?

(a) ANOVA.

(b) The χ^2 test of independence.

(c) The χ^2 test of goodness of fit.

(d) The Mann–Whitney test.

(e) The between-subjects t-test.

Q11.7*

Which of the following statements is false?

(a) Distribution-free tests can be useful when the assumptions of other tests are violated.

(b) Distribution-free tests are useful when handling categorical data.

(c) Non-parametric tests are useful when handling categorical data.

(d) Non-parametric tests have very few uses.

(e) Non-parametric tests and distribution-free tests both make relaxed assumptions about the parameters of population distributions.

Q11.8*

Which of the following is the main limitation of tests with relaxed assumptions?

(a) Their assumptions are generally too relaxed.

(b) They are usually very difficult to conduct.

(c) They can only be used effectively in applied settings.

(d) They provide information about odds rather than probabilities.

(e) They generally have less power than parametric tests.

The correct answer to 11.6 is (d), though this is controversial. Because one of the variables of interest here is categorical (company has/does not have pension plan), and the other has many levels (proportion of employees retained) the two potential tests the researcher could use are the Mann–Whitney and the between-subjects t-test. However, (e) is wrong because the distribution of data violates one of the assumptions of the t-test (that data are normally distributed). (a) is wrong because this same line of reasoning makes ANOVA inappropriate (noting too that this is identical to the between-subjects t-test where one variable has two categories). (b) and (c) are wrong because χ^2 tests require all data to be categorical.

The correct answer to 11.7 is (d). As we have shown in this chapter, non-parametric tests have a large number of uses and they are often both practical and easy to use. All of the other statements are true. As (a) and (e) suggest, non-parametric and distribution-free tests both make relaxed assumptions about population distributions, so they can be useful when the assumptions of other tests are violated. As (b) and (c) suggest, non-parametric and distribution-free tests are also both very useful when dealing with categorical data.

The correct answer to 11.8 is (e). The main limitation of tests with relaxed assumptions is that they tend to have less power than their parametric counterparts. Accordingly, *provided that the assumptions of parametric tests hold*, it is usually best to use these if possible. Having said that, tests with relaxed assumptions are generally very easy to conduct (so (b) is wrong), the fact that their assumptions are relaxed is one of their useful features (so (a) is wrong), and they can be used in a wide range of settings (not just applied ones, so (c) is wrong). (d) is wrong because not all such tests involve the use of odds, and those that do still provide information about probability.

Discussion/essay questions

(a) What reasons might a researcher have for using tests with relaxed assumptions?

(b) Which research practices have contributed to distribution-free tests being used less widely than other statistical techniques in psychology?

(c) Should psychologists use distribution-free tests more than they do?

(d) What are the limitations of distribution-free and non-parametric tests?

Practical problems

(a) An organizational researcher looks at the composition of company boards and finds that although 40% of these companies' employees are female, only 44 of 138 board members are women.

   (i) What is the expected frequency of female board members?

   (ii) Do these data provide statistical support for the hypothesis that women might be underrepresented at this level?

(b) A cognitive neuropsychologist conducts a study in which she investigates whether embedding words in song improves amnesic patients' memory. To do this, she gives 30 amnesiacs and 30 controls a poem to remember and another 30 amnesiacs and 30 controls a song to remember in which the words of that poem are sung. She then tests each group's recognition by presenting participants with one segment that was in the poem and one segment that was not, and asking them to correctly identify which of the two segments was in the original material they had learned. The numbers of participants who identify the correct segment are as follows:

	Poem	Song
Controls	28	29
Amnesiacs	16	27

(i) What is the expected frequency of correct identification in each sample of participants?

(ii) Is there any evidence that the amnesiacs' memory for poems is any better than chance?

(iii) Is there any evidence that the amnesiacs' memory is better when they learn the material in song rather than poem form?

(iv) Is there any evidence that learning the material in song rather than poem form has more impact on the amnesiacs' memory than on the memory of controls?

(v) To the extent that there is a relationship between learning context (song or poem) and participant type (control or amnesiac), what is its effect size?

(vi) Do the data suggest that there may be problems interpreting the impact of the independent variable on the recognition of the controls in this study?

(c) Educational psychologists are interested in seeing whether students' scores in final-year school exams were higher in 2002 than in 2001. To examine this, they obtain the scores from a random sample of 15 students in each of the two years. These are as follows (each mark is out of 100):

2001: 27.1, 44.5, 58.9, 70.4, 73.2, 84.2, 85.1, 88.2, 89.3, 90.2, 92.2, 93.2, 94.0, 94.5, 95.2

2002: 59.3, 74.2, 86.4, 86.7, 90.3, 93.3, 94.4, 94.6, 94.7, 95.3, 95.7, 96.6, 96.7, 97.1, 98.8

The researchers initially conduct a *t*-test to examine these data, but some critics of their research point out that this procedure is inappropriate because the distribution of scores is very skewed and hence it is inappropriate to assume that they are drawn from a normally distributed population.

(i) How should the researchers respond?

(ii) Would they reach a different conclusion if they used a distribution-free test to analyse their data?

Qualitative Methods

Despite the many differences between the statistical techniques that we have discussed in the previous five chapters, it is clear that they all have one thing in common: they involve the collection and manipulation of *quantitative data*. This means that when we thought about potential research questions (e.g., 'Does absence make the heart grow fonder?' 'Does attributional style affect psychological well-being?'), answers were provided that relied upon numbers rather than words and we had to devise scales or tests to measure things as varied as physical attraction, attributional style, anxiety, memory, and intelligence.

Moreover, having collected data in this form, we can see that the methods for analysing them could be understood in terms of a series of well-defined decisions that led to readily interpretable outcomes. Amongst psychologists in general there is also a high degree of agreement about the nature of these decisions and the sorts of products they should lead to. For example, having asked two independent groups of participants to rate the attractiveness of their partners on nine-point rating scales, almost all researchers would recommend that the data be examined by means of a *t*-test (providing that certain statistical assumptions are not violated).

This is all well and good. However, it is possible to object to these practices on the grounds that they misrepresent the underlying subject matter of psychology. Indeed, criticism of this form may have already occurred to you. Thus you might be prepared to accept that quantitative methods are elegant and coherent, but still be troubled by a feeling that numerical solutions do not really capture the world as you (and the participants in psychological research) know it. More specifically, you might point out that circling a number on a scale can never come close to capturing what it *means* to be in love, that a score on a test can never do justice to the *experience* of depression, or that when we say someone has a good memory we mean much more than that they can recall a lot of items from a meaningless list. In saying these things, you will be asking for examination of these phenomena that is *qualitative* rather than (just) quantitative and which does a better job of understanding them (a) as they are experienced by, and have meaning for, the people involved and (b) as they occur naturally 'in the real world'.

In this chapter we will look closely at some of the alternative ways of doing research that represent an attempt to respond to these sorts of objections. As we will see, beyond the details of the methods we discuss, a number of features distinguish the chapter from those that have preceded it. First amongst these is the fact that the choice of *which* qualitative method to use is made more difficult by the sheer variety of methods available. In a recent book, Tesch (1990) identifies nearly 30 such methods, and this is definitely an underestimate. Related to this point, while the procedures for handling quantitative data are relatively circumscribed and easy to codify (e.g., as in Appendix A), those for handling qualitative data are much more indeterminate and varied. There is only one correct way to perform a *t*-test, but an infinite number of ways in which most qualitative methods can be deployed. And finally, for both of these reasons there is much less agreement among researchers about exactly how qualitative analysis should be conducted. So, although there is some dispute about how to perform quantitative analysis (e.g., about whether the hypothesis-testing approach is appropriate; see Chapter 9), this is relatively mild compared to the heated debates that surround many aspects of qualitative research. Indeed, it is not too much of an exaggeration to suggest that the only thing that really unites the various strands of qualitative research is a shared recognition amongst those who do it of the limitations of a purely quantitative approach.

For all the above reasons, this chapter is therefore more an illustrative survey of qualitative methods than an attempt to provide a comprehensive grounding in their many features and uses. Indeed, to help structure the chapter we have chosen to focus on four different types of analysis. These serve to convey the range of options available to researchers and differ considerably in the extent to which they depart from, and present arguments against, the various quantitative approaches we have discussed in previous chapters.

However, before considering these methods and ideas in some detail, we will start by clarifying the basis of their proponents' misgivings about quantitative methods. This exercise has a dual purpose. On the one hand, it helps us to understand the basic motivations that underpin the various methods and to understand where those who use them are 'coming from'. On the other, it also raises a number of issues that *all* researchers need to consider carefully in developing a response to the challenge laid down by qualitative research. This is important because (as we intimated at the end of Chapter 5) there is a tendency for many researchers to advocate the exclusive use of quantitative methods and, in the process, to dismiss altogether the potential for qualitative approaches to contribute to psychological knowledge (usually on grounds that they are non-cumulative, non-generalizable, subjective, atheoretical and unscientific). This response is misguided, we suggest, because an appreciation of the issues raised by qualitative studies has the potential to enrich *all* psychological research – including that which is exclusively quantitative. For this reason, far from being incidental to psychological enquiry or being on the wane, qualitative methods have played a major role in the development of *all* branches of the discipline and interest in them is very much on the increase. Please bear in mind, though, that to some degree researchers are able to pick and choose among the methods on offer. A researcher does not need to accept every aspect of a particular critique in order to use most of the methods we describe.

Standard and radical critiques of quantitative approaches

The basis of what we can refer to as the standard critique of quantitative research is suggested by the introductory comments above and has probably already occurred to you either on reading the previous chapters or on exposure to research in lectures and laboratory practicals. Stated simply, researchers who expose themselves to 'real-world' psychological processes and states, such as love, hate, attachment, pride, uncertainty, depression, intelligence, attention and memory, often come to the view that there is 'more' to these phenomena than can be conveyed by mere numbers and by crude attempts to manipulate discrete aspects of the environment one at a time. Thinking, for example, about our hypothetical study in which we tried to test between the theories that 'absence makes the heart grow fonder' and 'absence leads the heart to wander', we can see that it is possible to object to this at a number of levels. First, one can argue that the study is limited by the fact that feelings of the heart were transposed into numbers on a scale when, in reality, their positive and negative aspects encompass emotions as varied (and with distinctions as subtle) as fondness, pleasure, affection, love, and lust as opposed to hate, dissatisfaction, distrust, pique, jealousy, and boredom. On a scale ranging from 1 (do not like at all) to 9 (like a great deal), when a participant circles '6', we might treat this as if it communicated reasonably strong liking, but could it not also be an indication of mild attraction, mild passion, mild warmth or mild fondness? Or perhaps it signifies something altogether different – like a sense of dutiful but ambivalent obligation. Did the person circle '6' because they really quite liked the target or because they felt some responsibility to express a certain degree of liking? Difficult as this question can be to answer, we can see that the problem becomes more serious if it is the case that circling a '6' means different things for different people. This is because these diverse meanings are necessarily conflated and unrecoverable when one makes a summary statement of the form 'the mean rating of participants in this condition was 6.40'. Moreover, dismissing this variation as statistical error or noise is problematic – not least because it does not actually show up as variation in the data set.

Beyond these problems with the dependent variable, a further problem relates to the practice of experimentally manipulating the independent variable. In our attraction study we did this by varying participants' exposure to a target and then measuring the impact of this manipulation on ratings of that target. Stop and think for a minute, though, about what the participants in the study were actually going through, and how they might have experienced this manipulation. Did they find the exposure pleasant, stimulating, or unusual? And did they find repeated exposure especially pleasant, increasingly tedious, or just plain weird? We discussed some of these issues in Chapter 4 when considering the problem of confounding – the fact that when an experimenter attempts to manipulate one thing (in this case interaction) they may actually be manipulating another (e.g., familiarity, boredom or weirdness). However, even if a researcher is sensitive to this issue, we can see that a more nuanced problem is that the same manipulation can mean different things to different people. So one person may have found repeated interaction with a stranger increasingly stimulating, while another found it increasingly bizarre.

One possible (and quite common) response to these observations is that while they pose problems for researchers in social areas of psychology which deal with 'warm and soft' phenomena such as emotions and feelings, they are of much less concern to experimenters in more cognitive areas who deal with 'cold and hard' questions of visual perception, verbal memory and the like. In fact, though, it is clear that this critique can be applied to these areas too.

Consider, for example, a cognitive experiment in which participants have to assign objects made of different shapes to different categories and the researcher measures the time it takes to complete the task as a function of stimulus complexity (e.g., by manipulating the number of different shapes that the object contains). While this dependent measure can be characterized as objective, it is nonetheless clear that it will be affected by the meaning that the task assumes for the participants. If they think the experiment is an intelligence test they may be motivated to respond quickly and in a way that is intended by the experimenter; but if they see it as 'another one of those pointless tasks designed to trick me' they may respond quite differently. In other words, the participants' *subjective orientation* to the task (i.e., the way they approach it) may vary and this will impact upon the meaning of both the independent and dependent variables. With one mindset the independent variable manipulates stimulus complexity and the dependent variable measures speed, but with the other mindset the independent variable may manipulate annoyance and the dependent variable may measure frustration or bloody-mindedness.

Faced with this dual problem relating to the indeterminate meaning of independent and dependent variables, one key recommendation of qualitative researchers is to adopt research practices that (a) focus on the meaning that particular behaviours have for participants them-selves (this is commonly referred to as a **hermeneutic approach**) and (b) actively involve participants in the research process (a principle referred to as **participant involvement** or **user involvement**). Even where participants are required to complete quantitative meas-ures, this usually means that they will be asked *individually* to discuss and explain *in their own words* what a particular response means and why they are making it. As a result, where quantitative approaches involve the cold, bare statistical analysis of numerical data, qualitative research focuses on words or other ways of capturing the warmer, richer elaboration of experience.

Differences of the above form constitute the standard critique of, and response to, quantitative research. Having said that, as we will see below, many of the actual methods in which these ideas are realized sit quite happily alongside the quantitative methods we have already discussed in previous chapters and can be used for very similar purposes. In this capacity qualitative methods can, for example, be used to embellish or question an empirical point, to demonstrate the relevance and utility of quantitative findings, or to formulate theore-tical and empirical objections to a particular body of work. Indeed Gilbert and Mulkay (1984) make the point that researchers often adopt a hermeneutic approach when explaining why their results have not come out as expected but a mainstream empiricist approach when dealing with results that they did expect.

There is, however, a more radical position than this which suggests that qualitative research needs to be doing something altogether incompatible with quantitative goals and practices. There are different components of this radical critique that not all researchers subscribe to, but three are widely discussed in various forms and arenas. First amongst these is an objection to the philosophies of **realism** or **positivism** that can be seen to underpin most quantitative research. Realism and positivism reflect the view, which is usually implicit in psychological research, that there is a set of objective psychological facts 'out there' awaiting 'discovery' by suitably trained researchers. For example, if a researcher sets out to test the theory that 'absence makes the heart grow fonder' or that 'memory declines with reduced attention' he or she implicitly assumes that there is something in the world which corresponds straightforwardly to 'fondness' or 'memory' (i.e., that these are DVs which can be measured objectively), and, by the same token, that there is something that he or she can do in the world that corresponds straightforwardly to a manipulation of 'absence' or 'attention' (i.e., that these are IVs which can be manipulated objectively).

Radical critics of quantitative methods reject these assumptions. In particular, they argue that features of the world only exist as a result of a set of meanings which are actively *constructed* by communities within it (e.g., scientists, students, Westerners). From this perspective, what 'counts' as 'fondness', 'memory', 'absence' or 'attention' can be seen to depend on who you are and where you fit into the social structure. Fondness, for example, might mean something different to a young person and an old person, and attention might mean something different to a cognitive psychologist and a soldier. Amongst other things, this means that fondness and attention are things which can be displayed and achieved in different ways by different communities and that to understand whether or not they have been achieved one must understand and take the perspective of the particular community in question.

From this viewpoint, then, there is no such thing as an objective psychological fact, and the process of discovery is essentially one which involves conferring novel meanings on particular experiences. Having found that people react negatively to strong advertising campaigns a researcher may claim to have discovered evidence of a 'rebound process', but one could actually argue that they (and those who accept their discovery) have merely come to interpret a particular set of events in a new way and that other equally valid interpretations of this finding are possible (e.g., that it is an example of a 'threat process' or a 'denial process'). One can also suggest that these alternative interpretations have just as much claim to validity and indeed are just as likely to find favour at some time in the future – for example, if people from a different sector of the research community become powerful. Indeed, this argument is consistent with Kuhn's view that science moves forward through paradigm shifts, rather than progress-in-the-abstract, and through the development of *different* understandings, not necessarily *better* ones (see Chapter 2).

The above objections are consistent with philosophies of **idealism, constructionism, constructivism, relativism**, or (more loosely) **postmodernism**. Broadly speaking, these are united by the view that no uniquely valid interpretation of the world is possible, for the simple reason that multiple interpretations of it exist and each appears equally valid when looked at from the perspective of the interpreter. If it is true that 'one man's meat is another man's poison', how can psychological reactions to a piece of pork be understood other than by reference to the subjective reality of the person who is asked to eat it? In other words, we cannot know whether pork is meat or poison without endeavouring to find out something about the cultural world of the would-be consumer.

Arguments of this form contribute to a second component of the radical critique which involves a rejection of researchers' general drive to develop universal laws of cause and effect (what is sometimes referred to as a **nomothetic approach**). Against this, and for reasons which follow from the above arguments, there are researchers who argue instead for an approach which attempts to understand behaviour *in the contexts where it occurs* without seeking to elevate any such understanding to the status of a law (this is sometimes referred to as an **idiographic approach**).

We can illustrate this point with reference to a team of researchers who reject the 'standard' goal of striving to conduct studies which might ostensibly allow them to conclude that 'absence makes the heart grow fonder'. As a qualitative alternative, these researchers might conduct a study of two groups of people who were separated from their partners (e.g., overseas students and workers on an oil rig) and try (a) to identify the different meaning that separation assumed for each group (or subgroups within them) and (b) to show how these different meanings are an aspect of different conceptions of what love is and what relationships are for. On the basis of such investigation, rather than concluding that absence makes the heart grow fonder (or that it does so only for a particular group in particular circumstances, as a more complex ANOVA design might suggest), the researchers might conclude instead that the ability to feel fondly towards one's partner when separated from him or her is dependent upon an ability to experience absence in a particular way and that this ability is constructed or avoided within particular communities in order to achieve particular objectives (e.g., to be seen to be being 'doing romantic love' or 'doing masculinity'). Expressing a feeling that absence does or does not makes one's heart grow fonder (as one might do by circling either '7' or '2' on a questionnaire) might therefore be understood as a way of constructing oneself as a 'sensitive new age guy' or a 'hard man' in order to have a particular sort of relationship with one's partner (which might then be used to legitimate or explain a whole host of other behaviours).

This, we can see, is an altogether different answer to that which emerges from 'standard' quantitative research – in form, content and function. Amongst other things, it means that while a quantitative researcher might feel qualified on the basis of his or her research to give you a very short answer to the question 'if my partner goes overseas will she love me more or less when she returns?', a qualitative researcher is more likely to sit you down and start by asking 'well, what exactly do you mean by "love"?'. The qualitative researcher might also want to move away from considering love as a variable and start thinking about the ways in which the idea of 'love' is used in everyday interaction.

Developing these arguments, a third and final point on which the radical critique argues against quantitative approaches is in its explicit recognition of the researcher's *involvement* in the research process and the interpretation of its outcomes, together with an associated belief that the products of scientific enquiry may only have *subjective*, not objective, validity. Such objections are targeted at a range of practices commonly associated with quantitative methods but are most clearly expressed in an opposition to the standard practices for writing up research findings. If, for example, one reads the sample research report in Appendix B (entitled 'The role of children's perceived sex in judgements of their emotions'), it is clear that it is written in a very clinical style and tells the story of what was done and what was found in a dispassionate and seemingly disinterested way. As a result 'the facts' appear to emerge as the result of a cold scientific process from which the wishes, beliefs, and values of the researcher have been totally expunged. In fact, though, it seems reasonable to assume that these wishes, beliefs and values had a considerable role to play in the research and that, as aspects of the scientific process, they are just as important as the ones we conventionally report (and may be even more important; see Spears & Smith, 2001). For example, the fact that we chose to test a particular theory in a particular way might have depended upon our relationship with the proponents of that theory (do we see them as allies or opponents?), our personal ambitions (will doing this research help us to get promotion?), and our political views (do we object to the theory on ideological grounds?). However, none of these issues is addressed in the report and a reader who was familiar with conventions in psychology would not expect them to be.

In important ways such factors mean that the outcomes of research *are* contingent upon researchers' own perspectives and objectives, and the apparent denial of this is something that many qualitative researchers object to. Amongst other things, this means that they are motivated to discover new ways of reporting psychological research that clearly identify their own role in the research process and which explicitly present their conclusions as *an* interpretation of the data, not *the only* interpretation. These points of divergence between quantitative and qualitative research are summarized in Table 12.1.

Table 12.1 Distinguishing features of quantitative and qualitative research

	Quantitative	Qualitative
Standard distinguishing features		
Form of data	Numbers	Situated practices
Form of analysis	Statistical	Illustrative
'Feel' of analysis	Cold, bare	Warm, rich
Radical distinguishing features		
Underlying philosophy	Positivist, realist	Relativist, constructionist
Goals of analysis	Nomothetic (oriented to discovery of universal causal laws)	Idiographic (oriented to understanding behaviour in its local context)
Products of analysis	Reliable, stable relationships between variables	Potentially variable meanings and rules
Application of findings	General	Particular
Stance assumed by researchers	Detached	Involved
Assumed status of analytical products	Objective	Potentially subjective

As presented in Table 12.1, the differences between quantitative and qualitative research appear to be rather stark. However, it is important to note that in practice the distinction between the two is not so black and white. This is for at least three reasons. First, not all qualitative researchers endorse a radical critique (or, if they do, they only embrace certain parts of it). Second, many quantitative researchers are sympathetic to the issues that this critique raises and try to display sensitivity to it in their research practice and theorizing. And finally, as we discuss in the next sections, while qualitative and quantitative methods are definitely different, most are grounded in the same basic activities and rest upon broadly similar analytical principles.

Q12.1*

> Which of the following is *not* associated with a postmodern approach to psychological research?
>
> (a) Idealism.
> (b) Positivism.
> (c) Constructivism.
> (d) Relativism.
> (e) Constructionism.

The correct answer is (b). In general, a postmodern approach to psychological research is *anti*-positivist, which is to say it rejects the idea that science can produce objective knowledge about the world. In contrast, a postmodern approach can encompass idealism (suggesting that scientific activity and knowledge are subjective; so (a) is wrong), constructivism and constructionism (suggesting that meaning is actively constructed by members of a particular community; so (c) and (e) are wrong), and relativism (suggesting that there is no such thing as universal objective truth; so (d) is wrong).

constructionism/constructivism Philosophies which suggest that meaning and reality do not exist in a fixed form external to the perceiver but rather are actively constructed by members of a particular community in order to achieve particular objectives. Although very similar, these two philosophies have slightly different nuances. In particular, constructivism can refer to an analytic approach which is based on examination of the way in which different realities are created.

hermeneutic approach An approach to research which focuses on the particular meaning that specific actions have for those who engage in them.

idealism A philosophy which suggests that features of the world are created through the subjective act of perceiving the world and hence are not amenable to measurement or definitive characterization.

idiographic approach An approach to research which attempts to understand phenomena in the particular context in which they arise and which is not oriented to the discovery of universal causal laws (of the form 'A always leads to B').

nomothetic approach An approach to research which is oriented to the discovery of universal causal laws (of the form 'A always leads to B').

participant involvement Research practice which acknowledges the role that participants play in research and which seeks to involve them in as much of the research process as possible.

positivism An approach to science which assumes that scientific activity produces (and should aim to produce) knowledge about objectively present and knowable features of the world.

postmodernism In popular (and rather loose) usage, a philosophy which embraces the tenets of idealism, relativism and constructivism in arguing that the constructs of value and worth are entirely dependent on the perspective of the judge and therefore that they are impossible to establish objectively.

realism A philosophy which suggests that features of the world exist in an objective form which makes them amenable to measurement and definitive characterization.

relativism A philosophy which asserts that there is no such thing as universal objective truth. Instead it is asserted that different interpretative frameworks and perspectives create their own truths and that no absolute criteria exist for differentiating between these in order to establish their validity.

user involvement Research practice which acknowledges the need to do research which is of benefit to particular communities and which seeks to involve potential users in as much of the research process as possible.

Methods of collecting qualitative data

As suggested above, although quantitative methods are different from qualitative ones, the methods and principles that guide data collection are often very similar. Indeed, almost all of the techniques that are typically used to collect quantitative data can also be used to collect qualitative data. This is particularly true of a number of the main methods of data collection that we have discussed in previous chapters – including interviews, case studies, archival studies and observational studies. In all of these settings, rather than seeking to gather numerical data (e.g., by using a survey instrument) a researcher can choose to gather verbal data from interviews (structured or unstructured), group discussion (e.g., using **focus groups** or **delphi groups**), written communication (e.g., letters, memos, public documents), recorded material (e.g., radio programmes, television interviews, documentaries, chat-shows), and a whole range of other sources (e.g., the Internet, transcripts of court or legislative proceedings).

As well as these generic methods for data collection, qualitative researchers have also devised a number of tools that enable them to collect data in specific forms. We will look at a few of these in more detail below, but some of the best known tools are the **Q-sort**, the **verbal protocol** and the **repertory grid**. Each of these has particular features which allow researchers to abstract theoretically relevant forms of information from more complex material (in the same way that a mean summarizes particular information about a response distribution).

Considered as a whole, qualitative methods of data-gathering vary in three key respects. First, the data can be structured or unstructured. Broadly speaking, the more structured data are, the more likely they are to be handled in clearly and consensually agreed ways after having been collected. This is clearest in the case of the tools alluded to above where widely accepted practices exist for managing data and reporting the results of their analysis. Against this, data from less structured sources (e.g., open-ended interviews, websites) are much more likely to be handled in idiosyncratic ways that are tailored to the specific goals of the researcher.

Second, data can be gathered *explicitly for research purposes* or can exist *independently of research*. For example, a researcher who seeks to gain insight into processes of political leadership could either examine the content of politicians' television interviews or conduct interviews with them themselves (Reicher & Hopkins, 1996, 2001).

A third difference, related to the second, is that researchers themselves can either be internal or external to the data. For example, they can choose to conduct an interview themselves or to examine an interview that has been conducted by someone else.

In any of these scenarios the researcher will always be in control of the analytic process, but the researcher's proximity to the data and the purposes for which they were produced both have a bearing upon issues of *reactivity* (as discussed in Chapters 4 and 5). This is not because reactivity is an issue in some situations and not in others, but rather because the **reactive focus** of research differs across different data-gathering contexts. Specifically, where the researcher is internal to data-gathering the participant will generally be reacting directly to the researcher (and to his or her assumed agenda), but where he or she is external to data-gathering the participant will usually be reacting to the perceived agenda of a different audience.

Although external agents may have interests that are independent of the researcher (and hence those data are less likely to be affected by participants' sensitivity to the researchers' goals), none of these options is inherently 'better' than any other. Instead, reactive focus represents one potential source of variation in the data. Indeed, this variation often becomes a *topic* for investigation, as may happen if a researcher compares the things that a person says to a researcher in private with those that they say to a public audience.

A good example of this strategy is provided by Gilbert and Mulkay's (1984) examination of biochemists' accounts of the scientific process. In their research articles and in descriptions of their own research activities the scientists drew upon what Gilbert and Mulkay refer to as an **empiricist repertoire.** This presented science as a completely objective activity in which progress was driven simply by the accumulation of critical data. However, in their private discussions with the researchers a **contingent repertoire** emerged in which the activities of competing scientists were dismissed for being driven by forces as varied as fashion, personal taste, luck, pig-headedness, blindness, prejudice and sheer stupidity. It is interesting to note, in passing, that the content of Gilbert and Mulkay's (1984) research is clearly relevant to the broad issues discussed in this chapter as it is possible to argue that quantitative methods in psychology (and the products with which it is associated; e.g., empirical reports like the one in Appendix B) are examples of the empiricist repertoire, while qualitative methods are generally more compatible with the contingent repertoire in serving to emphasize the subjective, human aspects of the research process (Potter, 1996; Woolgar, 1996).

---

contingent repertoire A way of accounting for scientific endeavour and progress which draws attention to the role played by subjective, human factors beyond the realm of the empirical phenomena under investigation.

delphi groups Methods for collecting qualitative and quantitative data in which members of a group respond individually to questionnaires on a given topic, their responses are collated and discussed by the group as a whole, and members then complete a second questionnaire. The method is often used to generate and evaluate ideas in organizational and clinical settings.

empiricist repertoire A way of accounting for scientific endeavour and progress which focuses on the empirical phenomena under investigation and suggests that scientific activity serves as a neutral medium through which these are understood (i.e., that the data 'speak for themselves').

focus groups Methods for collecting qualitative data in which groups of participants discuss a series of questions pertaining to a particular topic. In this way, data emerge from the interaction of the participants rather than simple question-and-answer sequences. The technique is often used to see how people resolve differences and disagreement and how consensus about a particular issue emerges.

Q-sort A qualitative research tool in which participants sort cards containing statements into piles associated with different points on a response dimension. In its original form participants placed 100 cards with statements about personal characteristics into piles ranging from 'not characteristic of me' to 'very characteristic of me', and did so using a forced sort so that the number of cards in the piles corresponded to a normal distribution (i.e., so that 2 cards were placed in pile 0, 4 in pile 1, 6 in pile 2, 12 in pile 3 and so on).

reactive focus Those aspects of a situation to which a research participant is sensitive when engaging in a particular behaviour (e.g., responding to a question). Accordingly, these aspects constitute the basis for any concerns about reactivity that a researcher might have.

repertory grid A qualitative research tool used to gain access to participants' personal constructs. Participants are first asked to identify similarities and differences between elements that are relevant to an aspect of their life. Regularities in the content of these similarities and differences are then used to gain an understanding of the way in which the participant subjectively organizes their world.

verbal protocol A qualitative research tool in which participants introspectively comment on a particular topic and their responses are coded using pre-established guidelines. The most common of these is the 'thinking-aloud protocol' used to gain insight into participants' cognitive processes while performing particular tasks (e.g., playing chess or map reading).

Some general principles for collecting and analysing qualitative data

In light of the radical critique discussed above, there are some particular dangers in attempting to identify general principles that guide the collection and analysis of qualitative data. This is because some researchers explicitly reject the idea that there might be any one way of approaching a research question that is inherently superior to others. For example, when discussing constructionist approaches to qualitative analysis, Potter (1996, p. 129) remarks:

> If anything, there is even more variation of method than there is of theory in constructionism. For many of these approaches indeed, it is not clear that there is anything that would correspond to what psychologists traditionally think of as 'method'.

Nonetheless, most handbooks of qualitative analysis do attempt to provide some guidelines to help researchers make certain sorts of decisions (or at least realize what sorts of decisions they have to make). For example, Yin (1994), discusses five steps for carrying out qualitative case studies and, with some minor adaptation, these can be seen as principles that could reasonably be used to guide most qualitative research. These steps are as follows:

1. *Develop appropriate research questions.* For obvious reasons qualitative research is not particularly useful if a researcher is seeking an answer to an essentially quantitative question (e.g., of the form 'How much?', 'How often?' or 'What proportion?'). Instead qualitative research is far better attuned to 'How do?' and 'Why do?' questions. The rationale for asking such questions also usually rests on assumptions (a) that research participants are in a position to comment verbally on issues pertaining to the research topic, and/or (b) that their comments are in some way relevant to understanding that topic. This would mean, for example, that qualitative research makes much more sense if one's research question is 'How do people feel about being separated from their partners?' rather than 'How do people repress unwanted thoughts?'

2. *Identify key propositions for the study.* In Chapter 2, we discussed the idea that all research is driven (explicitly or implicitly) by a desire to test (or explore) a set of hypotheses that derive from a particular theory or approach to a topic. Although the focus may change over time (e.g., as a result of participant involvement), the same is generally true of qualitative research. This is because, even where it is exploratory, such research is usually conducted with some scientific purpose or outcome in mind. Stating the purpose of any

study in advance is an important means by which its success can ultimately be judged. This is true even if the aims or goals of research are very minimal.

3. *Specify the unit(s) and context(s) of interest.* Although qualitative research typically focuses on the responses of individuals, the goal of research is rarely to find out more about those particular individuals or about individuals in general. Instead, research typically aims to make statements about *classes* of individuals (e.g., older daughters, scientists, chess players) or situations (e.g., organizational cultures, learning regimes, hospital wards). For example, in Reicher and Hopkins's (1996) studies of political leaders, the objective was to make statements about political leadership in general and about the way in which leaders tried to mobilize particular constituents (e.g., by appealing to shared national identity). Specifying the unit(s) and context(s) of interest (in this case political leaders discussing national identity) helps readers to understand the relationship between a particular piece of data (e.g., a response in an interview) and the research project as a whole.

4. *Establish the logic linking the data to the propositions.* Explaining how and why particular pieces of data help achieve particular research objectives is again a vital step in allowing the consumers of research to evaluate its success. The nature of these explanations will vary substantially as a function of the approach to research that is adopted (e.g., whether it is informed by a realist or constructionist philosophy). For example, in realist research a scientist's statement 'If you are an experimenter you know what is important and what is not important' might be used as an indication of the skills that experimenters are believed to have, but in constructionist research this statement could be used to make a claim about the situations in which scientists resort to an empiricist repertoire. Clearly, though, in order for a reader to know what status a particular piece of data has for the researcher, his or her analytical logic needs to be spelled out.

5. *Explain the criteria for interpreting the findings.* In previous chapters we discussed the idea of an alpha level as a benchmark which researchers use in order to decide whether or not to reject a null hypothesis. Even though no such benchmark exists in qualitative research it is still necessary for researchers to indicate why they favour particular interpretations of their data and why they draw particular conclusions. Usually (but not always) these claims will rely on the detection of *regularities and patterning*

within the data (e.g., repeated references to particular events, attempts to give indirect answers to questions under particular circumstances, the use of particular forms of sentence construction by particular groups). These regularities and patterns also usually rely on the detection of similarities and differences (e.g., within and between individuals and situations). In such circumstances the researcher should attempt to explain why any set of regularities and patterns has been singled out for attention. Amongst other things, this can help to offset claims that these patterns do not exist or that other interpretations of the data are more plausible.

Although the above steps play an important role in qualitative research, it is worth noting that each has a clear analogue in quantitative research. At the same time, as they are presented here, these steps appear to be much more indeterminate than those we have discussed in previous chapters. The idea of an alpha level, for example, represents an evidential criterion that runs through almost all quantitative research, but in the qualitative realm variation in the nature and form of interpretative criteria is immense. In order to illustrate this point, and to show how the above principles can be translated into different forms of research activity, it is therefore useful to consider in more detail some varied examples of qualitative research methods.

Q12.2*

Which of the following procedures would *not* be included in a programme of qualitative research?

(a) Assessment of effect size.
(b) Development of appropriate research questions.
(c) Clarification of the logic linking the data to research propositions.
(d) Explanation of criteria for data interpretation.
(e) Identification of key propositions.

The correct answer is (a). As noted in Chapters 8, 9 and 10, measurements of effect size are used to make statements about the outcomes of statistical analysis and so they are quantitative rather than qualitative procedures. The other four answers are incorrect, not least because Yin (1994) identifies them as key steps in the process of conducting and reporting qualitative case studies.

Examples of qualitative research methods

Along the lines of the scheme suggested by Henwood and Pigeon (1994), qualitative methods can be roughly classified as falling into three main groupings: (a) **constructionist methods**, which reject most of the objectives and assumptions of quantitative methods; (b) **contextualist methods**, which differ from quantitative methods in placing more emphasis on the subjective experience and goals of researchers and participants; and (c) **realist methods**, which share many of the same objectives and assumptions as quantitative methods (Henwood and Pigeon, 1994, refer to these as empiricist methods). In order to illustrate the differences between these methods, in this section we will consider at least one example of each type.

> **constructionist/constructivist methods** Approaches to
>   psychological research which embrace a philosophy of
>   constructionism/constructivism. Amongst other things, they (a) reject
>   the scientific method as a means of developing psychological
>   knowledge and (b) involve research and theorizing which attempt to
>   understand, but not go beyond, the perspective and experience of
>   participants.
> **contextualist methods** Approaches to psychological research in
>   which reliance on scientific method is tempered by an emphasis on
>   developing theory that is sensitive to the perspective and experience of
>   both participants and researchers as well as to the context in which
>   research takes place.
> **realist methods** Approaches to psychological research which
>   (a) accept the utility of the scientific method and (b) endorse a
>   philosophy of realism which suggests that it is possible to accurately
>   detect and characterize features of psychological reality.

Constructionist methods: Discourse analysis

As suggested above, constructionist approaches are among the most controversial in psychology for the simple reason that they are founded upon a rejection of the scientific method as it is typically understood and applied in research. Indeed, rather than developing hypotheses about psychological states and processes and seeking to test these in empirical studies, constructivists see the empirical method itself as a means of constructing particular meanings in order to achieve particular objectives – for example, to be seen as a scientist and to be seen to be 'doing science'. In this way, where another psychologist might seek to abstract meaning from quantitative or qualitative data in order to test and develop theory (so that the data are essentially a theoretical *resource*), constructivists see the process of abstracting meaning as a *topic* in itself. For this reason, constructivist methods focus very much on the fine-grained qualities of language itself, rather than seeking to abstract other forms of data from it.

Discourse analysis is a clear example of this practice. Amongst other things, it is commonly used to inspect the character of naturally occurring discourse in order to discover subtle (and typically un-detected) features of it that allow people to achieve particular ends. Almost any form of language can be used for this purpose: conversa-tions, discussions, speeches, advertising campaigns, the text of a dog licence, the instructions for using a food processor.

Where the analytical material takes the form of spoken language, this is usually reported using a standardized transcription system. Aspects of this system are illustrated by the following text reported by Potter (1997, p. 151) and transcribed from a famous BBC interview between Princess Diana and Martin Bashir:

Bashir:	Did you (.) allow your ↑friends, >your close friends,<
	to speak to °Andrewo Morton°?
Princess:	Yes I did. ⌈Yes I did
Bashir:	⌊°Why°?
Princess:	I was (.) at the end of my tether (.)
	I was (.) desperate (.)
	>I think I was so fed up with being< (.)
	seen as someone who was a ba:sket case (.)
	because I am a very strong person (.)
	and I know (.) that causes complications, (.)
	in the system (.) that I live in.
	(1.0) ((smiles and purses lips))
Bashir:	How would a book change that?
Princess:	→ I ↑dunno. ((raises eyebrows, looks away))
	Maybe people have a better understanding (.)
	maybe there's a lot of women out there
	who suffer (.) on the same level
	but in a different environment (.)
	who are unable to: (.) stand up for themselves (.)
	because (.) their self-esteem is (.) cut into two.
	→ I dunno ((shakes head))

369

In this text (.) refers to a pause of less than 0.2 seconds, (1.0) refers to a pause of 1 second, ↑ indicates raised pitch, > and < surround talk that is noticeably faster, ° ° surround talk that is noticeably lower in volume, : indicates a lengthening of the preceding sound, [indicates where talk starts to overlap, underlining indicates stress or emphasis, ((and)) surround transcriber's comments, and → points to lines that are referred to in the researcher's commentary on the text.

We can see that the transcription system makes the text relatively hard to read. At the same time, though, once the reader is reasonably familiar with transcription conventions, the system makes it possible to recover precise features of dialogue (e.g., intonation, pitch, speed) that would otherwise be unavailable for scrutiny. And in this particular case, the method allows the researcher (Potter) to make a detailed examination of the role that the two instances of 'I dunno' play for the person who uttered them.

Two points are relevant here. First, it is clear that the utterance 'I dunno' could easily pass undetected if it had not been subjected to detailed transcription of this form. This would be particularly true if the researcher who was recording the dialogue was concerned only to note its substantive content, as an 'I dunno' could easily be seen as trivial and irrelevant. Second, though, even if the researcher did note the presence of 'I dunno', from a realist perspective it is likely that it would be interpreted as a *literal* representation of the speaker's cognitions. In effect, then, it could be treated in the same way as a response of '1' on a 5-point scale which asked the question 'Do you know why this book would help your cause?' and 1 represented a response of 'not at all' and 5 a response of 'very definitely'.

Against such literal interpretations of data (whether qualitative or quantitative), discourse analysts note that any single response can have a range of potential meanings. For example, when asked the question 'Did you enjoy yourself?', the response 'Oh, absolutely!' (a '5' on a 5-point scale perhaps) could be meant to be taken literally, but it could also be intended to be ironic, sarcastic, witty or half-hearted. How can quantitative (or empiricist qualitative) methods differentiate between these various meanings? Constructionists argue that they cannot and therefore insist that attempts at interpreting language and behaviour need to be tied firmly to the contexts of production. Their methods therefore focus on identifying those various features which ensure that responses and interaction have the particular meanings that they do.

Here, too, any hypotheses are intended to emerge *from* the data rather than to be *taken into* the data-gathering exercise. For example, in the case of 'I dunno' Potter suggests that this serves as a form of 'stake inoculation' in which the speaker expresses ignorance in order to deflect potential accusations that she engaged in particular behaviour (telling her friends to contribute to a book which was critical of the royal family) for self-serving or malicious reasons. Having made this assertion, the researcher can then examine other transcripts to find evidence (a) of the same construction ('I dunno') being used for the same purposes, (b) of the same construction being used for different purposes, or (c) of different constructions being used for the same purposes. Other aspects of the same or different transcripts – especially those which are contradictory or inconsistent – can also be used to shed light on the meaning and function of such a construction. For example, were Diana to indicate in some other discourse that she knows exactly why Andrew Morton's book would help her cause this might suggest that her use of 'I dunno' in the interview transcribed above was not a reflection of genuine ignorance (although it is worth noting in passing that this logic in fact embodies some realist assumptions – specifically that ignorance, or anything else for that matter, can be authenticated as 'genuine').

The broad function of such analysis is to show how language is used actively and creatively by participants to achieve complex social goals (e.g., representing oneself positively and other people negatively), and, as a corollary, to show that an understanding of how those goals are achieved is impossible without detailed analysis of discourse. At a theoretical level it also serves to critique psychological (and other) research which treats language as a uniform, neutral and literal conduit for the transmission of information.

There is no finite set of ways in which discourse analysis can be performed and no prescribed set of methods by which means it should be conducted. Indeed, some (but not all) of its proponents suggest that providing such prescriptions may lead them into the positivist trap of privileging one interpretation of a text or an interaction when many are usually possible and valid. For this reason, discourse analysts describe the method as a 'craft skill' akin to riding a bicycle: hard to learn and hard to describe (e.g., Potter, 1997, pp. 147–148). Nonetheless, like riding a bicycle, discourse analysis is seen as something that one can do badly or do well, and it is very definitely not a method where 'anything goes'. The question of whether this fact is incompatible with the idealist philosophy that often informs the approach is one we will return to below.

Q12.3[**]**

Which of the following activities might be carried out as part of discourse analysis?

(a) Transcription of a conversation between two people at a breakfast table.

(b) Identification of changes in pitch when a person is speaking.

(c) Interpretation of linguistic features in the context of their production.

(d) Both (b) and (c).

(e) All of the above.

The correct answer is (e). All of the practices here are ones that discourse analysts might engage in. In particular, they are concerned with naturally occurring language (so (a) is correct), with recording detailed features of that language (so (b) is correct), and with tying the analysis of language to the context of its production (so (c) is correct).

discourse analysis A constructionist practice which involves the fine-grained analysis of language. By this means researchers focus on how language does more than merely describe the world or relay information, but is used instead to achieve complex social objectives in particular contexts.

Contextualist methods: Grounded theory

One of the ways in which constructionist approaches differ from conventional quantitative methods is in taking seriously the perspective of participants and in focusing on their understandings of the world rather than seeking to impose the (often different) understandings of the experimenter on the data that those participants provide. Contextualist approaches share an emphasis on the perspective and interests of participants, but seek to *reconcile* this with the scientific goals of the researcher rather than to see the scientific process of theory development as inherently flawed or restrictive.

The clearest example of this is probably provided by **grounded theory**, in which (as the name suggests) researchers attempt to develop analyses of psychological topics which are *grounded* in participants' localized experiences of relevant phenomena. A particular concern of researchers who use this method is to attempt to lay bare the various processes through which psychological theory is developed. They attempt, in particular, to identify any biases, prejudices, predispositions or hunches that they bring into the experiment and to document how these are supported or challenged by particular research findings. In this way, analysis of a particular phenomenon is presented as it emerges through what Pigeon and Henwood (1997, p. 255) describe as the dynamic ' "flip flop" between ideas and research experience'.

It is worth noting that there are a number of different ways of working with grounded theory, ranging from those which are more realist (and treat participants' input as relatively unproblematic) to those which are more constructionist (and, as in discourse analysis, are sensitive to the multiple meanings and purposes that participants' input can have). In all cases though, the research involves discrete phases of (a) data collection, (b) data storage, (c) coding and (d) analysis. The last of these phases focuses on refinement, manipulation and management of the data.

To provide a concrete example of the method, we can look at some pertinent aspects of an examination by Pigeon of engineers' assessment and management of risk during a project that involved the handling of hazardous waste (for more detail, see Pigeon & Henwood, 1997). Here data-gathering was proceeded by an attempt to gather a rich and varied set of materials that related to the issue in question. In particular, these took the form of semi-structured interviews with various people working on the project which were subsequently transcribed in detail. An example of a paragraph from one such transcript is as follows:

```
A. Paragraph from an interview relating to
Hazardous Waste case-study
Interview S, 27 April
Paragraph 8
I don't think there is any doubt that on this job I
readily accepted the advice of the civil engineer-
ing consultant, L, and didn't have the experience
to question that advice adequately. I was not aware
of the appropriate site investigation procedure,
and was more than willing to be seduced by the idea
that we could cut corners to save money.
```

Having gathered data in this form, the researcher's next task is to develop an appropriate **coding system** for it. This involves identifying key concepts in the text that are perceived (a) to be relevant to the issue at hand and (b) to be useful for the purpose of cross-referencing ideas and ultimately abstracting key themes and ideas. In the above example such indexing might take the following form:

```
B. Significant concepts identified within
paragraphs
Interview S
Paragraph 8
ACCEPTING PROFESSIONAL ADVICE
CRITICIZING OTHERS' WORK
CUTTING CORNERS
EXPERIENCE
```

The most important feature of such concepts is that they should **fit** the data by providing an appropriate representation of it. For this reason the concepts are not predetermined, but devised in an ongoing way as the research progresses through a process of **open coding**. After multiple pieces of data have been indexed in this way, the researcher is then able to examine the different ways in which concepts (e.g., 'cutting corners') are used across the data set as a whole. This can be done on a new concept card which lists *variants* of concept use across the data set as a whole. For this to occur, though, the concepts have to have been defined at an appropriate level of abstraction (not too specific, not too general), and, where necessary, the researcher has to go back to refine the coding system he or she has employed. In this case, a coding card (which need not be a card at all but could be a computer record) might have the following form:

```
CARD 22 CUTTING CORNERS
S Para 8        S said he was not aware of the appropri-
                ate site investigation procedures,
                and was willing to be seduced by the
                idea of cutting corners to save money.
T Para 12       G said he couldn't be bothered taking
                the time to do a neat job with the labels
                as nobody appreciated it anyway.
W Para 29       W's recollection of an instruction
                from a manager that he should save
                time by not checking whether concrete
                was permeable.
```

Precisely because this process of refining data-handling is a subjective one (i.e., one that is based on the researcher's own interpretations of the data), and this subjectivity will clearly have a role to play in the conclusions that the researcher eventually draws, grounded theorists recommend that records be kept of the processes that guide data management and interpretation. These can take the form of memos or a **reflexive journal** which explains why particular decisions were made and allows these to be retrieved at a later date. An example of such a memo might be as follows:

```
MEMO
18 July 2002 by A. Researcher on Splitting CUTTING
CORNERS
I decided to split the concept Cutting corners into
two concepts: Cutting corners due to external pres-
sure (Card 232), and Cutting corners as a personal
```

choice (Card 233) because the original concept
was too cumbersome and broad. It also appeared
that this distinction could be useful analytically
because cutting corners due to external pressure
seemed to be associated with decisions that related
to core aspects of the project (e.g., chemical
tests of concrete) whereas cutting corners due to
personal choice seemed to relate to more superfi-
cial decisions (e.g., putting labels on neatly).
This is seen in a comparison of T para 12 with T para
32 and W para 22 with W para 29.

Having completed a concept card (perhaps because adding more
entries no longer adds any richness to the information it contains and
the category it describes is said to have become *saturated*), the researcher
then attempts to develop the analysis further by identifying the
particular features that give a particular card its coherence. This can
be done by attempting to define the coding concept itself, again in the
form of a memo. In our engineering example, this might take the
following form:

DEFINITION FOR CARD 232
CUTTING CORNERS DUE TO EXTERNAL PRESSURE
Many participants (particularly junior ones)
refer to a perceived need to cut corners on vital
parts of the project due to external pressure.
This generally occurred in order to save either
time or money. Pressure is usually implicit and
only rarely explicit. Implicit pressure is seen to
be part of a general culture of economy that the
project managers reinforce in various ways (e.g.,
through timesheets, costings, budget meetings).
It is also reflected in references to fear of being
ridiculed (e.g., for being slow or fussy). External
pressures are thus subtle, and hard to pin down but
easy for managers to deny.

Having attempted to summarize the data on one card (possibly by
defining the concept that it relates to), advanced stages of analysis then
involve the researcher attempting to draw links between cards and to
integrate the emergent concepts at a higher level. This can involve at
least three things: (a) the identification of general themes that unite and
distinguish between multiple concepts; (b) the development of analytic

taxonomies (i.e., classification schemes that help to organize concepts); or (c) the clarification of relationships among concepts. In developing any or all of these products, three core goals remain paramount: (a) *documentation* of decisions relating to the analysis that allow that process to be interrogated and audited; (b) sensitivity to issues of *reflexivity* (i.e., awareness of the role that subjective decisions play in analysis); and (c) maximization of *fit* (i.e., ensuring that any analysis adequately describes the data).

In relation to all of these activities and goals, a residual question that you may be asking yourself is 'How will I know when any analysis is good enough?'. In other words, when does any analysis contain enough documentation, enough reflexivity and enough fit? Partly because it incorporates some of the idealist philosophy of constructionists, these questions are hard to answer in the abstract (in the way that we could when performing a *t*-test, say). Nonetheless, grounded theorists do assert that the method has the potential to take researchers' understanding of psychological processes forward and that whether or not it does can be established with reference to a number of criteria. Amongst other things, these can include assessment of whether the research (a) leads to the development of *novel* understanding of relevant issues, (b) helps develop understanding that is (to some extent) *transferable* from one content domain to another, and (c) is validated, and perceived to be useful, by the research participants themselves. For example, the study of risk management in engineering projects might be perceived to have been worthwhile if it suggests that a particular type of organizational culture is a major contributor to accidents and this is perceived to be useful by engineers themselves and helps them to eliminate accidents across a range of industries in future.

Q12.4[**]

What is the role of a reflexive journal in grounded theory?

(a) To record data that are collected in the field, but that need to be analysed at a later stage, once the researcher has had an opportunity to reflect on them.

(b) To allow participants to record their own thoughts and feelings about the research process – in particular, aspects of it that they are uncomfortable with and that they can discuss with the researcher later.

(c) To allow researchers to record their thoughts about the research process, so that the rationale for their decisions is recoverable at some later stage.

(d) To allow researchers and participants to reflect upon each other's activity so that differences in their perspective can be reconciled by a third party.

(e) To record specific features of the physical environment that reflect on the research process as a whole, but which might be omitted from quantitative analysis.

The correct answer is (c). Reflexive journals are used by researchers so that the processes that lead them to collect and interpret data in particular ways are available for examination at a later stage. This is intended to ensure that decisions and activities that have a bearing on research outcomes (and which can help to explain why data have a particular form), are recoverable after data have been collected. Although they all sound plausible, each of the other answers is wrong. (a) is wrong because reflexive journals are not used to record data. (b) and (d) are wrong because they are not used by participants (though other forms of research journals or diaries may be). (e) is wrong because, while it might discuss features of the environment that bear upon a researcher's decisions, those features are not its primary focus.

coding system In qualitative analysis, the categories used to summarize key features of a data set.

fit In *grounded theory*, the degree to which any aspect of analysis is an appropriate and recognizable description of the phenomena under investigation.

grounded theory A qualitative research practice in which understanding of a phenomenon is inductively derived from studying that phenomenon from the perspective of those to whom it is relevant. In this way, the researcher does not begin with a theory and then test it, instead theory is discovered, developed and provisionally verified as it emerges from systematic examination of data.

open coding In *grounded theory*, the process of developing coding concepts and categories that fit the data as closely as possible. For this reason, such concepts are not predetermined but evolve over the course of the coding process.

reflexive journal A researcher's record of thoughts and activities that relate to the research process. Amongst other things, this is intended to provide insight into the decisions that guide data management.

taxonomy A classification scheme used to summarize and organize information.

Realist methods: Repertory grid analysis and content analysis

Despite their differences, a common feature of constructionist and contextualist methods is that in attending to the meanings that participants give to their own behaviour they are generally sceptical about the prospects of using *pre-existing tools* to uncover that meaning. Instead, as a result of the idealistic philosophy they embrace, both approaches suggest that research methodology needs to be flexible and *participant-driven*, rather than prescribed formula or set of rules. In contrast to this view, in this subsection we consider examples of realist methodologies in which researchers bring to their research both a specified set of tools and an explicit framework for interpreting the data they produce.

We can start by looking at **repertory grid analysis**. This shares with discourse analysis and grounded theory a belief that it is important for psychological research in a number of domains to tap into the *subjective perspective* or **personal constructs** of participants. Indeed, the repertory grid was devised by the founder of personal construct theory, George Kelly (1955), in order to examine and try to understand how people feel about, and represent, themselves and key features of their world. This methodology has a range of applications that are pertinent to psychological research (and associated psychological interventions). For example, a counselling psychologist may want to understand the way a person feels about their family and friends in order to understand (and manage) family conflict, a social psychologist may want to know how a person feels about people from different cultures or ethnic backgrounds in order to understand (and reduce) prejudice, and an organizational psychologist may want to know how a worker feels about various groups at their place of work in order to understand (and modify) aspects of organizational culture.

We can illustrate how these techniques work by considering the example of an organizational psychologist who wants to understand how clinical psychologists in a hospital represent that work environment. A first stage in the analysis requires construction of a grid in which (a) the various aspects of the psychologists' world that the researcher wants to focus on (referred to as *elements*) are listed on the left, (b) different combinations of three elements are identified in separate rows underneath, and (c) two blank columns on the right correspond to each row (these are then used to identify *constructs*). In our example this exercise involves five elements: clients, peers, managers, other health professionals and doctors, as in the following grid:

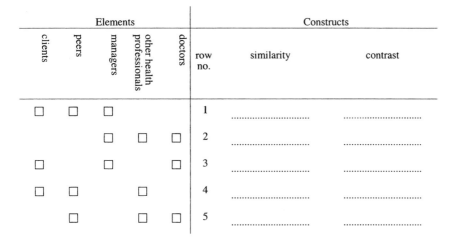

Importantly, grids can be used to examine many different types of element (e.g., people, places, objects) but the elements that are included in any one grid all need to be of a similar type (e.g., all groups, as in the above example). Note, though, that a normal grid would also contain about 10 elements and many more three-element combinations, so the above example is somewhat simplified.

Having created a grid in this fashion (where the boxes identify the elements in each combination of three), the participant, our clinical psychologist, is first asked to think about the three elements and indicate which two are most similar and which one is most different. For example, in the case of the row 1 comparison between clients, peers and management, the psychologist might indicate that managers were the 'odd one out', with peers and clients being most similar. Having done this (and marked the responses in the appropriate cells of the grid; e.g., with a tick for the two similar elements and a cross for the one contrast element), the participant is asked to explain what makes the two elements similar to each other and what makes them different from the third element. These explanations can be given simplifying labels and these labels are then written into the blank spaces in the relevant columns on the right (one being the *similarity construct*, the other being the *contrast construct*). In this example, the psychologist might indicate that they think clients and peers are similar in having healthcare goals, and that they differ from managers who have financial goals. This process could then be repeated for all the remaining sets of three elements, as follows:

clients	peers	managers	other health professionals	doctors	row no.	similarity (✓)	contrast (✗)
✓	✓	✗			1	have healthcare goals	have financial goals
	✓	✗	✓		2	aloof	team-players
✗		✓	✓		3	powerful	powerless
✗	✓		✓		4	professional	non-professional
	✓		✓	✗	5	equal	superior

When each of the three-element combinations has been used as a basis for eliciting constructs, the participant is then asked to indicate which of the two constructs (similarity or contrast) most appropriately describes each of the blank elements in each row (i.e., the elements not included in the original three-element combinations). In our example, the clinical psychologist might indicate that other professionals and doctors both share healthcare goals (the similarity construct) and so a tick would be placed in both of these blank cells. This process can then be repeated for the remaining rows of the grid, as follows:

clients	peers	managers	other health professionals	doctors	row no.	similarity (✓)	contrast (✗)
✓	✓	✗	✓	✓	1	have healthcare goals	have financial goals
✗	✗	✓	✗	✓	2	aloof	team-players
✗	✓	✓	✗	✓	3	powerful	powerless
✗	✓	✗	✓	✓	4	professional	non-professional
✓	✓	✗	✓	✗	5	equal	superior

Having collected data in this way, the researcher's job is now to organize the grid in a coherent fashion. A first stage in this process is to see if there are any sets of rows in which either exactly the same or exactly the opposite pattern of ticks and crosses is found. This process of detecting similarity and difference can be assisted if all the contrast cells are shaded a dark colour as in the above grid. If we look at this, we can see that no two rows are identical but that row 2 has the opposite pattern of ticks and crosses to row 5. Effectively, then, these rows can be made identical by changing ticks into crosses and crosses into ticks and reversing the similarity and contrast constructs. We can perform this operation, and indicate that we have completed it by placing an '(R)' (for 'reversed') next to each construct.

The next task is to reorganize the rows *and columns* in the grid so that those that are adjacent to each other have as similar a pattern of crosses and ticks as possible. The result will be something like the grid below:

	Elements					Constructs	
peers	other health professionals	clients	doctors	managers	row no.	similarity (✓)	contrast (✗)
✓	✓	✓	✗	✗	5	equal	superior
✓	✓	✓	✗	✗	2	team-players (R)	aloof (R)
✓	✓	✓	✓	✗	1	have healthcare goals	have financial goals
✓	✓	✗	✓	✗	4	professional	non-professional
✓	✗	✗	✓	✓	3	powerful	powerless

If we look first at the columns in this grid we can see that on the left peers have all ticks and that they are most different from managers on the right (who have mainly crosses). Other health professionals, doctors and clients, with a mixture of ticks and crosses (but different patterns) are in the middle, but other health professionals are closest to peers because they share more identical cells or *matches* (4 rather than 3) and doctors are closer to managers as they share more matches (3 rather than 1). Turning then to the rows, those that share the smallest number of matches are at the top and bottom of the grid (i.e., rows 2 and 5 versus row 3). As we know, rows 5 and 2 are in fact identical (after reversing row 2) and these are at the top. Row 1 is next as it has most matches with rows 5 and 2 (i.e., 4 rather than 3 or 2). Row 4 follows as it has most matches with row 1 (4 rather than 3). Finally, row 3 (which has 3 matches with row 4 above it) is at the bottom.

This procedure leaves us with a grid that is coherently organized and which provides a readily interpretable 'map' of the clinical psychologist's understanding of the groups in her workplace. It may be the case, however, that there is some redundancy in this map – especially if multiple constructs appear to be structuring the elements in a very similar way. As a final (optional) stage in grid analysis the researcher can therefore attempt to reduce the number of constructs by *combining* those which have a similar pattern of ticks and crosses across the various elements. In this example this would definitely seem to be warranted in the case of the constructs 'equal–superior' and 'team players–aloof' (which share 100% of possible matches) and there might also be a case for combining the constructs 'professional–non-professional' and 'powerful–powerless' (which share 80% of possible matches). If we performed both combinations this would reduce the grid to three sets of constructs: 'equal/team players–superior/aloof', 'have healthcare goals–have financial goals' and 'powerful/professional–powerless/non-professional'.

Having seen how this process of grid reorganization works, you will probably not be surprised to discover that a well-defined set of mathematical operations can be used to guide you through it (these can also be performed using a computer program). Details are provided in Kelly's original book (Kelly, 1955) and more recent texts like that by Stewart, Stewart, and Fonda (1981). However, at least with simple grids like this, these formal operations can be approximated reasonably well by 'feel'. Incidentally, the procedures involved in structuring and simplifying the grid are very similar to those involved in a complex statistical procedure known as **factor analysis**. This is typically used as a method of **data reduction** – for example, when researchers want to combine those items in a psychological instrument (e.g., a survey or psychological test) that appear to be measuring similar things. Indeed, although we do not deal with factor analysis in this book, the process of reorganizing repertory grid data provides an excellent intuitive introduction to the operations that this involves (for more detail see Kline, 1994).

In any event, we can see from our example that repertory grid analysis has allowed us to achieve a number of interesting things. Most significantly, it has allowed us to explore some of the complexities of participants' subjective perceptions while at the same time making those complexities intelligible and manageable. In the case of our clinical psychologist we can see, for example, what affinities and oppositions she perceives between groups in her workplace and the core dimensions on which those are defined. The potential uses of such information are considerable, and the repertory grid has a range of theoretical and practical applications. As examples, a researcher (or practitioner) could compare the data above with those obtained from either (a) the same person at a different time (e.g., to assess the impact of some organizational intervention), (b) other members of her work group (e.g., to see if there is any consensus between personal constructs), or (c) members of other work groups (e.g., to try to characterize the hospital's culture as a whole).

In contrast to more idealist (contructionist or contextualist) methods, we can see that the repertory grid analysis has a flavour which is not dissimilar to that of the quantitative methods addressed in previous chapters. In large part this is because the method relies on formal operations that are agreed upon by the people who use the method and which can be specified in textbooks like this one. The same is true of most other realist methods. In the case of **content analysis** – the method we will now consider – this quantitative flavour is enhanced further by the fact that it serves to *transform* qualitative data into quantitative data which (if desired) can then be subjected to formal statistical analysis.

Content analysis is a method for analysing communication after it has been produced. There are no boundaries to the form of communication that can be studied – indeed, the method can be applied to the analysis of most forms of behaviour, as most behaviour has some communicative dimension. Importantly, though, records of the communication must exist in some concrete form. This means that if a researcher is interested in map-reading ability they might want to examine verbal protocols in which novices and experts are asked to think aloud while performing a map-reading task (e.g., Green & Gilhooly, 1996); if they are interested in gender stereotypes they might want to examine the status and roles of men and women in television advertisements (e.g., Manstead & McCulloch, 1991); and if they are interested in genius they might want to examine the memoirs or diaries of exceptional people (e.g., Howe, Davidson, & Sloboda, 1998). Despite the differences between these various sources of data, there are several discrete steps that researchers need to perform in order to analyse their content.

The first step is to specify clearly the **sampling domain** from which data are to be gathered. As noted above, the possibilities here are infinite, but a specific and theoretically relevant source of data needs to be identified before research can proceed. As an example, let us imagine that a research team is interested in establishing whether managers of hospitals and managers of industrial companies have different management styles. Their hypothesis might be that hospital managers have a more democratic style and that industrial managers have a more autocratic style, but that these differences have reduced over time.

To investigate this issue the researchers might decide that it would be useful to examine a broad range of managers' communications: their e-mails or memos to staff, the messages they place on noticeboards, the things they include in the minutes of staff meetings and so on. Whichever of these is selected, the *precise features* of the domain then need to be specified and justified on theoretical and methodological grounds. The considerations that guide this decision are much the same as those that we discussed in Chapters 4 and 5. In particular, the researcher must endeavour to ensure that the specification of a sampling domain does not introduce systematic bias into the research. If the researcher were to study managers' e-mails, for example, changes over time might be due to the novelty of the technology rather than management style per se. Some ingenuity is often called for here too. In this case, due to the availability of complete sets of recent and older data and the absence of obvious confounds, the researchers may decide to examine the articles that managing directors write in in-house company magazines. More specifically, they may decide to examine the first articles appearing in the magazines of the 20 largest hospitals and the 20 largest industrial companies in the years 1990 and 2000.

The next important stage of analysis is the development of a *coding system*. As with grounded theory, this involves deciding upon categories or **coding units** that can be used to summarize key features of the data set. In written communication, coding units are typically specific words, phrases or themes. In communication more generally, they may relate to aspects of interaction such as its duration or intensity or the place and space in which it occurs. In this vein, you are probably familiar with the coding units that are used widely in the content analysis of professional sport. For example, analysis of soccer games includes categories like 'assists', 'shots on goal', and 'tackles'. Similarly, in our study of managerial style, relevant coding units might include 'favourable references to management decisions', 'favourable references to employee participation' and 'favourable references to teamwork'.

Again (and in contrast to the procedures involved in grounded theory), <u>decisions about the nature of these categories will be devised before data analysis begins</u> (but usually on the basis of preliminary examination of the material to be coded) and be driven by both theoretical and methodological considerations. On the one hand, the categories need to be relevant to the theoretical ideas being tested, but at the same time they need to be defined at an appropriate level of abstraction and not to introduce systematic bias into the analysis. For example, if our study of managerial style included the coding unit 'references to share price', it would not be surprising to find more instances of this unit in articles about industrial companies than in articles about hospitals, for the simple reason that hospitals are not normally listed on the stock market. In this case any variation in instances of the coding unit across the two types of organization would therefore not necessarily have anything to do with leadership style.

Having specified the sampling domain and the coding system, the next phase of content analysis involves the actual coding of data. Here the material in the sampling domain is systematically analysed, with instances of a given coding unit being recorded in a predetermined manner – typically through an entry (e.g., a tick) in the appropriate cell of a coding sheet. Where possible, coding is usually performed blind to reduce the possibility of experimenter bias (see Chapter 4). This means that information about the source of data is removed so that it cannot influence coding decisions. In cases where coding systems are complex and the content of coding categories is open to multiple interpretations, coding will also usually be preceded by some form of coder training. During this the criteria for coding decisions are clarified and potentially difficult decisions are discussed. In such cases it is also customary for multiple coders to perform the coding exercise independently before discussing and resolving any disagreement. The level of prediscussion agreement between coders (generally the proportion of coding choices on which they agree) can then be reported as an indication of the reliability of the coding process. This measure is referred to as **inter-rater reliability** and, generally speaking, the higher this is the better the coding system is seen to have been.

Once the process of data coding is completed, its final outcomes can then be summarized in a range of ways. For example, in our study of leadership style the data might be presented in terms of either (a) the proportion of companies in which there was at least one instance of a given coding category, as follows:

	Hospitals		Industrial companies	
	1990	2000	1990	2000
Percentage of articles including favourable references to				
management decisions	35	65	50	60
employee participation	70	60	35	55
teamwork	15	40	25	45

or (b) the number of instances of a given coding category in each type of company, thus:

	Hospitals		Industrial companies	
	1990	2000	1990	2000
Number of favourable references to				
management decisions	11	21	15	17
employee participation	32	25	17	28
teamwork	5	14	9	13

As with other quantitative measures (see Chapter 6), it is clear that each of these forms of presentation reveals slightly different patterns and hence serves to tell us slightly different things about the data. Moreover, based on material covered in previous chapters, we can also see that the patterns here can be described in language associated with quantitative analysis and could indeed be subjected to standard forms of statistical analysis. For example, if we look at the data in the top row of the second table, there is evidence of a two-way interaction between organization type and year (a pattern discussed in Chapter 10) and the statistical significance of this could be formally established by performing a chi-square test of independence (Chapter 11).

Q12.5[**]

A team of researchers want to use content analysis to examine the behaviour of people in a crowd. Specifically, they want to examine whether the number of times a person displays anger or frustration depends on the number of other people that are in close proximity. Which of the following statements is *false*?

(a) The researchers would want to specify their sampling domain in advance.
(b) The researchers might want to use multiple coders to ensure that coding is reliable.

(c) The researchers might want to assess the level of inter-rater reliability in categorizing particular displays of emotion as anger or frustration.

(d) The researchers would seek to clarify the nature of the coding categories 'anger' and 'frustration' after they have collected their data.

(e) The researchers may want to perform statistical analysis on the data they obtain.

The correct answer is (d). This statement is false because in content analysis researchers seek to clarify the nature of coding categories *before* collecting data. In much the same way, as (a) suggests, they should determine in advance exactly where they will be collecting data. As (b) and (c) suggest, the researchers may want to use multiple coders to ensure that there is agreement in use of the coding categories, and then measure that agreement. After collecting their data the researchers are quite likely to want to analyse it statistically (e.g., using a chi-square test of association; so (e) is true). Note that the activities suggested by (b) and (c) will be of limited use *unless* coding categories are specified in advance. Note, too, that although the data here do relate to an aspect of communication, they could quite easily relate to other forms of behaviour that are not communicative. Indeed, the principal elements of content analysis are very similar to methods used in observational studies of behaviour that do not involve communication (e.g., as conducted by animal researchers).

coding units In qualitative analysis, the discrete features of any *sampling domain* (e.g., particular words or phrases) that form the basis of the coding system.

content analysis A method for abstracting meaningful quantitative data from qualitative data that relate to an aspect of communication.

data reduction The process of simplifying a data set by combining responses on one or more measures.

factor analysis. A statistical method of *data reduction* that identifies and combines sets of dependent variables that are measuring similar things. The method relies on assessment of the correlations between all dependent variables and extraction of a small number of underlying factors that can be viewed as independent sources of relationships among those variables.

inter-rater reliability The level of agreement between two or more raters when they use a particular coding system to code qualitative data. This is often reported as the number of coded items on which coders agree divided by the total number of items coded.

personal constructs The ways in which a person subjectively understands and represents important features of their world. These are typically elicited using ***repertory grid analysis***.

repertory grid analysis. A method for summarizing aspects of participants' ***personal constructs***. The core feature of this is a grid which identifies similarities and differences among elements that are judged with reference to dimensions (constructs) generated by the participant.

sampling domain The sources from which qualitative data are collected and upon which analysis is performed.

Critiques of qualitative methods

Despite the fact that we have considered details of only four methods, the previous section makes it clear that a broad range of options are available to the researcher who wants to collect and analyse qualitative data. These range from those which attempt to retain as much quality in the data as possible by focusing on meaning within them, to those which endeavour to transform qualitative data into quantitative information by abstracting meaning from them. For this reason it is misleading to speak of qualitative research as if it represented a homogenous approach to data collection and analysis. Nonetheless, it is still quite common for researchers to present blanket objections to qualitative methods on a number of grounds. In this section we will briefly examine the basis and justification for such criticism.

As we noted earlier, the criticism of qualitative methods that is probably encountered most frequently objects to them on grounds *that they are not scientific*. Researchers who hold this view typically argue that, compared to quantitative research, the procedures for quantifying and minimizing methodological and statistical uncertainty in qualitative research are vague and underdeveloped. For example, in experimental research it is possible to design studies that work within established experimental paradigms in which internal and external validity are maximized, and then to conduct statistical analysis through which the significance of those findings can be assessed. In the case of constructionist methods (e.g., discourse analysis), however, it is much less clear how the reliability and validity of findings are established and what methods and criteria should be used to assess them. How do we know, for example, that Princess Diana's use of 'I dunno' represents a stake inoculator rather than a statement of genuine ignorance, a habitual response to a difficult question, or a verbal tic? And on what basis would we use this finding as a basis for generalization to other contexts?

In response to this objection, it is possible, first, to suggest that realist qualitative methods (and an associated logic which is invoked in most qualitative research) *would* allow us to answer these questions in ways that are directly analogous to other quantitative methods. Such analysis might, for example, show that Princess Diana used the phrase 'I dunno' much more commonly after a question in which her personal motives were questioned than when other types of difficult question were posed. Such an approach (the logic of which is often implicit in constructionist analysis) could also tackle issues of validity and reliability in much the same way as quantitative methods (e.g., by eliminating confounds, by having sufficiently large data sets). And issues of generalization could also be addressed through the development of appropriate theory (as argued in Chapter 4).

More generally, though, it is possible to argue that the model of psychological science against which qualitative methods are judged to be deficient is actually misinformed. Indeed, based on detailed analysis of the practices in which research psychologists engage, Woolgar (1988, 1996) suggests that psychological science (in common with all other branches of science) is a much less orderly and formalized activity than idealized versions suggest (e.g., those encountered in research articles). Rather, then, than data 'speaking for themselves', it appears that the form and meaning of data are very much a product of social activity on the part of researchers and their collective decisions about what is important and what is not. Woolgar argues that by these practice-based standards, constructionist and other qualitative methods are no less scientific than quantitative ones.

A second criticism of qualitative methods is that *they do not tell us much about psychology*, but are really only useful as tools of philosophical, sociological or linguistic analysis. This criticism is targeted mainly at constructionist approaches, and it is one that many researchers in this tradition would themselves accept. However, as with debate about the scientific credentials of qualitative research, such researchers would also question whether standard quantitative approaches are really exploring underlying psychological processes in the unproblematic way that their proponents suggest. Rather, because almost all windows on to psychological states and processes involve the use of language of some form (either in participants' responses or researchers' interpretations) constructionists would argue that psychological research is essentially a social activity that serves merely to favour and formalize particular *accounts* of psychological processes. For this reason, constructionists would argue that it makes a lot more sense to draw on ideas from other fields that are concerned with understanding language (e.g., sociology, linguistics, philosophy) than to focus on psychology as if it were a self-contained island of knowledge and wisdom.

A third criticism of qualitative methods is that *they fall foul of their own logic*. Again, this criticism is focused mainly on constructionist methods, with critics here observing that, although they are not always perfect, quantitative methods at least lay down specific criteria by which research procedures and outcomes can be judged. In the case of discourse analysis, though, in light of the fact that all understandings of psychological processes are deemed to be equally valid, how would we know whether the method had been performed well or badly, successfully or unsuccessfully? And to which guidelines could we appeal if we disagreed with another researchers' assessment of our work? We alluded to this point above when noting that discourse analysts some- times compare the method with riding a bicycle – something for which the instructions cannot be spelled out but which nevertheless people clearly succeed or fail at (Potter, 1997). The problem here, though, is that this response appears to rely on a level of realism that the approach itself rejects. Certainly, in suggesting that meaning and validity are relative constructions that can be gauged only from the perspective of the participant, but that research products (like riding a bicycle) can be objectively defined as successful or unsuccessful, constructionists can be accused of wanting to have their cake and eat it.

A fourth critique of qualitative methods is that *they focus on the particular rather than the general* and that this undermines attempts to make far-reaching statements about psychology and behaviour. Human beings and other creatures understand many aspects of their lives by generalizing on the basis of repeated observation. For example, on the basis of repeated experience, we know that it hurts more when you fall over on concrete than on carpet. As we saw in previous chapters, the quantitative approach is an extension of this approach to the domain of scientific enquiry but it can be argued that qualitative researchers fail to capitalize on our potential to develop generalizations in this way. This is a reasonable point, but it is possible to make the counter-argument that many important behaviours are genuinely unique (e.g., there is only one Diana interview) and generalization therefore risks misinterpretation. Against this, though, it needs to be acknowledged that most qualitative researchers *are* attempting to achieve generalization of some form (e.g., by suggesting that stake inoculation is a common linguistic device), and that for this reason it is important that researchers take steps to ensure that their findings have more than just localized status and value. As with quantitative research (see Chapter 4), one way they do this is by developing appropriate *theory*.

A fifth and final critique of qualitative methods is that they are to be distrusted because *they are an easy option*. According to this view, qualitative research is for losers. It is for those who are simply not up to the challenging task of conducting rigorously designed studies and analysing complex numerical data. Unlike the four other criticisms discussed above, this view is completely and seriously mistaken. Indeed, in almost every respect, the task of doing good qualitative research is every bit as demanding as that of doing good quantitative research. For example, it takes approximately ten times as long to transcribe the dialogue from an interview as it does to conduct it, which means that a typical study which requires this procedure demands over 100 hours of data entry. By comparison, the data from many experiments can be entered in a matter of minutes. Similarly, where most quantitative data analysis can be conducted effortlessly and economically using step-by-step guides or computer programs, the analysis of qualitative data can be a tortuous and drawn-out procedure that relies upon extensive collaboration with multiple parties (e.g., if independent coders are used in content analysis).

Having said this, it is certainly true that some students turn to qualitative methods because they harbour fears about quantitative techniques and succumb to the myth that a qualitative approach is an easy 'out'. This, however, is the very worst reason for doing qualitative research and it is destined to end in disappointment of one form or another: either the research process will prove much more painful than expected or a fundamental lack of commitment will lead to substandard work.

In summary, then, we would suggest that all but the last of these five criticisms have some substance, but that in the case of the first two objections there are grounds for leveling similar objections against quantitative methods. Researchers who would fault qualitative research for being unscientific and affording limited psychological insight thus run the risk of having to defend their own work against the same accusations. However, in much the same way, the third of the above criticisms points to the fact that qualitative researchers who fault quantitative methods for imposing particular meanings and standards on data can also be accused of having double standards. For it is clear from the writings of discourse analysts that they, no less than experimentalists, favour *particular* interpretations of phenomena and *particular* methods for arriving at those interpretations – it is just that these interpretations and methods are relativist rather than realist. Indeed, it is worth pointing out that it is precisely because constructionist researchers are able to demonstrate some analytical expertise that their invitations for students to read and be influenced by their research are seen as justified rather than fraudulent. For *both* quantitative and qualitative researchers, there is thus some irony in the fact that in striving to dismiss other approaches, the charges they raise could ultimately be used to undermine their own.

Conclusion: The importance of responding to the challenge

Although it is common for textbooks like this one to address quantitative and qualitative research techniques in different chapters, the above discussion points to some of the serious problems of this strategy. First amongst these is the fact that the distinction between quantitative and qualitative approaches is much less clear than one might imagine. Indeed, as we have seen, the differences between discourse analysis and content analysis are in many ways much more marked than those between content analysis and standard experimental methods. For this reason any approach to psychological research which is informed by a conviction that quantitative research is uniformly good and qualitative research is uniformly bad (or vice versa) is very foolish.

The benefits of a multi-faceted approach to psychological enquiry are well illustrated by the work of Reicher and his colleagues on crowd behaviour. In order to develop a rounded theoretical analysis of this phenomenon, this research has involved experiments that manipulate key theoretical variables (Reicher, 1984a), observational studies of crowds (e.g., Reicher, 1984b), content analysis of participants' statements (e.g., Stott, Hutchinson, & Drury, 2001) and discourse analysis of such statements (Potter & Reicher, 1987).

This is not to say that a researcher should not have a preference for one or other approach, or that most (or all) of one's research should not rely on a single method. There is nothing wrong with preferring quantitative to qualitative research (or vice versa), or in doing research that is mainly or exclusively quantitative (or qualitative). What we would suggest, however, is that it is a mistake to advocate one or other approach without considering both (a) how your research might be enhanced by taking an alternative approach, and (b) how you would respond to criticism of your research that might be levelled against it by advocates of an alternative approach.

The latter reflections are important for two reasons. In the first instance they are important because it is likely that at some stage or other your work will be exposed to criticism from researchers who embrace a different philosophy and methodology than yours. At that time you will need to mount a careful defence of your research strategy. But this will be difficult to do convincingly if you have not reflected critically on the issues raised in this chapter – thorny though many of these are. Secondly, however, these considerations are important because the process of attempting to respond to such criticism by conducting research that addresses the issues it raises represents one of the best ways of taking your own research forward.

Science does not progress because its practitioners cocoon themselves from ideas that they find threatening and hard to deal with. Instead it progresses when (and if) researchers are prepared to rise to the challenges created by productive intellectual tension. Qualitative research plays an important role in psychological science by creating tensions of exactly this form. For this reason alone, the challenges it lays down are well worth responding to.

Further reading

In response to the growing interest in qualitative methods in the last few years, a number of edited texts have been put together to provide details and discussions of a range of key developments in this area. There is considerable overlap amongst these, but the following volumes are well worth reading.

Richardson, J. T. E. (Ed.) (1996). *Handbook of qualitative research methods for psychology and the social sciences.* Leicester: BPS Books.

Silverman, D. (Ed.) (1996). *Qualitative research: Theory, method and practice.* London: Sage.

Qualitative research: A checklist for research evaluation and improvement

Potential problem	Question to ask	Potential improvement
Descriptive uncertainty	Does quantitative analysis adequately capture features of the phenomenon that the researchers are investigating?	Consider using qualitative methods in addition to, or as an alternative to, quantitative analysis
Participant involvement	Do participants share and/or value the researchers' understanding of the phenomenon they are investigating?	Consider using qualitative methods in which the participants are more directly involved in the research process (e.g., grounded theory)

Potential problem	Question to ask	Potential improvement
Positivism/realism	Is it the case that features of the world do not exist in a form which makes them amenable to decontextualized description and measurement?	Consider using methods which attend to contextual variation in phenomena (including qualitative methods such as discourse analysis)
Idealism/constructivism/ relativism/ postmodernism	Is it the case that features of the world (including contextual variation) can be made amenable to description and measurement?	Consider using methods which involve description and measurement (including various qualitative methods such as content analysis and grounded theory)
Inter-rater reliability	How much correspondence is there in different raters' coding of qualitative data?	Measure inter-rater reliability using an appropriate index (e.g., the probability of agreement in the assignment of data to categories).

Q12.6*

A team of researchers investigating young people's attitudes to marriage favour a contextualist approach to qualitative research in which commitment to the scientific method places emphasis on (a) the perspective of participants and researchers and (b) features of the research context. Which of the following approaches is most likely to appeal to them?

(a) Content analysis.
(b) Analysis of contextual variance.
(c) Grounded theory.
(d) Discourse analysis.
(e) Repertory grid analysis.

Q12.7***

What is inter-rater reliability?

(a) A measure of the agreement between people who use a particular coding system.
(b) A strategy for ensuring that people who code data are honest.
(c) A measure of the degree to which the personal constructs of researchers have affected their coding.
(d) A measure of the degree to which raters are consistent over time.

(e) The outcome of a process in which reflexive journals are inspected to ensure that researchers have taken account of the subjective meaning of phenomena for participants.

Q12.8**

Which of the following statements is true?

(a) It is generally better for a researcher to use one method to collect and analyse data as this avoids confusion.
(b) Researchers who use different methods to examine the same issue are more likely to misrepresent features of the phenomena they are investigating.
(c) Good researchers do not have methodological preferences as they are aware that these encourage disagreement and conflict.
(d) Qualitative methods are interesting, but they have not had much impact on psychology.
(e) None of the above.

The correct answer to 12.6 is (c). Grounded theory is a contextualist approach that attempts to combine use of scientific method with sensitivity to human and environmental factors that bear upon the process of data collection and interpretation. (a) is wrong because content analysis is a realist method that does not place emphasis on participants' own views. (b) is wrong because, although it has an authentic ring to it, there is no such thing as analysis of contextual variance. (d) is wrong because discourse analysis is a constructionist method that questions the utility of scientific method. (e) is wrong because, while it tries to capture the participants' perspective on phenomena of interest (i.e., their personal constructs), repertory grid analysis is not generally concerned to place emphasis on the context in which such constructs are elicited.

The correct answer to 12.7 is (a). Inter-rater reliability is used to assess the amount of agreement between participants in their coding of qualitative data. (b) is wrong because it cannot measure whether coders are honest. (c) is wrong because the measure does not assess the factors which contribute to agreement or disagreement among coders. (d) is wrong because the measure examines consistency between raters, not within the same rater. (e) is a nonsense answer which sounds like a procedure that might be used by a grounded theorist but is not.

The correct answer to 12.8 is (e). All of these statements are false. (a) and (b) are wrong because using different methods can actually be a way of eliminating confusion as it allows researchers to develop a richer understanding of the issues in which they are interested and to reconcile apparently contradictory aspects of their analysis. At the same time, (c) is wrong because all researchers have methodological preferences, and the debate this leads to is often productive and healthy. (d) is wrong because qualitative methods have always been influential in psychology and they are now more popular than ever.

Discussion/essay questions

(a) Why have qualitative techniques increased in popularity in recent years?

(b) What are the main reasons for choosing to conduct qualitative analysis?

(c) Given the many different ways in which qualitative analysis can be performed, what factors determine a researcher's decision to use a specific technique?

(d) What are the main problems with qualitative analysis? Can these be avoided?

Practical problems

(a) *Content analysis*

Obtain copies of all the major national newspapers that are published on a particular day and identify any articles which are related to the topic of mental illness. Your task is to perform content analysis on these in order to see whether there is a difference in the way in which mental illness is characterized (a) in different sections of the papers (e.g., news articles, court reports, feature articles), and (b) in different categories of paper (e.g., broadsheet, tabloid).

  (i) What is the sampling domain here? How might it be improved?

  (ii) What coding units would you use to code your data?

  (iii) How would you ensure that your coding was reliable?

  (iv) How would you analyse your data?

(b) *Grounded theory*

Conduct a search of national newspapers to find articles on the topic of health, and specifically the question of how health funds are allocated (e.g., in cases where particular patients require expensive treatment). Analyse these articles using grounded theory in order to characterize the nature of this debate.

  (i) Use open coding to develop a coding system comprised of coding categories that capture the ways in which this topic is treated. Stay very close to the meaning of sentences – avoid too much abstraction at this stage. Note also that at this stage the label for coding categories will only be provisional. As other examples of a concept come up, you may find you need to change the label in order to provide a better 'fit' to the data.

(ii) Identify links between the coding categories and concepts that provide structure to debate in this area.

(iii) What conclusions emerge from this analysis concerning the way in which decisions about healthcare are represented in various sections of the media?

(iv) What implications do these representations have for academic analysis of economic decisions?

(v) How do representations of healthcare rationing affect public understanding of this issue as a whole?

(c) *Discourse analysis*

Consider the following text which is taken from President Clinton's testimony to the US grand jury, in which he was questioned about his relationship with Monica Lewinsky (from Hepburn, 2003, pp. 166–196). This is a response to questioning about a phone call with Lewinsky in which it has been suggested that Clinton asked her to lie about an impending court case.

(12.0)
Mister Wisenberg ((C raises an index finger at
Q)) I remember that she came in to visit that
day, (0.5) I remember that she was very upset.
(2.5)
I don't recall whether I talked to her on the
phone before she came in to visit, (.) but I
may well have. = I'm no- not denying that I did.
I just don't recall that.

(i) Identify as many different features of this transcript as possible (e.g., the words, the pauses, the sequencing of ideas).

(ii) Draw up a list of the various goals that Clinton appears to be trying to achieve in his statement.

(iii) Reflect on whether particular features of his statement correspond to particular goals.

(iv) Reflect on the way that these patterns shed light on the phenomenon of memory, and on their relationship to the analysis offered by researchers who study memory using different methodologies.

13

Research Ethics

Science and society

Some time ago (indeed, before the authors had even started studying psychology) a man offered $1000 to anyone who could prove that smoking causes lung cancer in humans. Of course, nobody has ever claimed the prize. Based on the principles you have already read about in this book you could help design research that would have a chance of winning that prize. But we hope that after reading this chapter on **research ethics** you will understand why nobody will ever claim the $1000. The reasons all revolve around the ethics of running the experiment that would prove that smoking causes lung cancer.

The question whether smoking causes lung cancer is really one for medical research. So instead, let us consider an issue that is just as important, but is one that psychologists are directly concerned with – patients' attitudes to their recovery from cancer. Most people have an opinion on this issue. Some believe that positive attitudes help patients recover from cancer (or to survive longer). Others believe that if you have cancer, that's that – you will either recover or not, regardless of your attitude. Still others believe that positive attitudes do not matter all that much, but that if you have negative attitudes you will tend not to recover. There is evidence to support all of these possibilities, and substantial research into the issue has been conducted by psychologists and medical scientists.

We have chosen this issue not just because it is something you probably have an opinion about, but also because it is an important question and one to which science has not yet provided all the answers. We could have chosen a trivial issue to explain research ethics, but to do so would have risked missing the point. Research ethics relates to *serious issues*, often issues that are deeply personal for many people. Two other features of this example are important too: the fact that most people have an opinion about recovery from cancer and that science has yet to answer all their questions. Research ethics often relates to *issues that people in many different communities have opinions about.* Moreover, if you asked us 'What are the effects of attitudes to cancer on recovery?', we would have to say 'The jury is still out'. There has been much progress, but nobody can confidently say 'The effect of a person's attitudes to cancer on recovery is...'. This is partly because research ethics affects *the ability of the science to answer difficult questions* about sensitive issues.

Let us consider why the question of the effects of attitudes to cancer on recovery has not yet been resolved by science. The reasons are much the same as the reasons why nobody has ever claimed the $1000 prize for proving that smoking causes lung cancer. Suppose that you believe negative attitudes to cancer reduce a patient's chance of recovery. Several simple experiments could test this idea, but they are all so obnoxious that nobody has ever carried them out. For example, researchers could randomly allocate a large sample of cancer patients to two groups and thoroughly convince one group they were not going to recover (assuming that this could be done effectively), while having no contact with the control group. A few months later they would measure the condition of the patients.

Now it is true that research even more offensive than this has been conducted – for example, by scientists in Nazi Germany. But the vast majority of people who discovered that such research was going to be carried out where they worked or studied would be shocked. Many would go to rallies, sign petitions and write to politicians. Some of the researchers' colleagues might give media interviews, and call for the researchers to be thrown out of their professional associations, and all this would occur in an effort to stop the research from going ahead. It is likely that the institution in question would forbid its researchers from carrying out the research, and if the research went ahead there could be an enormous legal quagmire, possibly leading to criminal charges.

Why would all this happen? It would happen because the science of psychology, like any science, is part of the society in which the scientists work. There are three reasons why society has a right to express opinions about how scientists should carry out their research. First, society pays the bills for research (through taxes and tuition fees). Secondly, members of society often participate in that research. Thirdly, the research is usually *about* society. For all these reasons, the bogus experiment that we discussed above would never be carried out because society – in the form of governments, students, other researchers, lawyers, university administrations and community action groups – would say 'Find another way to answer this important question'.

In reality there are no researchers we know of who would want to carry out the study we have described. Universities and research centres are not full of crazy psychologists who want to do research that would harm participants. Researchers are not opposed to society, they are part of society, and they generally stick to the standards and values of the society they live in. In particular, this is because researchers have ethical standards, both formal and informal. Formal codes of practice are explicitly designed to limit harm to participants. For example, participants must generally be told enough about the research so that they can decide whether they want to participate. If they do not follow the principles set out in these codes, researchers will not receive funds from research bodies and journals will not publish their research. Moreover, their research will almost certainly be forbidden by their institutional **ethics committee**.

How, then, could the researchers address the question about the effects of attitudes to cancer in another way? Not easily. One possibility would be to change the question. The researchers could run an experiment with an experimental group comprised of people whose attitudes were manipulated so that they became more positive. They could then compare this group with a control group (who could be assumed to have more negative attitudes). However, there is a major problem with this study. It would actually be testing the hypothesis that *positive* attitudes improve recovery. At the end of the day, if the research showed that attitudes did not affect cancer recovery this might be because the researchers were studying the wrong attitudes.

Another possibility would be to use a correlational or survey approach (as discussed in Chapters 5 and 9). The researchers could find a sample of cancer patients, measure their attitudes to recovery, and then follow them up 6 months later to see how they were doing. They could then correlate attitudes to cancer with a measure of health. Alternatively, the researchers could conduct a quasi-experiment where a group of patients with positive attitudes were matched with a group of patients with negative attitudes on variables such as the severity of cancer. Six months later the health of people in the two groups could be compared.

If you have read the previous twelve chapters of this book you will be able to see what the problems with these research strategies are. In the case of the quasi-experiment, any number of *extraneous* variables could compromise any interpretation of the findings. For example, matching people for severity of cancer may build in other differences between groups (such as amount of treatment or age). In short, there is no way that the researchers could *prove* that negative attitudes prevent recovery from cancer.

Thus, the often quite reasonable demands that society makes on researchers mean that important questions that could in principle be answered by simple research strategies are never addressed. Although this is most obvious for serious and controversial issues such as attitudes to cancer, it in fact applies to all areas of research in psychology. Whenever psychologists design research they have to consider the effects that the research will have on participants. We have argued that to design and understand research you need to know a lot about principles such as randomization, causal inference and so on. Ethical principles are *every bit as important* to the real business of doing psychological research as any of the other ideas that we have discussed in this book.

You may think that the example we have used seems a bit far-fetched. Would researchers really ever do something that could have very serious effects on research participants? Would people really ever care enough about psychological research to organize angry protests and write letters to politicians? The answer to both questions is 'yes'.

A striking illustration of the first point is provided by research conducted by Berkun, Bialek, Kern, and Yagi (1962) in which participants were soldiers who thought they were being shelled by artillery while they tried to repair a broken radio. The amount of time it took to repair the radio was the dependent variable. Certainly, this study was done some time ago, and it was done by psychologists working for the United States defence forces, but the fact remains that the research was done, and unless society had intervened, it is possible that psychologists would still be doing similar things.

Are there cases of strong popular reactions against psychological research? There have been many examples. One is provided by research on racial differences in intelligence which has been controversial for a long time and continues to cause heated debate (e.g., Fraser, 1995; Gould, 1981; Herrnstein & Murray, 1994). Some prominent researchers in the area have met angry protests in universities and other forums throughout the world when they have presented their views.

However, the area that provokes the greatest continuing controversy is research that uses animals. We will consider the rights and wrongs of animal research in a later section, but research with animals is now so controversial and produces such strong feelings in segments of the wider community that many researchers find that they can no longer perform

Q13.1*

the research they feel they need to do. All we would say for now is that the conflicts here can be quite different from those that arise in other areas of psychology.

Which of the following is true about the relationship between scientific research and society?

(a) Science exists outside society.
(b) Ethical principles are generally imposed by governments on psychologists against their will.
(c) Only scientists should decide what is ethical or not about research.
(d) Decisions about research ethics are always a matter of personal choice.
(e) None of the above.

The correct answer is (e). This is almost a trick question. The relationship between scientific research and society is so complex that anyone who tries to reduce it to a few simple statements is always going to risk making mistakes. Statement (a) is simply wrong. Science is part of society. Statement (b) is sometimes wrong, as many ethical principles have willingly been *introduced* by psychologists. If (a) is wrong, (c) must also be wrong, as by most standards members of a society have a right to say what they think is unacceptable in their society. If scientists disagree it is up to them to explain why. (d) is wrong because although people have personal views, decisions about research ethics are often made by relevant groups in society, for example, funding bodies and ethics committees.

ethics committee A body set up by a research institution such as a university to review ethical principles relating to the conduct of research at that institution. Such committees usually contain representatives from groups for whom research ethics is important and relevant (e.g., researchers, lawyers, medical practitioners, ministers of religion, members of the general community).

research ethics The principles by which researchers decide the best way to balance the contribution of their research to human knowledge against potential damage to human welfare. Researchers are obligated to have a knowledge of any code of ethics that applies to their research.

Participation in research

Many readers of this book will have already participated in psychological research. If you are doing an introductory psychology course you may have been required to take part in research, often in exchange for course credit. Exactly the same thing is going on right now in universities and colleges all over the world.

For this reason research ethics is not a dry, abstract concern for other people, or something you can file away until the exam comes around. Most people who read this book will participate in psychological research and many will conduct research themselves. In fact much (perhaps most) of the research that is conducted in psychology is done by students – either advanced undergraduates or postgraduates. So when you participate in research there is a good chance that you are actually helping another student. In any case you will be helping to advance the sum of psychological knowledge, as well as observing how research is done by real researchers. Some would also argue that if you are studying psychology you are consuming psychological knowledge and so it is only fair that you help to add to this knowledge. However, these arguments are not reasons to make light of ethical concerns and if you are asked to participate in research you should be aware of your rights as a participant.

It is extremely unlikely that anyone reading this book will experience actual harm from participating in psychological experiments. Many of you will find that research participation is interesting, engaging and informative. Even if this is not the case, research participation in psychology is probably a lot safer than attending a class or catching a bus. That is because researchers follow principles which should serve to prevent harm occurring. Indeed, the biggest risk most participants face is that they might have to spend a few less than scintillating hours watching a computer screen or filling in questionnaires.

So what exactly are the main risks to participants in research? These fall into four main categories: (a) stress; (b) breaches of confidentiality; (c) deception; and (d) invasive procedures.

Some research may cause *stress* for participants. Sometimes this cannot be avoided – especially if stress is what the researchers are actually investigating. This is quite a plausible scenario as stress is a major topic addressed by a range of psychologists (e.g., in clinical, organizational and cognitive areas). As an example of such research, take the researcher who wants to examine the hypothesis that fear or anxiety impairs intellectual performance. Clearly, there is no way for this researcher to study these issues experimentally without creating

403

some distress in the participants. However, the researcher must strive to ensure that the stress does not persist outside the experimental session, and the research in general must minimize unintended or unnecessary stress. The research that has probably generated the most concern about stress for participants is that by Milgram (1963, 1974) on obedience. We will look at his work in more detail shortly.

Confidentiality is important because participants often give sensitive information to researchers. Participants are remarkably willing to give researchers information about their relationships, religious beliefs, sexual orientations and political attitudes – information that they would not dream of giving to even their closest friends. This is part of a general inclination on the part of research participants to be co-operative and helpful. As Orne (1969) noted, if someone walked up to people in the street and asked them to do 10 push-ups, they would ask 'Why?'. But if a psychologist made the same request in an experiment, they would ask 'Where?'.

One reason why research participants are so helpful is that many of them are committed to the research process. They want to answer researchers' questions because they want to contribute to the advancement of the science. Whatever the reasons for participation, it is essential that researchers do not abuse the trust that is placed in them, and that they maintain the confidentiality of their participants. If someone tells a researcher something, that person should be able to assume that nobody else will ever know who gave the researcher that information, and this should be especially true for any sensitive or personal information. For example, this is why participants in clinical or neuropsychological research are identified by a pseudonym or their initials (as in the case of HM, the patient with no apparent long-term memory, whom we mentioned in Chapter 3). The only exception is where participants give the researcher explicit permission to reveal their identity. This is very rarely necessary.

Deception is one feature of psychological research that contributes to more than its fair share of ethical debate. As we discussed in Chapter 4, deception involves giving participants information that is false. You may wonder why it is necessary for researchers to deceive participants. The reason is that many experiments, especially in social psychology, involve elaborate set-ups where participants think that one thing is happening but actually something else is happening. This is because most social psychologists believe that people's behaviour is influenced not so much by what is actually happening as by what people *think* is happening. Deception is therefore used to control *reactivity* (Chapter 4).

Let us illustrate this point with an example. Imagine that we want to know whether people respond differently to emergency situations when they are alone rather than in a group. Latané and Darley (1970) investigated this important question by asking participants to complete a questionnaire in a small room. The experimenters then filled the room with smoke. They found that people were more likely to check on the problem if they were alone than if they were with a group of strangers who continued to fill out their questionnaires (these strangers were actually **confederates** of the experimenter). This experiment made an important contribution to our understanding of human behaviour, but psychologists only acquired this knowledge because the researchers tricked their participants. After all, the alternatives would be starting a *real* fire (which could never be considered for all sorts of reasons) or telling the participants that the fire was *not* real before the research started. The latter simply would not work – a fire does not affect behaviour unless people believe it to be real.

Note, however, that the use of deception is not confined to the laboratory and can be used in field studies where researchers do not want their identity and purpose to be revealed. For example, this was the case when Festinger and his colleagues wanted to infiltrate a cult to see how its members would cope when their prophecy about the world's end failed to come true – a case study we referred to in Chapter 3 (Festinger *et al.*, 1956). Similarly, researchers have examined the circumstances under which a person comes to the aid of a victim by having confederates pose as people in distress (e.g., Darley & Batson, 1973). The ethical dilemma here is clear, and is one we sometimes become aware of when exposed to similar techniques in television programmes that set out to play jokes on members of the general public by placing them in awkward situations.

The way we think about things can have a powerful effect on our behaviour. In some research psychologists use deception to *control* for these effects experimentally. Experimental control of this form occurs in **placebo** studies where participants in one condition think they receive a treatment but in fact receive no treatment. This occurs to control for any effects that might arise from the fact that when the participants think they are receiving a treatment they may get better just because they *expect* to get better. Placebo effects like this are complex and apply in many subtle ways. However, if a control were not put in place it would be impossible to know the extent to which placebo effects contributed to any treatment effects. Moreover, if participants know they are not receiving a proper treatment they might actually go looking for one and their withdrawal from the research could threaten its internal validity (this is the problem of *mortality* that we discussed in Chapter 4).

What are the arguments against deception? Understandably, some people simply feel that it is wrong for researchers to deceive participants whatever the reason. This is a moral issue, but the moral cost must be weighed against the gains to knowledge from the deceptive research. Some issues simply cannot be studied without using deception. The moral burden of deception is one that individual researchers may choose to bear or not to bear, after they have taken account of the reasons for and against the deception. Suffice it to say that most social psychologists see deception as a justifiable technique where there are appropriate safeguards.

The other major argument against deception is that being tricked by the experimenter can be stressful for the participants, not least because it can reveal to people unpleasant things about themselves. The research that illustrates this point best was conducted by Stanley Milgram (1963) on obedience. This really kicked off the major debate on ethics in psychology, largely because it was (and still is) among the most provocative and controversial research ever done.

Milgram was interested in the extent to which people were prepared to obey the unreasonable and cruel commands of authority figures. The people who participated in this research were asked to deliver electric shocks to another research participant who was performing poorly on a memory task. The participants were instructed by the experimenter to give increasingly large electric shocks to this person (a man located in the next room) every time he made a mistake. As instructed by the experimenter, most participants continued to administer the shocks even after the person being shocked started to complain and scream. Most continued doing this even when the person being shocked stopped responding altogether. It was obvious that when they reflected on what they had done, all participants experienced a great deal of stress. Many of them had questioned the experimenter's instructions, yet they had continued to administer what they thought were potentially lethal shocks. In fact no shocks were administered – the experimenter's cover story was an elaborate deception involving a confederate of the experimenter who only pretended to be shocked.

As you can imagine, this study has raised many questions about the effect it may have had on participants. Some psychologists argue that such research is harmful for the participants as it causes stress, embarrassment and guilt. They also add that deceptive research like this can have few benefits (Baumrind, 1964, 1985). Extending this point, it has been argued that it was actually Milgram's *assistants* who, by carrying out the deception, displayed the most destructive form of obedience in the research.

However, Milgram actually followed up his participants in order to find out whether they had been harmed (something only a small number of researchers do). Most participants (80%) reported that although the research had been stressful at the time, they were grateful that they had participated in the experiment as it had taught them about human behaviour and their own capacities. This was partly because after the experiment was over Milgram was careful to conduct extensive **debriefing** that informed the participants about the purpose of the experiment and explained to them why the deception was necessary. Only 1.3% reported negative effects, and interviews by a psychiatrist revealed no negative long-term effects for any participant. It is worth noting, however, that Milgram's participants were healthy adults. Exactly the same study would have been far more objectionable if the participants had been people who were more susceptible to harm (e.g., children, the elderly or the mentally ill). It is also possible that reactivity (in the form of a desire to please the interviewer, as discussed in Chapters 4 and 5) may have led Milgram's participants to downplay the extent of their stress in his post-experimental enquiries.

In the absence of evidence of harm, then, we must ask whether the risk to the participants was justified given the benefit to human knowledge from the research. In his own defence Milgram pointed out that he had asked psychiatrists to estimate the percentage of people who would obey the experimenter's instructions. Because they assumed that only mentally disturbed people would administer the shocks, their estimate was 1% of the participants, this being the level of serious mental illness in the general population. In fact, none of Milgram's participants was mentally ill, and the level of obedience was actually a staggering 63%. Obviously, if Milgram's research had never been carried out we would never have known how prepared people are to obey instructions to do destructive things to other people.

So, although Milgram's research has been severely criticized on ethical grounds, the study did provide illuminating insights into a particularly important aspect of human behaviour. These insights may, for example, help to explain why otherwise normal people are willing to commit atrocities when told to do so by their superiors. But *was it worth it?* Before you answer this question we should point out that even if this research had not already been conducted (so that the insights it provided still remained to be made), Milgram's work would not be approved by most ethics committees today. What would be the price of *not* having this knowledge?

Whatever your response to these questions, it is apparent that ethics committees are usually very sensitive to the problems caused by doing research, but are much less sensitive to the problems caused by not doing research (Pettit, 1992; Rosenthal, 1994). This is partly because if these committees were to permit harmful research to go ahead, the victims (or their representatives) would hold them responsible. In contrast, the victims of scientific ignorance hardly ever complain.

One other risk of deception is that participants may end up mistrusting all researchers (Baumrind, 1985). That is, after they have found out that the information provided in psychology experiments can be misleading, a person may come to believe that all psychological research involves tricks, even though this is not true (particularly outside social psychology). This is a problem for researchers (in so far as it is an instance of reactivity), but instilling a healthy scepticism into students who will have to read, interpret and perhaps one day conduct research may not be such a bad thing.

It is clear from these examples that research can have effects which change people. Features which produce these changes are called **invasive procedures**. Extreme examples might include giving participants drugs (under medical supervision), inserting some psychophysiological recording device into their bodies, or giving people information that they could not otherwise have obtained (e.g., their score on a personality test). Ethical research (e.g., that based on the principles of the American Psychological Association) always involves minimizing any long-term effects on participants to those absolutely necessary for the research, and eliminating long-term negative effects.

An interesting question that remains is whether there is actually any evidence of people being harmed by research. To address the issue in the undergraduate population, Smith and Richardson (1983) surveyed 464 undergraduates in North America. One-fifth of the participants reported some harm in terms of feeling very nervous, very humiliated, very angry, excessive physical discomfort or that they were very wrongly deceived as a result of participating in research. If we exclude those who felt very nervous without other sources of harm (reasoning that this is less serious than the other types of possible harm) this left a total of 15 people, or 3% of the sample, who reported experiencing harm. However, as in the case of Milgram's follow-up interviews, it is possible that these results may have been contaminated by participants' reactivity – leading either to an over- or underestimation of the actual incidence of harm.

In general, then, it seems that there is little evidence that psychology students are harmed by their participation in normal research in the main areas of psychology – for example, those that involve interaction with other people, working with computer-controlled equipment, or filling in questionnaires. Based on the available evidence, there are only two conclusions we can draw: either researchers have not looked hard enough for the harmful effects of research participation, or the harmful effects are not especially great.

The position taken on this debate depends a great deal upon how fragile research participants (and people in general) are perceived to be (West & Gunn, 1978). Those most concerned about **research risk** tend to see research participants as relatively fragile. Nevertheless, *all* psychologists would accept that the *potential* for harm does exist. This fact needs to be borne in mind at all stages of the research process.

Having considered various points, we are now in a position to summarize some of the key principles that guide ethical research with human participants in psychology. In short, the research should minimize risk to participants, and if there are any negative effects upon participants the researcher has the responsibility to correct those negative effects. Above all, participation should be based on **informed consent**, and participants should be aware of features of the research that could be expected to affect their decision to participate. It is impossible to obtain informed consent when using unobtrusive measurements (Chapter 5), so other techniques should be considered where there is a risk of harm to participants.

The principle that the participant is capable of **discontinuing participation** at any time is also extremely important. If participants feel uncomfortable or for any reason feel that they do not wish to continue taking part then they must be free to leave at any time. They do not have to give any reason to the researcher.

The other critical feature of all research involving a researcher working with human participants is debriefing. If the research process is to be of any educational benefit for the participants – and it certainly should be – it is only fair that participants are told what the research was about and what it was trying to achieve. This debriefing should occur at the end of the research session, and certainly no later than the end of the testing programme. Above all, it is essential for the dignity of the participants that the researchers explain the nature of any deception used. As Smith and Richardson (1983) found, good debriefing seems to prevent the negative effects of deception. Researchers should try to explain deceptions in a sensitive manner – after all, nobody likes to find out that they have been tricked. They should also explain why the deception was necessary. Poor and insensitive debriefing can often

turn relatively minor problems into major problems, while good
debriefing can turn potentially major problems into minor ones.

For research conducted with populations that are more vulnerable
to research risk (e.g., children, the mentally ill and the elderly),
researchers must make extra efforts to ensure that these principles are
upheld. For example, informed consent must also be provided by
parents or guardians when research involves children.

Q13.2*

Which of the following should ethical research with humans involve?

(a) Informed consent on the part of the participants where possible.
(b) Debriefing.
(c) Minimization of research risk.
(d) Justification of invasive procedures.
(e) All of the above.

The correct answer is (e). All of the features (a) to (d) are vital for ethical
research in psychology. Informed consent is not possible in studies that
involve non-obtrusive measurement.

confederate Someone who works for the experimenter and acts in a
certain predetermined way. Normally the confederate pretends to be
a genuine research participant, so the use of confederates involves
deception.

confidentiality In the research process, confidentiality means ensuring
that individual participants cannot be identified. This often means
making sure that responses are anonymous.

debriefing Explaining the purpose and procedures of research to
participants after its completion. Debriefing should include a sensitive
explanation and justification of any deceptions used.

discontinuing participation An ethical principle which guarantees
the right of all human participants to cease taking part in research at
any time.

informed consent The ethical principle that research participants
should be told enough about a piece of research to be able to make a
decision about whether to participate in it.

invasive procedures Research procedures which lead to changes in
participants.

placebo A device used to control for the effect of participants'
expectations about the effects of research participation or the

experimental treatment. An example would be giving a control group a sugar tablet rather than the real medical drug given to an experimental group. Neither group would know whether they were receiving the placebo or a real drug (i.e., the participants would be *blind* to the treatment). In other respects the groups would be treated the same.

research risk The possibility of harm to participants, usually in the form of long-term negative effects.

Research with animals

At one time a great deal of research in psychology involved animals. Indeed, in some circles the popular name for psychology was 'rats and stats'. As you have found out, the stats are still there, but there are not as many rats or other animals now. In the period from January 1990 to September 1996 there were 276 286 journal articles listed in *Psychological Abstracts* (the main database of psychology and related journal articles), and 28 337 of these involved research with animals. In other words, over that period around 10% of the total amount of published research in psychology involved animals (mainly rats). However, animal research raises more than its fair share of debates about ethics.

We must hasten to add that the ethical debate in this area does not arise because psychologists treat animals worse than do other scientists, or other people who work with animals. This is not necessarily because psychologists are more ethical than other scientists, but simply because the nature of psychologists' work means that fewer of them perform procedures that can be distressing to animals (such as surgery). Indeed, a lot of animal research in psychology only involves the *observation* of behaviour. Moreover, most psychologists support the principles of **animal welfare**. Ethical treatment of animals involves things such as housing them in clean cages with adequate food and water, ensuring that the pain and distress they suffer are minimized, and that if it becomes necessary to kill them this is done in a humane and painless way. Ethical treatment of animals is actually in the researchers' interest. This is because if psychologists want to study the normal behaviour of animals it makes no sense to mistreat them (some people would extend this point to argue that it makes no sense to study them in laboratory cages).

Why do psychologists need to study animals? Some psychologists are simply interested in animal behaviour, and these researchers have no choice but to use animal participants. Others study animals because they are interested in questions which studies using human participants cannot address. Imagine that psychologists wanted to know whether a particular part of the brain is essential for controlling the desire to eat. There are only two ways to address this question. The researchers could attempt to find people who have had this section of their brain destroyed in accidents and see whether they still have a desire to eat. The problem is that accidents tend not to destroy isolated regions of the brain. So if it was found that the brain-injured person did not want to eat then this could be due to some other effect of the injury. As in all quasi-experiments, the interpretation of results could be contaminated by these extraneous (uncontrolled) variables.

Given that deliberately destroying parts of humans' brains would render a researcher liable for an extended prison sentence, the only alternative is to take animals with brains that are similar to our own, and conduct invasive research on these animals and see whether the animal still eats. This invasive research might involve the use of electrical probes or the destruction of specific regions of their brain. If psychologists and other scientists did not conduct these studies then important questions (e.g., concerning the biological factors that contribute to dietary disorders) would never be answered. As members of society, all of us have a right to decide whether or not we are prepared to allow animals to be harmed so that these questions can be addressed.

The fact that the work of animal psychologists has come increasingly under attack is correlated with the rise of the **animal rights movement** after the publication of Peter Singer's influential book *Animal Liberation* in 1975 (Herzog, 1995). Many members of this movement believe that animals have the same rights as humans. From this point of view the idea of keeping animals in captivity to observe their behaviour is as offensive as it would be for the researchers to take you prisoner for the same purpose. Obviously, there is a complete conflict of opinions here. The researchers believe that it is essential to study animals in ways necessary to draw the strongest scientific conclusions. Advocates of animal rights believe that the research this entails is unjustifiable. Their argument is not so much that psychologists are not obeying the ethical principles of their science, but more fundamentally that all such research is completely unethical and should be stopped.

This debate will not go away, and will remain acrimonious for the foreseeable future. The clearest conclusion we can draw is that animal research provides a good example of society at large taking an interest in what science does. Although much of the attention is unwanted by the scientists, it has had a positive effect on the welfare of research animals, and virtually all psychologists using animals are now fully committed to the cause of animal welfare (even though most reject the animal rights point of view).

However, the focus on animal research in psychology remains ironic. Much worse treatment of animals can occur in abattoirs, farms, animal refuges, restaurants, commercial research laboratories and people's own homes than in any university psychology laboratory. Animal rights advocates argue that psychologists have a much greater responsibility to act ethically and to reflect community concerns than do other people. However, it seems clear that, regardless of whether research with animals is right or wrong, the attention that university research laboratories receive from the animal rights movement reflects the fact that universities are important and relatively easy targets to influence – not necessarily the fact that university researchers do more terrible things to animals than do other people. Ultimately, the debate on this issue is as much political as ethical, and it will never be resolved purely by an appeal to ethical principles. This is because ethics is an expression and instrument of society and not everybody in society has the same principles. Instead, like science itself, ethical principles are a source of continuing argument, conflict and struggle.

Q13.3*

Which of the following is true about ethical research using animals?

(a) It must ensure that discomfort to animals is minimized and harm only occurs where essential.
(b) Ethics is not a major issue because participants are not deceived.
(c) Because it is such a controversial topic, the issues it raises are only worth discussing in relation to medical research.
(d) It is not really relevant to psychology.
(e) None of the above.

The correct answer is (a). Answer (b) is wrong because deception is only an issue for human participants. (c) is wrong because animal research in psychology and other sciences addresses issues that are just as important as those in medical research. Answer (d) is wrong because although animal research has declined in popularity, that does not mean that it is not important – 10% of the research published in a big science like psychology is still a lot of research.

> **animal rights movement** Groups comprised of people who believe
>   that animals have similar or equal rights to those of human beings.
> **animal welfare** The set of principles that guide humane organizations
>   such as societies for the prevention of cruelty to animals and which
>   promote consideration for the well-being of animals.

Final comment

It is obvious that this chapter has dealt a lot more with opinions than
have the previous chapters in this book. Probably some of our own
opinions will have become obvious, too, although we have tried our
best to frame these in terms of the conflicting sets of arguments that
characterize ethical debates both inside and outside psychology.

The fact that conflicts in this area are so pronounced is one reason
why research ethics is such an intriguing and integral part of the
research process. The science of psychology cannot be separated from
society because at all times, whether they like it or not, researchers are a
part of society (and quite an important part, too). As such they are
guided by values that are *strong* but also *open to challenge*. It should be no
surprise, then, if you react more vigorously to the issues raised here than
to most of the others discussed in this book.

Further reading

Over the years, a range of studies have fuelled debate about ethics in society.
However, because Milgram's obedience studies set the agenda for much of
this debate, it is worth starting one's reading in this area by examining
Baumrind's critique of this research and Milgram's own response.

Baumrind, D. (1964). Some thoughts on ethics of research: After reading
   Milgram's 'Behavioral study of obedience'. *American Psychologist, 19*,
   421–423.
Milgram, S. (1964). Issues in the study of obedience: A reply to Baumrind.
   American Psychologist, 19, 848–852.

Research ethics: A checklist for research
evaluation and improvement

Potential problem	Question to ask	Potential improvement
Breach of confidentiality	Is participants' contribution to research confidential?	Take steps to ensure that as far as possible the identity of individual participants and the results of their participation

Potential problem	Question to ask	Potential improvement
Breach of anonymity	Is participants' contribution to research anonymous?	are kept private. This can often be achieved by referring to participants only by codenames or numbers and/or by keeping records of participants' identities separate from their data. If confidentiality and anonymity are breached this must be explicitly justified and participants need to be informed of this fact before agreeing to participate.
Deception	Have participants been deceived about the nature or purpose of research?	Endeavour to tell participants the truth about research and avoid making false or misleading statements or omitting important
Concealment	Has some important information about the research been kept from participants?	information. If any deception is deemed necessary, this must be explicitly justified and participants must be sensitively debriefed at the conclusion of the study. If deception or concealment could reasonably be expected to affect the decision to participate (and hence to compromise the principle of informed consent), then participants need to be informed of this fact before agreeing to participate.
Invasive procedures	Does the research change the participants in any way?	Research should be designed to ensure that, as far as possible, it has no long-term effects on participants and that there are no long-term negative effects.
Research risk	Does the research have any long-term negative effects?	Where there is a risk of this, participants should be informed of this fact and monitored beyond the end of the study to ensure that harm has not occurred and that, if it has, it is corrected.
Inadequate debriefing	At the conclusion of the research have participants been fully informed about the purpose of the research and the nature of, and reasons for, any deception?	At the end of any piece of research participants should be thanked for participating, and the nature and value of the research should be explained to them. Any questions that they have about the research should be answered, and, as far as possible, participants should

Potential problem	Question to ask	Potential improvement
		feel involved and respected in the broad research process (e.g., by being made aware of the scientific benefits associated with the research). This phase of research is particularly important if a study involves invasive procedures, research risk, deception or concealment.
Uninformed consent	Have the participants been told enough about the research to make an informed decision about whether to participate in it?	Ensure that participants are given enough information about a piece of research to make a reasonable decision about whether they want to participate in it. If participation involves deception or other factors that might reasonably be expected to impact on this decision (e.g., in a double-blind trial of a therapeutic technique) participants need to be made aware of this before participating. Where participants are unable to give informed consent (e.g., because they are children or impaired) special safeguards have to be set in place and consent obtained from their legal guardians.
Inability to discontinue participation	Are the participants free to withdraw from the research at any stage?	If participants do not want to continue taking part in a study they must be free to withdraw from it. They should not be placed under pressure to continue and they do not have to give reasons for withdrawing.
Harm to animals	Are animals harmed (psychologically or physically) by taking part in the study?	Animals should not be harmed in the process of conducting research. If they are, or there is a risk of harm, this must be very clearly justified and the scientific benefits of the research must also be very clear. Approval for research with animals is normally granted by a special ethics committee that has a brief to consider broad-ranging welfare issues.

Potential problem	Question to ask	Potential improvement
Failure to weigh risks against potential benefit	Have the ethical risks associated with any research been considered in light of potential scientific gains?	Even if it contravenes the ethical guidelines outlined above, research that has clear scientific value should not be rejected out of hand. Instead, the goal of minimizing ethical concern should be weighed against the potential for scientific gain. Different groups will use different scales in this process, but all must strike a workable and moral balance between these elements.
Failure to gain ethical approval	Has the research been approved by a relevant ethical committee or body?	Researchers cannot make decisions about the above issues on their own. Instead, they must present the case for conducting their research to relevant professional bodies (e.g., a university ethics committee). In the process they must justify any procedures which raise any ethical concerns. Only after gaining approval from such a body should the research proceed.

Q13.4**

Imagine that you are conducting a psychological experiment that has been approved by your institutional ethics committee and two participants object to answering some questions which they consider to be too personal. As a result, they decide they want to cease participating in the experiment. What are their responsibilities in this case?

(a) To complete the experimental session because you would not ask personal questions unless they were really important for science.
(b) To explain to you why they wish to leave so that you can conduct debriefing.
(c) The participants have no responsibilities, they can leave at any time.
(d) To report you to the institutional ethics committee.
(e) To discuss your experiment with other students.

Q13.5***

Informed consent means that researchers should tell participants about which of the following before they agree to participate in research?

(a) The hypotheses.
(b) Anything that is likely to affect the participants' decision to participate in the research.
(c) Details of any deception.
(d) The independent variable.
(e) Whether the experiment involves a placebo.

Q13.6**

Which of the following statements about Milgram's obedience-to-authority studies is (are) true?

(a) They violated the American Psychological Association's standards at the time because they used poor debriefing procedures.
(b) They led to important developments in ethical principles in psychological research.
(c) They have been criticized for putting participants at risk of harm.
(d) Both (b) and (c).
(e) They used inadequate follow-up procedures.

The correct answer to 13.4 is (c). Participants are always free to discontinue participation at any time, even if this would be inconvenient for the researcher. If participants feel strongly about an issue then (d) and (e) are options, but they are not *required* to do anything. It is possible, for example, that questions which are deeply personal for one person are not personal for most other people and there is no way the researcher can establish this in advance. (b) is a reasonable thing to do as it may be useful for participants to explain the problems they encountered with the research and to listen to the experimenter's response. However, participants are not required to do this.

The correct answer to 13.5 is (b), but this is quite a difficult question. This is mainly because the ethics of deception is complex. However, all ethical guidelines allow deception under some circumstances (so (c) and (e) are wrong), and making participants aware of the *details* of any deception is pointless as this will only ensure that the experiment does not work. There is no reason for the researcher to tell participants about the hypothesis (as (a) suggests) or about the independent variable (as (d) suggests) before the session. Any deception should be explained during debriefing.

The correct answer to 13.6 is (d). (a) is wrong because although Milgram's studies aroused a great deal of debate at the time, the debriefing was extensive and there were no guidelines on debriefing at the time. This means that (b) is true. (c) is also true (see Baumrind, 1964, 1985). (e) is incorrect because Milgram actually performed very extensive follow-ups of his participants.

Discussion/essay questions

(a) Do ethics committees have too little power or too much?
(b) Should researchers still be able to use research procedures like those employed by Milgram in the 1960s?
(c) To what extent have ethics committees influenced the way in which psychological knowledge has advanced in the last 30 years?
(d) Draft some ethical guidelines that you think any research you personally conduct should meet. Justify your decisions.
(e) How do you think ethical guidelines for conducting research in psychology will change in the next century? Will this change be for the better?

14

Conclusion: Managing Uncertainty in Psychological Research

'Where has all this got us?'

We started this book by asking the question 'Why do I have to do this?'. At that point we tried to give you some answers which would motivate you to read on and to try to master the material that we were going to present in the next 13 chapters. If you have stuck to this task (and we hope you have), you should have learned a lot and have a real sense of accomplishment. That being the case, it seems appropriate to conclude by taking stock of the journey and asking where it has brought us.

In this concluding chapter our aim is to summarize some of our ideas about the role that statistics play in the research process and about the relationship between statistics and other aspects of methodology and research design. Central to this summary is the idea that the *challenges* psychologists face when they conduct research largely concern *how to manage different types of uncertainty in the research process* (Haslam & McGarty, 2001). In many respects this analysis of uncertainty management is one of the most important ideas in this book. Although the emphasis in this chapter reflects our personal views, these observations should encourage you to reflect critically on the process of both producing and consuming research.

Managing uncertainty in psychological research

In Chapters 6 to 9 we made an important distinction between two types of statistic: those that describe the properties of particular sets of data and those that allow us to make inferences about the probable relationship between a set of data and the underlying reality to which the data relate. Each of these types of statistic is associated with a different form of **statistical uncertainty** – **descriptive uncertainty** and **inferential uncertainty**, respectively. It is for the purpose of quantifying statistical uncertainty that almost all psychological research involves the use of statistics.

As an example, researchers who are interested in the productivity of people in the workplace may want to examine the stress levels of employees who work under artificial light (e.g., factory workers or miners). Part of their investigation might involve administering some psychological tests to 25 workers, where those workers' stress is quantified by assigning them a score between 0 and 100. To summarize the level of stress in this sample the researchers may then compute the group's mean score on this scale. In this and any other psychological research, there will always be a certain amount of descriptive uncertainty arising from the fact that not everyone will produce the same score. Indeed, even if the *same* person completed the test on two consecutive days it is quite likely that he or she would obtain different scores. The different scores may be due to random error or to other factors (e.g., measurement error or individual differences).

Whether descriptive uncertainty arises from random error or not, it can be quantified by some measure of dispersion – most commonly, the amount of variance (or standard deviation) around a mean. The greater the dispersion in the scores obtained from the research participants, the greater the uncertainty and the less confident the researchers would be in the ability of a measure of central tendency to describe those participants appropriately. If the average stress score for participants in a study was 60 and their scores ranged between 30 and 90, the researchers would be less certain about describing the participants in terms of their average stress level than if the range were between 55 and 65. Descriptive uncertainty would only be completely removed if all participants obtained an identical score.

Descriptive uncertainty is random variation in the sample over which the experimenter has no control and for which no explanation is proposed. Inferential uncertainty, on the other hand, relates to a judgement about whether it is plausible that the results obtained could have been produced by a random process (e.g., drawing random samples from the same population). Inferential uncertainty prevails when any meaningful variation present cannot be distinguished from random variation expected in the population. When inferential uncertainty is low we suspect that something interesting *is* going on. Inferential uncertainty manifests itself in many different forms and the particular form depends largely on the research question that is being addressed. It depends upon three things: (a) the amount of information that we have to indicate that something interesting is going on; (b) random error; and (c) the sample size (or, more particularly, the square root of the sample size).

In the sort of research to which our artificial lighting example relates, researchers would almost definitely want to make a number of inferences and each of these would be associated with some uncertainty. For example, they would probably want to know whether people who work under artificial light differ in their levels of stress from those who work under natural light. Inferential uncertainty could be eliminated by sampling everyone in these two populations and seeing if they differ. In practice, though, what any half-sensible researchers would do is take a sample of the people from both working conditions. They would then set about quantifying the amount of uncertainty associated with a statement suggesting that the two samples were not drawn from the same population. As with all inferential statistics, this quantification of uncertainty would actually be an estimation. It would be stated as a probability, where a lower probability would signify greater certainty about the inference being made.

In dealing with descriptive and inferential uncertainty, a researcher is often able to quantify the uncertainty accurately, but unable to remove it. Statistics allow researchers to make very precise descriptive and inferential statements, but the elimination of statistical uncertainty is best achieved by methodological changes. Among other things, statistical uncertainty can be minimized by increasing the power of the tests – by increasing the sample size, or by reducing the amount of random variation. Random variation could be reduced by using a within-subjects rather than a between-subjects design or by developing a more reliable measure of the phenomenon under investigation.

However, if statistical uncertainty *were* completely removed from research, it is likely that the psychological issues being addressed by the researcher would be extremely uninteresting. This is because the research would have to involve *complete sampling* of a *completely uniform* population. It is actually hard to think of any research using psychological statistics that would satisfy these requirements and would not be utterly trivial.

The observation that eliminating statistical uncertainty can lead to research that is trivial points to an extremely important tension in psychological research. This arises from the fact that, contrary to the significance fallacy, *statistical significance is not the same as psychological or theoretical significance*. Obtaining a statistically significant result tells us that descriptive and inferential uncertainty are tolerably low. But in the most extreme case statistical significance can amount to a statement of the blindingly obvious (e.g., that all first-year psychology students have one head). As a general rule, psychologists are not (or should not be) interested in truisms – their role is to contribute to and extend knowledge, not just to reproduce it.

Accordingly, an obsession with the reduction of statistical uncertainty can be counter-productive. This is one reason why in recent years the wisdom of a hypothesis-testing approach to statistical inference has come into question (as we noted in Chapter 8). One response to the problem of how to handle statistical uncertainty is to accompany treatments of inferential uncertainty (significance) with treatments of effect size. The aim of including information about effect size is to be sure not only that chance is not a plausible cause of our results but also that they are of a sufficient size to be interesting or useful (criteria which will vary from area to area and problem to problem).

However, statistical uncertainty is only one form of uncertainty faced by researchers. A second form, in many ways more serious, relates to confidence that research procedures are directly addressing the question in which researchers are interested and allowing them to answer it. It was this second form of uncertainty that we discussed in the chapters on research methodology in the first half of this book. It can be referred to as **methodological uncertainty**.

As with statistical uncertainty, it is useful to distinguish between two forms of methodological uncertainty. **Internal uncertainty** relates to researchers' confidence in their ability to interpret the results of a study correctly. This term has most in common with the notion of internal validity – the idea that in experimental research the observed effect of a particular manipulation has been correctly interpreted. In Chapter 4 we noted that a large number of features of experimental design can contribute to uncertainty of this form. Our ability to understand why the manipulation of an independent variable brings about change in a dependent variable can be compromised by the effects of maturation, history, reactivity, selection and various other experimental confounds. So, in a study of occupational stress our confidence in interpreting the effects of making one randomly selected group of workers work under non-artificial light would be reduced if participants' behaviour were affected by their knowledge that they were taking part in psychological research (as it was in the Hawthorne studies that we discussed in Chapter 4).

However, unlike internal validity, the concept of internal uncertainty is not just relevant to experimental and quasi-experimental research. This form of uncertainty is also prevalent in survey research where independent variables are not directly manipulated. In survey research whenever a relationship between two variables is observed it is inappropriate to draw any conclusions about the effects which one

variable has on another. This means that internal uncertainty –
pertaining to the interpretation of that relationship – must remain
high. Nevertheless, such uncertainty can be reduced in cases where this
type of research fails to reveal a relationship between two variables. As
we discussed in Chapter 5, this is because a lack of correlation allows the
researcher conclusively to *rule out* certain interpretations. For example,
if research fails to find a relationship between lighting conditions and
stress then internal uncertainty about the psychological interpretation
of such a relationship is reduced. In this case if someone suggests that
workers become stressed because they get headaches from poor lighting,
we will be reasonably certain they are wrong.

The second type of methodological uncertainty is **external uncertainty**, and this arises where we are not sure that the results we have
obtained in our research can be generalized to the population of
interest. In many respects this is the most generic form of uncertainty
encountered in psychological research, partly because it is closely
related to all the other forms of uncertainty that we have already
considered. Obviously we do not want to generalize our results
unless inferential and internal uncertainty are low. That is, before
we can generalize a result we want to be confident that the result is
not due to chance, and that it is due to the independent variable
rather than some confound. However, it is also the case that we will
find it easier to generalize our result when descriptive uncertainty is
low (mainly because we will be more confident about what that
result is).

In the example of the effect of artificial light on stress, we will have
less external uncertainty if we show that the result applies under a wide
range of conditions. For example, we will be more confident that we
can generalize the results if they are obtained using representative
random sampling techniques and a wide range of testing conditions and
if they have been predicted on the basis of a well-developed theory (e.g.,
one which asserts that unnatural environments are psychologically
damaging). On the other hand, external uncertainty will be high if we
use naive empiricism to generalize research findings without recourse to
theory or if we draw conclusions on the basis of samples that are not
representative of the population of interest on theoretically relevant
variables (problems we discussed in Chapter 4).

The concept of methodological uncertainty that we have introduced
here does not replace the concept of validity, but rather complements it.
Studies themselves can have or lack validity, but it is researchers
and consumers of research who actually express uncertainty about
studies. This means that while the validity of a study must be constant

over time, methodological uncertainty about that research can change depending on the state of scientific knowledge in a field. For example, this is what happened in the Hawthorne studies as researchers started to question some of the early explanations of the effects of manipulating factory working conditions (e.g., lighting levels). Certain inferences about these findings *always were* invalid, only the researchers' uncertainty changed. However, it was the level of uncertainty about the research, not its validity, that best characterized the state of scientific knowledge at any particular point in time. This reflects the fact that scientific knowledge is contingent on human understanding (and ignorance), not on facts in the abstract.

Because the interpretation of scientific data is a human activity, we often cannot be entirely certain that any particular study is internally valid and we can never be entirely sure that a study is externally valid. However, we can *and do* express varying degrees of certainty about the validity of a piece of research. These statements will often reflect the degree of agreement among researchers about the validity of a particular conclusion. Accordingly, where disputes about methodology occur, these usually involve one group of researchers being confident that conclusions about a study are valid and another group having doubts. Indeed, where *everybody* agrees that the validity of a study is low then it is unlikely that the research would be conducted and it is very unlikely that it would be reported. For experienced researchers, most methodological errors occur when they make what are perceived to be inappropriate claims about the results or implications of studies. This usually means that they have managed uncertainty badly, often by expressing more confidence in their interpretation of the results than appears to be warranted.

You will recall that researchers' ability to quantify statistical uncertainty is high, but it is often difficult to control. The very opposite is true for methodological uncertainty. No procedures have ever been agreed upon for measuring or estimating methodological uncertainty, but a lot is known about how to reduce it. As we noted in earlier chapters, internal uncertainty can be minimized or eliminated by using appropriately controlled experimental designs, while external methodological uncertainty can be reduced through appropriate sampling and the development of psychological theory.

The big question that you may now be asking yourself is, 'If research involves all these forms of uncertainty, how should they be collectively managed?'. In practice, strategic decisions about the management of uncertainty always involve *trade-offs*. Being sure about some things increases uncertainty about others. For example, if we reduce descriptive uncertainty by using a very homogeneous sample of participants in our research, we may increase external uncertainty about the applicability of our findings to a broader population. The relevance–sensitivity trade-off, discussed in Chapter 4, is another example of this point. As descriptive uncertainty is reduced through measurement sensitivity and accuracy, the relevance of research findings to the topic of interest may also be reduced, thereby increasing external uncertainty. Information about all four of the above types of uncertainty is summarized in Table 14.1.

Table 14.1 Forms of uncertainty in psychological research

		Produced by	Estimated by	Reduced by
Statistical	Descriptive	Measurement error	Dispersion	Accurate measurement
		Individual differences		Using homogeneous samples
	Inferential	Chance/error	Probability	Increasing power
Methodological	Internal	Lack of control		Experimental control
	External	Sampling error		Appropriate sampling
		Naive empiricism		Theory development

One very important point to note about the above discussion is that because some of the terminology we have introduced here is novel (i.e., the terms in bold) you are unlikely to encounter it outside this book. That being the case, you may well ask why we have chosen to burden you with it at this late stage in proceedings. Surely, the last thing you need now is to be weighed down by even more terminology? Mindful of this question, there are three grounds on which we would justify this decision.

Our first justification is simply that we believe this attempted systematization provides a very useful way of summarizing, integrating and understanding the key concepts and procedures that we have been dealing with throughout the book. In short, thinking about doing psychological research as a process of uncertainty management allows us to draw together the many disparate elements of the research process. Managing uncertainty is what the practice of conducting any research is all about – people in different scientific fields simply have to deal with different forms of uncertainty and need to develop procedures and technology that allow them to do this adequately. As we have seen, psychologists have developed a number of statistical and methodological techniques that enable them to manage different forms of uncertainty in different ways. Yet the same is true for physicists, biologists and sociologists. Indeed, a large part of *any* researcher's skill relates precisely to knowledge about what form of management is appropriate for dealing with the particular types of uncertainty he or she confronts.

That being the case, a second justification for this way of thinking about psychological research is that it allows us to restate some core tenets of research practice quite straightforwardly. That is, it follows from the above analysis that twin goals of appropriate psychological research are to *minimize methodological uncertainty and to quantify statistical uncertainty*. This statement in fact covers most of what we have been concerned with in this book. Indeed, we would go so far as to suggest that this is the underlying message in almost all textbooks that attempt to deal with principles of research methodology and statistics. It should be noted, however, that the terms we have developed are not intended to replace the well-established technical jargon that we have used throughout the book. Instead they are simply intended to enable you to develop a more integrated understanding of the place which those terms (and the activities to which they relate) occupy in the research process.

The question you may now ask yourself is whether the management of statistical and methodological uncertainty is all there is to psychological enquiry. Is doing psychological research only a question of engaging in the perpetual struggle with these two, really quite circumscribed, problems? The answer, of course, is 'no'. There are actually many other forms of uncertainty that are relevant to psychological research. Indeed, this provides the third reason for thinking about research practice as we have. Our aim in fencing off these two forms of uncertainty is partly to make it clear that there are other 'bigger picture' forms of uncertainty that are not really addressed in standard prescriptions for doing psychological (or any other) research.

In philosophical terms, the uncertainties we have dealt with can be thought of as *ontological* (i.e., they relate to the tangible existence of research findings). However, as we hinted in Chapter 2, there are also other *epistemological* uncertainties that are far less tangible (e.g., whether the research produces genuine or worthwhile knowledge). Among other things, such uncertainties take both a *social* and a *political* form (e.g., whether a given form of knowledge is acceptable in a particular research community, and whether particular groups in society benefit from the research). For example, if we think about research into workers' productivity like that we discussed above, we might have uncertainty about whether the research agenda is appropriate and whether the approach taken on an issue ultimately serves particular political interests. In this way the research might be criticized for addressing topics from a position which ultimately serves the narrow economic interests of management rather than the broad interests of the community (e.g., by defining productivity and performance in financial rather than social terms). Although the research area is very different in nature, similar issues pervade enquiry into the biological basis of personality and intelligence as this must always incorporate assumptions about the impact of environmental factors on behaviour. Given that the approach researchers take on *any* psychological issue will always reflect a particular ideological slant (however implicit), it is often appropriate to consider how the answers their research provides are constrained by the questions that are *not* asked.

Along these lines, a number of researchers interested in the social psychology of science have argued that progress in research is often achieved by *creating uncertainty* rather than by reducing it (e.g., Campbell, 1986; McGuire, 1997; Moscovici, 1976; Smithson, 1993). Uncertainty can be created when researchers are forced to confront new uncertainties using new methods (Kuhn, 1962). It can also be created when a researcher goes against the grain by questioning received wisdom and challenging knowledge that has been taken for granted within a particular world-view. This is what happened when Copernicus suggested that the earth went round the sun and when Freud suggested that the unconscious plays a central role in human behaviour. In many ways uncertainty reduction is therefore the business of 'normal science' while uncertainty creation is the stuff of scientific revolution.

We addressed some issues relating to the management of non-tangible forms of uncertainty in Chapter 13 when we discussed research ethics. However, any attempt to deal comprehensively with issues of social and political uncertainty lies well beyond the scope of this book. It is also the case that these other forms of uncertainty are generally discussed much less openly by researchers than the two forms of uncertainty that we have focused on here. Nevertheless, they exert a very profound influence on the research process (see Spears & Smith, 2001). Moreover, every researcher has to deal with these uncertainties one way or another. Sadly, perhaps, this sometimes means ignoring them or simply pretending they do not exist.

Note: Several of the following terms have been introduced in earlier chapters. They are reproduced here to recap key points in the above discussion.

descriptive uncertainty *Statistical uncertainty* arising from variation in observations around any measure of central tendency and for which the researcher proposes no explanation. It is uncertainty in knowing or predicting individual scores on the basis of a measure of central tendency. This uncertainty is quantified by dispersion measures (e.g., standard deviation, variance, range).

external uncertainty A form of *methodological uncertainty* relating to researchers' ability to generalize their findings to a relevant population appropriately. This uncertainty can be reduced by appropriate sampling and theory development.

inferential uncertainty *Statistical uncertainty* relating to the possibility that an observed result is due to random error or chance. This uncertainty is estimated by a probability value, where a low probability indicates low uncertainty.

internal uncertainty A form of *methodological uncertainty* relating to researchers' ability to interpret the reasons for the relationship between two variables correctly. This uncertainty can be reduced through experimental control.

methodological uncertainty Doubt about the applicability of research findings arising from features of the research procedure. Generally speaking, this uncertainty is difficult to quantify but it can be minimized by appropriate research practice.

statistical uncertainty Doubt about statistics arising from the presence of random error. Generally speaking, such uncertainty is easier to estimate than to reduce.

Final comment

At the start of this book we stated that our objective was to provide a user-friendly introduction to research methodology and statistics. However, before we part company it is probably appropriate to acknowledge that this does not mean that our progress has been all smooth sailing. As the above overview makes clear, we have had to introduce and grapple with a large number of difficult concepts, terms and procedures. In our view none of these is trivial or expendable, and all need to be mastered (or at least addressed) at some stage by anyone who wants to conduct or to understand psychological research.

Despite this, we would go so far as to suggest that the researcher who is always completely on top of all the issues addressed in this book would be the exception rather than the rule. This is not because most researchers are stupid or lazy. The vast majority are neither. Rather it is because the issues themselves are extremely challenging and because things that we understand at one time can become hazy later. That being the case, we would like to think that once you feel confident handling all the material contained in this book you will be well on the way to becoming an extremely competent researcher. There are very many other complex and difficult issues that you still need to learn about and grapple with, but we have tried to ensure that your efforts to do so will be built upon a solid foundation. While we cannot promise that the new methodological and statistical issues you will encounter will always be easy to understand, we can guarantee that they will be much easier to cope with than would be the case if you had not already done the hard work of tackling the issues this book has introduced.

As you progress it is likely that you will develop views that diverge from our own and that you may become quite critical of some of the ideas we have presented. That, however, can only be a good thing. Psychological research is never passive and its underlying principles are never just 'given'. For that reason it is every researcher's first responsibility to *think critically*. If this book has helped to make you a more responsible and active participant in the research process, its most important goal has been achieved.

Further reading

Haslam and McGarty's paper provides a detailed elaboration of the arguments in this chapter, with specific reference to the way that uncertainty has been managed in the last 100 years of research in social psychology. Of course, having reached the end of this book, we hope that you will now be motivated and equipped to do a great deal more reading, in order to find out more about the process of conducting psychological research and about the fruits of that process in particular areas.

Haslam, S. A. & McGarty, C. (2001). A hundred years of certitude? Social psychology, the experimental method and the management of scientific uncertainty. *British Journal of Social Psychology, 40*, 1–21.

References

Abramson, L. Y., Seligman, M. E. P., & Teasdale, J. D. (1978). Learned helplessness in humans: Critique and reformulation. *Journal of Abnormal Psychology, 87*, 49–74.

American Psychological Association (2001). *Publication manual of the American Psychological Association* (5th ed.). Washington DC: Author.

Aronson, E. (1997). The theory of cognitive dissonance: The evolution and vicissitudes of an idea. In C. McGarty & S. A. Haslam (Eds.), *The message of social psychology: Perspectives on mind in society.* Oxford and New York: Blackwell.

Bandura, A., Ross, D., & Ross, S. (1961). Transmission of aggression through imitation of aggressive models. *Journal of Applied Social Psychology, 63*, 575–582.

Barber, T. X., & Silver, M. J. (1968). Fact, fiction, and the experimenter bias effect. *Psychological Bulletin, 70*, 1–29.

Baumrind, D. (1964). Some thoughts on ethics of research: After reading Milgram's 'Behavioral study of obedience'. *American Psychologist, 19*, 421–423.

Baumrind, D. (1985). Research using intentional deception: Ethical issues revisited. *American Psychologist, 40*, 165–174.

Berkun, M. M., Bialek, H. M., Kern, R. P., & Yagi, K (1962). Experimental studies of psychological stress in man. *Psychological Monographs: General and Applied, 76* (15, whole no. 534).

Burgoyne, C. B. (1997). Distributive justice and rationing in the NHS: Framing effects in press coverage of a controversial decision. *Journal of Community and Applied Social Psychology, 7*, 119–136.

Campbell, D. T., (1986). Science's social system of validity-enhancing collective belief change and problems of the social sciences. In D. W. Fiske & R. A. Schweder (Eds.), *Metatheory in social science: Pluralisms and subjectivities* (pp. 108–135). Chicago: University of Chicago Press.

Campbell, D. T., & Stanley, J. C. (1963). *Experimental and quasi-experimental designs for research.* Chicago: Rand McNally.

Chalmers, A. F. (1978). *What is this thing called science?* Milton Keynes: Open University Press.

Cochrane, R., & Duffy, J. (1974). Psychology and the scientific method. *Bulletin of the British Psychological Society, 27*, 117–121.

Cohen, J. (1988). *Statistical power analysis for the behavioral sciences* (2nd ed.). Hillsdale, NJ: Erlbaum.

Cohen, J. (1994). The earth is round ($p < .05$). *American Psychologist, 49*, 997–1003.

Cohen, J. (1995). The earth is round ($p < .05$): Rejoinder. *American Psychologist, 50*, 1103.

Cook, T. D., & Campbell, D. T. (1979). *Quasi-experimentation: Design and analysis issues for field settings.* Chicago: Rand McNally.

Darley, J. M., & Batson, C. D. (1973). From Jerusalem to Jericho: A study of situational and dispositional variables in helping behaviour. *Journal of Personality and Social Psychology, 42*, 497–505.

Dawes, R. M. (1996). The purpose of experiments: Ecological validity versus comparing hypotheses. *Behavioral and Brain Sciences, 19*, 20.

de Groot, A. D. (1965). *Thought and choice in chess.* The Hague: Mouton.

Ekman, P., Levenson, R. W., & Frieson, W. V. (1983). Autonomic nervous system activity distinguishes among emotions, *Science, 221*, 1208–1210.

Eysenck, H. J., & Eysenck, S. B. G. (1985). *Personality and individual differences.* London: Plenum Press.

Festinger, L., Riecken, H., & Schachter, S. (1956). *When prophecy fails.* Minneapolis: University of Minnesota Press.

Feyerabend, P. K. (1975). *Against method: Outline of an anarchistic theory of knowledge.* New Left Books.

Fraser, S. (Ed.) (1995). *The bell curve wars: Race, intelligence and the future of America.* New York: Basic Books.

Frazer, L., & Lawley, M. (2000). *Questionnaire design and administration.* Brisbane: Wiley.

Freud, S. (1933/1964). *New introductory lectures on psychoanalysis* (J. Strachy, trans.). New York: Norton.

Frick, R. W. (1995). A problem with confidence intervals. *American Psychologist, 50*, 1102–1103.

Gilbert, G. N., & Mulkay, M. J. (1984). *Opening Pandora's box: A sociological analysis of scientists' discourse.* Cambridge: Cambridge University Press.

Gould, S. J. (1981). *The mismeasure of man.* New York: Norton.

Gould, S. J. (1982, May 6). A nation of morons. *New Scientist*, 349–352.

Gould, S. J. (1997). *Life's grandeur: The spread of excellence from Plato to Darwin.* London: Vintage.

Green, C., & Gilhooly, K. (1996) Protocol analysis: Practical implementation. In J. T. E. Richardson (Ed.), *Handbook of qualitative research methods for psychology and the social sciences* (pp. 55–74). Leicester: BPS Books.

Gribbin, J., & Rees, M. (1990). *The stuff of the universe: Dark matter, mankind and the coincidences of cosmology.* London: Heinemann.

Hammond, G. (1996). The objections to null hypothesis testing as a means of analysing psychological data. *Australian Journal of Psychology, 46*, 104–106.

Haslam, S. A., & McGarty, C. (2001). A hundred years of certitude? Social psychology, the experimental method and the management of scientific uncertainty. *British Journal of Social Psychology, 40*, 1–21.

Haslam, S. A., & McGarty, C. (2003). Experimental design and causality in social psychological research. In C. Sansone, C. C. Morf, & A. T. Panter (Eds.), *Handbook of methods in social psychology* (pp. 237–64). Thousand Oaks, CA: Sage.

Hathaway, S. R., & McKinley, J. C. (1943). *Manual for the Minnesota Multiphasic Personality Inventory.* New York: Psychological Corporation.

Henwood, K. L., & Pigeon, N. F. (1994). Beyond the qualitative paradigm: A framework for introducing diversity within qualitative psychology. *Journal of Community and Applied Social Psychology, 4,* 225–238.

Hepburn, A. (2003). *An introduction to critical social psychology.* London: Sage.

Herrnstein, R. J., & Murray, C. (1994). *The bell curve: Intelligence and class structure in American life.* New York: Free Press.

Herzog, H. A. (1995). Has public interest in animal rights peaked? *American Psychologist, 50,* 945–947.

Howe, M. J. A., Davidson, J. W., & Sloboda, J. A. (1998). Innate talents: Reality or myth? *Behavioural and Brain Sciences, 21,* 399–342.

Huff, D. (1973). *How to lie with statistics.* London: Penguin.

Judd, C. M., McClelland, G. H., & Culhane, S. E. (1995). Data analysis: Continuing issues in the everyday analysis of psychological data. *Annual Review of Psychology, 46,* 433–465.

Kelly, G. A. (1955). *The psychology of personal constructs* (2 vols.). New York: Norton.

Keppel, G. (1982). *Design and analysis: A researcher's handbook* (2nd ed.). Englewood Cliffs, NJ: Prentice Hall.

Kline, P. (1994). *An easy guide to factor analysis.* London: Routledge.

Kuhn, T. (1962). *The structure of scientific revolutions.* Chicago: University of Chicago Press.

Lassen, N. A., Ingvar, D. H., & Skinhøj, E. (1978). Brain function and blood flow. *Scientific American, 239,* 50–59.

Latané, B., & Darley, J. M. (1970). *The unresponsive bystander: Why doesn't he help?* New York: Appleton Century Crofts.

Magee, B. (1974). *Popper.* London: Woburn Press.

Manstead, A. S. R., & McCulloch, C.(1991). Sex role stereotyping in British television adverts. *British Journal of Social Psychology, 20,* 171–180.

Maxwell, S. E., & Delaney, H. D. (1990). *Designing experiments and analyzing data: A model comparison perspective.* New York: Harper Collins.

McGuire, W. J. (1997). Going beyond the banalities of bubbapsychology: A perspectivist social psychology. In C. McGarty & S. A. Haslam (Eds.), *The message of social psychology: Perspectives on mind in society.* Oxford and New York: Blackwell.

Miles, J., & Shevlin, M. (2001). *Applying regression and correlation: A guide for researchers and students.* London: Sage.

Milgram, S. (1963). Behavioral study of obedience. *Journal of Abnormal and Social Psychology, 67,* 371–378.

Milgram, S. (1964). Issues in the study of obedience: A reply to Baumrind. *American Psychologist, 19,* 848–852.

Milgram, S. (1974). *Obedience to authority.* New York: Harper & Row.

Milner, B. (1966). Amnesia following operation on the temporal lobes. In C. M. W. Whitty & O. L. Zangwill (Eds.), *Amnesia* (pp. 109–133). London: Butterworth.

Moscovici, S. (1976). *Social influence and social change.* London: Academic Press.

Orne, M. (1962). On the social psychology of the psychological experiment with particular reference to demand characteristics and their implications. *American Psychologist, 17*, 776–783.

Orne, M. (1969). Demand characteristics and the concept of quasi-controls. In R. Rosenthal and R. Rosnow (Eds.), *Artifact in behavior research*. New York: Academic Press.

Paulos, J. A. (1990). *Innumeracy*. London: Penguin.

Pettit, P. (1992). Instituting a research ethic: Chilling and cautionary tales. *Bioethics, 6*, 89–112.

Piaget, J. (1952). *The origins of intelligence in children* (M. Gabain, trans.). New York: International Universities Press.

Pigeon, N. F., & Henwood, K. L. (1997). Using grounded theory in psychological research. In N. Hayes (Ed.), *Doing qualitative analysis in psychology* (pp. 245–273). Hove: Psychology Press.

Popper, K. (1968). *The logic of scientific discovery*. London: Hutchinson.

Potter, J. (1996). Discourse analysis and constructionist approaches: theoretical background. In J. T. E. Richardson (Ed.), *Handbook of qualitative research methods for psychology and the social sciences* (pp. 125–140). Leicester: BPS Books.

Potter, J. (1997). Discourse analysis as a way of analysing naturally occurring talk. In D. Silverman (Ed.), *Qualitative research: Theory, method and practice* (pp. 144–160). London: Sage.

Potter, J., & Reicher, S. (1987). Discourses of community and conflict: The organization of social categories in accounts of a riot. *British Journal of Social Psychology, 26*, 25–40.

Ray, W. J. (1993). *Methods: Towards a science of behavior and experience* (4th ed.). Pacific Grove, CA: Brooks/Cole.

Reicher, S. D. (1984a). Social influence in the crowd: Attitudinal and behavioural effects of deindividuation in conditions of high and low group salience. *British Journal of Social Psychology, 23*, 341–350.

Reicher, S. D. (1984b) The St. Paul's riot: An explanation of the limits of crowd action in terms of a social identity model. *European Journal of Social Psychology, 14*, 1–21.

Reicher, S. D., & Hopkins, N. (1996). Self-category constructions in political rhetoric: An analysis of Thatcher's and Kinnock's speeches concerning the British miners strike (1984–5). *European Journal of Social Psychology, 26*, 353–372.

Reicher, S. D., & Hopkins, N. (2001). *Self and nation: Categorization, contestation and mobilization*. London: Sage.

Richardson, J. T. E. (Ed.) (1996). *Handbook of qualitative research methods for psychology and the social sciences*. Leicester: BPS Books.

Roethlisberger, F. J., & Dickson, W. J. (1964). *Management and the worker*. Cambridge, MA: Harvard University Press.

Rosenthal, R. (1966). *Experimenter effects in behavioral research*. New York: Appleton Century Crofts.

Rosenthal, R., & Fode, K. L. (1963). The effect of experimenter bias on the performance of the albino rat. *Behavioural Science, 8,* 183–189.

Rosenthal, R. (1994). Science and ethics in conducting, analyzing, and reporting research. *Psychological Science, 5,* 127–133.

Schuman, H., & Kalton, G. (1985). Survey methods. In G. Linzey & E. Aronson (Eds.), *The handbook of social psychology* (3rd ed., Vol. 1, pp. 635–697). Reading, MA: Addison-Wesley.

Seligman, M. E. P., & Maier, S. F. (1967). Failure to escape traumatic shock. *Journal of Experimental Psychology, 74,* 1–9.

Sherif, M. (1956). Experiments in group conflict. *Scientific American, 195,* 54–58.

Siegel, S. (1956). *Nonparametric statistics for the behavioral sciences.* New York: McGraw-Hill.

Silverman, D. (Ed.) (1996). *Qualitative research: Theory, method and practice* (pp. 144–160). London: Sage.

Singer, P. (1975). *Animal liberation.* New York: Random House.

Smart, R. (1966). Subject selection bias in psychological research. *Canadian Psychologist, 7,* 115–121.

Smith, S. S., & Richardson, D. (1983). Amelioration of deception and harm in psychological research. *Journal of Personality and Social Psychology, 44,* 1075–1082.

Smithson, M. (1993). Ignorance and science: Dilemmas, perspectives and prospects. *Knowledge: Creation, Diffusion, Utilization, 15,* 133–156.

Smithson, M. (2000). *Statistics with confidence.* London and Thousand Oaks, CA: Sage.

Spears, R., & Smith, H. J. (2001). Experiments as politics. *Political Psychology, 22,* 309–330.

Sternberg, R. J. (1995). *In search of the human mind.* Orlando, FL: Harcourt Brace.

Stewart, V., Stewart, A., & Fonda, N. (1981). *Business applications of repertory grid.* London: McGraw-Hill.

Stott, C., Hutchinson, P., & Drury, J. (2001) 'Hooligans' abroad? Inter-group dynamics, social identity and participation in collective 'disorder' at the 1998 World Cup finals. *British Journal of Social Psychology, 40,* 359–384.

Svenson, O. (1981). Are we all less risky and more skilful than our fellow drivers? *Acta Psychologica, 47,* 143–148.

Svyantek, D. J., & Ekeberg, S. E. (1995). The earth is round (so we can probably get there from here). *American Psychologist, 50,* 1101.

Tabachnick, B. G., & Fidell, L. S. (1996). *Using multivariate statistics* (3rd ed.). New York: Harper Collins.

Tajfel, H. (1970). Experiments in intergroup discrimination. *Scientific American, 223,* 96–102.

Tesch, R. (1990). *Qualitative research: Analysis types and software tools.* New York: Falmer.

Tukey, J. W. (1991). The philosophy of multiple comparisons. *Statistical Science, 6,* 100–116.

Turner, J. C. (1981). Some considerations in generalizing experimental social psychology. In G. M. Stephenson & J. H. Davis (Eds.), *Progress in applied social psychology* (Vol. 1, pp. 3–34). Chichester: Wiley.

Tversky, A., & Kahneman, D. (1974). Judgement under uncertainty: Heuristics and biases. *Science, 185*, 1123–1131.

Valentine, E. R. (1982). *Conceptual issues in psychology*. London: Allen & Unwin.

West, S. G., & Gunn, S. P. (1978). Some issues of ethics and social psychology. *American Psychologist, 33*, 30–38.

West, S. G., Newsom, J. T., & Fenaughty, A. M. (1992). Publication trends in the *Journal of Personality and Social Psychology*: Stability and change in topics, methods and theories across two decades. *Personality and Social Psychology Bulletin, 18*, 473–484.

Woolgar, S. (1988). *Science: The very idea*. London: Tavistock.

Woolgar, S. (1996). Psychology, qualitative methods and the ideas of science. In J. T. E. Richardson (Ed.) *Handbook of qualitative research methods for psychology and the social sciences* (pp. 11–24). Leicester: BPS Books.

Yin, R. K. (1994). *Case study research design methods* (2nd ed.). Thousand Oaks, CA: Sage.

Appendix A: Step-by-Step Guides to Key Statistical Tests

A.1. Working out a within-subjects *t*-test using the hypothesis-testing method

This test (also known as a correlated samples *t*-test or dependent groups *t*-test) is used when a variable has been manipulated within subjects so that pairs of scores are obtained from the same source. The procedure is as follows:

1. State the null hypothesis ($H_0 : \mu_1 = \mu_2$) and the alternative hypothesis (for a two-tailed test, $H_1 : \mu_1 \neq \mu_2$).
2. Convert each pair of scores into a *difference score* (D) by subtracting the second score from the first.
3. Calculate the mean, $\bar{D}$, and standard deviation, s_D, of the N difference scores (do not ignore the sign).
4. Compute a *t*-value, using the formula:

$$t = \frac{\bar{D}}{s_D / \sqrt{N}}$$

5. Compute the *degrees of freedom* for the test from the number of participants, where $df = N - 1$.
6. Use Table C.2 in Appendix C to find the critical value of t for that number of degrees of freedom at the designated significance level (e.g., $\alpha = .05$ or $.01$).
7. If the absolute (i.e., unsigned) value of t that is obtained exceeds the critical value then reject the null hypothesis (H_0) and conclude that the difference between means is statistically significant. Otherwise conclude that the result is not statistically significant and make no inferences about differences between the means.

The following is a worked example of a within-subjects *t*-test where participants' pairs of scores have been obtained on two variables, *A* and *B*. The chosen alpha level is .05.

Participant	A	B	$D(A - B)$
1	71	53	18
2	62	36	26
3	54	51	3
4	36	19	17
5	25	30	-5
6	71	52	19
7	13	20	-7
8	52	39	13
$N = 8$			$\sum D = 84$

$$\bar{D} = 84/8 = 10.5$$

$$s_D = 12.07$$

$$H_0 : \mu_1 = \mu_2$$

$$H_1 : \mu_1 \neq \mu_2$$

$$t = \frac{\bar{D}}{s_D/\sqrt{N}}$$

$$= \frac{10.5}{12.07/\sqrt{8}}$$

$$= \frac{10.5}{12.07/2.83}$$

$$= 2.46$$

$$df = N - 1$$

$$= 7$$

The obtained *t*-value is greater than the tabulated value of *t* with 7 *df* for $p = .05$ (i.e., 2.365), so the difference between means is significant $(t(7) = 2.46, p < .05)$.

A.2. Working out a between-subjects *t*-test using the hypothesis-testing method

This test (also known as an independent groups *t*-test or a two-sample *t*-test) is used when a variable has been manipulated between subjects so that every score is obtained from a different source (normally a different person). It is carried out as follows:

1. State the null hypothesis ($H_0 : \mu_1 = \mu_2$) and the alternative hypothesis (for a two-tailed test, $H_1 : \mu_1 \neq \mu_2$).
2. Compute means ($\bar{X}_1$ and $\bar{X}_2$) and variances (s_1^2 and s_2^2) for the scores in each experimental condition (where there are N_1 scores in the first condition and N_2 scores in the second).
3. Compute a pooled variance estimate using the following formula:

$$s_{pooled}^2 = \frac{(N_1 - 1)s_1^2 + (N_2 - 1)s_2^2}{N_1 + N_2 - 2}$$

4. Compute a *t*-value using the following formula:

$$t = \frac{\bar{X}_1 - \bar{X}_2}{\sqrt{s_{pooled}^2 \left(\frac{1}{N_1} + \frac{1}{N_2} \right)}}$$

5. Compute the degrees of freedom for the test from the sample sizes, where $df = N_1 + N_2 - 2$.
6. Use Table C.2 in Appendix C to identify the critical value of *t* for that number of degrees of freedom at the designated significance level (e.g., $\alpha = .05$).
7. If the absolute (i.e., unsigned) value of *t* that is obtained exceeds the critical value then reject the null hypothesis (H_0) and conclude that the difference between means is statistically significant. Otherwise conclude that the result is not statistically significant, and make no inferences about differences between the means.

The following is a worked example of a between-subjects *t*-test where scores have been obtained from participants in an experimental and a control group. The chosen alpha level is .05.

Experimental	Control
21	12
34	27
24	21
37	17
27	24
25	19
29	22
33	31

Experimental	Control
17	9
24	

$N_1 = 10$	$N_2 = 9$
$\bar{X}_1 = 27.10$	$\bar{X}_2 = 20.22$
$s_1^2 = 38.54$	$s_2^2 = 48.19$

$$H_0 : \mu_1 = \mu_2$$

$$H_1 : \mu_1 \neq \mu_2$$

$$t = \frac{\bar{X}_1 - \bar{X}_2}{\sqrt{s_{pooled}^2 \left(\dfrac{1}{N_1} + \dfrac{1}{N_2} \right)}}$$

where

$$s_{pooled}^2 = \frac{(N_1 - 1)s_1^2 + (N_2 - 1)s_2^2}{N_1 + N_2 - 2}$$

$$= \frac{((10 - 1)38.54) + ((9 - 1)48.19)}{10 + 9 - 2}$$

$$= \frac{9 * 38.54 + 8 * 48.19}{17}$$

$$= (346.86 + 385.52)/17$$

$$= 43.09$$

So

$$t = \frac{27.10 - 20.22}{\sqrt{43.08 \left(\dfrac{1}{10} + \dfrac{1}{9} \right)}}$$

$$= 6.88/\sqrt{43.08 * .21}$$

$$= 6.88/\sqrt{9.05}$$

$$= 2.28$$

$$df = N_1 + N_2 - 2$$

$$= 17$$

The obtained *t*-value is greater than the tabulated value of *t* with 17 *df* for $p = .05$ (i.e., 2.110), so the difference between means is significant ($t(17) = 2.29, p < .05$).

A.3. Working out a correlation using both hypothesis-testing and effect-size methods

This procedure is used to assess the relationship between two variables where pairs of scores on each variable have been obtained from the same source. It is carried out as follows:

1. State the null hypothesis ($H_0 : \rho = 0$) and the alternative hypothesis (for a two-tailed test, $H_1 : \rho \neq 0$).
2. Draw a scatterplot, representing the position of each of the N pairs of scores on the two variables (X and Y).
3. Create a table which contains values of X^2, Y^2 and XY for each pair of scores, and sums values of X, X^2, Y, Y^2 and XY.
4. Compute Pearson's r, using the formula:

$$r = \frac{N \sum XY - \sum X \sum Y}{\sqrt{(N \sum X^2 - (\sum X)^2)(N \sum Y^2 - (\sum Y)^2)}}$$

5. Compute the *degrees of freedom* for the test from the number of participants, where $df = N - 2$.
6. Use Table C.3 in Appendix C to identify the critical value of r for that number of degrees of freedom at the designated significance level (e.g., $\alpha = .05$).
7. If the absolute (i.e., unsigned) value of r exceeds the critical value then reject the null hypothesis (H_0) that there is no relationship between the variables and conclude that the relationship between variables is statistically significant. Otherwise conclude that the relationship is not statistically significant.
8. Consider the statistical significance of $|r|$ (i.e., the absolute value of r) in the context of the effect size, noting that where $.1 \leq |r| < .3$ the correlation between variables is only weak, where $.3 \leq |r| < .5$ the correlation is moderate and where $|r| \geq .5$ the correlation is strong.

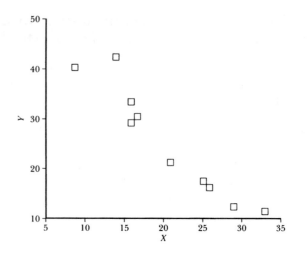

Figure A.1 Plot of data for worked example of correlation

The following is a worked example of a correlation where participants'
pairs of scores have been obtained on two variables, X and Y (see
Figure A.1). The chosen alpha level is .05.

Participant	X	X^2	Y	Y^2	XY
1	16	256	33	1089	528
2	29	841	12	144	348
3	14	196	42	1764	588
4	26	676	16	256	416
5	33	1089	11	121	363
6	25	625	17	289	425
7	16	256	29	841	464
8	17	289	30	900	510
9	9	81	40	1600	360
10	21	441	21	441	441

$N = 10 \quad \sum X = 206 \quad \sum X^2 = 4750 \quad \sum Y = 251 \quad \sum Y^2 = 7445 \quad \sum XY = 4443$

$H_0 : \rho = 0$

$H_1 : \rho \neq 0$

$$r = \frac{N \sum XY - \sum X \sum Y}{\sqrt{(N \sum X^2 - (\sum X)^2)(N \sum Y^2 - (\sum Y)^2)}}$$

$$= \frac{(10 * 4443) - (206 * 251)}{\sqrt{(10 * 4750 - (206)^2)(10 * 7445 - (251)^2)}}$$

$$= \frac{44\,430 - 51\,706}{\sqrt{(47\,500 - 42\,436)(74\,450 - 63\,001)}}$$

$$= \frac{-7276}{\sqrt{5064 * 11\,449}}$$

$$= \frac{-7276}{7614.31}$$

$$= -.96$$

The absolute value of r is greater than the tabulated value of r with 8 df for $p = .05$ (i.e., .632 – and for $p = .01$; i.e., .765) and $r > .5$, so there is a significant strong negative correlation between the variables ($r = -.96$, $p < .01$).

A.4. Procedures for conducting one-way ANOVA with equal cell sizes

This is a rough-and-ready guide to analyzing experiments that involve more than two experimental conditions. As you study further in statistics you will discover more sophisticated strategies for analysis but the following procedures will get you started and, importantly, teach you no bad habits. At the same time they should help you to understand some very important statistical principles. Please bear in mind, though, that the following procedures can only be followed if cell sizes are equal. More advanced texts show the procedures to use where cells sizes are unequal. Note also that many of the steps cannot be performed by a computer package. We have marked these here with an asterisk.

1. Draw up a table with one row and as many columns as there are conditions in the study. Leave a space for each cell mean, squared deviation from grand mean, variance, and for the grand mean (note that it is customary to report the standard deviation – the square root of the variance – and not the variance when results are submitted for publication and in lab reports). In the top left-hand corner of each cell write a number to identify it. Work out the sample size N, the cell size and the number of cells k and write these down.

*2. From your notes, work out which cells (if any) you wished to compare before you collected the data (these are your planned comparisons). Write down these comparisons below the table in the form 'Cell 2 > Cell 1' etc. As a rule of thumb, with four or fewer cells and a sample size of 50 or less allow yourself no more planned comparisons than the number of cells.

*3. If adopting the hypothesis-testing approach, write down the null hypothesis for each planned comparison and for the overall analysis. These should take the form:

$$H_0 : \mu_1 = \mu_2 = \mu_3 \text{ etc.}$$

and

$$H_1 : \text{not all } \mu\text{s are equal}$$

4. Calculate the cell means, grand mean, squared deviations from grand mean, and variances and fill them in the places provided.

5. Draw up an ANOVA table with columns for *Source, SS, df, U, F,* '$p <$' and R^2. Include a line in the ANOVA table for between cells, error (within cells) and total.

6. Calculate MS_W by pooling the within-cells variances. Add the variance for all cells and divide by the number of cells. Calculate df_W as $N-k$. Write these values in the ANOVA table.

7. Calculate df_B by subtracting one from the number of cells. Calculate MS_B by summing the total squared deviations of the cell means from the grand mean. Multiply this value by the cell size then divide by df_B. Write both values in the ANOVA table.

8. Calculate SS_B by multiplying MS_B by df_B. Calculate SS_W by multiplying MS_W by df_W. Write both values in the ANOVA table.

9. Calculate SS_T by adding SS_B and SS_W together. Write the value and $df_T = df_B + df_W$ in the ANOVA table.

10. Calculate the F ratio by dividing MS_B by MS_W.

11. If $F < 1$ then write ns (non-significant) in the '$p <$' column. Compare the F-value with the critical value for F with (df_B, df_W) degrees of freedom at the $\alpha = .05$ level. If the obtained F is larger than this value then continue to compare it to other critical values for F at the .01 and .001 levels. Write the smallest value of X for which the statement $p < X$ is true.

12. Calculate R^2 for the effect by dividing SS_B by SS_T.

*13 Evaluate the planned comparisons. First set the protected alpha level by dividing your alpha level by the number of comparisons you are making. Then conduct a t-test for each planned comparison. To do this calculate the difference between the means, and divide by (the square root of MS_W multiplied by the square root of $2/n$), where n is the number of people in each cell. If the obtained t-value is greater than the critical value given by the protected alpha level conclude that it is significant.

*14. Make the statistical inferences from your ANOVA table. If the value of '$p <$' in the table is less than your alpha level conclude that the effect is significant. Make some assessment of the size of the effect based on R^2.

The following is a worked example of a between-subjects one-way ANOVA where data have been obtained from four groups of four participants. Each group or cell represents a different experimental condition that a participant had been randomly assigned to.

Group 1	Group 2	Group 3	Group 4
7	5	3	2
6	7	6	3
4	3	4	5
5	4	3	3

$N = 16 \quad n = 4 \quad k = 4$

Let us assume that we hypothesize that Group 1 will have a higher mean than Group 2 (this suggests the planned comparison Group 1 > Group 2). For the ANOVA,

$$H_0 : \mu_1 = \mu_2 = \mu_3 = \mu_4.$$
$$H_1 : \text{not all } \mu\text{s are equal}$$

For planned comparison 1 > 2,

$$H_0 : \mu_1 = \mu_2$$
$$H_1 : \mu_1 > \mu_2$$

From these data we can construct a table showing means, squared deviations from the grand mean, and variances. Also shown is the grand mean (with equal cell sizes this is the mean of the cell means).

	Group 1	Group 2	Group 3	Group 4	Grand Mean
M	5.5	4.75	4.00	3.25	4.38
Squared deviations from grand mean	1.27	0.14	0.14	1.27	
Variance	1.67	2.92	2.00	1.58	

$$MS_W = (\Sigma s_i^2)/k$$
$$= (1.67 + 2.92 + 2.00 + 1.58)/4$$
$$= 2.04$$

$$df_W = N - k$$
$$= 16 - 4$$
$$= 12$$

$$SS_W = MS_W * df_W$$
$$= 2.04 * 12$$
$$= 24.50$$

$$df_B = k - 1$$
$$= 3$$

$$MS_B = \Sigma n(\bar{X}_i - \bar{X})^2/(k - 1)$$
$$= 4 * (1.25 + 0.14 + 0.14 + 1.28)/3$$
$$= 11.25/3$$
$$= 3.75$$

$$SS_B = MS_B * df_B$$
$$= 11.24$$

$$MS_F = MS_B / MS_W$$
$$= 3.75/2.04$$
$$= 1.84$$

$$F_{.05}(3, 12) = 3.49$$

Source	SS	df	· MS	F	p <	R²
Between cells (Condition)	11.25	3	3.75	1.84	ns	.31
Within cells	24.50	12	2.04			
Total	35.75	15				

The effect is of large size but the obtained F-value is smaller than the tabled or critical value of $F(3, 12)$ for $\alpha = .05$ (i.e., 3.49) so so we cannot reject H_0 that the means are different (note that our design has limited power to detect effects due to the very small sample size).

Our comparisons were planned so we proceed with them without worrying about the results of the ANOVA. We are conducting one comparison, Group 1 > Group 2, so our protected α is $.05/1 = .05$:

$$t = (\bar{X}_1 - \bar{X}_2)/\sqrt{MS_W * (2/n)}$$
$$= (5.5 - 4.75)/\sqrt{2.04 * 2/4}$$
$$= 0.74$$

This is smaller than the tabulated one-tailed value of t with 12 df for $\alpha = .05$ (i.e., 1.782) so we cannot reject the null hypothesis that the means of the two groups are equal.

A.5. Procedures for conducting two-way ANOVA with equal cell sizes

1. Draw up a table with as many columns as there are levels of one variable and as many rows as there are levels of the other variable. Leave a space for each cell mean, row mean, column mean and grand mean along with the cell variance (note that here it is customary to report the standard deviation – the square root of the variance – and not the variance). In the top left-hand corner of each cell give the cell a number to identify it.

*2. From your notes work out which cells, rows or columns (if any) you wished to compare before you collected the data (planned comparisons). Write down these comparisons below the table in the form 'Cell 2 > Cell 1' or 'Row 3 < Row 4'. As a rule of thumb, with four or fewer cells and a sample size of 50 or less allow yourself no more planned comparisons than the number of cells.

*3. If adopting the hypothesis-testing approach, state the null hypothesis for each planned comparison and each effect. For the row effect:

H_0 : Row means are equal

H_1 : Row means are not equal

for the column effect

H_0 : Column means are equal

H_1 : Column means are not equal

and for the interaction effect

H_0 : Cell means are equal to the values expected from the row and column effects

H_1 : Cell means are not equal to the values expected from the row and column effects.

4. Calculate the means and variances and fill them in the places provided.

5. Draw a line graph of the means, with one line representing the means of each column. Examine the plot. Do the lines appear to be coming closer at some point (i.e., do they deviate from the parallel)? If they do, this suggests an interaction. Is one line higher than the other? If it is, this suggests a row main effect. Are two points at one level of the column factor higher than two other points? If they are, this suggests a column main effect.

6. Draw up an ANOVA table with columns for *Source, SS, df, MS, F, 'p<'* and R^2. Include a line in the ANOVA table for between, interaction (row by column), row, column, error and total as sources.

7. Calculate MS_W by pooling the within-cells variances. Add the variance for all cells and divide by the number of cells. Calculate df_W as $N-k$, where N is the number of observations (normally participants) and k is the number of groups. Write these values in the ANOVA table.

8. Calculate df_B by subtracting one from the number of cells. Calculate MS_B by summing the total squared deviations of the cell means from the grand mean, multiply by the cell size and then divide by df_B. Write both values in the table.

9. Calculate SS_B by multiplying MS_B by df_B. Calculate SS_W by multiplying MS_W by df_W. Write both values in the table.

10. Calculate SS_R, SS_C and SS_{RC}: SS_R is the sum of the squared deviations between the row means and the grand mean, multiplied by the cell size; SS_C is the sum of the squared deviations between the column means and the grand mean, multiplied by the cell size; SS_{RC} is given by

$$SS_{RC} = SS_B - SS_R - SS_C.$$

For the 2×2 design the *df*s for row, column and row by column will all be 1.

11. Calculate SS_T by adding SS_B and SS_W together. Write the value in the ANOVA table.

12. Calculate MS_R by dividing SS_R by df_R. Calculate MS_C by dividing SS_C by df_C. Calculate MS_{RC} by dividing SS_{RC} by df_{RC}. Write all values in the ANOVA table.

13. Calculate the *F*-ratio for each effect by dividing each *MS* by MS_W.

14. If any $F < 1$ then write down *ns* (non-significant) in the *p<* column. Otherwise, compare the *F* value with the critical value for *F* with (df_B, df_W) degrees of freedom at the .05 level. If obtained *F* is larger than this value, then continue to compare it to other critical values for *F* at the .01 and .001, levels. Write the smallest value of *X* for which the statement $p < X$ is true. If this statement is not true for any tabled value, write *ns* in the table.

15. Calculate R^2 for every effect by dividing the relevant *SS* by SS_T.

*16. Evaluate the planned comparisons. First set the protected alpha level by dividing your alpha level by the number of comparisons you are making. Then conduct a *t*-test for each planned comparison. To do this, calculate the difference between the means, and divide by the square root of MS_W multiplied by the square root of $2/n$, where n is the number of people in each cell. If the obtained t-value is greater than the critical value given by the protected alpha level, conclude that it is significant.

*17. Make the statistical inferences from your ANOVA table. If the value of '$p <$' in the table is less than your alpha level, conclude that the effect is significant. Make some assessment of the size of the effect based on R^2.

A worked example of a between-subjects two-way ANOVA is available on the Sage website (http://www.sagepub.com/Haslam). This website also provides the instructions and spreadsheets necessary to perform all the above tests using standard computer packages (Excel and SPSS).

Appendix B: Writing Research Reports in Psychology

Overview

Writing laboratory reports is an essential skill that all psychology students must master. In the first instance this is because writing reports will be a major component of assessment in any course that you undertake. However, the same skills are involved in writing up any piece of psychological research professionally. Indeed, the guidelines below are based on those laid out in the *Publication Manual* of the American Psychology Association (APA, 2001). These (or very similar) guidelines must be followed by all researchers who attempt to publish work in psychology journals.

The overall goal of a laboratory report is to provide the reader with details of the rationale, methodology, results and conclusions of a specific piece of psychological research. The idea is to convey why the research was done, and how what was found contributes to the sum of knowledge in a given area. Psychologists and psychology students spend a considerable amount of time reading formal reports of this form (i.e., in journal articles), and these reports all have a common format to allow readers to access the specific material they are interested in as quickly and easily as possible. First and foremost, then, writing laboratory reports is an exercise in *effective and efficient scientific communication*.

Basic structure

All laboratory reports contain a title, an abstract, an introduction, a Method section, a Results section and a Discussion. At the end of the report there is also a references section and sometimes an appendix. In essence, the report tells two stories. The first is a succinct overview of the rationale for the research and its design, together with the key findings and conclusions. This is presented in a short *abstract* at the start of the report. The next four sections then tell essentially the same story in much more detail.

The *introduction* introduces (a) the general topic under investigation, (b) the theories that relate to that topic and relevant research that bears upon those theories, and (c) the specific hypotheses examined in the report, with an indication of exactly how these hypotheses are tested. Note that (a) leads to (b) and (b) to (c), in an *ever-narrowing* focus.

The *Method* section provides the reader with specific information about how the study was conducted – who the participants were, what materials or apparatus were used, and what the procedure for running the experiment was. This ensures that readers can be clear about exactly what the researcher did, so that if necessary they would be in a position to replicate that research themselves.

The *Results* section provides information about the data produced by the research, with details of all relevant descriptive and inferential statistics.

The *Discussion* then discusses (a) the fate of the hypotheses (whether or not they were supported), (b) the implications of this for relevant theories, and (c) the implication of these outcomes for the field as a whole. Limitations of the research are also noted and suggestions are made about important directions for future research. Note that here (a) leads to (b) and (b) to (c), in an *ever-broadening* focus.

These four sections represent the body of the report, and together they can be seen to have an hourglass structure, as indicated in Figure B.1. The introduction starts with broad issues and leads into

Figure B.1 Structure of a research report

the tight focus of the research at hand (a focus which is maintained through the Method and Results sections), while the Discussion starts with the issues at hand and leads back to the broad issues raised at the start of the report.

At the conclusion of the report, the *references* section provides information about the source of all the research which has been referred to in the report. An appendix then includes any supplementary material too bulky to incorporate in the Method or Results sections and not essential for the report to make sense.

The sections in detail

Title

The title of a report should provide a succinct statement (about 10 – 12 words) of the core purpose of the research, and for this reason it is usually framed in terms of the key independent and dependent variables and/or a key question that is to be addressed. Additional information which conveys important or distinctive information can be contained in a new clause separated by a colon. However, the title should be as punchy as possible, so avoid unnecessarily long or wordy titles and omit superfluous words. The following are some good and bad examples:

✓ The role of imagery and depth of processing in
  memory for words
✓ The effect of peer feedback on social behaviour: A study of dieting habits in adoles-
  cents
✗ A study of students' memory for words in the
  lab [No IV and irrelevant information]
✗ A survey asking why people diet [No IV]
✗ Lab Report 1 [No IV or DV]

Abstract

The abstract provides a short overview of research. It should be about 120 words long (no more than 960 characters) and is always presented on page 2 of the report. At a minimum it should state what the research involved (e.g., what the IVs and DVs were), who participated in it, and what the key results were. It should also say which theories or predictions were tested and whether these were supported.

The key here is that the abstract must present the most important information about the report. If research is published the abstract is usually the only information stored on databases and so in many instances a reader will make a decision about whether or not to read the entire article based on this information alone.

It is also worth noting that the process of writing the abstract is good preparation for writing the report as a whole, as it should clarify in your own mind what was important about the research and how the main features of the research fitted together. If you are having problems writing the abstract, this should warn you that you are not yet ready to write the report or that if you have already written the report your ideas may not be clearly structured.

> **Writing tip:**
>
> Writing the abstract 'cold' can be quite difficult and it is usually much easier to do if you have already written the rest of the report. However, if you write the draft abstract first, you can use this task to diagnose any problems in your report by highlighting sentences that you are having difficulty writing. If these sentences relate to your reasons for doing the study, problems in your introduction are likely and you may need to do more reading. If the problems relate to describing the mechanics of the study, problems in the Method section are likely, and so on.

Introduction

The Introduction needs to introduce the reader to the scientific problemthat is addressed by the reported research. This should be done in a number of steps. The introduction should start with a broad statement of why the particular topic being addressed is interesting and important. It should then progress to outline theories and other research relevant to that topic and to the research being conducted. It is important that this part of the introduction focuses on aspects of the existing literature that are relevant to material covered in the remainder of the report, so *be selective* and avoid unnecessary details. Finally, the introduction should clarify how these broad issues and theories are addressed in the research. This clarification will explain why the research incorporated the particular IVs and DVs that it did (e.g., which theories suggest they are important, which previous research has used them). All this should lead up to the final paragraph of the introduction which summarizes the aim of the research to be reported and clearly states the hypotheses that are to be tested in the research.

The introduction as a whole should thus tell an internally coherent story about 'why you did what you did'. This story should be accessible to as broad a scientific audience as possible and should make the research that is going to be presented in the report appear to be a balanced and reasonable attempt to deal with an important scientific issue. The point here is to provide a *platform* for the remainder of the report by setting up a framework within which the methodology and findings of the study make sense and can be interpreted.

Two additional points are worth making. First, a very common error in reports is that the link between theory and hypothesis is not fully elaborated in the introduction. Therefore *make sure that you always explain how an experimental hypothesis (or prediction) is derived from relevant theory*. Second, note that most research does not just address a single issue in isolation. However, the results of any piece of research often shed more light on some issues than on others, and so it is reasonable that the report as a whole focuses on those aspects of research where knowledge is advanced. Bearing this in mind, the introduction needs to be framed in terms of issues that are going to be important in the remainder of the report, rather than those that might have been important if the research had gone entirely as planned. This point becomes especially relevant as you start to take control of the research process yourself (i.e., as you start to write up projects that you have been responsible for designing and conducting). However, you must still form hypotheses before conducting the research.

Writing tips:

1. Ask yourself 'Why did we do this research?'. Your introduction needs to provide a sensible answer to this question, so you should not start writing it until you can provide one (at both a general and specific level).

2. When you have written the introduction, consider every paragraph in turn. Ask yourself 'How does this paragraph help me to explain why we did this research?'. If the answer is 'it doesn't' the material may be irrelevant and you should consider reworking or removing the paragraph.

Checklist for introduction

1. *Identify general issue/problem.*
2. *Outline theories that relate to the problem.*
3. *Summarize evidence for these theories that is relevant to the present study.*
4. *Explain how theories will be examined in this study.*
5. *Summarize the study's aims and hypotheses.*

Method

The point of the Method section is to provide enough information for readers to understand clearly what you actually did in the research so that they would be in a position to replicate it themselves if they wished. Here separate subsections usually provide details of the design of the research, the participants, the apparatus or materials involved in conducting the study and the exact procedure. To save space and avoid repetition, these subsections are sometimes combined (e.g., as 'Participants and Design' or 'Materials and Procedure'). If information is important for replication but unwieldy and not essential to understanding how the experiment was conducted, it can be placed in an appendix.

Participants. A short paragraph should indicate who participated in the research and report important demographic features of that research sample (i.e., their age and sex). Other descriptive characteristics of the sample relevant to the research should also be reported. For example, if the research is a study of visual perception it may be important to indicate how many of the participants wore glasses. The method for selecting the participants should also be identified, as well as details of any payment or reward they received in return for participation. The process by which participants were assigned to conditions should also be made clear and information provided about participants who did not complete the study or whose responses were not included in analysis (e.g., because they had participated in the study before).

Design. If the research is experimental, a short design statement is sometimes provided before describing the procedure more thoroughly (this section is optional and not required under APA guidelines). This indicates what the independent variables were, how many levels there were of each (and what the various treatments were) and how they were manipulated (within or between subjects). Key DVs can also be defined. A good design statement might read as follows:

> ```
> Mood was manipulated between subjects and par-
> ticipants were randomly assigned to one of three
> conditions (good mood, neutral mood or bad
> mood). Responses were obtained on two dependent
> measures: the Leeds Sadness Scale (LSS) and the
> Maudsley Mood Inventory (MMI).
> ```

Apparatus (or Materials). This subsection should provide information about important pieces of equipment that were necessary for the study's completion (e.g., a video recorder, computer or electroencephalograph). Details of questionnaires can also be provided. The maxim of relevance is important here: focus on those features of the research that are necessary for replication or which may have had a bearing on the results. For example, the fact that reaction time was measured by hand may be mentioned if you think that measurement error may have been a problem in the research.

Procedure. This subsection provides the reader with a step-by-step account of the participation process. It should describe all relevant events in the research from beginning to end (e.g., where the study took place, how assignment to conditions occurred, the order and timing of dependent measures, the nature of debriefing). However, avoid dwelling on irrelevant details or spending too long describing routine aspects of the research.

Writing tip:

Imagine that in ten years' time someone came to you and said 'I heard about that great study you did and I think it can make a great contribution to psychological science – but I'd like to see it replicated'. You have completely forgotten about the study and all other reports of the research have been lost. However, after rummaging around for a while, you come across the Method section of your report. Ask yourself 'Based on the information in my Method section, would I be able to faithfully reproduce my original research?'. If the answer is 'No', think about why this is the case and set about providing the information that would enable you to answer 'Yes'.

Results

The Results section summarizes the data obtained in the research and the outcomes of statistical analyses. The section often starts with an overview outlining the basic strategies used to analyse data (e.g., providing information about data aggregation and procedures used to make statistical inferences). It then goes on to report the results of those statistical analyses which relate to the goals of the research outlined in the introduction, and will be used to draw conclusions in the upcoming Discussion section. The Results section should present the results of statistical analysis and say what those results mean in empirical terms rather than attempting to draw broader practical or theoretical implications from them.

✓ Judgements on the ten trials were averaged for each participant. Mean scores for participants in the two experimental conditions were then compared using a between-subjects t-test. Participants in the fixation condition judged the variable line to be longer than did those in the scanning condition ($Ms = 4.23$, 2.31, respectively), $t(24) = 2.31$, $p < .05$. This result indicates that the Müller—Lyer illusion was stronger for participants in the fixation condition.

✓ Participants displayed greater need for achievement in the individual condition than in the group condition ($Ms = 5.43$, 3.21, respectively), $t(18) = 2.31$, $p < .05$.

✗ The difference between means was significant, $t(18) = 2.31$, $p < .05$, a result that supports the social relations model but which is inconsistent with the trait model.

If the pattern of relevant results is difficult to grasp when described in written text, it may help to place them in *either* a table *or* a figure (i.e., a graph). The table or graph should then be referred to at a relevant point in the text. If you need to provide details of statistical calculations or raw data, these should be provided in an appendix.

Statistical notation in Results sections should generally follow the examples provided in the chapters above. To summarize: M = mean, SD = standard deviation, N = sample size, n = a subsample (e.g., the number of participants in one condition).

Writing tips:

1. When you have written the Results section look back at what you wrote in the introduction and ask yourself 'Does my Results section provide simple and clear information relating to the questions raised in my introduction?'. This information is absolutely vital (and should represent the core of the Results section) so if it is missing or hidden away, you must take steps to revise the Results section accordingly.
2. Instructors have differing views about referring to the original hypotheses in the Results section. Many say you should never do this. Others believe that it can be helpful, especially when the results are complex. However, only refer to hypotheses if your instructor considers this appropriate.

Discussion

The Discussion mirrors the introduction in starting with a summary of the key findings of the research, then broadening to consider how those findings fit with previous research and theory, and their implications for understanding of the research topic as a whole. The overall aim of this section is to provide a satisfactory conclusion to the *research story* that was introduced at the start of the paper. As far as possible all loose ends should be tied up, and the reader should be left with a feeling that the research has advanced understanding of the psychological issues it addresses. Note that in order to be useful research does not need to support all (or any) of the researcher's hypotheses (see Chapter 2).

It is often appropriate to start the Discussion by restating the aim of the experiment and the hypotheses that were under investigation. This helps to refresh the reader's memory and contextualize what follows. The section must then summarize the research findings as they relate to these aims and consider the relationship between the findings and the hypotheses presented at the end of the introduction. Do the findings support these hypotheses or not?

The Discussion should then continue by clarifying the implications of the results for theories relevant to the topic that is being addressed and for the literature on that topic in general. These considerations should point out any inconsistencies or anomalies between the present and previous findings as well as potential ways of reconciling or making sense of them. It is important here that your observations are guided by the findings at hand, so avoid making unsubstantiated claims or going beyond the available information. It is acceptable to speculate about the broader meaning of your findings, but when these speculations are *post hoc* (i.e., after the fact) you must make this clear.

Any limitations of the study should also be discussed, as well as methodological changes which might be implemented in future research as a means of surmounting them and taking research forward. The Discussion then typically concludes with a simple summary of the significance of the reported research. If possible, try to end on a positive note that conveys some enthusiasm for the issues at hand. Here and throughout the Discussion you need to indicate to the reader that you have engaged critically and constructively with the research findings. For this reason you should try to avoid banal, clichéd or platitudinous comments that generally suggest a lack of engagement on your part (e.g., 'further research into this important topic will help advance knowledge').

Writing tip:

Make a list in point form of the things that you want the reader to have learned from reading your report. These represent the novel contribution of the research. Now take a working draft of your Discussion and mark the sections that deal with each point. Ask yourself whether all the points are covered and all given appropriate treatment. If you answer 'Yes' to both questions, your Discussion may be close to completion. However, also check the sections that are *not* marked. Ask yourself whether these are all essential to the story that your report tells. If they are not, you have some more thinking to do.

Checklist for Discussion

1. *Briefly restate the study's aim and summarize the results in relation to hypotheses.*
2. *Remark on the consistency of the findings with previous literature.*
3. *Clarify theoretical implications of the findings.*
4. *Note methodological or applied implications, including limitations of the study.*
5. *Make suggestions for future research.*
6. *Draw conclusions related to the general issue/problem identified at the outset.*

References

This section provides an alphabetical listing of all research papers referred to in the report (for formatting details, see below). Note that this is *not* a bibliography, and so the section should not list material unless it has been explicitly referred to.

Appendices

It may be appropriate (or for assessment purposes you may be required) to include appendices at the end of your report which present bulky and non-essential material that the reader may wish to inspect (e.g., complete questionnaires, details of statistical calculations, raw data). Each appendix should have a descriptive title and must be referred to in the body of the report.

General stylistic issues

A research report is a formal piece of work like an essay or a literature review. For this reason, it needs to be as well written and polished as any other piece of scholarly writing. Sentences should therefore be grammatical and complete, tenses and parts of speech should be used appropriately, and the report as a whole must read well and flow lucidly from one section to another. As well as this, though, the report needs to present information economically and concisely, so you should avoid any temptation to write in a florid or gushing style. Use words carefully and precisely (thinking carefully about the meaning of what you write and whether it is what you intend to say), and avoid colloquial expressions. You should also avoid sexist language. This includes using sex-specific terms (e.g., 'he', 'she', 'his', 'her') when a statement is equally applicable to both men and women.

The following examples illustrate some common stylistic errors:

✓ The experiment was done in a big lab. [informal/colloquial]

✗ The experiment was conducted in a large laboratory.

✓ It is not unreasonable to suppose that this result is indicative of bias on the part of participants. [florid language]

✗ This result suggests that participants were biased.

✗ The results reject the hypothesis. [imprecise: experimenters reject hypotheses, not results]

✓ The results are inconsistent with the hypothesis.

✗ Each participants responses were coded by a
  computer and participant's global scores were
  recorded on it's hard disk. [incorrect use of apos-
  trophes; note *it's* = *it is*]
✓ Each participant's responses were coded by
  a computer and participants' global scores
  were recorded on its hard disk.

✗ When a participant responded in this way he
  showed bias. [sexist language, if the participants could
  be either male or female]

✓ When participants responded in this way they
  showed bias. *or* This type of response reveals
  bias.

✗ The affect of alcohol is deleterious because
  it effects people's reaction times. [confusion
  of effect and affect: note *affect* as a noun
  refers to a feeling or emotion, as a transitive
  verb it means to act upon; *effect* as a noun
  refers to a result or consequence, as a transitive verb it means to bring about]
✓ The effect of alcohol is deleterious because
  it affects people's reaction times. [here 'effect'
  is a noun and 'affect' a transitive verb]

Reports are descriptions of studies that have already been conducted,
and so they should be written primarily in the past tense. However, at
some points in the report it may be appropriate to write in the present
tense (e.g., when describing the results of the experiment) or in the
future tense (e.g., when discussing issues that subsequent experiments
might address). Generally, though, write in the past tense unless there is
a good reason not to:

✓ The experiment tested the hypothesis that
  group interaction is stressful. [past tense]
✓ These results are consistent with predictions. [present tense]
✓ Future research will need to explore this
  issue further. [future tense]

Many psychologists also prefer reports to be written in the *passive voice* rather than the *active voice*. This is the difference between writing 'The participants were given a standard IQ test to complete' and 'The participants completed a standard IQ test'. The APA actually advocates use of the active voice, so it is a good idea to get guidance from your instructors on this point.

Finally, one extremely important feature of a report (like a psychology essay) is that it must *reference previous research and ideas appropriately*. As noted above, at various stages in the report (especially in the introduction and Discussion) you will need to refer to work that has previously been conducted by other researchers. Here you must cite the source of that work appropriately (see below), and (b) acknowledge the source of any of your own ideas that are based on that previous research. This is necessary for a number of reasons: most obviously so that readers can find that source for themselves if they are interested in checking or following up on the observations you make, and so that you do not inappropriately pass off someone else's ideas as your own.

It is important to note here that there is no shame in using and developing other people's ideas (indeed, this is an essential part of scientific progress; see Chapter 2). However, it is wrong to do so dishonestly, either by under-referencing or, in the most extreme cases, by *plagiarizing* (copying the work of others – an academic crime that will be dealt with severely).

Presentational issues

As with the structure and style of the report, a clear set of guidelines cover the way in which the report is presented on the printed page. These guidelines cover a broad range of issues, and it is a good idea to take a look at the *Publication Manual of the American Psychology Association* to see the various areas that are covered. Here though, we will focus on four important areas: (a) the overall presentation of the report; (b) section headings; (c) figures and tables; (d) numbers in text; and (e) referencing.

Overall presentation
The report as a whole should be typed single-sided on good-quality paper using double spacing and a single, simple and legible font (e.g., 12 point Times). A wide margin (at least 2.5 cm) should be left around the text (providing room for the reader's/marker's comments).

Section headings
These should be placed in all reports as follows (_____ = necessary page break; .... = text):

1

Title   [around 10–12 words]

Author Name
Other information (as required)

———————————————————————

2

Abstract

....   [around 120 words]

....

....

....

———————————————————————

3

Title

....   [NB: Introduction
                                                         has no heading]
....

....

Method

Participants

....

....

....

Design

....

....

....

Materials

....

....

....

Procedure

....

....

....

Results

....

....

....

Figure 1. Figure caption

....
....
....

Table 1

Table Title

....
....
....

Notes: (if required)

....
....
....

Discussion

....
....
....
....
....

_____

References

....
....
....
....

_____

Appendices

Appendix A: Title

....
....
....

Appendix B: Title

....

....

....

Tables and figures

These should be numbered consecutively through the report (starting with Table 1 and Figure 1), they should have a simple and clear explanatory title, and should be positioned as close as possible to the place in the text where they are first referred to. Table titles are positioned at the top of each table, with the first letter of all key words capitalized. Figure captions are presented below each figure, and only the first letter of the first word is capitalized. All features of the tables and figures (e.g., columns, rows, axes) should be appropriately labelled so that the meaning of any given number or data point is unambiguous. Columns in tables should be separated by appropriate spacing rather than vertical lines, although horizontal lines can be used to separate rows where necessary. APA guidelines suggest that labels on the y-axis of graphs should be typed vertically (going upward) unless they are very short.

Examples are as follows:

Table

Table 1 Mean Reaction Time (in milliseconds) as a Function of Alcohol Use

Alcohol use	M	SD	n
High	173	16.1	11
Low	124	12.4	23
None	120	10.9	14

Figure

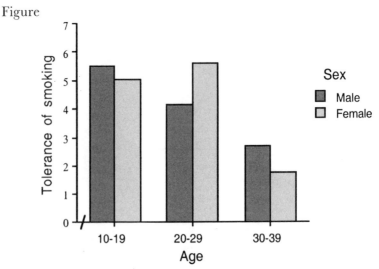

Figure 3 Students' tolerance of smoking as a function of their sex and age

Numbers in text

The APA rules for writing numbers in the text of a report are very complex. We recommend that students follow the following relatively simple rule that corresponds to APA dictates most of the time. Write numbers less than 10 in words and all others in digits. There are two important exceptions: (a) if numbers less than 10 are grouped for comparison with numbers greater than or equal to 10 then write them all as digits (e.g., 'one or two'; '3 vs. 11'; '265 and 102'); (b) use digits for all numbers which represent measurements of units (e.g., for time, age, and positions in a series); and (c) always write numbers in words at the start of a sentence.

Referencing

As noted above, where the work of other researchers is relevant to ideas or findings you refer to in the report, this needs to be referenced appropriately (note that referencing in psychological reports is not done using footnotes). At the relevant point in the text this involves identifying the relevant publication using the researcher's (or researchers') last name(s) and the date of publication. This information is contained in brackets and if multiple papers are referred to these are ordered alphabetically based on the first author's last name. If a paper has more than two authors and the paper is referred to more than once, then when cited for a second time the last names of the second and subsequent authors are truncated to 'et al.'. Examples are as follows:

> ✓ Previous research has shown that people favour members of their own group (Brewer, 1979; Tajfel, Flament, Billig, & Bundy, 1971).
> ✓ The work of Tajfel and colleagues (Tajfel, Flament, Billig, & Bundy, 1971) has shown that people favour members of their own group.

then later

> ✓ This point is confirmed by findings from the minimal group studies (Tajfel et al., 1971).
> ✓ This point is confirmed by findings reported by Tajfel et al. (1971).

In psychological reports it is not customary to include extensive direct quotes from other sources. However, when quoting the work of another researcher, the relevant text needs to be surrounded by quotation marks and accompanied by a page reference. Modifications to the text (e.g., to correct errors, regularize grammar or clarify meaning) are indicated by square brackets as in the following example:

> In their seminal text, Katz and Kahn (1966, p. 16) note that organizations have classically been defined as "social device[s] for efficiently accomplishing some stated purpose".

Whenever a reference to the work of researchers is made in the text, the full reference to that citation is then provided in an alphabetical list of such references provided in the reference section at the end of the report. Here journal articles, book chapters, edited books and authored books are referenced as follows:

Journal article

✓ Bate, P. (1984). The impact of organizational culture on approaches to organizational problem solving. *Organizational Studies*, *5*, 43–66.

Authored book

✓ Adorno, T. W., Frenkel-Brunswik, E., Levinson, D. J., & Sanford, R. N. (1950). *The authoritarian personality.* New York: Harper.

Edited book

✓ Cartwright, D., & Zander, A. (Eds.) (1960). *Group dynamics: Research and theory* (2nd ed.). Evanston, IL: Row Peterson.

Book chapter

✓ Brown, R. J. (1978). Divided we fall: Analysis of relations between different sections of a factory workforce. In H. Tajfel (Ed.), *Differentiation between social groups: Studies in the social psychology of intergroup relations* (pp. 395–429). London: Academic Press.

When modelling your own reference list on the above examples, pay careful attention to the order in which each element of the reference is placed, the punctuation, capitalization and underlining.

Further reading

The APA *Publication Manual* (as it is commonly known) is the standard reference text for writing in psychology. Its guidelines on issues of style and formatting have changed quite considerably over the years and any changes always arouse keen debate. Nonetheless, it is an authority whose strictures researchers and students cannot afford to ignore.

American Psychological Association (2001). *Publication manual of the American Psychological Association* (5th ed.). Washington, DC: Author.

Sample laboratory report

The following is a sample 1500-word report of an experiment which attempted to replicate a study conducted by Condry and Condry (1976). It is designed to give you an example to refer to when writing your own reports. Be warned that it is tailored to this particular experiment – you will need to make changes to the structure of the argument (as well as to the content) to suit the study you are writing up. Borders indicate separate pages.

```
Perceived sex and emotional judgement   1


The role of children's perceived sex in judgements of
                 their emotions

                  A. Student

             University of Yourtown


                 Word count
```

```
Perceived sex and emotional judgement   2


                  Abstract

  Many studies have identified sex differences in
children's behaviour. However, some of these dif-
ferences may be the result of stereotypic expecta-
tions about the behaviour of girls and boys. The
purpose of this study was to determine whether the
```

perceived sex of a child does in fact affect perceptions of its emotional reactions. Undergraduate
students ($N = 215$) viewed a videotape of an infant's
emotional responses to various stimuli. Half were
told the infant was a boy, half that it was a girl.
Participants were then asked to rate the emotional
reactions of the child. Consistent with the findings
of Condry and Condry (1976), the child was generally
perceived to be more emotional when it was thought to
be a boy. Findings suggest that sex differences
revealed by observational studies in which the
raters know the sex of the child should be treated
with caution.

The role of children's perceived sex in judgments
of their emotions

Several studies of children have shown that the
behavioural and emotional characteristics of young
boys differ from those of girls. For example, Fagot
(1974) found that boys exhibited a higher degree of
motor activity and object manipulation than girls,
while girls engaged in more verbal communication.
Cramer (1970) observed that 3- to 7-year-old boys
were more aggressive and impulsive than girls, who
displayed a greater degree of self-control. Jerseld
and Holmes (1935, as cited in Condry & Condry, 1976)
found that toddler girls expressed a higher degree of
fear in response to fear-provoking stimuli than did
boys.
    Maccoby and Jacklin (1974) have proposed that some
of these sex differences may be due to a process of
shaping whereby adults only encourage behaviour
seen to be appropriate for the child's sex. This
explanation assumes that adults have differential
expectations regarding the appropriate behaviour
for boys and girls. However, it has also been argued

that the existence of such differential expectations may also bias observers so that they exaggerate the extent to which boys and girls behave
differently (Cooper, 1974).

As with most findings of sex differences, the studies mentioned above used observational methods to
rate the behaviour of the child. With this technique, the child's sex is usually known to the observer. Accordingly, it is possible that ratings may be
influenced

Perceived sex and emotional judgement   4

by the observer's own expectations of sex-appropriate behaviour (Cooper, 1974).

In order to determine whether rated sex differences are influenced by the expectations of the
observer, Condry and Condry (1976) asked observers
to make judgements of the behaviour of a single child.
Observers watched a videotape of the child's
responses to a number of stimuli and then rated the
degree to which they thought each of three different
emotions (fear, anger, and pleasure) was present in
the child's response. Half the participants were
told that they were watching a boy, and half were
told that they were watching a girl. When the ratings
were aggregated across stimuli and type of emotion,
it was found that the child was rated as showing a
higher overall level of emotional response if
thought to be a boy. Evidence that perceptions of
behaviour are influenced by sex stereotypes was
also found. When the child was presented with a
stimulus which produced a negative, but ambiguous,
emotion, the child was rated as more aggressive
if perceived to be a boy, but as more fearful if
perceived to be a girl.

This experiment attempted to replicate the basic
pattern of findings reported by Condry and Condry
(1976). Following their results, it was predicted

that the perceived sex of the child would influence
observers' ratings of its emotional reactions. Specifically, it was hypothesized that a child believed
to be a boy would be perceived to be more emotional
than one believed to be a girl.

Method

Participants

The participants were 226 undergraduate psychology students attending scheduled laboratory sessions. Of these 139 were women and 87 were men. Data
from 11 students (7 women, 4 men) who had read the
course manual before the class were not included in
subsequent analysis.

Design

The independent variable was the sex attributed to
the child (male or female). This factor was manipulated between-subjects, with participants randomly
assigned to groups. The dependent variable was the
rated level of emotional reactivity.

Perceived sex and emotional judgement   5

Materials and Procedure

Participants were randomly allocated to one of two
groups, with each group receiving a different
instruction sheet (see Appendix A). Half of the participants were informed that the child was a girl,
the other half were told it was a boy. Participants
were required to transfer information about the
child, including its sex, from their instruction
sheet to a rating sheet. This allowed the attributed
sex of the child to be manipulated without the
experimenter having to state the child's sex
publicly.

When they had all done this, participants watched a
video depicting a 9-month-old child reacting to five
presentations of each of five emotionally arousing

stimuli. The stimuli were a toy wombat, a toy rabbit, a toy bear, a jack-in-the-box, and a strange noise. Immediately following the five presentations of each stimulus, participants rated the child's response to that stimulus on three dimensions indicating the amount of pleasure, anger, and fear displayed by the child. Responses were made on 11-point rating scales ranging from 0 (indicating that no emotion was displayed) to 10 (indicating a great deal of emotion).

Results

The data consisted of ratings of the degree of fear, anger, and pleasure shown by the child in response to each stimulus. Ratings were averaged across the presented objects and types of emotion to give a global measure of emotional reaction. Means and standard deviations for these global ratings are presented in Table 1 as a function of the attributed sex of the child.

Table 1 *Global Ratings of Emotional Reaction as a Function of Child's Attributed Sex*

Attributed sex	M	SD	n
Male	4.20	1.31	106
Female	2.43	1.02	109

From this table it can be seen that ratings of emotion were higher when the child was thought to be a boy ($M = 4.20$) than when it was thought to be a girl ($M = 2.43$). A between-subjects t-test indicated that this difference was significant, $t(213) = 10.92, p < .001$. Details of t-test calculations are presented in Appendix B.

Perceived sex and emotional judgement   6

Discussion

The aim of this experiment was to see whether ratings of a child's emotionality would be affected by its perceived sex. As hypothesized, the results

indicate that a child was rated as more emotional
when it was thought to be a boy than when it was
thought to be a girl. This pattern replicates
Condry and Condry's (1976) findings and supports
their conclusion that the perceived sex of a child
can influence ratings of its behaviour.

There are two key implications of this finding.
First, it serves to question the validity of sex differences reported in rating studies where the observers are aware of a child's sex (e.g., Cramer, 1970;
Fagot, 1974). The present results raise the possibility that such findings may reflect observers'
expectations, based on sex stereotypes, rather
than genuine behavioural differences. Evidence
that this stereotypic biasing can occur is also provided by Condry and Condry's (1976) finding that,
when presented with a buzzer as a stimulus, their
"boy" was rated as showing anger, while their
"girl" was rated as showing fear. It is possible
that similar results would be obtained from more
fine-grained analysis of the data collected in the
present study (i.e., based on separate analysis of
scores on different measures rather than a global
measure of emotional reaction) and this should be
examined in future studies.

Second, the present findings suggest that biases
in the interpretation of a child's behaviour may
contribute to subsequent shaping of that behaviour
into sex-appropriate forms, along lines suggested
by Maccoby and Jacklin (1974). For example, a boy who
cries may be treated by his parents as if he is angry,
while a girl may be treated as if she is afraid. It is
worth noting that Rothbart and Maccoby (1966) actually found that the pattern of such shaping also
depended on the sex of the observer: fathers were
more permissive with a child they thought was a
girl, while mothers were more permissive with a
child they thought was a boy. In future research it
might therefore also be interesting to see whether
the pattern of results obtained in the present study
varies as a function of the observer's sex.

In conclusion, the apparent sex of a child has been found to influence adults' perception of that child's behaviour. This casts doubt on findings of sex differences in studies where the observer

---

Perceived sex and emotional judgement 7

knows the sex of the child and raises the possibility that sex-based biases in the interpretation of behaviour may contribute to shaping of children's behaviour. Clearly this suggests that it might be necessary for future research to replicate important findings of sex differences in studies where the observer remains unaware of the child's sex in order to establish the reliability of those effects and the validity of received interpretations of them.

However, it is worth noting that one important limitation of this study was that the participants were students who on average may have had limited previous experience as observers of children's behaviour. This fact may reduce the study's external validity because similar results might not emerge if participants had greater expertise. For this reason, it would seem prudent to conduct further research to see whether the same biases that emerged in this study also emerge in ratings provided by participants with more direct experience of young children's behaviour. To this end, future studies might attempt to replicate the present study using parents and/or developmental experts as participants.

8

References

Condry, J., & Condry, S. (1976). Sex differences: A study of the eye of the beholder. *Child Development, 7,* 812–819.

Cooper, E. S. (1974). Direct observation? *Bulletin of the British Psychological Society, 27,* 3–7.

Cramer, B. (1970). Some sex differences in children between three and seven. *Psychosocial Processes, 6,* 60–76.

Fagot, B. I. (1974). Sex differences in toddlers' behaviour and parental reaction. *Developmental Psychology, 10,* 554–558.

Maccoby, E. M., & Jacklin, C. N. (1974). *The psychology of sex differences.* Stanford, CA: Stanford University Press.

Rothbart, M. K., & Maccoby, E. E. (1966). Parents' differential reactions to sons and daughters. *Journal of Personality and Social Psychology, 4,* 237–243.

9

Appendix A: Instruction sheets
Appendix B: t-test calculations

[You would place an exact copy of relevant material here. In this instance this would include details of the materials provided to participants and calculations from statistical tests.]

Appendix C: Statistical Tables

Areas under the standard normal curve

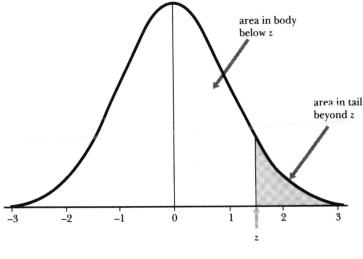

area in body below z

area in tail beyond z

total area under curve = 1 $\mu = 0, \sigma = 1$

Table C.1 provides details of the proportion of the area under the standard normal curve lying in the body below and in the tail beyond particular z-scores. The table can be used either (a) to identify probability levels associated with particular z-scores or (b) to identify z-scores associated with particular probabilities.

For example, to find out the probability of events associated with a z-score greater than 1.46, look for 1.46 in the left-hand column of the table labelled 'z' and read off the area that lies in the tail beyond that z-score in the adjacent column. In this case the value is .072. This means that 1.46 cuts off .072 * 100% of the total area. In other words, 7.2% of scores will be greater (and 92.8% will be equal to or lower) than 1.46 standard deviations above the mean.

On the other hand, to find out what z-value has to be exceeded to cut off 5% of the area, look for the first value that is equal to, or is less than, .05 in the column labelled 'Area in tail beyond z' and read off the associated z-score. In this case the required value is 1.65. This means that in order to cut off 5% or less of the population, a z-score has to be greater than or equal to 1.65. The value for a two-tailed test would be the value that cuts off .025 (i.e., .05 / 2) of the population in each tail. The corresponding value of z is 1.96.

Table C.1 Areas under the standard normal curve

z	Area in body below z	Area in tail beyond z	z	Area in body below z	Area in tail beyond z	z	Area in body below z	Area in tail beyond z
0.00	.500	.500	0.38	.648	.352	0.76	.776	.224
0.01	.504	.496	0.39	.652	.348	0.77	.779	.221
0.02	.508	.492	0.40	.655	.345	0.78	.782	.218
0.03	.512	.488	0.41	.659	.341	0.79	.785	.215
0.04	.516	.484	0.42	.663	.337	0.80	.788	.212
0.05	.520	.480	0.43	.666	.334	0.81	.791	.209
0.06	.524	.476	0.44	.670	.330	0.82	.794	.206
0.07	.528	.472	0.45	.674	.326	0.83	.797	.203
0.08	.532	.468	0.46	.677	.323	0.84	.800	.200
0.09	.536	.464	0.47	.681	.319	0.85	.802	.198
0.10	.540	.460	0.48	.684	.316	0.86	.805	.195
0.11	.544	.456	0.49	.688	.312	0.87	.808	.192
0.12	.548	.452	0.50	.691	.309	0.88	.811	.189
0.13	.552	.448	0.51	.695	.305	0.89	.813	.187
0.14	.556	.444	0.52	.698	.302	0.90	.816	.184
0.15	.560	.440	0.53	.702	.298	0.91	.819	.181
0.16	.564	.436	0.54	.705	.295	0.92	.821	.179
0.17	.567	.433	0.55	.709	.291	0.93	.824	.176
0.18	.571	.429	0.56	.712	.288	0.94	.826	.174
0.19	.575	.425	0.57	.716	.284	0.95	.829	.171
0.20	.579	.421	0.58	.719	.281	0.96	.831	.169
0.21	.583	.417	0.59	.722	.278	0.97	.834	.166
0.22	.587	.413	0.60	.726	.274	0.98	.836	.164
0.23	.591	.409	0.61	.729	.271	0.99	.839	.161
0.24	.595	.405	0.62	.732	.268	1.00	.841	.159
0.25	.599	.401	0.63	.736	.264	1.01	.844	.156
0.26	.603	.397	0.64	.739	.261	1.02	.846	.154
0.27	.606	.394	0.65	.742	.258	1.03	.848	.152
0.28	.610	.390	0.66	.745	.255	1.04	.851	.149
0.29	.614	.386	0.67	.749	.251	1.05	.853	.147
0.30	.618	.382	0.68	.752	.248	1.06	.855	.145
0.31	.622	.378	0.69	.755	.245	1.07	.858	.142
0.32	.626	.374	0.70	.758	.242	1.08	.860	.140
0.33	.629	.371	0.71	.761	.239	1.09	.862	.138
0.34	.633	.367	0.72	.764	.236	1.10	.864	.136
0.35	.637	.363	0.73	.767	.233	1.11	.867	.133
0.36	.641	.359	0.74	.770	.230	1.12	.869	.131
0.37	.644	.356	0.75	.773	.227	1.13	.871	.129

Table C.1 Continued

Appendix C:
Statistical Tables

z	Area in body below z	Area in tail beyond z	z	Area in body below z	Area in tail beyond z	z	Area in body below z	Area in tail beyond z
1.14	.873	.127	1.64	.949	.051	2.14	.984	.016
1.15	.875	.125	1.65	.951	.049	2.15	.984	.016
1.16	.877	.123	1.66	.952	.048	2.16	.985	.015
1.17	.879	.121	1.67	.953	.047	2.17	.985	.015
1.18	.881	.119	1.68	.954	.046	2.18	.985	.015
1.19	.883	.117	1.69	.954	.046	2.19	.986	.014
1.20	.885	.115	1.70	.955	.045	2.20	.986	.014
1.21	.887	.113	1.71	.956	.044	2.21	.986	.014
1.22	.889	.111	1.72	.957	.043	2.22	.987	.013
1.23	.891	.109	1.73	.958	.042	2.23	.987	.013
1.24	.893	.107	1.74	.959	.041	2.24	.987	.013
1.25	.894	.106	1.75	.960	.040	2.25	.988	.012
1.26	.896	.104	1.76	.961	.039	2.26	.988	.012
1.27	.898	.102	1.77	.962	.038	2.27	.988	.012
1.28	.900	.100	1.78	.962	.038	2.28	.989	.011
1.29	.901	.099	1.79	.963	.037	2.29	.989	.011
1.30	.903	.097	1.80	.964	.036	2.30	.989	.011
1.31	.905	.095	1.81	.965	.035	2.31	.990	.010
1.32	.907	.093	1.82	.966	.034	2.32	.990	.010
1.33	.908	.092	1.83	.966	.034	2.33	.990	.010
1.34	.910	.090	1.84	.967	.033	2.34	.990	.010
1.35	.911	.089	1.85	.968	.032	2.35	.991	.009
1.36	.913	.087	1.86	.969	.031	2.36	.991	.009
1.37	.915	.085	1.87	.969	.031	2.37	.991	.009
1.38	.916	.084	1.88	.970	.030	2.38	.991	.009
1.39	.918	.082	1.89	.971	.029	2.39	.992	.008
1.40	.919	.081	1.90	.971	.029	2.40	.992	.008
1.41	.921	.079	1.91	.972	.028	2.41	.992	.008
1.42	.922	.078	1.92	.973	.027	2.42	.992	.008
1.43	.924	.076	1.93	.973	.027	2.43	.992	.008
1.44	.925	.075	1.94	.974	.026	2.44	.993	.007
1.45	.926	.074	1.95	.974	.026	2.45	.993	.007
1.46	.928	.072	1.96	.975	.025	2.46	.993	.007
1.47	.929	.071	1.97	.976	.024	2.47	.993	.007
1.48	.931	.069	1.98	.976	.024	2.48	.993	.007
1.49	.932	.068	1.99	.977	.023	2.49	.994	.006
1.50	.933	.067	2.00	.977	.023	2.50	.994	.006
1.51	.934	.066	2.01	.978	.022	2.51	.994	.006
1.52	.936	.064	2.02	.978	.022	2.52	.994	.006
1.53	.937	.063	2.03	.979	.021	2.53	.994	.006
1.54	.938	.062	2.04	.979	.021	2.54	.994	.006
1.55	.939	.061	2.05	.980	.020	2.55	.995	.005
1.56	.941	.059	2.06	.980	.020	2.56	.995	.005
1.57	.942	.058	2.07	.981	.019	2.57	.995	.005
1.58	.943	.057	2.08	.981	.019	2.58	.995	.005
1.59	.944	.056	2.09	.982	.018	2.59	.995	.005
1.60	.945	.055	2.10	.982	.018	2.60	.995	.005
1.61	.946	.054	2.11	.983	.017	2.61	.995	.005
1.62	.947	.053	2.12	.983	.017	2.62	.996	.004
1.63	.948	.052	2.13	.983	.017	2.63	.996	.004

Table C.1 Continued

z	Area in body below z	Area in tail beyond z	z	Area in body below z	Area in tail beyond z	z	Area in body below z	Area in tail beyond z
2.64	.996	.004	2.76	.997	.003	2.88	.998	.002
2.65	.996	.004	2.77	.997	.003	2.89	.998	.002
2.66	.996	.004	2.78	.997	.003	2.90	.998	.002
2.67	.996	.004	2.79	.997	.003	2.91	.998	.002
2.68	.996	.004	2.80	.997	.003	2.92	.998	.002
2.69	.996	.004	2.81	.998	.002	2.93	.998	.002
2.70	.997	.003	2.82	.998	.002	2.94	.998	.002
2.71	.997	.003	2.83	.998	.002	2.95	.998	.002
2.72	.997	.003	2.84	.998	.002	2.96	.998	.002
2.73	.997	.003	2.85	.998	.002	2.97	.999	.001
2.74	.997	.003	2.86	.998	.002	2.98	.999	.001
2.75	.997	.003	2.87	.998	.002	2.99	.999	.001

Critical values of the *t*-distribution

Table C.2 provides critical values of the *t*-distribution to be used in conjunction with calculation of a *t*-value. To use the table, follow the steps below:

1. Look for the row with the appropriate number of degrees of freedom (*df*). If the exact number does not appear in the table look for the next smaller value of the degrees of freedom (e.g., 43 degrees of freedom does not appear in the table – so look up 42 degrees of freedom instead).
2. Look across the columns until you find the largest value of *t* in that row which is smaller than the value obtained from calculation. The value at the very top of that column is the *p*-value that you should report, but. . . .
3. If you are using a one-tailed test then use the *p*-value in the row that is labelled 'one tail'. Generally speaking, you should only do a one-tailed test if you have a directional hypothesis and are certain that this is the appropriate test.

Note: in the table the columns in bold highlight commonly used alpha levels.

For example, if the calculated *t* is 2.41, with 57 degrees of freedom, then to find the *p*-value for a two-tailed test, go to the row with $df = 55$ and look along this to find the first value that 2.41 exceeds. In this case this value is 2.396 and this corresponds to a two-tailed *p*-value of .02. Full results of this *t*-test could then be reported as $(t(57) = 2.41, p < .02)$.

The relevant lines in the table are reproduced below, with relevant numbers in boxes:

two tails	.5	.4	.3	.2	.1	.09	.08	.07	.06	.05	.04	.03	.02	.01	.005	.001
df																
55	0.679	0.848	1.046	1.297	1.673	1.726	1.784	1.848	1.920	2.004	2.104	2.228	2.396	2.668	2.925	3.476

Table C.2 Critical values of the t-distribution

									Probability levels (p)							
two tails	.5	.4	.3	.2	**.1**	.09	.08	.07	.06	**.05**	.04	.03	.02	**.01**	.005	**.001**
one tail	.25	.2	.15	.1	**.05**	.045	.04	.035	.03	**.025**	.02	.015	.01	**.005**	.0025	**.0005**
df																
1	1.000	1.376	1.963	3.078	**6.314**	7.026	7.916	9.058	10.579	**12.706**	15.895	21.205	31.821	**63.657**	127.321	**636.619**
2	0.816	1.061	1.386	1.886	**2.920**	3.104	3.320	3.578	3.896	**4.303**	4.849	5.643	6.965	**9.925**	14.089	**31.599**
3	0.765	0.978	1.250	1.638	**2.353**	2.471	2.605	2.763	2.951	**3.182**	3.482	3.896	4.541	**5.841**	7.453	**12.924**
4	0.741	0.941	1.190	1.533	**2.132**	2.226	2.333	2.456	2.601	**2.776**	2.999	3.298	3.747	**4.604**	5.598	**8.610**
5	0.727	0.920	1.156	1.476	**2.015**	2.098	2.191	2.297	2.422	**2.571**	2.757	3.003	3.365	**4.032**	4.773	**6.869**
6	0.718	0.906	1.134	1.440	**1.943**	2.019	2.104	2.201	2.313	**2.447**	2.612	2.829	3.143	**3.707**	4.317	**5.959**
7	0.711	0.896	1.119	1.415	**1.895**	1.966	2.046	2.136	2.241	**2.365**	2.517	2.715	2.998	**3.499**	4.029	**5.408**
8	0.706	0.889	1.108	1.397	**1.860**	1.928	2.004	2.090	2.189	**2.306**	2.449	2.634	2.896	**3.355**	3.833	**5.041**
9	0.703	0.883	1.100	1.383	**1.833**	1.899	1.973	2.055	2.150	**2.262**	2.398	2.574	2.821	**3.250**	3.690	**4.781**
10	0.700	0.879	1.093	1.372	**1.812**	1.877	1.948	2.028	2.120	**2.228**	2.359	2.527	2.764	**3.169**	3.581	**4.587**
11	0.697	0.876	1.088	1.363	**1.796**	1.859	1.928	2.007	2.096	**2.201**	2.328	2.491	2.718	**3.106**	3.497	**4.437**
12	0.695	0.873	1.083	1.356	**1.782**	1.844	1.912	1.989	2.076	**2.179**	2.303	2.461	2.681	**3.055**	3.428	**4.318**
13	0.694	0.870	1.079	1.350	**1.771**	1.832	1.899	1.974	2.060	**2.160**	2.282	2.436	2.650	**3.012**	3.372	**4.221**
14	0.692	0.868	1.076	1.345	**1.761**	1.821	1.887	1.962	2.046	**2.145**	2.264	2.415	2.624	**2.977**	3.326	**4.140**
15	0.691	0.866	1.074	1.341	**1.753**	1.812	1.878	1.951	2.034	**2.131**	2.249	2.397	2.602	**2.947**	3.286	**4.073**
16	0.690	0.865	1.071	1.337	**1.746**	1.805	1.869	1.942	2.024	**2.120**	2.235	2.382	2.583	**2.921**	3.252	**4.015**
17	0.689	0.863	1.069	1.333	**1.740**	1.798	1.862	1.934	2.015	**2.110**	2.224	2.368	2.567	**2.898**	3.222	**3.965**
18	0.688	0.862	1.067	1.330	**1.734**	1.792	1.855	1.926	2.007	**2.101**	2.214	2.356	2.552	**2.878**	3.197	**3.922**
19	0.688	0.861	1.066	1.328	**1.729**	1.786	1.850	1.920	2.000	**2.093**	2.205	2.346	2.539	**2.861**	3.174	**3.883**
20	0.687	0.860	1.064	1.325	**1.725**	1.782	1.844	1.914	1.994	**2.086**	2.197	2.336	2.528	**2.845**	3.153	**3.850**
22	0.686	0.858	1.061	1.321	**1.717**	1.773	1.835	1.905	1.983	**2.074**	2.183	2.320	2.508	**2.819**	3.119	**3.792**
24	0.685	0.857	1.059	1.318	**1.711**	1.767	1.828	1.896	1.974	**2.064**	2.172	2.307	2.492	**2.797**	3.091	**3.745**
26	0.684	0.856	1.058	1.315	**1.706**	1.761	1.822	1.890	1.967	**2.056**	2.162	2.296	2.479	**2.779**	3.067	**3.707**
28	0.683	0.855	1.056	1.313	**1.701**	1.756	1.817	1.884	1.960	**2.048**	2.154	2.286	2.467	**2.763**	3.047	**3.674**
30	0.683	0.854	1.055	1.310	**1.697**	1.752	1.812	1.879	1.955	**2.042**	2.147	2.278	2.457	**2.750**	3.030	**3.646**
32	0.682	0.853	1.054	1.309	**1.694**	1.748	1.808	1.875	1.950	**2.037**	2.141	2.271	2.449	**2.738**	3.015	**3.622**
34	0.682	0.852	1.052	1.307	**1.691**	1.745	1.805	1.871	1.946	**2.032**	2.136	2.265	2.441	**2.728**	3.002	**3.601**
36	0.681	0.852	1.052	1.306	**1.688**	1.742	1.802	1.867	1.942	**2.028**	2.131	2.260	2.434	**2.719**	2.990	**3.582**
38	0.681	0.851	1.051	1.304	**1.686**	1.740	1.799	1.864	1.939	**2.024**	2.127	2.255	2.429	**2.712**	2.980	**3.566**
40	0.681	0.851	1.050	1.303	**1.684**	1.737	1.796	1.862	1.936	**2.021**	2.123	2.250	2.423	**2.704**	2.971	**3.551**
45	0.680	0.850	1.049	1.301	**1.679**	1.733	1.791	1.856	1.929	**2.014**	2.115	2.241	2.412	**2.690**	2.952	**3.520**
50	0.679	0.849	1.047	1.299	**1.676**	1.729	1.787	1.852	1.924	**2.009**	2.109	2.234	2.403	**2.678**	2.937	**3.496**
55	0.679	0.848	1.046	1.297	**1.673**	1.726	1.784	1.848	1.920	**2.004**	2.104	2.228	2.396	**2.668**	2.925	**3.476**
60	0.679	0.848	1.045	1.296	**1.671**	1.723	1.781	1.845	1.917	**2.000**	2.099	2.223	2.390	**2.660**	2.915	**3.460**
65	0.678	0.847	1.045	1.295	**1.669**	1.721	1.778	1.842	1.914	**1.997**	2.096	2.219	2.385	**2.654**	2.906	**3.447**
70	0.678	0.847	1.044	1.294	**1.667**	1.719	1.776	1.840	1.912	**1.994**	2.093	2.215	2.381	**2.648**	2.899	**3.435**
75	0.678	0.846	1.044	1.293	**1.665**	1.718	1.775	1.838	1.910	**1.992**	2.090	2.212	2.377	**2.643**	2.892	**3.425**
80	0.678	0.846	1.043	1.292	**1.664**	1.716	1.773	1.836	1.908	**1.990**	2.088	2.209	2.374	**2.639**	2.887	**3.416**
85	0.677	0.846	1.043	1.292	**1.663**	1.715	1.772	1.835	1.906	**1.988**	2.086	2.207	2.371	**2.635**	2.882	**3.409**
90	0.677	0.846	1.042	1.291	**1.662**	1.714	1.771	1.834	1.905	**1.987**	2.084	2.205	2.368	**2.632**	2.878	**3.402**
95	0.677	0.845	1.042	1.291	**1.661**	1.713	1.770	1.833	1.904	**1.985**	2.082	2.203	2.366	**2.629**	2.874	**3.396**
100	0.677	0.845	1.042	1.290	**1.660**	1.712	1.769	1.832	1.902	**1.984**	2.081	2.201	2.364	**2.626**	2.871	**3.390**
105	0.677	0.845	1.042	1.290	**1.659**	1.711	1.768	1.831	1.901	**1.983**	2.080	2.200	2.362	**2.623**	2.868	**3.386**
110	0.677	0.845	1.041	1.289	**1.659**	1.710	1.767	1.830	1.900	**1.982**	2.078	2.199	2.361	**2.621**	2.865	**3.381**
115	0.677	0.845	1.041	1.289	**1.658**	1.710	1.766	1.829	1.900	**1.981**	2.077	2.197	2.359	**2.619**	2.862	**3.377**
120	0.677	0.845	1.041	1.289	**1.658**	1.709	1.766	1.828	1.899	**1.980**	2.076	2.196	2.358	**2.617**	2.860	**3.373**
∞	0.674	0.842	1.036	1.282	**1.645**	1.695	1.751	1.812	1.881	**1.960**	2.054	2.170	2.326	**2.576**	2.807	**3.291**

Critical values of Pearson's *r*

Table C.3 provides critical values of Pearson's *r* to be used in conjunction with calculation of a correlation coefficient. To use the table, follow the steps below:

1. Look for the row with the appropriate number of degrees of freedom (*df*). If the exact number does not appear in the table look for the next smaller value of the degrees of freedom (e.g., 33 degrees of freedom does not appear in the table – so look up 30 degrees of freedom instead).
2. Look across the columns until you find the largest value of *r* in that row which is smaller than the absolute (unsigned) value obtained from calculation. The value at the top of that column is the *p*-value that you should report.

For example, if the calculated *r* is −.27, with 84 degrees of freedom, then to find the *p*-value, go to the row with *df* = 80 and look along this to find the first value that .27 exceeds. In this case this value is .257 and this corresponds to a two-tailed *p*-value of .02 (and a one-tailed *p*-value of .01). In this case full results of the correlation could then be reported as (*r*(84) = −.27, *p* < .02).

The relevant lines in the table are reproduced below, with relevant numbers in boxes:

df	.10	.05	.02	.01
80	.183	.217	.257	.283

Table C.3 Critical values of Pearson's *r*

	Probability levels for two-tailed test (*p*)			
df	.10	.05	.02	.01
1	.988	.997	.9995	.9999
2	.900	.950	.980	.990
3	.805	.878	.934	.959
4	.729	.811	.882	.917
5	.669	.754	.833	.875
6	.621	.707	.789	.834
7	.582	.666	.750	.798
8	.549	.632	.715	.765
9	.521	.602	.685	.735
10	.497	.576	.658	.708
11	.476	.553	.634	.684
12	.458	.532	.612	.661
13	.441	.514	.592	.641
14	.426	.497	.574	.623
15	.412	.482	.558	.606

Table C.3 Continued

df	Probability levels for two-tailed test (p)			
	.10	.05	.02	.01
16	.400	.468	.543	.590
17	.389	.456	.529	.575
18	.378	.444	.516	.561
19	.369	.433	.503	.549
20	.360	.423	.492	.537
21	.352	.413	.482	.526
22	.344	.404	.472	.515
23	.337	.396	.462	.505
24	.330	.388	.453	.496
25	.323	.381	.445	.487
26	.317	.374	.437	.479
27	.311	.367	.430	.471
28	.306	.361	.423	.463
29	.301	.355	.416	.456
30	.296	.349	.409	.449
35	.275	.325	.381	.418
40	.257	.304	.358	.393
45	.243	.288	.338	.372
50	.231	.273	.322	.354
60	.211	.250	.295	.325
70	.195	.232	.274	.302
80	.183	.217	.257	.283
90	.173	.205	.242	.267
100	.164	.195	.230	.254
200	.116	.138	.164	.181
500	.073	.088	.104	.115
1000	.052	.062	.073	.081

Critical values of the *F*-distribution

Table C.4 provides critical values of the *F*-distribution to be used in conjunction with calculation of a *F*-value. To use the table, follow the steps below:

1. Look for the row with the appropriate number of degrees of freedom for the denominator and then the column with the appropriate number of degrees of freedom for the numerator. If the exact number does not appear in the column or row, look for the column or row with the next smallest value of the degrees of freedom (e.g., there is no row for 62 degrees of freedom, so instead look at the row for 60 degrees of freedom).
2. For each pair of degrees of freedom three *F*-values are listed. These correspond to three commonly used alpha levels $((\alpha = .05, .01$ and $.005)$. Find the largest of these three values which is smaller than the *F*-value obtained from calculation. The value in the second column at the left of the table corresponding to the critical value found is the *p*-value that you should report.

For example, if the calculated *F* is 5.32, with (2,62) degrees of freedom, then to find the *p*-value, go to the column with $df = 2$ and the row with $df = 60$. Look down the three listed values to find the largest value that 5.32 exceeds. In this case this value is 4.98 and this corresponds to an *F*-value of .01. Full results of this *F*-test could then be reported as $F(2,62) = 5.32, p < .01$.

The relevant lines in the table are reproduced below, with relevant numbers in boxes:

Denominator *df*	α	Numerator *df*		
		1	2	3
55	0.05	4.02	3.16	2.77
	0.01	7.12	5.01	4.16
	0.005	8.55	5.84	4.77
60	0.05	4.00	3.15	2.76
	0.01	7.08	4.98	4.13
	0.005	8.49	5.79	4.76
65	0.05	3.99	3.14	2.75
	0.01	7.04	4.95	4.10
	0.005	8.44	5.75	4.69

Table C.4 Critical values of the *F*-distribution (Smithson 2000, pp. 426–429)

Denominator degrees of freedom	α	Numerator degrees of freedom																						
		1	2	3	4	5	6	7	8	9	10	11	12	13	14	15	20	25	30	40	50	60	80	100
1	0.05	161.45	199.50	215.71	224.58	230.16	233.99	236.77	238.88	240.54	241.88	242.98	243.90	244.69	245.36	245.95	248.02	249.26	250.10	251.14	251.77	252.20	252.72	253.04
	0.01	4052	4999	5404	5624	5764	5859	5928	5981	6022	6056	6083	6107	6126	6143	6157	6209	6240	6260	6286	6302	6313	6326	6334
	0.005	16212	19997	21614	22501	23056	23440	23715	23924	24091	24222	24334	24427	24505	24572	24632	24837	24959	25041	25146	25213	25254	25306	25339
2	0.05	18.51	19.00	19.16	19.25	19.30	19.33	19.35	19.37	19.38	19.40	19.40	19.41	19.42	19.42	19.43	19.45	19.46	19.46	19.47	19.48	19.48	19.48	19.49
	0.01	98.50	99.00	99.16	99.25	99.30	99.33	99.36	99.38	99.39	99.40	99.41	99.42	99.42	99.43	99.43	99.45	99.46	99.47	99.48	99.48	99.48	99.48	99.49
	0.005	198.50	199.01	199.16	199.24	199.30	199.33	199.36	199.38	199.39	199.39	199.41	199.42	199.42	199.42	199.43	199.45	199.45	199.48	199.48	199.48	199.48	199.48	199.48
3	0.05	10.13	9.55	9.28	9.12	9.01	8.94	8.89	8.85	8.81	8.79	8.76	8.74	8.73	8.71	8.70	8.66	8.63	8.62	8.59	8.58	8.57	8.56	8.55
	0.01	34.12	30.82	29.46	28.71	28.24	27.91	27.67	27.49	27.34	27.23	27.13	27.05	26.98	26.92	26.87	26.69	26.58	26.50	26.41	26.35	26.32	26.27	26.24
	0.005	55.55	49.80	47.47	46.20	45.39	44.84	44.43	44.13	43.88	43.68	43.52	43.39	43.27	43.17	43.08	42.78	42.59	42.47	42.31	42.21	42.15	42.07	42.02
4	0.05	7.71	6.94	6.59	6.39	6.26	6.16	6.09	6.04	6.00	5.96	5.94	5.91	5.89	5.87	5.86	5.80	5.77	5.75	5.72	5.70	5.69	5.67	5.66
	0.01	21.20	18.00	16.69	15.98	15.52	15.21	14.98	14.80	14.66	14.55	14.45	14.37	14.31	14.25	14.20	14.02	13.91	13.84	13.75	13.69	13.65	13.61	13.58
	0.005	31.33	26.28	24.26	23.15	22.46	21.98	21.62	21.35	21.14	20.97	20.82	20.70	20.60	20.51	20.44	20.17	20.00	19.89	19.75	19.67	19.61	19.54	19.50
5	0.05	6.61	5.79	5.41	5.19	5.05	4.95	4.88	4.82	4.77	4.74	4.70	4.68	4.66	4.64	4.62	4.56	4.52	4.50	4.46	4.44	4.43	4.41	4.41
	0.01	16.26	13.27	12.06	11.39	10.97	10.67	10.46	10.29	10.16	10.05	9.96	9.89	9.82	9.77	9.72	9.55	9.45	9.38	9.29	9.24	9.20	9.16	9.13
	0.005	22.78	18.31	16.53	15.56	14.94	14.51	14.20	13.96	13.77	13.62	13.49	13.38	13.29	13.21	13.15	12.90	12.76	12.66	12.53	12.45	12.40	12.34	12.30
6	0.05	5.99	5.14	4.76	4.53	4.39	4.28	4.21	4.15	4.10	4.06	4.03	4.00	3.98	3.96	3.94	3.87	3.83	3.81	3.77	3.75	3.74	3.72	3.71
	0.01	13.75	10.92	9.78	9.15	8.75	8.47	8.26	8.10	7.98	7.87	7.79	7.72	7.66	7.60	7.56	7.40	7.30	7.23	7.14	7.09	7.06	7.01	6.99
	0.005	18.63	14.54	12.92	12.03	11.46	11.07	10.79	10.57	10.39	10.25	10.13	10.03	9.95	9.88	9.81	9.59	9.45	9.36	9.24	9.17	9.12	9.06	9.03
7	0.05	5.59	4.74	4.35	4.12	3.97	3.87	3.79	3.73	3.68	3.64	3.60	3.57	3.55	3.53	3.51	3.44	3.40	3.38	3.34	3.32	3.30	3.29	3.27
	0.01	12.25	9.55	8.45	7.85	7.46	7.19	6.99	6.84	6.72	6.62	6.54	6.47	6.41	6.36	6.31	6.16	6.06	5.99	5.91	5.86	5.82	5.78	5.75
	0.005	16.24	12.40	10.88	10.05	9.52	9.16	8.89	8.68	8.51	8.38	8.27	8.18	8.10	8.03	7.97	7.75	7.62	7.53	7.42	7.35	7.31	7.25	7.22
8	0.05	5.32	4.46	4.07	3.84	3.69	3.58	3.50	3.44	3.39	3.35	3.31	3.28	3.26	3.24	3.22	3.15	3.11	3.08	3.04	3.02	3.01	2.99	2.97
	0.01	11.26	8.65	7.59	7.01	6.63	6.37	6.18	6.03	5.91	5.81	5.73	5.67	5.61	5.56	5.52	5.36	5.26	5.20	5.12	5.07	5.03	4.99	4.96
	0.005	14.69	11.04	9.60	8.81	8.30	7.95	7.69	7.50	7.34	7.21	7.10	7.01	6.94	6.87	6.81	6.61	6.48	6.40	6.29	6.22	6.18	6.12	6.09
9	0.05	5.12	4.26	3.86	3.63	3.48	3.37	3.29	3.23	3.18	3.14	3.10	3.07	3.05	3.03	3.01	2.94	2.89	2.86	2.83	2.80	2.79	2.77	2.76
	0.01	10.56	8.02	6.99	6.42	6.06	5.80	5.61	5.47	5.35	5.26	5.18	5.11	5.05	5.01	4.96	4.81	4.71	4.65	4.57	4.52	4.48	4.44	4.41
	0.005	13.61	10.11	8.72	7.96	7.47	7.13	6.88	6.69	6.54	6.42	6.31	6.23	6.15	6.09	6.03	5.83	5.71	5.62	5.52	5.45	5.41	5.36	5.32
10	0.05	4.96	4.10	3.71	3.48	3.33	3.22	3.14	3.07	3.02	2.98	2.94	2.91	2.89	2.86	2.85	2.77	2.73	2.70	2.66	2.64	2.62	2.60	2.59
	0.01	10.04	7.56	6.55	5.99	5.64	5.39	5.20	5.06	4.94	4.85	4.77	4.71	4.65	4.60	4.56	4.41	4.31	4.25	4.17	4.12	4.08	4.04	4.01
	0.005	12.83	9.43	8.08	7.34	6.87	6.54	6.30	6.12	5.97	5.85	5.75	5.66	5.59	5.53	5.47	5.27	5.15	5.07	4.97	4.90	4.86	4.80	4.77

Table C.4 Continued

Numerator degrees of freedom

Denominator degrees of freedom	α	1	2	3	4	5	6	7	8	9	10	11	12	13	14	15	20	25	30	40	50	60	80	100
11	0.05	4.84	3.98	3.59	3.36	3.20	3.09	3.01	2.95	2.90	2.85	2.82	2.79	2.76	2.74	2.72	2.65	2.60	2.57	2.53	2.51	2.49	2.47	2.46
	0.01	9.65	7.21	6.22	5.67	5.32	5.07	4.89	4.74	4.63	4.54	4.46	4.40	4.34	4.29	4.25	4.10	4.01	3.94	3.86	3.81	3.78	3.73	3.71
	0.005	12.23	8.91	7.60	6.88	6.42	6.10	5.86	5.68	5.54	5.42	5.32	5.24	5.16	5.10	5.05	4.86	4.74	4.65	4.55	4.49	4.45	4.39	4.36
12	0.05	4.75	3.89	3.49	3.26	3.11	3.00	2.91	2.85	2.80	2.75	2.72	2.69	2.66	2.64	2.62	2.54	2.50	2.47	2.43	2.40	2.38	2.36	2.35
	0.01	9.33	6.93	5.95	5.41	5.06	4.82	4.64	4.50	4.39	4.30	4.22	4.16	4.10	4.05	4.01	3.86	3.76	3.70	3.62	3.57	3.54	3.49	3.47
	0.005	11.75	8.51	7.23	6.52	6.07	5.76	5.52	5.35	5.20	5.09	4.99	4.91	4.84	4.77	4.72	4.53	4.41	4.33	4.23	4.17	4.12	4.07	4.04
13	0.05	4.67	3.81	3.41	3.18	3.03	2.92	2.83	2.77	2.71	2.67	2.63	2.60	2.58	2.55	2.53	2.46	2.41	2.38	2.34	2.31	2.30	2.27	2.26
	0.01	9.07	6.70	5.74	5.21	4.86	4.62	4.44	4.30	4.19	4.10	4.02	3.96	3.91	3.86	3.82	3.66	3.57	3.51	3.43	3.38	3.34	3.30	3.27
	0.005	11.37	8.19	6.93	6.23	5.79	5.48	5.25	5.08	4.94	4.82	4.72	4.64	4.57	4.51	4.46	4.27	4.15	4.07	3.97	3.91	3.87	3.81	3.78
14	0.05	4.60	3.74	3.34	3.11	2.96	2.85	2.76	2.70	2.65	2.60	2.57	2.53	2.51	2.48	2.46	2.39	2.34	2.31	2.27	2.24	2.22	2.20	2.19
	0.01	8.86	6.51	5.56	5.04	4.69	4.46	4.28	4.14	4.03	3.94	3.86	3.80	3.75	3.70	3.66	3.51	3.41	3.35	3.27	3.22	3.18	3.14	3.11
	0.005	11.06	7.92	6.68	6.00	5.56	5.26	5.03	4.86	4.72	4.60	4.51	4.43	4.36	4.30	4.25	4.06	3.94	3.86	3.76	3.70	3.66	3.60	3.57
15	0.05	4.54	3.68	3.29	3.06	2.9	2.79	2.71	2.64	2.59	2.54	2.51	2.48	2.45	2.42	2.40	2.33	2.28	2.25	2.20	2.18	2.16	2.14	2.12
	0.01	8.68	6.36	5.42	4.89	4.56	4.32	4.14	4.00	3.89	3.80	3.73	3.67	3.61	3.56	3.52	3.37	3.28	3.21	3.13	3.08	3.05	3.00	2.98
	0.005	10.80	7.70	6.48	5.80	5.37	5.07	4.85	4.67	4.54	4.42	4.33	4.25	4.18	4.12	4.07	3.88	3.77	3.69	3.59	3.52	3.48	3.43	3.39
16	0.05	4.49	3.63	3.24	3.01	2.85	2.74	2.66	2.59	2.54	2.49	2.46	2.42	2.40	2.37	2.35	2.28	2.23	2.19	2.15	2.12	2.11	2.08	2.07
	0.01	8.53	6.23	5.29	4.77	4.44	4.20	4.03	3.89	3.78	3.69	3.62	3.55	3.50	3.45	3.41	3.26	3.16	3.10	3.02	2.97	2.93	2.89	2.86
	0.005	10.58	7.51	6.30	5.64	5.21	4.91	4.69	4.52	4.38	4.27	4.18	4.10	4.03	3.97	3.92	3.73	3.62	3.54	3.44	3.37	3.33	3.28	3.25
17	0.05	4.45	3.59	3.20	2.96	2.81	2.70	2.61	2.55	2.49	2.45	2.41	2.38	2.35	2.33	2.31	2.23	2.18	2.15	2.10	2.08	2.06	2.03	2.02
	0.01	9.40	6.11	5.19	4.67	4.34	4.10	3.93	3.79	3.68	3.59	3.52	3.46	3.40	3.35	3.31	3.16	3.07	3.00	2.92	2.87	2.83	2.79	2.76
	0.005	10.38	7.35	6.16	5.50	5.07	4.78	4.56	4.39	4.25	4.14	4.05	3.97	3.90	3.84	3.79	3.61	3.49	3.41	3.31	3.25	3.21	3.15	3.12
18	0.05	4.41	3.55	3.16	2.93	2.77	2.66	2.58	2.51	2.46	2.41	2.37	2.34	2.31	2.29	2.27	2.19	2.14	2.11	2.06	2.04	2.02	1.99	1.98
	0.01	8.29	6.01	5.09	4.58	4.25	4.01	3.84	3.74	3.60	3.51	3.43	3.37	3.32	3.27	3.23	3.08	2.98	2.92	2.84	2.78	2.75	2.70	2.68
	0.005	10.22	7.21	6.03	5.37	4.96	4.66	4.44	4.28	4.14	4.03	3.94	3.86	3.79	3.73	3.68	3.50	3.38	3.30	3.20	3.14	3.10	3.04	3.01
19	0.05	4.38	3.52	3.13	2.90	2.74	2.63	2.54	2.48	2.42	2.38	2.34	2.31	2.28	2.26	2.23	2.16	2.11	2.07	2.03	2.00	1.98	1.96	1.94
	0.01	8.18	5.93	5.01	4.50	4.17	3.94	3.77	3.63	3.52	3.43	3.36	3.30	3.24	3.19	3.15	3.00	2.91	2.84	2.76	2.71	2.67	2.63	2.60
	0.005	10.07	7.09	5.92	5.27	4.85	4.56	4.34	4.18	4.04	3.93	3.84	3.76	3.70	3.64	3.59	3.40	3.29	3.21	3.11	3.04	3.00	2.95	2.91
20	0.05	4.35	3.49	3.10	2.87	2.71	2.60	2.51	2.45	2.39	2.35	2.31	2.28	2.25	2.22	2.20	2.12	2.07	2.04	1.99	1.97	1.95	1.92	1.91
	0.01	8.10	5.85	4.94	4.43	4.10	3.87	3.70	3.56	3.46	3.37	3.29	3.23	3.18	3.13	3.09	2.94	2.84	2.78	2.69	2.64	2.61	2.56	2.54
	0.005	9.94	6.99	5.82	5.17	4.76	4.47	4.26	4.09	3.96	3.85	3.76	3.68	3.61	3.55	3.50	3.32	3.20	3.12	3.02	2.96	2.92	2.86	2.83

Table C.4 Continued

Numerator degrees of freedom

Denominator degrees of freedom	α	1	2	3	4	5	6	7	8	9	10	11	12	13	14	15	20	25	30	40	50	60	80	100
21	0.05	4.32	3.47	3.07	2.84	2.68	2.57	2.49	2.42	2.37	2.32	2.28	2.25	2.22	2.20	2.18	2.10	2.05	2.01	1.96	1.94	1.92	1.89	1.88
	0.01	8.02	5.78	4.87	4.37	4.04	3.81	3.64	3.51	3.40	3.31	3.24	3.17	3.12	3.07	3.03	2.88	2.79	2.72	2.64	2.58	2.55	2.50	2.48
	0.005	9.83	6.89	5.73	5.09	4.68	4.39	4.18	4.01	3.88	3.77	3.68	3.60	3.54	3.48	3.43	3.24	3.13	3.05	2.95	2.88	2.84	2.79	2.75
22	0.05	4.30	3.44	3.05	2.82	2.66	2.55	2.46	2.40	2.34	2.30	2.26	2.23	2.20	2.17	2.15	2.07	2.02	1.98	1.94	1.91	1.89	1.86	1.85
	0.01	7.95	5.72	4.82	4.31	3.99	3.76	3.59	3.45	3.35	3.26	3.18	3.12	3.07	3.02	2.98	2.83	2.73	2.67	2.58	2.53	2.50	2.45	2.42
	0.005	9.73	6.81	5.65	5.02	4.61	4.32	4.11	3.94	3.81	3.70	3.61	3.54	3.47	3.41	3.36	3.18	3.06	2.98	2.88	2.82	2.77	2.72	2.69
23	0.05	4.28	3.42	3.03	2.80	2.64	2.53	2.44	2.37	2.32	2.27	2.24	2.20	2.18	2.15	2.13	2.05	2.00	1.96	1.91	1.88	1.86	1.84	1.82
	0.01	7.88	5.66	4.76	4.26	3.94	3.71	3.54	3.41	3.30	3.21	3.14	3.07	3.02	2.97	2.93	2.78	2.69	2.62	2.54	2.48	2.45	2.40	2.37
	0.005	9.63	6.73	5.58	4.95	4.54	4.26	4.05	3.88	3.75	3.64	3.55	3.47	3.41	3.35	3.30	3.12	3.00	2.92	2.82	2.76	2.71	2.66	2.62
24	0.05	4.26	3.40	3.01	2.78	2.62	2.51	2.42	2.36	2.30	2.25	2.22	2.18	2.15	2.13	2.11	2.03	1.97	1.94	1.89	1.86	1.84	1.82	1.80
	0.01	7.82	5.61	4.72	4.22	3.90	3.67	3.50	3.36	3.26	3.17	3.09	3.03	2.98	2.93	2.89	2.74	2.64	2.58	2.49	2.44	2.40	2.36	2.33
	0.005	9.55	6.66	5.52	4.89	4.49	4.20	3.99	3.83	3.69	3.59	3.50	3.42	3.35	3.30	3.25	3.06	2.95	2.87	2.77	2.70	2.66	2.60	2.57
25	0.05	4.24	3.39	2.99	2.76	2.60	2.49	2.40	2.34	2.28	2.24	2.20	2.16	2.14	2.11	2.09	2.01	1.96	1.92	1.87	1.84	1.82	1.80	1.78
	0.01	7.77	5.57	4.68	4.18	3.85	3.63	3.46	3.32	3.22	3.13	3.06	2.99	2.94	2.89	2.85	2.70	2.60	2.54	2.45	2.40	2.36	2.32	2.29
	0.005	9.48	6.60	5.46	4.84	4.43	4.15	3.94	3.78	3.64	3.54	3.45	3.37	3.30	3.25	3.20	3.01	2.90	2.82	2.72	2.65	2.61	2.55	2.52
26	0.05	4.23	3.37	2.98	2.74	2.59	2.47	2.39	2.32	2.27	2.22	2.18	2.15	2.12	2.09	2.07	1.99	1.94	1.90	1.85	1.82	1.80	1.78	1.76
	0.01	7.72	5.53	4.64	4.14	3.82	3.59	3.42	3.29	3.18	3.09	3.02	2.96	2.90	2.86	2.81	2.66	2.57	2.50	2.42	2.36	2.33	2.28	2.25
	0.005	9.41	6.54	5.41	4.79	4.38	4.10	3.89	3.73	3.60	3.49	3.40	3.33	3.26	3.20	3.15	2.97	2.85	2.77	2.67	2.61	2.56	2.51	2.47
27	0.05	4.21	3.35	2.96	2.73	2.57	2.46	2.37	2.31	2.25	2.20	2.17	2.13	2.10	2.08	2.06	1.97	1.92	1.88	1.84	1.81	1.79	1.76	1.74
	0.01	7.68	5.49	4.60	4.11	3.78	3.56	3.39	3.26	3.15	3.06	2.99	1.13	2.87	2.82	2.78	2.63	2.54	2.47	2.38	2.33	2.29	2.25	2.22
	0.005	9.34	6.49	5.36	4.74	4.34	4.06	3.85	3.69	3.56	3.45	3.36	3.28	3.22	3.16	3.11	2.93	2.81	2.73	2.63	2.57	2.52	2.47	2.43
28	0.05	4.20	3.34	2.95	2.71	2.56	2.45	2.36	2.29	2.24	2.19	2.15	2.12	2.09	2.06	2.04	1.96	1.91	1.87	1.82	1.79	1.77	1.74	1.73
	0.01	7.64	5.45	4.57	4.07	3.75	3.53	3.36	3.23	3.12	3.03	2.96	2.90	2.84	2.79	2.75	2.60	2.51	2.44	2.35	2.30	2.26	2.22	2.19
	0.005	9.28	6.44	5.32	4.70	4.30	4.02	3.81	3.65	3.52	3.41	3.32	3.25	3.18	3.12	3.07	2.89	2.77	2.69	2.59	2.53	2.48	2.43	2.39
29	0.05	4.18	3.33	2.93	2.70	2.55	2.43	2.35	2.28	2.22	2.18	2.14	2.10	2.08	2.05	2.03	1.94	1.89	1.85	1.81	1.77	1.75	1.73	1.71
	0.01	7.60	5.42	4.54	4.04	3.73	3.50	3.33	3.20	3.09	3.00	2.93	2.87	2.81	2.77	2.73	2.57	2.48	2.41	2.33	2.27	2.23	2.19	2.16
	0.005	9.23	6.40	5.28	4.66	4.26	3.98	3.77	3.61	3.48	3.38	3.29	3.21	3.15	3.09	3.04	2.86	2.74	2.66	2.56	2.49	2.45	2.39	2.36
30	0.05	4.17	3.32	2.92	2.69	2.53	2.42	2.33	2.27	2.21	2.16	2.13	2.09	2.06	2.04	2.01	1.93	1.88	1.84	1.79	1.76	1.74	1.71	1.70
	0.01	7.56	5.39	4.51	4.02	3.70	3.47	3.30	3.17	3.07	2.98	2.91	2.84	2.79	2.74	2.70	2.55	2.45	2.39	2.30	2.25	2.21	2.16	2.13
	0.005	9.18	6.35	5.24	4.62	4.23	3.95	3.74	3.58	3.45	3.34	3.25	3.18	3.11	3.06	3.01	2.82	2.71	2.63	2.52	2.46	2.42	2.36	2.32

Table C.4 Continued

Denominator degrees of freedom	α	Numerator degrees of freedom																						
		1	2	3	4	5	6	7	8	9	10	11	12	13	14	15	20	25	30	40	50	60	80	100
32	0.05	4.15	3.29	2.90	2.67	2.51	2.40	2.31	2.24	2.19	2.14	2.10	2.07	2.04	2.01	1.99	1.91	1.85	1.82	1.77	1.74	1.71	1.69	1.67
	0.01	7.50	5.34	4.46	3.97	3.65	3.43	3.26	3.13	3.02	2.93	2.86	2.80	2.74	2.70	2.65	2.50	2.41	2.34	2.25	2.20	2.16	2.11	2.08
	0.005	9.09	6.28	5.17	4.56	4.17	3.89	3.68	3.52	3.39	3.29	3.20	3.12	3.06	3.00	2.95	2.77	2.65	2.57	2.47	2.40	2.36	2.30	2.26
34	0.05	4.13	3.28	2.88	2.65	2.49	2.38	2.29	2.23	2.17	2.12	2.08	2.05	2.02	1.99	1.97	1.89	1.83	1.80	1.75	1.71	1.69	1.66	1.65
	0.01	7.44	5.29	4.42	3.93	3.61	3.39	3.22	3.09	2.98	2.89	2.82	2.76	2.70	2.66	2.61	2.46	2.37	2.30	2.21	2.16	2.12	2.07	2.04
	0.005	9.01	6.22	5.11	4.50	4.11	3.84	3.63	3.47	3.34	3.24	3.15	3.07	3.01	2.95	2.90	2.72	2.60	2.52	2.42	2.35	2.30	2.25	2.21
36	0.05	4.11	3.26	2.87	2.63	2.48	2.36	2.28	2.21	2.15	2.11	2.07	2.03	2.00	1.98	1.95	1.87	1.81	1.78	1.73	1.69	1.67	1.64	1.62
	0.01	7.40	5.25	4.38	3.89	3.57	3.35	3.18	3.05	2.95	2.86	2.79	2.72	2.67	2.62	2.58	2.43	2.33	2.26	2.18	2.12	2.08	2.03	2.00
	0.005	8.94	6.16	5.06	4.46	4.06	3.79	3.58	3.42	3.30	3.19	3.10	3.03	2.96	2.90	2.85	2.67	2.56	2.48	2.37	2.30	2.26	2.20	2.17
38	0.05	4.10	3.24	2.85	2.62	2.46	2.35	2.26	2.19	2.14	2.09	2.05	2.02	1.99	1.96	1.94	1.85	1.80	1.76	1.71	1.68	1.65	1.62	1.61
	0.01	7.35	5.21	4.34	3.86	3.54	3.32	3.15	3.02	2.92	2.83	2.75	2.69	2.64	2.59	2.55	2.40	2.30	2.23	2.14	2.09	2.05	2.00	1.97
	0.005	8.88	6.11	5.02	4.41	4.02	3.75	3.54	3.39	3.26	3.15	3.06	2.99	2.92	2.87	2.82	2.63	2.52	2.44	2.33	2.27	2.22	2.16	2.12
40	0.05	4.08	3.23	2.84	2.61	2.45	2.34	2.25	2.18	2.12	2.08	2.04	2.00	1.97	1.95	1.92	1.84	1.78	1.74	1.69	1.66	1.64	1.61	1.59
	0.01	7.31	5.18	4.31	3.83	3.51	3.29	3.12	2.99	2.89	2.80	2.73	2.66	2.61	2.56	2.52	2.37	2.27	2.20	2.11	2.06	2.02	1.97	1.94
	0.005	8.83	6.07	4.98	4.37	3.99	3.71	3.51	3.35	3.22	3.12	3.03	2.95	2.89	2.83	2.78	2.60	2.48	2.40	2.30	2.23	2.18	2.12	2.09
42	0.05	4.07	3.22	2.83	2.59	2.44	2.32	2.24	2.17	2.11	2.06	2.03	1.99	1.96	1.94	1.91	1.83	1.77	1.73	1.68	1.65	1.62	1.59	1.57
	0.01	7.28	5.15	4.29	3.80	3.49	3.27	3.10	2.97	2.86	2.78	2.70	2.64	2.59	2.54	2.50	2.34	2.25	2.18	2.09	2.03	1.99	1.94	1.91
	0.005	8.78	6.03	4.94	4.34	3.95	3.68	3.48	3.32	3.19	3.09	3.00	2.92	2.86	2.80	2.75	2.57	2.45	2.37	2.26	2.20	2.15	2.09	2.06
44	0.05	4.06	3.21	2.82	2.58	2.43	2.31	2.23	2.16	2.10	2.05	2.01	1.98	1.95	1.92	1.90	1.81	1.76	1.72	1.67	1.63	1.61	1.58	1.56
	0.01	7.25	5.12	4.26	3.78	3.47	3.24	3.08	2.95	2.84	2.75	2.68	2.62	2.56	2.52	2.47	2.32	2.22	2.15	2.07	2.01	1.97	1.92	1.89
	0.005	8.74	5.99	4.91	4.31	3.92	3.65	3.45	3.29	3.16	3.06	2.97	2.89	2.83	2.77	2.72	2.54	2.42	2.34	2.24	2.17	2.12	2.06	2.03
46	0.05	4.05	3.20	2.81	2.57	2.42	2.30	2.22	2.15	2.09	2.04	2.00	1.97	1.94	1.91	1.89	1.80	1.75	1.71	1.65	1.62	1.60	1.57	1.55
	0.01	7.22	5.10	4.24	3.76	3.44	3.22	3.06	2.93	2.82	2.73	2.66	2.60	2.54	2.50	2.45	2.30	2.20	2.13	2.04	1.99	1.95	1.90	1.86
	0.005	8.70	5.96	4.88	4.28	3.90	3.62	3.42	3.26	3.14	3.03	2.94	2.87	2.80	2.75	2.70	2.51	2.40	2.32	2.21	2.14	2.10	2.04	2.00
48	0.05	4.04	3.19	2.80	2.57	2.41	2.29	2.21	2.14	2.08	2.03	1.99	1.96	1.93	1.90	1.88	1.79	1.74	1.70	1.64	1.61	1.59	1.56	1.54
	0.01	7.19	5.08	4.22	3.74	3.43	3.20	3.04	2.91	2.80	2.71	2.64	2.58	2.53	2.48	2.44	2.28	2.18	2.12	2.02	1.97	1.93	1.88	1.84
	0.005	8.66	5.93	4.85	4.25	3.87	3.60	3.40	3.24	3.11	3.01	2.92	2.85	2.78	2.72	2.67	2.49	2.37	2.29	2.19	2.12	2.07	2.01	1.97
50	0.05	4.03	3.18	2.79	2.56	2.40	2.29	2.20	2.13	2.07	2.03	1.99	1.95	1.92	1.89	1.87	1.78	1.73	1.69	1.63	1.60	1.58	1.54	1.52
	0.01	7.17	5.06	4.20	3.72	3.41	3.19	3.02	2.89	2.78	2.70	2.63	2.56	2.51	2.46	2.42	2.27	2.17	2.10	2.01	1.95	1.91	1.86	1.82
	0.005	8.63	5.90	4.83	4.23	3.85	3.58	3.38	3.22	3.09	2.99	2.90	2.82	2.76	2.70	2.65	2.47	2.35	2.27	2.16	2.10	2.05	1.99	1.95

Table C.4 Continued

Denominator degrees of freedom	α	Numerator degrees of freedom																						
		1	2	3	4	5	6	7	8	9	10	11	12	13	14	15	20	25	30	40	50	60	80	100
55	0.05	4.02	3.16	2.77	2.54	2.38	2.27	2.18	2.11	2.06	2.01	1.97	1.93	1.90	1.88	1.85	1.76	1.71	1.67	1.61	1.58	1.55	1.52	1.50
	0.01	7.12	5.01	4.16	3.68	3.37	3.15	2.98	2.85	2.75	2.66	2.59	2.53	2.47	2.42	2.38	2.23	2.13	2.06	1.97	1.91	1.87	1.82	1.78
	0.005	8.55	5.84	4.77	4.18	3.80	3.53	3.33	3.17	3.05	2.94	2.85	2.78	2.71	2.66	2.61	2.42	2.31	2.23	2.12	2.05	2.00	1.94	1.90
60	0.05	4.00	3.15	2.76	2.53	2.37	2.25	2.17	2.10	2.04	1.99	1.95	1.92	1.89	1.86	1.84	1.75	1.69	1.65	1.59	1.56	1.53	1.50	1.48
	0.01	7.08	4.98	4.13	3.65	3.34	3.12	2.95	2.82	2.72	2.63	2.56	2.50	2.44	2.39	2.35	2.20	2.10	2.03	1.94	1.88	1.84	1.78	1.75
	0.005	8.49	5.79	4.73	4.14	3.76	3.49	3.29	3.13	3.01	2.90	2.82	2.74	2.68	2.62	2.57	2.39	2.27	2.19	2.08	2.01	1.96	1.90	1.86
65	0.05	3.99	3.14	2.75	2.51	2.36	2.24	2.15	2.08	2.03	1.98	1.94	1.90	1.87	1.85	1.82	1.73	1.68	1.63	1.58	1.54	1.52	1.49	1.46
	0.01	7.04	4.95	4.10	3.62	3.31	3.09	2.93	2.80	2.69	2.61	2.53	2.47	2.42	2.37	2.33	2.17	2.07	2.00	1.91	1.85	1.81	1.75	1.72
	0.005	8.44	5.75	4.69	4.11	3.73	3.46	3.26	3.10	2.98	2.87	2.79	2.71	2.65	2.59	2.54	2.36	2.24	2.16	2.05	1.98	1.93	1.87	1.83
70	0.05	3.98	3.13	2.74	2.50	2.35	2.23	2.14	2.07	2.02	1.97	1.93	1.89	1.86	1.84	1.81	1.72	1.66	1.62	1.57	1.53	1.50	1.47	1.45
	0.01	7.01	4.92	4.07	3.60	3.29	3.07	2.91	2.78	2.67	2.59	2.51	2.45	2.40	2.35	2.31	2.15	2.05	1.98	1.89	1.83	1.78	1.73	1.70
	0.005	8.40	5.72	4.66	4.08	3.70	3.43	3.23	3.08	2.95	2.85	2.76	2.68	2.62	2.56	2.51	2.33	2.21	2.13	2.02	1.95	1.90	1.84	1.80
80	0.05	3.96	3.11	2.72	2.49	2.33	2.21	2.13	2.06	2.00	1.95	1.91	1.88	1.84	1.82	1.79	1.70	1.64	1.60	1.54	1.51	1.48	1.45	1.43
	0.01	6.96	4.88	4.04	3.56	3.26	3.04	2.87	2.74	2.64	2.55	2.48	2.42	2.36	2.31	2.27	2.12	2.01	1.94	1.85	1.79	1.75	1.69	1.65
	0.005	8.33	5.67	4.61	4.03	3.65	3.39	3.19	3.03	2.91	2.80	2.72	2.64	2.58	2.52	2.47	2.29	2.17	2.08	1.97	1.90	1.85	1.79	1.75
90	0.05	3.95	3.10	2.71	2.47	2.32	2.20	2.11	2.04	1.99	1.94	1.90	1.86	1.83	1.80	1.78	1.69	1.63	1.59	1.53	1.49	1.46	1.43	1.41
	0.01	6.93	4.85	4.01	3.53	3.23	3.01	2.84	2.72	2.61	2.52	2.45	2.39	2.33	2.29	2.24	2.09	1.99	1.92	1.82	1.76	1.72	1.66	1.62
	0.005	8.28	5.62	4.57	3.99	3.62	3.35	3.15	3.00	2.87	2.77	2.68	2.61	2.54	2.49	2.44	2.25	2.13	2.05	1.94	1.87	1.82	1.75	1.71
100	0.05	3.94	3.09	2.70	2.46	2.31	2.19	2.10	2.03	1.97	1.93	1.89	1.85	1.82	1.79	1.77	1.68	1.62	1.57	1.52	1.48	1.45	1.41	1.39
	0.01	6.90	4.82	3.98	3.51	3.21	2.99	2.82	2.69	2.59	2.50	2.43	2.37	2.31	2.27	2.22	2.07	1.97	1.89	1.80	1.74	1.69	1.63	1.60
	0.005	8.24	5.59	4.54	3.96	3.59	3.33	3.13	2.97	2.85	2.74	2.66	2.58	2.52	2.46	2.41	2.23	2.11	2.02	1.91	1.84	1.79	1.72	1.68
120	0.05	3.92	3.07	2.68	2.45	2.29	2.18	2.09	2.02	1.96	1.91	1.87	1.83	1.80	1.78	1.75	1.66	1.60	1.55	1.50	1.46	1.43	1.39	1.37
	0.01	6.85	4.79	3.95	3.48	3.17	2.96	2.79	2.66	2.56	2.47	2.40	2.34	2.28	2.23	2.19	2.03	1.93	1.86	1.76	1.70	1.66	1.60	1.56
	0.005	8.18	5.54	4.50	3.92	3.55	3.28	3.09	2.93	2.81	2.71	2.62	2.54	2.48	2.42	2.37	2.19	2.07	1.98	1.87	1.80	1.75	1.68	1.64
160	0.05	3.90	3.05	2.66	2.43	2.27	2.16	2.07	2.00	1.94	1.89	1.85	1.81	1.78	1.75	1.73	1.64	1.57	1.53	1.47	1.43	1.40	1.36	1.34
	0.01	6.80	4.74	3.91	3.44	3.13	2.92	2.75	2.62	2.52	2.43	2.36	2.30	2.24	2.20	2.15	1.99	1.89	1.82	1.72	1.66	1.61	1.55	1.51
	0.005	8.10	5.48	4.44	3.87	3.50	3.24	3.04	2.88	2.76	2.66	2.57	2.50	2.43	2.38	2.33	2.14	2.02	1.93	1.82	1.75	1.69	1.62	1.58
200	0.05	3.89	3.04	2.65	2.42	2.26	2.14	2.06	1.98	1.93	1.88	1.84	1.80	1.77	1.74	1.72	1.62	1.56	1.52	1.46	1.41	1.39	1.35	1.32
	0.01	6.76	4.71	3.88	3.41	3.11	2.89	2.73	2.60	2.50	2.41	2.34	2.27	2.22	2.17	2.13	1.97	1.87	1.79	1.69	1.63	1.58	1.52	1.48
	0.005	8.06	5.44	4.41	3.84	3.47	3.21	3.01	2.86	2.73	2.63	2.54	2.47	2.40	2.35	2.30	2.11	1.99	1.91	1.79	1.71	1.66	1.59	1.54

Table C.4 Continued

Denominator degrees of freedom	α	1	2	3	4	5	6	7	8	9	10	11	12	13	14	15	20	25	30	40	50	60	80	100
400	0.05	3.86	3.02	2.63	2.39	2.24	2.12	2.03	1.96	1.90	1.85	1.81	1.78	1.74	1.72	1.69	1.60	1.53	1.49	1.42	1.38	1.35	1.31	1.28
	0.01	6.70	4.66	3.83	3.37	3.06	2.85	2.68	2.56	2.45	2.37	2.29	2.23	2.17	2.13	2.08	1.92	1.82	1.75	1.64	1.58	1.53	1.46	1.42
	0.005	7.97	5.37	4.34	3.78	3.41	3.15	2.95	2.80	2.68	2.57	2.49	2.41	2.35	2.29	2.24	2.06	1.93	1.85	1.73	1.65	1.60	1.52	1.47
∞	0.05	3.84	3.00	2.60	2.37	2.21	2.10	2.01	1.94	1.88	1.83	1.79	1.75	1.72	1.69	1.67	1.57	1.51	1.46	1.39	1.35	1.32	1.27	1.24
	0.01	6.63	4.61	3.78	3.32	3.02	2.80	2.64	2.51	2.41	2.32	2.25	2.18	2.13	2.08	2.04	1.88	1.77	1.70	1.59	1.52	1.47	1.40	1.36
	0.005	7.88	5.30	4.28	3.72	3.35	3.09	2.90	2.74	2.62	2.52	2.43	2.36	2.29	2.24	2.19	2.00	1.88	1.79	1.67	1.59	1.53	1.45	1.40

Numerator degrees of freedom

Critical values of the χ^2-distribution

Table C.5 provides critical values of the χ^2-distribution to be used in conjunction with calculation of a χ^2-value. To use the table, follow the steps below:

1. Look for the row with the appropriate number of degrees of freedom (df).
2. Look across the columns until you find the largest value of χ^2 in that row which is smaller than the value obtained from calculation. The value at the very top of that column is the p-value that you should report.

Note: The columns in the table represent the most commonly used alpha levels.

For example, if the calculated χ^2 is 16.41, with 7 degrees of freedom, then to find the p-value go to the row with $df = 7$ and look along this to find the largest value that 16.41 exceeds. In this case this value is 14.0671 and this corresponds to a p-value of .05. Full results of this χ^2-test could then be reported as χ^2 (7) = 16.41, $p < .05$.

The relevant lines in the table are reproduced below, with relevant numbers in boxes:

Areas beyond χ^2

df	0.99	0.95	0.9	0.8	0.2	0.1	0.05	0.01	0.005	0.001
7	1.2390	2.1673	2.8331	3.8223	9.8032	12.0170	14.0671	18.4753	20.277	24.3213

Table C.5 Critical values of the chi-square distribution (Smithson, 2000, pp. 43–431)

					Area beyond χ^2					
df	0.99	0.95	0.9	0.8	0.2	0.1	0.05	0.01	0.005	0.001
1	0.0002	0.0039	0.0158	0.0642	1.6424	2.7055	3.8415	6.6349	7.8794	10.8274
2	0.0201	0.1026	0.2107	0.4463	3.2189	4.6052	5.9915	9.2104	10.5965	13.8150
3	0.1148	0.3518	0.5844	1.0052	4.6416	6.2514	7.8147	11.3449	12.8381	16.2260
4	0.2971	0.7107	1.0636	1.6488	5.9886	7.7794	9.4877	13.2767	14.8602	18.4662
5	0.5543	1.1455	1.6103	2.3425	7.2893	9.2363	11.0705	15.0863	16.7496	20.5147
6	0.8721	1.6354	2.2041	3.0701	8.5581	10.6446	12.5916	16.8119	18.5475	22.4575
7	1.2390	2.1673	2.8331	3.8223	9.8032	12.0170	14.0671	18.4753	20.2777	24.3213
8	1.6465	2.7326	3.4895	4.5936	11.0301	13.3616	15.5073	20.0902	21.9549	26.1239
9	2.0879	3.3251	4.1682	5.3801	12.2421	14.6837	16.9190	21.6660	23.5893	27.8767
10	2.5582	3.9403	4.8652	6.1791	13.4420	15.9872	18.3070	23.2093	25.1881	29.5879
11	3.0535	4.5748	5.5778	6.9887	14.6314	17.2750	19.6752	24.7250	26.7569	31.2635
12	3.5706	5.2260	6.3038	7.8073	15.8120	18.5493	21.0261	26.2170	28.2997	32.9092
13	4.1069	5.8919	7.0415	8.6339	16.9848	19.8119	22.3620	27.6882	29.8193	34.5274
14	4.6604	6.5706	7.7895	9.4673	18.1508	21.0641	23.6848	29.1412	31.3194	36.1239
15	5.2294	7.2609	8.5468	10.3070	19.3107	22.3071	24.9958	30.5780	32.8015	37.6978
16	5.8122	7.9616	9.3122	11.1521	20.4651	23.5418	26.2962	31.9999	34.2671	39.2518
17	6.4077	8.6718	10.0852	12.0023	21.6146	24.7690	27.5871	33.4087	35.7184	40.7911
18	7.0149	9.3904	10.8649	12.8570	22.7595	25.9894	28.8693	34.8052	37.1564	42.3119
19	7.6327	10.1170	11.6509	13.7158	23.9004	27.2036	30.1435	36.1908	38.5821	43.8194
20	8.2604	10.8508	12.4426	14.5784	25.0375	28.4120	31.4104	37.5663	39.9969	45.3142
21	8.8972	11.5913	13.2396	15.4446	26.1711	29.6151	32.6706	38.9322	41.4009	46.7963
22	9.5425	12.3380	14.0415	16.3140	27.3015	30.8133	33.9245	40.2894	42.7957	48.2676
23	10.1957	13.0905	14.8480	17.1865	28.4288	32.0069	35.1725	41.6383	44.1814	49.7276
24	10.8563	13.8484	15.6587	18.0618	29.5533	33.1962	36.4150	42.9798	45.5584	51.1790
25	11.5240	14.6114	16.4734	18.9397	30.6752	34.3816	37.6525	44.3140	46.9280	52.6187
26	12.1982	15.3792	17.2919	19.8202	31.7946	35.5632	38.8851	45.6416	48.2898	54.0511
27	12.8785	16.1514	18.1139	20.7030	32.9117	36.7412	40.1133	46.9628	49.6450	55.4751

Table C.5 Continued

df					Area beyond χ^2					
	0.99	0.95	0.9	0.8	0.2	0.1	0.05	0.01	0.005	0.001
28	13.5647	16.9279	18.9392	21.5880	34.0266	37.9159	41.3372	48.2782	50.9936	56.8918
29	14.2564	17.7084	19.7677	22.4751	35.1394	39.0875	42.5569	49.5878	52.3355	58.3006
30	14.9535	18.4927	20.5992	23.3641	36.2502	40.2560	43.7730	50.8922	53.6719	59.7022
31	15.6555	19.2806	21.4336	24.2551	37.3591	41.4217	44.9853	52.1914	55.0025	61.0980
32	16.3622	20.0719	22.2706	25.1478	38.4663	42.5847	46.1942	53.4857	56.3280	62.4873
33	17.0735	20.8665	23.1102	26.0422	39.5718	43.7452	47.3999	54.7754	57.6483	63.8694
34	17.7891	21.6643	23.9522	26.9383	40.6756	44.9032	48.6024	56.0609	58.9637	65.2471
35	18.5089	22.4650	24.7966	27.8359	41.7780	46.0588	49.8018	57.3420	60.2746	66.6192
36	19.2326	23.2686	25.6433	28.7350	42.8788	47.2122	50.9985	58.6192	61.5811	67.9850
37	19.9603	24.0749	26.4921	29.6355	43.9782	48.3634	52.1923	59.8926	62.8832	69.3476
38	20.6914	24.8839	27.3430	30.5373	45.0763	49.5126	53.3835	61.1620	64.1812	70.7039
39	21.4261	25.6954	28.1958	31.4405	46.1730	50.6598	54.5722	62.4281	65.4753	72.0550
40	22.1642	26.5093	29.0505	32.3449	47.2685	51.8050	55.7585	63.6908	66.7660	73.4029
41	22.9056	27.3256	29.9071	33.2506	48.3628	52.9485	56.9424	64.9500	68.0526	74.7441
42	23.6301	28.1440	30.7654	34.1574	49.4560	54.0902	58.1240	66.2063	69.3360	76.0842
43	24.3976	28.9647	31.6255	35.0653	50.5480	55.2302	59.3035	67.4593	70.6157	77.4184
44	25.1480	29.7875	32.4871	35.9744	51.6389	56.3685	60.4809	68.7096	71.8923	78.7487
45	25.9012	30.6123	33.3504	36.8844	52.7288	57.5053	61.6562	69.9569	73.1660	80.0776
46	26.6572	31.4390	34.2152	37.7955	53.8177	58.6405	62.8296	71.2015	74.4367	81.3998
47	27.4158	32.2676	35.0814	38.7075	54.9056	69.7743	64.0011	72.4432	75.7039	82.7198
48	28.1770	33.0981	35.9491	39.6205	55.9926	60.9066	65.1708	73.6826	76.9689	84.0368
49	28.9406	33.9303	36.8182	40.5344	57.0786	62.0375	66.3387	74.9194	78.2306	85.3499
50	29.7067	34.7642	37.6886	41.4492	58.1638	63.1671	67.5048	76.1538	79.4898	86.6603

Appendix D: Answers to Exercises

Chapter 4. Experimental design

(i) We cannot know whether the treatment only works when participants have a pre-test. The interaction between treatment and testing is also a threat to internal validity.

(ii) History and maturation effects are key threats. In fact this design really only examines the impact of the pre-test.

(iii) This design avoids some external validity problems and is a good choice. Note though, that sometimes researchers want to examine the effects of treatment on the *same* participants, and this design would not allow them to do this.

(iv) As with (i), pre-testing effects can interact with treatment.

(v) This is actually a very good design as it allows John to look at change in the same participants between the pre-test and post-test – something (iii) did not – but controls for problems associated with (i). However, it uses a lot of participants and experimental resources.

(vi) This design has no treatment, so it can tell John nothing about the effects of the teaching technique.

Chapter 5. Survey design

A. (i) This is convenience sampling.

(ii) This is not a random sample, but there is a good chance that it could be representative of the population (however, to fully answer this question you would need to have some knowledge about human vision rather than statistics). This is because the colour vision of shoppers is unlikely to differ from that of other members of the population (though note that the sample might well be unrepresentative if the researchers were interested in people's income level or their spending habits).

(iii) Yes, for the reason given above (though note that it would not be appropriate for all psychological research).

B. (i) There are several problems with this question. Most obviously, the unit of measurement is not specified, so it is unclear whether respondents should provide details of their annual, monthly or hourly income. As it is stated, the question also appears to be very confronting, and respondents may have concerns about revealing private information in this form. A better item would be:

```
What is your annual salary (before tax)? (circle one)
   $0-9,999   $10,000-19,999   $20,000-29,999
      $30,000-39,999   above $40,000
```

Here responding is not as threatening, and the categories can be constructed in a way that provides the researcher with useful information.

(ii) As it is presented here, this question is very vague. It is also likely that, if they took the question literally, almost everyone would answer 'yes', so it is going to provide very little useful information. A better question might be:

```
Do you worry about being able to pay your bills? (circle one)
      never   rarely   sometimes   often   always
```

(iii) This question actually contains two questions, and so if a person answers 'yes', it is unclear which component he or she is agreeing with. Accordingly, the question would be better if it was decoupled into two separate questions:

```
Are you in a pension plan? (tick one) yes  no
Are you in a superannuation scheme? (tick one)  yes  no
```

(iv) This question contains an acronym which is likely to confuse respondents. In general, technical language, jargon and acronyms should be avoided unless you are very confident that respondents will be very familiar with these. The question would therefore be improved if it was spelled out as follows:

```
Do you have an Independent Savings Agreement (ISA)?
(tick one) yes no
```

(v) This question has a number of problems. First, it is phrased in the negative, which means that if the person disagrees their response is actually a double negative, and this can be very confusing. Second, the end-points of the scale are not particularly discriminating and so they might not yield the optimal amount of information. Third, like question (ii), the question is rather vague and unspecified. A better item would be:

```
On the scale below indicate your level of agreement
with the following statement (circle one number):
I organize my finances well
disagree completely 1 2 3 4 5 6 7 agree completely
```

(vi) This item is badly worded and badly spelled. When preparing a questionnaire it is *very* important to attend to details of content and presentation in order to create a positive impression. If it looks as if you have not put much effort into constructing a questionnaire, why would anyone put any effort into responding? Tidied up, this question might read as follows:

```
How much do you agree with the following statement?
(circle one number)
I organize my finances well
disagree completely 1 2 3 4 5 6 7 agree completely
```

Chapter 6. Descriptive statistics

A. (i)

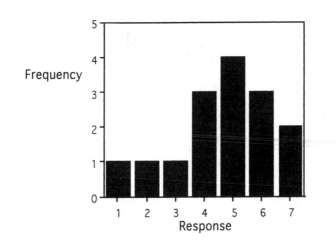

A. (ii)

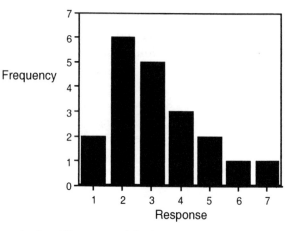

B. (i) yes, negatively; (ii) yes, positively
C. (i) mean = 4.67, median = 5, mode = 5
   (ii) mean = 3.20, median = 3, mode = 2
D. (i) range = 6, mean deviation = 1.33, variance = 2.95, standard deviation = 1.72
   (ii) range = 6, mean deviation = 1.26, variance = 2.59, standard deviation = 1.61
E. (i) In the case of a floor the mean will tend to be greater than the median. The mode will often be very low.
   (ii) This is because a floor produces positive skew (as only the positive end of the distribution can have a tail). This point is illustrated in Figure D.1.

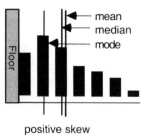

positive skew

Figure D.1 Effect of a floor on the skewness of a distribution

F. (i) The mean number of cars Americans own should exceed the median because there is a floor at 0 precluding a negative tail to the distribution.
   (ii) The mean score on the exam should be lower than the median because there is a ceiling of 100% ruling out a positive tail to the distribution.

G. In his book (which is well worth reading), Gould goes to great
    lengths to explain why the reduced performance of the best hitters
    is actually associated with an *increase* in overall batting perfor-
    mance. As Figure D.2 shows, his argument hinges on the fact that
    despite an overall increase in mean performance, it is still possible
    for the largest scores to be reduced if variance in hitting perfor-
    mance decreases a great deal as well. Gould's point, and one that
    we emphasize in this chapter, is that the meaning of single scores
    (whether they represent a typical score or an extreme one) depends
    upon the distribution of *all other* scores. In effect, then, *a single score
    is only given meaning by the distribution from which it is obtained.* Thus, the
    fact that the best baseball hitters have lower batting averages than
    they did at the turn of the century *does not* necessarily mean that the
    standard of baseball batting is declining (contrary to the argu-
    ments of a number of media commentators).

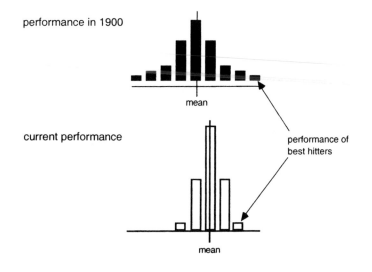

Figure D.2 Baseball averages in 1900 and today (Gould, 1997)

Chapter 7. Some principles of statistical inference

A. 1.08
B. 14%
C. 2.12
D. 1.7%

E. (i) 18

(ii) If both groups are drawn from the same population we should expect them to appear in the top 20 in the same ratio as they do in the population (though there will be variability around the expected values).

(iii) If you get this one correct, you're doing very well! Go to Table C.1. The 10th fastest runner in the red team is at the 10th percentile. Look in the body of the table for the z that cuts off 10% (.10). This is 1.28, indicating that the 10th fastest runner has a z-score of 1.28. Multiply 1.28 by 60 seconds and subtract it from 420 seconds to get his/her time ($= 343.2$ seconds). The 10th fastest runner in the blue team is at the 1.1th percentile. Look in the body of the table for the value of z that cuts of 1.1% (.011). This is 2.30 and indicates that the 10th fastest runner has a z-score of 2.30. Multiply 2.30 by 60 seconds and subtract it from 420 seconds to get his/her time ($= 267.6$ seconds).

(iv) The law of large numbers tells us the contest is unfair (as does common sense). If the red team were to beat the odds and win the race we would suspect that something extraordinary was going on – perhaps that the red team were more motivated as a result of being placed in a small team.

F. (i) Adam appears to be the best candidate as he has the highest z-score of 2.33. Bill's z-score is 2.0. Charles' z-score is 2.14.

(ii) 1% (looking at Table C.1, the area in the tail beyond z associated with a z-score of 2.33 is .01)

(iii) If the ability of architecture students in all cities is the same and is always normally distributed with the same variance then we can assume that all three are drawn from the standard normal distribution ($\mu = 0$, $\sigma = 1$). To calculate the proportion of groups with a mean z-score greater than 2.0 (Bill's score) we need to use the sampling distribution of the mean for this distribution. The sampling distribution of the mean for groups of three architects drawn from the three cities will have a mean of 0.0 and will have a standard deviation of 1.0 divided by the square root of 3. The score of 2.0 therefore differs from the population mean of 0.0 by 2 * 1.73 standard error units. This corresponds to a z-score of 3.46, which (based on information contained in Table C.1) means that less than 1 group in 1000 will have a mean greater than this value.

(iv) The candidates represent an exceptional group of architects.

Chapter 8. Examining differences between two means: The *t*-test

A. (Note: Milk $M = 7.00$, $SD = 1.15$, Alcohol $M = 5.70$, SD $= 1.25$)
    (i)   Between-subjects
    (ii) 2.41
    (iii) Yes (with 18 degrees of freedom the critical value of t for $\alpha = .05$ is 2.101)

B. (Note: $\bar{D} = 1.30$, $S_D = 1.83$)
    (i)   Within-subjects
    (ii) 2.25
    (iii) No (with 9 degrees of freedom the critical value of t for $\alpha = .05$ is 2.26)

C. As illustrated in Chapter 6, the scores from throws of a single die have a *uniform* or flat-rectangular distribution. The distribution obtained from adding the sum of many dice throws is approximately normal. The *t*-test is a normal theory test and works most efficiently when the data analysed are drawn from a normally distributed population. This point underpins the *assumption of normality*.

D. (i)   Both tests would use a within-subjects *t*-tests
    (ii) The alpha level chosen for each test would reflect the level of uncertainty that was acceptable. If we wished to be sure that there were no side-effects we might use a very large alpha level like .25. That is, we would not want to use a therapy unless we were very confident that there were no side-effects (note that in a real study we would actually look at the proportion of participants who experience side-effects rather than just whether there were side-effects on average!). Before we use the expensive therapy though we would want to be very confident that it was effective. We might use a stringent alpha level for this purpose such as .001.
    (iii) The fact that participants discussed their responses before making them means that those responses are not independent. This violates the *assumption of independence*, so these data should be treated with caution. Indeed, there may not even be much point in analysing the data because they may be contaminated by the exchange of information.

E. Yes. Using a one-sample *t*-test (with α set at .05) the mean score is significantly greater than 100, $t(9) = 3.03$, $p < .02$.

Chapter 9. Examining relationships between variables: Correlation

A.

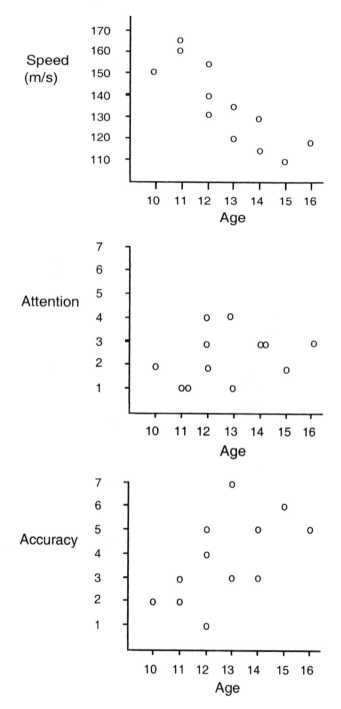

Age and Speed: $r = -.82$, Age and Attention: $r = .34$, Age and
Accuracy: $r = .59$.

B.   Only the correlation between Age and Speed is significant at the
.01 level (with 10 degrees of freedom, the critical value of r for
$\alpha = .01$ is .708).

C.   Age and Speed: large effect size, Age and Attention: moderate
effect size, Age and Accuracy: large effect size.

D.   68% (i.e., $-.82^2 * 100$)

E.   (i)   The within-subjects t-test shows that the reading ability scores
increase from age 9 to age 12, $(D = -2.7,\ SD = 2.06,\ t(9) = -4.15,\ p < .01)$. Using the formula for effect size given
on page 231, $r = .81$. This is a strong effect.

(ii)   The correlation between reading ability at age 9 and age 12 is
.689 ($p < .05$). This is also a strong effect.

(iii)   It is possible, and indeed common, for there to be a sizeable
difference between the mean score on two variables and for
there to be a sizeable correlation between them because
repeated measures t-tests and correlation actually answer
different questions. In this case it is possible for there to be
an increase in reading ability and for ability at the different
ages to be related to each other if the change in reading ability
is relatively similar for all participants. This is because the
correlation between two variables is not affected at all by
making a constant change (a transformation) to all of the
scores on one or both variables. For example, if we divided *all*
of the reading ability scores by two we would find that we still
obtained the same correlation and t-test score. However, if
we only divided the scores at age 12 by two we would find
that the correlation between reading ability at the different
times would remain the same but that the within-subjects
t-value would be very different. If you think about it, correlations would be a lot less useful if they did change when we
made a constant change to one or the other variable. It would
mean, for example, that the correlation between age and
intelligence would be different when you measured age in
years rather than months. Clearly this would be very confusing and it would make the statistic meaningless.

Chapter 10. Examining differences between more than two means: Analysis of variance

A. (i)

Source	SS	df	MS	F	p<	R²
Between groups (Age)	6831.4	3	2277.13	37.59	.01	.758
Within groups	2181.0	36	60.58			
Total	9001.6	39				

(ii) From this ANOVA table it is clear that the F-value for the between-groups age effect exceeds the tabled value of $F(3,36)$ with α set at .01 (4.38) and so there are strong grounds for rejecting the null hypothesis that the level of moral reasoning is the same in all age groups. Moreover, the effect would appear to be psychologically, not just statistically, significant as the size of this effect was large (i.e., $R^2 > .5$).

B. (i)

Source	SS	df	MS	F	p<	R²
Between groups (Age)	4536.9	1	4536.90	74.89	.01	.50
Between groups (Area)	1537.6	1	1537.60	25.38	.01	.17
Between groups (Age X Area)	756.9	1	756.90	12.49	.01	.08
Within groups	2181.0	36	60.58			
Total	9012.4	39				

(ii) From this ANOVA table it is clear that the F-value for the between-groups age effect exceeds the tabled value of $F(1,36)$ with α set at .01 (7.40) and so there are strong grounds for rejecting the null hypothesis that the level of moral reasoning is the same in all age groups. The between-groups area effect also exceeds the same tabulated value and so there are strong grounds for rejecting the null hypothesis that the level of moral reasoning is the same in areas of high and low crime. As well as this, the between-groups interaction effect exceeds the same tabulated value and so there are strong grounds for rejecting the null hypothesis that the effects of age and area are additive. This can be seen from the line graph of these data, in which the non-parallel lines provide evidence of an interaction between these two variables. However, it can be seen from the values of R^2 that these effects were of varying size, with a large effect for age (i.e., $R^2 > .25$), a moderate effect for area (i.e., $.09 > R^2 > .25$) and a small interaction effect (i.e., $R^2 < .09$).

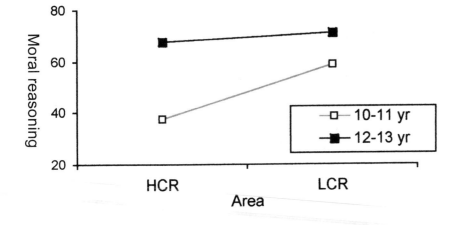

Chapter 11. Analysing other forms of data: χ^2 and distribution-free tests

A. (i) The expected frequency of female board members $= Np = 138 * .4 = 55.2$.

(ii) As $N > 25$, we can use the normal approximation to the binomial distribution to find out how likely it is that a distribution of board members as skewed as this would arise from a random process. Here the base-rate information tells us that p (the probability of an employee being female) $= .4$ and q (the probability of an employee being male) $= .6$. Thus:

$$z = \frac{x - Np}{\sqrt{Npq}}$$
$$= (44 - (138^*.4)/\sqrt{138^*.4^*.6}$$
$$= (44 - 55.2)/\sqrt{33.12}$$
$$= -11.2/5.75$$
$$= -1.95$$

We can see from Table C.1 that this z-score corresponds to a one-tailed probability of .026. The researchers would therefore be entitled to reject the null hypothesis (that the observed deviation from the expected frequency occurred by chance), and to claim support for their alternative hypothesis. Note, too, that the decision to use a one-tailed test could be justified on grounds that this hypothesis had been specified in advance.

B. (i) The expected frequency (f_e) of correct identification $= np$ (where n is the number of participants in each condition (30) and p is the probability of correct identification (.5)). Thus $f_e = 30*.5 = 15$.

(ii) To answer this question we need to compare the observed frequency ($f_e = 16$) with the expected frequency ($f_e = 15$). Because $N > 25$, we can use the normal approximation of the binomial distribution to find out how likely it is that a number of correct identifications as high as this would arise from a random process. Here p and $q = .5$, so:

$$z = \frac{x - Np}{\sqrt{Npq}}$$
$$= (16 - 15)/\sqrt{30*.5*.5}$$
$$= 1/\sqrt{7.5}$$
$$= 0.36$$

From Table C.1 we see that this z-score corresponds to a one-tailed probability of .641. There are thus no grounds for rejecting the null hypothesis that the observed deviation from the expected frequency occurred by chance.

(iii) We can answer this question using the chi-square test for goodness of fit, where

$$\chi^2 = \Sigma(f_0 - f_e)^2/f_e$$

Here $f_e = (16 + 27)/2 = 21.5$. So

$$\chi^2 = ((21.5 - 16)^2 + (21.5 - 27)^2)/20.5$$
$$= (5.5^2 + 5.5^2)/20.5$$
$$= 2.95$$

Here $df = k-1 = 1$. From Table C.5 we can see that with 1 df this value of χ^2 corresponds to a value of p between .1 and .05. With conventional levels of α (i.e., .05) there are therefore no grounds for concluding that learning context (song or poem) had an impact on recognition.

(iv) We can answer this question using the chi-square test of independence. Here row totals, column totals and expected frequencies are as follows:

	Male	Female	(Row totals)
Controls	28 (25.1)	29 (31.9)	57
Amnesiacs	16 (18.9)	27 (24.1)	43
(Column totals)	44	56	$N = 100$

So

$$\chi^2 = \Sigma(f_0 - f_e)^2/f_e = ((28 - 25.1)^2 + ((29 - 31.9)^2/31.9)$$
$$+ ((16 - 18.9)^2/18.9) + ((27 - 24.1)^2/24.1)$$
$$= ((2.9)^2/25.1) + ((2.9)^2/31.9) + ((2.9)^2/18.9)$$
$$+ ((2.9)^2/24.1) = 0.34 + 0.27 + 0.45 + 0.35 = 1.41$$

Here $df = (k-1)(k-1) = 1$. From Table C.5 we can see that with 1 df this value of χ^2 corresponds to a value of p between .25 and .10. With conventional levels of α (i.e., .05) there are therefore no grounds for concluding that learning context (song or poem) has more impact on the amnesiacs' memory than on the memory of controls. In other words, the results provide no basis for rejecting the null hypothesis that learning context (song or poem) is unrelated to participant type (control or amnesiac).

(v) Effect size can be measured by a phi-coefficient where $\phi = \chi^2/N = 1.41/100 = 0.14$. This is therefore a small effect (i.e., less than .1).

(vi) If there had been evidence of a relationship between learning context and participant type, the data for controls suggest that their responses might have been affected by a ceiling effect (see Chapter 9). This is because there was no opportunity for learning material in song form to improve recognition as the participants who learned the material in poem form were already performing the task almost perfectly. This suggests that in a future study, it might therefore be a good idea to make the task harder. Note, though, that as a result of a relevance–sensitivity trade-off (see Chapter 4), this might in turn mean that the manipulation of learning context has less impact on amnesiacs.

C. (i) Noting that the criticism is worth considering, the researchers could reanalyse their data using a distribution-free test. The obvious candidate here is the Mann–Whitney test (although the researchers should note that this can tell them whether there are differences in the distributions of sample data, not necessarily whether these differences are in central tendency).

(ii) The Mann–Whitney test is conducted as follows:

2001	Score	27.1	44.5	58.9	70.4	73.2	84.2	85.1	88.2	89.3	90.2	92.2	93.2	94.0	94.5	95.2	U_1
	Rank	30	29	28	26	25	23	22	19	18	17	15	14	12	10	7	295
2002	Score	59.3	74.2	86.4	86.7	90.3	93.3	94.4	94.6	94.7	95.3	95.7	96.6	96.7	97.1	98.8	U_2
	Rank	27	24	21	20	16	13	11	9	8	6	5	4	3	2	1	170

$$U_e = N_1((N_1 + N_2 + 1)/2) = 15((15 + 15 + 1)/2)$$
$$= (15 * 31)/2 = 232.5$$
$$S_U = \sqrt{((N_1 N_2 (N_1 + N_2 + 1))/12)}$$
$$= \sqrt{((15 * 15(15 + 15 + 1)/12)} = \sqrt{(6975/12)} = 24.11$$
$$z = (U_1 - U_e)/S_U = (295 - 232.5)/24.11$$
$$= 63.5/24.11 = 2.59$$

From Table C.1 we can see that this z-value cuts off only a small proportion of the normal curve, corresponding to a probability of .005. This suggests that such a difference in rankings is very unlikely to be the result of chance. Accordingly, we have a sound basis for concluding that performance had improved in 2002. Note that in this case a t-test would have led us to the same conclusion.

Chapter 12. Qualitative methods

A. (i) The sampling domain is the major national newspapers published on one particular day. Obviously, this domain could be enlarged in various ways (e.g., by including magazines or regional newspapers). Whether or not this would constitute an improvement depends on the questions being asked and the types of conclusions one wishes to draw. For example, including magazines would represent an improvement if one wanted to make arguments related to the range of forms in which people are exposed to written material about mental illness.

(ii)   Coding units could take any number of forms and these would depend on the research question you were interested in. Depending on this, they might, for instance, identify references that (a) are favourable or unfavourable, (b) treat mental illness as curable or incurable, or (c) advocate or oppose drug treatment.

(iii) The best way to ensure that your coding is reliable is to use multiple independent coders and then examine the correspondence in their assignment of material to particular categories. This can be done by measures of inter-rater reliability.

(iv)   Again, this would depend on the goals of the study, but in principle the data could be subjected to either qualitative analysis (e.g., using grounded theory) or quantitative analysis (e.g., using methods described in Chapter 11).

B. *Grounded theory*

This example is based on research conducted by Burgoyne (1997), and so it is instructive to read the report of this research to see how she tackles the problem. Amongst other things, Burgoyne:

(i)   develops a coding system in which the coding categories focused on representations of (a) issues and orientations (whether the article had a patient-centred view or a service-centred view), (b) who should make allocation decisions (e.g., doctors, patients, authorities), and (c) what the decision criteria should be (e.g., cost, care, individual rights, age).

(ii)   identifies links between particular orientations (e.g., a patient-centred view) and an emphasis on particular decision criteria (e.g., care, individual rights).

(iii) suggests that particular links (e.g., between being patient-centred and making decisions on the basis of individual rights) were more likely to be made in certain forms of newspaper (tabloid vs. broadsheet).

(iv)   concludes that representations of healthcare rationing were unrelated to the conceptions developed by economic theorists to describe issues surrounding resource allocation.

(v)   argues that the lack of consensus in the representation of healthcare rationing contributed to, and was symptomatic of, difficulties in having informed public debate on the topic.

C. *Discourse analysis*

This text is discussed by Hepburn (2003), who also examines the general issue of public displays of memory. In relation to this and other similar data, she notes that the act of remembering is a public one and that it has many purposes. Amongst other things, her analysis:

(i)   identifies a number of distinctive features of this text, including (a) the long pauses, (b) the contrast between being able to remember some things but not others, and (c) the differentiation between accepting a statement and not being able to deny it.

(ii)   notes that Clinton here is trying (a) to appear co-operative, (b) to appear honest and trustworthy, but (c) not to perjure himself (i.e., by telling a lie).

(iii)   argues that to achieve these various goals, Clinton has to steer a very difficult path between (a) saying that he remembers the phone call (in which case he might have to answer difficult questions about it) and (b) denying memory of it (which might seem uncooperative and implausible). To do this, he needs to give the impression of someone who is *trying* to remember but isn't able to – and it can be argued that this is what the various features of the account are designed to do.

(iv)   argues that this example illustrates the way in which, ultimately, memory and cognition are public acts and that, as such, they are far more nuanced than traditional approaches (e.g., in social and cognitive psychology) might suggest. So, rather than being able to say that a given memory is right or wrong, available or unavailable (as a quantitative analysis might require us to do), we see that natural acts of remembering often require people to avoid these binary choices.

Author Index

Abramson, L. Y., 68
American Psychological
   Association, 44, 216,
   408, 418, 451, 463,
   466–69
Aronson, E., 26
Austin, J. T., 62

Bandura, A., 36
Barber, T. X., 92
Batson, C. D., 405
Baumrind, D., 406, 408, 414
Berkun, M. M., 401
Bialek, H. M., 401
Burgoyne, C. B., 508

Campbell, D. T., 51, 87, 95,
   428
Chalmers, A. F., 27
Cochrane, R., 76
Cohen, J., 216, 231, 259, 266
Cook, T.D., 51
Culhane, S. E., 216

Darley, J. M., 405
Davidson, J. W., 383
Dawes, R. M., 93
de Groot, A. D., 61
Delaney, H. D., 293, 296, 310
Dickson, W. J., 83
Drury, J., 392
Duffy, J., 76

Ekeberg, S. E., 216
Ekman, P., 36
Eysenck, H. J., 36
Eysenck, S. B. G., 36

Fenaughty, A. M., 76
Festinger, L., 58, 405
Feyerabend, P. K., 14
Fidell, L. S., 145
Fode, K. L., 91
Fonda, N., 382
Fraser, S., 401
Frazer, S., 125
Freud, S., 58
Frick, R. W., 229
Frieson, W. V., 36

Gilbert, G. N., 355, 363
Gilhooly, K., 383
Gould, S. J., 165, 401, 498
Green, C., 383
Gribbin, J., 16, 23, 31
Gunn, S. P., 409

Hammond, G., 216
Haslam, S. A., 95, 420, 430
Hathaway, S. R., 36
Henwood, K. L., 368, 372, 373
Hepburn, A., 508
Herrnstien, R. J., 401
Herzog, H. A., 412
Hopkins, N., 362, 366

Howe, M. J. A., 383
Huff, D., 162
Hutchinson, P., 392

Ingvar, D. H., 37

Judd, C. M., 216

Kahneman, D., 36, 85
Kalton, G., 125
Kelly, G. A., 378, 382
Keppel, G., 293, 310
Kern, R. P., 401
Kline, P., 382
Kuhn, T., 22, 428

Lassen, N. A., 37
Latané, B., 405
Lawley, M., 125
Leong, T.L., 62
Levenson, R.W., 36

McClelland, G. H., 216
McCulloch, C., 383
McGarty, C., 95, 420, 430
McGuire, W. J., 428
McKinley, J. C. 36
Magee, B., 18
Maier, S. F., 68
Manstead, A. S. R., 383
Maxwell, S. E., 293, 296, 310
Miles, J., 266
Milgram, S., 404, 406–408, 414, 418, 419
Milner, B., 58
Morf, C. C., 62
Moscovici, S., 428
Mulkay, M. J., 355, 363
Murray, C., 401

Newsom, J. T., 76

Orne, M., 91, 404

Panter, A. T., 62
Paulos, J. A., 162

Pettit, P., 408
Piaget, J., 36
Pigeon, N. F., 368, 372, 373
Popper, K., 18
Potter, J., 363, 365, 369–71, 390, 392

Ray, W. J., 21
Rees, M., 16, 23, 31
Reicher, S. D., 362, 366, 392
Richardson, D., 408, 409
Richardson, J. T. E., 393
Riecken, H., 58, 405
Roethlisberger, F. J., 83
Rosenthal, R., 91, 408
Ross, D., 36
Ross, S., 36

Sansone, C., 62
Schachter, S., 58, 405
Schuman, H., 125
Seligman, M. E. P., 68
Sherif, M., 61
Shevlin, M., 266
Siegel, S., 340, 345
Silver, M. J., 92
Silverman, D., 393
Singer, P., 412
Skinhøj, E., 37
Skinner, B. F., 35
Sloboda, J. A., 383
Smart, R., 76
Smith, H. J., 359, 428
Smith, S. S., 408, 409
Smithson, M., 192, 239, 305, 310, 320, 345, 428, 485, 492
Spears, R., 359, 428
Stanley, J. C., 87, 95
Sternberg, R. J., 21
Stewart, A., 382
Stewart, V., 382
Stott, C., 392
Svyantek, D. J., 216

Tabachnick, B. G., 145
Tajfel, H., 36

Teasdale, J. D., 68
Tesch, R., 352
Tukey, J.W., 171
Turner, J. C., 77, 93
Tversky, A., 36, 85

Valentine, E. R., 27

Watson, J. B., 35
West, S. G., 76, 409
Woolgar, S., 363, 389

Yagi, K., 401
Yin, R. K., 365, 367

Subject Index

Note: This index lists all terms for which glossary definitions are provided. Page numbers of these definitions are in **bold.**

a priori (comparisons) 293–94, **296**

absolute difference 146, **151**

additive model *see* main effects model

alpha level 219–**24**, 225, 274, 294, 366–7

alternative hypothesis 218, 220–1, **226**, 257 288–9

animal rights movement 412–**14**

animal welfare 411, **414**–16

ANOVA 273–315, 319, 344, 444–50, 503

ANOVA table 286–**87**

archival records 115, **119**, 361

assumption of equal variance 234–**38**, 241, 277, 309

assumption of independence 234–**38**, 241, 309

assumption of normality 234–5, **238**, 241, 277, 309

assumptions 234–**38**, 259–263, 277, 309, 317–19, 335–36, 343, 365

barchart 136, **140**

base rate 322, **323**, 329

behavioural measures 35, **41**, 44

behavioural trace measures 37, **41**, 115

behaviourism 35, **41**

betting odds 331, **334**

between-cells mean square (MS_B) 280, **283**

between-subjects manipulation 71, **72**, 86–7, 89, 116–7, 209–10, 309, 422

binomial distribution 173, **175**, 320–22, 341

bivariate **247**

bivariate normal distribution 259–**262**, 265

blind (experimental) 92, **94**

Bonferroni adjustment 294–**96**

case study 58–**60**, 361

causal inference 45, 47, **50**, 56, 105, 124

causal relationship 16, **20**, 74, 105, 108, 124, 264–65

ceiling effect 264, **265**, 268

cells 278–79, 281–**83**, 295, 444–50

central limit theorem 185, **190**, 278

chance 170, **175**

chi-square distribution 325–**327**, 328, 346, 491–93

circular argument *see* reification

code 103, **107**

coding system 373, **377**, 384–85

coding units 384, **387**

cohort 117–**119**

column mean 298–303, **308**

column variable 298–99, **308**

common variance 256–57, **259**

computational formula 149, **151**, 253

computer-aided interviewing 113, **119**

concealment 92, **94**, 415

condition 44, 46–7, **50**

conditional odds 332, **334**

confederate 405, **410**

confidence interval 228–30, **233**, 289

confidence interval approach 228–30, **233**

confidentiality 404, **410**, 414

confounding 48, **50**, 58, 62, 116–17, 124, 166, 423–24

constructionism 357–**60**, 365, 394

constructionist methods 365, **368**, 369–73, 383, 388–90

constructivism *see* constructionism

constructivist methods *see* constructionist methods

content analysis 383–**87**, 392, 394, 396

contextualist methods **368**, 372–76, 383, 394

contingencies 328, **334**, 335

contingency table 328–30, **334**

contingent repertoire **363**

continuous variable 133, **134**, 136, 154

control group 44, **50**

convenience sampling 109, **112**

correlation 54, 56, **57**, 69, 74, 85, 106, 116, 246–72, 342, 424, 501–2

correlation coefficient 250–**54**, 256–58, 331

correlational fallacy 63, 264–**65**, 266, 268.

correlational method 54, **57**, 265, 400

counterbalancing 86, **88**

covariance 251–**54**

cover story 92, **94**, 406

critical psychologists 118, **119**

critical value(s) 219–**26**, 228, 229, 258, 277, 289, 480–93

crossover interaction 302–3, **308**

cross-sectional studies 116–**119**

curvilinear relationship 260–**66**

data reduction 382, **387**

data set 130, **131**

debriefing 407–**10**, 415

deception 92, **94**, 404–7, 409, 415

degrees of freedom (*df*) **202**, 204–12, 258, 276–80, 285–86, 326, 330, 437–49, 476–93

delphi groups 362, **363**

demand characteristics 91–2, **94**, 97

dependent variable (DV) 45, **50**, 51, 68, 70, 72–75, 82, 84, 86, 95, 102, 115–16, 123, 246–47, 273, 309, 354–56

descriptive statistics 130, **131**–65, 254, 196–98

descriptive uncertainty 169–71, **175**, 193, 195, 275, 393, 420–22, **429**

developmental surveys 116, **119**

dimension 35, **42**

directional test 221–**26**

discontinuing participation 409, **410**, 416

discourse analysis 368–**72**, 378, 392, 394, 397

discrete variable 133, **134**, 136

distribution 135, **140**

distribution-free statistics 335–**36**, 343–45

distribution-free tests 237, **238**, 335–43, 504–7

dynamic mental processes 35, **42**, 104–5

effect size 231–**33**, 255, 289, 291, 331

effect size approach 230–32, **233**, 258, 441–43

effects model 289–**92**, 297

empirical method 13, **15**, 27

empiricist repertoire 363, **364**

error term 172, **175**, 178, 188, 192, 204, 277, 282, 294–95
estimate 182, **190**, 199, 228
ethics committee 400, **402**, 407
expected frequency 153, **161**, 324–29, 330, 346
expected value 172, **175**, 192, 199, 217
experiment 43, **50**, 67–106
experimental control 47, **51**, 53, 62, 71, 80–92, l04–6, 117, 124, 170, 404–5, 423–26
experimental design 67, **68**–101, 494
experimental group 44–7, **51**
experimenter bias 91, **94**, 114
experimentwise alpha level 294, **296**
external uncertainty 424–**29**
external validity **68**, 89–94, 98, 109, 388
extraneous variable 37, **42**, 48, 50, 53, 62, 93, 123, 400

factor analysis 382, **387**
factors 273–**74**, 309
falsification 18, **20**
fatigue effects 81, 86, **88**, 96
F-distribution 276–**277**, 484–90
field study 60, **61**, 405
fit (in grounded theory) 374, **377**
flat-rectangular distribution 156, **161**–62
floor effect 264, **266**, 268
focus groups 362, **364**
forced-choice responses 121, **123**
frequency graph 135, **140**
frequency table 135, **140**
Friedman test **342**
fully factorial designs 300, **308**

gambler's fallacy 234, **238**
generalization 39–**42**, 48, 56, 77–8, 80, 89–94, 104–5, 152, 389–90, 424–26
goodness of fit 325–**27**
grand mean 279, 281–**83**, 284, 288, 289–303

grounded theory 372–**77**, 378, 384–85, 393, 394, 396

H_0 217, **226**, 257
H_1 218, 221, **226**, 257
Hawthorne effect 83, **88**, 423, 425
hermeneutic approach 355–56, **360**
histogram 136, **140**
history effects 81, **88**, 96
hypothesis 16, **20**
hypothesis-testing approach 216–**26**, 258, 326, 352, 437–43

idealism 357, **360**, 394
idiographic approach 357–**61**
independence 234–**38**
independent variable (IV) 45, 48, **51**, 68–72, 104, 247, 273, 296–307, 323, 354–56, 421
induction 17, **20**, 28, 77
inferential statistics 130, **131**, 166–97
inferential uncertainty 170–**75**, 191, 193, 195, 204, 240, 267, 420–22, 426, **429**, 310, 346
information term 172, **175**, 188, 191, 204, 277, 282
informed consent 409–**10**
instrument 35, **42**
instrumentation effects 84, **89**, 96
interaction 89, **94**, 97, 297–98, 301–6 308, 386
interaction sum of squares main effects 303, **308**
internal uncertainty 423–**29**
internal validity 45, 48, **51**, 68, 80–89, 264, 388, 423
inter-rater reliability 385, **387**, 394
interval measure 132–**34**, 141
interview 113–**19**, 361–62
invasive procedures 408, **410**, 412, 415

Kruskal-Wallis test **342**, 344

law of large numbers 180–**90**, 191–92, 200

loglinear analysis 333, **334**
longitudinal studies 116–19

main effects 298, **309**
main effects model 299–301, 307, **309**
manipulation 43, **51**, 58, 68–72, 124
manipulation check 70–**72**, 95
Mann-Whitney test 318, 337–**40**, 344, 347
marginal totals 329, **334**, 335
matching 78–**80**, 86, 400
maturation effects 81–**89**, 95, 116–18
McNemar test **341**
mean 137–**140**, 141–43, 198–245, 277, 292, 335, 343, 362
mean deviation 146–**51**
mean squares (*MS*) 280, **283**, 284
measurement error 159, **161**, 169, 421, 426
measures of central tendency 134–**40**, 141–44, 339
median 138–**40**
methodological uncertainty 189, 388, 423–**29**
mode 138–**40**, 141–143
mortality effects 85–**89**, 96, 111
multivariate statistics 316, **319**

N 138–**40**
naïve empiricism 77–**80**, 95, 424
naturalistic observational studies 113, **119**
negative correlation 249–**50**
negative skew 142–**44**
nominal measure 131, **134**
nomothetic approach 357–**61**
non-obtrusive measures 115 16, **119**
nonparametric statistics 335–**36**
non-parametric tests 237–**39**
non-probability sampling 110–**12**
non-reactive techniques 115–16, **119**
non-response 111–**12**
normal distribution 156–60, **161**, 177–78, 276

normal theory tests 234–35, **238**
null hypothesis 217–23, **226**, 257, 278–79, 288–89, 297, 330

observed distribution 152–**61**, 162, 335
observed frequency 324–**27**, 328–30, 346
odds 331, **334**
odds ratio 332–33, **334**
one-tailed test 221–22, **226**, 257–58, 477, 480, 481–82
open-coding 374, **377**
operationalization 67, **68**, 74, 123
order effects 83, 86, **89**, 96, 124
ordinal measure 132–**34**, 141, 254
outliers 145, **152**, 163, 235–36, 242, 260–61, 267, 311
overlap of distributions 209, **215**

pairwise comparisons 293, **296**
parsimony 23–**25**, 27, 29
participant involvement 355, **361**, 393
participants 44, **51**, 398–414
partitioning the sum of squares 284–**87**
Pearson's product-moment correlation 250–**55**, 316, 319, 344
Pearson's *r* 251–**55**, 482–83
personal constructs 378, **388**
phi 331, 333, **334**, 146
physiological measures 36–37, **42**, 44, 131, 408
placebo 405, **410**
point biserial correlation **342**
point estimate 228, **233**
pooled variance estimate 210–**15**, 278, 281
population 38–**42**, 48, 108–10, 152–61, 182–87
population parameter 154–**61**, 182, 189, 198–200, 228, 257–58
positive correlation 249–**50**
positive skew 142–**44**, 276

positivism 356–57, **361**, 371, 394
post hoc comparisons 293, **296**
post-modernism 357–**61**, 394
post-test 80–**89**, 90, 97
power 223–**26**, 343
practice effects 81, 86, **89**, 96, 117
prediction 16, 55, **247**
pre-test 80–**90**
probability (*p*) 153, 161, 320–22,
331–32
probability sampling 109–**112**
probability-level approach 227, **233**
psychological significance 231, **233**,
422–23
psychological tests 35–**42**
purposive sampling 110–**12**

Q-sort 362, **364**
qualitative research methods 118,
119, 351–97, 507–9
quasi-experiment 51–**4**, 56, 106, 266,
400
questionnaire 103–**07**, 120–23

random assignment 40–**51**, 52–54,
78–79, 84–87, 103, 113
random error 105, 158–60, 170–72,
175, 169, 251–52, 275, 278,
421–42
random event 166–67, 181–82, **190**
random process 171–**75**, 182, 191,
218–20
random sample 38–**42**, 104, 110, 124,
275, 424
range 144–**52**
ratio measure 132, **134**, 135
raw data 135–**40**
reactive focus 362–**64**
reactivity 82–**89**, 91, 96, 111,
114–15, 126, 362, 405–8
realism 356–57, **361**, 366, 394
realist methods **368**, 378–86, 373
redescription 18, **20**, 28
reflexive journal 374–75, **377**
refutation 18, **20**, 59

regression coefficient 259, **266**
regression to the mean 85, **89**, 97,
263–64
rejection region 218–22, **226**
reification 18, **20**, 28
relativism 357–**61**, 392, 394
relevance-sensitivity trade-off 73–**5**,
426
reliability 21–**5**, 29, 35, 38, 388–89
repertory grid 362, **364**
repertory grid analysis 378–83, **388**
replication 21, **26**, 58, 231
representative random sample 104,
107, 110, 124, 159, 424
representative sample 39–41, 48–9,
51, 62, 76, 108, 109
research ethics 52, 69–70, 73, 106,
115, 124, 398–419, **402**
research risk 409–**11**, 415
response scale 121–**23**, 353–54
restricted range 262–**66**, 268
reversed scoring 122–**23**
robust test 237–**39**
rounding (up) 137, **140**
row mean 298–303, **309**
row variable 298–9, **309**

sample 38, 39, **40**, 42, 75–80,
108–111
sample size (*N*) 110–**112**, 126, 421
sampling distribution 183–**90**, 276
sampling distribution of the
difference between means 199–**202**
sampling distribution of the mean
184–**90**
sampling domain 384, **388**
sampling error 159, **162**, 169–70,
424–26
sampling frame 110–**112**
scale 70, **72**
scatterplot 248–**50**, 255, 259
scientific method 12, 14, **15**–27, 368
selection effects 84, **89**, 97
self-report measures 36, 37, **42**, 44,
114, 131

sign test **341**, 344, 347

significance fallacy 231, **234**, 267, 311, 346, 422

significance-testing approach 217–**26**, 257–58, 274, 288–89, 437–50

significant figures 137, **140**

simple random sample 110–**112**

skewness 141–**44**

social desirability 114–115, **119**

sources of variation 284, 286–**87**

Spearman's correlation (r_s) **342**

split-ballot technique 106, **107**, 113, 124

stable psychological characteristics 35, **42**, 104

standard deviation 150–**152**, 155–56, 162, 275

standard deviation units 176–**80**

standard error 185–**90**, 192

standard error of the mean 185–**90**

standard error units 187–**90**

standard normal distribution 177–**80**, 476–79

standardization 176–**80**, 196, 198

statistical model 172, **175**–99

statistical odds 332–**34**

statistical significance 219–**26**, 256–58, 437–50

statistical uncertainty l69–**75**, 191–92, 388, 420, 426, **429**

statistics 130, **131**

straight-line relationship 249, **250**, 260

study 21, **26**

subjects 44, **51**

successive cross-sectional studies 117–**19**

sum of the squared deviations between cells (SS_B) 284–86, **288**, 289–90

sum of the squared deviations within cells (SS_W) 284–86, **288**, 289–90

survey 54–**57**, l02–29, 246–47

survey instrument 111–**12**

survey method 54–**57**, 58, 102–29, 246–47, 265–66, 400, 423–24, 494–96

systematic sampling 109–**112**

taxonomy 376, **377**

t-distribution 199–**203**, 228, 230, 276, 480–1

t-test 198, **199**–245, 273, 277, 281, 294, 316–19, 343, 437–40, 500

test statistic 171–74, 176, 198–202, 204, 207, 211, 257–58, 335

testing effects 82, **89**, 90, 117

tests with relaxed assumptions **336**, 337–43

theoretical distribution 152–**62**

theory 15–**20**, 23, 26–28, 59, 68–69, 77–78, 93, 372, 424–25

total sum of squares 284, 287–**88**, 289–90

transformation 145, **152**, 235

treatment 44–**51**

2 X 2 factorial design 300–**8**

two-tailed test 221–**27**, 257–58, 477, 481–83

Type I error 221–**27**, 274

Type II error 221–**27**, 274

uniform distribution 156–57, **162**

univariate 247

user involvement 355, **361**

validity 21, 22, **26**, 29, 38, 45–49, 68, 80–93, 388–89

variable 43–**51**, 68–79, 131–34, 316–17, 319, (324–335), 343

variance 147–**52**, 155–6, 274–77, 303, 306 (273–315)

verbal protocol 362, **364**

violation of assumptions 234–**39**, 259–65, 309, 311, 335, 343

weighted average 210, **215**

Wilcoxon matched-pairs signed-ranks test **341**

within-cells mean square (MS$_W$) 280, 282, **283**

within-subjects manipulation 71, **72**, 85, 205, 309

X 138, **141**

$\bar{X}$ (x bar) 138, **141**

Yates correction 330, **335**

z-score 177–**80**, 194–95, 322–324, 476–79

ΣX (sigma X) 138, **141**

Σ (sigma) 138, **141**